Android

BlackBerry

iPhone / iPad

⊚Harden's

UK Restaurant Survey
2014

"The UK's most helpful
and informative guide"
The Sunday Times

Survey driven reviews of nearly 3,000 restaurants

our pocket!

one and Android.

.com/mobile/android for more details.

Twitter – @hardensbites

013

26-1

in-Publication data: a catalogue record for this book is available from the British Library.

estar Wheatons

ith (cover) Margaret Vanschaemelhout
n Teschauer
n Ashpole, Gilles Talarek
lodagh Kinsella, Alexander Larman

The UK's 100 Best Restaurants

1   Gidleigh Park, Chagford

2   Andrew Fairlie, Gleneagles Hotel, Auchterarder

3   Yorke Arms, Ramsgill-in-Nidderdale

4   Restaurant Nathan Outlaw, The St Enodoc Hotel, Rock

5   Restaurant Martin Wishart, Edinburgh

6   Fraiche, Oxton

7   Le Manoir aux Quat' Saisons, Great Milton

8   The Ledbury, London W11

9   L'Enclume, Cartmel

10   Restaurant Sat Bains, Nottingham

11   The Kitchin, Edinburgh

12   The Fat Duck, Bray

13   Mr Underhill's, Ludlow

14   Waterside Inn, Bray

15   Le Gavroche, London W1

16   One-O-One, Sheraton Park Tower, London SW1

17   Pied à Terre, London W1

18   Midsummer House, Cambridge

19   Drakes, Ripley

20   Hambleton Hall, Hambleton

21   Viajante, London E2

22   The Square, London W1

23   Pétrus, London SW1

24   HKK, London EC2

25   Rasoi, London SW3

THE SUNDAY TIMES

The UK's 100 Best Restaurants

THE SUNDAY TIMES

The UK's 100 Best Restaurants

51   Assaggi, London W2

52   Story, London SE1

53   Hélène Darroze, The Connaught Hotel, London W1

54   The Harrow at Little Bedwyn, Marlborough

55   Bath Priory Hotel, Bath

56   Purnells, Birmingham

57   Lumière, Cheltenham

58   Wheelers Oyster Bar, Whitstable

59   Paul Ainsworth at Number 6, Padstow

60   La Petite Maison, London W1

61   The Five Fields, London SW3

62   The Peat Inn, Cupar

63   Umu, London W1

64   Le Champignon Sauvage, Cheltenham

65   Morston Hall, Morston

66   Holbeck Ghyll, Windermere

67   Great House, Lavenham

68   The French Restaurant, Midland Hotel, Manchester

69   The Castle Terrace, Edinburgh

70   Gauthier Soho, London W1

71   L'Atelier de Joel Robuchon, London WC2

72   Seven Park Place, London SW1

73   Amaya, London SW1

74   Artichoke, Amersham

75   L'Ortolan, Shinfield

THE SUNDAY TIMES

The UK's 100 Best Restaurants

Eat Well

If issues such as climate change, animal welfare and treating people fairly matter to you, look out for the SRA Sustainability Ratings next to restaurant listings.

The Sustainable Restaurant Association (SRA) is a not for profit body helping restaurants achieve greater sustainability. To help diners, it has developed Sustainability Ratings to assess restaurants in 14 key areas across three main sustainability categories of Sourcing, Environment and Society.

In a 2013 consumer survey for the SRA, more than 80% of diners said they knew little or nothing about the sustainable things restaurants are doing despite the same number wanting restaurants to communicate that information. Harden's has partnered with the SRA to include its Sustainability Ratings, giving diners the information to identify those restaurants doing great things. For example, we know diners want to know restaurants are sourcing from local producers, using high welfare meat and dairy and served sustainable fish. Improving waste energy and water efficiency are more ways for restaurants to be sustainable. The most sustainable restaurants engage with their communities.

By choosing a sustainable restaurant, you can be sure that your meal isn't costing the earth.

Chefs, restaurateurs and diners can make the difference by embracing sustainable values and in doing so create a better food chain. We hope diners will consider these ideals when choosing to dine out.

– Raymond Blanc OBE, President of the SRA

We're proud to support the SRA, and hope that by including SRA Sustainability Ratings to the restaurants we include, we can help set diners' expectations as to which of their choices will ensure the trade thrives for many years to come.

– Harden's

More than 50% = Good Sustainability
More than 60% = Excellent Sustainability
More than 70% = Exceptional Sustainability

CONTENTS

Berners Tavern

Tramshed

RATINGS & PRICES

Ratings

Our rating system does not tell you – as most guides do – that expensive restaurants are often better than cheap ones! What we do is compare each restaurant's performance – as judged by the average ratings awarded by reporters in the survey – with other similarly-priced restaurants.

This approach has the advantage that it helps you find – whatever your budget for any particular meal – where you will get the best 'bang for your buck'.

The following qualities are assessed:

F — Food
S — Service
A — Ambience

The rating indicates that, *in comparison with other restaurants in the same price-bracket*, performance is…

❶ — Exceptional
❷ — Very good
❸ — Good
④ — Average
⑤ — Poor

In the **UK section**, some restaurants are worth a mention but, for some reason (typically low feedback) we do not think a rating is appropriate. These are indicated as follows:

❶ —Tip

Prices

The price shown for each restaurant is the cost for one (1) person of an average three-course dinner with half a bottle of house wine and coffee, any cover charge, service and VAT. Lunch is often cheaper. With BYO restaurants, we have assumed that two people share a £6 bottle of off-licence wine.

Telephone number – within London all numbers should be prefixed with '020' if dialling from outside the London area.

Map reference – London after the telephone number; UK next to location.

Rated on Editors' visit – indicates ratings have been determined by the Editors personally, based on their visit, rather than derived from the survey.

Website – the first entry in the small print (after any note about Editors' visit)

Last orders time – listed after the website (if applicable); Sunday may be up to 90 minutes earlier.

Opening hours – unless otherwise stated, restaurants are open for lunch and dinner seven days a week.

Credit and debit cards – unless otherwise stated, Mastercard, Visa, Amex and Maestro are accepted.

Dress – where appropriate, the management's preferences concerning patrons' dress are given.

Special menus – if we know of a particularly good value set menu we note this (e.g. "set weekday L"), together with its formula price (FP) calculated exactly as in 'Prices' above. Details change, so always check ahead.

FROM THE EDITORS

For the second year, we're pleased to bring you what we believe to be the UK's most useful restaurant guide in its new 'glovebox' format. As ever, it is written 'from the bottom up' – we don't dictate the establishments listed, but base the selection on the results of our unique annual survey of thousands of restaurant-goers, in which you are most welcome to take part. (Further details of this are given overleaf.)

This guide includes the full content of our separately-published London guide, as well as coverage of cities, towns and villages across the whole of the UK. We recognise that the result is a guide somewhat skewed to London. We urge readers, though, to think of this extensive London coverage as a bonus rather than a defect. After all, our out-of-London coverage alone is broadly equivalent to the total content of the UK's longest-published UK guide, The Good Food Guide (including the restaurants of the metropolis).

It is certainly no longer true, as one could have said as recently as five years ago, that large areas of the UK are pretty much restaurant deserts, devoid of almost anything of interest to the discerning visitor. This ongoing transformation is perhaps most obvious in the great regional centres – even Manchester, a 'second city' which has been a laggard until very recently, seems finally to be getting its act together!

We urge all our readers to help us do even better justice to the restaurant scene outside the capital. If you think your area is under-represented, the answer is largely in your own hands – take part in our annual survey, and make sure your friends do too!

We are very grateful to each of our thousands of reporters, without whose input this guide could not have been written. Many reporters express views about a number of restaurants at some length, knowing full well that – given the concise format of the guide – we can seemingly never 'do justice' to their observations. We must assume that they do so in the confidence that the short – and we hope snappy – summaries we produce are as fair and well-informed as possible.

You, the reader, must judge – restaurant guides are not works of literature, and should be assessed on the basis of utility. This is a case where the proof of the pudding really is in the eating.

Our relationship with the Sunday Times continues to develop. For the fourth year, we are pleased to record, in the front section of the guide, the list we prepare for them of the Top 100 restaurants in the UK. As the years roll on, the risers and fallers – and the 'stayers' – in this tabulation are taking on an interest all of their own.

All restaurant guides are the subject of continual revision, and the more input we have, the more accurate and comprehensive future editions will be. If you are not already signed up, please do join the www.hardens.com mailing list – we will then ensure that you are invited to take part in future surveys.

Richard Harden   **Peter Harden**

HOW THIS BOOK IS ORGANISED

The guide begins in *London*, and contains the full text of the guide already published as *London Restaurants 2014*. Thereafter, the guide is organised strictly alphabetically by location, without regard to national divisions – Beaumaris, Belfast and Birmingham appear together under 'B'.

For *cities and larger towns*, you should therefore be able to turn straight to the relevant section. In addition to the entries for the restaurants themselves, cities which have significant numbers of restaurants also have a brief introductory overview.

In *less densely populated areas*, you will generally find it easiest to start with the relevant map at the back of the book, which will guide you to the appropriate place names.

If you are looking for a specific restaurant, the alphabetical index at the very back of the book lists all of the restaurants – London and UK – in this guide.

YOUR CONTRIBUTION

This book is the result of a research effort involving thousands of 'reporters'. As a group, you are 'ordinary' members of the public who share with us summary reviews of the best and the worst of your annual dining experiences. This year, over 9,000 of you gave us some 80,000 reviews in total.

The density of the feedback on London (where many of the top places attract several hundred reviews each) is such that the ratings for the restaurants in the capital are almost exclusively statistical in derivation. (We have, as it happens, visited almost all the restaurants in the London section, anonymously, and at our own expense, but we use our personal experiences only to inform the standpoint from which to interpret the consensus opinion.)

In the case of the more commented-upon restaurants away from the capital, we have adopted an essentially statistical approach very similar to London. In the case of less-visited provincial establishments, however, the interpretation of survey results owes as much to art as it does to science.

In our experience, smaller establishments are – for better or worse – generally quite consistent, and we have therefore felt able to place a relatively high level of confidence in a lower level of commentary. Conservatism on our part, however, may have led to some smaller places being under-rated compared to their more-visited peers.

LONDON INTRODUCTION & SURVEY RESULTS

RANKED BY THE NUMBER OF REPORTERS' VOTES

These are the restaurants which were most frequently mentioned by reporters. (Last year's position is given in brackets.) An asterisk* indicates the first appearance in the list of a recently-opened restaurant.

1	J Sheekey (1)
2	Le Gavroche (4)
3	Scott's (2)
4	Clos Maggiore (6)
5	Brasserie Zédel*
6	Chez Bruce (3)
7	Dinner (5)
8	The Ledbury (7)
9	The Wolseley (9)
10	Pollen Street Social (8)

J Sheekey

11	The Delaunay (16)
12	The Square (15)
13=	La Trompette (14)
13=	Medlar (26)
15	Marcus Wareing (10)
16	Bleeding Heart (13)
17	The Cinnamon Club (20)
18	Galvin Bistrot de Luxe (11)
19	The River Café (18)
20=	Galvin La Chapelle (17)

Dabbous

20=	Le Caprice (22)
22	La Poule au Pot (24)
23=	Benares (34)
23=	Bocca Di Lupo (26)
25	Amaya (34)
26	The Ivy (21)
27	Dabbous*
28	Trinity (-)
29	MEATLiquor (32)
30	Gordon Ramsay (31)

Balthazar

31	Balthazar*
32	Bar Boulud (23)
33	Terroirs (19)
34	Zuma (26)
35	Tayyabs (-)
36	Colbert*
37	Andrew Edmunds (32)
38	Gauthier Soho (-)
39	Hunan (-)
40	Pied à Terre (-)

Colbert

Top gastronomic experience

1   Le Gavroche (3)
2   The Ledbury (2)
3   Dinner (1)
4   Chez Bruce (5)
5   Pollen Street Social (6)
6   Marcus Wareing (4)
7   Dabbous*
8   The Square (7)
9   Medlar*
10 Pied à Terre (8)

Favourite

1   Chez Bruce (1)
2   Le Gavroche (5)
3   The Wolseley (6)
4   Le Caprice (7)
5   J Sheekey (3)
6   The Delaunay (-)
7   Trinity (9)
8   The Ledbury (-)
9   Pollen Street Social (4)
10 The River Café (10)

Best for business

1   The Wolseley (1)
2   The Square (2)
3   The Delaunay (7)
4   Galvin La Chapelle (5)
5   The Don (3)
6   Bleeding Heart (4)
7   L'Anima (8)
8   Scott's (9)
9   1 Lombard Street (-)
10 Savoy Grill (-)

Best for romance

1   Clos Maggiore (1)
2   La Poule au Pot (2)
3   Andrew Edmunds (3)
4   Bleeding Heart (4)
5   Le Gavroche (7)
6   Galvin at Windows (5)
7   Chez Bruce (6)
8   The Ritz Restaurant (-)
9   Le Caprice (8)
10 Café du Marché (-)

Best breakfast/brunch

1   The Wolseley (1)
2   The Delaunay (-)
3=   Roast (2)
3=   Cecconi's (4)
5   Riding House Café (-)
6   Granger & Co (-)
7   The Modern Pantry (-)
8   Duck & Waffle*
9   Smiths (Ground Floor) (3)
10   Dean Street Townhouse (-)

Best bar/pub food

1   The Anchor & Hope (1)
2   The Bull & Last (3)
3   The Harwood Arms (2)
4   The Thomas Cubitt (8)
5   The Anglesea Arms (7)
6   The Grazing Goat*
7   The Canton Arms (4)
8   The Gun (6)
9   The Orange (5)
10   The Ladbroke Arms (-)

Most disappointing cooking

1   Oxo Tower (Rest') (1)
2   Balthazar*
3   Gordon Ramsay (5)
4   Brasserie Zédel*
5   Colbert*
6   Dinner (-)
7   The Wolseley (7)
8   The Ivy (3)
9   Alain Ducasse (-)
10   Ametsa with Arzak Instruction*

Most overpriced restaurant

1   Oxo Tower (Rest') (1)
2   Gordon Ramsay (3)
3   The River Café (5)
4   Dinner (-)
5   Alain Ducasse (7)
6   Cut (-)
7   Marcus Wareing (4)
8   Le Gavroche (8)
9   The Ivy (-)
10   Pollen Street Social (-)

SURVEY HIGHEST RATINGS

FOOD

£85+

1	The Ledbury
2	Le Gavroche
3	One-O-One
4	Pied à Terre
5	Viajante

£65-£84

1	Chez Bruce
2	Story
3	Assaggi
4	Zuma
5	Hunan

£50-£64

1	Sushi Tetsu
2	Dinings
3	Gauthier Soho
4	St John Bread & Wine
5	Dabbous

£40-£49

1	Jin Kichi
2	Babur
3	Il Bordello
4	Corner Room
5	Zucca

£39 or less

1	Ganapati
2	Santa Maria
3	José
4	Taiwan Village
5	Paradise Hampstead

SERVICE

£85+

1	Le Gavroche
2	The Ledbury
3	Pied à Terre
4	Pétrus
5	The Square

£65-£84

1	The Goring Hotel
2	Chez Bruce
3	Story
4	Trinity
5	Alyn Williams

£50-£64

1	Sushi Tetsu
2	About Thyme
3	Oslo Court
4	Outlaw's
5	Caraffini

£40-£49

1	Il Bordello
2	Lamberts
3	Quality Chop House
4	The Crooked Well
5	Indian Zilla

£39 or less

1	Paradise Hampstead
2	Taiwan Village
3	Carob Tree
4	José
5	Ganapati

AMBIENCE

1 The Ritz Restaurant
2 Galvin at Windows
3 Le Gavroche
4 Hélène Darroze
5 Sketch (Lecture Rm)

1 The Bingham
2 Rules
3 The Goring Hotel
4 Bibendum
5 Galvin La Chapelle

1 La Poule au Pot
2 Clos Maggiore
3 Randall & Aubin
4 Bob Bob Ricard
5 Grazing Goat

1 Andrew Edmunds
2 The Atlas
3 The Swan
4 Pizarro
5 Spuntino

1 Gordon's Wine Bar
2 José
3 Brasserie Zédel
4 Barrica
5 Chicken Shop

OVERALL

1 Le Gavroche
2 The Ledbury
3 Pied à Terre
4 Pétrus
5 The Greenhouse

1 Chez Bruce
2 The Bingham
3 Story
4 The Goring Hotel
5 J Sheekey

1 Sushi Tetsu
2 Clos Maggiore
3 J Sheekey Oyster Bar
4 Gauthier Soho
5 L'Aventure

1 Il Bordello
2 The Atlas
3 Babur
4 Lamberts
5 The Swan

1 José
2 Paradise Hampstead
3 Ganapati
4 Barrica
5 Taiwan Village

SURVEY BEST BY CUISINE

These are the restaurants which received the best average food ratings (excluding establishments with a small or notably local following).

Where the most common types of cuisine are concerned, we present the results in two price-brackets. For less common cuisines, we list the top three, regardless of price.

For further information about restaurants which are particularly notable for their food, see the cuisine lists starting on page 172. These indicate, using an asterisk*, restaurants which offer exceptional or very good food.

British, Modern

£50 and over
1   The Ledbury
2   Chez Bruce
3   Story
4   Trinity
5   Kitchen W8

Under £50
1   Lamberts
2   The Clove Club
3   Abbeville Kitchen
4   10 Greek Street
5   The Ladbroke Arms

French

£50 and over
1   Le Gavroche
2   Gauthier Soho
3   Pied à Terre
4   Pétrus
5   The Square

Under £50
1   Charlotte's Bistro
2   Brawn
3   Charlotte's Place
4   Green Man & Fr Horn
5   Mill Lane Bistro

Italian/Mediterranean

£50 and over
1   Assaggi
2   Al Boccon di'vino
3   Murano
4   The River Café
5   Quirinale

Under £50
1   Il Bordello
2   Zucca
3   Dehesa
4   Pentolina
5   Portobello Ristorante

Indian & Pakistani

£50 and over
1   Amaya
2   Rasoi
3   The Cinnamon Club
4   Tamarind
5   Benares

Under £50
1   Ganapati
2   Babur
3   Paradise Hampstead
4   Potli
5   Tayyabs

Chinese

Japanese

British, Traditional

Vegetarian

Burgers, etc

Pizza

Fish & Chips

Thai

Steaks & Grills

Fish & Seafood

Fusion

Spanish

Turkish

Lebanese

TOP SPECIAL DEALS

The following menus allow you to eat in the restaurants concerned at a significant discount when compared to their evening à la carte prices.

The prices used are calculated in accordance with our usual formula (i.e. three courses with house wine, coffee and tip).

Special menus are by their nature susceptible to change – please check that they are still available.

Weekday lunch

£80+ Gordon Ramsay

£70+ Hélène Darroze

£65+ Alain Ducasse
Apsleys
Cut
Dinner
Pied à Terre
Wiltons

£60+ L'Atelier de Joel Robuchon
Benares
Hibiscus
The Ledbury
Marcus Wareing
Oxo Tower (Rest')

£55+ Le Gavroche
Murano
Pollen Street Social
Seven Park Place
Theo Randall
Thirty Six
Tom Aikens
Viajante

£50+ Babbo
Bibendum
Bo London
Corrigan's Mayfair
Cotidie
HKK
Lutyens
One-O-One
Oxo Tower (Brass')
Pétrus
Le Pont de la Tour
Sumosan

£45+ Alyn Williams
L'Autre Pied
The Cinnamon Club
Club Gascon
Criterion
Dabbous
Galvin at Windows
Galvin La Chapelle
Gauthier Soho
Koffmann's
Launceston Place
Mari Vanna
maze
maze Grill
Orrery
The Providores
Spice Market
Trinity

£40+ Angelus
L'Anima
Babylon
Bar Boulud
Belvedere
Bonds
Cambio de Tercio
Chor Bizarre
Le Colombier
Hix
Kitchen W8
Lucio
Morgan M
Novikov (Italian restaurant)
La Poule au Pot
Quirinale
Sale e Pepe
Tamarind
Zaika

£35+ Albannach
The Almeida
aqua kyoto
L'Aventure
Benihana
Bradley's
Butlers Wharf Chop House
Caffè Caldesi
La Collina
Les Deux Salons
Dorchester Grill
The Enterprise
Essenza
L'Etranger
Franco's
Frederick's
Galvin Bistrot de Luxe
High Timber
Magdalen
The Malt House
Mint Leaf
Momo
Moti Mahal
Odette's
Pellicano
Quo Vadis
Racine
Red Fort
Les Trois Garçons
Villa Bianca

£30+	Archipelago		Mazi		Indian Zing
	Bistrotheque		Mediterraneo		Ishtar
	Bluebird		Mon Plaisir		Polish Club
	La Bouchée		Osteria dell'Arancio		The Orange Tree
	Boudin Blanc		Pissarro		The Palmerston
	Chez Patrick		Sam's Brasserie		Tierra Peru
	Cinnamon Kitchen		Sonny's Kitchen		
	Cinnamon Soho		Sophie's Steakhouse	£20+	Cellar Gascon
	E l l even Park Walk		Verru		Empress of Sichuan
	Formosa Dining Room		The Victoria		Joe Allen
	Franklins				Le Sacré-Coeur
	The Frontline Club	£25+	Alquimia		Sichuan Folk
	The Gun		Chabrot Bistrot des Halles		Yum Yum
	The Hoxton Grill		Chapters		
	Lamberts		China Tang	£15+	Chelsea Bun Diner
	Latium		Daquise		
	The Lockhart		Le Deuxième	£10+	Sree Krishna
	Market		Grumbles		

Pre/post theatre (and early evening)

£80+	Marcus Wareing		Indigo		Odette's
			maze		Orso
£60+	L'Atelier de Joel		maze Grill		Quo Vadis
	Robuchon		Tamarind		Red Fort
	Thirty Six				Trishna
		£40+	Bar Boulud		
£55+	Theo Randall		L'Etranger	£30+	Bistrotheque
	Wiltons		Hix		La Bouchée
			Kitchen W8		Cinnamon Soho
£50+	Bentley's		Morgan M		Harrison's
	The Ivy		Quirinale		Latium
	Koffmann's	£35+	Albannach		Mele e Pere
	Oxo Tower (Brass')		The Almeida		
			The Avenue	£25+	Le Deuxième
£45+	Axis		The Balcon		Grumbles
	Brasserie Max		Bradley's		Mon Plaisir
	Le Caprice		Christopher's		
	The Cinnamon Club		Dean Street Townhouse	£20+	Joe Allen
	Criterion		L'Escargot		
	Galvin La Chapelle		Frederick's	£15+	Carom at Meza
	Homage		Galvin Bistrot de Luxe		

Sunday lunch

£45+	Bradley's	£40+	The Almeida	£30+	Les Associés
	Le Colombier		Garnier		
	Galvin Bistrot de Luxe		MASH Steakhouse	£25+	Grumbles
	Koffmann's				Malabar
		£35+	Maggie Jones's		Polish Club
			Sonny's Kitchen		
			The Wells		

THE RESTAURANT SCENE

No change... but all change

This year we record 125 openings, a little down on last year (134), but comfortably within the range – 120 to 142 – which history suggests is normal in the current century. Closings, at 56, are well down on the previous year (74), and very low by historical standards – the lowest, in fact, since 2000. (See lists of openings and closings on pages 26 and 27.)

In fact, so low is the number of closings this year that the number of net openings (openings minus closings), 69, is not far short of the all-time record net openings figure of 75, which was in our 2006 guide.

This same impression of robustness is conveyed by a bellwether ratio we track each year: the ratio of openings to closings, which tends to follow a clear cycle. This year's ratio (2.2:1) emphatically continues the rebound which was apparent last year (1.8) from the low point of the cycle (1.5) recorded the year before that.

These numbers suggest that the market is in an up phase, which impression is confirmed if we look at our annual best-of-crop selection. Every year, we choose what seem to us to be the ten most significant openings of the year, and our selection for this year is as follows:

Balthazar	The Clove Club
Five Fields	Grain Store
HKK	Kitchen Table
Shiori	Story
Tartufo	White Rabbit

The initial impression is of continuity: last year was a very strong year, and this is too. The impression of steady-as-she-goes is, however, misleading. Of our selection last year, no fewer than seven of the ten were in the key West End postcode, W1. And this year... just one!

Next stop: the doughnut

Historically, London restaurants have had a homeland. Pre War, it was those ill-matched W1 twins, Soho and Mayfair. In the '60s, then-bohemian Chelsea began to take over. In 1992, when we published our first guide, the heartland was still the SWs. Many readers under 30 will be surprised to know that it was only in the late-'90s that a restaurant scene of any note re-emerged in W1 itself!

And now? Well, the interesting thing about our top ten of the year is that not only are they largely non-central, but they come from all points of the compass – a sort of doughnut, if you like, of which the West End is the hole.

As the new skyscrapers and tower cranes looming over many non-central areas of London suggest, London is well on the way to becoming a city with many nodes of economic and cultural activity, rather in the style of a Tokyo or Shanghai. (And less and less like the Parisian model, where more or less everything still – more than two centuries on from the Revolution – radiates from the Place de la Concorde.) London's restaurant scene – or rather, now, scenes – cannot help reflecting this, and ever more so over coming years.

New York, of course, has already been through all this – Greewich Village, to Midtown, to Downtown, over the bridge to Brooklyn… and now people even talk of Queens as the next frontier!

Perhaps the fact that NYC has 'been through it all before' to some extent explains the ongoing popularity of American, and especially NYC, concepts and influences in London at the moment. These include:

- the opening of new operations by US-based operators (*Balthazar, Chop Shop, Five Guys, Hoi Polloi* and *Shake Shack)*
- explicitly US-inspired culinary concepts, such as *Jackson & White, The Lockhart* and *Soho Diner*
- meat-based cooking generally, and particularly the ongoing obsession with steaks and burgers
- a general desire to imitate New York (and especially Brooklyn) styling, even in non-US restaurants.

It would not be unfair to note that much of the American inspiration has had much more to do with style than content! Reporters' (and press critics') poor reception of the long-awaited *Balthazar* is a case in point.

We observed this American trend last year, and many of the other macro-trends currently apparent are also by and large a continuation of what has gone before. Small plates presentation, for example, is now almost the new normal. South American and Hispanic influences continue to be important. The idea that London has 'no good Japanese restaurants' recedes ever further into history.

One new significant trend: very small restaurants, such as *Marianne* and *Kitchen Table at Bubbledogs*. Such ventures, which might once have been dismissed as bizarre, are signs that London's restaurant goers should be ready for pretty much anything. Alongside the huge expansion of the geographical area of restaurant-going London, we are seeing, and will see in the future, more and more different and exciting concepts from all parts of the globe. And – who knows? – perhaps even some generated here in London!

Prices

The average price of dinner for one at establishments listed in the guide is £47.68 (compared to £46.55 last year). Prices have risen by 3.5% in the past 12 months – exactly the same as last year's increase and, once again, a whisker ahead of the rise in consumer prices more generally.

OPENINGS AND CLOSURES

Openings (125)

A Wong
Albion, SE1
Alquimia
Ametsa with
  Arzak Instruction
Amica Bio, WC1
Assiette Anglaise
Beard to Tail
The Berners Tavern
Big Easy WC2
Bird in Hand
Bird of Smithfield
Bo London
Bone Daddies
Bonnie Gull
Bouchon Fourchette
Boulestin
Brasserie Chavot
Bubbledogs, Kitchen Table
Bumpkin SW3
Burger & Lobster
  SW1 & EC4

Bush Dining Hall
Caffe Vegnano WC1
Il Calcio W1 & SW5
Carom @ Meza
Casse-Croute
Chabrot Bistrot des Halles
Chop Shop
Chotto Matte
The Clove Club
Le Coq
Coya
The Dairy
Dirty Burger
Dishoom E2
Duke's Brew & Que
Eat Tokyo W6
The Fish & Chip Shop
The Five Fields
Five Guys
Flat Iron
Flesh & Buns
Foxlow

Garufin
Gin Joint
Grain Store
Greenberry Café
Grillshack
Gymkhana
Haché EC1
Hoi Polloi
Honest Burgers
  W11 & NW1
Honey & Co
Hummus Bros EC1
Hutong
Jackson & Whyte
The Jam Tree SW4
John Salt
Jubo
K10 Appold Street
Kaspar's Seafood & Grill
The Keeper's House
Kerbisher & Malt W5
Kirazu

Keeper's House

Koya-Ko
Little Social
The Lockhart
Made in Italy, James Street
The Magazine Restaurant
The Malt House
Marianne
Maxela
Meat Mission
MEATmarket
Michael Nadra NW1
Moxon's Fish Bar
Natural Kitchen EC3
Newman Street Tavern
Notes N7
Notting Hill Kitchen
No 11 Pimlico Road
The Oak W12
Obika, W1, SW3, E14
Oblix

Olivocarne
One Canada Square
Ostuni
Patty & Bun
Picture
Pig & Butcher
Pizza Pilgrims
Plum + Spilt Milk
Prawn on the Lawn
Il Ristorante, Bulgari Hotel
Rossopomodoro
   N1, NW1, SW18
Sager & Wilde
Season Kitchen
Shake Shack
The Shed
The Shiori
Shoryu Ramen SW1 & W1
The Sign of the Don
Smiths Brasserie

The Smokehouse Islington
Social Eating House
Soho Diner
Sticks & Sushi
Story
Sweet Thursday
Tartufo
Toasted
Tom's Kitchen E14
Tommi's Burger Joint
Tozi
Tramontana Brindisa
28-50 W1
White Rabbit
Whyte & Brown
Wright Brothers E1
Yashin SW7
Zoilo

Closures (56)

The Ark
Aurelia
Back to Basics
Bar Trattoria Semplice
Bincho Yaktori, EC1
Butcher & Grill, SW19
Cantinetta
Casa Batavia
Le Cassoulet
The Chelsea Brasserie
Chez Liline
Chrysan
Cicada
Daphne
Delfina
La Delizia SW18
The Ebury
Fig
Fish Place

The Forge
Frankies Italian
Gordon Ramsay at
Claridges
Great Eastern Dining
Room
Green's, EC3
Hix Belgravia
Langan's Bistro
The Luxe
Mar I Tera, W1
The Markham Inn
Mennula
Moolis
Nahm
North Road
Notting Hill Brasserie
Odin's
L'Oranger

Prism
Ransome's Dock
Ristorante Semplice
Roganic
Le Saint Julien
Sardo Canale
Savoy, River Restaurant
Searcy's Brasserie
Serafino
Le Suquet
Sushi of Shiori
Tapasia
Tempo
Tom Ilic
Trojka
Uli
Verta
Wabi
Waterloo Brasserie

EATING IN LONDON FAQs

How should I use this guide?

You will often wish to use this guide in a practical way. At heart, the issue will usually be geographical – where can we eat near...? To answer such questions, the Maps (from page 224) and Area Overviews (from page 186) are the place to start. The latter tell you all the key facts about the restaurants – perhaps dozens of 'em – in a particular area in the space of a couple of pages. These Area Overviews are unique, so please do spend a second to have a look!

This section, though, is about seeking out restaurants for the joy of it – a few thoughts to lead you to London's best restaurants for particular types of events, or to lead you down byways you might not otherwise have considered.

What makes London special?

Cosmopolitanism has always been part of London's make-up, but in recent years this diversity has more and more been allied with quality. A 'virtuous' circle has set in, with London becoming an acknowledged destination for chefs and restaurateurs from all over the word, which has further reinforced the capital's name as the 'place to be', which has then sucked in further talent. This process has now gone on for long enough that London is often identified (and not just by Londoners) as one of the world's great restaurant cities.

This process has been accompanied and in part sustained by another virtuous circle – a greater interest in dining out by the capital's under-35s than was traditionally the case. This has encouraged a greater provision of dining out opportunities suited to that demographic. Younger people being, generally speaking, more novelty-seeking than silver haired types, the whole restaurant scene has become much buzzier.

The result is that there is no restaurant scene in the world today which is more exciting – and deservedly so – than the one we enjoy in London.

Which is London's best restaurant?

In a restaurant scene as diverse and interesting as London's, 'best' – more and more – means different things to different people, so it gets ever harder to give a single answer. If the question is translated to mean 'which is the best grand French restaurant in town', the answer is pretty clearly – still! – *Le Gavroche*. London's original grand restaurant of recent times has been performing particularly strongly of late. If you're looking for a more modern – and informal – take on the grand dining experience, *The Ledbury* is probably the place to go. For other truly tip-top suggestions, please use the lists on pages 20-21.

What about something a little more reasonably priced?

There is a reason that *Chez Bruce* has just been voted London's favourite restaurant for an amazing 9th consecutive year – if you're looking for a top quality all-round experience at a level which, if not inexpensive, is less than ruinous, it is a destination it's hard to beat. The only downside is that you have to make the schlep to Wandsworth to enjoy it.

A step down in the price-and-grandeur stakes, how about the excellent *Lambert's*... but that's even further out, in Balham. Just too far? A formula rather similar to Chez Bruce (if not yet quite as good) can be enjoyed, somewhat more conveniently for many people, at Chelsea's rising *Medlar*. Or, for an all-round foodie treat of a much trendier type, head to Shoreditch's former Town Hall, now home to *The Clove Club*.

What about some really good suggestions in the heart of the West End?

It is becoming less the case than once it was that you need to head out of the West End for a really good meal without breaking the bank. Witness such possibilities as *Little Social*, cutely hidden away in Mayfair, and *Gauthier Soho*. You have to ring for entry to the latter's townhouse premises, adding to the sense of occasion.

What about a big night out?

Sometimes, of course, the food is just part of the package, and you're looking for theatre and people-watching as much as a meal. The obvious choice for such a trip, especially if you are entertaining visitors from out-of-town, is *The Wolseley* – the food may not be that remarkable, but the 'package' – which includes a remarkable Edwardian interior and a location right next to the Ritz – is very hard to beat. The food may not be earth-shattering, but no one seems to mind.

Other West End establishments offering a grand all-round formula, of which the food is just one part of the whole, albeit an important one, include such stand-outs as *Scott's* (Mayfair), *Le Caprice* (St James's), *The Delaunay* (Covent Garden) and *J Sheekey* – the long-established fish restaurant, hidden-away in Theatreland, which was once again this year the survey's most commented-on restaurant.

Small is beautiful

Much of the gastronomic excitement of recent years has come from 'tapas' specialists, inspired not just by Spain but by SW France and beyond. Such concepts have brought sophisticated yet affordable formats to the heart of the West End. *Barrafina* represents the classic tapas ideal, with outfits such as *Bocca di Lupo, Ceviche, Copita, Dehesa, Lima* and *Salt Yard* all offering their own variations on the theme.

EATING IN LONDON FAQs

What about British cooking?

Until recently, the idea of British restaurants (other than simple grill or roast houses) was pretty much unknown, as most restaurants were French or Italian, or, in more recent times, Indian or Chinese.

It was the Smithfield restaurant *St John*, established in 1994, whose dedication to old-fashioned (and usually offal-heavy) British cooking captured the zeitgeist and re-awakened an interest in traditional food culture. Other notable British restaurants often trace their roots back to St John, including *Magdalen* (South Bank), *Great Queen Street* (Covent Garden), *Hereford Road* (Bayswater) and, of course – currently best of all – *St John Bread & Wine* (Shoreditch).

A couple of years ago, the trend reached a zenith, at least in a media-friendly sense, with the opening of Heston Blumenthal's good-but-pricey *Dinner* (Knightsbridge). But a lot of the 'British' cooking is taking place in gastropubs…

What are gastropubs?

Essentially, bistros in pub premises. They come in many styles. What many people think of as the original gastropub (*The Eagle*, 1991) still looks very much like a pub with a food counter. Few of the best gastropubs are particularly central. The handy location of the *Anchor & Hope*, on the South Bank, is part of the reason for its great popularity. Other stars include the *Bull & Last* (Kentish Town), the *Canton Arms* (Stockwell) and the *Harwood Arms* (Fulham).

Isn't London supposed to be a top place for curry?

Many visitors come to London wanting to 'try Indian'. The choice of 'Indians' – a term including Pakistani and Bangladeshi restaurants in this context – is so great, however, that you then need to decide what sort of Indian you want to try.

You want value? Two top names in the East End (and hence relatively accessible from central London) are almost legendary 'experiences' – the *Lahore Kebab House* and *Tayyabs*. The predominantly veggie *Rasa* group also includes some very good value options. Or, for an immersive experience, go down to Tooting, and check out a fixture like *Sree Krishna*.

At the other end of the scale (and, for the most part, right in the heart of town) are the 'nouvelle Indians', where spicy dishes are presented with a heavy European influence. *Amaya*, *Benares*, *The Cinnamon Club*, *The Painted Heron*, *Quilon*, *Rasoi*, *Trishna*, *Veeraswamy* and *Zaika* are all examples of plush restaurants just as suited to business (and in many cases romance) as their European price-equivalents.

In fact, wherever you are in London, you should be in reach of an Indian restaurant of more-than-average note – search out the asterisked restaurants in the Indian and Pakistani lists commencing on pages 181 and 182 respectively.

Any money-saving tips?

- If you have the luxury of being in charge of your own timetable, there are some extraordinary bargains to be had simply by lunching rather than dining, and the more reasonably priced menus often available at the lunch service give you the opportunity to check out establishments which might otherwise be simply unattainable. See the spread on pages 22 and 23.

- Think ethnic – for a food 'experience' at modest cost, you're likely to be better off going Indian, Thai, Chinese or Vietnamese (to choose four of the most obvious cuisines) than English, French or Italian. The days when there was any sort of assumption that ethnic restaurants were – in terms of comfort, service and décor – in any way inferior to European ones is long gone, but they are still often somewhat cheaper.

- Don't assume the West End is the obvious destination. It is becoming less and less true anyway that the best and most interesting London restaurants are necessarily to be found within the confines of the Circle Line, so don't be reluctant to explore! Use the maps at the back of this book to identify restaurants near tube stations on a line that's handy for you.

- If you must dine in the West End, try to find either pre-theatre (generally before 7 pm) or post-theatre (generally after 10 pm) menus. You will generally save at least the cost of a cinema ticket, compared to dining à la carte. Many of the more upmarket restaurants in Theatreland do such deals. For some of our top suggestions, see page 23.

- Use this book! Don't take pot luck, when you can benefit from the pre-digested views of thousands of other diners-out. Choose a place with a ❶ or ❷ for food, and you're very likely to eat much better than if you walk in somewhere 'on spec' – this is good advice anywhere, but is most particularly so in the West End.

- Once you have decided that you want to eat within a particular area, use the Area Overviews (starting on p186) to identify the restaurants that are offering top value. We have gone to a lot of trouble to boil down a huge amount of data into the results which are handily summarised in such lists. Please use them! You are unlikely to regret it.

- Visit our website, www.hardens.com for the latest reviews, news and offers, and to sign up for our annual spring survey.

Gauthier

Grain Store

Bubbledogs

Marianne

LONDON DIRECTORY

A Cena TW1 £50 ❸❷❸
418 Richmond Rd   8288 0108   1–4A
For "the best Italian food around Richmond",
many locals would seek out this "always convivial"
St Margaret's spot – the cooking "maintains high
standards", and "you can always find something
different on the wine list". / TW1 2EB;
www.acena.co.uk; @acenarestaurant; 10 pm; closed
Mon L & Sun D; booking: max 6, Fri & Sat.

A Wong SW1 NEW £33 ❸❸❸
70-71 Wilton Rd   7828 8931   2–4B
"Not your standard Chinese menu!" – this "noisy"
café-style newcomer has made quite a splash
in under-provided Pimlico (though it's rather less
of a hit with reporters than it has been with the
critics); "particularly good" dim sum is a highlight.
/ SW1 1DE; www.awong.co.uk/; 10.15 pm; closed
Mon L & Sun.

The Abbeville SW4 £44 ❹❸❷
67-69 Abbeville Rd   8675 2201   10–2D
"Just as good for a pint and a packet of crisps as a
three-course meal", this "busy" Clapham back street
boozer is invariably hailed as an "enjoyable"
destination. / SW4 9JW; www.renaissancepubs.co.uk;
@renaissancepubs; 10.30 pm, Sun 9 pm; SRA-56%.

**Abbeville Kitchen
SW4** £46 ❷❷❸
47 Abbeville Rd   8772 1110   10–2D
"An exceptional neighbourhood restaurant" –
with its "genuinely interesting" British fare,
"fantastic" staff and "very convivial" setting,
this Clapham yearling is a real all-round crowd-
pleaser. / SW4 9JX; www.abbevillekitchen.com;
@abbevillek; 10.30 pm, Sun 9.30 pm; closed Mon L,
Tue L & Wed L.

Abeno £40 ❸❸❸
47 Museum St, WC1   7405 3211   2–1C
17-18 Great Newport St, WC2
7379 1160   4–3B
"Unique" and "fun", these West End 'okonomi-yaki'
(Japanese omelette) parlours – where the cooking
takes place at your table – make entertaining
venues for a light bite. / www.abeno.co.uk;
10 pm-11 pm; WC2 no booking.

The Abingdon W8 £55 ❸❸❷
54 Abingdon Rd   7937 3339   5–2A
"The best local ever" – this "buzzy" backstreet
Kensington fixture may be on the "expensive" side,
but it's "always popular", thanks to its "solid"
standards and "welcoming" style; the cute booths
at the back suit "small groups or romance".
/ W8 6AP; www.theabingdon.co.uk; 10.30 pm, Fri & Sat
11 pm, Sun 10 pm; set Sun L £39 (FP).

Abokado £17 ❹❹❹
16 Newman St, W1   7636 9218   2–1B
160 Drury Ln, WC2   7242 5600   4–2D
The Lexington, 40-56 City Rd, EC1
7608 2620   12–1A
63 Cowcross St, EC1   7490 4303   9–1A
33 Fleet St, EC4   7353 8284   9–2A
"Fresh choices for a light lunch, and a quick
turnaround", especially "a nice range of cheap
sushi" – most reports on this small (mainly) take-
away chain are complimentary. / www.abokado.com;
7.30 pm Mon-Fri, NW1 9 pm, 5 pm Sat & Sun;
no Amex; no booking.

About Thyme SW1 £55 ❷❶❸
82 Wilton Rd   7821 7504   2–4B
"By far the best restaurant round Victoria", say fans
– this "charming and welcoming" Pimlico stalwart
is "not cheap", but its "hearty" Iberian-influenced
food is "consistently good and interesting".
/ SW1V 1DL; www.aboutthyme.co.uk; 10.30 pm;
closed Sun.

L'Absinthe NW1 £45 ❹❷❸
40 Chalcot Rd   7483 4848   8–3B
"Très francais!"; the owners "delight in their Gallic
roots", and offer a "warm welcome" to this "closely-
packed" Primrose Hill corner bistro, which serves
a "limited" menu of "well-presented" classic dishes.
/ NW1 8LS; www.labsinthe.co.uk; @absinthe07jc;
10.30 pm, Sun 9.30 pm; closed Mon.

Abu Zaad W12 £23 ❸❸❹
29 Uxbridge Rd   8749 5107   7–1C
"A delightful Syrian landmark, in buzzing Shepherd's
Bush" – a café/takeaway near the market, where
"the prices are excellent, and the food's even
better!" / W12 8LH; www.abuzaad.co.uk; 11 pm;
no Amex.

Adams Café W12 £30 ❸❶❷
77 Askew Rd   8743 0572   7–1B
A (very good) Shepherd's Bush greasy spoon by day
which, as it "turns Tunisian" by night, develops
a "warm family atmosphere"; the owners are
"delightful", and offer "generous" portions of North
African grills, couscous and tagines, plus some "well-
priced" wines (or BYO). / W12 9AH;
www.adamscafe.co.uk; 10 pm; closed Sun.

**Addie's Thai Café
SW5** £31 ❷❸❸
121 Earl's Court Rd   7259 2620   5–2A
"Top-value Bangkok street cooking, with genuine
flavours" – this "Earl's Court staple" continues
to please all who comment on it... "when you can
get a table", that is. / SW5 9RL; www.addiesthai.co.uk;
11 pm, Sun 10.30 pm; no Amex.

Admiral Codrington
SW3 **£53** ❸④④
17 Mossop St   7581 0005   5–2C
*"Tucked away" in a back street, a "fun" (and noisy)
Chelsea stalwart that's "always packed";
menu highlight? – the burgers are "unexpectedly
brilliant".* / SW3 2LY; www.theadmiralcodrington.co.uk;
@TheAdCod; 10 pm, Thu-Sat 11 pm, Sun 9.30 pm.

Afghan Kitchen N1 **£26** ❷④④
35 Islington Grn   7359 8019   8–3D
*A tiny café, in the heart of Islington – "the menu
only has a few items", but they're "all delicious, fresh
and incredibly tasty".* / N1 8DU; 11 pm; closed
Mon & Sun; no credit cards.

Aglio e Olio SW10 **£41** ❸❸④
194 Fulham Rd   7351 0070   5–3B
*"Crazy-cramped" and "amazingly noisy",
this "efficient" little café, by the Chelsea
& Westminster Hospital, offers "large portions
of hearty and fresh Italian staples"
at "very reasonable prices".* / SW10 9PN; 11.30 pm.

Akari N1 **£38** ❷❸❸
196 Essex Rd   7226 9943   8–3D
*"You don't expect amazing sushi to be served in a
converted pub", but this family-run Japanese
in Islington does just that – "everything is delicious".*
/ N1 8LZ; 11 pm; closed Mon, Tue-Fri D only, Sat & Sun
open L & D; no Amex.

Al Duca SW1 **£45** ④④⑤
4-5 Duke of York St   7839 3090   3–3D
*Fans say it offers "good modern cooking
at reasonable prices", but this St James's Italian has
quite a few critics too – they find the style
"nondescript" and service "cold".* / SW1Y 6LA;
www.alduca-restaurant.co.uk; 11 pm; closed Sun.

Al Forno **£37** ④❸❷
349 Upper Richmond Rd, SW15
8878 7522   10–2A
2a King's Rd, SW19   8540 5710   10–2B
*These "buzzing" Italians are classic examples of the
"old school", complete with "friendly", if sometimes
"chaotic", service; they don't delight everyone though
– doubters say they're "like a step back into the
'80s".* / SW15 11 pm; SW19 11.30 pm, Sun & Mon
10.30 pm.

Al Hamra W1 **£53** ④④④
31-33 Shepherd Mkt   7493 1954   3–4B
*A "pricey" Lebanese stalwart, once regarded
as quite an 'institution', but which is mainly of note
nowadays for its charming al fresco tables
in Mayfair's Shepherd Market.* / W1J 7PT;
www.alhamrarestaurant.co.uk; 11.30 pm.

Al Sultan W1 **£45** ❸❷④
51-52 Hertford St   7408 1155   3–4B
*This rather nondescript Lebanese, just off Mayfair's
Shepherd Market, inspires only modest survey
commentary; most reporters, though, would say the
food is at least "good".* / W1J 7ST; www.alsultan.co.uk;
11 pm.

Al-Waha W2 **£46** ❷④④
75 Westbourne Grove   7229 0806   6–1B
*"Everyone we take loves its high quality!" – a low-
key Bayswater fixture, serving "authentic" Lebanese
cuisine.* / W2 4UL; www.alwaharestaurant.com; 11 pm;
no Amex.

Alain Ducasse
Dorchester W1 **£121** ④❸④
53 Park Ln   7629 8866   3–3A
*"The three Michelin stars are for the Ducasse
name, not anything achieved here!" – this "bland"
Mayfair super-chef outpost is a "lazy" sort
of operation; it's not that "exquisite" dishes are
unknown, but they are not sufficiently prevalent
to justify the "extortionate" prices.* / W1K 1QA;
www.alainducasse-dorchester.com; 9.30 pm; closed Mon,
Sat L & Sun; jacket; set weekday L £68 (FP).

Alba EC1 **£46** ❸❷④
107 Whitecross St   7588 1798   12–2A
*"Hearty and rustic" Piedmontese cooking is the
speciality at this veteran restaurant, in a side street
near the Barbican – a "high-quality" establishment
that's "great for a business lunch"; "lovely" staff add
life to the rather "airport lounge" interior.*
/ EC1Y 8JH; www.albarestaurant.com; 10.45 pm;
closed Sun.

Albannach WC2 **£58** ④④❸
66 Trafalgar Sq   7930 0066   2–3C
*Bang on "Tourist Central", a large Scottish-themed
bar/restaurant; it's a "noisy", quite "fun" venue,
but the food is "missing something".* / WC2N 5DS;
www.albannach.co.uk; 10.45 pm, Sun 6 pm; closed
Sun D; set weekday L & pre-theatre £37 (FP).

Albertine W12 **£33** ④❷❷
1 Wood Ln   8743 9593   7–1C
*"Boldly resisting the rise of Westfield over the road",
this wine bar "oasis" is a "reliable" old-timer, where
"a wonderful wine list", "competitively priced",
accompanies the "simple but tasty fare".*
/ W12 7DP; 10.30 pm; closed Sat L & Sun; no Amex.

The Albion N1 **£45** ❸❸❶
10 Thornhill Rd   7607 7450   8–3D
*"It'll redeem your faith in gastropubs!"; fans adore
the "lovely", "cosy" style (and beautiful garden)
of this "quintessential North London boozer", where
the "wonderful Sunday roasts" are a particular
highlight.* / N1 1HW; www.the-albion.co.uk;
@thealbionpub; 10 pm, Sun 9 pm; SRA-63%.

Albion £44 ④④❸
NEO Bankside, Holland St, SE1
7827 4343 9–3B NEW
2-4 Boundary St, E2 7729 1051 12–1B
Especially for breakfast, Sir Terence Conran's "airy"
and "buzzy", "'50s-style" café, in an "über-cool"
part of Shoreditch, can make a "fabulous"
destination; service, though, is "not that effective",
and other meals can seem decidedly
"unremarkable"; now also on the South Bank.
/ 11 pm.

Ali Baba NW1 £23 ❸②④
32 Ivor Pl 7723 5805 2–1A
"Authentic Egyptian food in an authentic Egyptian
restaurant" – this living-room-style Marylebone café
(behind a takeaway) is "not very atmospheric"
(unless you like the TV blaring much of the time),
but it makes an interesting budget destination; BYO.
/ NW1 6DA; midnight; no credit cards.

All Star Lanes £46 ④❸❸
Victoria Hs, Bloomsbury Pl, WC1
7025 2676 2–1D
Whiteley's, 6 Porchester Gdns, W2
7313 8363 6–1C
Old Truman Brewery, 95 Brick Ln, E1
7426 9200 12–2C
Westfield Stratford City, E20
3167 2434 1–1D
"Like being in Happy Days!" – these American
diners attached to bowling alleys may not be places
of culinary pilgrimage, but they're undoubtedly
"fun", and they dish up "reasonable" burgers and
other staples. / www.allstarlanes.co.uk; WC1 10.30 pm,
Fri & Sat midnight, Sun 9 pm; E1 10 pm; W2 10.30 pm,
Fri-Sun 11 pm; E2 9.30 pm; WC1 & W2 closed
L Mon-Thu.

Alloro W1 £59 ❸❸④
19-20 Dover St 7495 4768 3–3C
"A discreet location for a snappy business lunch" –
this Mayfair Italian is almost invariably touted as an
"utterly reliable" destination, where the food
is "good, if a touch forgettable". / W1S 4LU;
www.alloro-restaurant.co.uk; 10.30 pm; closed
Sat L & Sun.

The Almeida N1 £58 ❸④④
30 Almeida St 7354 4777 8–2D
Fans of this D&D group operation near Islington's
eponymous theatre tout it as a "straightforwardly
good" option with "a little more style than the local
norm"; critics though still see it as "uninspired" –
"it could be so much better". / N1 1AD;
www.almeida-restaurant.co.uk; 10.30 pm; closed
Mon L & Sun D; set weekday L & pre-theatre £37
(FP); SRA-65%.

Alounak £29 ❸④❸
10 Russell Gdns, W14 7603 1130 7–1D
44 Westbourne Grove, W2 7229 0416 6–1B
"Tasty kebabs and the best meze" inspire high
loyalty to these "authentic", "easy-going" and
"incredibly cheap" Persian cafés in Bayswater and
Olympia; BYO is another bonus. / 11.30 pm; no Amex.

Alquimia SW15 NEW £54 ❷❷❷
Putney Wharf 8785 0508 10–2B
"A new local favourite that deserves to do well" –
a tapas bar in Putney Wharf, which impresses early-
days visitors with its "quality" cooking and its
"charming" service; the setting is "attractive" too
(though only the window/al fresco tables have
views). / SW15 2JX; www.alquimiarestaurant.co.uk;
11.30, Sun 10.30 pm; set weekday L £28 (FP).

Alyn Williams
Westbury Hotel W1 £73 ❷⓪④
Bond St 7078 9579 3–2C
Alyn Williams creates some "sophisticated" and
"stunningly executed" dishes at this "well-spaced"
chamber, hidden away inside a Bond Street hotel;
while "stylish", its decor lacks va va voom, but the
"fantastically unstuffy" service offers much
compensation; "unbeatable" set lunch. / W1S 2YF;
www.westburymayfair.com; 10.30 pm; closed
Sat L & Sun; jacket; set weekday L £45 (FP).

Amaranth SW18 £30 ❷❸❷
346 Garratt Ln 8874 9036 10–2B
"Amazing food at incredible-value prices, and BYO
too!" – that's the deal at this "cramped" but
"very friendly" Earlsfield Thai. / SW18 4ES; 10.30 pm;
D only, closed Sun; no Amex.

Amaranto
Four Seasons Hotel
W1 £83 ④④⑤
Hamilton Pl 7319 5206 3–4A
A shadow of its one-time gastronomic self;
this Mayfair hotel boasts a "spacious" dining room
in "James-Bond-goes-Arabic" style – it inspires few
reports, too many of the "absolutely awful" variety.
/ W1J 7DR; www.fourseasons.com; @amarantolondon;
10.30 pm; jacket.

Amaya SW1 £73 ⓪❸❷
Halkin Arc, 19 Motcomb St 7823 1166 5–1D
"Chef Karunesh Khanna is a magician!";
his "very clever" tapas-style dishes – cooked on an
open grill, and offering "clean and aromatic flavours
across the board" – make this sleek and "tucked
away" Belgravian arguably "the best of London's
aspirational Indians". / SW1X 8JT;
www.realindianfood.com; 11.30 pm, Sun 10.30 pm.

Ametsa with Arzak Instruction
Halkin Hotel SW1 NEW £85 ⑤④⑤
5 Halkin St 7333 1234 2–3A
"A pig's ear!"; for fans, the "invigorating" cuisine at Juan Mari Arzak's Basque import to Belgravia may offer a "superlative" culinary fantasy, but many critics just report a "dismal" experience, and at "mad" prices too; the room that was Nahm (RIP) remains as "cold and clinical" as ever. / SW1X 7DJ; www.comohotels.com/thehalkin/dining/ametsa; @COMOHotels; 10 pm.

Amico Bio £37 ❸④❸
43 New Oxford St, WC1
7836 7509 4–1C NEW
43-44 Cloth Fair, EC1 7600 7778 9–2B
"Nourishing" veggie Italian fare is "an excellent concept", say fans, and it's one that's realised well at the Smithfield original of these "inviting" low-key spots; good early reports on the new Holborn branch too. / EC1 10.30pm; EC1 closed Sat L & Sun.

Anarkali W6 £33 ❸❸④
303-305 King St 8748 1760 7–2B
"The chef really looks after you", at this age-old Hammersmith Indian; it certainly appears "basic", but fans insist the food is "great". / W6 9NH; midnight, Sun 11.30 pm; no Amex.

The Anchor & Hope
SE1 £45 ❶❸❸
36 The Cut 7928 9898 9–4A
"The crème de la crème of gastropubs!"; this "always jam-packed" institution, near the Old Vic, is again voted London's No. 1, thanks to its "hearty" British fare at "unbeatable" prices; "just a shame you can't book" – "arrive early". / SE1 8LP; 10.30 pm; closed Mon L & Sun D; no Amex; no booking.

Andrew Edmunds W1 £46 ❸❷❶
46 Lexington St 7437 5708 3–2D
"The quintessence of shabby chic" – this "quirky", "candlelit" Soho phenomenon is "the kind of place you find in Paris not London", and "incredibly romantic"; its "simple", "refreshingly honest" cooking is "good (but not knock-out)", but the "eclectic, encyclopaedic list of wines is truly wonderful"; "sit upstairs if you can". / W1F 0LW; 10.45pm, Sun 10.30 pm; no Amex; booking: max 6.

The Angel & Crown
WC2 £44 ❸④④
58 St Martin's Ln 7748 5244 4–3B
"Unpretentiously good" cooking makes this year-old Covent Garden pub a handy destination, especially for "good-value" pre-theatre sustenance; by the standards of the Martin brothers' gastropub empire, though, it's only made a modest splash. / WC2N 4EA.

Angels & Gypsies
Church Street Hotel
SE5 £41 ❷❸❷
29-33 Camberwell Church St
7703 5984 1–3C
"Very cool", "hip" and "buzzing", a Camberwell bar which offers "a welcome taste of Spain" with its "cleverly worked" tapas – "not the standard stuff" at all. / SE5 8TR; www.angelsandgypsies.com; @angelsngypsies; 10.30 pm, Fri & Sat 11 pm.

Angelus W2 £74 ❸❷❸
4 Bathurst St 7402 0083 6–2D
"Thierry Tomassin is a star", whose "wine choice can be totally relied upon" – so say fans of the ex-Gavroche sommelier's conversion of a former Bayswater boozer, which is nowadays a "traditional" Gallic restaurant, where the fare is "artery-clogging but delicious". / W2 2SD; www.angelusrestaurant.co.uk; 11 pm, Sun 10 pm; set weekday L £44 (FP).

Angler
South Place Hotel
EC2 £69 ❸❷❷
3 South Pl 3503 0000 12–2A
A "stunning, lovely and bright top floor room" (over a trendy City hotel, and with an exceptional terrace) is the venue for this D&D group yearling, often praised for "really lovely" fish-centric cuisine. / EC2M 2AF; www.southplacehotel.com.

The Anglesea Arms
SW7 £47 ④④❷
15 Selwood Ter 7373 7960 5–2B
"A proper pub", in a leafy South Kensington location, whose attractions include "fine beer", and a "great terrace"; the food is "competent", but "it isn't cheap, and you can wait a long time to be served". / SW7 3QG; www.angleseaarms.com; @angleseaarms; 10 pm, Sun 9.30 pm.

The Anglesea Arms
W6 £50 ❷❸❷
35 Wingate Rd 8749 1291 7–1B
"Best in the West!" – thanks to its "simple but superbly executed" British dishes, and its "successful balance between gastro and pub", this Ravenscourt Park fixture is "always rammed"; the food rating, though, no longer hits the dizzying heights it once did. / W6 0UR; www.anglesea-arms.co.uk; Mon 10 pm, Tue-Sat 10.30 pm, Sun 9.30 pm; no Amex; no booking.

Anglo Asian
Tandoori N16 £35 ❸❷❸
60-62 Stoke Newington Church St
7254 3633 1–1C
Stoke Newington's "stalwart curry house" par excellence – an impressive all-rounder that's still "always dependable". / N16 0NB; 11 pm; no Amex.

L'Anima EC2 **£77** ❷❷❸
1 Snowden St 7422 7000 12–2B
"Thoroughly professional" and "sharp", in a rather
"NYC" sort of way – this major "City lunch
favourite" serves "understated but superior" Italian
dishes, alongside a "creative wine list" in a
"spacious" setting; not everyone loves the "goldfish
bowl" of an interior, though. / EC2A 2DQ;
www.lanima.co.uk; 11 pm, Sat 11.30 pm; closed
Sat L & Sun; set weekday L £44 (FP).

Annie's **£45** ❹❷❷
162 Thames Rd, W4 8994 9080 1–3A
36-38 White Hart Ln, SW13
8878 2020 10–1A
Really "fun" and "cosy", these Barnes and Strand
on the Green local restaurants are handy all-
rounders – "very welcoming with kids, but also good
for a romantic dinner", they offer food which
is decent and "reasonably priced".
/ www.anniesrestaurant.co.uk; 10 pm, Sat 10.30 pm,
Sun 9.30 pm.

Antelope SW17 **£40** ❸❷❷
76 Mitcham Rd 8672 3888 10–2C
"A rare non-Indian gem in Tooting"; this "eclectic"
and "really engaging" gastropub wins plaudits all
round, not least for its "hearty" scoff; "no wonder
the Antic chain are taking over south London"!
/ SW17 9NG; www.theantelopepub.com;
@theantelopesw17; 10.30 pm; closed
Mon-Fri L & Sun D; no Amex.

Antepliler **£34** ❸❹❸
139 Upper St, N1 7226 5441 1–1C
46 Grand Pde, N4 8802 5588 1–1C
A particular "gem" amidst the overpriced
restaurants of Islington's Upper Street, this "above-
average" Turkish operation impresses with its sheer
consistency; the Newington Green outlet is just the
same. / www.anteplilerrestaurant.com; 11 pm.

The Anthologist EC2 £41 ❸❸❷
58 Gresham St 465 0101 9–2C
A "casual", "large" and "busy" hang-out,
near Guildhall, serving a "wide-ranging" menu –
"it looks like it should be a case of style-over-
substance, but they actually manage to pull off
doing a lot of things at once". / EC2V 7BB;
www.theanthologistbar.co.uk; 10 pm; closed Sat & Sun;
SRA-73%.

Antico SE1 **£47** ❸❸❹
214 Bermondsey St 7407 4682 9–4D
A "reliable", if occasionally "frantic", Bermondsey
yearling offering "well thought-out" Italian dishes.
/ SE1 3TQ; www.antico-london.co.uk; 10.30 pm;
closed Mon.

Antidote W1 **£50** ❸❹❸
12a Newburgh St 7287 8488 3–2C
Just off Carnaby Street, a cramped Gallic operation
offering "tasty" bistro staples; star of the show,
however, is the "fantastic selection of wines".
/ W1F 7RR; www.antidotewinebar.com;
@AntidoteWineBar; 11 pm; closed Sun D.

Antipasto & Pasta
SW11 **£40** ❸❷❹
511 Battersea Park Rd 7223 9765 10–1C
A "safe local favourite" par excellence; as all
Battersea folk know, "you can't beat the half-price
nights" at this long-established Italian. / SW11 3BW;
11.30 pm, Sun 11 pm; need 4+ to book.

Apollo Banana Leaf
SW17 **£20** ❶❷⑤
190 Tooting High St 8696 1423 10–2C
"The interior isn't great, the service is competent...
but the food, for the price, is simply brilliant" –
all reports confirm the "sublime" quality of the
cuisine at this inauspicious-looking Tooting BYO.
/ SW17 0SF; 10.30 pm; no Amex.

Apostrophe **£18** ❸❸❸
Branches throughout London
"Decadent hot chocolate, sparky coffee and real
chai" are all highlights of these "cheerful" and
"efficient" Gallic cafés, which sell some "very good
sandwiches" too. / www.apostropheuk.com;
most branches 6 pm, Sat 5.30 pm; no booking.

Applebee's Cafe SE1 **£42** ❸❸❹
5 Stoney St 7407 5777 9–4C
The "great selection of fresh fish" – "simply grilled
or fried" – can come as a "nice surprise" to first-
time visitors to this "noisy" outfit, in the heart
of Borough Market. / SE1 9AA; www.applebeesfish.com;
@applebeesfish; 10 pm, Fri 10.30 pm; closed Sun;
no Amex.

Apsleys
Lanesborough Hotel
SW1 **£109** ❹❹❸
1 Lanesborough Pl 7333 7254 5–1D
Shame that this lavish and "calming" Belgravia
outpost of a top Roman chef undermines its appeal
with such "terrifying" prices – the food is often
"fabulous"; change may be afoot in 2014 as a
major refurb is planned. / SW1X 7TA;
www.apsleys.co.uk; 10.30 pm; jacket; booking: max 12;
set weekday L £65 (FP).

aqua kyoto W1 £71 ④④❸
240 Regent St (entrance 30 Argyll St) 7478
0540 3–2C
"Lovely" terraces apart, this nightclubby fusion-restaurant, six floors above Regent Street, inspires notably mixed reports – all the way from "outstanding", via "not a patch on the HK original", to "what a disaster"! / W1B 3BR; www.aqua-london.com; @aqualondon; 10.45 pm, Thu-Sat 11.15 pm; closed Sun D; set weekday L £39 (FP).

aqua nueva W1 £66 ⑤⑤④
240 Regent St (entrance 30 Argyll St) 7478
0540 3–2C
The design of this nightclubby sixth-floor Spanish operation, up above Regent Street, may be "amazing", but it again drew flak this year for "tiny" portions and "inflated" prices; it's the service, though, which attracts particular ire. / W1B 3BR; www.aqua-london.com; @aqualondon; 11 pm.

Arbutus W1 £49 ❸④④
63-64 Frith St 7734 4545 4–2A
"Interesting food with an edge" (plus an "excellent choice of wines by the glass and 250ml carafe") has won renown for this "slightly bland and cramped" bistro; "it's not the bargain it once was", however, and the Soho market has got a lot more competitive of late… / W1D 3JW; www.arbutusrestaurant.co.uk; 10.45 pm, Fri & Sat 11.15 pm, Sun 10.30 pm.

**Archduke Wine Bar
SE1** £52 ⑤⑤④
Concert Hall Approach, South Bank 7928
9370 2–3D
Incredibly convenient for the Royal Festival Hall, this outpost of steak 'n' burger chain Black & Blue occupies a series of characterful railway arches; it rarely excels, but it's still "better than some of the places on the South Bank". / SE1 8XU; www.blackandbluerestaurants.com; 10.30 pm, Sun 10 pm.

Archipelago W1 £54 ④④❸
110 Whitfield St 7383 3346 2–1B
OTT decor helps lend a romantic ambience to this tiny spot, near the Telecom Tower; the cooking from the bizarrely exotic menu (wildebeest, ostrich…) only intermittently lives up. / W1T 5ED; www.archipelago-restaurant.co.uk; 10.15 pm; closed Sat L & Sun; set weekday L £30 (FP).

Ark Fish E18 £41 ❶②④
142 Hermon Hill 8989 5345 1–1D
"The freshest fish you can hope for" – the raison d'être of this popular (expect to queue later in the week), if "rather noisy", South Woodford spot; friendly and efficient service too. / E18 1QH; www.arkfishrestaurant.co.uk; 9.45 pm, Fri & Sat 10.15 pm, Sun 8.45 pm; closed Mon; no Amex.

**L'Art du Fromage
SW10** £49 ❷❸❸
1a Langton St 7352 2759 5–3B
In World's End, this "small and cosy paradise for cheese-lovers" has acquired a modest reporter following; its rather "away-from-it-all" charms, however, seduce all who comment on it. / SW10 0JL; www.artdufromage.co.uk; 10.30 pm; closed Mon L, Tue L, Wed L & Sun.

Artigiano NW3 £45 ❸④❸
12a Belsize Ter 7794 4288 8–2A
"Simply-prepared food, in a smart but relaxed atmosphere" – the enduring formula for this "very agreeable" Belsize Park Italian. / NW3 4AX; www.etruscarestaurants.com; 10 pm; closed Mon L.

L'Artista NW11 £34 ④❸❸
917 Finchley Rd 8731 7501 1–1B
"Under the arches by Golders Green Station since forever!" – this "enthusiastic" Italian institution thrives on its "lively" ("impossibly noisy") style, and its "ridiculously large" lashings of pizza and other fare. / NW11 7PE; www.lartistapizzeria.com; 11.30 pm.

L'Artiste Musclé W1 £43 ④④❸
1 Shepherd Mkt 7493 6150 3–4B
"An affordable gem in the heart of Mayfair"; this "old-fashioned" Gallic bistro certainly has "no gastronomic pretensions", but fans claim it as a "a perfect piece of Paris", transported to Shepherd Market. / W1J 7PA; 10 pm, Fri-Sun 10.30 pm.

Asadal WC1 £39 ❸④④
227 High Holborn 7430 9006 2–1D
A "solid" subterranean operation, implausibly located below Holborn tube; "it makes no bones about being high end, but for Korean food with bite at a good price, you can't go too far wrong". / WC1V 7DA; www.asadal.co.uk; 10.30 pm; closed Sun L.

Asakusa NW1 £35 ❶④④
265 Eversholt St 7388 8533 8–3C
"Fantastic sushi at amazingly cheap prices" ensures that this "unassuming" operation, in the shadow of Euston station, is often "incredibly busy", largely with Japanese people; "try it once – I guarantee you'll be back!" / NW1 1BA; 11.30 pm, Sat 11 pm; D only, closed Sun.

Asia de Cuba
St Martin's Lane
Hotel WC2   **£89**   ④⑤④

45 St Martin's Ln   7300 5588   4–4C

"Fusion that hits the spot" can still wins fans for this "atmospheric" but often "noisy" Theatreland veteran (one of the very first upmarket 'trendy' restaurants to open in the West End); service, though, is patchy and prices "stratospheric", especially when "not all of the eclectic combinations work out". / WC2N 4HX; www.morganshotelgroup.com; @asiadecuba; midnight, Sun 10 pm.

Ask   **£40**   ④④④

Branches throughout London

"Passable", "wholesome", "nothing wrong with it"… – it may rarely excite, but this pizza/pasta chain is generally hailed as a pretty decent stand-by. / www.askcentral.co.uk; most branches 11 pm, Fri & Sat 11.30 pm; some booking restrictions apply.

Assaggi W2   **£72**   ①①③

39 Chepstow Pl   7792 5501   6–1B

"The best Italian food anywhere… and that includes Italy!" – this "simply furnished" (and "noisy") room, above a former Bayswater boozer, has rightly won fame for its "incredibly fresh" cooking, supplied by "entertaining" staff. / W2 4TS; 11 pm; closed Sun; no Amex.

Assiette Anglaise
N7 NEW   **£45**   ②③③

489 Liverpool St   7609 0300   8–2D

"Slightly incongruous at the less salubrious end of Islington", this "wonderful" Gallic neighbourhood newcomer has taken up where Morgan M (re-located to Clerkenwell) left off, but in a simpler vein and at "amazing value" prices; "the word got out very quickly and it can be hard to get a table". / N7 8NS; www.assietteanglaise.co.uk; @AAnglaise; 10 pm, Sat 10.30 pm; closed Mon, Tue L, Wed L, Thu L, Fri L & Sun D.

Les Associés N8   **£45**   ③②④

172 Park Rd   8348 8944   1–1C

"Run by a Frenchman, who is the real McCoy!" – this perennially popular Crouch End bistro is a local favourite, where "reasonable prices" compensate for decor that's on the shabby side of chic. / N8 8JT; www.lesassociesn8.co.uk; @lesassociesn8; 10 pm; closed Mon, Tue L, Sat L & Sun D; 24 hr notice for L bookings; set Sun L £32 (FP).

Atari-Ya   **£31**   ❶④⑤

20 James St, W1   7491 1178   3–1A
7 Station Pde, W3   8896 1552   1–2A
1 Station Pde, W5   8896 3175   1–3A
595 High Rd, N12   8446 6669   8–1B
31 Vivian Ave, NW4   8202 2789   1–1B
75 Fairfax Road, London, NW6   7328 5338   8–2A

Some of "the best and most authentic Japanese food in London" – these no-frills cafés offer "sparklingly fresh" sushi that's "the real deal"; the menu, though, is "not especially easy to follow" ("and some of the staff don't seem that keen to clarify"). / www.atariya.co.uk; W1 8 pm, NW4 & NW6 9.30 pm, W9 9 pm; NW4, NW6 closed Mon.

L'Atelier de Joel
Robuchon WC2   **£84**   ❷❷❷

13-15 West St   7010 8600   4–2B

OK, prices are "sky high", but the "divine little morsels" on offer at the Parisian über-chef's "very sleek" and "seductive" Theatreland outpost are a total "wow" for most reporters (especially at lunch, which is "tremendous value"); "sit at the bar, so you can see what's going on in the open kitchen". / WC2H 9NE; www.joelrobuchon.co.uk; @latelierlondon; midnight, Sun 10 pm; no trainers; set weekday L & pre-theatre £62 (FP).

Athenaeum
Athenaeum Hotel W1   **£78**   ❷❶❸

116 Piccadilly   7499 3464   3–4B

Looking for an "excellent-value set lunch" or a "wonderful afternoon tea"? – this "lovely" low-key hotel delivers "five-star" service, and attracts much more consistent feedback than many of its flashier Mayfair peers. / W1J 7BJ; www.athenaeumhotel.com; 10.30 pm.

The Atlas SW6   **£45**   ❷❷❷

16 Seagrave Rd   7385 9129   5–3A

A "very chilled" backstreet stalwart, near Earl's Court 2, that's "just how a pub should be"; it offers "Mediterranean-inspired food far superior to the average", and has a "nice garden" too. / SW6 1RX; www.theatlaspub.co.uk; @theatlasfulham; 10 pm.

Aubaine   **£57**   ⑤⑤④

4 Heddon St, W1   7440 2510   3–2C
260-262 Brompton Rd, SW3   7052 0100   5–2C
37-45 Kensington High St, W8   7368 0950   5–1A

Perhaps "more refined" than many rivals, but these Gallic café/bistros are increasingly seen as a "wasted opportunity" – for the "indifferent" overall experience, critics find prices "absurd". / www.aubaine.co.uk; @balanslondon; SW3, SW19 10 pm, Sun 9.30 pm; Heddon St 11 pm, Oxford St 9 pm, Sun 6 pm, W8 10 pm, Sun 6 pm, Dover St 10 pm, Sun 9.30 pm; W8 no booking.

Aurora W1   £47   ❸❷❶
49 Lexington St   7494 0514   3–2D
*"Perfect for informal intimacy", this Soho stalwart
is "the epitome of cosiness", and it has a secret
weapon – "a wonderful little courtyard for al fresco
dining"; the food (from "a small menu")
is "good too". / W1F 9AP; www.aurorasoho.co.uk;
10 pm, Wed-Sat 10.30 pm, Sun 9 pm.*

Automat W1   £61   ④④④
33 Dover St   7499 3033   3–3C
*"A classic American diner in the heart of Mayfair",
where the "top breakfast (and lots of it)" and
"excellent" burgers are highlights of the menu
of "high-quality US comfort food"; prices, though,
fully reflect the location. / W1S 4NF;
www.automat-london.com; 11.45 pm, Sat 10.45 pm,
Sun 9.45 pm.*

L'Autre Pied W1   £78   ❷❷④
5-7 Blandford St   7486 9696   2–1A
*"Each plate is like performance art", say fans
of Pied à Terre's Marylebone sibling, where the
tasting menu in particular is "imaginative and
sublime"; the room, though, can feel rather "bland".
/ W1U 3DB; www.lautrepied.co.uk; 10 pm; closed Sun D;
set weekday L £47 (FP).*

Avalon SW12   £41   ④④❸
16 Balham Hill   8675 8613   10–2C
*On the way to Balham, a "huge" and "hectic"
gastropub which is "great for families or large
groups"; food and service, though, can be "hit -and-
miss". / SW12 9EB; www.theavalonlondon.com;
10.30 pm, Sun 9 pm; SRA-56%.*

L'Aventure NW8   £58   ❷❶❶
3 Blenheim Ter   7624 6232   8–3A
*With its "charmingly arrogant service", "fashionably
outdated decor", and "absolutely gorgeous" Gallic
cooking, this "delightful" St John's Wood classic
offers a perfect combination "for a memorable
night", and it is "as romantic as its name suggests"
too. / NW8 0EH; 11 pm; closed Sat L & Sun;
set weekday L £38 (FP).*

The Avenue SW1   £55   ❸❸❸
7-9 St James's St   7321 2111   3–4D
*A "very good value" lunch menu is the stand-out
attraction at this "slick" and "airy" (but sometimes
"noisy") D&D group venue; its "roomy" (and slightly
"cavernous") modern interior is well suited to its
primary role as a St James's business rendezvous.
/ SW1A 1EE; www.avenue-restaurant.co.uk; 10.30 pm;
closed Sat L & Sun; set weekday L £28 (FP), set
pre-theatre £37 (FP); SRA-62%.*

Axis
One Aldwych Hotel
WC2   £63   ④④④
1 Aldwych   7300 0300   2–2D
*"Relaxed" and "classy", or "cold" and "impersonal"?
– as ever, views on the decor of this large Covent
Garden basement are mixed; it's undeniably
a "handy" location, however, and a "good value" one
pre-theatre. / WC2B 4RH; www.onealdwych.com;
10.30 pm; closed Mon, Sat L & Sun; set pre theatre
£46 (FP).*

Azou W6   £41   ❸❷❷
375 King St   8563 7266   7–2B
*"Compared favourably to our actual trip
to Morocco!" – this sweet little café is a
Hammersmith "favourite", thanks to its friendly
service and tasty fare. / W6 9NJ; www.azou.co.uk;
@azourestaurant; 11 pm.*

Ba Shan W1   £48   ❷④④
24 Romilly St   7287 3266   4–3A
*"Sensational" Hunanese cooking that's
"much hotter than the Chinatown norm" helps
make this "unpretentious" Soho café – a sibling
to Bar Shu, just over the road – a "great-value"
destination. / W1D 5AH; 11 pm, Fri & Sat 11.30 pm.*

Babbo W1   £76   ⑤④④
39 Albermarle St   3205 1099   3–3C
*Despite its handy location and "nice premises",
near the Ritz, this Mayfair Italian attracts relatively
few reports – it can't help that the food is pricey
and "not that distinguished". / W1S 4JQ;
www.babborestaurant.co.uk; @BabboRestaurant; 11 pm,
Sun 10.30 pm; closed Sun L; set weekday L £50 (FP).*

Babur SE23   £50   ❶❶❷
119 Brockley Rise   8291 2400   1–4D
*A "gastronomic jewel"; this "unfailingly impressive"
Honor Oak Park Indian attracts a huge amount
of feedback, almost all of which tends to confirm
it as "the best restaurant in SE London". / SE23 1JP;
www.babur.info; @BaburRestaurant; 11.30 pm.*

Babylon
Kensington Roof
Gardens W8   £72   ④④❷
99 Kensington High St   7368 3993   5–1A
*"What girl doesn't like a flamingo?" – they're
sometimes to be spotted in the extraordinary 8th-
floor roof garden overlooked by this Kensington
eyrie; "the menu is workmanlike and perhaps a little
uninspiring, but with views like this who cares?"
/ W8 5SA; www.virgin.com/roofgardens; 10.30 pm; closed
Sun D; set weekday L £44 (FP); SRA-75%.*

Il Bacio £42 ❸❸❸
61 Stoke Newington Church St, N16 7249
3833 1–1C
178-184 Blackstock Rd, N5 7226 3339 8–1D
"Yummy, thin-crust, wood-fired pizza" is served
"with gusto" at these "cosy" Sardinian spots,
in Stoke Newington and Highbury.
/ www.ilbaciohighbury.co.uk; 10 pm-11 pm; Mon-Fri L;
no Amex.

Baker & Spice £40 ④④④
54-56 Elizabeth St, SW1 7730 5524 2–4A
47 Denyer St, SW3 7225 3417 5–2D
20 Clifton Rd, W9 7289 2499 8–4A
Good but "absurdly expensive" – same verdict
as ever on this chichi pâtisserie/deli chain, which
continues to disenchant some reporters with service
that's "slow" or "off-hand".
/ www.bakerandspice.uk.com; 7 pm, Sun 6 pm; closed
D; no Amex; no booking.

Balans £47 ⑤④④
34 Old Compton St, W1 7439 3309 4–3A
60-62 Old Compton St, W1 7439 2183 4–3A
239 Old Brompton Rd, SW5 7244 8838 5–3A
Westfield, Ariel Way, W12 8600 3320 7–1C
214 Chiswick High Rd, W4 8742 1435 7–2A
187 Kensington High St, W8 7376 0115 5–1A
Westfield Stratford, Westfield Startford, E20
8555 5478 1–1D
"Watch the hive of activity that is Soho" from the
most central branch of this "buzzing" diner chain,
which is especially popular for brunch; critics,
though, feel the food has "gone from adequate
to mediocre". / www.balans.co.uk; midnight-2 am;
34 Old Compton St 24 hrs, E20 11pm; some booking
restrictions apply.

The Balcon
Sofitel St James SW1 £60 ❸❸❸
8 Pall Mall 7968 2900 2–3C
"Large", "airy" and "relaxed", and just by Trafalgar
Square too – this "reliable" brasserie certainly
makes a handy West End rendezvous; the pre-
theatre menu, in particular, is "hard to beat".
/ SW1Y 5NG; www.thebalconlondon.com; 10.45 pm,
Sun 9.45 pm; set pre theatre £36 (FP).

Bald Faced Stag N2 £47 ❸④❸
69 High Rd 8442 1201 1–1B
"One of the few East Finchley places worth visiting"
– it offers "all that you expect from a good
gastropub", including "well-executed" fare. / N2 8AB;
www.thebaldfacedstagn2.co.uk; @thebaldfacestagn2;
10.30 pm, Sun 9.30 pm.

The Balham Bowls Club
SW12 £40 ❸❸❷
7-9 Ramsden Rd 8673 4700 10–2C
The dining room at this spacious haunt (which has
nothing to do with bowls) serves "decent home-
made food", and fans say this is "the best pub
in Balham". / SW12 8QX; www.balhambowlsclub.com;
11 pm, Fri & Sat midnight; closed weekday L; no Amex.

Balthazar WC2 £64 ⑤④❸
4-6 Russell St 3301 1155 4–3D
"Oh dear!"; Keith McNally's "very disappointing"
Manhattan-comes-to-Covent-Garden import wows
reporters as little as it did the press; the room may
be "beautiful, buzzy, fun, and very NYC", but it's
"greedily packed-in", and the food is "like a glorified
Café Rouge". / WC2E 7BN; www.balthazarlondon.com.

Baltic SE1 £50 ❸❸❷
74 Blackfriars Rd 7928 1111 9–4A
A "claustrophobic" front bar gives little hint of the
attractions of this "spacious" bar/restaurant lying
behind a small Borough frontage – a "slick",
"crowded" and "fun" operation, where the "Polish-
fusion" fare rarely disappoints. / SE1 8HA;
www.balticrestaurant.co.uk; 11.15 pm, Sun 10.15 pm;
closed Mon L.

Bam-Bou W1 £54 ❸❸❷
1 Percy St 7323 9130 2–1C
"They've mastered the art of casual dining", at the
Caprice group's "lovely" French colonial-style
Fitzrovia townhouse – a "fun" venue, offering "high-
quality" pan-Asian food and "amusing" cocktails.
/ W1T 1DB; www.bam-bou.co.uk; midnight; closed Sun;
booking: max 6.

The Banana Tree
Canteen £34 ④④❸
103 Wardour St, W1 7437 1351 3–2D
21-23 Westbourne Grove, W2 7221 4085
6–1C
166 Randolph Ave, W9 7286 3869 8–3A
237-239 West End Ln, NW6 7431 7808 1–1B
75-79 Battersea Rise, SW11 7228 2828
10–2C
412-416 St John St, EC1 7278 7565 8–3D
"Always popular and busy" – these pan-Asian
canteens have a "pleasing upbeat" style, and offer
food that's "decent for a chain"; "a recent revamp
has improved the SW11 branch".
/ @bananatree247; 11 pm, Sun 10.30 pm; booking:
min 6.

Bangalore Express **£38** ④④❸
103-105 Waterloo Rd, SE1   7021 0886   9–4A
1 Corbet Ct, EC3   7220 9195   9–3C
"Indian food with a western twist" (and "a hint of wit" too) wins majority approval for these contemporary-style establishments, in the City and Waterloo (the latter with funky, double-decker seating); for sceptics, though, the supposed wackiness is all a bit "stereotyped". / www.bangaloreuk.com; 10.30 pm.

Bangkok SW7 **£39** ❷❷❸
9 Bute St   7584 8529   5–2B
"Forty years on, and still the same delicious food, friendly owner, chef…and clientele!" – London's original Thai restaurant, near South Kensington tube, soldiers on magnificently. / SW7 3EY; 10.45 pm; no Amex.

**Bank Westminster
St James Court
Hotel SW1** **£61** ④④④
45 Buckingham Gate   7630 6644   2–4B
Handy for Buckingham Palace, a bar/restaurant with the surprise attraction of a "large glass gazebo"; its "well-spaced" tables make it particularly useful as a business lunch venue. / SW1E 6BS; www.bankrestaurants.com; @bank_westmin; 11 pm; closed Sat L & Sun.

Banners N8 **£45** ❸❸❶
21 Park Rd   8348 2930   1–1C
It may look a bit "like a US burger joint", but this Crouch End "perennial" in fact offers an "eclectic" (Caribbean-tinged) menu that's especially "great for breakfast or brunch" (particularly en famille); "it can be hard to get a table". / N8 8TE; www.bannersrestaurant.com; 11.30 pm, Fri & Sat midnight, Sun 11 pm; no Amex.

Baozi Inn WC2 **£18** ❸④④
25 Newport Ct   7287 6877   4–3B
"Don't plan on making an evening of it", but this "respectable" Chinatown Sichuanese is a handy spot for "cheap and tasty steamed buns", plus a "limited" range of soups, noodles and so on. / WC2H 7JS; 10 pm, Fri-Sat 10.30 pm; no credit cards; no booking.

**Bar Boulud
Mandarin Oriental
SW1** **£60** ❸❷❸
66 Knightsbridge   7201 3899   5–1D
"A perfect combination of posh and casual!" – this "buzzy" Knightsbridge basement outpost of a top NYC chef offers "'stylish" Gallic bistro fare (plus some "out-of-this-world" burgers); no denying a growing feeling, though, that standards here are now "good, rather than exceptional". / SW1X 7LA; www.barboulud.com; 10.45 pm, Sun 9.45 pm; set weekday L & pre-theatre £44 (FP).

Bar Italia W1 **£28** ④❷❶
22 Frith St   7437 4520   4–2A
"The only place in Britain where the espresso tastes like a proper Italian one!" – this 24/7 Soho landmark retains its cult status; "you don't lack entertainment" either, especially from the "interesting clientele" in the early hours. / W1D 4RT; www.baritaliasoho.co.uk; @TheBaristas; open 24 hours, Sun 4 am; no Amex; no booking.

Barbecoa EC4 **£67** ④④④
20 New Change Pas   3005 8555   9–2B
"Make sure you get a view of St Paul's", if you visit Jamie's "cavernous" and "loud" City BBQ; for business, it can provide an "impressive" destination – given the "crazy" prices, though, those paying their own way may find standards "uninspiring". / EC4M 9AG; www.barbecoa.com; @barbecoa; 10.45 pm.

La Barca SE1 **£56** ④❷❷
80-81 Lower Marsh   7928 2226   9–4A
"The last of the old-school Italians"? – this "friendly and cosy" Waterloo veteran has more claim than most, and it retains "a huge regular clientele" with its "well-executed" (if "expensive") menu. / SE1 7AB; www.labarca-ristorante.com; 11.15 pm; closed Sat L & Sun.

Il Baretto W1 **£63**
43 Blandford St   7486 7340   2–1A
"Completely Italian" in style, this "good but expensive" Marylebone basement has many fans; it also inspires an impressive array of niggles, though, including "hit-and-miss" cuisine, "patchy" or "arrogant" service, and, of course, the "din"; it relaunches in late-2013 after a major refurbishment. / W1U 7HF; www.ilbaretto.co.uk; 10.30 pm, Sun 10 pm.

Barrafina **£41** ❶❶❷
54 Frith St, W1   7813 8016   4–2A
10 Adelaide St, WC2   awaiting tel   4–2D
"The best tapas bar in London"… "possibly the world!"; "it's worth the hour's wait" to nab a perch at this tiny (23-seat) and "too busy" Soho phenomenon, where there's an "intimacy" to having "incredible" dishes "entertainingly prepared" before your very eyes; a WC2 branch opens in early-2014. / www.barrafina.co.uk; 11 pm, Sun 10 pm; no booking.

Barrica W1 **£39** ❷❷❶
62 Goodge St   7436 9448   2–1B
"You could almost be in Madrid!" – such is the "hustle and bustle" at this "fun and friendly" Fitzrovia haunt, where the "gorgeous" tapas are "the real deal". / W1T 4NE; www.barrica.co.uk; 10.30 pm; closed Sun.

Bar Shu W1 £51 ❷⑤④
28 Frith St 7287 6688 4–3A
If you like it "really hot", this Soho café – with its "fiery" and "fragrant" Sichuanese cuisine – is, say fans, "a revelation"; service, though, "needs getting used to", and the odd sceptic feels the place is "overrated". / W1D 5LF; www.bar-shu.co.uk; 11 pm, Fri-Sat 11.30 pm.

Basilico £35 ❸❷④
690 Fulham Rd, SW6 0800 028 3531 10–1B
26 Penton St, N1 0800 093 4224 8–3D
51 Park Rd, N8 8616 0290 1–1C
515 Finchley Rd, NW3 0800 316 2656 1–1B
175 Lavender Hill, SW11 0800 389 9770 10–2C
178 Upper Richmond Rd, SW14 0800 096 8202 10–2B
"Simply the best pizza delivery!" – "tasty thin-crusts with imaginative toppings", plus "prompt" service, please all who comment on this small chain. / www.basilico.co.uk; @basilicopizzas; 11 pm; no booking.

Bayee Village SW19 £45 ❸④④
24 High St 8947 3533 10–2B
"As good as any Soho Chinese", say fans, this Wimbledon Village fixture is a "dependable" sort of destination, where the fare is "more authentic than you might expect". / SW19 5DX; www.bayee.co.uk; 10.45 pm.

Beach Blanket Babylon £61 ⑤④❸
45 Ledbury Rd, W11 7229 2907 6–1B
19-23 Bethnal Green Rd, E1 7749 3540 12–1C
"Great for cocktails and hen nights!"; the decor at these Gaudi-esque Notting Hill and Shoreditch hang-outs is wonderful, but the notably "average" and "highly-priced" food is not. / www.beachblanket.co.uk; 10.30 pm; W11 booking advisable Fri-Sat.

Beard to Tail EC2 £49 ④❸④
77 Curtain Rd 7739 4781 12–1B
Still few and uneven reports on this "manly" ('nose-to-tail') and rather barely furnished Shoreditch yearling; some reporters "have never been disappointed", but our own experience chimed with those who find it "average all-round"; "good selection of beers and whiskies", though. / EC2A 3BS; www.beardtotail.co.uk.

Bedford & Strand WC2 £47 ④④❸
1a Bedford St 7836 3033 4–4D
Handily located just off the Strand, a sometimes "noisy" basement offering "good food, for what's basically a wine bar"; "nice staff" too. / WC2E 9HH; www.bedford-strand.com; 10.30 pm; closed Sat L & Sun.

Bedlington Café W4 £30 ❷❸④
24 Fauconberg Rd 8994 1965 7–2A
This Chiswick fixture has had a bit of a "spruce up" of late; however, the main attraction – the "rustic, spicy and authentic" Thai dishes – remains much the same as ever; BYO. / W4 3JY; 10 pm; closed Sun L; no credit cards.

The Begging Bowl SE15 £38 ❶❷❸
168 Bellenden Rd 7635 2627 1–4D
"Phenomenal" Thai cooking – that's "really the whole story" on this Peckham yearling, which occupies a light and airy corner site. / SE15 4BW; www.thebeggingbowl.co.uk.

Beirut Express £42 ❷④④
65 Old Brompton Rd, SW7 7591 0123 5–2B
112-114 Edgware Rd, W2 7724 2700 6–1D
"Amazing fresh juices" and "authentic" meze and wraps win praise for this Lebanese duo, in Bayswater and South Kensington. / www.maroush.com; W2 2 am; SW7 midnight.

Beiteddine SW1 £51 ❸❷④
8 Harriet St 7235 3969 5–1D
A "first-rate" Lebanese whose "nice, quiet and leisurely" ambience, in the old style, seems ever more at odds with its location, just off Euro-glittery Sloane Street. / SW1X 9JW; www.beiteddinerestaurant.com; midnight.

Belgo £42 ④④④
50 Earlham St, WC2 7813 2233 4–2C
67 Kingsway, WC2 7242 7469 2–2D
72 Chalk Farm Rd, NW1 7267 0718 8–2B
44-48 Clapham High Rd, SW4 7720 1118 10–2D
The appeal may have "diluted" over the years, but these "monastic" Belgian brasseries – majoring in moules-frites and Continental lagers – are still "lively" ("noisy") and "reasonably priced", and notably good with kids too. / www.belgo-restaurants.co.uk; most branches 10.30 pm-11.30 pm; SW4 midnight, Thu 1 am, Fri & Sat 2 am, Sun 12.30 am.

Bellamy's W1 £65 ❸❷❷
18-18a Bruton Pl 7491 2727 3–2B
Run by the ex-MD of nearby Annabel's nightclub, this Mayfair mews operation is a "discreet" and "well-spaced" rendezvous, where "the quality of the cooking is disguised by its simplicity". / W1J 6LY; www.bellamysrestaurant.co.uk; 10.30 pm; closed Sat L & Sun.

**Bellevue
Rendez-Vous SW17   £47   ❸❷❷**
218 Trinity Rd   8767 5810   10–2C
*"A haven of romantic calm away from the not-so-
beautiful Trinity Road" – this "absolute gem" offers
a "short menu bursting with well-cooked traditional
dishes"; top tip – "the cheese board is second only
to Chez Bruce" (round the corner). / SW17 7HP;
www.bellevuerendezvous.com; 10.30 pm; closed Mon L;
no Amex.*

Belvedere W8   £69   ④④❷
Holland Pk, off Abbotsbury Rd
7602 1238   7–1D
*"Want to feel special, with someone who is special?"
– this "chic, spacious and classy" veteran not only
has "a beautiful park location", but is "one of the
best dining rooms in London" too; notwithstanding
a "top-value Sunday lunch", however, the food
is "ordinary". / W8 6LU;
www.belvedererestaurant.co.uk; 10.30 pm; closed Sun D;
set weekday L £40 (FP).*

Ben's Canteen SW11   £48   ④④④
140 St John's Hill   7228 3260   10–2C
*"Comfort food, well-cooked" has made this
Wandsworth spot a popular local destination;
"brunch is the meal", though – at other times,
prices for what's on offer can seem "very full".
/ SW11 1SL; www.benscanteen.com; @benscanteen;
10 pm.*

Benares W1   £82   ❷❷❸
12a Berkeley Square Hs, Berkeley Sq
7629 8886   3–3B
*Atul Kochhar's "impressive" cuisine ("exciting tasting
menu" a highlight) maintains this Mayfair operation
as one of London's foremost 'nouvelle Indians';
the windowless first-floor space is "impersonal"
to some, but fans insist it's "spacious" and "stylish".
/ W1J 6BS; www.benaresrestaurant.co.uk; 10.30 pm;
closed Sun; no trainers; set weekday L £60
(FP); SRA-68%.*

Bengal Clipper SE1   £40   ❸❸❷
Shad Thames   7357 9001   9–4D
*This grand and long-established Indian is certainly
a "good neighbourhood standby" for those who live
near Tower Bridge; indeed, the worst anyone can
find to say about it is that it's "always reliable"!
/ SE1 2YR; www.bengalclipper.co.uk; 11.30 pm,
Sun 11 pm.*

Benihana   £65   ④④④
37 Sackville St, W1   7494 2525   3–3D
77 King's Rd, SW3   7376 7799   5–3D
*Children (of all ages) "love the show" (which involves
much knife-wielding) at these long-established,
and not inexpensive, teppanyaki parlours, which can
make quite a "treat" as a party destination;
lunchtime menus include less drama, but can
be surprisingly "good value". / www.benihana.co.uk;
@Benihanauk; 10.30 pm, Sun 10 pm; set weekday L
£37 (FP).*

Benito's Hat   £26   ❸❸④
12 Great Castle St, W1   7636 6560   3–1C
56 Goodge St, W1   7637 3732   2–1B
19 New Row, WC2   7240 5815   4–3C
King's Cross Station, N1   7812 1304   8–3C
*These self-service Mexicans are especially worth
visiting for a great-value Happy Hour cocktail; while
you're there, pick up a "great" and "filling" burrito –
one of the range of "tasty" bites.
/ www.benitos-hat.com; 10 pm, Thu-Sat 11 pm; Great
Castle St closed Sun.*

Bentley's W1   £74   ❷❸❷
11-15 Swallow St   7734 4756   3–3D
*"Always first-class", this "beautifully elegant"
Mayfair fish "institution" wins high acclaim for its
"super, no-nonsense seafood" – the "down-to-earth"
ground floor champagne and oyster bar (with nice
al fresco tables) is often preferred to the "quieter"
upstairs. / W1B 4DG; www.bentleys.org;
@bentleys_london; 10.30 pm; no jeans; booking: max 8;
set pre theatre £53 (FP).*

Bento Cafe NW1   £36   ❷❷④
9 Parkway   7482 3990   8–3B
*"A real find"; all reports attest to the standards
of this Camden Town spot, where "both the Chinese
and Japanese menus are very good"; "excellent"
sashimi is a highlight, and the Bento boxes offer
"terrific value" too. / NW1 7PG; bentocafe.co.uk;
10.15 pm, Fri-Sat 10.45 pm.*

Benugo £35 ④④❷
14 Curzon St, W1 7629 6246 3–4B
23-25 Gt Portland St, W1 7631 5052 3–1C
V&A Museum, Cromwell Rd, SW7
7581 2159 5–2C
Natural History Museum, Cromwell Rd, SW7
7942 5011 5–2B
Westfield, Unit 1070 Ariel Way, W12
8746 9490 7–1C
St Pancras International, , NW1
7833 0201 8–3C
BFI Southbank, Belvedere Rd, SE1
7401 9000 2–3D
Museum Of Childhood, Cambridge Heath Rd, E2
8983 5215 1–2D
116 St John St, EC1 7253 3499 9–1A
82 City Rd, EC1 7253 1295 12–1A
*Generally improving standards of late at this
"friendly" fast-food chain, which inhabits some
"stunning" sites; it's a mixed bag, though – the V&A
outlet is quite a "hidden gem", but the prominent
BFI Southbank branch has "gone downhill" in recent
times. / www.benugo.com; 4 pm-10 pm; W1 & EC1
branches closed Sat & Sun; W1 & EC1 branches,
no credit cards.*

**The Berners Tavern
London EDITION
W1** NEW £65
10 Berners St 7908 7979 3–1D
*Local hero Jason Atherton has teamed up with
seminal boutique hotelier Ian Schrager to launch
this spectacular all-day dining room, near Oxford
Circus; early-days press reports suggest it looks set
to become quite a 'scene'. / W1T 3NP.*

Best Mangal £35 ❷❸❸
619 Fulham Rd, SW6 7610 0009 5–4A
104 North End Rd, W14 7610 1050 7–2D
66 North End Rd, W14 7602 0212 7–2D
*"I go back again and again for the great,
and cheap, food" – especially "if it's protein you
need", these west London Turkish BBQs are
"the business". / www.bestmangal.com; midnight,
Sat 1 am; no Amex.*

Bevis Marks E1 £65 ④④④
3 Middlesex St 7247 5474 9–2D
*It may still be "the best kosher restaurant in the
City", but since this business-friendly venue shifted
from the synagogue to this new site, its ratings have
dived; fans feel it's still "superb", but critics say:
"if this is gourmet kosher, I'd rather eat at home!"
/ E1A 7AA; www.bevismarkstherestaurant.com; 9 pm;
closed Fri D, Sat & Sun.*

Beyoglu NW3 £39 ❸❸④
72 Belsize Ln 7435 7733 8–2A
*"A great small Turkish restaurant", in Belsize Park;
the decor can seem a bit "tired", but it does offer
"better-than-average food at cheaper-than-average
prices". / NW3 4XR; www.beyoglu.co.uk; 11 pm;
no Amex.*

Bianco43 SE10 £42 ❸❸④
43 Greenwich Church St 8858 2668 1–3D
*Still rather mixed commentary on this two-year-old
Greenwich Italian – pizzas often come
"recommended", but the same can't be said about
the "hot" and "crowded" setting, or the "intrusive
funky music". / SE10 9BL; www.bianco43.com;
@bianco_43; 11.30 pm; no Amex.*

Bibendum SW3 £79 ❸❷❶
81 Fulham Rd 7581 5817 5–2C
*"Full of elegance and light" – the "peaceful"
first floor of this Brompton Cross landmark is,
for fans, "still London's most beautiful restaurant",
and "always a safe bet" for "superior" cuisine
matched by a "biblical" wine list; sceptics, however,
find prices excessive. / SW3 6RD;
www.bibendum.co.uk; 11 pm, Sun 10.30 pm; booking:
max 12 at L, 10 at D; set weekday L £50 (FP).*

**Bibendum Oyster
Bar SW3** £58 ❷❸❸
81 Fulham Rd 7589 1480 5–2C
*"For a crab, or a dozen oysters and a bottle
of vino", this swish seafood bar, off the entrance
to the Chelsea Conran Shop, is just the job –
now that nearby Le Suquet has closed, where else
would you go for "top fruits de mer"? (as we go to
press, the bar is set to re-open after a major
refurb). / SW3 6RD; www.bibendum.co.uk; 10 pm;
no booking.*

Bibimbap Soho W1 £29 ❸❸④
11 Greek St 7287 3434 4–2A
*A Korean pit stop in Soho, named after its speciality
– "a DIY stir-fry in a hot stone bowl, with or without
fried egg on top"; "does what it says on the tin,
and does it well". / W1D 4DJ; www.bibimbapsoho.com;
@bibimbapsoho; 11 pm; closed Sun; no Amex.*

**Big Apple Hot Dogs
EC1** £12 ❷❷–
239 Old St 387441 12–1B
*"No brains, no bones and no butts!" – the inspiring
promise of the quality of meat sold at this
"passionate" little cart, near Old Street Tube, which
sells "amazing franks", with "light and fluffy buns"
and "inspiring" sauces. / EC1V 9EY;
www.bigapplehotdogs.com.*

Big Easy £50 ❸❸❷
12 Maiden Ln, WC2 awaiting tel 4–3D **NEW**
332-334 King's Rd, SW3 7352 4071 5–3C
*"New Orleans was never closer!"; in the face of all
the upstart competition, this ever-"lively" Chelsea
surf 'n' turf shack still offers "excellent ribs and
burgers, and other stuff that isn't too healthy
either", plus the "best-value" lobster in town.
/ www.bigeasy.co.uk; @bigeasytweet; Mon-Thu 11 pm,
Fri-Sat 11.30 pm, Sun 10.30 pm.*

Bill's £38 ❸❸❷
Branches throughout London
*The "buzzy" branches of this fast-expanding chain
– "decked out like an old-fashioned produce store"
– make great standbys for "easy-going" occasions;
"fantastic" breakfast and brunches are a highlight.
/ most branches 11 pm.*

Bincho Yakitori W1 £37 ❸❸❸
16 Old Compton St 7287 9111 4–2A
*"A winner for a quick eat"; now bereft of its former
sibling, this "buzzing" Soho venue serves "very tasty
small bites". / W1D 4TL; www.bincho.co.uk; 11.30 pm,
Sun 10.30 pm; closed Mon L.*

The Bingham TW10 £70 ❷❷❶
61-63 Petersham Rd 8940 0902 1–4A
*"Stunning Thames views plus wonderful food served
with style" – that's the formula that wins huge
acclaim for this "sophisticated" Richmond hotel
dining room; indeed, since the removal of the
dreaded Michelin star, reporters are clearer than
ever that it's "always a delight! / TW10 6UT;
www.thebingham.co.uk; 10 pm; closed Sun D; no trainers;
SRA-58%.*

**Bird in Hand
W14** **NEW** £42 ❸❸❸
Brook Green 7371 2721 7–1C
*"Transformed from a second-rate pub to a first-rate
Italian restaurant" – a family-friendly Brook Green
newcomer offering "a generous range of freshly-
prepared pizzas, and an interesting wine list".
/ W14 0LR; www.thebirdinhandlondon.com;
@TBIHLondon; 10 pm.*

**Bird of Smithfield
EC1** **NEW** £51 ❹❹❸
26 Smithfield St 7559 5100 9–2B
*A very mixed survey reception for this ex-Ivy chef's
"brasserie-style" Smithfield newcomer; fans say it's
a "wonderful" place with an "excellent and simple"
menu, while others cite "teething problems" – let's
hope they can sort them out. / EC1A 9LB;
www.birdofsmithfield.com; @BirdoSmithfield; 10.15 pm;
closed Sun D; SRA-57%.*

Bistro 1 £23 ❹❷❸
27 Frith St, W1 7734 6204 4–3A
75 Beak St, W1 7287 1840 3–2D
33 Southampton St, WC2 7379 7585 4–3D
*"A good choice when you're in a hurry"; these
"basic" – but "efficient" and "friendly" – bistros
have handy West End locations, and offer
a "good selection" of dishes at "reasonable" prices.
/ www.bistro1.co.uk; @bistro1_london; midnight.*

Bistro Aix N8 £53 ❷❶❷
54 Topsfield Pde, Tottenham Ln 8340 6346
8–1C
*A "little piece of Paris", in Crouch End –
"a wonderful neighbourhood restaurant" where the
cuisine is "authentic", the service "very helpful",
and the setting "incredibly romantic". / N8 8PT;
www.bistroaix.co.uk; 10 pm, Fri & Sat 11 pm; no Amex.*

Bistro Union SW4 £44 ❸❷❸
40 Abbeville Rd 7042 6400 10–2D
*Adam Byatt's Clapham bistro yearling is "less formal
than its big sister Trinity", and is a "fun" and
"casual" venue for food that's "hearty" and
"satisfying"… if not quite as exciting as the
pedigree might suggest. / SW4 9NG;
www.bistrounion.co.uk; 10 pm; closed Sun D.*

**Bistrot Bruno Loubet
The Zetter EC1** £53 ❸❸❸
St John's Square 86-88 Clerkenwell Rd
7324 4455 9–1A
*Fans of Bruno Loubet's "airy" Clerkenwell three-
year-old still laud his creative "take on classic bistro
cuisine", all "at a non-astronomical price"; quite
a few reports of late, however, suggest "the spirit
has gone out of the place" – the strain of opening
Grain Store, perhaps? / EC1M 5RJ;
www.bistrotbrunoloubet.com; 10.30 pm, Sun 10 pm;
SRA-73%.*

Bistrotheque E2 £52 ❸❸❷
23-27 Wadeson St 8983 7900 1–2D
*"The absence of a sign" is all part of the "intrigue"
that's made this "great East End local", in a former
warehouse, a major boho hit – a "buzzy" and
"bright" space, sometimes with a pianist, where the
food has "definitely improved in recent times".
/ E2 9DR; www.bistrotheque.com; @BISTROTHEQUE;
10.30 pm, Fri & Sat 11 pm; closed weekday L;
set weekday L & pre-theatre £33 (FP).*

Black & Blue   **£52**   ❸❸④
37 Berners St, W1   7436 0451   2–1B
90-92 Wigmore St, W1   7486 1912   3–1A
215-217 Kensington Church St, W8
7727 0004   6–2B
1-2 Rochester Walk, SE1   7357 9922   9–4C
*"Can't be beaten for quality, price and consistency";
these "no-frills" steakhouses generally make a virtue
of being "predictable", although the odd "average
all-round" experience is not unknown.
/ www.blackandbluerestaurant.com; @BlackBlueGroup;
most branches 11 pm, Fri & Sat 11.30 pm; W1 closed
Sun; no booking.*

BLEEDING HEART
EC1   **£62**   ❸❷❶
Bleeding Heart Yd, Greville St
7242 8238   9–2A
*"Tucked-away on the edge of the City", this hugely
popular and immensely characterful warren –
combining bistro, tavern and restaurant –
is, "curiously, as suited to romance as it is to power
dining"; its "stereotypically Gallic" staff offer "a gem
of a wine list" to complement the "classic" bourgeois
fare. / EC1N 8SJ; www.bleedingheart.co.uk; 10.30 pm;
closed Sun.*

Blue Elephant SW6   **£49**   ❸❸❷
The Boulevard   7751 3111   10–1B
*Fans do vaunt the "lovely location overlooking
Chelsea Harbour", but it's difficult to avoid the
conclusion that this grand Thai institution has
"lost its mojo" since it moved to the fringes
of Fulham; the Sunday buffet, in particular,
"just doesn't taste the same". / SW6 2UB;
www.blueelephant.com; @BlueElephantLon; 11.30 pm,
Sun 10.30 pm.*

Blue Legume   **£40**   ④❷❷
101 Stoke Newington Church St, N16
7923 1303   1–1C
177 Upper St, N1   7226 5858   8–2D
130 Crouch Hill, N8   8442 9282   8–1C
*"Find a space amongst the buggies", if you visit
these "bright" and "welcoming" north London diners
– "super places for brunch", where "growth doesn't
seemed to have compromised quality".
/ www.thebluelegume.co.uk; 10.30 pm; N8 closed
L, N16 closed Sun D.*

Bluebird SW3   **£64**   ⑤④④
350 King's Rd   7559 1000   5–3C
*The D&D group's Chelsea landmark has the
occasional fan, but, given its size and prominence,
inspires remarkably limited survey feedback –
"it has such potential", bemoans one reporter,
"but only the location makes it popular".
/ SW3 5UU; www.bluebird-restaurant.co.uk; 10.30 pm,
Sun 9.30 pm; set weekday L £32 (FP); SRA-64%.*

Bluebird Café SW3   **£42**   ⑤⑤④
350 King's Rd   7559 1000   5–3C
*"Oh dear, even the chips were appalling" – like its
parent restaurant, this prominently-sited café seems
to rely very heavily on the charms of its fashionable
King's Road location; at least it's "great for people-
watching". / SW3 5UU; www.bluebird-restaurant.co.uk;
@bluebirdchelsea; 10 pm, Sun 9.30 pm; no reservations.*

Blueprint Café
Design Museum SE1   **£47**   ④④❶
28 Shad Thames, Butler's Wharf
7378 7031   9–4D
*You'll be "bowled over by the views" of Tower Bridge
("they put binoculars on every table"), at this South
Bank D&D group restaurant; it's striking how little
survey feedback it has inspired since its longtime
former chef departed – this averages out
somewhere round "OK". / SE1 2YD;
www.blueprintcafe.co.uk; 10.30 pm; closed Sun D;
SRA-61%.*

Bo London W1 NEW   **£80**   ❸❷④
4 Mill St   7493 3886   3–2C
*Alvin Leung's new Mayfair restaurant, on the former
site of Patterson's (RIP), specialises in "incredible"
("don't-try-this-at-home") Chinese dishes at "second
mortgage" prices; fans (the majority) say you
"you must try it once", but the doubters just "can't
see the point". / W1S 2AX;
www.bolondonrestaurant.com; @Bo_London; 11 pm;
closed Sat L & Sun; set weekday L £52 (FP).*

Bob Bob Ricard W1   **£63**   ❸❷❶
1 Upper James St   3145 1000   3–2D
*"Frankly ridiculous decor" – complete with boothed
seating, and a champagne call-button on every table
– sets the decadent tone of this "quirky" but
"glamorous" Soho venue, where "high-end comfort
food" is twinned with "wonderful bargains on top-
end wine". / W1F 9DF; www.bobbobricard.com;
10.30 pm; closed Sat L & Sun; jacket.*

Bocca Di Lupo W1   **£59**   ❶❷❷
12 Archer St   7734 2223   3–2D
*"Inspired", "regional" Italian tapas – "matched
by no other Italian restaurant in London",
and served by "passionate" and "unpretentious"
staff – win adulation for this "bustling" venture,
tucked away near Piccadilly Circus; "get a counter
seat to watch the brigade in action". / W1D 7BB;
www.boccadilupo.com; 11 pm, Sun 9.15 pm; booking:
max 10.*

Al Boccon di'vino
TW9   **£64**   **❶❷❷**
14 Red Lion St   8940 9060   1–4A
"You eat what the owner bought in the market"
("you have no option but to go with the flow")
at this slightly "wacky", old-fashioned Italian,
in Richmond town centre; pratically all reporters are
"bowled over" by it – an "always fun, interesting,
and filling" experience with "wonderful" food.
/ TW9 1RW; www.nonsolovinoltd.co.uk; 8 pm; closed
Mon, Tue L & Wed L.

Bodean's   **£44**   **❸④❸**
10 Poland St, W1   7287 7575   3–1D
4 Broadway Chambers, SW6   7610 0440   5–4A
169 Clapham High St, SW4   7622 4248   10–2D
16 Byward St, EC3   7488 3883   9–3D
"It certainly feels like you're in the US of A", if you
visit these "OTT sports-bar-style" BBQ joints; "ribs,
wings, fries and slaw", and "delicious beers" too –
"ain't nothing fancy, but boy do you get fed!"
/ www.bodeansbbq.com; 11 pm, Sun 10.30 pm;
8 or more.

La Bodega Negra W1   **£47**   **④❸❷**
13-17 Moor St   7758 4100   4–2B
This "busy" and "dimly-lit" Soho basement Mexican
can be "a fun night out"; it's "quite pricey for what
it is", though, and critics dismiss it as "all gimmicks".
/ W1D 5NH; www.labodeganegra.com; 1 am,
Sun 11.30 pm.

Boisdale SW1   **£55**   **❸❸❷**
13-15 Eccleston St   7730 6922   2–4B
"A superb cigar terrace" is amongst the manly
attractions of this Belgravia "bastion" of Scottish
Baronial sensibility; it is also known for its "perfect"
steak, "excellent" wine, and "splendid" whiskies,
all at prices some find "a bit OTT". / SW1W 9LX;
www.boisdale.co.uk; 11.30 pm; closed Sat L & Sun.

Boisdale of Canary
Wharf E14   **£60**   **④④❸**
Cabot Pl   7715 5818   11–1C
"Panoramic views of Cabot Square" underpin the
"power-lunch" (or "power dinner with jazz") appeal
of this Caledonian-themed restaurant, where "great
steaks and burgers" are the stock-in-trade; no huge
surprise, though, that it can seem a bit "investment
banker-pricey". / E14 4QT; www.boisdale.co.uk;
10.30 pm; closed Sun.

The Bolingbroke
SW11   **£43**   **④❸❸**
174 Northcote Rd   7228 4040   10–2C
"Lots of kids create a happy atmosphere" for the
"great breakfasts", and lunches too, at this reliable
Battersea boozer; it is, however, "not the place for
a quiet supper". / SW11 6RE;
www.renaissancepubs.co.uk; 10.30 pm, Sun 9 pm;
SRA-56%.

Bombay Brasserie
SW7   **£56**   **❸④④**
Courtfield Close, Gloucester Rd   7370 4040
5–2B
This "cavernous" South Kensington subcontinental
is a "top tip" for some reporters, who particularly
praise the "excellent weekend buffet"; it also has
plenty of critics, though, who find it "overpriced,
pretentious, and living on past glories". / SW7 4QH;
www.bombaybrasserielondon.com; 11.30 pm,
Sun 10.30 pm.

Bombay Palace W2   **£55**   **❶❶❸**
50 Connaught St   7723 8855   6–1D
"By far the best, putting all other Indians to shame!"
– this "warm" and "friendly" Bayswater "hidden
gem", recently refurbished, dazzles all reporters with
its "classic" dishes, realised "to a standard rarely
found". / W2 2AA; www.bombay-palace.co.uk;
11.30 pm.

Bonds
Threadneedles
Hotel EC2   **£67**   **④④❸**
5 Threadneedle St   7657 8088   9–2C
This "refined" dining room, in a former banking hall,
inspires surprisingly little comment, given its heart-
of-the-City location; with its "good-value lunch
menu" and "well spaced tables", though,
some reporters find it a handy business rendezvous.
/ EC2R 8AY; www.bonds-restaurant.co.uk; 10 pm; closed
Sat & Sun; set weekday L £44 (FP).

Bone Daddies W1 **NEW** **£22**   **❷④❸**
30-31 Peter St   7287 8581   3–2D
"Delicious and innovative ramen, with rock 'n' roll
as the soundtrack" – the unlikely formula that's
made this "well-priced" Soho noodle-soup
newcomer an instant hit; needless to say,
it's "not the place for a relaxing dinner". / W1F 0AR;
www.bonedaddiesramen.com; @bonedaddiesRbar;
10 pm, Tue-Wed 11 pm, Thu-Sat midnight, Sun 9 pm.

Bonnie Gull W1 **NEW**   **£48**   **❷❸❷**
21a, Foley St   7436 0921   2–1B
"Small but perfectly formed" – this "hip" but
"friendly" Fitzrovia fish specialist (on the site of Back
to Basics, RIP) has made itself an instant hit.
/ W1W 6DS; www.bonniegull.com; @BonnieGull;
9.45 pm.

Boqueria SW2   **£33**   **❷❷❷**
192 Acre Ln   7733 4408   10–2D
"A hidden gem between Clapham and Brixton",
this "fantastic" funky yearling serves "really
excellent" tapas alongside a "small but decent"
selection of wines and sherries; even fans note,
though, it can get "very loud". / SW2 5UL;
www.boqueriatapas.com; @BoqueriaTapas; 11 pm,
Fri-Sat 12 am, Sun 10 pm; closed weekday L.

Il Bordello E1　　£48　　❷❶❷
81 Wapping High St　7481 9950　11–1A
*"On a quiet Wapping street", a "chaotic" and
"very friendly" pizza and pasta stop that's "always
heaving", thanks to its "outstanding" all-round value
(and "huge" portions). / E1W 2YN; www.ilbordello.com;
11 pm, Sun 10.30 pm; closed Sat L.*

La Bota N8　　£32　　❸❹❹
31 Broadway Pde　8340 3082　1–1C
*"Well-prepared classic dishes, no fuss, decent
portions and low prices" – this Crouch End favourite
is "just what a neighbourhood tapas restaurant
should be". / N8 9DB; www.labota.co.uk; 11 pm, Fri-Sun
11.30 pm; closed Mon L; no Amex.*

The Botanist SW1　　£61　　⑤⑤⑤
7 Sloane Sq　7730 0077　5–2D
*Thanks perhaps to its first-rate "people-watching"
possibilities, this "heaving" Sloane Square
bar/restaurant has become a self-perpetuating local
hub – it seems to have little to do with the actual
quality of the food or service! / SW1W 8EE;
www.thebotanistonsloanesquare.com; 10.45 pm.*

La Bottega　　£17　　❸❸❷
20 Ryder St, SW1　7839 5789　3–4C
25 Eccleston St, SW1　7730 2730　2–4B
65 Lower Sloane St, SW1　7730 8844　5–2D
97 Old Brompton Rd, SW7　7581 6622　5–2B
*"Perfect cappuccinos", "inexpensive lunchtime
snacks", "good wine" and "friendly" service – what's
not to like about these smart Italian café/delis?
/ www.labottega65.com; Lower Sloane St 8 pm, Sat 6 pm,
Sun 5 pm; Eccleston St 7 pm; Old Brompton Rd 8 pm;
Ryder St closed Sat & Sun; no booking.*

La Bouchée SW7　　£47　　❹❹❸
56 Old Brompton Rd　7589 1929　5–2B
*With its "petit coin de Paris" charm, this "dark,
cosy and romantic" (and "cramped") South
Kensington cellar remains a "safe bet" for a "tasty"
meal. / SW7 3DY; 11 pm, Sun 10.30 pm; set weekday
L & pre-theatre £31 (FP).*

**Bouchon Fourchette
E8 NEW**　　£36　　❷❷❸
171 Mare St　8986 2702　1–2D
*"You could be in Paris", at this "totally French"
newcomer… "which feels a bit odd, in Hackney!";
its "tiny kitchen" produces a "very simple menu"
of "good-value" classics. / E8 3RH; @BFourchette;
10 pm, Fri & Sat 11 pm; closed Mon L.*

Boudin Blanc W1　　£60　　❹❹❷
5 Trebeck St　7499 3292　3–4B
*"Busy, cramped, and with bags of atmosphere",
this "very French" bistro remains a "reliable" old-
favourite for most reporters (and it has some great
al fresco tables in Shepherd Market); critics,
however, find the cuisine "undemanding",
and complain of "Parisian attitude" on the service
front. / W1J 7LT; www.boudinblanc.co.uk; 11 pm;
set weekday L £30 (FP).*

Boulestin SW1 NEW　　£66　　❸❷❸
5 St James's St　7930 2030　3–4D
*On the former St James's site of L'Oranger (RIP),
an elegant new French restaurant offering
a straight-down-the-line comfort formula de luxe,
of a type rarely found nowadays; it was already well
into its swing on our early-days visit. / SW1A 1EF;
www.boulestin.co.uk.*

Boulevard WC2　　£44　　❹❹❸
40 Wellington St　7240 2992　4–3D
*This stereotypical but "attractive" Theatreland
brasserie divides opinion; to cynics,
it's "the worst sort of tourist trap", but it also has its
fans who say it offers "no-nonsense" fare
at reasonable prices. / WC2E 7BD;
www.boulevardbrasserie.co.uk; 11 pm, Fri & Sat
11.30 pm, Sun 10.30 pm.*

The Boundary E2　　£62　　❷❷❷
2-4 Boundary St　7729 1051　12–1B
*Sir Terence Conran's "luxurious" basement
restaurant, in trendy Shoreditch, offers Gallic dining
in a surprisingly "classic" (and "pricey") style –
"ideal for power dining", with "attentive" service and
an "excellent wine selection"; "in summer, have a
drink at the rooftop bar first". / E2 7DD;
www.theboundary.co.uk; 10.30 pm; D only, ex Sun L only.*

**The Bountiful Cow
WC1**　　£53　　❹❹❹
51 Eagle St　7404 0200　2–1D
*"Big, bloody and juicy" – the burgers at this
Bloomsbury basement are "amazing", say fans;
overall, though, there's less survey commentary than
we'd like, not all of it especially complimentary.
/ WC1R 4AP; www.thebountifulcow.co.uk; 10.30 pm;
closed Sun.*

Bradley's NW3　　£57　　❹❸❹
25 Winchester Rd　7722 3457　8–2A
*"Tucked away in a Swiss Cottage backstreet",
this ambitious local is, say fans, "a real gem"; while
all reporters agree the pre-(Hampstead)-theatre
deals are great, however, sceptics find standards
"erratic". / NW3 3NR; www.bradleysnw3.co.uk; 10 pm;
closed Sun D; set weekday L & pre-theatre £35 (FP).*

Brady's SW18 £33 ❷❷❷
513 Old York Rd 8877 9599 10–2B
The burghers of Battersea are very excited about their favourite chippy, which has been "very much improved" by its move to new riverside premises, where the fish 'n' chips are "superb"; "there are still queues, but now there's a smart bar to wait in!". / SW18 1TF; www.bradysfish.co.uk; @Bradyfish; 10 pm, Sun 8.30 pm; closed Mon, Tue L, Wed L & Thu L; no Amex; no booking.

La Brasserie SW3 £56 ❸❹❷
272 Brompton Rd 7581 3089 5–2C
"Yes, the prices are high, but the food is terrific", says one of the fans of this "perennial favourite" Gallic brasserie, on a prominent Chelsea corner; it's "always buzzy" – most famously for breakfast. / SW3 2AW; www.labrasserielondon.co.uk; 11.30 pm; no booking, Sat L & Sun L.

Brasserie Blanc £52 ❹❸❹
8 Charlotte St, W1 7636 4975 2–1C
119 Chancery Ln, WC2 7405 0290 2–2D
35 The Mkt, WC2 7379 0666 4–3D
9 Belvedere Rd, SE1 7202 8470 2–3D
60 Threadneedle St, EC2 7710 9440 9–2C
14 Trinity Sq, EC3 7480 5500 9–3D
1 Watling St, EC4 7213 0540 9–2B
With its "simple" Gallic staples and "helpful" service, Raymond Blanc's brasserie chain makes a "reliable" fall-back; last year, it absorbed the old Chez Gérard outlets, including the WC2 branch, which – with many al fresco tables on the first floor of Covent Garden Market – has one of London's best locations. / www.brasserieblanc.com; most branches close between 10 pm & 11 pm; SE1 closed Sun D, most City branches closed Sat & Sun; SRA-64%.

Brasserie Chavot
W1 NEW £70 ❷❸❸
41 Conduit St 7078 9577 3–2C
Eric Chavot is a chef with a long-term fan base, and it's turned out in force to acclaim the "spectacular", "classic" Gallic fare on offer at his new Mayfair dining room; the spacious interior – inherited from the Gallery (RIP) – is somewhere between "beautiful" and "blingy". / W1S 2YQ; www.brasseriechavot.com; @brasseriechavot; 10.30 pm, Sun 9 pm.

Brasserie Max
Covent Garden
Hotel WC2 £73 ❹❹❸
10 Monmouth St 7806 1000 4–2B
An attractive hotel brasserie which offers a retreat from the hustle and bustle of Covent Garden; even foes concede it's a "buzzy spot", and even fans acknowledge it's "not the cheapest". / WC2H 9HB; www.coventgardenhotel.co.uk; 11 pm; set pre theatre £47 (FP).

Brasserie on St John
Street EC1 £41 ❸❹❹
360-362 St John's St 7837 1199 8–3D
"Well situated for Sadler's Wells" – almost invariably the context in which reporters note this "noisy" brasserie; the food is not the main point, but it rarely seems to disappoint. / EC1V 4NR; www.the-brasserie.com; 11 pm, Fri-Sat 11.30 pm, Sun 10.30 pm; closed Mon.

Brasserie Toulouse-
Lautrec SE11 £39 ❸❷❷
140 Newington Butts 7582 6800 1–3C
This wine bar offshoot of Kennington's nearby Lobster Pot is as "authentically Gallic" an affair as you'll find, and the food, say local supporters, is "better than ever" – "well worth supporting". / SE11 4RN; www.btlrestaurant.co.uk; 10.30 pm, Sat & Sun 11 pm.

BRASSERIE ZÉDEL W1 £38 ❺❸❶
20 Sherwood St 7734 4888 3–2D
For an "opulently Parisian" experience on the cheap, you can't beat Corbin & King's vast and "dazzling" Art Deco basement, near Piccadilly Circus; views divide, however, on the overall verdict – for a majority the "democratised" prices make it "remarkable value", but a large minority finds the "clichéd" brasserie fare "underwhelming". / W1F 7ED; www.brasseriezedel.com; @brasseriezedel; 11.45 pm; SRA-74%.

Brawn E2 £48 ❷❷❸
49 Columbia Rd 7729 5692 12–1C
"So different, so fresh, so quirky" – this "cool" East End offshoot of the Terroirs empire has won renown with its "terrific, imaginative" food, its "brilliant selection of really interesting wines", and its all-round "attention to detail". / E2 7RG; www.brawn.co; @brawn49; 11 pm; closed Mon L & Sun D; no Amex.

Bread Street Kitchen
EC4 £62 ❹❹❹
1 New Change 3030 4050 9–2B
"Warehouse-y", "cavernous" and "noisy", this City shopping mall dining room gives no particular hint of being owned by the world-famous Gordon Ramsay; the food – "nothing special" – likewise. / EC4M 9AF; www.breadstreetkitchen.com; 11 pm, Sun 8 pm.

Briciole W1 £39 ❸❸❸
20 Homer St 7723 0040 6–1D
"Wonderful ingredients are served very simply", at this "transformed" former pub, in a "quiet Marylebone backwater" – now a "bustling", "welcoming" and "good-value" Italian bar/deli. / W1H 4NA; www.briciole.co.uk; @briciolelondon; 10.15 pm.

Brick Lane Beigel Bake E1   **£7**   ❶❷④
159 Brick Ln   7729 0616   12–1C
The "world-famous East End bakery", open 24/7;
"you can't beat a salt beef beigel from here,
any time of day or night"… but "they taste
best at 2am!" / E1 6SB; open 24 hours; no credit cards;
no booking.

The Bright Courtyard W1   **£55**   ④④④
43-45 Baker St   7486 6998   2–1A
"Top dim sum" are a highlight at this grand and airy
Marylebone Chinese (part of a Shanghai-based
chain); "the only problem is the price"… especially
with Royal China just over the road. / W1U 8EW;
www.lifefashiongroup.com; 10.45 pm, Thu-Sat 11.15 pm.

Brilliant UB2   **£37**   ❷❷❸
72-76 Western Rd   8574 1928   1–3A
An "amazing eatery", deep in the suburb
of Southall, rightly renowned for "authentic Punjabi
food that's always first class". / UB2 5DZ;
www.brilliantrestaurant.com; @BRILLIANTRST; 11 pm,
Fri-Sat 11.30 pm; closed Mon, Sat L & Sun L.

Brinkley's SW10   **£51**   ⑤④❸
47 Hollywood Rd   7351 1683   5–3B
Home from home for the "Made in Chelsea crowd"
– this "atmospheric" stalwart wins a loyal following
with its "great value-for-money wines", and "lovely"
garden; critics, however, dismiss the "basic" scoff
as "rah-rah rubbish". / SW10 9HX;
www.brinkleys; 11 pm; closed weekday L.

Brinkley's Kitchen SW17   **£51**   ④④❸
35 Bellevue Rd   8672 5888   10–2C
"A fab local that never disappoints"; John Brinkley's
Wandsworth brasserie is a "buzzy" sort of place
offering a "really well chosen" and "good-value"
wine list, plus "sensibly-priced" food that plays a bit
of a supporting role. / SW17 7EF; www.brinkleys.com;
@BrinkleysR; 11 pm; closed Mon & Sun D.

Brompton Bar & Grill SW3   **£56**   ❸❷❸
243 Brompton Rd   7589 8005   5–2C
"Professional", "businesslike", "reliable", "relaxing",
and "reasonably-priced"; this well-spaced bistro –
on the Knightsbridge site which old-stagers will
recall as the Brasserie St Quentin – attracts nothing
but positive reports. / SW3 2EP;
www.bromptonbarandgrill.com; 10.30 pm, Sun 10 pm.

The Brown Cow SW6   **£42**   ❸❸❷
676 Fulham Rd   7384 9559   10–1B
Heart-of-Fulham locals are lucky that the Sands
End team has taken over the former premises
of Manson (RIP), which now trades as a "fun"
gastroboozer, offering food that's "good, if not
gastronomic". / SW6 5SA; www.thebrowncowpub.co.uk.

The Brown Dog SW13 £48   ❸❸❷
28 Cross St   8392 2200   10–1A
A "hidden-away gem", in Barnes's super-cute Little
Chelsea – a "really welcoming and cosy local pub"
where the cooking is "a cut above standards
gastropub pub fare"; "dog-friendly too!" / SW13 0AP;
www.thebrowndog.co.uk; @browndogbarnes; 10 pm,
Sun 9 pm.

(Hix at Albemarle) Brown's Hotel W1   **£78**   ④❸❸
Albemarle St   7518 4004   3–3C
With its spacious layout, and its secluded tables and
booths, this "discreet" Mayfair dining room
is certainly "well-placed for business lunches";
despite Mark Hix's involvement, though, standards
remain "ordinary, for a place of this price and
type". / W1S 4BP; www.thealbemarlerestaurant.com;
11 pm, Sun 10.30 pm.

Browns   **£46**   ⑤④④
2 Cardinal Pl, SW1   7821 1450   2–4B
47 Maddox St, W1   7491 4565   3–2C
82-84 St Martin's Ln, WC2   7497 5050   4–3B
9 Islington Grn, N1   7226 2555   8–3D
Butler's Wharf, SE1   7378 1700   9–4D
Hertsmere Rd, E14   7987 9777   11–1C
8 Old Jewry, EC2   7606 6677   9–2C
These "buzzy" English brasseries often occupy
"fantastic" old buildings, and fans say they make
"reliable" venues for many occasions; there are still
too many reports, though, of meals where "every
dish disappointed… and always in a different way!"
/ www.browns-restaurants.co.uk; most branches
10 pm-11 pm; EC2 closed Sat D & Sun; W1 closed
Sun D.

Brula TW1   **£52**   ❷❶❷
43 Crown Rd   8892 0602   1–4A
"Brula is brilliant!" – St Margaret's locals adore this
"great little French-style neighbourhood restaurant";
it can get "noisy", though, and tables are "rather
close". / TW1 3EJ; www.brula.co.uk; 10.30 pm; closed
Mon & Sun D.

Brunswick House Cafe SW8   **£42**   ❸④❷
30 Wandsworth Rd   7720 2926   10–1D
You eat "surrounded by architectural salvage" at this
"quirky" venue – a listed Georgian house packed
with "bric-a-brac", right next to the "hideous"
Vauxhall traffic system; it makes for a "wonderful,
if unlikely" experience – surprisingly "comfortable",
and with some "delicious" British grub. / SW8 2LG;
www.brunswickhousecafe.co.uk; 10 pm; closed Sun D.

Bubbledogs W1 £30 ④❸❷
70 Charlotte St   7637 7770   2–1C
"Great champagne plus tasty hot dogs" – it's sure
a "novel" concept, and the queues testify to the
success of this unlikely Fitzrovia "dude food" hit…
and critics duly insist that this
is "the most overhyped place in town"; (see also
Kitchen Table @ Bubbledogs). / W1T 4QG;
www.bubbledogs.co.uk; 9 pm; closed Sun.

**(Kitchen Table)
Bubbledogs W1** NEW £91 ❶❷❷
70 Charlotte St   7637 7770   2–1C
"My most exciting restaurant experience in years!"
– enter via the hot dog place to eat at this
horseshoe-shaped chef's table (19 seats), where
James Knappett and his "brilliantly choreographed"
chefs deliver a "stunning" 12-14 course dinner
that's "full of invention", with wines from the
"passionate" sommelier. / W1T 4QG;
www.kitchentablelondon.co.uk; 9.30 pm (6 & & 7.30 pm
seatings only); D only, closed Mon & Sun.

Buen Ayre E8 £51 ❶④④
50 Broadway Mkt   7275 9900   1–2D
"A small, humble, crowded and insanely popular
Argentinian steakhouse, in the East End"; regulars
say it "laughs in face of more sophisticated rivals
like Hawksmoor", by serving "life-changing hunks
of meat" (cooked on an open fire) at "great-value"
prices. / E8 4QJ; www.buenayre.co.uk; 10.30 pm;
no Amex.

Buenos Aires Cafe £51 ❸④❸
86 Royal Hill, SE10   8488 6764   1–3D
17 Royal Pde, SE3   8318 5333   1–4D
"A steak-eater's delight"; this busy Argentinian –
in an "atmospheric location overlooking the Heath"
– is one of the best bets in Blackheath village;
the Greenwich spin-off is more café-like.
/ www.buenosairesltd.com; SE3 10.30 pm; SE10 7 pm,
Sat & Sun 6 pm; no Amex.

**The Builders Arms
SW3** £44 ④❸❸
13 Britten St   7349 9040   5–2C
"Good gastropub, very relaxing, not too noisy
or packed" – all you need to know about this
notably consistent Chelsea gastroboozer, hidden
away behind Waitrose. / SW3 3TY;
www.geronimo-inns.co.uk; 10 pm, Thu-Sat 11 pm,
Sun 9 pm; no booking; SRA-60%.

Bull & Last NW5 £61 ❷❸❸
168 Highgate Rd   7267 3641   8–1B
"Setting the gastropub benchmark", this "perfect"
Kentish Town phenomenon offers "quality food in a
real pub setting"; OK, nowhere's actually perfect –
it's "a bit too loud". / NW5 1QS;
www.thebullandlast.co.uk; @thebullandlast; 10 pm,
Sun 9 pm.

Bumpkin £51 ⑤⑤④
119 Sydney St, SW3   3730 9344   5–2B NEW
102 Old Brompton Rd, SW7   7341 0802   5–2B
209 Westbourne Park Rd, W11   7243 9818
6–1B
Westfield Stratford City, 105-106 The Street, E20
8221 9900   1–1D
This faux-"rustic" British chain has its fans,
who praise its "freshly cooked fare" and
"very relaxed" style; "well-meaning but incompetent"
service, however, is a perennial bugbear – "it would
have been comical, if they hadn't been charging for
it!" / www.bumpkinuk.com; 11 pm.

Buona Sera £38 ④❸❸
289a King's Rd, SW3   7352 8827   5–3C
22 Northcote Rd, SW11   7228 9925   10–2C
"Reliable" and reasonably-priced, this Italian café
in Battersea has quite a name as a "kid-friendly"
destination (if sometimes a "hellishly noisy" one);
its Chelsea spin-off, with its "perennially fascinating"
two-level layout, is "hard to beat for impromptu pre-
cinema dining". / midnight; SW3 11.30 pm,
Sun 10 pm; SW3 closed Mon L.

Burger & Lobster £43 ❷❸❸
Harvey Nichols, SW1   7235 5000   5–1D NEW
29 Clarges St, W1   7409 1699   3–4B
36 Dean St, W1   7432 4800   4–2A
40 St John St, EC1   7490 9230   9–1B
Bow Bells Hs, 1 Bread St, EC4   7248 1789
9–2B NEW
"Dead simple" but "divine", a formula of lobster,
lobster brioche or burger powers the growth
of these "fun" and "casual" hang-out; they are
"always packed" and "noisy", though, and waits can
be "infuriating". / www.burgerandlobster.com;
@Londonlobster; 10.30 pm; Clarges St closed Sun D,
Bread St & St John St closed Sun.

Busaba Eathai £38 ❸❸❷
35 Panton St, SW1   7930 0088   4–4A
106-110 Wardour St, W1   7255 8686   3–2D
8-13 Bird St, W1   7518 8080   3–1A
22 Store St, WC1   7299 7900   2–1C
44 Floral St, WC2   7759 0088   4–2D
358 King's Rd, SW3   7349 5488   5–3B
Westfield, Ariel Way, W12   3249 1919   7–1C
Westfield Stratford, E20   8221 8989   1–1D
313-319 Old St, EC1   7729 0808   12–1B
"A lovely relaxed vibe" is created by the dark and
"funky" decor at these large-communal-table
'Thai Wagamamas' (same creator, but better
ratings) – "a great cheap eat", with dishes offering
"lovely vivid flavours". / www.busaba.co.uk; 11 pm,
Fri & Sat 11.30 pm, Sun 10 pm; W1 no booking;
WC1 booking: min 10.

Bush Dining Hall
W12 NEW   £42   ❸❹❸
304 Uxbridge Rd   8749 0731   7–1B
"A welcome addition to Shepherd's Bush" – this new
"oasis" is an add-on to the characterful music
venue, offering a "short" modern British menu,
which critics find a touch "overpriced". / W12 7LJ;
www.bushhalldining.co.uk; @BushHallDining; 10.30 pm,
Fri-Sat 10 pm; closed Sun D.

Butcher & Grill SW11 £47   ❹❸❸
39-41 Parkgate Rd   7924 3999   5–4C
A Battersea local restaurant with a deli and butcher
attached; sceptics say there's "room for all-round
improvement", but "the beef is of high standard",
and the place has something of a reputation as a
family brunch spot; the SW19 branch is no more.
/ SW11 4NP; www.thebutcherandgrill.com; 11 pm,
Sun 4 pm; closed Sun D.

Butcher's Hook SW6 £41   ❸❷❸
477 Fulham Rd   7385 4654   5–4A
A "great local gastropub", opposite Stamford Bridge
– "a top place for an interesting lunch before the
footie". / SW6 1HL; www.thebutchershook.co.uk;
10.30 pm; no Amex.

Butlers Wharf
Chop House SE1   £60   ❹❹❹
36e Shad Thames   7403 3403   9–4D
Mixed views on this D&D group South Bank fixture
– fans praise the "beautiful location by Tower
Bridge", and the "meaty feasts" on offer, but critics
find standards "variable", and caution that "the bar
offers much better value than the restaurant".
/ SE1 2YE; www.chophouse.co.uk; 10.45 pm,
Sun 9.45 pm; set weekday L £37 (FP); SRA-63%.

La Buvette TW9   £44   ❸❷❷
6 Church Walk   8940 6264   1–4A
"A treasure in the heart of Richmond", this "quietly
hidden-away" and "cosy" ("cramped") bistro offers
Gallic fare that's "old-fashioned" but "reliable";
for the summer, it has "lovely" tables in a leafy
courtyard too. / TW9 1SN; www.labuvette.co.uk;
@labuvettebistro; 10 pm.

Byron   £35   ❸❸❸
11 Haymarket, SW1   7925 0276   4–4A
97-99 Wardour St, W1   7297 9390   3–2D
24-28 Charing Cross Rd, WC2   7557 9830
4–4B
33-35 Wellington St, WC2   7420 9850   4–3D
300 King's Rd, SW3   7352 6040   5–3C
242 Earl's Court Rd, SW5   7370 9300   5–2A
75 Gloucester Rd, SW7   7244 0700   5–2B
93-95 Old Brompton Rd, SW7   7590 9040
5–2B
Westfield, Ariel Way, W12   8743 7755   7–1C
222 Kensington High St, W8   7361 1717   5–1A
341 Upper St, N1   7704 7620   8–3D
46 Hoxton Sq, N1   3487 1230   12–1B
22 Putney High St, SW15   8246 4170   10–2B
Cabot Place East, E14   7715 9360   11–1C
7 Upper Cheapside Pas, One New Change, EC2
7246 2580   9–2B
"Not been to a bad'un yet!"; this phenomenal
chain's growth remains "hectic", but it continues
to impress with its "proper" burgers, its "fantastic"
milkshakes, and its "attractive" (if sometimes
"incredibly noisy") branches; can it last though? –
ratings are, slowly, inching south.
/ www.byronhamburgers.com; -most branches 11 pm;
SRA-63%.

C London W1   £97   ⑤⑤④
25 Davies St   7399 0500   3–2B
Even as a "fun" night out for rubbernecking the
Eurotrash, this Mayfair Italian circus seems to be
running out of steam – critics say food that's
"inferior to your typical trattoria" comes at "insane"
prices, and service is "catastrophic". / W1K 3DE;
www.crestaurant.co.uk; 11.45 pm.

C&R Cafe   £29   ❸④④
3-4 Rupert Ct, W1   7434 1128   4–3A
52 Westbourne Grove, W2   7221 7979   6–1B
Looking for a "cheap" but "inspiring" bite? –
this "cramped" but "fun" Indonesian/Malaysian
café, tucked-away in Chinatown, "consistently
delivers the goods"; no feedback on the Bayswater
branch. / www.cnrrestaurant.com; 11 pm.

The Cabin W4   £48   ④④④
148 Chiswick High Rd   8994 8594   7–2A
"Good grills, good seafood, good variety" – this solid
(if perhaps "not spectacular") surf 'n' turf diner
in Chiswick wins a steady local following. / W4 1PR;
www.cabinrestaurants.co.uk; 10.30 pm, Fri & Sat 11 pm;
No toddlers after 6pm.

**The Cadogan Arms
SW3**   **£48**   ❸❹❸
298 King's Rd   7352 6500   5–3C
*"An underrated gem" – this King's Road corner
boozer, handy for the UGC cinema, offers "simple
but well cooked school food in a traditional pub
atmosphere". / SW3 5UG;
www.thecadoganarmschelsea.com; @TheCadoganArms;
10.30 pm, Sun 9 pm.*

Café 209 SW6   **£23**   ❹❸❶
209 Munster Rd   7385 3625   10–1B
*Zany owner Joy ensures "it's always a hilarious
experience" to dine at this tiny, squashed-in BYO
caff in deepest Fulham, where the Thai chow
is "inexpensive" but tasty. / SW6 6BX; 10.30 pm;
D only, closed Sun, closed Dec; no Amex.*

**Le Café Anglais
Whiteley's W2**   **£58**   ❸❹❷
8 Porchester Gdns   7221 1415   6–1C
*"Like a cruise ship's main dining room" – Rowley
Leigh's "light" and "well-spaced" Deco-ish brasserie
(with oyster bar) floats serenely on the top floor
of Whiteleys, and its cuisine is "very competent";
"inept" service can let it down (but they are
"very kid friendly"); Monday nights BYO, no corkage!
/ W2 4DB; www.lecafeanglais.co.uk; 10.30 pm, Fri & Sat
11 pm, Sun 10pm.*

Café Below EC2   **£33**   ❹❹❸
St Mary-le-Bow, Cheapside   7329 0789   9–2C
*"Home-made food in the City", all "at very
reasonable prices", underpins the appeal of this
simple self-service café, which occupies the
atmospheric crypt of St Mary le Bow. / EC2 6AU;
www.cafebelow.co.uk; 3 pm; L only, closed Sat & Sun.*

Café Bohème W1   **£45**   ❸❸❷
13 Old Compton St   7734 0623   4–2A
*At "atmospheric" café/bar/brasserie at the heart
of Soho – an ideal spot for a West End rendezvous,
and offering pretty dependable food at "reasonable
prices". / W1 5JQ; www.cafeboheme.co.uk;
@CafeBoheme1; 2.45 am, Sun midnight; no reservations.*

Café del Parc N19   **£35**   ❷❶❷
167 Junction Road   7281 5684   8–1C
*"Superb hosts" win a devoted small fan club for this
"tapas-with-a-twist" culinary oasis, "in the desert
that is Tufnell Park". / N19 5PZ; www.delparc.com;
10.30 pm; open D only, Wed-Sun; no Amex.*

Café des Amis WC2   **£57**   ❹❹❹
11-14 Hanover Pl   7379 3444   4–2D
*With its "handy" location, down a cute alley near
the Royal Opera House, this "busy" Covent Garden
landmark is well-known as a "useful pre-theatre
or post-opera" operation; the "overpriced" food
"could be better", though, and service too often
"goes awry". / WC2E 9JP; www.cafedesamis.co.uk;
11.30 pm, Sun 7pm.*

Café du Marché EC1   **£54**   ❷❷❶
22 Charterhouse Sq   7608 1609   9–1B
*"Be transported from Clerkenwell to a village
in France", at this "side ally secret" –
an "old faithful" that's "everything a French
restaurant ought to be"; "solid" bourgeois cuisine
is "charmingly" served in a "cosy and candle-lit"
setting, that's business-friendly at lunch,
but seductive by night. / EC1M 6DX;
www.cafedumarche.co.uk; 10 pm; closed Sat L & Sun.*

Cafe East SE16   **£22**   ❷❹❹
100 Redriff Rd   7252 1212   11–2B
*"The best pho in London" headlines the "very fresh"
and "authentic" menu on offer at this "basic" and
"silly-cheap" Bermondsey café; no wonder it's
"always packed" (often "with Vietnamese people").
/ SE16 7LH; www.cafeeast.foodkingdom.com; 10.30 pm,
Sun 10 pm; closed Tue.*

**Café in the Crypt
St Martin's in the
Fields WC2**   **£31**   ❹❹❹
Duncannon St   7766 1158   2–2C
*"Reliable", "cheap" and "cheerful" – the self-service
canteen below Trafalgar Square's great church is no
gourmet destination, but it's a "useful" option in the
very "heart" of town. / WC2N 4JJ; www.smitf.org; 8 pm,
Thu-Sat 9 pm, Sun 6 pm; no Amex; no booking.*

Café Japan NW11   **£41**   ❷❹❹
626 Finchley Rd   8455 6854   1–1B
*"Superb sushi in a busy part of Golders Green";
the setting may be "cramped" and "sterile", but this
very "authentic" and "reasonably-priced" stalwart
is "always full". / NW11 7RR; 10 pm, Sun 9.30 pm;
closed Mon; no Amex; only D.*

Café Pacifico WC2   **£43**   ❹❹❷
5 Langley St   7379 7728   4–2C
*"Loud and bustling", this Mexican cantina, in Covent
Garden, dates from long before the current Latino
wave hit town; fans say it still offers a good night
out, with food that's "cheap and full of flavour".
/ WC2 9JA; www.cafepacifico-laperla.com; 11.45 pm,
Sun 10.45 pm.*

Café Rouge   **£37**   ❺❹❹
Branches throughout London
*As a "reliable staple", some reporters do tip this
formulaic Gallic bistro chain, touting its good
breakfasts, and its "suitability for families"; as ever,
though, the volume of feedback dissing it as
"horrific" is impressive – "why do we put up with
it?" / www.caferouge.co.uk; 11 pm, Sun 10.30 pm.*

**Café Spice Namaste
E1**   **£54**   ❷❷❸
16 Prescot St   7488 9242   11–1A
*Cyrus Todiwala "continues to weave his magic",
at this "quirky" City-fringe veteran – his trademark
Parsee cooking is "sophisticated" and "different",
and it's charmingly served in a "funky" and*

"colourful" high-ceilinged room. / E1 8AZ;
www.cafespice.co.uk; 10.30 pm; closed Sat L & Sun.

Caffè Caldesi W1   £58   ❸❷❸
118 Marylebone Ln   7487 0754   2–1A
For "straightforwardly good" meal, in "old-school,
Italian fine dining" style, fans think it worth seeking
out this "friendly" and "respectful" Marylebone
stalwart. / W1U 2QF; www.caldesi.com; 10.30 pm, Sun
10 pm; set weekday L £35 (FP).

Caffè Nero   £13   ❹❸❸
Branches throughout London
"You can taste the coffee, not an American
facsimile" – and it's "strong-tasting" and "universally
good" – at this "staple" Italian chain; "tasty wraps
and paninis" too. / most branches 7 pm; City branches
earlier; most City branches closed all or part of weekend;
some branches no credit cards; no booking.

Caffé Vergnano   £31   ❹❸❷
Staple Inn, High Holborn, WC1   7242 7119
9–2A **NEW**
62 Charing Cross Rd, WC2   7240 3512   4–3B
Royal Festival Hall, SE1   7921 9339   2–3D
2 New Street Sq, EC4   7936 3404   9–2A
"Exemplary coffee" is to be had from both branches
of this Italian café group, whose original outlet is in
the heart of Theatreland; the South Bank branch
also serves "wonderful cakes", and more substantial
snacks too. / www.caffevergnano1882.co.uk;
EC4 11 pm; SE1 midnight; WC2 8 pm, Fri & Sat
midnight; EC4 Sat & Sun; no Amex.

La Cage Imaginaire
NW3   £41   ❹❹❸
16 Flask Walk   7794 6674   8–1A
A small Gallic bistro, with a "wonderful location"
on a cute heart-of-Hampstead lane; even those not
thrilled by the food may find a visit an "agreeable"
experience overall. / NW3 1HE;
www.la-cage-imaginaire.co.uk; 11 pm.

Cah-Chi   £36   ❷❷❸
394 Garratt Ln, SW18   8946 8811   10–2B
34 Durham Rd, SW20   8947 1081   10–2B
These buy Asian outlets in Earlsfield and Raynes
Park, serve up "delicious and fresh" fare at "cheap"
prices; beware, though – "we never know what
to order, and the Koreans at the next table always
seem to have something more interesting!"; BYO.
/ www.cahchi.com; SW20 11 pm; SW18 11 pm, Sat &
Sun 11.30 pm; SW20 closed Mon; cash only.

Il Calcio   £55
33 North Audley St, W1   7629 7070   3–2A
NEW
241 Old Brompton Rd, SW5   7835 0050   5–3A
NEW
A rather baffling new Romanian-backed Italian in a
prime Mayfair location (and also with a presence
in Earl's Court); of the few early-days reports,
we agree with the one that says that – with its

"overpriced" food offer and its "erratic" service –
it "feels like the wrong venture in the wrong place".
/ W1 10.45 pm.

Cambio de Tercio
SW5   £61   ❷❷❷
161-163 Old Brompton Rd   7244 8970   5–2B
Still "the star of London's Spanish restaurants" –
this Earl's Court fixture serves "deliciously inventive"
cooking, plus a "breathtaking" wine list, in a setting
that's "noisy and exciting, and always full".
/ SW5 0LJ; www.cambiodetercio.co.uk; 11.15 pm,
Sun 11 pm; set weekday L £41 (FP).

Camino N1   £46   ❷❷❷
3 Varnishers Yd, Regent Quarter   7841 7331
8–3C
"Tucked-away in a King's Cross courtyard",
this "buzzy" and "convivial" venue ("too noisy"
at times) makes "a good find for tasty Spanish
tapas". / N1 9FD; www.camino.uk.com; 11 pm; closed
Sun D; SRA-70%.

Cannizaro House
SW19   £62   ❹❹❷
West Side, Wimbledon Common   8879 1464
10–2A
"The new conservatory has added another
dimension" to this "charming" country house,
by Wimbledon Common; its dining offer is still
inconsistent, though – fans say it's "first-class",
but others talk of "inexperienced" staff, "miserly
portions" and "horrendous" prices. / SW19 4UE;
www.cannizarohouse.com; 9.30 pm.

Canta Napoli   £37   ❸❸④
9 Devonshire Rd, W4   8994 5225   7–2A
136 High St, TW11   8977 3344   1–4A
"Really cheerful" service and very "dependable"
pizzas (plus other staple dishes) underpin high local
satisfaction with this Chiswick Italian; there is also
a branch in Teddington. / 10.30 pm; no Amex.

Canteen   £41   ⑤⑤⑤
55 Baker St, W1   0845 686 1122   2–1A
Royal Festival Hall, SE1   0845 686 1122   2–3D
Park Pavilion, 40 Canada Sq, E14   0845 686
1122   11–1C
Crispin Pl, Old Spitalf'ds Mkt, E1   0845 686
1122   12–2B
As a breakfast staple, these "basic" cafés have their
fans; ratings remain at rock-bottom, though, as too
many reporters find them to be "bleak" places with
"nondescript" food and "bad" service – "there's
no need to re-create '70s-retro as accurately
as this!" / www.canteen.co.uk; 11 pm, E14 & W1 Sun
7 pm; no booking weekend L.

Cantina Laredo WC2 £52   ❸❷⑤
10 Upper St Martin's Ln   7420 0630   4–3B
This Covent Garden Mexican (part of
an international chain) may offer "authentic US-
Mex" dishes, and "excellent margaritas", but it looks

and feels like a hotel brasserie. / WC2H 9FB; www.cantinalaredo.co.uk; @CantinaLaredoUK; 11.30 pm, Sat midnight, Sun 10.30 pm.

Cantina Vinopolis
Vinopolis SE1   £52   ④④❸
1 Bank End   7940 8333   9–3C
In atmospheric railway arches, within London's museum of wine, this South Bank café has long given the impression of "trading on its location"; it does, however, offer "a great selection of wines by the glass". / SE1 9BU; www.cantinavinopolis.com; 10 pm; closed Sun.

Canton Arms SW8   £43   ❷❷❷
177 South Lambeth Rd   7582 8710   10–1D
"A privilege to have it in my 'hood"; with its "robust and delicious" cooking, this sibling to the fabled Anchor & Hope has become the brightest light of Stockwell gastronomy – it's "worth the trip". / SW8 1XP; www.cantonarms.com; 10 pm; closed Mon L & Sun D; no Amex; no booking.

Cape Town Fish
Market W1   £47   ④④❸
5 & 6 Argyll St   7437 1143   3–1C
Prominently-sited by the Palladium, a "no-nonsense" (and rather "touristy") fish and seafood outlet that some reporters find an "enjoyable destination before a show" (or "if you can get an offer"); service, though, can be "very slow". / W1F 7TE; www.ctfm.com; @ctfmlondon; 10.45 pm.

Capote Y Toros SW5   £43   ❷❸❸
157 Old Brompton Rd   7373 0567   5–2B
Cambio de Tercio's nearby "little sister" offers some "very good" tapas (albeit "a bit pricey"), and its South Kensington premises are quite "atmospheric" too. / SW5 0LJ; www.cambiodetercio.co.uk; @CambiodTercio; 11.15 pm; D only, closed Mon & Sun.

LE CAPRICE SW1   £71   ❸❷❷
Arlington Hs, Arlington St   7629 2239   3–4C
"Still with its old pizzazz and magic" – Richard Caring's '80s-minimalist "super-staple", behind the Ritz, "continues to deliver at a very high level"; old-timers, though, can't quite avoid the feeling that "standards have fallen" since yesteryear. / SW1A 1RJ; www.le-caprice.co.uk; midnight, Sun 11 pm; set pre theatre £47 (FP).

Caraffini SW1   £51   ❸❶❷
61-63 Lower Sloane St   7259 0235   5–2D
"Wonderfully reliable" and with "superlative" service, this "stalwart" Italian, near Sloane Square, is "almost like a club" – an "unpretentious", "fun" and "noisy" place where "many locals come to entertain their friends". / SW1W 8DH; www.caraffini.co.uk; 11.30 pm; closed Sun.

Caravan   £45   ❸❸❷
1 Granary Sq, N1   7101 7661   8–3C
11-13 Exmouth Mkt, EC1   7833 8115   9–1A
"Amazing" brunches – with "hard-to-beat" coffee

(roasted in-house) – is the highlight at these funky eateries, which at other times serve "a modern British/global take on tapas"; while still ultra "hip", the Exmouth original is nowadays eclipsed by the "exciting" King's Cross spin-off (housed in an "incredible" former grain store).
/ www.caravanonexmouth.co.uk; EC1 10.30 pm, Sun 4 pm; EC1 Sun D.

Carluccio's   £41   ⑤⑤④
Branches throughout London
"We expected better" – too often the verdict on the "wishy-washy" food and "hit 'n' miss" service at this glossy, faux-Italian chain; staff can be "unbelievably helpful" where kids are concerned however, and "breakfasts are great value".
/ www.carluccios.com; most branches 11 pm, Sun 10.30 pm; no booking weekday L; SRA-62%.

Carob Tree NW5   £32   ❸❷❷
15 Highgate Rd   7267 9880   8–1B
"The closest you can get to a seaside Greek cafe in London!" – this "buzzy" and "friendly" Dartmouth Park spot has made quite a name with its "excellent" meze and its "wonderful" fish, all in "gigantic" portions. / NW5 1QX; 10.30 pm, Sun 9 pm; closed Mon; no Amex.

The Carpenter's
Arms W6   £47   ❸❸❸
91 Black Lion Ln   8741 8386   7–2B
"A cut above your average gastropub", this "cute" and tucked-away Hammersmith spot offers "reliable" dishes in "relaxing" surroundings; "lovely" garden too. / W6 9BG; 10 pm, Sun 9 pm.

Carvosso's W4   £46   ④❸❷
210 Chiswick High Rd   8995 9121   7–2A
"There's something for everyone" at this large and rambling venture, in Chiswick's former police station, where the star feature is a "lovely summer courtyard"; the food, though is "variable". / W4 1PD; www.carvossosat210.co.uk; 11 pm.

Casa Brindisa SW7   £43   ④④④
7-9 Exhibition Rd   7590 0008   5–2C
"Superb" tapas draw quite a following to this "buzzing" and "chaotic" spot, by South Kensington tube; it also draws a fair amount of flak, though, from those who find its whole performance rather "unconvincing". / SW7 2HE; www.casabrindisa.com; 11 pm, Sun 10 pm.

Casa Malevo W2   £52   ❸❸❸
23 Connaught St   7402 1988   6–1D
"Good hearty fare" maintains the popularity of this "friendly" and "good-value" Bayswater Argentinian; "meat-eaters will love it!" / W2 2AY; www.casamalevo.com; @casamalevo; 10.30 pm.

Casse-Croute SE1   NEW £36
109 Bermondsey St   7407 2140   9–4D
We're really sorry we didn't get to visit this new

Bermondsey bistro before this guide went to press –
it's been widely reviewed as a top-value destination
'of the sort you don't get in France any more'.
/ SE1 3XB.

Cattle Grid £43 ❸④④
35-37 Battersea Rise, SW11   7228 4690
10–2C
1 Balham Station Rd, SW12   8673 9099   10–2C
Few reports on these Battersea and Balham
steakhouses; fans proclaim "good quality belying the
prices", but the experience can also seem rather
"neutral". / www.cattlegridrestaurant.com; 10 pm, Fri &
Sat 10.30 pm; no Amex.

Cây Tre £38 ❸④❸
42-43 Dean St, W1   7317 9118   4–2A
301 Old St, EC1   7729 8662   12–1B
"There's always a queue out of the door", at the
original (and better) branch of this Vietnamese duo
– a tiny café in Shoreditch, with "authentic and
delicious" scoff; its more "polished" Soho sibling
is slowly beginning to measure up.
/ www.vietnamesekitchen.co.uk; 11 pm, Fri-Sat 11.30 pm,
Sun 10.30 pm.

Cecconi's W1 £73 ④④❷
5a Burlington Gdns   7434 1500   3–3C
"Hedgies wine and dine… (that said) for breakfast (especially),
lunch and dinner", at this "entertaining", "slick" and
"incredibly busy" all-day Mayfair corner linchpin;
service needs to "sharpen" up, though, and the
"simple" Italian fare has too often been
an "anticlimax" of late. / W1S 3EP;
www.cecconis.co.uk; @SohoHouse; 11.30 pm,
Sun 10.30 pm.

Cellar Gascon EC1 £37 ❷❸❷
59 West Smithfield   7600 7561   9–2B
A "wonderful" wine list complements the "delicious
tapas style food from SW France" on offer at this
offshoot from nearby Club Gascon; "slightly random"
Gallic service "just adds to the atmosphere".
/ EC1A 9DS; www.cellargascon.com; midnight; closed
Sat & Sun; set weekday L £20 (FP).

Le Cercle SW1 £54 ❸❷❸
1 Wilbraham Pl   7901 9999   5–2D
Hidden-away in a (deep) basement near Sloane
Square, this Gallic venture is "a class act", serving
"small plates with surprising flavour combinations";
the "subtle lighting and drapes" can make
it "unbeatably romantic", but when it's "quiet"
(perhaps more often of late?), the ambience can
be rather "subdued". / SW1X 9AE; www.lecercle.co.uk;
10.45 pm; closed Mon & Sun.

Ceviche W1 £45 ❸❸❷
17 Frith St   7292 2040   4–2A
"Delicious" ceviche and other "interesting" Peruvian
dishes help make this "bustling" Soho yearling
"a great place to meet friends for casual eats";
it can, however, seem "pricey" for what it is.

/ W1D 4RG; www.cevicheuk.com; 11.30 pm,
Sun 10.15 pm; SRA-56%.

Chabrot Bistrot
d'Amis SW1 £59 ❸❷❸
9 Knightsbridge Grn   7225 2238   5–1D
"An antidote to more impersonal places";
this "traditional bistro", hidden-away in the heart
of Knightsbridge, champions an approach that's less
common than it should be – "very French",
"simple", "unpretentious" and "fun". / SW1X 7QL;
www.chabrot.co.uk; 10.45 pm, Sun 9.45 pm.

Chabrot Bistrot
des Halles EC1 NEW £41 ❷❷❸
62-63 Long Ln   7796 4550   9–1B
"A straightforward menu, in an attractive room with
pleasant service" – Chabrot's new offshoot, near the
Barbican, does the whole 'Gallic bistro' thing properly
– a trick which always seemed to elude its
predecessor, St Julien (RIP). / EC1A 9EJ;
www.chabrot.co.uk; @ChabrotSmith; 11 pm; closed Sun;
set weekday L £27 (FP).

Chakra W11 £64 ❸④④
157-159 Notting Hill Gate   7229 2115   6–2B
Despite the "OTT" décor ("more club than
restaurant"), the atmosphere can seem "a bit dull"
at this Indian yearling in Notting Hill – "a pity,
as the food tastes great". / W11 3LF;
www.chakralondon.com; 11 pm, Sun 10.30 pm.

Chamberlain's EC3 £70 ❸④④
23-25 Leadenhall Mkt   7648 8690   9–2D
A long-established fish restaurant, in the heart
of Leadenhall Market, that's been winning more
positive reviews of late; its "mainstream" food may
come at decidedly "upmarket" prices, but fans
proclaim this "one of the City's few reliable business
lunch locations"! / EC3V 1LR; www.chamberlains.org;
@chamberlainsldn; 9.15 pm; closed Sat & Sun.

Champor-Champor
SE1 £49 ❷❸❶
62 Weston St   7403 4600   9–4C
"Tucked away near the Shard", a "weird-looking but
fun" (and "romantic") little gem, where reporters
are "knocked sideways" by the "interesting and
different South East Asian cuisine". / SE1 3QJ;
www.champor-champor.com; @ChamporChampor;
10 pm; D only, closed Sun.

The Chancery EC4 £51 ❸❸④
9 Cursitor St   7831 4000   9–2A
With its "professional" attitude and "beautifully
presented" cuisine, this "hidden-away" spot,
near Chancery Lane, often makes "a good quiet
option for a business lunch"; some feedback,
however, suggests a "slip in standards" of late.
/ EC4A 1LL; www.thechancery.co.uk; 10.30 pm; closed
Sat L & Sun.

Chapters SE3 £49 ④❸④
43-45 Montpelier Vale 8333 2666 1–4D
*"West End, no thanks", say fans of this Blackheath
brasserie, who applaud its "very good all-day
dining"; breakfasts apart, however, the survey finds
standards "nothing to write home about". / SE3 0TJ;
www.chaptersrestaurants.com; 11 pm, Sun 9 pm;
set weekday L £29 (FP).*

Charles Lamb N1 £43 ❸❸❶
16 Elia St 7837 5040 8–3D
*Gallic ownership helps add a superb, "fun"
dimension to this "favourite" Islington gastropub,
which serves a "small but perfectly formed" menu
of "utterly satisfying" pub grub with a Gallic twist";
it can get "very crowded". / N1 8DE;
www.thecharleslambpub.com; @Thecharleslamb;
9.30 pm; closed Mon L & Tue L; no Amex; no booking.*

**Charlotte's Bistro
W4** £47 ❷❷❷
6 Turnham Green Ter 8742 3590 7–2A
*Fast becoming a "Chiswick staple", this "buzzy
brasserie" is inspiring ever-stronger support, thanks
to its "well put-together" food and its "friendly"
service; kick off with a cocktail in the "stylish bar".
/ W4 1QP; www.charlottes.co.uk; @CharlottesW4;
10 pm, Fri-Sat 10.30 pm, Sun 9 pm; SRA-56%.*

Charlotte's Place W5 £47 ❸❷❸
16 St Matthew's Rd 8567 7541 1–3A
*"Back on top form", this mega-popular bistro, on the
Common, "definitely offers the best food in Ealing";
even fans may concede, though, that it's "probably
not a 'destination'". / W5 3JT; www.charlottes.co.uk;
10.30 pm, Fri & Sat 11 pm, Sun 9 pm; SRA-56%.*

**Chelsea Bun Diner
SW10** £29 ❸④④
9a Lamont Rd 7352 3635 5–3B
*A "workman's café"-style operation, by a bus stop,
offering "massive portions for minimum cost in an
area of fabulous wealth" (Chelsea, that is);
not least as a hangover cure, the famous all-day
breakfast is "hard to beat"; BYO. / SW10 0HP;
www.chelseabun.co.uk; 6 pm; L only; no Amex;
no booking, Sat & Sun; set weekday L £19 (FP).*

**The Chelsea Kitchen
SW10** £28 ④④❸
451 Fulham Rd 3055 0088 5–3B
*"For nostalgia alone" fans of this re-located "no-
frills" '50s veteran, nowadays near Brompton
Cemetery, are "glad it was revived"; it can, however,
also seem "lame" – "it's cheap, with lots of choice,
but I'd rather pay more, for something a bit nicer!"
/ SW10 9UZ; www.chelseakitchen.com; 11.30 pm,
Sun 11 pm.*

**The Chelsea Ram
SW10** £40 ④❸❷
32 Burnaby St 7351 4008 5–4B
*A characterful gastroboozer that's nowadays part
of the Geronimo Inns portfolio – "a useful
outpost on the Chelsea borders". / SW10 0PL;
www.chelsearam.com; 10 pm, sun 8 pm; no Amex;
SRA-60%.*

Chettinad W1 £31 ❸❸④
16 Percy St 3556 1229 2–1C
*The "café-like" decor may be "quite bland", but you
couldn't say the same about the "real South Indian
dishes" on offer at this Fitzrovia yearling; a "great-
value lunch thali" is especially worth seeking out.
/ W1T 1DT; www.chettinadrestaurant.com.*

**Cheyne Walk
Brasserie SW3** £69 ④④❸
50 Cheyne Walk 7376 8787 5–3C
*A bit of a missed opportunity, this attractive
Thames-side pub-conversion is nowadays a Gallic
brasserie for Chelsea plutocrats; the style
is "convivial", and the wood-fired grill produces some
delicious dishes, but "the quality doesn't begin to live
up to the prices". / SW3 5LR;
www.cheynewalkbrasserie.com; 10.30 pm, Sun 9.30 pm;
closed Mon L.*

CHEZ BRUCE SW17 £68 ❶❶❷
2 Bellevue Rd 8672 0114 10–2C
*For the 9th year, Bruce Poole's formidably consistent
neighbourhood legend, by Wandsworth Common,
is the survey's No 1. favourite – its straightforward
but unbeatable formula combines "incredible-value"
cooking, "amazing" wine and "helpful and
welcoming" service. / SW17 7EG;
www.chezbruce.co.uk; 10 pm, Fri & Sat 10.30 pm,
Sun 9.30 pm.*

Chez Marcelle W14 £32 ❶⑤④
34 Blythe Rd 7603 3241 7–1D
*Friendly proprietor Marcelle provides "tremendous"
dishes – "some of the best Lebanese food
anywhere" – at her "jolly" café, behind Olympia;
be braced, though, for "incredibly slow" service…
so "just chill, and have a good time". / W14 0HA;
10 pm; closed Mon, Tue-Thu D only, Fri-Sun open L & D;
no credit cards.*

Chez Patrick W8 £46 ❸❶❸
7 Stratford Rd 7937 6388 5–2A
*"Patrick continues to charm and amuse", at his
"quirky" and "cramped" Gallic stalwart, hidden away
in Kensington; it remains ever popular with a loyal
fan club for its "sound" cooking ("especially
of fish"). / W8 6RF; www.chez-patrick.co.uk; 10.30 pm;
closed Sun D; set weekday L £30 (FP).*

Chicken Shop NW5 £30 ❸❷❷
79 Highgate Rd 3310 2020 8–1B
*"Chirpy chirpy… cheap cheap!"; this "vibrant"
Kentish Town yearling – a sort of "upmarket*

Nando's"– is "a great idea, well-executed"; "go early to avoid the queues". / NW5 1TL; www.chickenshop.com; SRA-60%.

Chilango £15 ❷❷❸
76 Chancery Ln, WC2 7430 1323 2–1D
27 Upper St, N1 7704 2123 8–3D
32 Brushfield St, E1 3246 0086 12–2B **NEW**
64 London Wall, EC2 7628 7663 9–2C **NEW**
142 Fleet St, EC4 7353 6761 9–2A
"Totally addictive" burritos "bursting with flavour" underpin the high esteem of these "great alternatives to sandwich tedium".
/ www.chilango.co.uk; @Chilango_uk; EC4, EC2, EC1 9 pm; N1 10 pm, Fri & Sat midnight; EC4, EC2, E1 closed Sat & Sun; no booking.

Chilli Cool WC1 £30 ❸⑤⑤
15 Leigh St 7383 3135 2–1D
"Most of the clientèle are Chinese", at this Bloomsbury café, which offers "proper hot and oily Sichuanese cooking" to "blow your socks off" – almost makes it worthwhile braving the dingy décor and sometimes "rude" service. / WC1H 9EW; www.chillicool.com; 10.15 pm.

China Tang
Dorchester Hotel W1 £72 ④④❸
53 Park Ln 7629 9988 3–3A
"There are dozens of oriental eateries better than this!" – David Tang's "self-important" Mayfair hotel basement offers "bland" cooking at "top dollar" prices; the lavishly styled bar, though, is undoubtedly "great". / W1K 1QA; www.thedorchesterhotel.com; 11.45 pm; set weekday L £29 (FP).

Chinese Cricket Club
EC4 £54 ④④⑤
19 New Bridge St 7438 8051 9–3A
A potentially handy business-restaurant, in a hotel by Blackfriars Bridge; recent reports, however, range quite irreconcilably – from "brilliant cooking and good value" to "my very worst meal of the year"! / EC4V 6DB; www.chinesecricketclub.com; 10 pm; closed Sat & Sun L.

Chipotle £17 ❸❸④
101-103 Baker St, W1 7935 9881 2–1A
181-185 Wardour St, W1 7494 4156 3–1D
114-116 Charing Cross Rd, WC2 7836 8491 4–1A
92-93 St Martin's Ln, WC2 7836 7838 4–4B
334 Upper St, N1 7354 3686 8–3D **NEW**
40 Wimbledon Hill, SW19 8946 6360 10–2B **NEW**
"The best burritos", and other "distinct and tangy" Mexican dishes, help win consistent support for this "fairly authentic" chain; oddly, though, it's never become big news here, as it is in the US.
/ www.chipotle.com; 10 pm - 11 pm.

Chisou £50 ❷❸④
4 Princes St, W1 7629 3931 3–1C
31 Beauchamp Pl, SW3 3155 0005 5–2D
1-4 Barley Mow Pas, W4 8994 3636 7–2A
"Authentic" Japanese dishes (including "top-notch sushi") and a "comprehensive sake list" all reward "adventurous selection" at this small chain; the "utilitarian" Mayfair original is still top for food, with Knightsbridge more atmospheric; Chiswick is the "cute" one. / www.chisourestaurant.com; Mon-Sat 10.30 pm, Sun 9.30 pm.

Chiswell Street Dining
Rooms EC1 £60 ④❸④
56 Chiswell St 7614 0177 12–2A
The name says it all – this relatively ambitious gastropub-style operation, near the Barbican, makes a handy business rendezvous, from breakfast onwards. / EC1Y 4SA; @chiswelldining; 11 pm; closed Sat & Sun.

Cho-San SW15 £41 ❷❷❸
292 Upper Richmond Rd 8788 9626 10–2A
"Just like being in Tokyo!"; this Putney stalwart offers "freshly-prepared", "homely" and "delicious" Japanese food from a "wide and interesting" menu (including excellent sushi); "hopefully it will keep its character after a recent refurb". / SW15 6TH; 10.30 pm; closed Mon.

Chop Shop SW1 NEW £49 ❸❸④
66 Haymarket 7842 8501 4–4A
In the heart of Theatreland, a new steakhouse concept from an outfit based in NYC; it might be useful enough pre-show, but our early-days visit hinted at no positive reason actively to seek it out. / SW1Y 4RF; www.chopshopuk.com.

Chor Bizarre W1 £57 ❷❷❷
16 Albemarle St 7629 9802 3–3C
"Terrific thalis" are a menu highlight at this "pleasantly surprising" Mayfair Indian – a "posh" but "unstuffy" venue, packed with bric-à-brac, which deserves to be better-known. / W1S 4HW; www.chorbizarre.com; 10.45 pm, Sun 10.15 pm; set weekday L £40 (FP).

Chotto Matte W1 NEW £55
11 Frith St 7042 7171 4–2A
From the man behind Ping Pong, an ambitious, multi-level Soho newcomer, where the fare is Japanese/Peruvian, and for rather less than it costs at Nobu – sounds as if it could be interesting. / W1D 4RB; www.chotto-matte.com.

Choys SW3 £46 ④❸④
172 King's Rd 7352 9085 5–3C
The 'Last Emperor' of the Chelsea Chinese dining scene? – this "bright" King's Road classic (est. 1952) can seem "a little expensive for what it is", but remains a valued standby for most reporters who comment on it. / SW3 4UP; 11 pm.

Ametsa with Arzack Instruction

Bone Daddies

Brawn

Carom @ Meza

Christopher's WC2 **£70** ❸❸❷
18 Wellington St 7240 4222 4–3D
The recent refit "has added glamour and a sense
of space" to this "delightful" (and business-friendly)
Covent Garden townhouse; early reports
suggest that, as ever, it's "not cheap", but that
realisation of the surf 'n' turf cuisine has improved
since the re-launch. / WC2E 7DD;
www.christophersgrill.com; @christopherswc2; 11.30 pm,
Sun 10.30 pm; booking: max 14; set pre theatre
£39 (FP).

Chuen Cheng Ku W1 **£37** ❸④④
17 Wardour St 7437 1398 4–3A
"Ever-circling" dim sum trolleys are the key feature
of a "cracking-value" lunchtime visit to this
"old Chinatown warhorse" – a particularly good
experience "with kids"; à la carte, however, the food
is "very average". / W1D 6DJ;
www.chuenchengku.co.uk; 11.45 pm.

Churchill Arms W8 **£34** ❸❷❶
119 Kensington Church St 7792 1246 6–2B
"At the back of a truly original, quirky pub,
off Notting Hill Gate", a "really fun", "plant-filled"
conservatory, where the Thai dishes on offer are
"the very definition of cheap and cheerful".
/ W8 7LN; 10 pm, 9.30 pm.

Chutney SW18 **£31** ❷❸❸
11 Alma Rd 8870 4588 10–2B
"A great local Indian with its own unique style
of cooking and some fantastic deals" –
the worst thing any reporter has to say about this
"friendly" Wandsworth fixture! / SW18 1AA;
www.chutneyrestaurant.co.uk; 11.30 pm; D only.

Chutney Mary SW10 **£55** ❷❶❷
535 King's Rd 7351 3113 5–4B
"A real aristocrat of the Indian restaurant world" –
this "long-term favourite", at the far end of Chelsea,
boasts a "very atmospheric conservatory", and is
a "totally charming" destination, offering
"wonderfully aromatic" dishes, and "tip top" service
too. / SW10 0SZ; www.realindianfood.com; 11.45 pm,
Sun 10.45 pm; closed weekday L; booking: max 8.

Chutneys NW1 **£30** ④❸④
124 Drummond St 7388 0604 8–4C
"The lunchtime and weekend buffet is very tasty
and truly excellent value", say fans of this "airy"
café – long a "cheap 'n' cheerful" staple of the Little
India, near Euston; you can BYO too. / NW1 2PA;
www.chutneyseuston.co.uk; 11 pm; no Amex; need 5+
to book.

Ciao Bella WC1 **£41** ④❷❷
86-90 Lamb's Conduit St 7242 4119 2–1D
It's not just the "back-to-the-70s" time warp
experience that wins fans for this "buzzy", "no-
frills" family-run Bloomsbury Italian – its "solid" scoff
comes at "value-for-money" prices. / WC1N 3LZ;
www.ciaobellarestaurant.co.uk; 11.30 pm, Sun 10.30 pm.

Cibo W14 **£51** ❷❶❸
3 Russell Gdns 7371 6271 7–1D
"The forgotten star of west London" –
this "marvellous local Italian", on the
Kensington/Olympia border, is an "authentic" and
"unassuming" stalwart, where the cooking is still
often "superb". / W14 8EZ; www.ciborestaurant.net;
11 pm; closed Sat L & Sun D.

Cigala WC1 **£49** ❸❸④
54 Lamb's Conduit St 7405 1717 2–1D
With its "genuine" Spanish food (plus "a very good
wine list"), this "bustling" operation, on a quiet
Bloomsbury street, impresses many reporters;
the decor is a touch "sterile", though, and service
can be erratic. / WC1N 3LW; www.cigala.co.uk;
10.45 pm, Sun 9.45 pm.

Le Cigalon WC2 **£47** ❸❷❷
115 Chancery Ln 7242 8373 2–2D
Built as a Victorian auction house, these "very bright
and airy" premises, now specialising in the cuisine
of Provençe, are "something of an oasis in the
restaurant-starved legal district" – "great for
a business lunch", obviously, but equally suited
to "dinner with friends". / WC2A 1PP;
www.cigalon.co.uk; 10 pm; closed Sat & Sun.

**THE CINNAMON
CLUB SW1** **£69** ❷❸❷
Old Westminster Library, Great Smith St 7222
2555 2–4C
In the "beautiful" setting of Westminster's former
library, near the Abbey, Iqbal Wahhab's
"outstanding" venture is one of London's
most impressive destinations; its "haute take"
on Indian cuisine often achieves an "absolutely
sublime" standard. / SW1P 3BU;
www.cinnamonclub.com; @CinnamonClub; 10.30 pm;
closed Sun; no trainers; set weekday L & pre-theatre £48
(FP); SRA-68%.

**Cinnamon Kitchen
EC2** **£55** ❷❷❸
9 Devonshire Sq 7626 5000 9–2D
"Exciting" Indian fusion cuisine combines with
"attentive" service and an "elegant" setting
(with airy seating in the atrium) to make the
Cinnamon Club's "business-like" spin-off a top City
destination – it even offers a "good-value set
lunch". / EC2M 4YL; www.cinnamon-kitchen.com;
@cinnamonkitchen; 11 pm; closed Sat L & Sun;
set weekday L £34 (FP); SRA-61%.

Cinnamon Soho W1 **£43** ④④④
5 Kingly St 7437 1664 3–2D
Soho's "stripped-down version of the Cinnamon
Club" pleases most reporters with its "small menu
of well-spiced Indian dishes" (and its "fantastic-
value" set lunch deals too); for a voluble minority,
though, the whole performance is "a bit lacklustre".
/ W1B 5PE; www.cinnamon-kitchen.com/soho-home;

@cinnamonsoho; 11 pm, Sun 4.30 pm; closed Sun D; set weekday L & pre-theatre £32 (FP).

Circus WC2 £65 ④④❷
27-29 Endell St 7420 9300 4–2C
OK, it's "the unique ambience" and "enjoyable showmanship" you go for, but this Covent Garden cabaret wins surprisingly upbeat feedback on its "high-quality Asian food". / WC2H 9BA; www.circus-london.co.uk; @circus_london; midnight, Fri-Sat 2 am; D only, closed Mon & Sun.

City Càphê EC2 £14 ❶❸⑤
17 Ironmonger St no tel 9–2C
"Get there by noon", to nab a seat at this "great little restaurant/take-away" – the quality of its "fabulous" and "great value" Vietnamese dishes (in particular the báhn mi) has become the stuff of local City legend. / EC2V 8EY; www.citycaphe.com; 3 pm; L only, closed Sat & Sun.

City Miyama EC4 £52 ❸④⑤
17 Godliman St 7489 1937 9–3B
This City stalwart attracts a steady "Japanese-corporate" clientele, thanks to its very decent cuisine (particularly sushi), and in spite of its "tired décor and lack of atmosphere". / EC4 5BD; www.miyama-restaurant.co.uk; 9.30 pm; closed Sat & Sun.

Clarke's W8 £69 ❸❷–
124 Kensington Church St 7221 9225 6–2B
Preparing to celebrate 30 years in business in 2014, Sally Clarke's "civilised" Californian-inspired Kensington fixture had a major refurbishment after our survey for the year had concluded; the restaurant was path-breaking in its day, so here's hoping that the revamp marks an era of renewed vigour. / W8 4BH; www.sallyclarke.com; 10 pm; closed Sun D; booking: max 14.

The Clissold Arms N2 £49 ④❸❸
Fortis Grn 8444 4224 1–1C
This Muswell Hill boozer (known for its associations with The Kinks) is one of the better gastropubs in these parts, and consistently well-rated; "the garden is wonderful in summer". / N2 9HR; @ClissoldArms; 10 pm, Sat 10.30 pm, Sun 9 pm.

CLOS MAGGIORE WC2 £59 ❷❶❶
33 King St 7379 9696 4–3C
"So romantic, you could say yes to anyone!"; this "womb-like" Covent Garden wonderland is again London's No.1 passion-magnet – "the best tables are in the conservatory"; the food is often "excellent", but it's eclipsed by the "encyclopaedic" wine list. / WC2E 8JD; www.closmaggiore.com; @ClosMaggioreWC2; 11 pm, Sun 10 pm.

The Clove Club
EC1 NEW £65 ❷❶❷
Shoreditch Town Hall, 380 Old St 7729 6496 12–1B
"Stunning" food ("a real adventure for the senses!") twinned with "really knowledgeable" service has made an instant hit of the former Ten Bells pop-up, now translated to an "exciting and buzzing" setting in Shoreditch's erstwhile town hall – "definitely worth the hype". / EC1V 9LT; www.thecloveclub.com; 9.30 pm.

Club Gascon EC1 £71 ❷❸❸
57 West Smithfield 7600 6144 9–2B
"Unusual" SW French regional cuisine is prepared with "imagination and verve" – and "fabulous wine to match" – at this very "classy" City-fringe haven, renowned for "London's best foie gras". / EC1A 9DS; www.clubgascon.com; @club_gascon; 10 pm, Fri-Sat 10.30 pm; closed Sat L & Sun; set weekday L £45 (FP).

Cocum SW20 £30 ❷❷❸
9 Approach Rd 8540 3250 10–2B
An "authentic" and "reliable" Raynes Park south Indian… "not much else to say, really!" / SW20 8BA; www.cocumrestaurant.co.uk; 10.30 pm; closed Fri L.

Colbeh W2 £26 ❷④④
6 Porchester Pl 7706 4888 6–1D
It's nothing to look at, and the menu never changes, but this pint-sized Bayswater Iranian majors in "spicy kebabs" and "the best flatbread in town". / W2 2BS; 11 pm.

Colbert SW1 £60 ④④❸
51 Sloane Sq 7730 2804 5–2D
Come back Oriel (RIP), all is forgiven? – the Wolseley team really needs to "get a grip" on their long-awaited Belgravia brasserie project; it has its fans, but the proportion of reporters who find it "charmless, overblown and overpriced" is little short of astonishing. / SW1W 8AX; www.colbertchelsea.com.

Colchis W2 £55 ❷❸❸
39 Chepstow Pl 7221 7620 6–1B
"A real eye-opening experience"; the ground floor of this former Bayswater boozer (of which the upstairs is Assaggi) is still little-known, but it offers some "very interesting" Georgian dishes, and some intriguing Georgian wines to go with them. / W2 4TS; www.colchisrestaurant.co.uk; 11 pm, Sun 10 pm; closed weekday L.

La Collina NW1 £54 ❸❸❷
17 Princess Rd 7483 0192 8–3B
"A small gourmet Italian in a Primrose Hill side street", where the food (Piedmontese) is "unusual and always good"; summer visits are best, as you can sit in the garden. / NW1 8JR; www.lacollinarestaurant.co.uk; 10.15 pm, Sun 9.45 pm, Mon 9.30 pm; closed Mon L; set weekday L £35 (FP).

Le Colombier SW3 £59 ❸❷❷
145 Dovehouse St 7351 1155 5–2C
"The perfect formula for a super-agreeable dining experience", say fans, this "uncomplicated" Chelsea Gallic "classic" is a "warm and personal" sort of place in a "smart", rather "old-fashioned" style; "it helps if your French is adequate!" / SW3 6LB; www.le-colombier-restaurant.co.uk; 10.30 pm, Sun 10 pm; set weekday L £40 (FP), set Sun L £46 (FP).

Como Lario SW1 £47 ❹❹❸
18-22 Holbein Pl 7730 2954 5–2D
This "jolly" and "reasonably-priced" Italian used to be quite a Sloane Square staple; nowadays, its "old-fashioned" charms inspire few reports, but all are reasonably positive. / SW1W 8NL; www.comolario.co.uk; 11.30 pm, Sun 10 pm; set Sun L £31 (FP).

Comptoir Gascon EC1 £44 ❸❹❸
63 Charterhouse St 7608 0851 9–1A
The "duck burger de luxe is not to be missed", if you visit this "no-fuss" (but quite "romantic") bistro, by Smithfield Market; it offers a "simple" but "interesting" French (SW) menu, and "excellent wines" too. / EC1M 6HJ; www.comptoirgascon.com; 10 pm, Thu-Fri 10.30 pm; closed Mon & Sun.

Comptoir Libanais £28 ❹❹❸
59 Broadwick St, W1 7434 4335 3–2C
65 Wigmore St, W1 7935 1110 3–1A
1-5 Exhibition Rd, SW7 7225 5006 5–2C
Westfield, The Balcony, W12 8811 2222 7–1C
Westfield Stratford City, 2 Stratford Pl, E20 8555 6999 1–1D
A "cosmopolitan" atmosphere (at South Kensington in particular) – plus "a great range of Lebanese staples" (meze, wraps, juices) at "decent prices" – win many recommendations for this "useful" chain. / www.lecomptoir.co.uk; W12 9 pm, Thu & Fri 10 pm, Sun 6 pm; W1 9.30 pm; W12 closed Sun D; no bookings.

Constancia SE1 £49 ❸❸❸
52 Tanner St 7234 0676 9–4D
A "cosy and bustling" Argentinian, near Tower Bridge, which serves "fantastic steaks, cooked on an open grill", and "great wines" to go with 'em too. / SE1 3PH; www.constancia.co.uk; 10.30 pm; D only; no Amex.

Il Convivio SW1 £55 ❷❷❸
143 Ebury St 7730 4099 2–4A
"Stylish, quiet and agreeable", this "hidden treasure", in Belgravia, offers "consistently good" Italian cooking, and "impeccable" service too; so why isn't it better known? – "the atmosphere doesn't match the rest of the experience". / SW1W 9QN; www.etruscarestaurants.com; 10.45 pm; closed Sun.

Coopers Restaurant & Bar WC2 £49 ❸❸④
49a Lincolns Inn Fields 7831 6211 2–2D
Hidden away in Lincoln's Inn Fields, a "reasonably-priced" midtown standby that's especially useful as a lunchtime rendezvous, "popular with local lawyers, and university academics too"; upstairs is slightly grander. / WC2A 3PF; www.coopers-restaurant.com; 11 pm; closed Sat & Sun.

Copita W1 £43 ❸❹❸
27 D'Arblay St 7287 7797 3–1D
"Why isn't this place rammed?", say fans of the "novel flavours and combinations" on offer at this Soho tapas yearling; the results are "not universally outstanding", however, and "pricey" too. / W1F 8EP; www.copita.co.uk; 10.30 pm; closed Sun.

Le Coq N1 🆕 £39
292-294 St Paul's Rd 7359 5055 8–2D
A new Islington rôtisserie chicken specialist; sadly, we didn't have the opportunity to visit before this guide went to press, but some media commentary has been very positive indeed. / N1 2LH; www.le-coq.co.uk.

Coq d'Argent EC2 £60 ❹❹❸
1 Poultry 7395 5000 9–2C
The "fantastic" top-floor location, complete with a "great summer terrace", makes this "slick" D&D group restaurant a perennial favourite for City dining (and for breakfast too); critics dismiss the cooking as "by numbers", though, and the wine list can seem "insanely overpriced". / EC2R 8EJ; www.coqdargent.co.uk; 9.45 pm; closed Sun D; SRA-65%.

Cork & Bottle WC2 £48 ❹❹❷
44-46 Cranbourn St 7734 7807 4–3B
So retro it's now "cool", this "hidden gem" of a wine bar, in a seedy corner of Leicester Square, manages "never to be overrun with tourists"; it's "the wide and exciting wine list", though, which draws the locals – the scoff doesn't have much to do with it. / WC2H 7AN; www.thecorkandbottle.co.uk; @corkbottle1971; 11.30 pm, Sun 10.30 pm; no booking after 6.30 pm.

Corner Room E2 £48 ❶❷❸
Patriot Sq 7871 0461 1–2D
Fans are "blown away" by the "weird but perfect flavour combinations" on offer at this "quirky" spin-off from Viajante; "much cosier" than big brother, and "tremendous value" to boot, it's "well worth the trip to Bethnal Green!" / E2 9NF; www.viajante.co.uk/corner-room/; @townhallhotel; 10.30 pm.

Corrigan's Mayfair W1 £86 ❹❹❹
28 Upper Grosvenor St 7499 9943 3–3A
Fans still find Richard Corrigan's Mayfair dining room "an absolute British gem", but its performance slid dramatically this year; "heavy-handed" cooking and "eye-watering" prices were key complaints, but "shambolic" service, and a "subdued" ambience also played their part; Monday nights BYO,

no corkage! / W1K 7EH; www.corrigansmayfair.com;
10.45 pm, Sun 9.30 pm; closed Sat L; booking: max 10;
set weekday L £54 (FP).

Côte £43 ④❸④
124-126 Wardour St, W1 7287 9280 3–1D
17-21 Tavistock St, WC2 7379 9991 4–3D
45-47 Parsons Green Ln, SW6 7736 8444
10–1B
98 Westbourne Grove, W2 7792 3298 6–1B
50-54 Turnham Green Ter, W4 8747 6788
7–2A
47 Kensington Ct, W8 7938 4147 5–1A
Hays Galleria, Tooley St, SE1 7234 0800 9–4D
8 High St, SW19 8947 7100 10–2B
26 Ludgate Hill, EC4 7236 4399 9–2A
"Usually reliable", this "accommodating" and
"buzzy" Gallic brasserie chain makes an ideal
"standby", and one offering "value for money" too,
especially at lunch (and early-evening); Richard
Caring, le patron, has just made a(nother) mint,
selling the business to a private equity firm.
/ www.cote-restaurants.co.uk; 11 pm.

Cotidie W1 £78
50 Marylebone High St 7258 9878 2–1A
This ambitious Marylebone Italian was relaunched,
with a new chef, in the summer of 2013; let's hope
he can improve on the formerly "hit-and-miss"
standards! / W1U 5HN; www.cotidierestaurant.com;
11.30 pm, Sun 11 pm; set weekday L £52 (FP).

The Courtauld Gallery Café
The Courtauld
Gallery WC2 £30 ④❸❸
Somerset Hs, Strand 7848 2527 2–2D
"Convenient", if too often crowded, this café
on Somerset House's main courtyard is of note for
a lower-level al fresco dining area all of its own –
a surprise 'find' just a few metres from the Strand.
/ WC2R 0RN; L only; no Amex.

The Cow W2 £54 ❸❸❶
89 Westbourne Park Rd 7221 0021 6–1B
"Great Guinness and oysters" headline the menu
at Tom Conran's hip Notting Hill-fringe boozer
(which has a marginally grander dining room
upstairs); on the downside, it's "quite pricey for
a non-booking establishment with small and slightly
cramped tables". / W2 5QH; www.thecowlondon.co.uk;
10.30 pm, Sun 10 pm; no Amex.

Coya W1 NEW £70 ❷❷❶
118 Piccadilly 7042 7118 3–4B
"Suitable for romance, a celebration, or a big table
with friends", this "excellent" ("and expensive") new
Mayfair Peruvian is not just a "fun" place, but offers
"fabulous food" as well; "cool" bar too. / W1J 7NW;
www.coyarestaurant.com; @coyarestaurant.

Crazy Bear W1 £62 ❸④❷
26-28 Whitfield St 7631 0088 2–1C
With its sexy basement bar and mega-lavish decor,

this ever-"trendy" Fitzrovia haunt still pleases
most reporters, and its "pricey" pan-Asian fare
generally hits the spot too; service, however, can be
somewhat "idiosyncratic". / W1T 2RG;
www.crazybeargroup.co.uk; 10.30 pm; closed
Sat L & Sun; no shorts.

Criterion W1 £69 ④④❶
224 Piccadilly 7930 0488 3–3D
"Spectacular", "truly magnificent", "beautiful" –
it's the architecture and ambience of this
extraordinary neo-Byzantine "oasis", right
on Piccadilly Circus, that "makes a visit worthwhile";
the food, however, can be a touch "institutional".
/ W1J 9HP; www.criterionrestaurant.com; 11.30 pm,
Sun 10.30 pm; set weekday L & pre-theatre £48 (FP).

The Crooked Well SE5 £47 ❷❷❷
16 Grove Ln 7252 7798 1–3C
"A neighbourhood joint that's a real favourite";
this "large" but "friendly" Camberwell two-year-old
is an all-round hit, thanks not least to its "succulent"
British fare. / SE5 8SY; www.thecrookedwell.com;
@crookedwell; 10.30 pm; closed Mon L; no Amex.

Crussh £17 ❸❷④
Branches throughout London
"A great place for a healthy lunch of soup, wraps
or salads, and the juices are very good too" –
this "extremely helpful" chain pulls off the hard act
of being "virtuous without being dull".
/ www.crussh.com; 4.30 pm-8 pm; many branches closed
all or part of weekend; no credit cards in many branches.

Cumberland Arms
W14 £42 ❷❷❸
29 North End Rd 7371 6806 7–2D
"Really good food every time" – reason to seek out
this pleasing, if no-frills, pub in the no man's land
near Olympia (run by the same team as The Atlas).
/ W14 8SZ; www.thecumberlandarmspub.co.uk;
@thecumberland; 10 pm, Sun 9.30 pm.

Cut
45 Park Lane W1 £98 ⑤⑤⑤
45 Park Ln 7493 4545 3–4A
"Smell the money!"; the steaks may often
be "indulgent", but prices (especially of wine) at LA
restaurateur Wolfgang Puck's steakhouse are
so "stupefying" that the whole operation strikes
critics as plain "vulgar"; the view – "Park Lane
traffic" – is no great plus either. / W1K 1PN;
www.45parklane.com; 10.30 pm; set weekday L
£68 (FP).

Cyprus Mangal SW1 £31 ❷❸④
45 Warwick Way 7828 5940 2–4B
"OK it's cheap, OK it's not luxurious, but the food
is extraordinary value", say fans of the "good fresh
grills and salads" on offer at this "cramped and
dive-y" Pimlico BBQ; BYO. / SW1V 1QS; 10.45 pm,
Fri & Sat 11.45 pm.

Da Mario SW7   £41   ❸❸❸
15 Gloucester Rd   7584 9078   5–1B
A "friendly" and "lively" South Kensington pizzeria
veteran, where "children are always given a typically
Italian welcome"; "great pre-Albert Hall". / SW7 4PP;
www.damario.co.uk; 11.30 pm.

Da Mario WC2   £45   ❸❷❸
63 Endell St   7240 3632   4–1C
This "lovely, neighbourhood, family-run Italian"
makes a rather "unusual" find, slap bang in the
middle of Covent Garden – "always good value",
and always offering "a welcoming reception for
returning customers". / WC2H 9AJ;
www.da-mario.co.uk; 11.15 pm; closed Sun.

DABBOUS W1   £63   ❶❶❸
39 Whitfield St   7323 1544   2–1C
A tiny minority may proclaim "the emperor's new
clothes", but – for a crushing majority – Ollie
Dabbous's "industrial"-style foodie Fitzrovia
sensation fully "lives up to the hype" – service may
be "with the minimum of fuss", but "every magical
mouthful is a wonder"; book for next year now.
/ W1T 2SF; www.dabbous.co.uk; @dabbous; 11.30 pm;
closed Mon & Sun; set weekday L £47 (FP).

Daddy Donkey EC1   £16   ❷❸–
100 Leather Ln   448448   9–2A
A grand-daddy of the streetfood world, this "cool"
Clerkenwell outfit specialises in "burritos as they
should be served"; let's hope they don't spoil it all,
now they have an actual shop! / EC1N 7TE;
www.daddydonkey.co.uk/.

The Dairy SW4 NEW   £39
15 The Pavement   7622 4165   10–2D
Oddly located on a busy corner by Clapham
Common tube, this wine-bar-style newcomer –
whose chef used to work at Raymond Blanc's
'Manoir' – has been a 'rave' for almost all of the
many press critics who have visited. / SW4 0HY;
www.the-dairy.co.uk.

Dalchini SW19   £36   ④❸④
147 Arthur Rd   8947 5966   10–2B
The "interesting" menu at this "charming spot",
opposite Wimbledon Park tube, features Hakka
(Indian/Chinese) cuisine; not everyone's wowed,
but fans insist this is "a great local". / SW19 8AB;
www.dalchini.co.uk; 10.30 pm, Fri & Sat 11 pm,
Sun 10 pm; no Amex.

Dans le Noir EC1   £77   ④④④
29 Clerkenwell Grn   7253 1100   9–1A
"A mystery menu, eaten in total darkness,
how exciting can you get?" – that's the more positive
view on this bizarre Farringdon venture; others,
though, dismiss it as a "gimmick" – "the pitch black
supposedly heightens your senses… but it certainly
heightens the bill!" / EC1R 0DU; www.danslenoir.com;
9.30 pm, Sun 7.30 pm; closed weekday L.

Daphne's SW3   £68   ④❷❷
112 Draycott Ave   7589 4257   5–2C
"A perennial favourite"; this "elegant and
comfortable" ("slightly '80s") Chelsea stalwart –
with its "personal" service – is "always busy and
lively"; no one really minds that its "comfort-Italian"
dishes are rather middle of the road. / SW3 3AE;
www.daphnes-restaurant.co.uk; 11.30 pm, Sun 10.30 pm.

Daquise SW7   £45   ④❸④
20 Thurloe St   7589 6117   5–2C
"New owners have done a brilliant job", at this
revived Polish bistro, by South Kensington tube,
which "has gone up in the world since its days as a
'50s café"; it serves us "solid, authentic cooking"
at "reasonable prices". / SW7 2LT; daquise.co.uk;
11 pm; no Amex; set weekday L £26 (FP).

**The Dartmouth
Arms SE23**   £37   ④❸❸
7 Dartmouth Rd   8488 3117   1–4D
A "very cosy" gastropub in Forest Hill; there is the
occasional suggestion that it has "gone slightly
downhill this year", but it still attracts mainly positive
reports. / SE23 3HN; www.thedartmoutharms.com;
10 pm, Sun 9 pm; no Amex.

**The Dartmouth
Castle W6**   £42   ④❸❸
26 Glenthorne Rd   8748 3614   7–2C
"A great little find in Hammersmith" –
an atmospheric and "busy" pub, north of King
Street, offering "good, solid" cooking. / W6 0LS;
www.thedartmouthcastle.co.uk; 10 pm, Sun 9.30 pm;
closed Sat L.

Daylesford Organic   £42   ④⑤④
44b Pimlico Rd, SW1   7881 8060   5–2D
208-212 Westbourne Grove, W11   7313 8050
6–1B
More even standards of late at this "bright" and
"airy" deli/café de luxe, five minutes' walk from
Sloane Square; it's often hailed as a "really good"
venue for breakfast or for brunch.
/ www.daylesfordorganic.com; SW1 & W11 7 pm,
Sun 4 pm; W1 9 pm, Sun 6.15 pm; W11 no booking L.

**Dean Street
Townhouse W1**   £56   ④④❷
69-71 Dean St   7434 1775   4–2A
"Slick" and happening, this Soho brasserie seduces
the punters with its "comfortable" gent's-club décor,
which "harks back to a bygone era of luxury";
the food, though, is decidedly "ordinary" – only the
"fabulous" brunch really stands out. / W1D 3SE;
www.deanstreettownhouse.com; 11.30 pm, Fri & Sat
midnight, Sun 10.30 pm; set pre theatre £37 (FP).

Defune W1   £63   ❷❸⑤
34 George St   7935 8311   3–1A
This "old-school" Japanese ("a world away from the
glitz of Nobu or Zuma") is "as cold as ice" on the
decor front, but fans feel its "incredible" sushi and

"terrific" other fare "makes it all worthwhile"; critics, though, can find bills "outrageous". / W1U 7DP; www.defune.com; 10.45 pm, Sun 10.30 pm.

Dehesa W1 £49 ❶❷❷
25 Ganton St 7494 4170 3–2C
"Truly heavenly" tapas and an "excellent wine list" fuel the "busy buzz" of this stylish haunt, a sibling to Salt Yard, just off Carnaby Street; "despite its initial pokey appearance", it's "a lovely place to spend a long afternoon". / W1F 9BP; www.dehesa.co.uk; @SaltYardGroup; 10.45 pm; closed Sun D; SRA-63%.

THE DELAUNAY WC2 £60 ❸❷❶
55 Aldwych 7499 8558 2–2D
"Like The Wolseley, only smaller" – this "beautiful" Aldwych celeb-magnet is "another triumph" for Corbin & King (and likewise a business and power breakfast mainstay); the food – "Viennese/Alsatian cooking with a smattering of British dishes" – is "good, but always a secondary attraction". / WC2B 4BB; www.thedelaunay.com; @TheDelaunayRest; midnight, Sun 11 pm; SRA-66%.

Delfino W1 £51 ❷❸❹
121 Mount St 7499 1256 3–3B
A Mayfair Italian claimed by fans to offer "the best pizza in central London" (with a "thin base and crust, and very flavourful toppings"), and "efficient and charming" service too – the consistency of the many reports is impressive. / W1K 3NW; www.finos.co.uk; 11 pm; closed Sun.

Delhi Grill N1 £33 ❷❷❸
21 Chapel Mkt 7278 8100 8–3D
"Zingy flavours… amazing kebabs… terrific value" – that's the deal at this "addictive" little "gem" of a curry shop, near Angel tube, and "so easy on the wallet" too. / N1 9EZ; www.delhigrill.com; 10.30 pm.

La Delizia Limbara SW3 £39 ❸❹❹
63-65 Chelsea Manor St 7376 4111 5–3C
The thin-crust pizza at this "busy" Chelsea side street stalwart are amongst "the most authentic" in town; the "no-frills" setting, however, can seem a little too "clinical". / SW3 5RZ; 11 pm, Sun 10.30 pm; no Amex.

Department of Coffee EC1 £15 ❸❷❷
14-16 Leather Ln 7419 6906 9–2A
"The coffee and the feel are excellent"; the food may not excite, but fans still insist this City spot "leads the coffee-shop pack". / EC1N 7SU; www.departmentofcoffee.co.uk; 6 pm, Sat-Sun 4 pm; L only.

The Depot SW14 £41 ❸❷❷
Tideway Yd, Mortlake High St 8878 9462 10–1A
"Perfect, if you get a table by the river" – this "spacious" and "informal" Barnes haunt can be "magical when the sun sets", and is a major family favourite at weekends; the food's never been the main event, but is currently on something of a high. / SW14 8SN; www.depotbrasserie.co.uk; @TheDepotBarnes; 10 pm, Sun 9.30 pm.

Les Deux Salons WC2 £50 ❹❹❸
40-42 William IV St 7420 2050 4–4C
"A wonderful take on a posh Parisian brasserie", say fans of Will Smith & Anthony Demetre's "useful" and "vibrant" Theatreland spot; others think that – while it "seems to tick all the boxes" – the food is "uninspired", the decor "boring", and the service so-so. / WC2N 4DD; www.lesdeuxsalons.co.uk; 10.45 pm, Sun 5.45 pm; closed Sun D; set weekday L £35 (FP).

Le Deuxième WC2 £57 ❹❹❺
65a Long Acre 7379 0033 4–2D
An "always reliable" standby, handy for the Royal Opera House – a "popular" and "busy" spot, especially pre-theatre and for lunch; the décor is "rather sparse", though, and the food is "reasonable, rather than exciting". / WC2E 9JH; www.ledeuxieme.com; Mon-Thu 11 pm, Fri-Sat 11.30 pm, Sun 10 pm; set weekday L & pre-theatre £28 (FP).

dim T £34 ❹❹❹
56-62 Wilton Rd, SW1 7834 0507 2–4B
32 Charlotte St, W1 7637 1122 2–1C
1 Hampstead Ln, N6 8340 8800 8–1B
3 Heath St, NW3 7435 0024 8–2A
Tooley St, SE1 7403 7000 9–4D
A modern, pan-Asian chain whose performance is "not ground breaking in any way"; the SE1 branch, however, boasts "a nice upstairs with views of Tower Bridge and the Thames". / www.dimt.co.uk; @dim_t; most branches 11 pm, Sun 10.30 pm.

Diner £33 ❹❸❷
18 Ganton St, W1 7287 8962 3–2C
190 Shaftesbury Ave, WC2 3551 5225 4–1C
105 Gloucester Rd, SW7 7244 7666 5–2B **NEW**
21 Essex Rd, N1 7226 4533 8–3D
64-66 Chamberlayne Rd, NW10 8968 9033 1–2B
2 Jamestown Rd, NW1 7485 5223 8–3B
128 Curtain Rd, EC2 7729 4452 12–1B
"My US friends thought I'd flown them home!" – these "buzzy" hang-outs offer "a decent slice of Americana", including all the "classic" dishes (burgers, ribs, chilli dogs, shakes…). / www.goodlifediner.com; most branches 11 or 11.30 pm; booking: max 10.

Dinings W1 £53 ❶❷❺
22 Harcourt St 7723 0666 8–4A
"An odd, even ugly place but WOW!!"; the sushi Tomonari Chiba offers at this Marylebone bunker is "off-the-scale-good" (and rivalled only by Sushi Tetsu for the crown as 'best in London'); shame

about the "dark and uncomfy" interior. / W1H 4HH; www.dinings.co.uk; 10.30 pm; closed Sun.

DINNER
MANDARIN
ORIENTAL SW1   £94   ❸❸❸
66 Knightsbridge   7201 3833   5–1D
"Heston's done it again", say fans of his Knightsbridge production, extolling "incredible" dishes, with an "amusing" and "superbly inventive" olde-English twist; but not everyone's dazzled – to sceptics its merely "a smart hotel place", with nice park views and "ludicrous" bills. / SW1X 7LA; www.dinnerbyheston.com; 10.30 pm; set weekday L £65 (FP).

Dirty Burger   £14   ❷❸❸
78 Highgate Rd, NW5   3310 2010   8–2B
Arch 54, 6 South Lambeth Rd, SW8   7074 1444 2–4D **NEW**
"Don't be fooled by the downtrodden exterior"; this "not-so-secret-burger shack", in Kentish Town, is one of the best "no-nonsense" burger joints in town – "lip-smackingly good" scoff, and "a lot of fun" too; now with a new Vauxhall sibling. / www.eatdirtyburger.com; NW5, Mon-Thu midnight, Fri & Sat 1 am, Sun 11 pm – SW8 Mon-Thu 11 pm, Fri & Sat 2 am, Sun 8 pm.

Dishoom   £40   ❸❸❶
12 Upper St Martins Ln, WC2   7420 9320 4–3B
7 Boundary St, E2   7420 9324   12–1B **NEW**
"A real change from most Indians"; this "vibrant" Covent Garden café – a superb "recreation of the numerous Parsi cafés in Mumbai"– has many fans for its unusually "cool" ambience, and "delicious contemporary cuisine"; now in Shoreditch too. / www.dishoom.com; @Dishoom; 11 pm, Sun 10 pm.

Diwana Bhel-Poori
House NW1   £30   ④④⑤
121-123 Drummond St   7387 5556   8–4C
The characterfully knackered canteen decor may evoke "a '70s sauna", but this "marvellous" survivor, near Euston is still celebrated for its "cheap lunchtime buffet" and "great dosas" – twin highlights of its "delicious veggie Indian menu", which is priced "as cheap as chips"; BYO. / NW1 2HL; 11.45 pm, Sun 11 pm; no Amex; need 10+ to book.

The Dock Kitchen
Portobello Dock W10 £54   ❸❸❶
344 Ladbroke Grove, Portobello Dock 8962 1610   1–2B
"An extraordinary variety of cuisines delivered with great panache" wins fans for Steve Parle's "exciting" venture, in an "urban-romantic" canalside setting in deepest Notting Hill; it does have its critics, though, who feel "it's too eclectic to get any one thing particularly right". / W10 5BU;

www.dockkitchen.co.uk; @TheDockKitchen; 10 pm; closed Sun D.

Dockmaster's House
E14   £53   ❷❸④
1 Hertsmere Rd   7345 0345   11–1C
"Unexpected and under-utilised", this "posh" Indian, in an "historic" Georgian building near West India Quay, is well worth seeking out for its "tasty, well-balanced and different" dishes, "efficiently" served too. / E14 8JJ; www.dockmastershouse.com; @DockmastersHous; 10.30 pm; closed Sat L & Sun.

The Don EC4   £64   ❸❷❸
20 St Swithin's Ln   7626 2606   9–3C
This "City oasis", tucked-away near Bank, remains one of the Square Mile's top lunch spots – it's "that rare spot where business can be done in attractive surroundings" (especially in the "fun" basement wine "caves"); the cuisine, though, risks "resting on its laurels" a bit. / EC4N 8AD; www.thedonrestaurant.com; @thedonlondon; 9.45 pm; closed Sat & Sun; no shorts.

don Fernando's TW9 £43   ④❷④
27f The Quadrant   8948 6447   1–4A
"Unchanging, but always popular"; this "efficient" tapas bar is a "jolly" and "bustling" fixture, where the food comes in "hearty" portions; handy for the Richmond Theatre too. / TW9 1DN; www.donfernando.co.uk; 11pm, Sun 10pm; no Amex; no booking.

Donna Margherita
SW11   £42   ❷❸④
183 Lavender Hill   7228 2660   10–2C
"Naples on a plate"; "the pizzas are to die for", at this "chilled" and "authentic" Battersea spot; it's a "family-friendly" destination, naturally, "but even babies who arrive crying are soothed by the joyful welcome!" / SW11 5TE; www.donna-margherita.com; 10.30 pm, Fri-Sat 11 pm; Mon-Thu D only, Fri-Sun open L & D.

Donostia W1   £44   ❸❷❷
10 Seymour Pl   3620 1845   2–2A
For many reporters, this popular yearling near Marble Arch offers "tapas with a Basque influence" which are "far superior to that of most rivals"; the occasional sceptic, though, tends to the view that it's "not worth a special trip". / W1H 7ND; www.donostia.co.uk; @DonostiaW1; 11 pm; closed Mon L.

Dorchester Grill
Dorchester Hotel W1 £95   ❸❷④
53 Park Ln   7629 8888   3–3A
This grand Mayfair hotel's grill-room has been dishing up some "outstanding" dishes of late... so it's a shame about the "OTT" décor ("odd having all that tartan!") and "outrageous" prices. / W1K 1QA; www.thedorchester.com; 10.15 pm, Sat 10.45 pm, Sun 10.15 pm; no trainers; set weekday L £37 (FP).

Dose EC1 £13 ❷❸④
70 Long Ln 7600 0382 9–1B
A "fantastic" caffeine high, plus a sandwich that's
"worth a journey" – this Antipodean coffee shop,
in Smithfield, still gets an enthusiastic thumbs-up
from its small fan club. / EC1A 9EJ;
www.dose-espresso.com; L only, closed Sun; no Amex.

Dotori N4 £28 ❷④④
3 Stroud Green Rd 7263 3562 8–1D
A "tiny" Finsbury Park Asian that "always rammed
to the rafters"; your order can take "ages" to come,
but it's "worth the wait", as the Korean/Japanese
fare is "always tasty" and "definitely good value for
money". / N4 2DQ; 10.30 pm; closed Mon; no Amex.

**Downtown Mayfair
W1** £92 ④④④
15 Burlington Pl 3056 1001 3–2C
This Mayfair Italian lacks even the 'charm' some
discern in its elder sibling, C London; reports,
few, suggest it's a "cold" and "soulless" sort of place,
that's "very overpriced for the food it offers".
/ W1S 2HX; www.downtownmayfair.com;
@downtownmayfair; 11.45 pm; closed Fri D,
Sat D & Sun.

Dragon Castle SE17 £37 ❷❸④
100 Walworth Rd 7277 3388 1–3C
It may sometimes seem a bit of a "cavern", but this
Elephant & Castle fixture is, for some reporters,
"still the best Chinese restaurant in London",
with "really good" dim sum a highlight of the often-
"memorable" cooking. / SE17 1JL;
www.dragon-castle.com; 11 pm.

**The Drapers Arms
N1** £46 ❸❸❸
44 Barnsbury St 7619 0348 8–3D
An "excellent neighbourhood pub", in Islington, that's
"still going strong"; it's a "friendly" sort of place,
whose attractions include "seasonal" British menus,
and "great craft ales". / N1 1ER;
www.thedrapersarms.com; @DrapersArms; 10.30 pm;
no Amex.

Duck & Waffle EC2 £68 ④④❶
110 Bishopsgate 3640 7310 9–2D
With its "incredible" 40th-floor views (plus a
"terrifying" lift ride to get there), this City yearling
would have made quite a splash anyway, so it's
surprising how many reporters also applaud its
"unexpectedly great" British food… especially when
it's served 24/7. / EC2N 4AY; www.duckandwaffle.com.

Ducksoup W1 £50 ④④④
41 Dean St 7287 4599 4–2A
"So cool it hurts"; this "narcissistic" bare-bones Soho
bistro is a "cramped" but "expensive" venue, where
the food is "not bad… just not as good as they
think it is!" / W1D 4PY; www.ducksoupsoho.co.uk;
@ducksoup.

**The Duke of
Cambridge N1** £50 ❸❸❷
30 St Peter's St 7359 3066 1–2C
"Creative organic cooking" ("from an ever-changing
blackboard menu") has made quite a name for this
"lovely" Islington back street boozer, which inspires
impressively consistent reviews all-round. / N1 8JT;
www.dukeofcambridge.com; 10.30 pm, Sun 10 pm;
no Amex.

Duke of Sussex W4 £44 ❸④❷
75 South Pde 8742 8801 7–1A
On the Chiswick/Acton border, an "airy" and
"appealing" Victorian pub (with "a lovely garden
tucked away at the back"), serving an "interestingly
different menu with a Spanish bias"; "always
buzzing", it gets "rammed" at peak times. / W4 5LF;
@thedukew4; 10.30 pm, Sun 9.30 pm.

**Duke's Brew & Que
N1** NEW £43 ❷❸④
33 Downham Rd 3006 0795 1–2D
"Amazing, huge and tasty beef ribs", "incredible
burgers" and "an excellent choice of beers"
(they brew their own) – all star dishes at this
"cool BBQ", in Dalston. / N1 5AA;
www.dukesbrewandque.com; @DukesJoint; 10.30 pm,
Sun 9.30 pm.

Durbar W2 £32 ❷❷❷
24 Hereford Rd 7727 1947 6–1B
"Top-quality Indian food, at decent prices" – it may
be prehistoric in origin (1956), but this Bayswater
veteran still draws a "loyal crowd" with its "refined
but unfussy" cuisine. / W2 4AA;
www.durbartandoori.co.uk; 11.30 pm; closed Fri L.

E&O W11 £52 ❷❸❶
14 Blenheim Cr 7229 5454 6–1A
"After 10 years, I still get excited!" – this "social,
buzzy and groovy" Notting Hill hang-out is still
serving "Asian-fusion dishes at their finest", and still
"always fun". / W11 1NN; www.rickerrestaurants.com;
11 pm, Sun 10.30 pm; booking: max 6.

**El leven Park Walk
SW10** £59 ❸❸④
11 Park Wk 7352 3449 5–3B
"Calm", "nice", perhaps "a bit bland" –
this contemporary Chelsea Italian doesn't always set
the pulse racing, but it's "traditional food with
a modern twist" is prepared to a very "steady"
standard. / SW10 0AJ;
www.atozrestaurants.com/11parkwalk; midnight;
set weekday L £33 (FP), set dinner £41 (FP).

The Eagle EC1 £32 ❸④❷
159 Farringdon Rd 7837 1353 9–1A
"The first, and still among the best"; this "vibe-filled"
Farringdon boozer helped coin the term 'gastropub',
and still offers "imaginative" Med-inspired dishes
from its blackboard menu. / EC1R 3AL; 10.30 pm;
closed Sun D; no Amex; no booking.

Earl Spencer SW18   **£46**   ❸④❸
260-262 Merton Rd   8870 9244   10–2B
It may look "like a roadhouse" (and "on a busy
road" too), but this Wandsworth fixture is really
"a pub in name only" nowadays – the food
is "consistently good" and sometimes "excellent".
/ SW18 5JL; www.theearlspencer.co.uk; 11 pm;
Mon-Thu D only, Fri-Sun open L & D; no booking Sun.

Eat   **£14**   ④❸④
Branches throughout London
"A fab selection of interesting soups" remains
a highlight at this grab-and-go chain; as always,
fans say it's "taken on Pret and won", but, as ever,
survey ratings still lag its arch-rival's. / www.eat.co.uk;
4 pm-8 pm; most City branches closed all or part
of weekend; no credit cards; no booking.

Eat Tokyo   **£23**   ❸❸④
50 Red Lion St, WC1   7242 3490   2–1D
15 Whitcomb St, WC2   7930 6117   4–4A
169 King St, W6   8741 7916   7–2B **NEW**
18 Hillgate St, W8   7792 9313   6–2B
14 North End Rd, NW11   8209 0079   1–1B
NEW
The "intimate and stylish" new Holborn branch
(on the former site of Eddoko, RIP) is a highlight
of this small Japanese chain, where the food
is "inexpensive but high on quality and authenticity".

**Ebury Restaurant
& Wine Bar SW1**   **£53**   ④④④
139 Ebury St   7730 5447   2–4A
This "old-time" (1959) Belgravia wine bar-cum-
restaurant is never going to set the world on fire,
but its "reliable" food – and, more particularly,
its "superb" and "good-value" wines – can still make
it "a good destination for a reasonably-priced
meal". / SW1W 9QU; www.eburyrestaurant.co.uk;
10.15 pm.

Eco SW4   **£34**   ❷❸❷
162 Clapham High St   7978 1108   10–2D
"Improved" by its recent major refurbishment,
this perennially trendy Clapham haunt remains
a "friendly" outfit that's "always reliable" for
an "excellent pizza". / SW4 7UG;
www.ecorestaurants.com; @ecopizzaLDN; 11 pm, Fri &
Sat 11.30 pm.

Ed's Easy Diner   **£31**   ④④❸
12 Moor St, W1   7434 4439   4–2A
Trocadero, 19 Rupert St, W1   7287 1951
3–3D
Sedley Pl, 14 Woodstock St, W1   7493 9916
3–2B
London's original US diner chain is a riot of '50s
kitsch; a visit can still be "great fun" (especially with
kids), even if there's no doubt "you can find a better
burger in town these days". / www.edseasydiner.co.uk;
Rupert St 10.30 pm, Fri & Sat 11.30 pm, Sun 10 pm;
Moor St 11.30 pm, Thu-Sat midnight, Sun 10 pm, Sedley

Place 9 pm, Thu-Sat 10 pm, NW1 Mon-Sat 10 pm,
Sun 9 pm; Moor St no booking.

Edera W11   **£61**   ❷0④
148 Holland Park Ave   7221 6090   6–2A
"First-rate" Sardinian food and notably "charming"
service win very solid support for this "reliable"
Holland Park fixture; it's no bargain, though,
and "the menu seems slow to change". / W11 4UE;
www.atoz.co.uk; 11 pm, Sun 10 pm.

Eight Over Eight SW3 **£57**   ❸❷❸
392 King's Rd   7349 9934   5–3B
A "humming star of Chelsea"; Will Ricker's hang-out
at World's End is always "vibrant and fun", and it
offers some "excellent" pan-Asian nibbles;
no denying, though, that it's "pricey, for what you
get". / SW3 5UZ; www.rickerrestaurants.com; 11 pm,
Sun 10.30 pm.

Elena's L'Etoile W1   **£52**   ④④④
30 Charlotte St   7636 7189   2–1C
Traditionalists still warm to the "good old-fashioned
French fare" and "uncorporate" vibe at this faded
Fitzrovia fixture (est 1896); since Elena retired,
however, it seems rather to have lost its way.
/ W1T 2NG; www.elenasletoile.co.uk; 10.30 pm; closed
Sat L & Sun.

**Elephant Royale
Locke's Wharf E14**   **£49**   ❸④❸
Westferry Rd   7987 7999   11–2C
"A lovely location by the river" (nice terrace too,
with stunning views of Greenwich) helps ensure that
this remote Thai, on the Isle of Dogs, is "always
busy"; it's on the pricey side, but the food is of
a "high standard". / E14 3WA;
www.elephantroyale.com; 10.30 pm, Fri & Sat 11 pm,
Sun 10 pm.

Elliot's Cafe SE1   **£51**   ❸④④
12 Stoney St   7403 7436   9–4C
"A welcome addition to Borough Market" –
this "casual" café yearling wins much praise for its
"inventive" and "seasonal" cooking, and its
"welcoming style"; consistency can be an issue,
though, and the odd "disappointing" meal is not
unknown. / SE1 9AD; www.elliotscafe.com; @elliotscafe;
10 pm; closed Sun.

Emile's SW15   **£44**   ❸❷④
96-98 Felsham Rd   8789 3323   10–2B
"Tucked away" in a Putney back street, a "friendly"
and "romantic" stalwart bistro, where the beef
Wellington (in particular) is the stuff of local legend.
/ SW15 1DQ; www.emilesrestaurant.co.uk; 11 pm;
D only, closed Sun; no Amex.

The Empress E9   **£44**   ❷❸❷
130 Lauriston Rd   8533 5123   1–2D
"A stone's throw from beautiful Victoria Park",
this "atmospheric" boozer is one of East London's
top gastropubs; the menu is divided into small plates
and more standard options, and results are often

"excellent". / E9 7LH; www.empresse9.co.uk; @elliottlidstone; 10 pm, Sun 9.30 pm; closed Mon L; no Amex.

Empress of Sichuan WC2 £36 ❷❸❷
6 Lisle St 7734 8128 4–3A
"Spicy treats in the heart of Chinatown!" – this "authentic" Sichuanese is well worth seeking out… assuming you like your dishes hot, of course. / WC2H 7BG; 11 pm; set weekday L £23 (FP).

The Engineer NW1 £58 ④④❸
65 Gloucester Ave 7722 0950 8–3B
"It's everything a gastropub should be", say devotees of this "lovely" Primrose Hill boozer, especially known for its "great garden"; since it changed hands a year or two ago, however, some reporters feel "it's not what it was". / NW1 8JH; www.the-engineer.com; 10.30 pm, Sun 10 pm; no Amex.

Enoteca Turi SW15 £56 ❷⓪❸
28 Putney High St 8785 4449 10–2B
The "rustic" cooking is eclipsed only by the "spellbinding" all-Italian wine list at Giuseppe and Pamela Turi's "hidden gem", near Putney Bridge – a "welcoming" stalwart, run in "convivial" family-run style. / SW15 1SQ; www.enotecaturi.com; 10.30 pm, Fri-Sat 11 pm; closed Sun.

The Enterprise SW3 £57 ④❸❷
35 Walton St 7584 3148 5–2C
The food is "never spectacular", but that does little to dent the appeal of this "long-term-favourite" Chelsea local – a "tightly-packed" but "fun" haunt that "appeals to all age-groups". / SW3 2HU; www.theenterprise.co.uk; 10 pm, Sat 10.30 pm; no booking, except weekday L; set weekday L £36 (FP).

Entrée SW11 £52 ❸❷❷
2 Battersea Rise 7223 5147 10–2C
"A cracking little basement cocktail bar" adds life to this "small but well-conceived" Battersea venue – "a step up from other locals", with "cheerful" staff and an "interesting and varied" menu. / SW11 1ED; www.entreebattersea.co.uk/; 10.30 pm; closed weekday L.

Eriki NW3 £39 ❷❸④
4-6 Northways Pde, Finchley Rd 7722 0606 8–2A
"The hidden gem of Swiss Cottage!" – this ambitious Indian serves an "interesting" menu of "fresh"-tasting, dishes of high quality; despite their best efforts on the décor front, however, the atmosphere "does not hum". / NW3 5EN; www.eriki.co.uk; 10.45 pm; closed Sat L.

Esarn Kheaw W12 £33 ❷❸⑤
314 Uxbridge Rd 8743 8930 7–1B
"Authentic Esarn (North Eastern) Thai cuisine" has long been a feature of this family-run shop-conversion in Shepherd's Bush… but "don't go in search of atmosphere". / W12 7LJ;

www.esarnkheaw.co.uk; @esarn_kheaw; 11 pm; closed Sat L & Sun L; no Amex.

L'Escargot W1 £59 ❸❷❷
48 Greek St 7439 7474 4–2A
This Soho "classic" is certainly well suited to a "delightful set lunch", and it offers a "good-value pre-theatre menu" too; some reporters also tip it for romance or as a top foodie destination, but the volume of feedback of late has been surprisingly limited. / W1D 4EF; www.whitestarline.org.uk; 11.15 pm; closed Sat L & Sun; set pre theatre £36 (FP).

Essenza W11 £57 ❸❸④
210 Kensington Park Rd 7792 1066 6–1A
A "casual" and "friendly" Notting Hill spot fans like for being "not quite as heaving as some other places" nearby; it offers "consistent" cooking, too, at prices that are "very reasonable, for the area". / W11 1NR; www.essenza.co.uk; 11.30 pm; set weekday L £36 (FP).

L'Etranger SW7 £69 ❸④❸
36 Gloucester Rd 7584 1118 5–1B
"Very interesting French-Asian fusion cuisine" is twinned with "astonishing" (if "extraordinarily expensive") wine list at this "sexily lit" (but somewhat "subdued") South Kensington fixture. / SW7 4QT; www.etranger.co.uk; 11 pm, Sun 10 pm; set weekday L £38 (FP), set pre-theatre £42 (FP).

Euphorium Bakery N1 £13 ❸④❸
26a Chapel Mkt 7837 7010 8–3D
"The antidote to high street coffee chains" – this "genuinely Continental" café/bakery offers "fine sarnies and cakes at fair prices". / N1 9EN; www.euphoriumbakery.com; 6.15 pm; L only; no Amex.

Everest Inn SE3 £34 ❷❷❸
41 Montpelier Vale 8852 7872 1–4D
"Fresh", "innovative" and "big-flavoured" north Indian cuisine – with some "outstanding Nepalese dishes" – wins more-than-local applause for this "helpful and efficient" Blackheath fixture. / SE3 0TJ; www.everestinn.co.uk; midnight, Sun 11 pm.

Eyre Brothers EC2 £57 ❸❸❸
70 Leonard St 7613 5346 12–1B
A "sophisticated" Hispanic venture, which was launched long before anyone ever called this area 'Silicon Roundabout'; it draws a steady business following, but – thanks not least to its "expertly assembled" wine list – arguably "deserves to be busier". / EC2A 4QX; www.eyrebrothers.co.uk; 10 pm; closed Sat L & Sun.

Faanoos £27 ❸④❸
472 Chiswick High Rd, W4 8994 4217 7–2A
481 Richmond Road, SW14 8878 5738 1–4A
"Amazing" flatbread, straight from the oven, is a highlight of dining at these "accommodating" west London Persians – a top cheap 'n' cheerful

choice, where the cooking is "always fresh"; BYO.
/ SW14 11 pm; W4 11 pm; Fri & Sat midnight.

Fabrizio EC1 £52 ❷❶⑤
30 Saint Cross St 7430 1503 9–1A
"Fabrizio the charming and genial patron keeps
up high standards", at this "unpretentious" trattoria,
near Hatton Garden, which serves up "comforting"
and "unfussy" dishes ("like your Sicilian grandma
might make") at "top-value" prices. / EC1N 8UH;
www.fabriziorestaurant.co.uk; 10 pm; closed Sat L & Sun.

Fabrizio N19 £31 ❸❷④
34 Highgate Hill 7561 9073 8–1C
Fabrizio "is such a welcoming host", at this "no-
frills" neighbourhood Italian, "in the leafy environs
of Highgate Hill"; it serves "delicious and
straightforward pizza and pasta". / N19 5NL.

Fairuz W1 £49 ❸❷❸
3 Blandford St 7486 8108 2–1A
"Possibly Marylebone's best-kept secret";
the Lebanese fare at this popular spot is "a cut
above", and "reasonably priced" too (especially
at lunch); the only real complaint? – some tables are
a touch "cramped". / W1H 3DA; www.fairuz.uk.com;
11 pm, Sun 10.30 pm.

La Famiglia SW10 £60 ④④❸
7 Langton St 7351 0761 5–3B
"Retaining some of its old magic", this long-
established trattoria "all-rounder" (with legendary
garden) still pleases the faithful with its
"comfortable" charms; critics, though, say it's
"overpriced, even for Chelsea", and find standards
"very average" nowadays. / SW10 0JL;
www.lafamiglia.co.uk; 11.45 pm.

Fat Boy's £34 ④④❸
10a-10b Edensor Rd, W4 8994 8089 10–1A
33 Haven Grn, W5 8998 5868 1–2A
201 Upper Richmond Rd, SW14 8876 0644
1–4A
431 Richmond Rd, TW1 8892 7657 1–4A
68 High St, TW8 8569 8481 1–3A
A "reliable" chain of neighbourhood Thais, where
the food's "consistently good", if "not exciting".
/ www.fatboysthai.co.uk; 11 pm.

Faulkner's E8 £29 ❷④④
424-426 Kingsland Rd 7254 6152 1–1D
A long-standing Dalston chippy, still winning praise
for its "wonderful, traditional fried fish". / E8 4AA;
10 pm, Fri-Sun 11 pm; no Amex; need 8+ to book.

The Fellow N1 £45 ❸④④
24 York Way 7833 4395 8–3C
"Just around the corner from King's Cross",
this "solid" gastropub is certainly "a boon for
travellers", and in a still "pretty barren area"; "throw
in the roof terrace, and you have to call it a hidden
gem!" / N1 9AA; www.thefellow.co.uk; @24yorkway;
9.45pm.

The Fentiman Arms SW8 £46 ❸❸❷
64 Fentiman Rd 7793 9796 10–1D
One of the best of the Geronimo Inns,
this "pleasant" Kennington gastroboozer is a notably
consistent performer; it particularly benefits from its
"great" garden (which offers an "excellent" summer
BBQ). / SW8 1LA; www.geronimo-inns.co.uk;
@fentmanarms; 10 pm, Sun 9 pm; SRA-60%.

Fernandez & Wells £33 ❸❸❷
16a, St Anne's Ct, W1 7494 4242 3–1D
43 Lexington St, W1 7734 1546 3–2D
73 Beak St, W1 7287 8124 3–2D
Somerset Hs, Strand, WC2 7420 9408 2–2D
"A brilliant little chain", whose artfully "scruffy" Soho
origins are somewhat at odds with the "light and
airy" branch in Somerset House; all are "bustling
and fun", serving "outstanding coffee, sandwiches
and cake", plus other "well-sourced" bites,
and "interesting" wines. / www.fernandezandwells.com;
Lexington St & St Anne's court 10 pm; Beak St 6 pm,
Somerset House 11 pm; St Anne's Court closed Sun.

Fez Mangal W11 £22 ❶❷❸
104 Ladbroke Grove 7229 3010 6–1A
"Not fancy, but the food is excellent"; this "honest"
Turkish charcoal grill, in Notting Hill, inspires
impressively consistent reports; BYO. / W11 1PY;
www.fezmangal.co.uk; 11.30 pm; no Amex.

Ffiona's W8 £53 ④❸❸
51 Kensington Church St 7937 4152 5–1A
Fiona presides with aplomb over this "dinner-party-
like" Kensington bistro veteran, where the food
is "relatively simple" but "consistent", and "a great
night out is guaranteed"; recent innovation – a "fab"
brunch. / W8 4BA; www.ffionas.com; @ffionasnotes;
11 pm, Sun 10 pm; closed Mon; no Amex.

Fifteen N1 £61
15 Westland Pl 3375 1515 12–1A
Jamie's philanthropic Hoxton bistro may do its
trainees a favour, but the poor old punters have
been paying through the nose for its often
"unattractive" and "poorly cooked" dishes;
the first report of the spring 2013 relaunch,
however, relates "improvements all round" – about
time! / N1 7LP; www.fifteen.net; 10 pm; booking:
max 12.

**The Fifth Floor Restaurant
Harvey Nichols SW1** £57 ❸❸❸
109-125 Knightsbridge 7235 5250 5–1D
It's surprising the way this late-'90s-hotspot,
up above Knightsbridge, has faded from view
in recent times… especially as the very
modest feedback it inspires is all positive, praising
an airy "oasis", with "surprisingly good food and
service", and an "exceptional" wine list. / SW1X 7RJ;
www.harveynichols.com; 10.45 pm; closed Sun D;
SRA-63%.

La Figa E14 £40 ❸❷④
45 Narrow St 7790 0077 11–1B
"Family-friendly and often packed", this long-
established Limehouse Italian has a big name for
"generous portions" and *"great value"* – *"worth
a detour!"* / E14 8DN; www.lafigarestaurant.co.uk;
11 pm, Sun 10.30 pm.

Fino W1 £49 ❸❸❸
33 Charlotte St 7813 8010 2–1C
"A modern take on classic tapas" has helped win
major popularity for the Hart brothers' *"hidden-
away"* and *"classy"* Fitzrovia basement; is it *"stuck
in a bit of a rut"*, though? – there's a feeling *"it's not
as good as it was"*, and *"bills are quite high"*.
/ W1T 1RR; www.finorestaurant.com; 10.30 pm; closed
Sat L & Sun; booking: max 12.

Fire & Stone £41 ④④④
31-32 Maiden Ln, WC2 08443 712550 4–3D
Westfield, Ariel Way, W12 0844 371 2551
7–1C
4 Horner Sq., E1 0844 371 2554 12–2B
A *"different spin on pizzas"* (*"some quite inspiring"*)
– and at *"reasonable prices"* too – wins fans for
these large and *"hectic"* chain outlets; *"if you have
to eat at Westfield, this may be one of the better
choices"*. / www.fireandstone.com; WC2 11 pm;
W12 11.15 pm; E1 11pm, Sun 8 pm.

First Floor W11 £46 ❸④❶
186 Portobello Rd 7243 0072 6–1A
As a *"superb venue for a party"*, this high-ceilinged
Portobello fixture, with its sense of *"faded
grandeur"*, is ideal; it's a romantic spot too, and the
food is never less than *"dependable"*. / W11 1LA;
www.firstfloorportobello.co.uk; 10.30 pm.

**The Fish & Chip
Shop N1** `NEW` £43 ❶❷❷
189 Upper St 3227 0979 8–2D
"A new stand-out in an area spoilt for choice!";
this *"lovely"* newcomer – run by the ex-supremo
of the Caprice group – is *"everything you want from
a fish 'n' chip shop"*, and its *"brilliant"* food includes
some *"nostalgic"* puds. / N1 1RQ;
www.thefishandchipshop.uk.com; 11 pm, Sun 10 pm.

Fish Central EC1 £29 ❸❷④
149-155 Central St 7253 4970 12–1A
"Unbeatable value and flavour" draw many fish 'n'
chip fans to this *"busy"* but *"welcoming"* spot, 'twixt
Old Street and Islington. / EC1V 8AP;
www.fishcentral.co.uk; 10.30 pm, Fri & Sat 11 pm;
closed Sun.

Fish Club £38 ❷❷④
189 St John's Hill, SW11 7978 7115 10–2C
57 Clapham High St, SW4 7720 5853 10–2D
"Fish 'n' chips as they should be", served battered
or grilled – plus oysters, fish pie, sweet potato
wedges and so on – win all-round praise for these
"upmarket" south London chippies.

/ www.thefishclub.com; 10 pm; closed Mon L;
no bookings.

Fish in a Tie SW11 £36 ④❷❷
105 Falcon Rd 7924 1913 10–1C
"Always reliable and budget-friendly", this super-
inexpensive bistro, tucked away behind Clapham
Junction, offers *"really good food"*; it's invariably
"full and lively". / SW11 2PF; www.fishinatie.co.uk;
midnight, Sun 11 pm; no Amex; set always available
£20 (FP).

Fish Market EC2 £53 ❸❷❸
16 New St 3503 0790 9–2D
A *"businessy"* D&D group yearling, near Liverpool
Street; it's been instantly hailed as a handy set-up
offering *"simple"* but *"expertly-cooked"* fish.
/ EC2M 4TR.

fish! SE1 £54 ④④❸
Cathedral St 7407 3803 9–4C
This striking all-glass brasserie, by Borough Market,
can seem *"a victim of its own success"* – the fish
can be *"excellent"*, but the overall experience often
seems *"a bit pricey for what it is"*, especially when
it's so *"crammed-in"*. / SE1 9AL; www.fishkitchen.com;
@fishborough; 10.45 pm, Sun 10.30 pm.

Fishworks £50 ❸④④
7-9 Swallow St, W1 7734 5813 3–3D
89 Marylebone High St, W1 7935 9796 2–1A
*"It's a little formulaic, but for all that you get good
fish"* – and a *"wonderful selection"* too – at these
low-key fishmongers-cum-restaurants, in Mayfair
and Marylebone (and also Richmond).
/ www.fishworks.co.uk; 10.30 pm.

**Fitou's Thai
Restaurant W10** £26 ❷❸④
1 Dalgarno Gdns 8968 0558 6–1A
"A hidden neighbourhood gem"; this *"great-value"*
BYO café, by Little Wormwood Scrubs, serves Thai
scoff of *"very good quality"*. / W10 5LL;
www.fitourestaurant.co.uk; 10.30 pm; closed Sun L.

**The Five Fields
SW3** `NEW` £70 ❷❶❷
8-9 Blacklands Ter 7838 1082 5–2D
"The most assured new opening" of recent times,
say fans – this Chelsea newcomer (on the site of El
Blason, RIP) is *"a great addition to the London
scene"* – the interior is *"beautiful"* (if quite tightly-
packed) and service *"attentive"*; ex-NYC chef Taylor
Bonnyman's *"very interesting"* dishes deliver some
"mind-blowing" flavours too. / SW3 2SP;
www.fivefieldsrestaurant.com; @The5Fields; 10.30 pm.

Five Guys WC2 `NEW` £13
1-3 Long Acre 0833 005 4–3C
This major US burger chain recently established its
first European bridgehead in Covent Garden;
it caused much excitement on opening, but we'll
look forward to next year's survey to see what

people really think of it. / WC2E 9LH;
www.fiveguys.co.uk.

500 N19 £44 ❸❸④
782 Holloway Rd 7272 3406 8–1C
An Archway phenomenon, this "fabulous family-run
place" has made a big name for its "genuine"
Sicilian cooking; it still attracts much praise,
not least for its "sensible prices", but quite a few
reporters this year found it "failed to deliver".
/ N19 3JH; www.500restaurant.co.uk; 10.30 pm, Sunday
9.30 pm; Mon-Thu D only, Fri-Sun open L & D.

The Flask N6 £43 ④④❷
77 Highgate West Hill 8348 7346 1–1C
A "lovely" (and extensive) ancient inn, in Highgate,
most recommended as "a cracking place for Sunday
lunch". / N6 6BU; www.theflaskhighgate.com; @flaskn6;
10 pm, Sun 9 pm.

Flat Iron W1 🆕 £22 ❸❷❷
17 Beak St no tel 3–2D
"Simple" and "straightforward", this steak-for-a-
tenner newcomer offers "serious value, by the
standards of Soho's often overpriced no-bookings
eateries"; "squeezing onto benches" at communal
tables doesn't seem to be a problem. / W1F 9RW;
www.flatironsteak.co.uk; @flatironsteak.

Flat White W1 £11 ❷❷❷
17 Berwick St 7734 0370 3–2D
"The granddaddy of Antipodean coffee shops";
this Soho fixture "still packs the smoothest,
creamiest coffee punch", and "the breakfasts are
delicious too". / W1F 0PT; www.flat-white.co.uk; L only;
no credit cards; no booking.

Fleet River Bakery
WC2 £20 ❷④❸
71 Lincolns Inn Fields 7691 1457 2–1D
"In a side alley near Holborn tube", an "original"
and "delightful" café, where the menu offers not
just delectable cakes, but other "interesting" dishes,
as well as "expert" coffee; beware queuing at peak
times, though, and service which can be "very slow".
/ WC2A 3JF; www.fleetriverbakery.com; 5 pm, Sat 3 pm;
L only, closed Sun.

Flesh and Buns
WC2 🆕 £50
41 Earlham St 7632 9500 4–2C
A new izakaya (informal Japanese) restaurant, in a
Covent Garden basement, from the team behind
Soho's trendy Bone Daddies; early press reviews
have been very positive. / WC2H 9LX;
www.fleshandbuns.com.

Florence SE24 £41 ④④❷
131-133 Dulwich Rd 7326 4987 10–2D
"If you don't have kids, you may wish to stay away",
but if you do, this "very child-friendly" Brockwell
Park boozer may seem like a gift from the gods,
"standard pub fare" notwithstanding. / SE24 0NG;

www.florencehernehill.com; @theflorencepub; 10 pm,
Sun 9.30 pm.

Food for Thought
WC2 £23 ❸❸④
31 Neal St 7836 0239 4–2C
A dear old basement veggie in Covent Garden
which, for its many loyal fans, remains "a unique
and amazing centrally-located gem"… "basic"
presentation, "harassed" staff and "overcrowding"
are all just part of the formula; BYO. / WC2H 9PR;
www.foodforthought-london.co.uk; 8 pm, Sun 5 pm; closed
Sun D; no credit cards; no booking; set always available
£15 (FP).

Forman's E3 £54 ❷❸④
Stour Rd, Fish Island 8525 2365 1–1D
The "light and airy" canalside dining room
of London's sole salmon-smokery – with its
"amazing views" of the Olympic Stadium – makes
"a good spot… once you find it", and the "best-of-
British" cuisine can be "surprisingly imaginative" too.
/ E3 2NH; www.formans.co.uk; 9 pm; Closed Mon-Wed,
Thu & Fri D only, Sat open L & D, closed Sun D.

Formosa Dining Room
The Prince Alfred W9 £49 ④④❸
5a Formosa St 7286 3287 6–1C
"Handily attached to a great pub" (one of London's
most imposing), this Maida Vale dining room is a
"solid" sort of destination, that's often "busy";
"the specials tend to be good". / W9 1EE;
www.theprincealfred.com; @theprincealfred; 10 pm, Fri &
Sat 11 pm, Sun 9 pm; no Amex; set weekday L £33 (FP).

(1707)
Fortnum & Mason W1 £45 ❸❷❸
181 Piccadilly 7734 8040 3–3D
"Browse the whole of the Fortnum's list, at cost plus
£10 corkage – that's the unbeatable (for the
West End) proposition that makes this basement
wine bar especially worth seeking out; "tapas-style
snacks and platters" too. / W1A 1ER;
www.fortnumandmason.co.uk; @fortnumandmason;
8 pm, Sun 6 pm; closed Sun D.

(The Diamond Jubilee Tea Salon)
Fortnum & Mason
W1 £50 ❸❶❶
181 Piccadilly 7734 8040 3–3D
"A splendid venue for a sumptuous afternoon tea" –
this "light, airy, spacious and very comfortable dining
room" is proving a tremendous addition to the
store… "fresher and more serene" than the nearby
Ritz! / W1A 1ER; www.fortnumandmason.com.

(The Fountain)
Fortnum & Mason W1 £62 ④❸❸
181 Piccadilly 7734 8040 3–3D
"Definitely a place to take your favourite aunt" –
the buttery of the Queen's grocer remains
"a beautiful oasis of calm and manners" (if one with
"prices to match the location"); the menu offers

"choice in abundance" too, with the top option being the "spectacular Full English breakfast". / W1A 1ER; www.fortnumandmason.com; @fortnumandmason; 7.45 pm; closed Sun D.

Fortune Cookie W2 £28 ❷④⑤
1 Queensway 7727 7260 6–2C
Right by Queensway tube, a "good old-reliable", where an "authentic Cantonese fix" can be had at "reasonable prices". / W2 4QJ; 11 pm.

40 Maltby Street SE1 £40 ❷❸❸
40 Maltby St 7237 9247 9–4D
"Basic, but totally cool", this wine bar – located "under the arches" of "the 'new' Borough Market" – offers "excellent" tapas-style dishes, complemented by "adventurous" natural wines that are "always interesting". / SE1 3PA; www.40maltbystreet.com; 9.30 pm; closed Mon, Tue, Wed L, Thu L, Sat D & Sun; no Amex; no bookings.

Four Regions TW9 £43 ❸❷④
102-104 Kew Rd 8940 9044 1–4A
"The local Chinese everyone loves of!" – a Richmond mainstay, which owes its enduring popularity to its "enjoyable" cooking, and the often "excellent" service. / TW9 2PQ; 11.30 pm, Sun 11 pm.

The Four Seasons £31 ❷⑤⑤
12 Gerrard St, W1 7494 0870 4–3A
23 Wardour St, W1 7287 9995 4–3A
84 Queensway, W2 7229 4320 6–2C
"The best roast duck this side of Beijing" is the headline attraction at this "ridiculously inexpensive" Bayswater fixture; the Chinatown outpost is equally "great, rough and ready". / www.fs-restaurants.co.uk; Queensway 11 pm, Sun 10h45 pm; Gerrard St 1 am; Wardour St 1am, Fri-Sat 3.30 am.

Fox & Grapes SW19 £55 ④④❸
9 Camp Rd 8619 1300 10–2A
Claude Bosi's pub certainly has a "good location", right by Wimbledon Common, and fans say its "imaginative" cooking has made it "a great additional" locally; it takes a lot of flak too, however, for a menu that's "dull" and "vastly overpriced". / SW19 4UN; foxandgrapeswimbledon.co.uk; 9.30 pm, Sun 8.15 pm; no Amex.

The Fox & Hounds
SW11 £47 ❷❷❷
66 Latchmere Rd 7924 5483 10–1C
A "really friendly" Battersea gastroboozer, where most reporters find the food – with its "definite Mediterranean theme" – "never fails to deliver". / SW11 2JU; www.thefoxandhoundspub.co.uk; @thefoxbattersea; 10 pm; Mon-Thu D only, Fri-Sun open L & D.

The Fox and Anchor
EC1 £49 ❷❷❶
115 Charterhouse St 7250 1300 9–1B
A marvellously "cosy" and "historic" inn, "tucked away" in Clerkenwell, where British dishes are

executed with a "creativity and lightness of touch rarely found"; breakfast is a famous highlight – "a full cholesterol fry-up washed down with a pint of Guinness". / EC1M 6AA; www.foxandanchor.com; @MeetMeAtTheFox; 9.30 pm.

Foxlow EC1 NEW £48
St John St awaiting tel 9–2A
On the former Clerkenwell site of North Road (RIP), the latest outpost of the – now venture-capitalist-backed – Hawksmoor steakhouse empire opens in late 2013. / EC1; www.foxlow.co.uk.

Foxtrot Oscar SW3 £55 ④④⑤
79 Royal Hospital Rd 7352 4448 5–3D
Perhaps the most eloquent commentary on the Chelsea bistro, just a few doors from Ramsay HQ and nowadays owned by him, is the scant survey feedback it inspires – such as there is suggests a visit is a "very flat" experience. / SW3 4HN; www.gordonramsay.com/foxtrotoscar/; 10 pm, Sun 9 pm.

Franco Manca £22 ❷❸❸
144 Chiswick High Rd, W4 8747 4822 7–2A
76 Northcote Rd, SW11 7924 3110 10–2D
Unit 4 Market Row, SW9 7738 3021 10–2D
Westfield Stratford, E20 8522 6669 1–1D
Thanks to their "awesome" sourdough crusts, and their "beautiful toppings", these "really Neapolitan" pizza stops (SW9 in particular) are hailed as "the best in the country"; as the venture-capital-backed roll-out gathers pace, however, ratings are beginning to go just a little bit soggy. / www.francomanca.co.uk; SW9 10.30, Mon 5 pm; W4 11 pm; E20 9 pm, Thu-Sat 10 pm, Sun 6 pm; SW9 no bookings.

Franco's SW1 £74 ❸❸❸
61 Jermyn St 7499 2211 3–3C
A "lush" St James's Italian, under the same ownership as nearby Wilton's, which has been inspiring impressively consistent reports of late; its "well-spaced" tables make it a handy business destination, if not a bargain one. / SW1Y 6LX; www.francoslondon.com; 10.30 pm; closed Sun; set weekday L £38 (FP).

Franklins SE22 £49 ❸④❸
157 Lordship Ln 8299 9598 1–4D
"A local institution", down East Dulwich way – this "comfortable" pub-conversion wins praise for an "interesting" menu (especially for carnivores); it does have the odd critic, though, who says "it's never quite as good as it thinks it is". / SE22 8HX; www.franklinsrestaurant.com; @frankinsse22; 10.30 pm; no Amex; set weekday L £30 (FP).

Frantoio SW10 £57 ④❷❷
397 King's Rd 7352 4146 5–3B
"More like a club", this very "local"-feeling World's End Italian is a "welcoming" sort of place offering

"genuine" food at "reasonable" prices; "more menu variety", however, might not go amiss. / SW10 0LR; www.frantoio.com; 11.15 pm, Sun 10.15 pm.

Frederick's N1 £62 ❸❷❷
106 Islington High St 7359 2888 8–3D
Critics may still find the food "more reliable than exciting", and prices "somewhat inflated", but this (surprisingly) grand and "charming" Islington veteran is "as popular as ever"; the conservatory is undoubtedly a "special venue". / N1 8EG; www.fredericks.co.uk; 11 pm; closed Sun; set weekday L & pre-theatre £37 (FP).

Freemasons Arms NW3 £41 ⑤⑤④
32 Downshire Hill 7433 6811 8–2A
This Hampstead Heath-side boozer looks "promising", but it "relies too much on its location" – too often the food's "nondescript" and "overpriced", and service can be "abominable". / NW3 1NT; www.freemasonsarms.co.uk; @Freemasons_Arms; 11 pm, Sat 10.30 pm, Sun 10.30 pm.

Frizzante at City Farm Hackney City Farm
E2 £31 ❷④④
1a Goldsmiths Row 7729 6381 12–1D
"Restaurant-standard food in a ramshackle school classroom, or at least that's what it feels like!" – this family-friendly spot, between Columbia Road and Broadway Market, remains particularly popular as a breakfast destination. / E2 8QA; www.frizzanteltd.co.uk; @frizzanteltd; D only, closed Mon; no Amex.

Frizzante Cafe Surrey Docks Farm
SE16 £34 ❸❷❸
South Whf, Rotherhithe St 7231 1010 11–2B
The "very friendly" café of this Thames-side farm, in deepest Rotherhithe, has a "tolerance for kids" which makes it a natural weekend destination... most particularly for a brunch using "tasty organic produce". / SE16 5ET; www.frizzanteltd.co.uk; 4.30 pm; closed Mon, Tue-Sun D; no Amex.

La Fromagerie Café W1 £38 ❷④❷
2-6 Moxon St 7935 0341 3–1A
"Much improved, now it's bigger"; the café of the famous Marylebone cheese shop offers "interesting" light bites – "everything tastes deliciously fresh, and of itself!" / W1U 4EW; www.lafromagerie.co.uk; @lafromagerieuk; 6.30 pm, Sat 6 pm, Sun 5 pm; L only; no booking.

The Frontline Club W2 £54 ❸④❸
13 Norfolk Pl 7479 8960 6–1D
"Eclectic dishes, cooked well" and an "unusual, great-value wine list" win consistent praise for this

professional dining room "on Paddington's doorstep"; it's part of a club for war-reporters, and the photography on display is often "very striking". / W2 1QJ; www.frontlineclub.com; 10.30 pm; closed Sat L & Sun; set weekday L £34 (FP).

Fryer's Delight WC1 £13 ❸④⑤
19 Theobald's Rd 7405 4114 2–1D
This "greasy-spoon-type" Bloomsbury chippy may be "scrappy-looking", but it certainly inspires loyalty – "I have a visitor from NYC, in his 70s, who always insists we go: it's his corner of England, serving fish 'n' chips as he remembers it from 50 years ago!". BYO. / WC1X 8SL; 10.30 pm; closed Sun; no credit cards.

Fujiyama SW9 £28 ❸④④
5-7 Vining St 7737 2369 10–2D
"Better than Wagamama!"; though it's "overshadowed by the trendy new places" down Brixton way, this cheap 'n' cheerful Japanese canteen remains a "very solid option". / SW9 8QA; www.newfujiyama.com; 11 pm.

Fulham Wine Rooms SW6 £52 ❸❸❸
871-873 Fulham Rd 7042 9440 10–1B
It's sometimes "too busy", but this contemporary-style wine bar pleases most reporters with its interesting vintages from "atmosphere-controlled cabinets"; the food's not bad, and there's a pleasant terrace too. / SW6 5HP; www.greatwinesbytheglass.com; 11 pm.

Fuzzy's Grub £14 ❸④④
6 Crown Pas, SW1 7925 2791 3–4D
10 Well Ct, EC4 7236 8400 9–2B
62 Fleet St, EC4 7583 6060 9–2A
Curious that these British-themed diners haven't caught on more; they offer "a good deal" – especially for a "top breakfast" – and their generous sandwiches (packed with quality, traditional roast meats) are in a style that's currently rather à la mode. / www.fuzzysgrub.co.uk; most branches between 3 pm and 5 pm; closed Sat & Sun; no Amex; no booking.

Gaby's WC2 £34 ❸❸④
30 Charing Cross Rd 7836 4233 4–3B
"Holding out against the chains and redevelopers of the West End!" – this grungy deli, by Leicester Square tube, has won a stay of execution from its landlords; still time, then, to enjoy "the best falafel and salt beef"! / WC2H 0DE; midnight, Sun 10 pm; no Amex.

Gail's Bread £27 ④④❸
138 Portobello Rd, W11 7460 0766 6–1B
282 Chiswick High Rd, W4 8995 2266 7–2A
64 Hampstead High St, NW3 7794 5700 8–1A
5 Circus Rd, NW8 7722 0983 8–3A
64 Northcote Rd, SW11 7924 6330 10–2C

33-35 Exmouth Mkt, EC1   7713 6550   9–1A
"You can't fault Gail's for its great bread, coffee, cakes and take-out salads" – it may be "noisy" and a bit "chaotic", but a visit to this upmarket café/bakery chain rarely disappoints.
/ www.gailsbread.co.uk; W11 & WC1 7 pm; NW3 & NW6 8 pm, W1 10 pm, SW7 9 pm, Sun 8 pm; no booking.

Galicia W10   **£39**   ❸❸❷
323 Portobello Rd   8969 3539   6–1A
Surprisingly little survey comment on this age-old North Kensington tapas bar – all tends to confirm, though, that it remains a "great local". / W10 5SY; 11.15 pm; closed Mon.

Gallery Mess
Saatchi Gallery SW3   **£51**   ④④④
Duke of Yorks HQ, Kings Rd   7730 8135   5–2D
Near Sloane Square, and with many tables al fresco, this large café attached to the gallery certainly has a "great" location; no huge surprise, then, that the food can be "uninspired", and service "slow" – "a decent bet, but it could aim a bit higher". / SW3 4RY; www.saatchigallery.com/gallerymess; @gallerymess; 9.30 pm, Sun 6.30 pm; closed Sun D.

Gallipoli   **£35**   ④❷❸
102 Upper St, N1   7359 0630   8–3D
107 Upper St, N1   7226 5333   8–3D
120 Upper St, N1   7226 8099   8–3D
"For a buzzy cheap eat", it's hard to beat these "basic" but brilliant Turkish bistros, in the heart of Islington. / www.cafegallipoli.com; 11 pm, Fri & Sat midnight.

Galvin at Windows
Park Lane London
Hilton Hotel W1   **£93**   ④❸❶
22 Park Ln   7208 4021   3–4A
"Talk about a room with a view!" – the Galvins' 28th-floor Mayfair eyrie boasts the most "amazing panorama"; away from the windows, though, the ambience can fall flat, making the prices of the "good but unremarkable" cuisine hard to stomach. / W1K 1BE; www.galvinatwindows.com; 10.30 pm, Thu-Sat 11 pm; closed Sat L & Sun D; no shorts; set weekday L £49 (FP).

GALVIN BISTROT DE LUXE
W1   **£63**   ❷❷❷
66 Baker St   7935 4007   2–1A
"A very slick and dependable operation"; the original Marylebone Galvin "has all the virtues of a good Parisian bistro, with a few British ones thrown in" – "excellent-value" cuisine, "unobtrusive" service and a "convivial" (if slightly "formal") setting. / W1U 7DJ; www.galvinrestaurants.com; @galvin_brothers; Mon-Wed 10.30 pm, Thu-Sat 10.45 pm, Sun 9.30 pm; set weekday L £37 (FP), set pre-theatre £39 (FP), set Sun L £48 (FP).

GALVIN LA
CHAPELLE E1   **£74**   ❷❷❶
35 Spital Sq   7299 0400   12–2B
"Stunning food in a stunning location" makes for a "superb experience" at the Galvin brothers' cathedral-like dining hall, by Spitalfields Market – a "courteous" operation, with cuisine that's "modern enough to be interesting, but classic enough to stay uncontentious". / E1 6DY; www.galvinrestaurants.com; 10.30 pm, Sun 9.30 pm; set weekday L & pre-theatre £49 (FP).

Ganapati SE15   **£43**   ❶❶❷
38 Holly Grove   7277 2928   1–4C
"Consistently superior to flashy Indians you find in the West End!" – with its "divine" Keralan cooking, this "unassuming" diner is held out as "Peckham's claim to being a dining destination"; it's a "fun" and "chilled" experience too. / SE15 5DF; www.ganapatirestaurant.com; 10.30 pm, Sun 10 pm; closed Mon; no Amex.

Gandhi's SE11   **£28**   ❸④❸
347 Kennington Rd   7735 9015   1–3C
"Popular with the locals, so book ahead" – this old-school Kennington Indian may offer an "unchanging" menu, but it's realised to an "above-average" standard. / SE11 4QE; www.gandhis.co.uk; 11.30 pm.

Garnier SW5   **£55**   ❸❷④
314 Earl's Court Rd   7370 4536   5–2A
"A most welcome addition to Earl's Court" – the Garnier brothers' local restaurant serves "the sort of simple, classic French food you can't get in France any more", and with aplomb; it does, however, "lack the ambience" of its sibling, Le Colombier. / SW5 9BQ; Mon-Sat 10.30 pm, Sun 10 pm; set Sun L £43 (FP).

Le Garrick WC2   **£41**   ④④❸
10-12 Garrick St   7240 7649   4–3C
A "pleasant" Covent Garden fixture with a decidedly "quaint" lay-out; its "classic" French staples are on the "predictable" side of "solid". / WC2E 9BH; www.garrickrestaurantbar.co.uk; @le_garrick; 10.30 pm; closed Sun.

Garrison SE1   **£48**   ❸❸❷
99-101 Bermondsey St   7089 9355   9–4D
A "very busy" Bermondsey gastroboozer, with a "lovely interior" and a "great vibe"; the food in general is "very decent", with the "dependable" brunch a particular highlight. / SE1 3XB; www.thegarrison.co.uk; 10 pm, Fri-Sat 10.30 pm, Sun 9.30 pm.

Garufa N5   **£48**   ❷④❸
104 Highbury Pk   7226 0070   8–1D
"Marvellous for meat-lovers!" – "terrific" steaks and "the best" chips are what this Argentinian grill, near the Emirates Stadium, is all about. / N5 2XE; www.garufa.co.uk; @GarufaLondon; 10.30 pm; no Amex.

Garufin WC1 🆕 **£48** ❸❷❸
8b, Lamb's Conduit Pas   7430 9073   2–1D
Just south (NB) of Holborn, a "scruffy" but
"very friendly" new basement operation, offering
"Argentinian comfort food" and a "cracking" wine
list to go with it; we enjoyed our visit, but reports are
a bit up-and-down. / WC1R 4RH; 10.30 pm;
closed Sun.

Gastro SW4 **£42** ④④❷
67 Venn St   7627 0222   10–2D
"Toujours français!"; for authenticity alone,
this "stalwart" café/bistro, by the Clapham Picture
House, is hard to beat; service this year, though,
has seemed less stereotypically Gallic. / SW4 0BD;
midnight; no Amex.

The Gate **£43** ❸④④
51 Queen Caroline St, W6   8748 6932   7–2C
370 St John St, EC1   7278 5483   8–3D
"A welcome addition to Islington" – the new
N1 branch of this veggie duo wins praise for its
"calm" style and "fresh and interesting" cooking;
it's not yet as highly rated as the stellar
Hammersmith original, however (reopening, after
a major refurb, in late-2013).
/ www.thegaterestaurants.com; @gaterestaurant;
EC1 10.30 pm, W6 10.30, Sat 11 pm.

Gaucho **£70** ❸④④
25 Swallow St, W1   7734 4040   3–3D
60a, Charlotte St, W1   7580 6252   2–1C
125 Chancery Ln, WC2   7242 7727   2–2D
89 Sloane Ave, SW3   7584 9901   5–2C
64 Heath St, NW3   7431 8222   8–1A
02 Centre, Peninsular Sq, SE10   8858 7711
11–2D
Tooley St, SE1   7407 5222   9–4D
Tow Path, TW10   8948 4030   1–4A
29 Westferry Circus, E14   7987 9494   11–1B
93a Charterhouse St, EC1   7490 1676   9–1B
5 Finsbury Ave, Broadgate, EC2   7256 6877
12–2B
1 Bell Inn Yd, EC3   7626 5180   9–2C
"Good, but at a price…"; this "slick" and "funky"
chain is still a "winner" for a business rendezvous
(and has "the best Argentinian wine list in London"
too); in an ever more competitive steakhouse world
however, it risks seeming "overpriced", especially
as standards seem "increasingly patchy".
/ www.gaucho restaurants.co.uk; 11 pm, Fri & Sat
11.30 pm, SE10, Piccadilly midnight, Sun 11 pm;
EC3 & EC1 closed Sat & Sun; WC2 & EC2 closed
Sat L & Sun.

Gauthier Soho W1 **£63** ❶❶❷
21 Romilly St   7494 3111   4–3A
Alexis Gauthier's "inspired" modern French cuisine
goes from strength to strength, at his "quirky" and
"faultlessly charming" Soho townhouse (where
"ringing the door to get in adds novelty"); "I can't
understand why they lost their Michelin star!"

/ W1D 5AF; www.gauthiersoho.co.uk; 10.30 pm; closed
Mon L & Sun; set weekday L £46 (FP); SRA-52%.

LE GAVROCHE W1 **£131** ❶❶❷
43 Upper Brook St   7408 0881   3–2A
"As relevant today as it ever was!" – M Roux Jr's
"timeless classic", in Mayfair, won this year's vote
as "London's finest gastronomic experience";
"the bill's stratospheric, but so's the performance!",
with "sublime" Gallic cuisine and magisterial
"old school" service; "unbelievably good" set lunch
(book months ahead). / W1K 7QR;
www.le-gavroche.co.uk; 11 pm; closed Sat L & Sun; jacket
required; set weekday L £59 (FP).

Gay Hussar W1 **£47** ④❸❷
2 Greek St   7437 0973   4–2A
The "snug" and "unchanging" charms of this
"iconic" (socialist) haunt make it, for diehard fans,
"Soho's best restaurant" – the "old-fashioned"
Hungarian fodder is "not wonderful, but who
cares?" / W1D 4NB; www.gayhussar.co.uk; 10.45 pm;
closed Sun.

Gaylord W1 **£50** ❸❸④
79-81 Mortimer St   7580 3615   2–1B
A grand old Indian, just north of Oxford Street –
the food is "delicious", but critics can find prices
"startling". / W1W 7SJ; www.gaylordlondon.com;
10.45 pm, Sun 10.30 pm; no Amex.

Gazette **£38** ④④❷
79 Sherwood Ct, Chatfield Rd, SW11
7223 0999   10–1C
100 Balham High St, SW12   8772 1232   10–2C
"Very good food" plus "typically Gallic service" –
that's the formula that's made quite a hit of these
"good-value" Balham and Battersea brasseries.
/ www.gazettebrasserie.co.uk; 11 pm.

Geales **£47** ④④④
1 Cale St, SW3   7965 0555   5–2C
2 Farmer St, W8   7727 7528   6–2B
A tale of two (upmarket) chippies – reports from
the heart-of-Chelsea branch suggest a "chaotic"
performance of late, while the original, off Notting
Hill Gate, continues on its usual dependable course.
/ www.geales.com; @geales1; 10.30 pm, Sun 9.30 pm;
Mon L.

Gelupo W1 **£10** ❶❷❸
7 Archer St   7287 5555   3–2D
"Exquisite" ices – "from far-out flavours to classics"
– are on offer at this "simply fabulous" gelataria,
tucked-away in Soho, opposite Bocca di Lupo
(same owners). / W1D 7AU; www.gelupo.com; 11 pm,
Fri & Sat 12.30 am; no Amex; no booking.

Gem N1 **£30** ❸❷❸
265 Upper St   7359 0405   8–2D
"Mezze are particularly good" (and there are some
"excellent" Kurdish grill dishes on offer too), at this
"low-key" bolthole – an "always-reliable" Islington

"staple". / N1 2UQ; www.gemrestaurant.org.uk; 11 pm, Fri-Sat midnight, Sun 10.30 pm; no Amex.

La Genova W1 £59 ④④④
32 North Audley St 7629 5916 3–2A
This "shamelessly retro" Mayfair Italian is one of a dying breed; it doesn't please everyone, but fans praise its "comfortable" virtues. / W1K 6ZG; www.lagenovarestaurant.com; 11 pm; closed Sun.

George & Vulture EC3 £48 ④❸❷
3 Castle Ct 7626 9710 9–3C
An "old-style City place" – yes, it really is in Dickens – which sells itself "on not having been updated"; "go for the experience, not the food!" / EC3V 9DL; 2.45 pm; L only, closed Sat & Sun.

The Giaconda Dining Rooms WC2 £51 ❸❷④
9 Denmark St 7240 3334 4–1A
The relaunch of this "friendly" bistro, in the shadow of Centre Point, has proved a mixed blessing; fans say its looks are "improved", and that it offers "adventurous" cooking that's "as good as ever" – others feel that it's "lost its way". / WC2H 8LS; www.giacondadining.com; @giacondadining; 9.15 pm; closed Sat L & Sun.

Gifto's Lahore Karahi UB1 £18 ❷❸④
162-164 The Broadway 8813 8669 1–3A
A "buzzy, Formica-top delight" – this popular Southall diner draws in the weekend crowds with its "excellent range" of "delicious" dishes, particularly meat, at "very good prices". / UB1 1NN; www.gifto.com; 11.30 pm, Sat-Sun midnight.

Gilak N19 £35 ❸❷④
663 Holloway Rd 7272 1692 8–1C
"Huge and incredibly fresh salads", followed by "interesting stews and kebabs, loaded with herbs" – that's the sort of meal you might enjoy at this "courteous and efficient" Archway gem, specialising in the cuisine of Northern Iran. / N19 5SE; www.gilakrestaurant.co.uk; @Gilakrestaurant; 11 pm; no Amex.

Gilbert Scott St Pancras Renaissance NW1 £61 ④④❷
Euston Rd 7278 3888 8–3C
A "glorious" neo-Gothic setting is the backdrop to Marcus Wareing's airy (but tightly-packed) St Pancras dining room; fans applaud its "superb" British cuisine too, but service is "mixed", and for a large minority of sceptics the food is "underwhelming" or "poor value". / NW1 2AR; www.thegilbertscott.co.uk; @Thegilbertscott; 10.45 pm.

Gilgamesh NW1 £70 ❸❸❷
The Stables, Camden Mkt, Chalk Farm Rd
7428 4922 8–3B
"A bit like visiting an Asian leisure park attraction

in Blackpool"; this gigantic Camden Town venue, with ultra-lavish wood-carved decor, doesn't attract a huge amount of feedback, but its pan-Asian cuisine is surprisingly well-rated – worth a go "for a special occasion". / NW1 8AH; www.gilgameshbar.com; 11 pm, Fri-Sat 11.30 pm.*

Gin Joint EC2 NEW £50
Barbican Centre, Silk St 7588 3008 12–2A
Opening as this guide was going to press, Searcy's have rebranded their former Brasserie (RIP) within the Barbican, with this hipper concept, where food comes on small plates, and the drinks list is themed around mother's ruin. / EC2Y 8DS; www.searcys.co.uk/venues/gin-joint.

Ginger & White £17 ❸❷❷
2 England's Ln, NW3 7722 9944 8–2A
4a-5a, Perrins Ct, NW3 7431 9098 8–2A
A brunch-friendly duo of cafés in Hampstead and Belsize Park; they offer "tempting cakes and great coffee" too. / www.gingerandwhite.com; 5.30 pm, W1 6 pm; W1 closed Sun.

Giraffe £41 ⑤⑤⑤
120 Wilton Rd, SW1 7233 8303 2–4B
6-8 Blandford St, W1 7935 2333 2–1A
19-21 The Brunswick Centre, WC1 7812 1336 8–4C
120 Holland Park Ave, W11 7229 8567 6–2A
270 Chiswick High Rd, W4 8995 2100 7–2A
7 Kensington High St, W8 7938 1221 5–1A
29-31 Essex Rd, N1 7359 5999 8–3D
196-198 Haverstock Hill, NW3 7431 3812 8–2A
46 Rosslyn Hill, NW3 7435 0343 8–2A
Royal Festival Hall, Riverside, SE1 7928 2004 2–3D
1 Crispin Pl, E1 3116 2000 12–2B
Recently acquired by Tesco, this "easy-going" world food chain is "built for families", and "brilliant for breakfast" too – perhaps that's another way of saying it's "ideal for people who don't care about food that much"! / www.giraffe.net; 10.45 pm, Sun 10.30 pm; no booking, Sat & Sun 9 am-5 pm.

The Glasshouse TW9 £67 ❷❷❸
14 Station Pde 8940 6777 1–3A
This "light and airy" (if "noisy") Kew sibling of the fabled Chez Bruce still wins acclaim for its "first-class" food, "superb" wine and "enormously professional" service; ratings, though, slipped this year from their traditional peaks – let's hope it's just a blip. / TW9 3PZ; www.glasshouserestaurant.co.uk; @The_Glasshouse; 10.30 pm, Sun 10 pm.

Gold Mine W2 £33 ❸④⑤
102 Queensway 7792 8331 6–2C
"Roast duck to die for" – top of the bill at this "inexpensive" Bayswater Chinese. / W2 3RR; 11 pm.

Golden Dragon W1   £33   ❸❹❸
28-29 Gerrard St   7734 1073   4–3A
For "a reliable-quality Chinese in the heart
of Chinatown", this (relatively) smart but "brusque"
fixture is just the job; it serves up "all the standard
dishes, and plenty of unusual ones", plus "excellent"
dim sum. / W1 6JW; 11 pm, Fri & Sat 11.30 pm,
Sun 10.20 pm.

Golden Hind W1   £26   ❸❶❸
73 Marylebone Ln   7486 3644   2–1A
"A winner on every visit"; this "welcoming"
Marylebone chippy is "brilliant at what it does" –
"BYO, and enjoy!" / W1U 2PN; 10 pm; closed
Sat L & Sun.

Good Earth   £56   ❷❸❸
233 Brompton Rd, SW3   7584 3658   5–2C
143-145 The Broadway, NW7   8959 7011
1–1B
"The food is exceptionally good, but it's a shame the
prices are so high" – the story from these
"upmarket" Chinese veterans, in Knightsbridge and
Mill Hill, never really changes.
/ www.goodearthgroup.co.uk; 11 pm, Sun 10.30 pm.

Goode & Wright W11   £54   ❸❹❹
271 Portobello Rd   7727 5552   6–1A
An Anglo-French Notting Hill spot that "doesn't look
like a pub or bar, but has that sort of feel about it"
– breakfasts are "excellent", but standards at other
times can be a touch "variable". / W11 1LR;
www.goodeandwright.co.uk; 10 pm; closed Mon & Sun L.

Goodman   £63   ❷❷❸
24-26 Maddox St, W1   7499 3776   3–2C
3 South Quay, E14   7531 0300   11–1D
11 Old Jewry, EC2   7600 8220   9–2C
"Just getting the edge over Hawksmoor"; these
"high-powered" and "male-dominated" Mayfair,
City and Canary Wharf locations are "probably the
closest London has to a proper US steakhouse" –
"incredibly consistent" standards, plus that "genuine
NYC/London feel"! / www.goodmanrestaurants.com;
10.30 pm; W1 & E14 closed Sun; EC2 closed Sat & Sun.

Gopal's of Soho W1   £30   ❸❸❹
12 Bateman St   7434 1621   2–2A
An "authentic" Indian, in the traditional sense of the
word, hidden-away in Soho – still probably the
West End's top old-style subcontinental. / W1D 4AH;
www.gopalsofsoho.co.uk; 11.30 pm, Sun 11 pm.

Gordon Ramsay SW3 £126   ❹❹❹
68-69 Royal Hospital Rd   7352 4441   5–3D
Clare Smyth's "classic" cuisine is, say fans,
"outstanding", and helps to make the Sweary One's
rather "stuffy" Chelsea HQ a "peerless" destination;
too many critics, though complain of "mundane"
cooking served in a "sterile" ambience... and all
at "piss-take" prices! / SW3 4HP;
www.gordonramsay.com; 10.15 pm; closed Sat & Sun;

no jeans or trainers; booking: max 8; set weekday L
£82 (FP).

**Gordon's Wine Bar
WC2**   £32   ⑤❹❶
47 Villiers St   7930 1408   4–4D
"Mad busy", for a reason!; this cellar wine bar,
by Embankment tube, has a wonderfully
"idiosyncratic" style, plus an "impressive" list that's
"a must for wine lovers" (and, in summer, one of
central London's largest terraces); the food
is incidental. / WC2N 6NE; www.gordonswinebar.com;
10 pm, Sun 9 pm; no booking.

**The Goring Hotel
SW1**   £78   ❸❶❶
15 Beeston Pl   7396 9000   2–4B
"Englishness at its best"; the "well spaced" dining
room of this family-owned hotel, near Victoria, is a
"supremely civilised" bastion where the food –
"generous" and "old school" – is exactly as you
would hope; it makes a great venue for
breakfast or for business (or for the two combined).
/ SW1W 0JW; www.thegoring.com; 10 pm; closed Sat L;
no jeans or trainers; table of 8 max.

**Gourmet Burger
Kitchen**   £29   ❹❹❹
Branches throughout London
Although the formula is "no longer novel",
many fans love the "super-juicy" burgers and
toppings on offer at this "WYSIWYG" chain; it was
rated only a hair's breadth behind Byron's this year.
/ www.gbkinfo.com; most branches close 10.30 pm;
no booking.

**Gourmet Pizza Company
Gabriels Wharf SE1**   £30   ❹❹❸
56 Upper Ground   7928 3188   9–3A
This Thames-side pizzeria (with great views from
the outside tables) is the only survivor of the former
chain which has not been re-branded by its owner,
PizzaExpress; it's generally held out as a "reliable"
option (and "crowded at weekends"), but there were
a couple of "below par" reports this year too.
/ SE1 9PP; www.gourmetpizzacompany.co.uk; 11.30 pm.

Gourmet San E2   £25   ❷⑤⑤
261 Bethnal Green Rd   7729 8388   12–1D
"Don't be put off by the décor" – this "unassuming"
Bethnal Green spot offers "some of the
best Sichuanese food in London", with "plenty
of spice" and "a fiery kick". / E2 6AH;
www.oldplace.co.uk; 11 pm; D only.

Gow's EC2   £57   ❸❸❹
81 Old Broad St   7920 9645   9–2C
"Staid" it may be, but this long-established cellar
operation, near Liverpool Street is, "still a good City
option if you like fish". / EC2M 1PR;
www.ballsbrothers.co.uk; 9 pm; closed Sat & Sun.

The Gowlett SE15　£31　❷❸❷
62 Gowlett Rd　7635 7048　1–4C
This "good honest local" is not prized only for its "interesting and regularly-changing selection of draught beers"; it's also world-famous in Peckham as the claimed supplier of "London's best pizza". / SE15 4HY; www.thegowlett.com; @theGowlettArms; 10.30 pm, Sun 9 pm; no credit cards.

Goya SW1　£44　❹❸❹
34 Lupus St　7976 5309　2–4C
The food "may not scale the heights", but this long-established tapas bar is nonetheless a "friendly" sort of place, prized by locals as "one of those few Pimlico establishments that's not a tourist trap!" / SW1V 3EB; www.goyarestaurant.co.uk; 11.30 pm.

Grain Store N1 NEW　£50　❷❷❶
1-3 Stable St, Granary Sq　7324 4466　8–3C
"An exciting new venture for Bruno Loubet and his team"; this King's Cross newcomer – "a fantastic warehouse space with open-plan kitchen" – promotes an "innovative" brand of vegetable-centric cuisine, which early-days reports rate as approaching the "sublime". / N1C 4AB; www.grainstore.com; @GrainStoreKX; 10.30 pm; closed Sun D; SRA-89%.

Gran Paradiso SW1　£46　❹❸❹
52 Wilton Rd　7828 5818　2–4B
"An excellent old-fashioned Italian" – this "comfortable" Pimlico fixture is the epitome of a "reliable" warhorse; younger bloods, though, feel a "make-over" would do no harm. / SW1V 1DE; 10.45 pm; closed Sat L & Sun.

The Grand Imperial Guoman Grosvenor Hotel SW1　£52　❸❷❷
101 Buckingham Palace Rd　7821 8898　2–4B
"Outstanding for dim sum, when it's a bargain too!"; at any time, though, this "very grand" dining room – almost part of Victoria Station – makes a "reliable" destination, and some reporters describe it as a surprise "gem"! / SW1W 0SJ; www.grandimperiallondon.com; 10.30 pm.

Granger & Co W11　£48　❹❺❸
175 Westbourne Grove　7229 9111　6–1B
Bill Granger's "buzzy and cool" Notting Hill outpost is "a decent effort at re-creating the Sydney original", and can make a good destination for a "delicious brunch"; queues can be "ludicrous" though, and the service "really bad". / W11 2SB; www.grangerandco.com; @grangerandco; 10.30 pm.

The Grapes E14　£42　❹❹❷
76 Narrow St　7987 4396　11–1B
This "Limehouse treasure" is perhaps the "smallest, oldest, and quaintest Docklands pub"; it has quite a name for its fish cooking too, but ratings have slipped significantly in recent times – "go for the history and the river setting". / E14 8BP;

www.thegrapes.co.uk; @TheGrapesLondon; 9.30 pm; closed Sat L & Sun D; no Amex.

Grazing Goat W1　£53　❸❹❸
6 New Quebec St　7724 7243　2–2A
Near Marble Arch, a notably "decent" gastroboozer, hailed in some reports for the "best pub food locally" – although it's not really a 'destination' to match its Belgravia cousins, the Thos Cubitt and so on, its survey ratings are actually rather higher! / W1H 7RQ; www.thegrazinggoat.co.uk; @TheGrazingGoat; 10 pm, Sun 9.30 pm; ; SRA-75%.

Great Nepalese NW1　£33　❸❷❺
48 Eversholt St　7388 6737　8–3C
"A long-enduring and welcoming retreat" from the Euston streetscape – this "friendly" stalwart serves a "somewhat exotic" menu, offering not just your standard curries, but also some "interesting Nepalese specialities". / NW1 1DA; www.great-nepalese.co.uk; 11.30 pm, Sun 10 pm.

Great Queen Street WC2　£45　❷❸❸
32 Great Queen St　7242 0622　4–1D
"Eclectic" British seasonal cooking that's "full of flavour and finesse" has made a runaway hit of this "pub-like", "cramped" and "incredibly noisy" Covent Garden operation; "the only real problem is getting a table!" / WC2B 5AA; @greatqueenstreet; 10.30 pm; closed Sun D; no Amex.

The Greedy Buddha SW6　£32　❸❹❹
144 Wandsworth Bridge Rd　7751 3311　10–1B
"Excellent" Nepalese dishes are a highlight of the menu at this "good local Indian", in Fulham; brace yourself, though, for sometimes "chaotic" service. / SW6 2UH; www.thegreedybuddha.com; 10.30 pm, Fri-Sat 11.30 pm; no Amex.

Green Cottage NW3　£40　❸❹❺
9 New College Pde　7722 5305　8–2A
"Still very much as it was 30 years ago", this "unpretentious" Swiss Cottage Cantonese continues to impress the locals with its "freshly-cooked" cuisine. / NW3 5EP; 10.30 pm, Sun 9.30 pm; no Amex.

Green Man & French Horn WC2　£44　❸❷❸
54 St Martin's Ln　7836 2645　4–4C
"The Terroirs empire goes from strength to strength", and this latest "cosy" offshoot in a converted Theatreland pub is, say fans, a "thrilling" West End début, where "superlative" biodynamic (Loire) wines are complemented by a "short" but slightly "different" menu. / WC2N 4EA; www.greenmanfrenchhorn.co.

Green Papaya E8   **£31**   ❷❸④
191 Mare St   8985 5486   1–1D
A "cheap 'n' cheerful" but "courteous", Hackney
spot, offering "crunchy" Vietnamese scoff with some
"amazing" flavours. / E8 3QT; www.green-papaya.com;
@goGreenPapaya; 10.30 pm; Closed L, Mon; no Amex.

Green's SW1   **£61**   ❸❸④
36 Duke St   7930 4566   3–3D
For "classic British nursery fare in the heart
of clubland", it's hard to match Simon Parker
Bowles's "marvellously old-fashioned" stalwart;
some change is afoot however – it may move
in 2014 to the old Wheeler's premises,
by St James's Palace; the EC3 branch is no more.
/ SW1Y 6DF; www.greens.org.uk; 10.30 pm; closed Sun;
no jeans or trainers.

**Greenberry Cafe
NW1** NEW   **£44**   ❸❸④
101 Regent's Park Rd   7483 3765   8–2B
"A great addition to Primrose Hill"; the proprietor
of Islington's former Lola's restaurant has set up a
"wonderful new café" on the site that was Troika
(RIP) – a "helpful" sort of all-day establishment,
offering "tasty food" at "reasonable prices",
and already very popular. / NW1 8UR;
www.greenberrycafe.co.uk.

The Greenhouse W1   **£107**   ❷❶❷
27a Hays Mews   7499 3331   3–3B
"An unparalleled wine list for sheer quality" is the
stand-out attraction at this "beautiful", "well-
spaced" and "very professional" Mayfair stalwart,
where Arnaud Bignon's "exquisite" cuisine is the
centrepiece of "a superb all-round gastronomic
experience". / W1J 5NX;
www.greenhouserestaurant.co.uk; 10.30 pm; closed
Sat L & Sun; booking: max 12.

Grillshack W1 NEW   **£21**   ❸❷④
61-63 Beak St   no tel   3–2D
On the former Alphabet site, Richard Caring's
latest venture is a Lower East Side-feeling parlour,
offering very simple American-style dishes; on our
early-days visit, we didn't find it very atmospheric,
but prices are impressively low. / W1R 3LF; Rated
on Editors' visit; www.grillshack.com; @grillshackuk;
10.30 pm, Sun 10 pm.

Grumbles SW1   **£42**   ④❸❸
35 Churton St   7834 0149   2–4B
Some say it's "past its sell-by date", but this "cosy"
Pimlico fixture mostly gets the thumbs-up as a
"great local bistro"; it must be doing something right
– it can be "hard to get a table". / SW1V 2LT;
www.grumblesrestaurant.co.uk; 10.45 pm; set weekday
L £26 (FP), set pre-theatre £27 (FP), set Sun L £28 (FP).

Guglee   **£32**   ❸❸④
7 New College Pde, NW3   7317 8555   8–2A
279 West End Ln, NW6   7317 8555   1–1B
"Very good for a local Indian, with more authentic

food than you'd normally find" – these
"accommodating" West Hampstead and Swiss
Cottage establishments continue to inspire only
positive reports; they're "always busy".
/ www.guglee.co.uk; 11 pm.

The Guinea Grill W1   **£67**   ❸❷❷
30 Bruton Pl   7499 1210   3–3B
It's the quaint (if perhaps "male-dominated")
atmosphere which makes this "smart" Mayfair
dining room – attached to a "classic, old-fashioned
pub" – so popular, but the steaks and pies can
be "excellent" too, if decidedly "not cheap".
/ W1J 6NL; www.theguinea.co.uk; @guineagrill;
10.30 pm; closed Sat L & Sun; booking: max 8.

The Gun E14   **£52**   ❸❸❷
27 Coldharbour   7515 5222   11–1C
"A perfect antidote to Canary Wharf!" –
this "classy" waterside pub has "lots of character"
and "a stunning panoramic view" (over the Thames
to the O2); the food is of "high quality" too.
/ E14 9NS; www.thegundocklands.com; 10.30 pm,
Sun 9.30 pm; set weekday L £33 (FP).

Gung-Ho NW6   **£39**   ❸❷❸
328-332 West End Ln   7794 1444   1–1B
A change of management has unsettled reports
on this West Hampstead stalwart; most, however,
are upbeat – it's "still one of the best local
Chineses". / NW6 1LN; www.stir-fry.co.uk; 11.30 pm;
no Amex.

The Gunmakers EC1   **£40**   ❷❷❸
13 Eyre Street Hill   7278 1022   9–1A
Hidden away in Farringdon, a boozer which "looks
pretty ordinary", but which invariably "hits the spot"
with its "classic" pub cuisine, realised to a
"surprisingly good" standard. / EC1R 5ET;
www.thegunmakers.co.uk; @thegunmakers; 10 pm;
closed Sat & Sun D; no booking Fri D.

**Gustoso Ristorante
& Enoteca SW1**   **£43**   ❸❶❸
33 Willow Pl   7834 5778   2–4B
"Tucked away" in a side street, just off Vauxhall
Bridge Road, this "friendly" Italian yearling has been
"a welcome addition" to a "thinly-provided" area;
"it has already gathered a good local following".
/ SW1P 1JH; 10.30 pm, Fri & Sat 11 pm, Sun 9.30 pm.

Gymkhana W1 NEW   **£65**
42 Albemarle St   3011 5900   3–3C
From the people who brought you Trishna,
this smart new Indian restaurant, not far from the
Ritz, opened shortly before this guide went to press;
the media have raved, including a very rare
5* award from the doyenne of critics, Fay Maschler.
/ W1S 3FE; www.gymkhanalondon.com.

Haché   **£36**   ❸❸❷
329-331 Fulham Rd, SW10   7823 3515   5–3B
24 Inverness St, NW1   7485 9100   8–3B
153 Clapham High St, SW4   7738 8760

10–2D NEW
147-149 Curtain Rd, EC2   7739 8396   12–1B
"Greasy-fingered heaven!"; this "excellent" and
"appealing" little chain outscores its bigger rivals
with its "wonderful" burgers – not only
do "they really taste of meat", but they can
be ordered rare too! / www.hacheburgers.com;
10.30 pm, Fri-Sat 11 pm, Sun 10 pm.

Hakkasan   **£86**   ❸⑤❷
17 Bruton St, W1   7907 1888   3–2C
8 Hanway Pl, W1   7927 7000   4–1A
"Oligarchs and their leggy girlfriends" party at the
newer Mayfair branch of these dimly-lit "beautiful-
people" haunts; regular folk, though, appear to be
finding them ever less attractive – even if the
Chinese cooking is "decent", prices seem ever-more
"ferocious", and service is sometimes "spectacularly
bad". / www.hakkasan.com; midnight, Sun 11 pm.

Halepi W2   **£43**   ❸⓿❸
18 Leinster Ter   7262 1070   6–2C
Critics find it a little "tired", but this long-established
Greek taverna, just north of Hyde Park, still delights
its loyal band of devotees. / W2 3ET;
www.halepi.co.uk; midnight.

The Hampshire Hog W6 £49   ④❸❸
227 King St   8748 3391   7–2B
With its "bright and pretty" styling, and huge
garden, this large gastropub brings no end of cheer
to the drab environs of Hammersmith Town Hall –
perhaps why it's "always busy", even if the "simple"
cooking can seem "expensive" for what it is.
/ W6 9JT; www.thehampshirehog.com;
@TheHampshireHog; 11 pm; closed Sun D; SRA-68%.

Haozhan W1   **£51**   ❷④⑤
8 Gerrard St   7434 3838   4–3A
"Bistro-style" in operation, this "now slightly shabby"
spot serves "interesting" cuisine that's "a step
up from the rest of Chinatown"; it's "speedily
served" too… not always a good thing. / W1D 5PJ;
www.haozhan.co.uk; @haozhan; 11.15 pm, Fri & Sat
11.45 pm, Sun 10.45 pm.

Harbour City W1   **£39**   ❸④⑤
46 Gerrard St   7439 7859   4–3B
"Terrific dim sum, very cheap" – the headline
attraction at this otherwise "OK-ish" Chinatown
"stalwart". / W1D 5QH; 11.30 pm, Fri-Sat midnight,
Sun 10 pm.

Hard Rock Café W1   **£48**   ❸❸❷
150 Old Park Ln   7629 0382   3–4B
The world's original Hard Rock continues to please
children of all ages, and surprisingly consistently too
– "you can't beat their burgers, ribs or even
steaks… provided you are willing to put up with the
music", and the "depressing" queue. / W1K 1QZ;
www.hardrock.com/london; @HardRockLondon; midnight;
need 20+ to book.

Hardy's Brasserie W1 £48   ❸④❸
53 Dorset St   7935 5929   2–1A
"A pleasant regular haunt for a quick lunch or a
lengthy dinner" – this Marylebone fixture always
impresses, thanks not least to its "comprehensive"
wine list and its "reasonable" prices. / W1U 7NH;
www.hardysbrasserie.com; @hardys_W1; 10 pm; closed
Sat & Sun.

Hare & Tortoise   **£29**   ❸❸❸
11-13 The Brunswick, WC1   7278 9799   2–1D
373 Kensington High St, W14   7603 8887
7–1D
38 Haven Grn, W5   8810 7066   1–2A
296-298 Upper Richmond Rd, SW15
8394 7666   10–2B
90 New Bridge St, EC4   7651 0266   9–2A
"Choice and efficiency"; these "bustling" pan-Asian
canteens offer an "always-enjoyable" combination
of "cheap, cheerful and healthy" dishes (sushi,
noodles, curries), and at a "speedy" pace too.
/ www.hareandtortoise-restaurants.co.uk; 10.45 pm, Fri &
Sat 11.15 pm; EC4 10 pm; EC4 closed Sun;
W14 no bookings.

Harrison's SW12   **£46**   ④④❸
15-19 Bedford Hill   8675 6900   10–2C
"The Balham Set" (there is such a thing, apparently)
is the core clientele at this laid-back brasserie;
it's "always buzzing", even if both food and service
are a bit up-and-down. / SW12 9EX;
www.harrisonsbalham.co.uk; @harrisonsbalham;
10.30 pm, Sun 10 pm; set pre theatre £30
(FP); SRA-71%.

Harry Morgan's NW8   **£39**   ❸❸④
31 St John's Wood High St   7722 1869   8–3A
"There isn't a great Jewish deli in Britain, but this
is the nearest", say fans of this St John's Wood
institution; it offers "all the classics",
not least a "very good salt beef sandwich".
/ NW8 7NH; www.harryms.co.uk; 10.30 pm.

Harwood Arms SW6   **£54**   ❶❷❸
Walham Grove   7386 1847   5–3A
"Consistently faultless seasonal British cooking"
(with "terrific" game a highlight) has made this
Fulham backstreet hostelry an "outstanding"
destination; you can still get a pint and Scotch egg
at the bar, but "you need to book weeks ahead for
a full meal". / SW6 1QP; www.harwoodarms.com;
9.15 pm, Sun 9 pm; closed Mon L.

Hashi SW20   **£35**   ❷❷❸
54 Durham Rd   8944 1888   10–2A
"Just as good as the most expensive places in the
West End!" – this "brilliant" (and "friendly") Raynes
Park Japanese impresses all who report on it.
/ SW20 0TW; 10.30 pm; closed Mon; no Amex.

The Havelock Tavern
W14   **£43**   ❷④❷
57 Masbro Rd   7603 5374   7–1C
*"Consistently great, despite the changes
of ownership and staff" – the main problem with
this "laid-back" gastroboozer, in the backstreets
of Olympia, is that it's often "hard to find a seat".
/ W14 0LS; www.havelocktavern.com; 10 pm,
Sun 9.30 pm; no booking.*

The Haven N20   **£49**   ④④⑤
1363 High Rd   8445 7419   1–1B
*For most reporters, this "noisy" Whetstone fixture
is an "always reliable" local favourite; there are also
quite a few critics, though, who find the place "over-
rated" and "overpriced". / N20 9LN;
www.haven-bistro.co.uk; 11 pm.*

Hawksmoor   **£62**   ❷❷❸
5a, Air St, W1   7406 3980   3–3D
11 Langley St, WC2   7420 9390   4–2C
157 Commercial St, E1   7426 4850   12–2B
10-12 Basinghall St, EC2   7397 8120   9–2C
*"The group that can do no wrong" (well for the
blogosphere anyway) – Huw Gott and Will Beckett's
"failsafe", "meat-paradises" mix "superlative" steaks
with "tantalising" cocktails; prices can seem
"hideous" however and – by a smidgeon – its overall
rating is pipped by rival Goodman.
/ www.thehawksmoor.com; all branches between
10 pm & 11 pm; EC2 closed Sat-Sun.*

Haz   **£36**   ④④❸
9 Cutler St, E1   7929 7923   9–2D
34 Foster Ln, EC2   7600 4172   9–2B
112 Hounsditch, EC3   7623 8180   9–2D
6 Mincing Ln, EC3   7929 3173   9–3D
*"Not bad for a quick bite"; no denying, though,
that this "crammed-in" Turkish chain, in the City,
is attracting increasing flak for "uninspiring" food
and "brusque" service. / www.hazrestaurant.co.uk;
11.30 pm; EC3 closed Sun.*

Hazev E14   **£34**   ④❸❸
2 South Quay Sq, Discovery Dock West
7515 9467   11–1C
*Worth knowing about in the E14 chain-hell,
a "striking" Turkish restaurant (including
an "affordable" cafeteria), near Surrey Quays DLR;
it's usually "busy", thanks not least to its "tasty"
cuisine. / E14 9RT; www.hazev.com; 11.30 pm,
Sun 10.30 pm, Mon 11 pm.*

Hazuki WC2   **£40**   ❸④④
43 Chandos Pl   7240 2530   4–4C
*"Like stepping into Tokyo, a genuine little Japanese
restaurant, informal, good value, and friendly" –
a handy place to know about, by the Trafalgar
Square post office. / WC2M 4HS;
www.hazukilondon.co.uk; 10.30 pm, Sun 9.30 pm.*

Hedone W4   **£78**   ❷❸❸
301 Chiswick High Rd   8747 0377   7–2A
*Mikael Jonsson's "incredibly original" two-year-old
("at the wrong end of Chiswick") is "like nothing
else in London", particularly in its "unsurpassed
sourcing" of ingredients; "given the hype in foodie
circles", however, it can strike the uninitiated
as "underwhelming", especially at the price.
/ W4 4HH; www.hedonerestaurant.com; 9.30 pm; closed
Mon, Tue L, Wed L, Thu L & Sun.*

Hélène Darroze
The Connaught Hotel
W1   **£127**   ❸❷❷
Carlos Pl   3147 7200   3–3B
*For "old world elegance", few hotel dining rooms
can match the "classic" allure of this Mayfair
legend; its star Parisian chef's reign remains
an inconsistent one – many "simply outstanding"
meals are reported, but even fans of the "refined"
cuisine can declare bills "ridiculous". / W1K 2AL;
www.the-connaught.co.uk; 10 pm; closed Mon & Sun;
jacket & tie; set weekday L £70 (FP).*

Hellenic W1   **£45**
45 Crawford St   7935 1257   6–1D
*The premises may be "new" and "smart", but this
"old gentleman" of a Marylebone restaurant
remains true to the "friendly" values which so long
sustained it in Thayer St; its "classic" Greek menu
seems as good as ever too, but there's too little
feedback as yet to make a rating appropriate.
/ W1H 1JT; 10.45 pm; closed Sun; no Amex.*

The Henry Root
SW10   **£52**   ④④❸
9 Park Walk   7352 7040   5–3B
*This "casual" Chelsea hang-out is "a useful
combination of bar and restaurant" – "not a fine
food destination", but a "very flexible format".
/ SW10 0AJ; www.thehenryroot.com; @thehenryroot;
10.45 pm, Sun 8.45 pm.*

Hereford Road W2   **£47**   ❷❸❸
3 Hereford Rd   7727 1144   6–1B
*Tom Pemberton's open-kitchen Bayswater bistro
"rarely disappoints" with its "regularly-changing" and
"good-value" seasonal fare, which spotlights "great
ingredients, simply cooked"; if you can, though, get a
booth at the front – the rear dining room can seem
"clinical". / W2 4AB; www.herefordroad.org; 10.30 pm,
Sun 10 pm.*

Hibiscus W1   **£120**   ④④④
29 Maddox St   7629 2999   3–2C
*Despite its "sterile" ambience, Claude Bosi's Mayfair
HQ is, say fans, a "showcase" for his "ground-
breaking and challenging" cuisine; ratings are
undercut, however, by the criticisms of "unreal"
pricing and "hit 'n' miss" results – perhaps, now he's
bought out his business partner, the place will finally
truly shine? / W1S 2PA; www.hibiscusrestaurant.co.uk;
11 pm; closed Sun; set weekday L £61 (FP).*

Clove Club

Dishoom

Five fields

Flesh & Buns

High Road Brasserie
W4   **£49**   ④④❸
162-166 Chiswick High Rd   8742 7474   7–2A
"A great spot for brunch and people-watching";
this Chiswick brasserie is certainly a "buzzing"
destination, with some nice tables al fresco, and can
certainly deliver a "great burger"; critics, however,
feel it "trades on its name". / W4 1PR;
www.brasserie.highroadhouse.co.uk; @sohohouse;
10.45 pm, Fri & Sat 11.45 pm, Sun 9.45 pm.

High Timber EC4   **£58**   ④❸❸
8 High Timber   7248 1777   9–3B
"Lovely views" of the Thames and Tate Modern,
plus "amazing" wines (mostly South African), score
points for this business-friendly spot; not everyone's
impressed, though – "nothing was outrageously
wrong, it's just that there's no wow-factor".
/ EC4V 3PA; www.hightimber.com; @HTimber; 10 pm;
closed Sat & Sun; set weekday L £38 (FP).

Hilliard EC4   **£28**   ❷❷❸
26a Tudor St   7353 8150   9–3A
"Packed out with barristers from the nearby
Temple" – a cramped all-day canteen serving "fresh,
simple dishes from high-quality ingredients"
(not least "the best sarnies in the City",
plus "a couple of hot options" at lunchtime); "great
coffee" too. / EC4Y 0AY; www.hilliardfood.co.uk; 6 pm;
L only, closed Sat & Sun; no booking.

Hix W1   **£66**   ④④⑤
66-70 Brewer St   7292 3518   3–2D
"His weekly column is better than his food!";
Mark Hix may have the blogosphere eating out
of his hand, but his "self-consciously chic" Soho diner
strikes reporters as ever-more "overpriced and overhyped" – the cooking can be "surprisingly bland",
service is disinterested, and there is "no atmosphere
to speak of". / W1F 9UP; www.hixsoho.co.uk;
@HixRestaurants; 11.30 pm, Sun 10.30 pm;
set weekday L & pre-theatre £44 (FP).

Hix Oyster & Chop
House EC1   **£58**   ④❸❸
36-37 Greenhill Rents, Cowcross St   7017 1930
9–1A
Fans of Mark Hix's "lively" eatery, near Smithfield
Market, say it's a "carnivore's heaven", offering
"interesting cuts of meat" alongside some
"excellent" fish; overall, however, the food is "below
the standard his name would lead you to expect".
/ EC1M 6BN; www.restaurantsetcltd.com; 11 pm,
Sun 9 pm.

HKK EC2   **£127**   ❷❷④
Broadgate West, 88 Worship St   3535 1888
12–2B
"As good as anything in Hong Kong";
this "exceptional" City-fringe newcomer, from the
Hakkasan group, may have a "sterile" ("monastic")
ambience, but its "refined" cuisine and "slick"
service have made it an immediate smash hit...

even if it is "very pricey". / EC2A 2BE;
www.hkklondon.com; 9.45 pm; closed Sat L & Sun;
set weekday L £52 (FP).

Hoi Polloi
Ace Hotel E1 NEW   **£59**
100 Shoreditch High St   8880 6100   12–1B
The dining room of the new ACE hotel in Shoreditch
opens as this guide goes to press; if it turns out
anything like the NYC ACE, it will quickly become in-
crowd central. / E1 6JQ.

Hole in the Wall W4   **£40**   ④❸❸
12 Sutton Lane North   8742 7185   7–2A
A spacious garden is the stand-out feature of this
cute Gunnersbury gastropub; it's just the place
"for those evenings when no one fancies cooking".
/ W4 4LD; 9.45 pm, Sun 9.15 pm; closed
Mon L & Tue L.

Holy Cow SW11   **£25**   ❷④❸
166 Battersea Pk Rd   7498 2000   10–1C
"First-rate Indian take-away food"; we don't
normally list delivery services, but we've made
an exception for this "reliable" Battersea operation,
where the dishes always tastes "freshly prepared".
/ SW11 4ND; www.holycowfineindianfood.com; 11 pm,
Sun 10.30 pm; D only.

Homage
Waldorf Hilton WC2   **£73**   ④④❸
22 Aldwych   7836 2400   2–2D
"Fairly unmemorable" but still "always bustling",
this grandly-housed Gallic brasserie, on the fringe
of Covent Garden, is relatively "reasonably priced",
and makes a "great stand-by" for lunch or pre-
theatre. / WC2B 4DD;
www3.hilton.com/en/hotels/united-kingdom/the-waldorf-hi
lton-london-LONWAHI/dining/index.html; Mon-Wed
10 pm, Thu-Sat 10.30 pm, Sun 9.30 pm; D only; set pre
theatre £46 (FP).

Honest Burgers   **£37**   ❶❷❸
4 Meard St, W1   3609 9524   4–2A
159 Portobello Rd, W11   awaiting tel
6–1B NEW
54-56 Camden Lock Pl, NW1   8617 3949
8–2B NEW
Brixton Village, Coldharbour Ln, SW9
7733 7963   10–2D
"AMAZING" burgers and fries "to which the word
'chip' does not do justice" – the original Brixton
branch of this growing small chain serves London's
No 1. burger; the queue, though, is "a total pain".
/ www.honestburgers.com; @honestburgers; 10 pm -
11 pm; SW9 closed Mon D.

Honey & Co W1 NEW   **£31**   ❷❷④
25a, Warren St   7388 6175   2–1B
"What a thrill to find a place like this!" – a "tiny"
instant smash hit, near Warren Street tube, where
"lovely people" serve "simple" but "high impact"
Middle Eastern-inspired dishes; it's a "cramped"

spot, though, which some reporters feel risks getting "overhyped". / WIT 5JZ; www.honeyandco.co.uk.

The Horseshoe NW3 £47 ❸❸❸
28 Heath St 7431 7206 8–2A
"Great ales" are a highpoint at this "friendly" microbrewery in "the very heart of Hampstead" – the origin of what's now Camden Town Brewery; to accompany them – "well-presented comfort food". / NW3 6TE; www.thehorseshoehampstead.com; @getluckyatthehorseshoe; 10pm, Fri-Sat 11 pm.

Hot Stuff SW8 £20 ❷❷❸
23 Wilcox Rd 7720 1480 10–1D
"Cheap 'n' cheerful, but so tasty and different!"; this BYO Vauxhall Indian feels like a "very genuine" sort of place and it offers "generous" dishes with "a glorious Asian/African fusion". / SW8 2XA; www.eathotstuff.com; 9.30 pm; closed Mon; no Amex.

The Hoxton Grill EC2 £51 ④④❷
81 Great Eastern St 7739 9111 12–1B
"Trendy", by the standards of dining areas off hotel lobbies – a "buzzy and comfortable" Shoreditch venue, offering "straightforward American-style diner food". / EC2A 3HU; www.hoxtongrill.co.uk; @hoxtongrill; 11.45 pm; set weekday L £33 (FP).

Hudsons SW15 £41 ④④❸
113 Lower Richmond Rd 8785 4522 10–1A
A "fantastic neighbourhood bistro"; this Putney fixture has quite a name locally as a "fun" hang out; "great brunch" a highlight. / SW15 1EX; www.hudsonsrestaurant.co.uk; @hudsonsw15; 10 pm, Sun 9.30 pm; closed Tue L.

Hummus Bros £17 ❸❸④
88 Wardour St, W1 7734 1311 3–2D
37-63 Southampton Row, WC1 7404 7079 2–1D
62 Exmouth Mkt, EC1 7812 1177 9–1A NEW
128 Cheapside, EC2 7726 8011 9–2B
"A great and very reasonable cheap eat"; "whatever it is they put in the hummus, I suspect it's addictive", says one fan of these cafeteria-style pit stops, which offer "a range of delicious toppings and wholesome pitta" to complement the main event. / www.hbros.co.uk; W1 10 pm, Thu-Sat 11 pm; WC1 9 pm, EC1 10 pm, Thu-Sat 11 pm, Sun 4 pm; WC1, EC2 closed Sat & Sun; no booking.

Hunan SW1 £65 ❶❸④
51 Pimlico Rd 7730 5712 5–2D
"Let Mr Peng feed you, and you won't go wrong!" – that's the way to go at this "unique" Pimlico veteran, regarded by many as "hands down, London's best Chinese"; the setting is "undistinguished", though, and service of late has been more "hit 'n' miss" than usual. / SW1W 8NE; www.hunanlondon.com; 11 pm; closed Sun.

Huong-Viet
An Viet House N1 £34 ❸④④
12-14 Englefield Rd 7249 0877 1–1C
In De Beauvoir, a "community-centre-turned-restaurant" – it offers "something different, even in an area with a lot of Vietnamese variety", and the food can be "superb"; BYO. / N1 4LS; 11 pm; closed Sun; no Amex.

Hush £57 ④❺④
8 Lancashire Ct, W1 7659 1500 3–2B
95-97 High Holborn, WC1 7242 4580 2–1D
"Nice to sit outside on a balmy summer evening… but that's about it" – this Mayfair restaurant, with its extensive terrace, is mainly "popular" because of its cute, tucked-away location; well, it can't be the "so-so" cooking and sometimes "pushy" service. / www.hush.co.uk; @Hush_Restaurant; W1 10.45 pm; WC1 10.30 pm, Sun 9.30 pm; WC1 closed Sun.

Hutong
The Shard SE1 NEW £75 ❸④❶
31 St Thomas St 7478 0540 9–4C
"Stunning" hardly does justice to the views from the 33rd floor of London's newest landmark; the grandest of the eateries opening in 2013 – this dark and dimly-lit Chinese dining room, serves food that's "surprisingly good". / SE1 9RY; www.hutong.co.uk; @HutongShard; 11 pm.

Ibérica £45 ❸❸❸
195 Great Portland St, W1 7636 8650 2–1B
12 Cabot Sq, E14 7636 8650 11–1C
With their "easy-going" style and their true "Spanish hospitality", these "relaxing" tapas bars "feel like the real deal"; the E14 branch is something of "a safe haven in Canary Wharf", but the Great Portland St original is more highly rated. / 11 pm; W1 closed Sun D.

Ikeda W1 £65 ❷❷❺
30 Brook St 7629 2730 3–2B
"Purist" and "expensive", this Mayfair veteran is known by aficionados for its very accomplished sushi; "like many long-lived Japanese operations, it feels very stiff", and it's interior – "stuck somewhere round 1988" – is a "let-down". / W1K 5DJ; 10.20 pm; closed Sat L & Sun.

Imli Street W1 £37 ❸❷❷
167-169 Wardour St 7287 4243 3–1D
Formerly called plain Imli, this "busy" street food operation in Soho is praised in all reports for its "delicious" and "authentic" Indian small plates, and at "reasonable prices" too. / W1F 8WR; www.imlistreet.com; 11 pm, Sun 10 pm.

Imperial China WC2 £44 ④④④
25a Lisle St 7734 3388 4–3B
"Dependable, and more spacious than most", this large and "busy" Chinatown fixture attracts particular praise for "the freshest dim sum".

/ WC2H 7BA; www.imperialchina-london.co.uk; 11 pm,
Sun 9.30 pm.

Imperial City EC3 £48 ④④④
Royal Exchange, Cornhill 7626 3437 9–2C
"Decent, but not remarkable"; this once-celebrated
Chinese – in the "spacious" and (potentially)
"atmospheric" vaults of the Royal Exchange –
is nowadays merely "a safe place for a working City
lunch or dinner". / EC3V 3LL;
www.orientalrestaurantgroup.co.uk; 10.15 pm; closed
Sat & Sun.

Inaho W2 £39 ❶⑤⑤
4 Hereford Rd 7221 8495 6–1B
A "little slice of Tokyo", oddly located in a tiny
Bayswater shack, where – despite "variable service
and basic decor" – you "always need to book";
why? – the food (especially sushi) is "top-grade".
/ W2 4AA; 10.30 pm; closed Sat L & Sun; no Amex
or Maestro.

Inamo £44 ④④④
4-12 Regent St, SW1 7484 0500 3–3D
134-136 Wardour St, W1 7851 7051 3–1D
These "wacky" West End Japanese outfits – where
"you order by tapping images projected onto your
table" – can be "fun", especially with children;
with their "average" food and "poor" service,
though, critics dismiss them as "a gimmick, and not
one to be repeated". / www.inamo-restaurant.com;
@InamoRestaurant; 11 pm, SW1 12 am.

Indali Lounge W1 £43 ❷❷④
50 Baker St 7224 2232 2–1A
"Very good for a low-fat Indian meal!"; this singularly
healthy Marylebone subcontinental "looks more like
a nightclub when you go in", but its "interesting"
cuisine pleases all who comment on it. / W1U 7BT;
www.indalilounge.com; 11.30, Sun 11 pm; closed Sat L.

**India Club
Strand Continental
Hotel WC2** £25 ❸❸⑤
143 Strand 7836 0650 2–2D
"Visit at least once, just for the experience!" –
this canteen near the Indian High Commission
offers a return to "a world of red-lino post-war
austerity"; it's a "dependable" place, though, where
the food is "surprisingly good", and "cheap" too;
BYO. / WC2R 1JA; www.strand-continental.co.uk;
10.50 pm; no credit cards; booking: max 6.

Indian Moment SW11 £34 ❸④④
44 Northcote Rd 7223 6575 10–2C
"A real breath of fresh air in the curry house world"
– this "ghee-free" Battersea Indian has quite a local
following for its "delicious" and "healthy" cuisine;
its "cramped" premises, however, sometimes seem
a mite "crowded". / SW11 1NZ; 11.30 pm, Fri & Sat
midnight; no Amex.

Indian Ocean SW17 £29 ❷❷❸
214 Trinity Rd 8672 7740 10–2C
"The best Indian, no argument!" – this "lively"
Wandsworth institution may have moved sites
in recent times, but it retains a devoted local
following for its "really delicious" cuisine.
/ SW17 7HP; www.indianoceanrestaurant.com;
11.30 pm.

Indian Rasoi N2 £37 ❷❷❸
7 Denmark Ter 8883 9093 1–1B
"Unusually good for this part of town"; this "buzzy"
Muswell Hill Indian offers "refreshingly different"
cuisine – the "delicate" and "nuanced" dishes can
be "extraordinarily good". / N2 9HG;
www.indian-rasoi.co.uk; 10.30 pm; no Amex.

Indian Zilla SW13 £45 ❶❶❸
2-3 Rocks Ln 8878 3989 10–1A
The Barnes offshoot of Indian Zing is, similarly,
"not your average curry house", and Manoj
Vasaikar's "original" and "distinctly flavoured" dishes
are "first-class". / SW13 0DB; www.indianzilla.co.uk;
11 pm, Sun 10.30 pm; closed Mon L, Tue L & Wed L.

Indian Zing W6 £46 ❶❷❸
236 King St 8748 5959 7–2B
"They must be missing Michael Winner", at what
used to be his favourite curry house,
near Ravenscourt Park; Manoj Vasaikar's "delicate"
and "original" cuisine is as "outstanding" as ever,
but the "well-appointed" dining room can get rather
"noisy". / W6 0RS; www.indianzing.co.uk; 11 pm,
Sun 10 pm; set weekday L £28 (FP).

**Indigo
One Aldwych WC2** £66 ④❸④
1 Aldwych 7300 0400 2–2D
"Good for a pre-theatre dinner", "great for
breakfast", "lovely for brunch" – these are the
occasions for which reporters seek out this Aldwych
hotel mezzanine; "for most buzz, get a table
overlooking the bar". / WC2B 4BZ;
www.onealdwych.com; 10.15 pm; set pre theatre
£46 (FP).

Inn the Park SW1 £49 ④❸❷
St James's Pk 7451 9999 2–3C
This architecturally striking venue certainly has
a stellar location, within St James's Park, and some
"wonderful al fresco tables"; standards, traditionally
lacklustre, have improved of late, and breakfast here
is always "an uplifting way to start the day".
/ SW1A 2BJ; www.peytonandbyrne.co.uk;
@PeytonandByrne; 8.30 pm; closed Sun D; no Amex.

Inside SE10 £42 ❷❷⑤
19 Greenwich South St 8265 5060 1–3D
"Still the best bet in Greenwich"; in a sea
of mediocrity, this is a "reliable neighbourhood
restaurant" which "aims high, and delivers", even if
it does have an interior that's "plain" and rather
"cramped". / SE10 8NW; www.insiderestaurant.co.uk;

@insideandgreenwich; 10.30 pm, Fri-Sat 11 pm; closed Mon & Sun D.

Isarn N1 £57 ❷❷④
119 Upper St 7424 5153 8–3D
"Streets ahead of most Thai restaurants", this rather corridor-like Islington spot is hailed in pretty much all reports for its "original" and "delicious" cuisine. / N1 1QP; www.isarn.co.uk; 11 pm, Sun 10.30 pm; no Amex.

Ishbilia SW1 £52 ❸❷⑤
9 William St 7235 7788 5–1D
Handy for Knightsbridge, a Lebanese café typically packed with customers from the Arab world, drawn by the "wide and authentic" menu; critics, though, do feel "it could do with a bit of a facelift". / SW1X 9HL; www.ishbilia.com; @Ishbilia; 11.30 pm.

Ishtar W1 £44 ❸❷❸
10-12 Crawford St 7224 2446 2–1A
Not far from Baker Street, a "fabulous" Turkish all-rounder, hailed by many reporters for its "unbeatable-value" set lunch menu. / W1U 6AZ; www.ishtarrestaurant.com; 11 pm, Sun 10.30 pm; set weekday L £26 (FP).

Isola del Sole SW15 £48 ④④④
16 Lacy Rd 8785 9962 10–2B
For some locals, an "unfavourable upgrade" knocked the gloss off this Putney Sicilian a couple of years ago; it has its fans, though, who praise its "home-made" fare, "sweet" service and "lovely" ambience. / SW15 1NL; www.isoladelsole.co.uk; @isoladelsoleuk; 10.30 pm; closed Sun.

Itsu £32 ④❸④
118 Draycott Ave, SW3 7590 2400 5–2C
100 Notting Hill Gate, W11 7229 4016 6–2B
Level 2, Cabot Place East, E14 7512 5790 11–1C
From "healthy" take-away options to conveyor-sushi (some branches only), this 21st-century chain wins praise for its "decent" grub and "fun" style; not everyone, though, is taken – "it's got the health", says one critic, "but not the happiness". / www.itsu.co.uk; 11 pm; E14 10 pm; some are closed Sat & Sun; no booking.

The Ivy WC2 £72 ④❸❷
1-5 West St 7836 4751 4–3B
"Forget the celeb label and enjoy!"; this "iconic" panelled dining room, at the heart of Theatreland, is still – for its huge fan club – a "vibrant" metropolitan lynchpin; critics, though, say it has "had its day", and offers "rather underwhelming" British dishes at "silly" prices. / WC2H 9NQ; www.the-ivy.co.uk; 11.30 pm, Sun 10.30 pm; no shorts; booking: max 6; set pre theatre £50 (FP).

Izgara N3 £33 ❸④⑤
11 Hendon Lane 8371 8282 1–1B
"Decent kebabs and stews" are the headline attraction at this "busy" Turkish establishment, in North Finchley; service is "efficient, but not especially friendly". / N3 1RT; www.izgararestaurant.net; 11.30 pm; no Amex.

Jackson & Whyte W1 NEW
56 Wardour St awaiting tel 3–2D
How many more 'American' restaurants can we bear/cope with? – the Grillshack team is to open this all-day restaurant, specialising in the food of the East Coast, in late-2013 on the former Soho site of Satsuma (RIP). / W1D 4JG.

Jai Krishna N4 £19 ❷④④
161 Stroud Green Rd 7272 1680 8–1D
A "friendly and cheap" South Indian BYO, in Stroud Green, hailed by locals for its "astonishing value". / N4 3PZ; 10.30 pm; closed Sun; no credit cards.

The Jam Tree £47 ❸❸❷
541 King's Rd, SW6 3397 3739 5–4B
13-19 Old Town, SW4 3397 4422 10–2D
NEW
Surprisingly little survey commentary on these Olympia and Fulham gastropubs, but they are almost invariably noted for their "generous" cuisine and their "friendly" service. / SW4 12 am, Sun-Wed 11 pm; SW6 11 pm, Fri-Sat 2 am.

Jamie's Italian £43 ⑤⑤④
11 Upper St Martin's Ln, WC2 3326 6390 4–3B
Westfield, Ariel Way, W12 8090 9070 7–1C
2 Churchill Pl, E14 3002 5252 11–1C
Jamie O's "basic and noisy" Italian chain undeniably pleases many fans with its "easy and fun" style; it has far too many detractors, however, who say "just don't go", on account of "very slack" service, and food that can be "really appalling". / www.jamiesitalian.com; @JamiesItalianUK; 11.30 pm, Sun 10.30 pm; over 6.

Jenny Lo's Tea House SW1 £34 ❸❷④
14 Eccleston St 7259 0399 2–4B
"A great, quick-bite option"; this "simple noodle house", by Victoria Coach Station, offers "better-than-average" chow, canteen-style, and at "amazingly reasonable prices". / SW1W 9LT; www.jennylo.co.uk; 9.55 pm; closed Sat & Sun; no credit cards; no booking.

Jin Kichi NW3 £41 ❶❷④
73 Heath St 7794 6158 8–1A
The ambience "may not be the best", but this "tiny and cramped" (and ultra-"authentic") Hampstead Japanese stalwart has offered "quality and consistency for over 20 years"; the speciality is "the best yakitori", but all the food (sushi

included) is "fantastic". / NW3 6UG;
www.jinkichi.com; 11 pm, Sun 10 pm; closed Mon L.

Joanna's SE19   **£44**   ❸❷❷
56 Westow Hill   8670 4052   1–4D
"A really good neighbourhood restaurant"; thanks
to its "lovely" ambience, "attentive" service and
"great" views of Canary Wharf, this Crystal Palace
fixture is a destination that's always "buzzing".
/ SE19 1RX; www.joannas.uk.com; @JoannasRest;
10.45 pm, Sun 10.15 pm.

Joe Allen WC2   **£53**   ⑤④❷
13 Exeter St   7836 0651   4–3D
It's still as "thespy" as ever, and the late-night
atmosphere is as "fabulous" as ever, but this
Theatreland basement changed hands this year
(after 35 years); the food? – the straightforward
American dishes (including an off-menu burger)
"have never been the point", but too often of late
they have been plain "awful". / WC2E 7DT;
www.joeallen.co.uk; Sun-Thu 11.45 pm, Fri & Sat
12.45 am; set weekday L & pre-theatre £24 (FP).

Joe's Brasserie SW6   **£42**   ❸❷❸
130 Wandsworth Bridge Rd   7731 7835
10–1B
"Standard but very reliable" staples, "strongly
supported by a very reasonable wine list" – still
a winning formula for John Brinkley's deepest-
Fulham veteran; it has a "super terrace" too, that's
"great for people-watching". / SW6 2UL;
www.brinkleys.com; 11 pm.

John Salt N1 NEW   **£35**   ④④❸
131 Upper St   7359 7501   8–3D
The blogosphere has been well impressed by this
"loud and echoey" new Islington hang-out,
and many reporters acclaim Neil Rankin's
"brilliant", BBQ-heavy menu as "taking pub food
up a level"; there's also a school of thought, though,
that it is "so over-rated". / N1 1QP; www.john-salt.com;
10 pm; no Amex.

José SE1   **£40**   ❷❷❶
104 Bermondsey St   7403 4902   9–4D
"The only serious competition for Barrafina"; with its
"divine" tapas, "wonderfully diverse" wines and
sherries, "super-efficient" service, and brilliant vibe,
José Pizarro's tiny Bermondsey corner-bar is "worth
the hype, the squeeze, and the inevitable wait".
/ SE1 3UB; @Jose_Pizarro; 10.30 pm, Sun 5.30; closed
Fri D, Sat D & Sun D.

Joy King Lau WC2   **£34**   ❸④④
3 Leicester St   7437 1132   4–3A
Just off Leicester Square, this "always-packed",
three-floor operation offers a classic Chinatown
experience… in a good way; "authentic dim sum"
(expect a queue) is the highlight of the "reliable"
Cantonese menu. / WC2H 7BL; www.joykinglau.com;
11.30 pm, Sun 10.30 pm.

Jubo EC2 NEW   **£18**
68 Rivington St   7033 0198   12–1B
A large new Korean canteen in Shoreditch, which
opened in mid-2013; early published reviews
suggests it will be a useful standby (no bookings) for
the local hipsters, rather than a destination in itself.
/ EC2A 3AY; www.jubolondon.com.

The Jugged Hare
EC1Y   **£50**   ④④❸
49 Chiswell St   7614 0134   12–2A
Near the Barbican, this former pub (now "themed
along hunting lodge lines") makes a "pleasant,
down-to-earth environment" for an "unfussy" meal;
many reporters are impressed by the "big-flavoured
and hearty" British fare, but sceptics can find
it "a bit pricey" for what it is. / EC1Y 4SA;
www.juggedhare.com; @juggedhare; 11 pm, Thu-Sat
midnight, Sun 10.30 pm.

Julie's W11   **£62**   ④④❶
135 Portland Rd   7229 8331   6–2A
"The home of countless romances" –
this "very lovely" semi-subterranean Holland Park
labyrinth is a time capsule of sexy '70s London;
as always, though, it's a "shame about the food".
/ W11 4LW; www.juliesrestaurant.com; 11 pm.

The Junction Tavern
NW5   **£43**   ❸❶❷
101 Fortess Rd   7485 9400   8–2B
"Trying hard, and doing a good job at a reasonable
price" – this Kentish Town fixture continues
to please with its "warm, welcoming and friendly"
style, and its "surprisingly good" pub grub.
/ NW5 1AG; www.junctiontavern.co.uk; 10.30 pm,
Sun 9.30 pm; Mon-Thu D only, Fri-Sun open L & D;
no Amex.

Juniper Dining N5   **£46**   ❷❸❸
100 Highbury Pk   7288 8716   8–1D
"A gem of a local restaurant", whose
"uncomplicated but imaginative" dishes delight
Highbury reporters; fish is a highlight. / N5 2XE;
www.juniperdining.co.uk; 9.30 pm; closed Mon & Sun D.

JW Steakhouse
Grosvenor House
Hotel W1   **£75**   ④④❸
86 Park Ln   7399 8460   3–3A
For "superb" USDA and British steaks,
this cavernous but "comfortable" Park Lane spot
is – say fans – "surprisingly good" for a hotel
operation; top tip? – the cheesecake is "easily the
best this side of the Atlantic!" / W1K 7TN;
www.jwsteakhouse.co.uk; 10.30 pm, Fri & Sat 11 pm.

K10   **£36**   ❷❷④
20 Copthall Ave, EC2   7562 8510   9–2C
3 Appold St, EC2   7539 9209   12–2B NEW
"It still rocks!"; this City conveyor-Japanese serves
an "unusually wide variety of dishes",
and "you could eat everything that whooshes by";

the new one on Appold/Sun St is "quick and really good" too. / www.k10.com; Appold 9 pm, Wed-Fri 9.30 pm; both branches Sat & Sun, Copthall closed Mon-Fri D.

Kaffeine W1 **£12** ❸❷⓿
66 Great Titchfield St 7580 6755 3–1C
"A real stand-out amongst London's thousands of coffee shops" – this "compact" Soho café combines "multi-award-winning" coffee with "exemplary" service, as superior sandwiches, cakes and salads. / W1W 7QJ; www.kaffeine.co.uk; L only; no Amex; no bookings.

Kai Mayfair W1 **£97** ④④④
65 South Audley St 7493 8988 3–3A
The cuisine at this swanky Mayfair Chinese really is "truly exceptional"; prices more than measure up, though, and its following among reporters is relatively modest. / W1K 2QU; www.kaimayfair.co.uk; 10.45 pm, Sun 10.15 pm.

Kaifeng NW4 **£59** ❷❷❸
51 Church Rd 8203 7888 1–1B
"There is no better kosher Chinese in London" than this "consistently busy" Hendon stalwart (which is also coeliac- and allergy-friendly); even fans concede it's "very expensive", but they do say it's "worth every penny". / NW4 4DU; www.kaifeng.co.uk; 10 pm; closed Fri & Sat.

Kaosarn **£26** ❷❷❷
110 St Johns Hill, SW11 7223 7888 10–2C
Brixton Village, Coldharbour Ln, SW9 7095 8922 10–2D
These "always-buzzing" cafés, in Brixton Village and Battersea, offer "snappy" service of "superb, home-cooked Thai food"; "be prepared to queue if you haven't booked"; BYO. / SW9 10 pm, Sun 9 pm; sw11 closed Mon L.

Karma W14 **£39** ❷⓿④
44 Blythe Rd 7602 9333 7–1D
An "overlooked" Indian, "off the beaten track in Olympia", which is well worth seeking out for its "exciting" cooking and "brilliant" service – even those who are "not so sure about the decor" say they "keep returning". / W14 0HA; www.k-a-r-m-a.co.uk; 11 pm; no Amex.

Karpo NW1 **£48** ❸④④
23 Euston Rd 7843 2221 8–3C
An "excellent" and "quirky" King's Cross find – "a little oasis of calm" with a "very airy" interior (complete with living wall), serving "surprisingly sophisticated" food. / NW1 2SD; www.karpo.co.uk; 10.30 pm.

Kaspar's Seafood and Grill The Savoy Hotel
WC2 NEW **£74** ❸❷❸
91 The Strand 7836 4343 4–3D
"Better than the reviews have generally suggested", this seafood-led relaunch of the former River Restaurant has pleased most early-days reporters, even if the décor is "a bit TOWIE" for some tastes. / WC2R 0EU; www.kaspars.co.uk; 11 pm.

Kateh W9 **£42** ❷❷❷
5 Warwick Pl 7289 3393 8–4A
"Small but perfectly formed"; this Little Venice outfit offers a "modern and elegant twist" on Persian cuisine "of a very high standard"; "shame it's so cramped", though. / W9 2PX; www.katehrestaurant.co.uk; 11 pm, Sun 9.30 pm; closed weekday L.

Kazan **£45** ❸❸④
77 Wilton Rd, SW1 7233 8298 2–4B
93-94 Wilton Rd, SW1 7233 7100 2–4B
"Don't be fooled by the plain exteriors!"; this duo of Turkish operations, in Pimlico, serve "quality" meze and other "reliable" fare – just the job for "a good light meal at a very reasonable price". / www.kazan-restaurant.com; 10 pm.

The Keeper's House
W1 NEW **£65**
Royal Academy Of Arts, Burlington Hs, Piccadilly 7300 5881 3–3D
A garden is, implausibly, among the attractions of the RA's major new bar/restaurant development, opening as this guide goes to press; let's hope it offers a step up from the standards at the RA's existing restaurant! / W1J 0BD; www.keepershouse.org.uk.

Ken Lo's Memories
SW1 **£62** ❸❸④
65-69 Ebury St 7730 7734 2–4B
Fans insist this "high-end" (but rather "clinical") Belgravia "old faithful" is "still London's best Chinese"; it's difficult, though, to avoid the conclusion that many ambitious recent openings have left it "outclassed". / SW1W 0NZ; www.memoriesofchina.co.uk; 10.45 pm, Sun 10 pm.

Ken Lo's Memories
of China W8 **£57** ❸④④
353 Kensington High St 7603 6951 7–1D
Fans say this upscale (and once-pre-eminent) establishment, on the Olympia/Kensington border, can still be "very good"; for an "expensive" place, though, it's sometimes seemed "nothing special" of late. / W8 6NW; www.memoriesofchina.co.uk; 10.45 pm.

Kennington Tandoori
SE11 £48 ❷❷❷
313 Kennington Rd 7735 9247 1–3C
"A cracking local Indian", offering "modern dishes
and old classics with a twist"; thanks not least to its
"very welcoming" service, it has an impressive local
following (including many politicos). / SE11 4QE;
www.kenningtontandoori.com; 11.30 pm; no Amex.

Kensington Place W8 £54 ❸❸④
201-209 Kensington Church St 7727 3184
6–2B
"Reincarnated as a fish restaurant", the seminal
'90s British brasserie seems to be slowly
"rediscovering its mojo"; some things don't change,
though – this goldfish bowl of a place gets
"very noisy" when it's full. / W8 7LX;
www.kensingtonplace-restaurant.co.uk;
@kprestaurantW8; 10.30 pm; closed Mon L & Sun D;
SRA-63%.

Kensington Square
Kitchen W8 £32 ❸❶❷
9 Kensington Sq 7938 2598 5–1A
Offering a warm welcome to "Kensington ladies
who lunch", a cute, if "slightly cramped", café on this
pretty square, providing an "amazingly good"
breakfast, and coffee and light meals all day.
/ W8 5EP; www.kensingtonsquarekitchen.co.uk;
@KSKRestaurant; 3.30 pm; L only; no Amex.

The Kensington
Wine Rooms W8 £50 ④❸❸
127-129 Kensington Church St 7727 8142
6–2B
"Stunning, esoteric, and wine-ranging", the wine
list (all available by the glass) at this pub-conversion,
near Notting Hill Gate, is ideal "for a liquid dinner";
indeed, "you probably wouldn't go there for the
food…" / W8 7LP; www.greatwinesbytheglass.com;
10.45 pm.

Kentish Canteen
NW5 £44 ④❸❸
300 Kentish Town Rd 7485 7331 8–2C
A "reliable and enjoyable" two-year-old; perhaps one
might "expect more flair", but overall it's "a lovely
local", most tipped for its "good family brunch".
/ NW5 2TG; www.kentishcanteen.co.uk; 10.30 pm.

(Brew House)
Kenwood House NW3 £32 ④❸❶
Hampstead Heath 8341 5384 8–1A
"Nothing beats sitting outside on the terrace", and a
Full English at this smart self-service café, at the top
of Hampstead Heath, makes a great way to start
the day; later on, you can "eat delicious sandwiches,
while sipping expensive coffee". / NW3 7JR;
www.companyofcooks.com; 6 pm (summer), 4 pm
(winter); L only.

Kenza EC2 £58 ④④❸
10 Devonshire Sq 7929 5533 9–2D
Surprisingly little feedback on this large basement
Lebanese, near Liverpool Street; it can be handy,
though, for a "good set lunch", and fans say the
raucous evening ambience – complete with belly
dancing – is "superb" too. / EC2 4YP;
www.kenza-restaurant.com; 10 pm; closed Sat L & Sun.

Kerbisher & Malt £19 ❸❸④
53 New Broadway, W5 8840 4418 1–3A
NEW
164 Shepherd's Bush Rd, W6 3556 0228
7–1C
"Spankingly fresh, traditional fish 'n' chips"
(plus "homemade sauces") have made quite a hit
of these Shepherd's Bush and (now) Ealing chippies;
the décor, though, strikes critics as on the "chilly"
side. / www.kerbisher.co.uk; 10 pm - 10.30pm, Sun 9 pm
- 9.30 pm; W6 Closed Mon.

Kettners W1 £56 ④❸❸
29 Romilly St 7734 6112 4–2A
"The room remains beautiful", the food "promises
more than it delivers", and the service is a bit
"hit 'n' miss" – in fact, plus ça change at this Soho
fixture, with its "excellent position in the heart
of Theatreland"; the top tip, as ever, is the swish
Champagne bar. / W1D 5HP; www.kettners.com;
11 pm, Fri & Sat 11.30 pm, Sun 9.30 pm.

Kew Grill TW9 £58 ❸❷❸
10b Kew Grn 8948 4433 1–3A
Antony Worrall Thompson's "warm" and "friendly"
home base seem to have benefited from his more
concentrated personal attention in recent times –
its "simple grills" are pricey, but can be "very good".
/ TW9 3BH; www.awtrestaurants.com; 10.30 pm, Fri-Sat
11 pm, Sun 10 pm; closed Mon L.

Khan's W2 £23 ❸④❸
13-15 Westbourne Grove 7727 5420 6–1C
A "legendary" Indian veteran, in Bayswater, offering
a selection of dishes at rock-bottom prices in a "no-
frills" setting, with an ambience sometimes likened
to a railway station; no booze. / W2 4UA;
www.khansrestaurant.com; 11.30 pm, Sat-Sun midnight.

Khan's of Kensington
SW7 £43 ❸❸④
3 Harrington Rd 7584 4114 5–2B
The name says it all – this is a very standard Indian
restaurant, but it's very handily located, by South
Kensington tube, and was consistently well-rated
by reporters this year. / SW7 3ES;
www.khansofkensington.co.uk; 11pm, Fri & Sat
11.30 pm, Sun 10.30 pm.

Kiku W1 £55 ❷❷⑤
17 Half Moon St 7499 4208 3–4B
"Authentic, all the way down to the quality of the
sushi… and the neon lighting!" – this "boring"-
looking Mayfair fixture makes "a great lunch/work

place", and the food is "very reliable". / W1J 7BE;
www.kikurestaurant.co.uk; 10.15 pm, Sun 9.45 pm;
closed Sun L.

Kikuchi W1   **£49**   ❶④⑤
14 Hanway St   7637 7720   4–1A
Food that's just "out of this world" makes it well
worth seeking out this "tucked-away" Japanese,
off Tottenham Court Road, which fans hail for some
of the best sushi in town; unless you're a native,
however, it's "not the friendliest place". / W1T 1UD;
10.30 pm; closed Sun.

Kimchee WC1   **£38**   ④④❸
71 High Holborn   7430 0956   2–1D
"A worthy competitor to Wagamama"; fans say this
"always humming" Holborn two-year-old offers
a "vast menu" of "enticing" Korean dishes,
and "great value" too; others, however are less
impressed, finding the food "uninspiring" and service
"haphazard". / WC1V 6EA; www.kimchee.uk.com;
@kimcheerest; 10.30 pm.

**Kings Road Steakhouse
& Grill SW3**   **£51**   ④④⑤
386 King's Rd   7351 9997   5–3B
"Quite swanky-looking, but uninspiring" – this MPW-
branded Chelsea steakhouse strikes too many
reporters for comfort as "very average" (or worse);
"be on the lookout for discounts!" / SW3 5UZ;
www.kingsroadsteakhouseandgrill.com; 10.30 pm,
Sun 10 pm.

Kipferl N1   **£43**   ❸④❸
20 Camden Pas   77041 555   8–3D
A "busy" Islington deli/restaurant, where "authentic"
(and "slightly unusual") Austrian treats – including
top cakes and pancakes – are served with
"fabulous" coffee. / N1 8ED; www.kipferl.co.uk; 9 pm;
closed Mon.

Kiraku W5   **£34**   ❶❷❸
8 Station Pde   8992 2848   1–3A
"Local Japanese residents flock" to this "laid-back"
café near Ealing Common tube; given the superb
standard of the "wide and varied menu" (which
incorporates, but is far from limited to, "fantastic
sushi"), prices are notably "competitive". / W5 3LD;
www.kiraku.co.uk; @kirakulondon; 10 pm; closed Mon;
no Amex.

Kirazu W1 NEW   **£35**
47 Rupert St   7494 2248   3–2D
A trendy Soho newcomer, offering Kyoto-style home
cooking at modest cost; it opened just too late
to attract survey commentary, but press reports
have been very encouraging. / W1D 7PD;
www.kirazu.co.uk.

Kitchen W8 W8   **£65**   ❶❷❸
11-13 Abingdon Road   7937 0120   5–1A
The part-backing of Phil Howard (of The Square)
helps explain the "surprisingly gourmet" cuisine,
"charmingly" served, at this "unheralded" local on a

Kensington side street; "its open-plan series of small
rooms", however, never seems to spark on the
atmosphere front. / W8 6AH; www.kitchenw8.com;
@KitchenW8; 10.15 pm, Sun 9.15 pm; set weekday
L £40 (FP), set pre-theatre £42 (FP).

Koba W1   **£43**   ❸❸④
11 Rathbone St   7580 8825   2–1C
"The excellent BBQ" is a "reliable" attraction of this
friendly Fitzrovia Korean; its ratings have slipped
a notch of late, though, as even fans note the
"prices are a little high". / W1T 1NA; 10.30 pm;
closed Sun L.

**Koffmann's
The Berkeley SW1**   **£80**   ❷❶❸
The Berkeley, Wilton Pl   7107 8844   5–1D
"A chance to savour the cooking of a culinary
legend!"; Pierre K ran '90s-London's best restaurant
(La Tante Claire) and the "rich" and "old-fashioned"
Gallic dishes on offer at this "cosy", if "low-
ceilinged", Knightsbridge basement are "sublime",
with wine and service to match. / SW1X 7RL;
www.the-berkeley.co.uk/top_restaurants.aspx; 10.30 pm;
set weekday L £48 (FP), set Sun L £49 (FP), set
pre-theatre £51 (FP).

Kolossi Grill EC1   **£32**   ④❷❷
56-60 Rosebery Ave   7278 5758   9–1A
"Unpretentious, reasonably-priced, pleasantly
located..." – this old-time Farringdon taverna
invariably pleases: "I've been eating meze here for
40 years, and they are still great value!" / EC1R 4RR;
www.kolossigrill.com; 11 pm; closed Sat L & Sun.

Konditor & Cook   **£27**   ❸④④
Curzon Soho, 99 Shaftesbury Ave, W1   854
9367   4–3A
46 Gray's Inn Rd, WC1   854 9365   9–1A
10 Stoney St, SE1   854 9363   9–4C
22 Cornwall Road, SE1   854 9361   9–4A
30 St Mary Axe, EC3   854 9369   9–2D
"Wonderful" coffee and cakes, and "first-rate
savouries" too – reporters find little to fault at the
"bustling" branches of this consistent small chain.
/ www.konditorandcook.com; 6 pm; W1 11 pm;
WC1 & EC3 closed Sat & Sun; SE1 closed Sun;
no booking.

Kopapa WC2   **£56**   ❸④④
32-34 Monmouth St   7240 6076   4–2B
"Peter Gordon does it again", says one of the many
fans of his "cramped" Theatreland dining room,
where "delicious and quirky small plates" are the
menu staple (and breakfasts are "fantastic" too);
service, though is sometimes "nowhere to be seen".
/ WC2H 9HA; www.kopapa.co.uk; @Kopapacafe;
10.45 pm, Sun 9.45 pm.

Koya W1 £34 ❷❸❸
49 Frith St 7434 4463 4–2A
"Queues, even in the depth of winter" advertise the charms of this "basic" but "brilliant" Soho Japanese, where the menu features not just "the best udon noodles in London", but also some notably "creative" specials. / W1D 4SG; www.koya.co.uk; @KoyaUdon; 10.30 pm; no booking.

Koya-Ko W1 NEW £33
50 Frith St awaiting tel 4–2A
Next to the mega-popular Soho udon restaurant, a fast-service all-day newcomer; special attractions? – such cross-cultural delights as an English breakfast soup! / W1D 4SQ.

Kulu Kulu £31 ④⑤④
76 Brewer St, W1 7734 7316 3–2D
51-53 Shelton St, WC2 7240 5687 4–2C
39 Thurloe Pl, SW7 7589 2225 5–2C
"They don't look much" ("like a hole in the wall"), the service is "basic", and the food quality "mixed", but this grungy conveyor-café chain is still hailed by fans as a "great place to satisfy a sushi-craving on the cheap". / 10 pm; SW7 10.30 pm; closed Sun; no Amex; no booking.

Kurumaya EC4 £41 ❸❸④
76-77 Watling St 7236 0236 9–2B
"Consistently good" food makes this "friendly" and "efficient" Japanese a handy City stand-by… not least the ground-floor kaiten (conveyor) operation, which serves "fantastic fresh sushi". / EC4M 9BJ; www.kurumaya.co.uk; @Kurumaya76; 9.30 pm; closed Sat & Sun.

The Ladbroke Arms
W11 £49 ❷❸❷
54 Ladbroke Rd 7727 6648 6–2B
"Well-cooked dishes, pretty people and dogs" – this smart Notting Hill boozer really leaves nothing to be desired; in fact, the only problem is that, "whether it's a sunny day, or a grey one", it can sometimes be "a bit too popular". / W11 3NW; www.capitalpubcompany.com; 9.30 pm; no booking after 8 pm.

Ladudu NW6 £35 ❸❸④
152 West End Ln 7372 3217 1–1B
"Great spicing" peps up the Vietnamese scoff on offer at this "busy but always accommodating" West Hampstead café. / NW6 1SD; www.ladudu.com; @ladudufood; 10.30 pm.

Ladurée £60 ❷④❸
Harrods, 87-135 Brompton Rd, SW1
3155 0111 5–1D
71-72 Burlington Arc, Piccadilly, W1 7491 9155
3–3C
1 Covent Garden Mkt, WC2 7240 0706
4–3D
14 Cornhill, EC3 7283 5727 9–2C
"The best macarons in a very plush setting" –

the essential features of these bijoux outposts of the famed Parisian pâtisserie, but they do also offer other "beautifully made" cakes plus superior coffee, omelettes and sandwiches (availability varies by branch). / www.laduree.com; SW1 8.45 pm, Sun 5.45 pm; W1 6.30 pm, Sun 5 pm, EC3 8 pm; EC3 closed Sat-Sun; W1 no booking, SW1 no booking 3 pm-6 pm.

The Lady Ottoline
WC1 £46 ④④❸
11a, Northington St 7831 0008 2–1D
This year-old relaunch of a characterful Victorian boozer is "a great addition to Bloomsbury", say fans; others, though, can go no further than finding it "decent enough". / WC1N 2JF; www.theladyottoline.com; @theladyottoline; 10 pm, Sun 8 pm.

Lahore Karahi SW17 £23 ❷④④
1 Tooting High Street, London 8767 2477
10–2C
"Still the best subcontinental café around!" – this "busy", "canteen-style" Tooting "favourite" has a big name for its "genuine Pakistani food at bargain prices"; BYO. / SW17 0SN; www.lahorekarahi.co.uk; midnight; no Amex.

Lahore Kebab House £26 ❶④④
668 Streatham High Rd, SW16 8765 0771
10–2D
2-10 Umberston St, E1 7488 2551 11–1A
"The best kebabs west of Lahore!"; with its "fantastic flavours at great prices", this "plain" Pakistani canteen in Whitechapel is nothing short of a "phenomenon" – even those who find the setting "depressing" concede the food is "spectacular"; SW16 is good too; BYO. / midnight.

Lamberts SW12 £47 ❶❶❷
2 Station Pde 8675 2233 10–2C
"What an outstanding restaurant in an unlikely place!" – this "unfailing" gem, near Balham station, is "excellent across the board"; indeed, locals claim it's a rival to nearby Chez Bruce, but it's no criticism to say it's not trying to play in quite the same league. / SW12 9AZ; www.lambertsrestaurant.com; @lamberts_balham; 10 pm, Sun 5 pm; closed Mon & Sun D; no Amex; set weekday L £33 (FP); SRA-60%.

(Winter Garden)
The Landmark NW1 £82 ❸❷❶
222 Marylebone Rd 7631 8000 8–4A
It's the "fabulous" Sunday jazz brunch – "not gourmet, but excellent for a buffet", and with "unlimited" champagne – which is the particular draw to this "relaxed" venue, in the soaring atrium of a Marylebone hotel; lunch and afternoon tea also have their fans. / NW1 6JQ; www.landmarklondon.co.uk; 10.30 pm; no trainers; booking: max 12.

**Langan's Brasserie
W1** £64 ④❷❷
Stratton St 7491 8822 3–3C
This "legendary" grand brasserie, near the Ritz,
may seem a little "dated", but its upbeat style has
proved amazingly enduring over the years
(especially for business); it's given a more
"professional" impression of late since recent
management changes – might this be the start of a
comeback? / W1J 8LB; www.langansrestaurants.co.uk;
11 pm, Fri & Sat 11.30 pm, Sun 10 pm.

Lantana Cafe W1 £34 ❸❸❷
13-14 Charlotte Pl 7323 6601 2–1C
"Laid-back", it may be, but this Oz café in Fitzrovia
– with its "amazing" cakes, its "top-notch" coffee
and its "interesting" other dishes – is becoming
quite a beacon; "shame they don't take
reservations!" / W1T 1SN; www.lantanacafe.co.uk;
3 pm; L only; no Amex; no booking.

Lardo E8 £38 ❸④❸
Richmond Rd 8533 8229 1–2D
A "hip crowd" Hackney yearling, offering a menu
of pizza, pasta and cured meats for which
"you won't have to re-mortgage"; what it arguably
"lacks in ambition", it makes up for with "fantastic
sourcing". / E8 3NJ; www.lardo.co.uk; 10.30 pm,
Sun 9.30 pm.

Latium W1 £49 ❷⓿❸
21 Berners St 7323 9123 3–1D
"Reminiscent of a top Rome restaurant" – Maurizio
Morelli's "civilised" venture, just north of Oxford
Street, is a "totally professional but genuinely warm"
operation, serving up an "elaborate" menu of "fine"
dishes (ravioli is the house speciality), plus a
"fabulous selection of wines". / W1T 3LP;
www.latiumrestaurant.com; 10.30 pm, Sat 11 pm; closed
Sat L & Sun; set weekday L & pre-theatre £34 (FP).

Launceston Place W8 £74 ❷❷❷
1a Launceston Pl 7937 6912 5–1B
With its "off-the-beaten track" location "in the
backstreets of Kensington", and its "elegant"
townhouse interior, this "intimate" and
"professional" D&D group all-rounder is a natural
romantic "oasis"; under chef Tim Allen, the cuisine
is returning to "superb" form too. / W8 5RL;
www.launcestonplace-restaurant.co.uk; 10 pm; closed
Mon L; set weekday L £48 (FP); SRA-63%.

**The Lawn Bistro
SW19** £57 ④❷④
67 High St 8947 8278 10–2B
"A necessary addition to the Wimbledon Village
scene, but overpriced for what it is" – a good
example of the somewhat ambivalent reception
to this "fancy" yearling; it is however "the best lunch
option in the village" (which is "not saying much!").
/ SW19 5EE; www.thelawnbistro.co.uk; 9.30 pm,
Sat 10 pm; closed Sun D.

THE LEDBURY W11 £113 ⓿⓿❷
127 Ledbury Rd 7792 9090 6–1B
"Brett Graham is a genius, whose
French/Australasian fusion still dazzles", and his
"impeccable" Notting Hill fixture was again rated
London's foodie No. 1, thanks to its "enchanting"
food and "silky smooth" service; can he push on for
the dreaded third Michelin star, though, without
succumbing to stuffiness and overpricing?
/ W11 2AQ; www.theledbury.com; 10.15 pm, Sun 10 pm;
closed Mon L; set weekday L £62 (FP).

Lemonia NW1 £46 ④❷⓿
89 Regent's Park Rd 7586 7454 8–3B
"Amazingly reliable through the decades",
this "unique" Primrose Hill mega-taverna is still
"always packed to the gills"; it can't be the food,
so it must be that this is an "always-fun" destination
that's become a "home from home" for many
locals. / NW1 8UY; www.lemonia.co.uk; 11 pm; closed
Sun D; no Amex.

Leon £26 ④❸❸
275 Regent St, W1 7495 1514 3–1C
35-36 Gt Marlborough St, W1 7437 5280
3–2C
73-76 The Strand, WC2 7240 3070 4–4D
7 Canvey St, SE1 7620 0035 9–3B
Cabot Place West, E14 7719 6200 11–1C
3 Crispin Pl, E1 7247 4369 12–2B
12 Ludgate Circus, EC4 7489 1580 9–2A
86 Cannon St, EC4 7623 9699 9–3C
"A saviour from boring lunches" – with their
"lovely", "clean-tasting" wraps, salads and juices,
these wholesome diners are still, for most reporters,
"a great alternative to typical fast food";
as expansion continues, though, ratings are heading
south. / www.leonrestaurants.co.uk; 10 pm;
W1 8.45 pm; E14 8 pm; EC4 closed Sun; W1 closed
Sat & Sun; no booking L.

Leong's Legends W1 £36 ❸④❸
3 Macclesfield St 7287 0288 4–3A
"A slightly more unusual Taiwanese take on the
typical Chinatown offering" – this budget diner
specialises in Xiao Long Bao (soup dumplings),
and offers "authentic" and "tasty" scoff at a "knock-
down price". / W1D 6AX; www.leongslegend.com;
11 pm, Sat 11.30 pm; no booking.

Levant W1 £54 ④❸❷
Jason Ct, 76 Wigmore St 7224 1111 3–1A
"You are no longer really in London", if you pay
a visit to this party-Lebanese, in a basement near
Selfridges; it has only attracted modest survey
feedback of late, but all positive. / W1U 2SJ;
www.levant.co.uk; 9.45pm, Fri-Sat midnight.

The Lido Cafe
Brockwell Lido SE24 £44 ❸❸❷
Dulwich Rd 7737 8183 10–2D
"Brilliant" breakfasts are a highlight of the dining
experience at this "spectacular" south London lido,
but its "good honest grub" is enjoyable at any time;
"book a table by the window, so you can watch the
swimmers". / SE24 0PA; www.thelidocafe.co.uk;
@thelidocafe; 9.30 pm; closed Mon D & Sun D;
no Amex.

The Light House
SW19 £49 ❹❸❸
75-77 Ridgway 8944 6338 10–2B
Mixed reports on this "bustling" Wimbledon spot;
fans insist that it "punches above its weight",
with "greatly improved" post-refurb décor, and a
menu that's "always interesting"; execution, though,
can be "variable". / SW19 4ST;
www.lighthousewimbledon.com; 10.30 pm; closed Sun D.

Lima W1 £56 ❸❹❹
31 Rathbone Pl 3002 2640 2–1C
"Ceviche to die for" is the highlight of the
"colourful" cuisine at the Fitzrovia yearling
sometimes acclaimed as "London's top Peruvian";
acoustics are "poor", though, and some reporters
just "can't see what everyone goes on about".
/ W1T 1JH; www.limalondon.com;
www.twitter.com/lima_london; 10.30 pm; closed Sun;
SRA-51%.

Lisboa Pâtisserie W10 £8 ❸❸❹
57 Golborne Rd 8968 5242 6–1A
"The best pasteis de nata (custard tarts) in the
world" – well, nearly – are served at this "stalwart"
North Kensington café. / W10 5NR; 7 pm; L & early
evening only; no booking.

Little Bay £31 ❹❷❶
228 Belsize Rd, NW6 7372 4699 1–2B
171 Farringdon Rd, EC1 7278 1234 9–1A
"Is there a better-value meal in London?", say fans
of these "gorgeous", "fun" and "romantic" budget
bistros, where the scoff "isn't fancy" but it is
"unbelievably reasonably priced"; live opera is a
"bonus" too. / www.little-bay.co.uk; @TheLittleBay;
11.30 pm, Sun 11 pm; no Amex, NW6 no credit cards.

Little Georgia Café £38 ❸❹❸
14 Barnsbury Rd, N1 7278 6100 8–3D
87 Goldsmiths Row, E2 7739 8154 1–2D
"A hidden gem, and you can BYO too!" – this "cosy"
café, in Bethnal Green, offers an interesting
Georgian menu; praise too for its year-old Islington
offshoot, though it takes some flak on the service
front. / www.littlegeorgia.co.uk.

Little Social W1 NEW £60 ❷❷❷
5 Pollen St 7870 3730 3–2C
"The very amicable new sibling of Pollen Street
Social" (over the road) "recreates the feel of a
French bistro", and fans find it "more relaxed",

"more personal" and "more atmospheric" than big
brother; the cooking is "lovely" too. / W1S 1NE;
www.littlesocial.co.uk.

LMNT E8 £36 ❹❸❶
316 Queensbridge Rd 7249 6727 1–2D
"Crazy" OTT classical decor (Sphinx, Greek urns,
hieroglyphics) makes it "always fun" to visit this
pharaoh-kitsch Dalston pub-conversion; it matters
not that the food is "a bit variable". / E8 3NH;
www.lmnt.co.uk; 10.30 pm; Mon-Thu D only, Fri-Sun open
L & D; no Amex.

Lobster Pot SE11 £61 ❷❸❹
3 Kennington Ln 7582 5556 1–3C
"A quirky little place that's stood the test of time" –
this family-run stalwart may have an "odd" location,
in deepest Kennington, plus surreal 'sunken
schooner' decor (complete with taped gulls),
but "it excels at what it does – traditionally-
prepared Gallic seafood". / SE11 4RG;
www.lobsterpotrestaurant.co.uk; 10.30 pm; closed
Mon & Sun; booking: max 8.

Locanda Locatelli
Hyatt Regency W1 £75 ❸❸❹
8 Seymour St 7935 9088 2–2A
Fans still extol Giorgio Locatelli's "elegant and
understated" Marylebone dining room for "perfect"
Italian cuisine "that both respects and pushes
tradition"; it can also seem "absurdly expensive"
though, and service occasionally "lets the place
down". / W1H 7JZ; www.locandalocatelli.com; 11 pm,
Thu-Sat 11.30 pm, Sun 10.15 pm; booking: max 8.

Locanda Ottomezzo
W8 £66 ❹❹❹
2-4 Thackeray St 7937 2200 5–1B
"Tucked-away", "intimate" and "idiosyncratic",
this "upmarket neighbourhood Italian" has
a devoted Kensington following; "if the prices were
lower, it would be amazing…" / W8 5ET;
www.locandaottoemezzo.co.uk; 10.30 pm, Fri & Sat
10.45 pm; closed Mon L & Sun.

Loch Fyne £44 ❹❸❹
2-4 Catherine St, WC2 7240 4999 2–2D
77-78 Gracechurch St, EC3 7929 8380 9–3C
Whether this comfy, if slightly sedate national
seafood chain is "highly dependable", or merely
"formulaic", has long been a matter of dispute;
this year, however, a number of reporters suggested
it's "trying hard to raise its game".
/ www.lochfyne-restaurants.com; 10 pm; WC2 10.30 pm.

The Lockhart W1 NEW £50
24 Seymour Pl 3011 5400 2–2A
Not far from Marble Arch, a summer 2013
newcomer specialising in the cuisine of the
American Southwest; we sadly didn't have the
opportunity to visit before this guide went to press.
/ W1H 7NL; www.lockhartlondon.com;
@LockhartLondon; 10.30 pm; set weekday L £33 (FP).

Lola & Simón W6   £48   ❸❷❸
278 King St   8563 0300   7–2B
*This "quirky" Argentinian/Kiwi café – run with
"energy and commitment" – is a "cosy" feature
of Hammersmith's main drag; it's open all day,
but particularly known locally as the "perfect
morning pit stop". / W6 0SP; www.lolaandsimon.co.uk;
@lola_simon; 10 pm; no Amex.*

Lola Rojo SW11   £42   ❸④④
78 Northcote Rd   7350 2262   10–2C
*Offering "a modern twist on tapas", this "lively" and
"friendly" Battersea spot is an almost invariable
crowd-pleaser. / SW11 6QL; www.lolarojo.net;
10.30 pm, Sat & Sun 11 pm; no Amex.*

**Look Mum No Hands!
EC1**   £29   ❸❸❷
49 Old St   7253 1025   9–1B
*"Where else can you have a snack and get your
bike repaired at the same time?" – this "hip" café-
cum-cycle-shop dishes up "delicious healthy food",
plus plenty of "super-friendly attitude too".
/ EC1V 9HX; www.lookmumnohands.co.uk;
@lookmumnohands; 10 pm.*

**The Lord Northbrook
SE12**   £35   ❸❷❷
116 Burnt Ash Rd   8318 1127   1–4D
*This Lea Green boozer – "beautifully done up" two
years ago – hasn't entirely gone 'gastro', but its
"friendly" staff serve up "surprisingly good" grub
from a "short and sensible menu". / SE12 8PU;
www.thelordnorthbrook.co.uk; 9 pm, Fri-Sat 10 pm.*

Lorenzo SE19   £41   ④❷❸
73 Westow Hill   8761 7485   1–4D
*A "cosy" fixture of Upper Norwood – a dependable
Italian that's "always full", thanks to its "simple" but
"great-value" pizza and pasta menu. / SE19 1TX;
www.lorenzo.uk.com; 10.30 pm.*

**Lotus Chinese Floating
Restaurant E14**   £42   ④④❸
9 Oakland Quay   7515 6445   11–2C
*Permanently-moored, near Canary Wharf, a boat
offering "really good dim sum" at lunchtime; as an
evening destination, though, it can feel pretty
"soulless". / E14 9EA; www.lotusfloating.co.uk;
10.30 pm; closed Mon.*

Lucio SW3   £64   ❸④④
257 Fulham Rd   7823 3007   5–3B
*"In the end, everyone in Chelsea will be seated next
to you!" – this "old-money" Italian certainly doesn't
lack local custom, but even fans may note that it's
"pricey", and a "distinct feeling of priority for the
regulars" irks some. / SW3 6HY; 10.45 pm;
set weekday L £42 (FP).*

Lucky Seven W2   £39   ❸❸❷
127 Westbourne Park Rd   7727 6771   6–1B
*Brace yourself to share a booth at Tom Conran's
funky, tightly-packed slice of Americana, on the
fringe of Notting Hill; it does a mean burger,
and some "pretty amazing chocolate malts" too.
/ W2 5QL; www.tomconranrestaurants.com; 10.15 pm,
Sun 10 pm; no Amex; no booking.*

Lupita WC2   £38   ④④❸
13-15 Villiers St   7930 5355   4–4D
*"So much better than your average Tex-Mex",
this "refreshing" corner Mexican, right by Charing
Cross, offers "proper food, like you find in Mexico".
/ WC2N 6ND; www.lupita.co.uk; @LupitaUK; 11 pm,
Fri-Sat 11.30 pm, Sun 10 pm.*

Lutyens EC4   £72   ④④④
85 Fleet St   7583 8385   9–2A
*Sir Terence Conran's large Fleet Street outpost is a
"noisy" and "impersonal" affair, where the food
is "rarely exciting" – no doubt why many reports
confirm it's "fine for a business lunch"! / EC4Y 1AE;
www.lutyens-restaurant.com; 10 pm; closed Sat & Sun;
set weekday L £50 (FP).*

Ma Cuisine TW9   £41   ❸❸❸
9 Station Approach   8332 1923   1–3A
*"The best middle-of-the-road restaurant in Kew!";
this slightly "middle-aged" Gallic venture, near the
tube, is currently in an "up-phase"; it serves classic
bistro fare at affordable prices. / TW9 3QB;
www.macuisinekew.co.uk; 10 pm, Fri & Sat 10.30 pm;
no Amex.*

Ma Goa SW15   £39   ❷0❷
242-244 Upper Richmond Rd   8780 1767
10–2B
*"Utterly reliable, and fantastic value";
this "consistently warm and friendly" family-fun
Putney local is well worth seeking out for its Goan
cuisine – "a revelation". / SW15 6TG;
www.ma-goa.com; @magoarestaurant; 11 pm,
Sun 10 pm; closed Mon L & Sat L.*

**Made In Camden
Roundhouse NW1**   £38   ❸❸❸
Chalk Farm Rd   7424 8495   8–2B
*It may be attached to Camden Town's Roundhouse,
but this "inventive" café is a destination in its own
right; it serves an "enterprising and cosmopolitan"
small plates menu that's "especially great for
brunch". / NW1 8EH; www.madeincamden.com;
10.15 pm.*

Made in Italy   £41   ❸④❸
14a, Old Compton St, W1   0011 1214   4–2B
50 James St, W1   7224 0182   3–1A **NEW**
249 King's Rd, SW3   7352 1880   5–3C
*"I love the metre-long pizzas!" – this "fun" Chelsea
outfit serves up stone-baked pizzas that consistently
satisfy, and it even has a terrace for sunny days;
good (if limited) feedback on Soho too.*

/ www.madeinitalygroup.co.uk; 11 pm, Sun 10 pm;
SW3 closed Mon L.

Madhu's UB1   **£34**   ❸❸❸
39 South Rd   8574 1897   1–3A
A pilgrimage to this landmark of Southall's curry
strip is the stuff of foodie legend; some devotees
do declare it "the best in town", but "enjoyable"
is the better mark of overall survey approval.
/ UB1 1SW; www.madhus.co.uk; 11.30 pm; closed Tue,
Sat L & Sun L.

Madsen SW7   **£48**   ❸④⑤
20 Old Brompton Rd   7225 2772   5–2B
A "simple" South Kensington Scandinavian,
recommended for a "slightly different but
reasonably-priced" meal of Smørrebrød
(open sarnies) and other "Danish staples"; on the
downside, however, it can all seem "rather bland".
/ SW7 3DL; www.madsenrestaurant.com;
@madsenlondon; 10 pm, Fri-Sat 10.45 pm; closed
Sun D; no Amex.

**The Magazine Restaurant
Serpentine Gallery W2** 🆕
Kensington Gdns   7402 6075   6–2D
Zaha Hadid, no less, is the architect of the
restaurant of this new gallery in the heart of Hyde
Park, opening as this guide goes to press; the chef,
Berlin-born Oliver Lange, apparently cooks in British
style. / W2 3XA.

Magdalen SE1   **£55**   ❷❸❸
152 Tooley St   7403 1342   9–4D
"Thoughtful" and "gutsy" seasonal British cuisine
at "sensible" prices, with a "wonderful wine list" too,
have helped win a large, loyal following for this
"hidden gem" – well "worth a detour" in the thin
area round City Hall. / SE1 2TU;
www.magdalenrestaurant.co.uk; 10 pm; closed
Sat L & Sun; set weekday L £35 (FP).

Maggie Jones's W8   **£55**   ④④❶
6 Old Court Pl   7937 6462   5–1A
"A blast from the past" – this "'70s throwback"
(named after a former fan, Princess Margaret,
who used to book in that name) is a
"very atmospheric" Kensington destination, serving
English cooking of a rather "solid" type; service can
be "patchy", but it is "with a smile". / W8 4PL;
www.maggie-jones.co.uk; 11 pm, Sun 10.30 pm; set Sun L
£39 (FP).

Maguro W9   **£37**   ❶❷❸
5 Lanark Pl   7289 4353   8–4A
With its growing reputation for "awesome" sushi
(in particular), this "consistently brilliant" Maida Vale
"hidden gem" isn't really so hidden any more –
its "tiny" premises are "always packed". / W9 1BT;
www.maguro-restaurant.com; 10.30 pm; no Amex.

Maison Bertaux W1   **£16**   ❷❸❶
28 Greek St   7437 6007   4–2A
"Delightfully unchanging" and "eccentric", this Soho

café (est 1871) may seem like a "bizarre throwback", but the cakes it offers are still "always
delicious". / W1D 5DQ; www.maisonbertaux.com;
10.15 pm, Sun 8 pm.

Malabar W8   **£44**   ❷❷❸
27 Uxbridge St   7727 8800   6–2B
"An old classic, still keeping the punters happy after
more than 25 years" – this "accommodating"
Indian, off Notting Hill Gate, is still a definite
"cut above", and offers some "thoughtfully-spiced"
dishes. / W8 7TQ; www.malabar-restaurant.co.uk;
11.30 pm, Sun 10.30 pm; set Sun L £29 (FP).

**Malabar Junction
WC1**   **£40**   ❸④❸
107 Gt Russell St   7580 5230   2–1C
"Behind an unprepossessing entrance, near the
British Museum", lurks this "surprisingly spacious,
light and airy" spot, in which to enjoy "classic"
Keralan cuisine; service here has long been of note,
but recently it has been rather up-and-down.
/ WC1B 3NA; www.malabarjunction.com; 11 pm.

The Mall Tavern W8   **£48**   ❸❸❸
71-73 Palace Gardens Ter   7229 3374   6–2B
The "famous Cow Pie" – twinned with other
"modern British classics" – has carved out quite
a name for this Kensington gastropub (particularly
the "fantastic chef's table"); the cooking, though,
is perhaps a touch "less exciting than it used
to be". / W8 4RU; www.themalltavern.com; 10 pm.

**The Malt House
SW6** 🆕   **£53**   ❷❸❸
17 Vanston Pl   7084 6888   5–3A
"This is not pub food, it is serious food!" – with its
"interesting" menu, this "friendly" Fulham newcomer
offers "a perfect combination of delicious food and
easy-going surroundings". / SW6 1AY;
www.malthousefulham.co.uk; @MalthouseFulham;
10 pm, Sun 9 pm; set weekday L £35 (FP).

Mandalay W2   **£27**   ❸❷⑤
444 Edgware Rd   7258 3696   8–4A
This family-run Burmese (Indian/Chinese) stalwart,
near Edgware Road tube "has had its ups and
downs", but it's "incredibly cheap", and generally
worth a try; "the interior is a bit rough-round-the-
edges, but the welcome is warm and attentive".
/ W2 1EG; www.mandalayway.com; 10.30 pm;
closed Sun.

Mandarin Kitchen W2 £40   ❷④⑤
14-16 Queensway   7727 9012   6–2C
"Undoubtedly the best lobster noodles" – highlight
of the "fantastic" Chinese seafood dishes on offer
at this Bayswater veteran; the "very '70s" décor,
though, "desperately needs work". / W2 3RX;
11.15 pm.

Mangal I E8　　　£30　　❶④④
10 Arcola St　7275 8981　1–1C
"Still the best Turkish grill in London despite the increasing number of imitators" – this Dalston marvel offers a "wonderful meat-fest" and "beautiful salads" too… all at "unbelievably low prices"; BYO. / E8 2DJ; www.mangal1.com; midnight, Sat-Sun 1 am; no credit cards.

Mangal II N16　　　£36　　❸❸④
4 Stoke Newington Rd　7254 7888　1–1C
"Notorious as Gilbert & George's go-to supper destination", this "cheap and cheerful" Dalston Ocakbasi "never fails to satisfy your cravings for grilled meat". / N16 8BH; www.mangal2.com; 1 am.

Mango & Silk SW14　　£34　　❷❷❸
199 Upper Richmond Rd　8876 6220　1–4A
"So much better than a lot of the 'standard' Indians… a bit more expensive, but you get what you pay for" – this East Sheen spot serves a "good selection of gourmet" dishes. / SW14 8QT; www.mangoandsilk.co.uk; @Mangoandsilk; 9.30 pm, Fri & Sat 10 pm; D only, closed Sun.

Mango Food of India SE1　　　£50　　❸❸④
5-6 Cromwell Buildings, Redcross Way　7407 0333　9–4C
"Busy, and with plenty of buzz", a tucked-away modern Indian, near Borough Market, offering "good-quality" cooking, and a "few 'different' dishes". / SE1 9HR; 11 pm.

Mango Room NW1　　£44　　❸❸❸
10-12 Kentish Town Rd　7482 5065　8–3B
"Unchanged in two decades", this buzzy haunt remains a well-rated Camden Town hang-out, serving "sophisticated" Caribbean grub with easy-going style. / NW1 8NH; www.mangoroom.co.uk; 11 pm.

Mango Tree　　　£53　　❸④④
46 Grosvenor Pl, SW1　7823 1888　2–4B
Harrods, 87-135 Brompton Rd, SW1　7730 1234　5–1D
Fans of these "busy" Thai outfits (part of an international chain) laud their "authentic" fare; critics, however, dismiss their regularly price-promoted cooking as "pretty uninteresting" – "even at 50% off it was too expensive!" / www.mangotree.org.uk; @MangoTreeLondon; Brompton Rd Mon-Sat 8.30 pm, Sun 7.30 pm; Grosvenor Pl Mon-Wed 11 pm, Thu-Sat 11.30 pm, Sun 10.30 pm.

Manicomio　　　£59　　❸④❸
85 Duke of York Sq, SW3　7730 3366　5–2D
6 Gutter Ln, EC2　7726 5010　9–2B
"Competent food with a light touch" helps make these "female-friendly" Italians popular with most Chelsea and City reporters; lots of outside tables make for "good people-watching" too.

/ www.manicomio.co.uk; SW3 10.30 pm, Sun 10 pm; EC2 10 pm; EC2 closed Sat & Sun.

Manna NW3　　　£52　　④④④
4 Erskine Rd　7722 8028　8–3B
The UK's longest-established veggie (1968) has put in an up-and-down performance in recent years; fans say it's "back on form", but sceptics say its Primrose Hill setting is too "Spartan", and that it "trades on its longevity". / NW3 3AJ; www.mannav.com; @mannacuisine; 10.30 pm; closed Mon, Tue-Fri D only, Sat & Sun open L & D.

The Manor Arms SW16　　　£37　　❷❸④
13 Mitcham Ln　3195 6888　10–2C
A huge success, down Streatham way; this "family-friendly" boozer is acclaimed in many reviews for its "high quality", with "superb" seafood and "brilliant Sunday lunches" among the highlights. / SW16 6LQ; www.themanorarms.com.

Mao Tai SW6　　　£63　　❷❷❷
58 New King's Rd　7731 2520　10–1B
A pricey pan-Asian veteran, in Fulham, offering "a good mixture of old favourites and more contemporary dishes"; "it's always been good, but it's got even better in recent times!" / SW6 4LS; www.maotai.co.uk; 11.30 pm, Sun 10.30 pm; D only, ex Sun open L & D.

Mar I Terra SE1　　　£31　　❸❸❷
14 Gambia St　7928 7628　9–4A
A long-established bar that's "slightly out of the way, but worth tracking down" as a "useful pre-theatre" (South Bank) destination, thanks not least to its "authentic" and "tasty" cuisine. / SE1 0XH; www.mariterra.co.uk; 10.30 pm; closed Sat L & Sun.

MARCUS WAREING THE BERKELEY SW1 £116　❸❷❷
Wilton Pl　7235 1200　5–1D
For "precision and perfection", fans still hail the "unbelievable experience" offered by Marcus Wareing's "elegantly relaxed" Knightsbridge dining room, vaunting "superlative" cuisine and "top drawer" service; prices are "eye-watering", however, and ratings support those who feel it's "not as tip-top as it used to be". / SW1X 7RL; www.marcus-wareing.com; 10.45 pm; closed Sun; no jeans or trainers; booking: max 8; set weekday L £63 (FP), set pre-theatre £82 (FP).

Mari Vanna SW1　　　£68　　④⑤❷
116 Knightsbridge　7225 3122　5–1D
A visit to this rustic-chic Russian yearling, by Knightsbridge tube, is just like "entering Chekhov's world" – the food is "average", but the atmosphere is "fantastic", and the people-watching is "fabulous"! / SW1X 7PJ; www.marivanna.co.uk; @marivannalondon; 11.30 pm; set weekday L £46 (FP).

Marianne W2 NEW **£82**
104 Chepstow Rd   3675 7750   6–1B
*A Bayswater newcomer of note for its sheer
(lack of) size; Marianne Lumb has an impressive
cv behind her, and just 14 seats in her restaurant;
early press reaction has been very positive.
/ W2 5QS; www.mariannerestaurant.com;
@marianne_w2.*

Marine Ices NW3 **£39**
8 Haverstock Hill   7482 9003   8–2B
*"Glorious Italian gelati" have served generations
of kids at this Camden Town "perennial", and the
pizzas are traditionally "pretty good too";
the founding family sold out this year, though, so we
don't think a rating is yet appropriate. / NW3 2BL;
www.marineices.co.uk; 11 pm, Sun 10 pm; closed Mon;
no Amex.*

Market NW1 **£49** ❸④④
43 Parkway   7267 9700   8–3B
*"A noughties update of the 1970s bistro format";
this "bare-brick" Camden Town haunt offers
a "short but intriguing" menu of "well-produced"
dishes, and a "relaxed" experience overall.
/ NW1 7PN; www.marketrestaurant.co.uk;
@MarketCamden; 10.30 pm, Sun 3 pm; closed Sun D;
set weekday L £31 (FP).*

Maroush **£47** ❷❸④
I) 21 Edgware Rd, W2   7723 0773   6–1D
II) 38 Beauchamp Pl, SW3   7581 5434   5–1C
V) 3-4 Vere St, W1   7493 5050   3–1B
VI) 68 Edgware Rd, W2   7224 9339   6–1D
'Garden') 1 Connaught St, W2   7262 0222
6–1D
*"Fresh, aromatic and tasty" dishes have long made
this Lebanese chain a London fixture; as well as the
grander dining rooms, the "busy, hustling and
bustling" café/take-aways at some branches (I, II
and IV) are "great for a light meal"; top tip –
ask for the 'wraps' menu. / www.maroush.com;
most branches close between 12.30 am-5 am.*

Masala Zone **£32** ❸❷❷
9 Marshall St, W1   7287 9966   3–2D
48 Floral St, WC2   7379 0101   4–2D
147 Earl's Court Rd, SW5   7373 0220   5–2A
583 Fulham Rd, SW6   7386 5500   5–4A
75 Bishop's Bridge Rd, W2   7221 0055   6–1C
80 Upper St, N1   7359 3399   8–3D
25 Parkway, NW1   7267 4422   8–3B
*"It's hard to be disappointed", at this "buzzy and
efficient" Indian street-food chain; "it may not be the
most adventurous cuisine-wise", but it's "reliable"
and very "sensibly priced" – for best value, grab a
Thali. / www.realindianfood.com; 11 pm, Sun 10.30 pm;
no Amex; booking: min 10.*

MASH Steakhouse
W1 **£75** ❸❸❸
77 Brewer St   7734 2608   3–2D
*Occupying a subterranean "Art Deco masterpiece",
near Piccadilly Circus, this new (from Denmark)
steakhouse concept has struck most, if not quite all,
early-days reporters as "pricey, but worth it", and it
makes a notably "well-spaced" destination for
a business rendezvous; BYO, no corkage
on Sundays. / W1F 9ZN;
www.mashsteak.dk/restaurants/london; 11.30 pm,
Sun 11 pm; closed Sun L; set Sun L £43 (FP).*

Massimo
Corinthia Hotel SW1 **£81** ⑤⑤④
10 Northumberland Ave   7998 0555   2–3D
*Since Massimo left in mid-2012, this unbelievably
opulent chamber, near Embankment, has given the
impression of "needing to be kicked into action" –
offering cooking of no more than "trattoria"
standard, is this perhaps the Most-Expensive-Least-
Exploited dining room in town? / SW1A 2BD;
www.massimo-restaurant.co.uk; 10.45 pm; closed Sun;
SRA-50%.*

Masters Super Fish
SE1 **£29** ❷④⑤
191 Waterloo Rd   7928 6924   9–4A
*"All those cabbies can't be wrong!" –
you "consistently get the best fish 'n' chips", at this
"seriously unpromising-looking" chippy, near the Old
Vic. / SE1 8UX; 10.30 pm; closed Sun, Mon L; no Amex;
no booking Fri D.*

Matsuba TW9 **£43** ❷④④
10 Red Lion St   8605 3513   1–4A
*This stalwart family-run Japanese is one
of Richmond's foodie stand-outs – "gorgeous
sashimi" a particular highlight. / TW9 1RW;
10.30 pm; closed Sun.*

Matsuri SW1 **£80** ❸❷⑤
15 Bury St   7839 1101   3–3D
*"Very good teppanyaki" is the prime draw to this
long-established St James's basement, where there
is also a high-quality sushi bar – both inspire pretty
solid feedback, but little in the way of excitement.
/ SW1Y 6AL; www.matsuri-restaurant.co.uk; 10.30 pm,
Sun 10 pm.*

Maxela SW7 NEW **£45** ❶❸④
84 Old Brompton Rd   7589 5834   5–2B
*"An Italian addition to the steakhouses in London" –
a South Kensington newcomer that's "a butcher's
shop with kitchen attached" where "magical"
imported meat is used to "divine" effect. / SW7 3LQ;
www.maxela.co.uk; @MaxelaUk; 11 pm.*

Maxim W13 **£38** ❸④❸
153-155 Northfield Ave   8567 1719   1–3A
*Who cares if it looks "dated"?; this Chinese stalwart
is prized by Ealing and Northfields locals for its*

"consistently reliability". / W13 9QT; 11.30 pm, Sun 11 pm.

maze W1 **£80** ④④④
10-13 Grosvenor Sq 7107 0000 3–2A
Gordon Ramsay's large Mayfair tapas-operation inspires mixed feelings; fans find the "numerous courses, beautifully presented" to be "tirelessly exquisite" – critics say you pay "huge money" for a formula that's simply "tired". / W1K 6JP; www.gordonramsay.com/maze; 10.30 pm; set weekday L & pre-theatre £48 (FP).

maze Grill W1 **£76** ④④④
10-13 Grosvenor Sq 7495 2211 3–2A
Somewhat steadied of late, Gordon Ramsay's Mayfair steakhouse can make a handy business lunch rendezvous (and for Saturday family lunching too); non-meat dishes, however, "can leave a lot to be desired", contributing to an experience that's often "underwhelming" overall. / W1K 6JP; www.gordonramsay.com; 11 pm; no shorts; set weekday L & pre-theatre £46 (FP).

Mazi W8 **£55** ❸④④
12-14 Hillgate St 7229 3794 6–2B
"Exciting Greek food with a twist" inspires rave reviews from fans of this "very cramped" restaurant off Notting Hill Gate (on the site which, for many years, was Costa's Grill); the odd sceptic, though, does find the cooking rather "average". / W8 7SR; www.mazi.co.uk; closed Mon L & Tue L; set weekday L £31 (FP).

**The Meat & Wine Co
Westfield W12** **£54** ④❸④
Unit 1026 Ariel Way 8749 5914 7–1C
Prominently sited at the main entrance to Westfield, this large operation won better feedback this year "for great steaks and quality wines"; it's not inexpensive, so the "great £10 lunch special" is a particular bonus. / W12 7GA; www.themeatandwineco.com; 11.30 pm, Sun 10.30 pm.

Meat Mission N1 NEW **£32** ❷④❸
14-15 Hoxton Mkt 7739 8212 12–1B
"The ability to book a table and avoid ridiculous queues" – a major bonus at this latest "grungy and cool" 'meat' outlet, on the way in to Hoxton Square, serving "ace monkey fingers" and "brilliant-value" burgers. / N1 6HG; www.meatmission.com/; @MEATmission; midnight, sun 10 pm

MEATLiquor W1 **£35** ❷④❸
74 Welbeck St 7224 4239 3–1B
"Finger-lickin' good!"; this "sinful" yearling, near Oxford Street, doles out "greasy, unhealthy, and absolutely wonderful" burgers, in a "stripped-back and grungy" setting; queues are a "nightmare", however, and all that "striving to be edgy and urban" can be a "turn-off" for some reporters. / W1G 0BA; www.meatliquor.com; @MEATliquor; 11 pm, Fri-Sat 1 am, Sun 9.30 pm; closed Sun; no booking.

**MEATmarket
WC2** NEW **£30** ❸④④
Jubilee Market Hall, 1 Tavistock Ct 7836 2139 4–3D
Fans of the "dirty" burgers and "grungy" looks of this latest MEAT, overlooking Covent Garden's Jubilee Market, proclaim it "an excellent addition to the empire"; the group's "decidedly non-fancy style", however, does not please everyone – "why can't the MEAT franchise clean up a bit?" / WC2E 8BD; 11 pm, Sun 10 pm; no Amex.

Mediterraneo W11 **£55** ❸❸❸
37 Kensington Park Rd 7792 3131 6–1A
"Always buzzy and welcoming", this corner Italian is a long-standing feature of the heart of Notting Hill; "the food is good… but the tiramisù is great!" / W11 2EU; www.mediterraneo-restaurant.co.uk; 11.30 pm, Sun 10.30 pm; booking: max 10; set weekday L £33 (FP).

MEDLAR SW10 **£65** ❷❷④
438 King's Rd 7349 1900 5–3B
"Chez Bruce in Chelsea, marvellous!" – fans of this "clone" of the Wandsworth icon (from a team who worked there) hail its "superlative" food, and "knowledgeable" service; it's a "cramped" site, however, and sceptics feel there's "still a way to go to eclipse the south London favourite". / SW10 0LJ; @medlarchelsea; 10.30 pm.

**Megan's Delicatessen
SW6** **£43** ❸❸❷
571 Kings Rd 7371 7837 5–4A
A "busy and bustling" Parson's Green spot, serving "simple and satisfying" fare – in particular, an excellent brunch; "get a table in the garden". / SW6 2EB; www.megansrestaurant.com; @meganscafe; 10 pm; closed Sun D; no Amex.

Mela WC2 **£41** ❸④④
152-156 Shaftesbury Avenue 7836 8635 4–2B
This "unprepossessing" Theatreland Indian, by Cambridge Circus, is certainly "nothing special in terms of ambience", but it dishes up some "tasty" scoff, and they "have some good offers" too. / WC2H 8HL; www.melarestaurant.co.uk; 11.30 pm, Sun 10.30 pm.

Mele e Pere W1 **£49** ❸❸④
46 Brewer St 7096 2096 3–2D
"Loud" and "cavernous", this Soho Italian basement yearling inspires up-and-down reports – supporters praise its "great bar area" and its "interesting" and "authentic" cuisine, but there's also a school of thought that standards are "adequate" at best. / W1F 9TF; @meleepere; 11 pm; set pre theatre £32 (FP).

Mem & Laz N1   £29   ④❸❸
8 Theberton St   7704 9089   8–3D
A "loud" and "cosy" budget operation, in Islington,
serving an "eclectic menu, which ranges across the
Mediterranean and (especially for puds) the UK";
"it just keeps getting bigger, so the formula
must be working!" / N1 0QX; www.memlazuk.com;
11.30 pm, Fri & Sat midnight; no Amex.

Menier Chocolate
Factory SE1   £48   ⑤④❸
51-53 Southwark St   7234 9610   9–4B
This quirky adjunct to a Southwark theatre certainly
has a "great atmosphere" for a pre-performance
meal; "sadly, the food doesn't match up", but the
"very cheap" show-'n'-dinner deal can still be good
value. / SE1 1RU; www.menierchocolatefactory.com;
10.45 pm; closed Mon & Sun D.

The Mercer EC2   £56   ❸❸❸
34 Threadneedle St   7628 0001   9–2C
For a "reliably good-quality City lunch" –
or "breakfast par excellence" – this former banking
hall is a safe all-round performer, "conveniently
located" in the heart of the Square Mile. / EC2R 8AY;
www.themercer.co.uk; 9.30 pm; closed Sat & Sun.

Le Mercury N1   £29   ④④❸
140a Upper St   7354 4088   8–2D
A "no-frills" Islingon bistro "institution", renowned for
its "criminally cheap" prices – it's "always buzzing,
whenever you go", and the grub's very "reasonable",
considering; a recent nearby offshoot, Deuxième,
has made a "very good start" too. / N1 1QY;
www.lemercury.co.uk; 12.30 am, Sun 11 pm.

Meson don Felipe SE1 £39   ④④❸
53 The Cut   7928 3237   9–4A
A "fantastic buzz" evidences the ongoing appeal
of this "noisy" and "squashed" tapas veteran,
near the Old Vic; it offers "an authentic Spanish
evening far cheaper than Ryanair", even if the food
really is "nothing special" nowadays; and as for the
guitarist… / SE1 8LF; www.mesondonfelipe.com; 11 pm;
closed Sun; no Amex; no booking after 8 pm.

Mestizo NW1   £41   ④④❸
103 Hampstead Rd   7387 4064   8–4C
"A wide range of tequilas and cocktails" adds to the
appeal of this Mexican restaurant, near Warren
Street Tube; some reporters "remain a bit
undecided" on the food, but almost everyone says
it's at least "reasonable". / NW1 3EL;
www.mestizomx.com; @mestizomx; 11 pm, Fri-Sat
11.30 pm, Sun 10 pm.

Mews of Mayfair W1 £61   ④❸❷
10 Lancashire Ct, New Bond St   7518 9388
3–2B
"Well-crafted cocktails" add to the vibe of this
trendified venue "tucked-away" off Bond Street
(and it's "great if you can sit outdoors in the alley");
the food, though, is relatively "ordinary". / W1S 1EY;

www.mewsofmayfair.com; @mewsofmayfair; 10.45 pm;
closed Sun D; SRA-67%.

Meza SW17   £15   ❷❸❸
34 Trinity Rd   111299   10–2C
"Simple, spectacularly good, and almost obscenely
cheap"; no wonder this "tiny but perfectly formed"
Wandsworth Lebanese is "always full" – "you need
to book quite a few weeks in advance". / SW17 7RE.

(Carom at Meza)
Meza W1 [NEW]   £32   ❷❷❸
100 Wardour St   7314 4002   3–2D
"Light and Fresh" Indian street-food "bursting with
flavour and colour" defies the dreary track record
of this "cavernous" D&D venue in Soho, which was
formerly just called 'Meza'. / W1F 0TN;
www.meza-soho.co.uk; 11 pm; closed Sat L & Sun; set pre
theatre £19 (FP); SRA-61%.

Mezzanine
Royal National
Theatre SE1   £50   ④④④
Royal National Theatre, Belvedere Rd
7452 3600   2–3D
"Convenient, willing service, dull food" – that's still
the majority verdict on the RNT's "soulless" in-house
dining facility; it does have its fans, though.
/ SE1 9PX; www.nationaltheatre.org.uk;
@NationalTheatre; 11 pm; closed Mon, Tue L & Fri;
SRA-55%.

Michael Nadra   £53   ❶❸④
6-8 Elliott Rd, W4   8742 0766   7–2A
42 Gloucester Ave, NW1   7722 2800   8–2B
[NEW]
Michael Nadra is now in two places at once, having
faithfully cloned his "memorably delicious" cuisine,
as seen in Chiswick, to Camden Town; his new
opening (on the site of Sardo Canale, RIP),
is "a fantastic addition to NW1", even if – as in
W4 – the ambience "needs work".
/ www.restaurant-michaelnadra.co.uk; W4 10 pm, Fri-Sat
10.30 pm, NW1 10.30 pm, Sun 9 pm; W4 closed
Sun D.

Mien Tay   £30   ❷④④
180 Lavender Hill, SW11   7350 0721   10–1C
122 Kingsland Rd, E2   7729 3074   12–1B
These family-run Vietnamese greasy spoons "do the
obvious things very well", alongside "a long menu
of more interesting stuff" (quail, goat, eel, frogs'
legs…); the décor is "rather utilitarian", though,
and service can be "haphazard"; BYO. / 11 pm, Fri &
Sat 11.30 pm, Sun 10.30 pm; cash only.

Mildreds W1   £40   ❷④❸
45 Lexington St   7494 1634   3–2D
This "unfailing favourite of many years' standing" is,
for its many fans, the "best veggie around" –
that must be why its cramped Soho premises are
generally "incredibly noisy and busy". / W1F 9AN;
www.mildreds.co.uk; 11 pm; closed Sun; no Amex;
no booking.

Mill Lane Bistro NW6 £47 ❸❷❷
77 Mill Ln 7794 5577 1–1B
*"Simple, suitably French and consistently good" –
all reports agree that this "lovely" West Hampstead
spot "does what it says, and does it well".
/ NW6 1NB; www.milllanebistro.com; @millanebistro;
10 pm, Fri-Sat 10.30 pm, Sun 9 pm; closed
Mon & Sun D; no Amex.*

**Mimmo la Bufala
NW3 £50 ❹❸❹**
45a South End Rd 7435 7814 8–2B
*"Mimmo brings a real sense of fun" to this Italian
spot near Hampstead Heath BR, although it attracts
some flak for its "Hampstead prices"; it changed its
name last year from Fratelli la Bufala – a global
chain, whose branches are popping up all over
town. / NW3 2QB; www.mimmolabufala.co.uk; 11 pm;
no credit cards.*

**Min Jiang
The Royal Garden
Hotel W8 £73 ❷❷❶**
2-24 Kensington High St 7361 1988 5–1A
*Probably the best Chinese all-rounder in town;
this 8th-floor dining room, with "beautiful" views
over Kensington Gardens, has very few obvious flaws
– highlights include "excellent" Peking duck (pre-
order) and "superb" lunchtime dim sum too.
/ W8 4PT; www.minjiang.co.uk; 10 pm.*

Mint Leaf £54 ❷❸❸
Suffolk Pl, Haymarket, SW1 7930 9020 2–2C
Angel Ct, Lothbury, EC2 7600 0992 9–2C
*Surprisingly little commentary on this style-conscious
duo of designer-Indians, in a large basement
by Trafalgar Square, and near Bank… especially
as almost all the feedback says their "different"
dishes are "good" or better.
/ www.mintleafrestaurant.com; SW1 11 pm,
Sun 10.30 pm; EC2 10.30 pm; SW1 closed Sat & Sun L;
EC2 closed Sat & Sun; set weekday L £35 (FP).*

Miran Masala W14 £23 ❶❷❸
3 Hammersmith Rd 7602 4555 7–1D
*"The best Pakistani food ever" – that's fans claim
as they truffle out this basic café, opposite Olympia;
BYO – "you'll have trouble to spend as much
as £30 for two". / W14 8XJ; www.miranmasala.com;
11.30 pm.*

Mirch Masala £24 ❷❹❺
171-173 The Broadway, UB1 8867 9222 1–3A
1416 London Rd, SW16 8679 1828 10–2C
213 Upper Tooting Rd, SW17 8767 8638
10–2D
111-113 Commercial Rd, E1 7377 0155
12–2D
*"Fantastically-flavoured" Pakistani curries
at "amazingly low prices" make these "basic" and
"busy" canteens well worth seeking out; unlicensed,
but you can BYO. / www.mirchmasalarestaurant.co.uk;
midnight.*

Mishkin's WC2 £43 ❺❹❸
25 Catherine St 7240 2078 4–3D
*Russell Norman's "cool" Covent Garden diner
delights fans with its menu of "NYC-Jewish comfort
food", and some "gorgeous" cocktails too; for critics,
though, "it feels like an experience dreamt up by
a branding consultant", and an "ultimately
uninspiring" one at that. / WC2B 5JS;
www.mishkins.co.uk; 11.30 pm, 10.30 pm Sun.*

Miyama W1 £54 ❷❷❺
38 Clarges St 7499 2443 3–4B
*A stalwart Mayfair Japanese whose "sterile" dining
room is sometimes "so quiet, you feel you have
to whisper"… so the fact the place has lasted
so long must be testament to the splendid quality
of its sushi, and other fare! / W1J 7EN;
www.miyama-restaurant.co.uk; 10.15 pm; closed
Sat L & Sun.*

**The Modern Pantry
EC1 £54 ❹❹❹**
47-48 St Johns Sq 7553 9210 9–1A
*Anna Hansen's "inventive" fusion cuisine divides
views on this "noisy" Clerkenwell venture; fans say
it's "one of the best", offering food that's "never
dull", but critics find it just "peculiar" – "seemingly
interesting on paper, then failing to deliver"; perhaps
try brunch first! / EC1V 4JJ;
www.themodernpantry.co.uk; 10.30 pm, Sun 10 pm;
SRA-82%.*

Momo W1 £62 ❹❹❶
25 Heddon St 7434 4040 3–2C
*"A great place for a lively night out" – Mourad
Mazouz's "lovely" Mayfair Moroccan is an
energetically "characterful", if "noisy" operation,
offering "quite authentic" cuisine. / W1B 4BH;
www.momoresto.com; 11.30 pm, Sun 11 pm; closed
Sun L; set weekday L £38 (FP).*

Mon Plaisir WC2 £59 ❹❸❸
19-21 Monmouth St 7836 7243 4–2B
*This "old-fashioned bistro" – a "very French"
Theatreland stalwart for over half a century –
continues to dish up "classic bourgeois cooking"
in its "bustling" warren of dining rooms; "some of
the food falls a little short" nowadays, but the
famous pre-theatre menu offers the same great
value as ever. / WC2H 9DD; www.monplaisir.co.uk;
11.15 pm; closed Sun; set pre-theatre £29 (FP), set
weekday L £33 (FP).*

Mona Lisa SW10 £28 ❸❷❷
417 King's Rd 7376 5447 5–3B
*"Like being transported back to the '70s" –
this "crowded and buzzy" Italian greasy spoon,
at the far end of Chelsea, offers "really good value";
"everything is freshly cooked", including the top
"builders' breakfasts" (often enjoyed, with due irony
of course, by the local toffs). / SW10 0LR; 11 pm,
Sun 5.30 pm; closed Sun D; no Amex.*

**Monmouth Coffee
Company** £12 ❶❶❷
27 Monmouth St, WC2 7379 3516 4–2B
Arches Northside, Dockley Rd, SE16
7232 3010 9–4D
2 Park St, SE1 7940 9960 9–4C
"Still the best coffee in town"; all of the many
reports confirm that these cult cafés are
"top quality", and that the bread 'n' jam breakfasts
at the Borough market branch are "a London
experience" (and, fortunately, one that's "worth
queuing for" too). / www.monmouthcoffee.co.uk;
6 pm-6.30 pm; SE16 12 pm; closed Sun; SE16 open Sat
only; no Amex; no booking.

Monty's £32 ❸❸❸
692 Fulham Rd, SW6 7371 5971 10–1B
54 Northfield Ave, W13 8567 6281 1–2A
1 The Mall, W5 8567 8122 1–2A
"The go-to curry" for many an Ealing resident –
these stalwart subcontinentals (whose 'branches' are
not in fact under common ownership) are
"perennial" favourites locally, thanks to their
"consistently fresh-flavoured dishes" (which include
some Nepali specials). / 11 pm.

The Morgan Arms E3 £46 ❸❸❷
43 Morgan St 8980 6389 1–2D
"What a delight of a neighbourhood pub"; this Bow
boozer impresses all who comment on it with its
"much better than average" food, its "friendly"
service and its "pleasant" atmosphere. / E3 5AA;
www.morganarmsbo.com; @TheMorganArms; 10 pm,
Sun 9 pm.

Morgan M EC1 £66 ❷❸⑤
50 Long Ln 3589 4521 9–2B
"The transfer of Holloway's only top-class restaurant
to Smithfield does not seem to have gone well…";
Morgan Meunier still produces some "creative and
beautiful" cuisine, but the wow factor has decidedly
gone AWOL; can't help that the interior is "dreary"
beyond all reason. / EC1A 9EJ; www.morganm.com;
10.30 pm; closed Sun; set weekday L & pre-theatre
£44 (FP).

Morito EC1 £35 ❷❷❸
32 Exmouth Mkt 7278 7007 9–1A
"The more Spanish, more bar-like little brother
of the always excellent Moro";
it's "the hippest of places", offering "yummy and
unusual" tapas… in a "really cramped" setting.
/ EC1R 4QE; www.morito.co.uk; 11 pm, Sun 4 pm; closed
Sun D; no Amex; no booking for D.

Moro EC1 £52 ❶❷❷
34-36 Exmouth Mkt 7833 8336 9–1A
"There's nowhere quite like Moro!" – this "joyous"
Exmouth Market perennial thrives on its "exciting"
Moorish/Andalucian cuisine, "massive and unusual
wine list", and "surprisingly good value";
the acoustics, though, are "challenging". / EC1R 4QE;
www.moro.co.uk; 10.30 pm; closed Sun D.

**Mosaica
The Chocolate Factory
N22** £46 ④④❸
Unit C005, Clarendon Rd 8889 2400 1–1C
"Eclectic and visually interesting", the interior of this
Wood Green venture (entered through a semi-
abandoned factory) certainly creates quite
a "surprise to newbies"; food reports have been
a bit up-and-down of late, but fans
insist it "just keeps getting better". / N22 6XJ;
www.mosaicarestaurants.com; @MosaicaChocFac;
9.30 pm, Sat 10 pm; closed Sat L & Sun D.

Motcombs SW1 £60 ④❸❷
26 Motcomb St 7235 6382 5–1D
"A good local"; now occupying one of the
glitziest corners in town, this long-established wine
bar/restaurant seems an ever more "real"
reminiscence of the very 'English' Belgravia of old –
the slightly "bland" food is entirely in keeping.
/ SW1X 8JU; www.motcombs.co.uk; 11 pm; closed
Sun D.

Moti Mahal WC2 £57 ❷❷④
45 Gt Queen St 7240 9329 4–2D
"Should be better known"; this "surprisingly good"
Covent Garden outpost of a Delhi-based empire
offers "refined and robust" North Indian cuisine
with "big and imaginative flavours", albeit in a
setting critics can find "a little unatmospheric".
/ WC2B 5AA; www.motimahal-uk.com; 10.45 pm; closed
Sat L & Sun; set weekday L £38 (FP).

**Moxon's Fish Bar
SW12** NEW £27 ❶❸⑤
7 Westbury Pde 8675 2468 10–2C
"Local fishmonger Robin Moxon really knows his
cod from his pollock" – his "tiny" (8 seats) new
Clapham chippy serves "sensational", "Billingsgate-
fresh" fish, plus "whale-size" chips. / SW12 9DZ;
www.moxonsfishbar.com; @moxonsfish; 10 pm; closed
Mon, Tue L, Wed L, Thu L, Sat L & Sun.

Mr Chow SW1 £87 ④④④
151 Knightsbridge 7589 7347 5–1D
"The one and only!" – fans of this Knightsbridge
Chinese veteran claim it's still "going just as strong
as back in the '70s… only they've replaced the
Americans with Russians"; survey feedback
is limited, but the cooking generally gets the thumbs-
up. / SW1X 7PA; www.mrchow.com; 11.45 pm; closed
Mon L.

Mr Kong WC2 £31 ④❸④
21 Lisle St 7437 7341 4–3A
It looks "rather average", but this "bustling"
Chinatown café – with its "good-humoured" service
and "dependable" cooking – is the "go-to Chinese"
for many reporters; that said, while "the specials
deserve high marks", the standard fare is "just OK".
/ WC2H 7BA; www.mrkongrestaurant.com; 2.45 am,
Sun 1.45 am.

Mr Wing SW5 £46 ④④❷
242-244 Old Brompton Rd 7370 4450 5–2A
Surprisingly few reports of late on the Earl's Court fixture once regarded as west London's premiere party/romantic Chinese; it's still "worth a trip just for the jazz brunch and the fish tank", explains one long-term fan, but "has lost some of its charm since the old manager retired". / SW5 0DE; www.mrwing.com; @MrWingLondon; 11.30 pm.

Mugen EC4 £47 ❸❸④
26 King William St 7929 7879 9–3C
This "efficient" outfit, by London Bridge, offers a wide variety of dishes, and is "very popular with the local Japanese community"; "arrive early if you want to eat at the bar, as the best options run out". / EC4R 9AW; 10.30 pm; closed Sat & Sun.

Murano W1 £95 ❸❷❸
20-22 Queen St 7495 1127 3–3B
"Still packing a punch", Angela Hartnett's "magnificent modern Italian", in Mayfair, is pleasing a growing proportion of reporters, not least with its "elegant" cuisine; critics, though, still find the performance rather "safe". / W1J 5PP; www.muranolondon.com; @muranolondon; 11 pm; closed Sun; set weekday L £55 (FP).

My Old Place E1 £38 ❷⑤④
88-90 Middlesex St 7247 2200 9–2D
"The real thing, just like Sichuan!"; this "authentic" and "busy" East End spot offers "mouth-watering" dishes ("pig's intestine, BBQ rabbit, frogs' legs"), in "massive" portions, and "with no frills and no pretentions". / E1 7EZ; www.oldplace.co.uk; 11 pm; no Amex.

Naamyaa Café EC1 £37 ④④❸
407 St John St 3122 0988 8–3D
Alan Yau's "very metropolitan and hip" Islington café has often seemed "rather overhyped" in its first year of operation – it has its fans, but too many reporters find the realisation of its Thai street food menu "terribly average". / EC1V 4AB; www.naamyaa.com; @Naamyacafe; 10.30 pm.

Nando's £30 ④④④
Branches throughout London
For "a quick, cheap eat", many reporters are "embarrassed to admit they like" this flame-roasted, peri-peri chicken chain – "easy", "reasonably healthy" and "reliable"... and if you "arrive with two hungry kids in tow, you'll be sat down and eating in 10 minutes flat". / www.nandos.co.uk; 11.30 pm, Sun 10.30 pm; no Amex; no booking.

Napulé SW6 £39 ❸❸❸
585 Fulham Rd 7381 1122 5–4A
"A relaxed" and "happy" outpost of the Made In Italy franchise, near Fulham Broadway – it inspires modest survey commentary, but all positive. / SW6 5UA; 11.30 pm, Sun 10.30 pm; closed weekday L; no Amex.

The Narrow E14 £48 ⑤④④
44 Narrow St 7592 7950 11–1B
Gordon Ramsay's Limehouse gastroboozer – with its "merely average" food, and its "higher than expected" prices – offers "nothing special, apart from a great river view". / E14 8DP; www.gordonramsay.com; @thenarrow; 10.30 pm, Sun 10 pm.

**The National Dining Rooms
National Gallery
WC2** £52 ⑤⑤④
Sainsbury Wing, Trafalgar Sq 7747 2525 2–2C
"A window table to enjoy the view" (if you can nab one) is the most certain attraction at this large first-floor dining room – sometimes "atrocious" service contributes to a performance critics otherwise brand a "disgrace". / WC2N 5DN; www.thenationaldiningrooms.co.uk; 7 pm; Sat-Thu closed D, Fri open L & D; no Amex.

**National Gallery Café
National Gallery
WC2** £45 ❸④❸
East Wing, Trafalgar Sq 7747 5942 4–4B
"An ideal location for exhausted tourists!" – this "haven of relative tranquility", right on Trafalgar Square, offers "classy" British snacks which "mainly succeed"; a "great-value" breakfast is the top tip. / WC2N 5DN; www.thenationaldiningrooms.co.uk; 11 pm, Sun 6 pm; closed Sun D; no Amex.

Natural Kitchen £36 ❸④❸
77-78 Marylebone High St, W1 3012 2123 2–1A
7 Pepys St, EC3 7702 4038 9–3D **NEW**
15-17 New Street Sq, Fetter Ln, EC4 7353 5787 9–2A
"Interesting, and decently priced" – the food at this "healthy" deli-diner duo usually satisfies; the setting, though, "can be a little noisy". / EC4 9 pm; EC3 4 pm; W1 8 pm, Sat & Sun 7 pm; EC4 & EC3 closed Sat & Sun.

Nautilus NW6 £42 ❶❷⑤
27-29 Fortune Green Rd 7435 2532 1–1B
"Yes, it is decked out in Formica", and "rather drab" too, but this West Hampstead chippy is "consistently superb" – "I first went 31 years ago, and it's still as good as ever!" / NW6 1DU; 10 pm; closed Sun; no Amex.

Navarro's W1 £42 ❸④❸
67 Charlotte St 7637 7713 2–1C
A "beautiful and very Spanish" tiled interior sets the scene at this Fitzrovia tapas veteran, where "high standards are maintained", and at "affordable prices" too. / W1T 4PH; www.navarros.co.uk; @SpanishEchelon; 10 pm; closed Mon L & Sun.

Nazmins SW18 £37 ❸❸❸
396-398 Garratt Ln 8944 1463 10–2B
In Earlsfield, an "excellent neighbourhood Indian"

which, say local fans, "never fails to deliver on price, quality and service". / SW18 4HP; www.nazmins.com; @nazmins; 11.30 pm.

Needoo E1   **£26**   ❷④④
87 New Rd   7247 0648   12–2D
Don't be put off by the queue outside this East End Pakistani (or by the noise within) – this is an "outstanding" grill and curry house, where "you can eat like a king for £15 a head"; BYO. / E1 1HH; www.needoogrill.co.uk; 11.30 pm.

New China Boulevard
SW18   **£48**   ❸④❸
1 The Boulevard, Smugglers Way   8871 3881
10–2B
Surprisingly little feedback on this river-view Cantonese, in a Wandsworth development; such as it is, however, confirms good standards all-round, with "great Sunday dim sum" a highlight. / SW18 1DE; www.chinaboulevard.com; 11 pm.

New Mayflower W1   **£39**   ❷❷④
68-70 Shaftesbury Ave   7734 9207   4–3A
It may look "tired", but this stalwart Chinatown Cantonese delivers some "quite authentic" flavours ("by London standards"), and the service is "speedier and smilier than it use to be"; late, late opening too. / W1D 6LY; 4 am; D only; no Amex.

New Street Grill EC2   **£60**   ④❷❷
16 New St   3503 0785   9–2D
Near Liverpool Street, a well-spaced D&D group yearling, created from the conversion of a splendid old 18th-century warehouse; it attracted surprisingly little feedback for such a business-friendly venue, where "very good steaks" headline the "varied" menu. / EC2M 4TR.

New World W1   **£36**   ④④❸
1 Gerrard Pl   7434 2508   4–3A
"A real HK experience!"; children, especially, just "love the trolleys" which whizz the lunchtime dim sum around this cavernous Chinatown fixture; evenings? – "don't bother!" / W1D 5PA; www.newworldlondon.com; 11.30 pm, Sun 11 pm.

Newman Street
Tavern W1 NEW   **£40**   ④④❸
48 Newman St   3667 1445   3–1D
"Deceptively plain", carefully sourced British dishes often realised to a "really lovely" standard have won acclaim for this "light and bright" Marylebone pub-conversion; ratings are undercut, however, by those who (mystifyingly, in our view) say it's "massively over-hyped". / W1T 1QQ;
www.newmanstreettavern.co.uk; @NewmanStTavern; 10.30 pm; closed Sun D; SRA-69%.

1901
Andaz Hotel EC2   **£60**   ④④❸
40 Liverpool St   7618 7000   12–2B
It can seem a touch "cavernous" on entry, but this "spacious" and "beautiful" hotel dining room, by Liverpool Street, makes "a reliable place for a business breakfast, lunch or dinner", even if the food is "forgettable". / EC2M 7QN; www.andazdining.com; 10 pm; closed Sat L & Sun; booking: max 20.

Nizuni W1   **£46**   ❷❷④
22 Charlotte St   7580 7447   2–1C
"A quality Korean-hybrid spin on Japanese cuisine" is the stock-in-trade of this "excellent-value" Fitzrovia two-year-old, whose styling is akin to "a sort of upmarket Itsu". / W1T 2NB; www.nizuni.com; 10.45 pm; closed Sun L.

No 11 Pimlico Road
SW1 NEW   **£40**   ④⑤④
11 Pimlico Rd   7730 6784   5–2D
Oh dear; only as a bar can reporters see any real reason to seek out this "very noisy" new occupant of the attractive former Ebury (RIP) site, on the fringe of Belgravia; rarely is the food rated better than "undistinguished". / SW1W 8NA; www.no11pimlicoroad.co.uk; @no11pimlicoroad.

Nobu
Metropolitan Hotel
W1   **£87**   ❷④④
19 Old Park Ln   7447 4747   3–4A
London's original Nobu still cranks out "wow" Japanese-fusion fare at "crazy-expensive" prices, still has "perfunctory" service, and still drags in a fair few "movers 'n' shakers"; "it's definitely past its glory days", though, and the atmosphere is "not what it was". / W1K 1LB; www.noburestaurants.com; 10.15 pm, Fri & Sat 11 pm, Sun 10 pm.

Nobu Berkeley W1   **£87**   ❸④④
15 Berkeley St   7290 9222   3–3C
The younger, showier (and nowadays better-known) of the two London outposts of the glamorous Japanese-fusion brand; it still offers "superlative" sushi and "great people-watching", but critics find it "extremely overpriced" for what it is. / W1J 8DY; www.noburestaurants.com; 11 pm, Sun 9.45 pm; closed Sat L & Sun L.

Noor Jahan   **£38**   ❷❷❸
2a, Bina Gdns, SW5   7373 6522   5–2B
26 Sussex Pl, W2   7402 2332   6–1D
"A classic Indian in all respects"; these "consistently high-quality" curry houses – with their dingily comfortable decor and "obligatory gruff service" – are "as good as it gets for standard subcontinental fare". / 11.30 pm, Sun 10 pm.

Nopi W1   **£56**   ❷❷❸
21-22 Warwick St   7494 9584   3–2D
Thanks to Yottam Ottolenghi's "wonderfully

colourful, fresh and inventively-flavoured small plates", this "beautiful" Soho two-year-old has quickly become a major destination; sceptics, though, can find prices "ludicrous" – "just go to Ottolenghi instead!" / W1B 5NE; www.nopi-restaurant.com; 10.15 pm, Sun 4 pm; closed Sun D.

Nordic Bakery £15 ❸❹❸
14a, Golden Sq, W1   3230 1077   3–2D
37b, New Cavendish St, W1   7935 3590   2–1A
48 Dorset St, W1   7487 5877   2–1A
"Fabulous cinnamon buns", "delicious rye bread sarnies" and "fine coffee" – all highlights of the "Scandinavian delights" on offer at this refreshing small group. / Golden Square 8 pm, Sat 7 pm, Sun 7 pm; Cavendish Street & Dorset Street 6 pm.

The Norfolk Arms
WC1 £45 ❸❹❹
28 Leigh St   7388 3937   8–4C
"Tucked-away near King's Cross", a boozer known for its "fantastic" tapas – "not in London's top tier, but a very solid performer". / WC1H 9EP; www.norfolkarms.co.uk; 10.15 pm.

North China W3 £40 ❷❷❷
305 Uxbridge Rd   8992 9183   7–1A
"Standards never drop", at this "good and reliable, if slightly-old-fashioned Chinese" – still Acton's greatest contribution to London gastronomy. / W3 9QU; www.northchina.co.uk; 11 pm, Fri & Sat 11.30 pm.

The North London
Tavern NW6 £45 ❹❹❸
375 Kilburn High Rd   7625 6634   1–2B
Near the Tricycle Theatre, a "somewhat noisy" Kilburn boozer, praised for its "attractive" interior, and for food that's "better than average for a pub". / NW6 7QB; www.northlondontavern.co.uk; @NorthLondonTav; 10.30 pm, Sun 9.30 pm; set dinner £28 (FP).

North Sea Fish WC1 £37 ❸❸❹
7-8 Leigh St   7387 5892   8–4C
"Still one of the most reliable – and most popular – chippies in London"; "reassuringly", this Bloomsbury veteran "hasn't changed in years", so such aspects as the "hideous" lighting have to be deemed part of the 'charm'. / WC1H 9EW; www.northseafishrestaurant.co.uk; 11 pm; closed Sun; no Amex.

The Northall WC2 £58 ❸❷❷
10a, Northumberland Ave   7321 3100   2–3C
The "spacious" dining room of this new hotel, near Embankment, hasn't made many waves, but – with its "competent cooking, pleasing service and impressive décor" – it makes a "can't-go-wrong" business rendezvous. / WC2N 5AE; www.thenorthall.co.uk; 10.45 pm.

Northbank EC4 £54 ❸❹❸
1 Paul's Walk   7329 9299   9–3B
A "stunning" riverside location – with "big windows overlooking the Millenium Bridge and Tate" – is the highlight at this City stalwart; the food (Cornish fish the speciality) can be a "knockout", but some reporters are unimpressed, and service can be "slow". / EC4V 3QH; www.northbankrestaurant.co.uk; @NorthbankLondon; 10 pm; closed Sun.

The Northgate N1 £42 ❷❷❸
113 Southgate Rd   7359 7392   1–1C
"If this is your local, lucky you!" – this "friendly" gastropub dishes up "excellent, reasonably-priced" grub to De Beauvoir residents, and the occasional 'visitor' too. / N1 3JS; 10 pm; D only, ex Sun open L & D; no Amex.

Notes £18 ❹❷❷
31 St Martin's Ln, WC2   7240 0424   4–4C
36 Wellington St, WC2   7240 7899   4–3D
6a, Tileyard Studios, N7   7700 0710
8–2C **NEW**
These handy Covent Garden cafés are most notable for the wonderfully atmospheric outlet by the Coliseum – "one of the best coffee bars in town", offering "excellent" brews, and snacks which are rather incidental. / Wellington St Mon-Wed 10 pm, Thu-Fri 11 pm, Sun 6 pm; St Martin's Ln Mon-Wed 9 pm, Thu-Sat 10 pm, Sun 6 pm; N7 closed Sat-Sun.

Notting Hill Kitchen
W11 **NEW** £30 ❷❸❷
92 Kensington Park Rd   7313 9526   6–2B
A star Portuguese chef is now installed in the rambling townhouse site most recently occupied by the Notting Hill Brasserie (RIP); our early-days visit suggested it could become a top-grade all-rounder, but initial press reaction has been mixed. / W11 2PN; Rated on Editors' visit; www.nottinghillkitchen.co.uk; @NottingHillKTN; 10 pm; closed Mon & Tue.

Noura £56 ❸❹❸
16 Hobart Pl, SW1   7235 9444   2–4B
17 Hobart Pl, SW1   7235 9696   2–4B
2 William St, SW1   7235 5900   5–1D
16 Curzon St, W1   7495 1050   3–4B
Generally "reliable", these Mayfair and Knightsbridge outlets dish up "good Lebanese food" in a "French brasserie atmosphere". / www.noura.co.uk; 11.30 pm, Sun 10 pm; 16 Hobart Place closed Sun.

Novikov (Asian restaurant)
W1 £76 ❸❹❸
50A Berkeley St   7399 4330   3–3C
"You can easily spend over £100/head, without wine", in the "crushed" pan-Asian section of this blingy Russian-backed Mayfair yearling; it's "fun" though (in its way), the food can be "memorable", and the people-watching is arguably

"the best in town". / W1J 8HD;
www.novikovrestaurant.co.uk; 11.15 pm.

Novikov (Italian restaurant)
W1   **£78**   ⑤⑤④
50 Berkeley St   7399 4330   3–3C
"Does Novikov think he's still in Moscow?" – prices
in the "ridiculously pricey" Italian dining room of this
Eurotrash-central Mayfair scene are just "off the
clock"… especially when you bear in mind the
"pedestrian" cooking and "slipshod" service, and an
atmosphere reminiscent of "a Hilton
breakfast room". / W1J 8HD;
www.novikovrestaurant.co.uk; 11.30 pm; set weekday L
£44 (FP).

Nozomi SW3   **£87**   ④④⑤
14-15 Beauchamp Pl   7838 1500   5–1C
"The only place I've been with music so loud the
table actually vibrates!" – this pricey Japanese joint
presumably hits the spot for Knightsbridge
scenesters, but reporters tend to find it a "soulless"
place that "trades on its location". / SW3 1NQ;
www.nozomi.co.uk; 11.30 pm, Sun 10.30 pm; closed
Mon L.

Numero Uno SW11   **£53**   ❸②②
139 Northcote Rd   7978 5837   10–2C
"A rock-solid Italian", popular with the denizens
of the Nappy Valley – "it's the sort of local everyone
would like to have", which is presumably why it can
get rather "crowded". / SW11 6PX; 11.30 pm;
no Amex.

Nuovi Sapori SW6   **£43**   ❸0❸
295 New King's Rd   7736 3363   10–1B
"A warm welcome" from the friendly owner sets the
tone at this "top local Italian", down Fulham way,
which serves up some "great dishes". / SW6 4RE;
11 pm; closed Sun.

Nusa Kitchen   **£12**   ②③④
9 Old St, EC1   7253 3135   9–1B
2 Adam's Ct, EC2   7628 1149   9–2C
"The queue is the only downside"; these City and
Farringdon pit stops offer a "wonderful variety"
of "filling and delicious" soups, with "lots of
interesting garnishes". / www.nusakitchen.co.uk; 4 pm;
Sat & Sun; no booking.

The Oak   **£50**   ❷❸0
243 Goldhawk Rd, W12   8741 7700
7–1B 🆕
137 Westbourne Park Rd, W2   7221 3355
6–1B
With its superbly "cool vibe" and its "brilliant wood-
fired" pizzas this former boozer has made itself
quite a Notting Hill fixture – don't miss the "funky
and relaxed" bar upstairs; on an early visit, its airy
new Shepherd's Bush sibling seems a tad less "self-
conscious" (but all things are relative).

Obika   **£46**   ❸❸❸
11 Charlotte St, W1   7637 7153   2–1C 🆕
96 Draycott Ave, SW3   7581 5208   5–2C 🆕
35 Bank St, E14   7719 1532   11–1C 🆕
We're slightly mystified by the success of these
"gimmicky" Italian operations, where many dishes
are based on Mozzarella; they now have three
locations, though, including the former Chelsea site
of Ilia (RIP). / www.obika.co.uk; 10 pm - 11 pm;
E14 Closed Sun.

Oblix
The Shard SE1 🆕   **£57**   ④❸0
31 St Thomas St   7268 6700   9–4C
"Killer views" through "floor to ceiling windows"
make it a "phenomenal" experience to visit this
32nd-floor South Bank eyrie (and the cocktails
"get full marks too"); the cuisine so far has been
"solid, but unspectacular", but optimists
insist it "shows promise". / SE1 9RY;
www.oblixrestaurant.com.

Odette's NW1   **£58**   ❸④❸
130 Regent's Park Rd   7586 8569   8–3B
For a "high quality" neighbourhood experience,
north London has few restaurants to rival this
"intimate" Primrose Hill veteran, with Bryn
Williams's deft cuisine; there are quibbles though –
service can be "amateurish", it can seem
"expensive", and it's still not a patch on Odette's
in days of yore. / NW1 8XL;
www.odettesprimrosehill.com; Mon-Thu 10 pm, Fri-Sat
10.30 pm, Sun 9 pm; no Amex; set weekday L &
pre-theatre £37 (FP).

Okawari W5   **£37**   ❸④❸
13 Bond St   8566 0466   1–3A
"A reliably good no-frills Japanese restaurant";
this Ealing café offers sushi that's "always of good
quality", and "excellent-value" Bento boxes too.
/ W5 5AP; www.okawari.co.uk; 11.15 pm, Sun 10.45 pm.

The Old Brewery
SE10   **£48**   ④④❷
The Pepys Building, Old Royal Naval College
3327 1280   1–3D
The impressive garden is usually "packed with
tourists", but any visitor to this historic Greenwich
site will be pleased by the formidable range
of home-brews, plus the decent, if "basic", dishes
to go with 'em. / SE10 9LW;
www.oldbrewerygreenwich.com; @OldBrewery; 10 pm,
Fri & Sat 10.30 pm; D only; no Amex.

The Old Bull & Bush
NW3   **£41**   ④④④
North End Rd   8905 5456   8–1A
Opposite Golder's Hill Park, a famous pub that's
quite a local favourite; at busy times, however,
it's seriously "hit-and-miss". / NW3 7HE;
www.thebullandbush.co.uk; 9.30 pm, Sat 10 pm;
Sun 9 pm; set weekday L £27 (FP).

Old Parr's Head W14 £23 ❸❸④
120 Blythe Rd 7371 4561 7–1C
*In the backstreets of Olympia, a pretty
undistinguished-looking pub – its menu of Thai
staples, however, offers "good value". / W14 0HD;
www.theoldparrshead.co.uk; 10 pm, Sat & Sun 9.30 pm;
no Amex.*

**The Old White
Bear NW3 £48** ❸❷❸
Hampstead 7794 7719 8–1A
*"A better-than-average gastropub", in an off-the-
beaten-track Hampstead location; a "cosy" and
"genuine" sort of place, it offers a menu that's both
"interesting and varied". / NW3 1LJ;
www.theoldwhitebear.co.uk; @OldWhiteBearNW3;
10.30 pm, Sun 9.30 pm; closed Mon L.*

Oliveto SW1 £51 ❷④④
49 Elizabeth St 7730 0074 2–4A
*"Incredibly busy" (and "very noisy" too), this "bright"
and "child-friendly" Sardinian serves up some
"superb" pizza and pasta; only by Belgravia
standards, however, could this be called a "cheap 'n'
cheerful" option! / SW1 9PP; www.olivorestaurants.com;
11 pm, Sun 10.30 pm; booking: max 7 at D.*

Olivo SW1 £57 ❷❷④
21 Eccleston St 7730 2505 2–4B
*A minimalist Sardinian fixture, near Victoria, which
is "always packed with regulars", thanks to its
"interesting" wines and "consistently good"
cooking… "dreadful acoustics and dated décor"
notwithstanding. / SW1 9LX; www.olivorestaurants.com;
10.30 pm; closed Sat L & Sun L.*

Olivocarne SW1 NEW £52 ❸❷④
61 Elizabeth St 7730 7997 2–4A
*"Go for steak – the rest of the food
is unremarkable"; by the standards of Belgravia's
impressive Olivo group, this meat-focused Italian
is rather lacklustre – "lacking the vibe" of its
siblings, and a touch "greedily priced" too.
/ SW1W 9PP; www.olivorestaurants.com; 10.30 pm;
closed Sun D.*

Olivomare SW1 £63 ❶❸❸
10 Lower Belgrave St 7730 9022 2–4B
*Hidden-away in Belgravia, an "astoundingly
authentic Sardinian seafood restaurant" ("the menu
groans with crab, sea urchin and sumptuous whole
fish"); not everyone, though, loves the "distinctly
odd" '60s Sci-fi decor (even if it is "less noisy now
they've changed the ceiling"). / SW1W 0LJ;
www.olivorestaurants.com; 11 pm, Sun 10.30 pm;
booking: max 10.*

Olley's SE24 £39 ❷❸❸
65-69 Norwood Rd 8671 8259 10–2D
*"You can't fault Olley's!"; this "very friendly" and
"keenly priced" Brockwell Park institution is one
of south London's best chippies. / SE24 9AA;
www.olleys.info; 10 pm, Sun 9.30 pm; closed Mon;
no Amex; SRA-70%.*

Olympus Fish N3 £33 ❷❸④
140-144 Ballards Ln 8371 8666 1–1B
*"Anyone who thinks the Two Brothers is Finchley's
best chippy is missing out", say supporters of this
"very popular" and "very friendly" – and now
higher-rated – rival. / N3 2PA; 11 pm; closed Mon.*

**One Blenheim Terrace
NW8 £60** ⑤④④
1 Blenheim Ter 7372 1722 8–3A
*An ambitious St John's Wood venture that inspired
a fair volume of feedback in its first year
of operation; unfortunately, much of this suggests it's
a "pretentious" place, where the food is "not as
good as they think it is". / NW8 0EH;
www.oneblenheimterrace.co.uk; 10.30 pm, Sun 3 pm;
closed Mon.*

**One Canada Square
E14 NEW £58**
1 Canada Sq 7559 5199 11–1C
*Opening as this guide goes to press, a new business-
friendly brasserie at the foot of one of the Canary
Wharf towers; if the Martin brothers get this one
right, it could become quite a destination. / E14 5AB;
www.onecanadasquarerestaurant.com;
@OneCanadaSquare.*

101 Thai Kitchen W6 £32 ❷❸⑤
352 King St 8746 6888 7–2B
*"It's not the most elegant place", and "service isn't
great", but this Hammersmith café has a loyal fan
club, which insists that the Thai scoff it offers
is "superb". / W6 0RX; www.101thaikitchen.com;
10.30 pm, Fri & Sat 11 pm.*

**1 Lombard Street
EC3 £69** ④④❸
1 Lombard St 7929 6611 9–3C
*This "airy" and "impressive" former banking hall,
opposite the Royal Exchange, remains a key City
rendezvous – "an excellent all-round
breakfast or lunch option" even if prices do reflect
the location"; for gravitas to the max, head for the
'fine-dining' room at the rear. / EC3V 9AA;
www.1lombardstreet.com; 10 pm; closed Sat & Sun;
6 max in main restaurant.*

**One-O-One
Sheraton Park Tower
SW1 £94** ❶❸⑤
101 Knightsbridge 7290 7101 5–1D
*Is it "the best seafood in Europe"? Pascal Proyart
"has a Midas touch with fish", and his
"tremendously imaginative" cuisine inspires foodie
adulation for his Knightsbridge HQ; pity about the
room, though – "a weird space in a weird building",
and "so soulless". / SW1X 7RN;
www.oneoonerestaurant.com; @oneoone; 10 pm;
booking: max 6; set weekday L £50 (FP).*

FSA

The Only Running Footman W1 £49 ❸④❷
5 Charles St 7499 2988 3–3B
A handy option in pricey Mayfair – this "cheerful and stylish" gastropub offers affordable scoff, and inspires consistently upbeat feedback. / W1J 5DF; www.therunningfootmanmayfair.com; @theorfootman; 10 pm.

Opera Tavern WC2 £40 ❷❸❸
23 Catherine St 7836 3680 4–3D
"Iberico and foie-gras mini-burgers are a must", on a visit to this "cool" but "friendly" Covent Garden pub-conversion (a sibling to Salt Yard), whose "splendid" tapas and "interesting wines and sherries" are "great pre-theatre", but also make it a "top central rendezvous" at any time. / WC2B 5JS; www.operatavern.co.uk; @saltyardgroup; 11.15 pm; closed Sun D; SRA-63%.

The Orange SW1 £53 ❸❸❷
37 Pimlico Rd 7881 9844 5–2D
"Warm, wooden decor" contributes to the "always-great atmosphere" at this "airy" Pimlico gastropub; the food (majoring in "fantastic pizza") is "surprisingly good", and it comes at prices which are "reasonable... for the area". / SW1W 8NE; www.theorange.co.uk; 10 pm, Sun 9.30 pm; SRA-75%.

Orange Pekoe SW13 £26 ❷❷❷
3 White Hart Ln 8876 6070 10–1A
"Very popular, and it deserves it!"; this Barnes "gem" serves a wide range of "fragrant" teas and "delectable" baked goods, plus other "super", "light" dishes. / SW13 0PX; www.orangepekoeteas.com; 5 pm; L only.

The Orange Tree N20 £43 ④⑤❸
7 Totteridge Ln 8343 7031 1–1B
This large and inviting Totteridge gastropub is clearly a top destination in a thin area; reports are few, however, and remain mixed. / N20 8NX; www.theorangetreetotteridge.co.uk; @orangetreepub; 9.45 pm, Fri-Sat 10.30 pm, Sun 9 pm; set weekday L £28 (FP).

Orchard WC1 £41 ❸❸❸
11 Sicilian Ave 7831 2715 2–1D
This prettily-located Bloomsbury café, with nice al fresco tables, is a "welcoming" sort of place, offering "wonderfully seasonal" cuisine (and "great-looking cakes, too"); "your friends will never even notice it's vegetarian!" / WC1A 2QH.

Orpheus EC3 £41 ❷❷④
26 Savage Gdns 7481 1931 9–3D
"A little corner of Greece", unexpectedly nestling in a railway arch near Tower Hill; the style may evoke "a City lunch room of the 1960s", but the "diverse selection of top-quality fish" on offer is "a real treat". / EC3N 2AR; L only, closed Sat & Sun.

Orrery W1 £74 ❸❷❷
55 Marylebone High St 7616 8000 2–1A
"Beautiful and light" decor creates "a lovely space" (with "good views" over a churchyard) at this "peaceful", first-floor venture, in Marylebone; it's sometimes seen as the culinary flagship of the D&D group, and its "serious" Gallic cuisine rarely disappoints. / W1U 5RB; www.orreryrestaurant.co.uk; @orrery; 10.30 pm, Fri & Sat 11 pm; set weekday L £48 (FP); SRA-61%.

Orso WC2 £58 ④❸④
27 Wellington St 7240 5269 4–3D
Long-term fans still proclaim the "reliable" charms of this sometimes "noisy" Italian post-opera favourite, in a discreet Covent Garden basement; critics, though, find its "unchanging" style is becoming simply "jaded". / WC2E 7DB; www.orsorestaurant.co.uk; 11.30 pm; set pre theatre £38 (FP).

Oscar Charlotte Street Hotel W1 £62 ④④❷
15 Charlotte St 7806 2000 2–1C
A "nice buzz" pervades this large and attractively decorated Fitzrovia haunt, whose bar is very popular with local media types; other than the "excellent breakfast", though, "the food is just average". / W1T 1RJ; www.charlottestreethotel.com; 10.45 pm, Sun 10 pm.

Oslo Court NW8 £60 ❷❷❷
Charlbert St, off Prince Albert Rd 7722 8795 8–3A
What "a hoot"!; this '70s-timewarp, at the foot of a Regent's Park apartment block, offers "an experience like no other"; it's the "terrific, old-fashioned service", and loyal north London clientele which really makes the place, but the food – with the almost surreal pudding trolley as the "climax" – is "surprisingly good" too. / NW8 7EN; 11 pm; closed Sun; no jeans or trainers.

Osteria Antica Bologna SW11 £40 ❸❸❸
23 Northcote Rd 7978 4771 10–2C
"A great local restaurant", near Clapham Junction – this "pleasant" fixture offers "classic Italian dishes at reasonable prices". / SW11 1NG; www.osteria.co.uk; 10.30 pm, Sun 10 pm.

Osteria Basilico W11 £55 ❸❸❷
29 Kensington Park Rd 7727 9957 6–1A
"A lively, fun and tasty Notting Hill stalwart!" – the "really busy, noisy and cramped" ground floor (where you can people-watch) is always the "preferred option" at this long-established "neighbourhood" Italian. / W11 2EU; www.osteriabasilico.co.uk; 11.30 pm, Sun 10.15 pm; no booking, Sat L.

Greenberry Cafe

Gymkhana

HKK

Il ristorante - Bulgari Hotel

Osteria Dell'Angolo
SW1   **£55**   ❸❷④
47 Marsham St   3268 1077   2–4C
Most reports on this Westminster Italian are of a
"very slick" establishment, where "the high
standards of food and service continue"; shame,
though, that the ambience is so determinedly
"sterile". / SW1P 3DR; www.osteriadellangolo.co.uk;
10.30 pm; closed Sat L & Sun.

Osteria dell'Arancio
SW10   **£54**   ❸❸❸
383 King's Rd   7349 8111   5–3B
"An unusual, almost entirely Italian wine list,
with many lesser known options" helps win fans for
this "always-friendly" World's End fixture; the food
is "dependable" too, if at "prices that match the
neighbourhood". / SW10 0LP;
www.osteriadellarancio.co.uk; 10.30 pm, Sun 9.30 pm;
closed Mon L; set weekday L £33 (FP).

Ostuni NW6 NEW   **£42**
43-45 Lonsdale Rd   7624 8035   1–2B
Out in Queen's Park, an impressively-scaled Italian
newcomer, with an unusual regional specialisation
(Puglia); sadly, we didn't have have the opportunity
to visit before this guide went to press, but early
critical reaction has been very favourable.
/ NW6 6RA; www.ostuniristorante.co.uk.

Otto Pizza W2   **£29**   ❷❷❷
6 Chepstow Rd   7792 4088   6–1B
"Tasty pizzas with a twist" (and a cornmeal crust) –
secret of the success of this "fantastic pizzeria",
on the Bayswater/Notting Hill border. / W2 5BH;
www.ottopizza.com; @OttoPizzaUk; 11 pm, Sun 10 pm.

Otto's WC1   **£55**   ❷❷❸
182 Grays Inn Rd   7713 0107   2–1D
"A wonderful surprise in an unprepossessing part
of Bloomsbury"; the "very cordial" Otto's
"wonderfully eclectic" yearling has made quite a hit
with its "determinedly old-fashioned" Gallic style
(and its "astonishing" wine list). / WC1X 8EW;
www.ottos-restaurant.com; 10 pm; closed Sat L & Sun.

Ottolenghi   **£47**   ❶❷❸
13 Motcomb St, SW1   7823 2707   5–1D
63 Ledbury Rd, W11   7727 1121   6–1B
1 Holland St, W8   7937 0003   5–1A
287 Upper St, N1   7288 1454   8–2D
Yotam Ottolenghi's Zeitgeisty deli/diners bewitch
a large following with the "zingy and unusual"
Middle Eastern flavours of their "colourful" and
"alluring" dishes (not least "the best desserts");
"just a shame about the queues!"
/ www.ottolenghi.co.uk; N1 10.15 pm; W8 & W11 8 pm,
Sat 7 pm, Sun 6 pm; N1 closed Sun D; Holland
St takeaway only; W11 & SW1 no booking, N1 booking
for D only.

Outlaw's Seafood and Grill
The Capital Hotel
SW3   **£80**   ❷❶❸
22-24 Basil St   7589 5171   5–1D
The relaunch of this small dining room,
near Harrods, under acclaimed Cornwall-based chef
Nathan Outlaw, has made a relatively minor splash,
but its "astounding" fish dishes are "top notch" and
lunch in particular is "fantastic value"; for some
tastes, though, the interior is a tad "Spartan" and
"hotel-y". / SW3 1AT; www.capitalhotel.co.uk.

(Brasserie)
Oxo Tower SE1   **£70**   ⑤⑤④
Barge House St   7803 3888   9–3A
"An unrivalled position overlooking the Thames"
is "entirely negated" by the "indescribably
lacklustre" standards at this South Bank landmark,
where service is "shockingly poor", and the food
is "average at best"… and all at "crazy" prices!
/ SE1 9PH;
www.harveynichols.com/restaurants/oxo-tower-london;
11 pm, Sun 10 pm; set weekday L & pre-theatre
£52 (FP).

(Restaurant)
Oxo Tower SE1   **£84**   ⑤⑤④
Barge House St   7803 3888   9–3A
"Words cannot describe how bad this restaurant is!"
– "overpriced" and "pompous", this top-floor South
Bank fixture once again takes no end of flak from
reporters; perhaps not entirely coincidentally, it does
have a "great view". / SE1 9PH;
www.harveynichols.com/restaurants/; 11 pm, Sun 10 pm;
set weekday L £60 (FP).

The Oyster Shed EC4 **£46**   ④④❸
1 Angel Ln, Ground Floor   7256 3240   9–3C
River views, and a "lovely and light" (if Identikit)
interior, justify a trip to this large Thames-side
Geronimo Inn, which in particular is "a worthy, post-
work, destination"; its fish and seafood can
be "great", but "simple things can let it down".
/ EC4R 3AB; www.geronimo-inns.co.uk/theoystershed;
9.30 pm; closed Sat & Sun; SRA-60%.

Ozer W1   **£48**   ④❷④
5 Langham Pl   7323 0505   3–1C
Right by Broadcasting House, this "semi-formal"
operation (flagship of the Sofra chain) certainly
makes a handy standby for BBC luvvies, and its
"wide-ranging Turkish, Middle Eastern and North
African menu" offers "good value, especially given
the location". / W1B 3DG; www.sofra.co.uk; 11 pm.

Le P'tit Normand
SW18   **£41**   ❸❷❸
185 Merton Rd   8871 0233   10–2B
"It's nothing to look at from outside", but this age-
old Southfields bistro has been on good form of late
– "a great local", it feels "very French", and offers
"welcoming" service and "fine" cooking too.

/ SW18 5EF; www.leptitnormand.co.uk; 10 pm,
Sun 3 pm; closed Mon, Tue L, Wed L, Thu L & Sun D.

The Paddyfield SW12 **£28** ❷❷❸
4 Bedford Hill   8772 1145   10–2C
"Great Balham value!" – this BYO hole-in-the-wall,
serves "excellent Thai/Vietnamese food"
at "low prices". / SW12 9RG; www.thepaddyfield.co.uk;
11 pm; D only, closed Mon; no credit cards.

Il Pagliaccio SW6 **£38** ❸❷❸
182-184 Wandsworth Bridge Rd   7371 5253
10–1B
"Wonderful fresh pizza" is the culinary highlight
of a visit to this family-friendly Sands End institution,
to which the characterful service adds much charm.
/ SW6 2UF; www.paggs.co.uk; @pagliaccipizza; midnight;
no Amex.

Le Pain Quotidien **£37** ④④❸
Branches throughout London
For their "delicious breads" and
"the best Continental breakfast in town",
fans applaud these very "attractive" faux-rustic
cafés; "I sat next to Pippa Middleton, so it must be a
good place!" / www.painquotidien.com; most branches
close between 7 pm-10 pm; no booking at some
branches, especially at weekends.

The Painted Heron
SW10 **£56** ❶❷❸
112 Cheyne Walk   7351 5232   5–3B
"Simply stunning" dishes, "singing with spices",
seem to have survived the change of ownership
at this surprisingly "superb" Indian, hidden away off
Chelsea Embankment; the ambience remains a little
bit "staid". / SW10 0DJ; www.thepaintedheron.com;
Mon-Sat 10.30 pm, Sun 10 pm; no Amex.

The Palm SW1 **£83** ④⑤④
1 Pont St   7201 0710   5–1D
An "overpriced" Belgravia outpost of a
US steakhouse chain where the food is often
as "boring" as the interior, and service is sometimes
in the style of "Fawlty Towers"; otherwise, it's fine.
/ SW1X 9EJ; www.thepalm.com/london; 11 pm,
Sun 10 pm; Mon-Thu D only, Fri-Sun open L & D.

The Palmerston SE22 £50 ❸④④
91 Lordship Ln   8693 1629   1–4D
A "consumate gastropub" – this East Dulwich
boozer is "a modest and over-achieving" fixture,
where the food is "genuinely consistent". / SE22 8EP;
www.thepalmerston.net; @ThePalmerston; 10 pm,
Sun 9.30 pm; set weekday L £28 (FP).

Palmyra TW9 **£41** ❷❷④
277 Sandycombe Rd   8948 7019   1–3A
"Tucked-away" in Kew, a Lebanese restaurant that
reporters reckon "deserves to be busier"; the setting
can seem "rather soulless", but the food is "really
tasty". / TW9 3LU; www.palmyrarestaurant.co.uk;
11 pm; no Amex.

The Pantechnicon
SW1 **£56** ❸❸❷
10 Motcomb St   7730 6074   5–1D
In the heart of Belgravia, this "posh gastropub" has
an impressively clubby upstairs dining room;
fans find the food "a cut above", but there's also
a school of thought that it is "forgettable".
/ SW1X 8LA; www.thepantechnicon.com; Weekdays
10 pm, Sun 9.30 pm; SRA-75%.

Pantry SW18 **£30** ❸❷❸
342 Old York Rd   8871 0713   10–2B
A popular deli/café, in the villagey part
of Wandsworth; "delicious breakfasts, cooked
to order" are the daily highlight. / SW18 1SS;
www.thepantrylondon.com; @pantrycafe@pantrycafe;
L only; no Amex.

Pappa Ciccia **£39** ❸❸❸
105 Munster Rd, SW6   7384 1884   10–1B
41 Fulham High St, SW6   7736 0900   10–1B
These "typical neighbourhood Italians" are "lively
and fun", and very "dependable" – they serve pizza
and other fare (with "fab specials") in "generous
portions", or you can "just pop in for a great
cappuccino and cake"; BYO. / www.pappaciccia.com;
11 pm, Sat & Sun 11.30 pm; Munster Rd no credit
cards.

Paradise by Way of Kensal Green
W10 **£47** ❸❸❷
19 Kilburn Ln   8969 0098   1–2B
A hugely atmospheric and perennially hip Kensal
Green fixture – this rambling, shabby-chic tavern
numbers amongst its many attractions a "quirky"
rear dining room, offering very "acceptable"
cooking. / W10 4AE; www.theparadise.co.uk;
@weloveparadise; 10.30 pm, Fri & Sat 11 pm;
Sun 9 pm; closed weekday L; no Amex.

Paradise Hampstead
NW3 **£30** ❶❷❸
49 South End Rd   7794 6314   8–2A
A "first-class" South End Green favourite; one of
north London's top Indians, it offers "novel and
delicious" curries, and the staff are prepared
to "go the extra mile". / NW3 2QB;
www.paradisehampstead.co.uk; 10.45 pm.

El Parador NW1 **£35** ❷❷❷
245 Eversholt St   7387 2789   8–3C
"A little gem", in Camden Town, where the
"outstanding" tapas "never fail to please";
"the terrace garden at the back is particularly
wonderful on a warm summer's evening".
/ NW1 1BA; www.elparadorlondon.com; 11 pm, Fri-Sat
11.30 pm, Sun 9.30 pm; closed Sat L & Sun L; no Amex.

Paramount
Centre Point WC1 **£65** ④④❷
101-103 New Oxford St   7420 2900   4–1A
For "superb views" and a cocktail, the 32nd floor
of Centre Point has its plus points; given the

"mediocre" food and service, though, its attractions for a full-blown meal are more dubious. / WC1A 1DD; www.paramount.uk.net; 11 pm.

Patara £54 ❷❸❸
15 Greek St, W1 7437 1071 4–2A
7 Maddox St, W1 7499 6008 3–2C
181 Fulham Rd, SW3 7351 5692 5–2C
9 Beauchamp Pl, SW3 7581 8820 5–1C
"Authentic Thai food, elegantly presented in a calm and pleasant atmosphere" – that's the deal that's long made a big hit of this "reliable" chain; given the prices, though, critics can find the style a touch "formulaic". / www.pataralondon.com; 10.30 pm; Greek St closed Sun L.

Paternoster Chop House EC4 £55 ⑤⑤⑤
Warwick Ct, Paternoster Sq 7029 9400 9–2B
For a busy steakhouse near St Paul's, this D&D group operation inspires amazingly little survey feedback; fans say it's a "buzzy" place with "good meat" – critics that the acoustics are "dreadful" ("like sitting in a tin can"), service "in need of improvement", and the food "disappointing". / EC4M 7DX; www.paternosterchophouse.co.uk; 10.30 pm; closed Sat & Sun D; SRA-72%.

Patio W12 £35 ④❷❶
5 Goldhawk Rd 8743 5194 7–1C
"Like sitting in someone's home, and that's how you are treated" – the food may be "heavy", but the vodka is cheap, at this "very cheerful" Polish stalwart, right on Shepherd's Bush Green, which offers an "outstanding-value" package overall. / W12 8QQ; www.patiolondon.com; 11 pm, Sat & Sun 11.30 pm; closed Sat L & Sun L.

Pâtisserie Valerie £27 ⑤⑤⑤
Branches throughout London
"Terrible, now it's a chain" – too often the verdict on the venture capital-backed roll-out of these "once-delightful" and "quirky" pâtisseries, which have been "formularised" and "had all charm squeezed from them"; growth, however, continues unabated. / www.patisserie-valerie.co.uk; most branches close between 5 pm-8 pm; no booking except Old Compton St Sun-Thu.

Patogh W1 £24 ❷❷④
8 Crawford Pl 7262 4015 6–1D
"One of the best meals you can find for under a tenner!" – this "modest"-looking pit stop, just off the Edgware Road, offers "some of the tastiest Persian food in town", and at "dead cheap" prices too; BYO. / W1H 5NE; 11 pm; no credit cards.

Patty and Bun W1 NEW £21 ❶❸❸
54 James St 7487 3188 3–1A
"I waited over an hour in the cold for this burger… and boy was it worth it!"; this "cramped" new

burger joint, near Selfridges, inspires lots of reports, all saying pretty much the same – "apart from the perma-queue, it's brilliant"! / W1U 1HE; www.pattyandbun.co.uk; @pattyandbunjoe; 10.15 pm, Sun 9.15 pm; closed Mon; no Amex.

Paul £27 ④⑤④
115 Marylebone High St, W1 7224 5615 2–1A
29-30 Bedford St, WC2 7836 3304 4–3C
"Pricier than others, but worth it" – these outposts of France's biggest café/pâtisserie chain impress with their "wonderful, freshly-made sandwiches", "great salads" and "delicious" pastries and coffee; shame about the "slow" service though; (only the largest branches are listed). / www.paul-uk.com; most branches close between 7 pm-8.30 pm; no booking.

Pearl Liang W2 £43 ❷❸❸
8 Sheldon Sq 7289 7000 6–1C
This smart but "hard-to-find" basement, stuck out in Paddington Basin, is known as "one of London's better Chinese options" (with "incredible" dim sum a highlight); service can be "haphazard", though, and the occasional reporter does sense "slippage" of late. / W2 6EZ; www.pearlliang.co.uk; 11 pm.

The Peasant EC1 £46 ❸❷❸
240 St John St 7336 7726 8–3D
In the '90s, the "very pleasant and comfortable" upstairs dining room of this "lovely old gin palace", in Clerkenwell, was at the vanguard of London's gastropub revolution; it still serves "solidly good, sophisticated comfort food". / EC1V 4PH; www.thepeasant.co.uk; @ThePeasant; 10.45 pm, Sun 9.30 pm.

Pellicano SW3 £58 ④❶④
19-21 Elystan St 7589 3718 5–2C
A "reliable Italian stalwart", in a Chelsea backstreet, where the staff are "very friendly and welcoming"; the food "keeps up a good standard, even if it does vary a bit from visit to visit". / SW3 3NT; www.pellicanorestaurant.co.uk; 11 pm, Sun 9.30 pm; set weekday L £38 (FP).

E Pellicci E2 £21 ④❷❶
332 Bethnal Green Rd 7739 4873 12–1D
It's not just the famous (and listed) Art Deco interior that makes this East End café a "classic" – "everyone is made to feel welcome and invited to join in the banter!" / E2 0AG; 4.15 pm; L only, closed Sun; no credit cards.

Pentolina W14 £43 ❷❷❸
71 Blythe Rd 3010 0091 7–1D
"The locals can't believe how lucky they are!" – this "simple and elegant" Olympia Italian, has "charming owners", and serves "fabulous" dishes made from "quality ingredients". / W14 0HP; www.pentolinarestaurant.co.uk; 10 pm; closed Mon & Sun; no Amex.

The Pepper Tree SW4 £27 ❸❷④
19 Clapham Common S'side 7622 1758
10–2D
*"Tasty food at reasonable prices" – the mainstay
of the "utterly dependable" formula that's long
sustained this once-pioneering Thai canteen,
near Clapham Common tube; service "in double-
quick time" too. / SW4 7AB; www.thepeppertree.co.uk;
10.45 pm, Sun-Mon 10.15 pm; no Amex; no booking.*

Pescatori £55 ❸❸④
11 Dover St, W1 7493 2652 3–3C
57 Charlotte St, W1 7580 3289 2–1C
*For "well prepared fish in the Italian style",
many more mature reporters find these slightly
"old-fashioned" West End eateries a "very useful
and reasonably-priced" option; the occasional
'off' report, however, is not unknown.
/ www.pescatori.co.uk; 11 pm; closed Sat L & Sun.*

Petek N4 £31 ❸❷❷
94-96 Stroud Green Rd 7619 3933 8–1D
*"The jewel of Finsbury Park!", say local fans;
it "doesn't look much", but it's a "no-nonsense",
"colourful" and "busy" operation serving "generous
and juicy Turkish dishes". / N4 3EN;
www.petekrestaurant.co.uk; 11 pm.*

**Petersham Hotel
TW10** £65 ④❸❷
Nightingale Ln 8940 7471 1–4A
*"Wonderful views of the River Thames" add lustre
to the "old-fashioned" ("slightly stuffy") style of this
Richmond hotel dining room; most reporters find
a visit a "comforting" experience, though critics can
find the approach a touch "complacent".
/ TW10 6UZ; www.petershamhotel.co.uk;
@ThePetersham; 9.45 pm, Sun 8.45 pm.*

**Petersham Nurseries
TW10** £72 ❸❺❸
Church Ln, Off Petersham Rd 8940 5230
1–4A
*"Primitive, scruffy, but oh-so-trendy" –
this "ramshackle" venue (in the glasshouse of an
upmarket garden centre) makes a famously
"quirky" setting; since Skye Gyngell's departure,
however, its performance seems ever more
"smug and overpriced". / TW10 7AG;
www.petershamnurseries.com; L only, closed Mon.*

La Petite Maison W1 £84 ❷❸❷
54 Brook's Mews 7495 4774 3–2B
*"Outstanding zest and freshness" characterise the
"sensational" but simple-sounding sharing plates
on offer at casually glamorous Nice-comes-to-
Mayfair scene; the prices, though, are "crazy",
and the whole "noisy" vibe is a bit "oligarchic" for
some tastes. / W1K 4EG; www.lpmlondon.co.uk;
10.30 pm, Sun 9 pm.*

Pétrus SW1 £92 ❷⓿❸
1 Kinnerton St 7592 1609 5–1D
*"Superb" ("if not especially innovative") food –
"especially desserts" – figures in almost all reports
on this "very professionally-run" Ramsay-outpost,
in Belgravia, and the wines are "splendid" too;
if there is a criticism, it is that the rather beige
dining room "lacks soul". / SW1X 8EA;
www.gordonramsay.com/petrus; 10.30 pm; closed Sun;
no trainers; set weekday L £53 (FP).*

Pham Sushi EC1 £37 ❶④⑤
159 Whitecross St 7251 6336 12–2A
*"The most amazing fresh sushi and sashimi" justify
the trip to this "very basic" diner, north of the
Barbican, and it's "so incredibly cheap" – "the dishes
are as good as Zuma or Nobu, but a third of the
price!" / EC1Y 8JL; www.phamsushi.co.uk; 10 pm; closed
Sat L & Sun.*

Pho £36 ❷❷❷
163-165 Wardour St, W1 7434 3938 3–1D
3 Great Titchfield St, W1 7436 0111 3–1C
Westfield, Ariel Way, W12 07824 662320
7–1C
48 Brushfield St, E1 7377 6436 12–2B
86 St John St, EC1 7253 7624 9–1A
*"A brilliant homage to Vietnamese street-food";
you "can't fault" this growing chain of "vibrant" pit
stops, where "irresistible, yummy and filling noodle
soups" are "efficiently served" in a "fun"
environment, at "honest prices". / www.phocafe.co.uk;
EC1 10 pm, Fri & Sat 10.30 pm; W1 10.30 pm;
W12 9 pm, Sat 7 pm, Sun 6 pm; EC1 closed
Sat L & Sun; W1 closed Sun; no Amex; no booking.*

Phoenix Palace NW1 £51 ❸④④
5-9 Glentworth St 7486 3515 2–1A
*"You could be in Hong Kong", at this glitzy-but-
gloomy venture, near Baker Street tube, which
is "very popular with the Chinese community",
thanks to its "un-Anglicised" cooking and its
"excellent dim sum"; in recent years, however,
"standards have slipped" a bit. / NW1 5PG;
www.phoenixpalace.co.uk; 11.15 pm, Sun 10.30 pm.*

Piccolino £51 ④❸④
21 Heddon St, W1 7287 4029 3–2C
11 Exchange Sq, EC2 7375 2568 12–2B
*"A friendly and flexible chain, welcoming to all
generations" – the general view on this "safe" Italian
group. / www.piccolinorestaurants.co.uk; 11 pm,
Sun 10 pm; EC2 closed Sat & Sun.*

Picture W1 **NEW** £32 ❷❷④
110 Great Portland St 7637 7892 2–1B
*Very handy for Broadcasting House (and, at
lunchtime, seemingly entirely full of BBC staff),
this cacophonous new restaurant offers enjoyable
small plates at reasonable prices. / W1W 6PQ; Rated
on Editors' visit; www.picturerestaurant.co.uk.*

PIED À TERRE W1   £104   **❸❹❸**
34 Charlotte St   7636 1178   2–1C
"An outstanding restaurant, with a team in full
song!"; David Moore's "sophisticated" Fitzrovia
fixture offers not just Marcus Eaves's "exquisite"
cuisine, but also a "brilliant" wine list (including
some "great global discoveries"), and notably
"discreet" and "friendly" service too. / W1T 2NH;
www.pied-a-terre.co.uk; 10.45 pm; closed Sat L & Sun;
booking: max 7; set weekday L £68 (FP).

Pig & Butcher N1 NEW £48   **❷❷❷**
80 Liverpool Rd   7226 8304   8–3D
"A really great addition to Islington's gastropubs";
this "beautiful" hostelry is a real pub (you can
just drink), with "a huge list of ales", but also turns
out "fantastic", "solid" staples – meat dishes
in particular are "peerless". / N1 0QD;
www.thepigandbutcher.co.uk; @pigandbutcher;
10.30 pm; closed Mon L, Tue L & Wed L.

The Pig's Ear SW3   £50   **❹❹❸**
35 Old Church St   7352 2908   5–3C
An Art Nouveau-themed Chelsea boozer, featuring
a "delightful, old-fashioned upstairs dining room";
fans still laud its "honest British fare", but a
worrying number of reports of late complain of food
of "poor quality". / SW3 5BS; www.thepigsear.info;
10 pm, Sun 9 pm.

Pilpel   £9   **❷❷❹**
38 Brushfield Street, London, E1   7247 0146
12–2B
Old Spitalfields Mkt, E1   7375 2282   12–2B
146 Fleet St, EC4   7583 2030   9–2A
Paternoster Sq, EC4   7248 9281   9–2B
"The best falafel this side of Tel Aviv" and "great
service" too! – expect "massive" (but "fast-moving")
queues if you make a lunchtime visit to a branch
of this "slick" small chain. / www.pilpel.co.uk.

ping pong   £32   **❹❷❸**
10 Paddington St, W1   7009 9600   2–1A
29a James St, W1   7034 3100   3–1A
45 Gt Marlborough St, W1   7851 6969   3–2C
48 Eastcastle St, W1   7079 0550   3–1C
74-76 Westbourne Grove, W2   7313 9832
6–1B
Southbank Centre, SE1   7960 4160   2–3D
St Katharine Docks, E1   7680 7850   9–3D
Bow Bells Hs, 1 Bread St, EC4   7651 0880
9–2B
"Fab, fresh fare and cocktails that really hit the
spot" – many reporters like these stylish and "laid-
back" dim sum hang-outs; service is "speedy" too
(and "they deal effortlessly with young kids").
/ www.pingpongdimsum.com; @pingpongdimsum;
10 pm-11.30 pm; EC2 & EC4 closed Sat & Sun; booking:
min 8.

El Pirata W1   £38   **❹❷❶**
5-6 Down St   7491 3810   3–4B
"A really lively tapas bar in the depths of Mayfair" –
a "fun" little dive, and one that's "surprisingly good
value" for the area too. / W1J 7AQ; www.elpirata.co.uk;
@elpirataw1; 11.30 pm; closed Sat L & Sun.

**El Pirata de Tapas
W2**   £41   **❸❸❷**
115 Westbourne Grove   7727 5000   6–1B
A "lovely" Bayswater bar; with its "finely flavoured"
tapas and its "consistent high standards" all-round,
it inspires only positive reports. / W2 4UP;
www.elpiratadetapas.co.uk; @Pirate_de_Tapas; 11 pm,
Sun 10 pm.

Pissarro W4   £49   **❹❹❶**
Corney Reach Way   8994 3111   10–1A
"Make sure you ask for a conservatory table",
at this "lovely" Chiswick location, which has
a "beautiful, peaceful setting, right on the Thames"
– "a wonderful place for a family weekend lunch",
in particular. / W4 2UG; www.pissarro.co.uk;
@pissarroW4; 9.45 pm; set weekday L £32 (FP).

Pitt Cue Co W1   £25   **❶❸❸**
1 Newburgh St   no tel   3–2D
"I actually enjoyed the queuing!" – such are the
"happy" vibes at this tiny and "crowded" Carnaby
Street BBQ – a "meaty-licious" heaven, where the
pulled pork in particular is a "must-try". / W1F 7RB;
www.pittcue.co.uk; SRA-57%.

Pizarro SE1   £47   **❷❷❶**
194 Bermondsey St   7407 7339   9–4D
"Wonderful on all levels" – José P's Bermondsey
"gem" is a "passionate" undertaking, serving tapas
"almost as good as in Barcelona", and "interesting"
wines too; unsurprisingly, it "can get very busy".
/ SE1 3TQ; www.josepizarro.com/restaurants/pizarro;
@Jose_Pizarro; 11 pm, Sun 10 pm.

Pizza East   £47   **❷❸❶**
310 Portobello Rd, W10   8969 4500   6–1A
79 Highgate Rd, NW5   3310 2000   8–1B
56 Shoreditch High St, E1   7729 1888   12–1B
"Skinny jeans and face fur are 'de rigueur'" at these
"warehousey" hang-outs (which now include
a "painfully trendy" Kentish Town branch);
its "reinvention of pizza", though, can come as a
"genuine surprise" – "spot on". / www.pizzaeast.com;
@PizzaEast; E1 Sun-Wed 11 pm, Thu 12 am, Fri-Sat
1am; W10 Mon-Thu 11.30 pm, Fri-Sat 12 am,
Sun 10.30 pm.

Pizza Metro SW11   £45   ❷④④
64 Battersea Rise   7228 3812   10–2C
*"As good as Naples' best!" – these "noisy" and
"friendly" haunts (London pioneers of pizza-by-the-
metre) are still sterling members of the capital's
pizza 'hall of fame'; Notting Hill is just as highly-
rated nowadays as the Battersea original.
/ SW11 1EQ; www.pizzametropizza.com; 11 pm; closed
weekday L; no Amex.*

Pizza Pilgrims W1 NEW £23
11-12 Dean St   667258   4–2A
*A former pizza pop-up, now with its own proper
base, in the heart of Soho; early-days press reviews
have been encouraging. / W1D 3RP; @pizzapilgrims;
10.30 pm; closed Sun; no Amex.*

Ciro's (Pizza Pomodoro)
SW3   £48   ❸④❷
51 Beauchamp Pl   7589 1278   5–1C
*An age-old Euro-hang-out, in a Knightsbridge
basement, where the special attraction is the "great
bar atmosphere" later on in the evening, with live
music; OK pizza too. / SW3 1NY;
www.pomodoro.co.uk; 1 am; D only.*

PizzaExpress   £38   ④④❸
Branches throughout London
*"A bigger, more intelligent menu" (including the
"lightweight pizzas with a hole in the middle"),
plus constant reinvention of the "bright" decor
maintain the benchmark status of this ever-faithful
stand-by, not least as "a guaranteed success with
kids". / www.pizzaexpress.co.uk; 11.30 pm-midnight;
most City branches closed all or part of weekend;
no booking at most branches.*

Pizzeria Oregano N1   £40   ❷❷❸
18-19 St Albans Pl   7288 1123   8–3D
*"Tucked-away down a side-alley off Islington's Upper
Street", this family-run café knocks out "superb,
crispy pizzas at great prices", plus other "delicious"
pasta dishes and salads. / N1 0NX; 11 pm,
Fri 11.30 pm, Sun 10.30 pm; closed weekday L.*

Pizzeria Pappagone
N4   £37   ❸❷❷
131 Stroud Green Rd   7263 2114   8–1D
*"They love to sing Happy Birthday", at this
"extremely noisy" Italian, in Stroud Green; a "fun"
place, offering very dependable pizza and pasta,
and which is "guaranteed always to be full".
/ N4 3PX; www.pizzeriapappagone.co.uk; midnight.*

Pizzeria Rustica TW9 £38   ❸❸④
32 The Quadrant   8332 6262   1–4A
*"Delicious thin-crust pizza" wins a fair-sized fan
club for this "cramped" Richmond Italian –
a notably "dependable" destination. / TW9 1DN;
www.pizzeriarustica.co.uk; 11 pm, Fri & Sat 11.30 pm,
Sun 10.30 pm.*

PJ's Bar and Grill
SW3   £53   ④❷❷
52 Fulham Rd   7581 0025   5–2C
*"Busy" and "buzzing" at all hours, a "festive"
Chelsea bar/restaurant that's most tipped as a
"brunch classic". / SW3 6HH; www.pjsbarandgrill.co.uk;
10.30 pm, Sun 10 pm.*

Plane Food TW6   £53   ④④④
Heathrow Airport, Terminal 5   8897 4545
1–3A
*"Decent airport food at last!"; Gordon Ramsay's
airside brasserie provides a "bit of peace and quiet"
within T5, and, by transport catering standards,
offers "good value", especially for breakfast.
/ TW6 2GA; www.gordonramsay.com; 9.30 pm.*

Plateau E14   £58   ⑤④⑤
Canada Pl   7715 7100   11–1C
*This "staid" Canary Wharf restaurant, part of the
D&D group, gives every impression of depending for
business on its "convenient" location and its
"fabulous" outlook – otherwise, it can seem
"insultingly average in every respect". / E14 5ER;
www.plateau-restaurant.co.uk; 10.15 pm; closed
Sat L & Sun; SRA-63%.*

Plum + Spilt Milk
Great Northern Hotel
N1 NEW   £45   ❸❸❷
King's Cross   3388 0800   8–3C
*This "nicely styled" new King's Cross dining room
makes a surprisingly funky 'find' for a railway station
hotel; in the early days, though, reports on the
(simple) food have spanned the whole range from
"excellent" to "below par". / N1C 4TB;
www.gnhlondon.com; @PlumSpiltMilk; 11 pm,
Sun 10 pm.*

Plum Valley W1   £45   ❷❸❷
20 Gerrard St   7494 4366   4–3A
*A "classy" Chinatown joint, in contemporary style,
where the cuisine is "truly different" from the local
mainstream, and often "very delicious" too.
/ W1D 6JQ; 11.30 pm.*

Pod   £14   ❸❸④
124 High Holborn, WC1   3174 0541   2–1D
Tooley St, SE1   3174 0374   9–4D
10 St Martin's Le Grand, EC1   3174 0399
9–2B
162-163 London Wall, EC2   7256 5506   9–2C
25 Exchange Sq, EC2   3174 0290   12–2B
Devonshire Sq, EC2   3174 0108   9–2D
5 Lloyds Ave, EC3   3174 0038   9–3D
1 Printer St, EC4   3174 0228   9–2A
75 King William St, EC4   7283 7460   9–3C
*"A revelation"; fans of these health-conscious pit
stops say their "homestyle and very wholesome"
scoff (wraps, salads, soups, small plates)
is "the best fast food on the high street".
/ www.podfood.co.uk; 3 pm-4 pm, WC2 7 pm, Sat 8 pm,*

Sun 5 pm; branches closed Sat & Sun, St Martin's & City Rd closed Sun.

Poissonnerie
de l'Avenue SW3 £69 ②②④
82 Sloane Ave 7589 2457 5–2C
This "old-fashioned" Brompton Cross veteran is a fixed point in a changing world; it generally appeals to a more mature crowd, who know that its fish and seafood are "dependably first-rate". / SW3 3DZ; www.poissonneriedelavenue.co.uk; 11.30 pm, Sun 10,30 pm.

(Ognisko Polskie)
The Polish Club SW7 £54 ④④②
55 Prince's Gate, Exhibition Rd 7589 4635 5–1C
For time-warp grandeur at reasonable cost, few venues rival this faded émigrés' club, in South Kensington; its dependable Polish fodder is best enjoyed in summer on the "lovely balcony". / SW7 2PN; www.ognisko.com; 11 pm; no trainers; set weekday L & Sun L £27 (FP).

POLLEN STREET
SOCIAL W1 £81 ②②③
8-10 Pollen St 7290 7600 3–2C
Jason Atherton's "genuinely exciting" cuisine – "fresh in every sense" – again inspires adulation for his Mayfair two-year-old (where the "amazing dessert bar" is a "highlight"); though, and some reporters can find dishes "over-engineered". / W1S 1NQ; www.pollenstreetsocial.com; 10.45 pm; closed Sun; set weekday L £55 (FP).

Polpo £36 ④③❶
41 Beak St, W1 7734 4479 3–2D
6 Maiden Ln, WC2 7836 8448 4–3D
2-3 Cowcross St, EC1 7250 0034 9–1A
A "cool NYC vibe" that's "easy, welcoming and democratic" – plus loads of savvy marketing – has raised Russell Norman's "cramped" Venetian-style tapas bars to cult status; "queueing is annoying", though, and the quality of the dishes "does vary". / www.polpo.co.uk; W1 & EC1 11 pm; WC2 11 pm, Sun 10.30 pm; W1 & EC1 closed D Sun.

Le Pont de la Tour
SE1 £72 ④④②
36d Shad Thames 7403 8403 9–4D
"Tower Bridge views to die for" (especially from outside tables) are the undoubted plus of a meal at this stalwart D&D group South Banker – a hotspot for business or romance; opinions on the cuisine, however, range all the way from "brilliant" to "disappointing", though the wine list is "second to none". / SE1 2YE; www.lepontdelatour.co.uk; @lepontdelatour; 11 pm, Sun 10 pm; no trainers; set weekday L £52 (FP); SRA-58%.

Popeseye £51 ④④⑤
108 Blythe Rd, W14 7610 4578 7–1C
277 Upper Richmond Rd, SW15 8788 7733 10–2A
These "basic" west London dives have long had a name for "steaks as good as you'll find", and "good-value" wines to go with 'em too; recent times, however, have seen a number of "disappointing" reports from former fans. / www.popeseye.com; 10.30 pm; D only, closed Sun; no credit cards.

La Porchetta Pizzeria £33 ❸❸❸
33 Boswell St, WC1 7242 2434 2–1D
141-142 Upper St, N1 7288 2488 8–2D
147 Stroud Green Rd, N4 7281 2892 8–1D
74-77 Chalk Farm Rd, NW1 7267 6822 8–2B
84-86 Rosebery Ave, EC1 7837 6060 9–1A
"Like a little outpost of chaotic Italian life" – these noisy, and "authentic" north London stalwarts are long on "jolly" atmosphere and "fast, family-friendly service"; they dish up "satisfyingly big" pizza plus other "decent and cheapish fare". / www.laporchetta.net; last orders varies by branch; WC1 closed Sat L & Sun; N1,EC1 & NW1 closed Mon-Fri L; N4 closed weekday L; no Amex.

Portal EC1 £56 ④④❸
88 St John St 7253 6950 9–1B
A potentially impressive Portuguese, in Clerkenwell, with a "light-filled conservatory" and an "interesting" menu (and wine list); service can be too "laissez-faire", however, and those who claim the food is "nothing special" were more in evidence this year. / EC1M 4EH; www.portalrestaurant.com; dine@portal; 10.15 pm; closed Sat L & Sun.

La Porte des Indes
W1 £63 ❸②②
32 Bryanston St 7224 0055 2–2A
"Wow!"; this "enormous" and lavish basement, near Marble Arch, certainly impresses first-timers, and its (French-colonial) "Indian food with a twist" has been on "excellent" form of late; Sunday brunch, in particular, is "well worth booking for". / W1H 7EG; www.laportedesindes.com; 11.30 pm, Sun 10.30 pm.

Porters English
Restaurant WC2 £44 ④❸❸
17 Henrietta St 7836 6466 4–3C
Amidst all the 'boutique-ification' of Covent Garden, Lord Bradford's English-themed diner seems ever-more retro nowadays (even despite its recent more modern refurb); critics find the food "stodgy"… but watch out for "excellent" pies, and "good-value special offers". / WC2E 8QH; www.porters.uk.com; 11.30 pm, Sun 10.30 pm; no Amex.

Il Portico W8   £49   ④❸❸
277 Kensington High St   7602 6262   7–1D
*"A large and loyal clientele" patronises this
"traditional" Kensington trattoria – "the very
epitome of an Italian family place"; doubters,
though, are mystified by its popularity – "clearly
there's a lot of people out there nostalgic for the
'60s!" / W8 6NA; www.ilportico.co.uk; 11 pm;
closed Sun.*

**Portobello
Ristorante W11**   £49   ❷❷❷
7 Ladbroke Rd   7221 1373   6–2B
*"Not just great for pizza!" (by the metre) –
this "friendly" spot, just off Notting Hill Gate, is also
of note for its "really good Italian home cooking"
and "charming" service; "sit on the patio
in summer". / W11 3PA; www.portobellolondon.co.uk;
10.30 pm, Sun 10.15 pm.*

**The Portrait
National Portrait
Gallery WC2**   £51   ④④❶
St Martin's Pl   7312 2490   4–4B
*"Everything is secondary" to the "terrific" views
("over the Trafalgar Square roofscape") of this
mega-central top-floor dining room; perhaps new
caterers Company of Cooks will be able to make
it a gastronomic destination in its own right.
/ WC2H 0HE; www.searcys.co.uk; Thu-Fri 8.30 pm;
Sat-Sun closed L, Sun-Wed closed D.*

Potli W6   £37   ❷④④
319-321 King St   7741 4328   7–2B
*It may look "shabby" from the outside, but this
"hospitable" Hammersmith Indian serves up some
"exciting and well-spiced" dishes (including
a "particularly delicious range of starters").
/ W6 9NH; www.potli.co.uk; 10.30 pm, Fri-Sat 11.30 pm.*

La Poule au Pot SW1   £59   ❸❸❶
231 Ebury St   7730 7763   5–2D
*"Home of Gallic cuisine, and amour" – for over half
a century, this "rustic" charmer (with its candle-light
and "dark nooks"), on a Pimlico corner, has been
one of London's top choices for romance; on the
food front, the prix-fixe lunch offers particularly
"amazing" value. / SW1W 8UT; www.pouleaupot.co.uk;
11 pm, Sun 10 pm; set weekday L £40 (FP).*

**Prawn On The Lawn
N1** [NEW]   £27
220 St Paul's Rd   3302 8668   8–2D
*Sadly, we didn't get the chance to visit this new
Canonbury seafood parlour before this guide went
to press; the media reception, however, has been
enthusiastic. / N1 2LY; prawnonthelawn.com.*

Pret A Manger   £15   ④❷④
Branches throughout London
*"Unbeatable for consistency", thanks to its "always-
fresh" snack range, and its "super-efficient" service,
this London-based sandwich chain (now also
in Paris, NYC and HK) is still the 'gold standard';
let's hope the bargain 99p coffee will survive the
economic upturn! / www.pret.com; generally
4 pm-6 pm; closed Sun (except some West End
branches); City branches closed Sat & Sun; no Amex;
no booking.*

Princess Garden W1   £59   ❶❷❸
8-10 North Audley St   7493 3223   3–2A
*"Always delicious, and not as expensive as it looks"
– this smart Mayfair Chinese veteran is hailed
in many reports for its "fresh" and "delicate"
cuisine, which includes some "fabulous and
authentic dim sum". / W1K 6ZD;
www.princessgardenofmayfair.com; 10.45 pm,
Sun 10.45 pm.*

**Princess of Shoreditch
EC2**   £46   ❸④❸
76 Paul St   7729 9270   12–1B
*"Full of Shoreditch luvvies", "a very pleasant" small
dining room, up a spiral staircase from "a very
popular pub". / EC2A 4NE;
www.theprincessofshoreditch.com; @princessofs; 10 pm,
Sun 8 pm; no Amex.*

**Princess Victoria
W12**   £46   ④❷❷
217 Uxbridge Rd   8749 5886   7–1B
*An "oasis" at the far end of Shepherd's Bush,
this "welcoming" gin palace, which has been
beautifully restored, has a big name locally for its
"refined" gastropub cuisine, and it offers
a "surprisingly good" wine selection too. / W12 9DH;
www.princessvictoria.co.uk; @pvwestlondon; 10.30 pm,
Sun 9.30 pm; no Amex.*

Princi W1   £33   ❸④❷
135 Wardour St   7478 8888   3–2D
*"Energetic" at all hours (and sometimes "hectic"),
this "upscale" Soho cafeteria-cum-bakery offers
"Italian fast food at its best" (now including table-
service pizza). / W1F 0UT; www.princi.com; midnight,
Sun 10 pm; no booking.*

Prix Fixe W1   £37   ❸❷❸
39 Dean St   7734 5976   4–2A
*A "cosy" and "reliable" Soho bistro, offering "great
food, reasonably priced" – no wonder it's always
"lively"; there was a major refurb in the summer
of 2013. / W1D 4PU; www.prixfixe.net; 11.30 pm.*

The Providores W1 £70 ❷④⑤
109 Marylebone High St 7935 6175 2–1A
"Challenging combinations producing amazing flavours" still inspire applause for Peter Gordon's "tightly-packed" first-floor Marylebone dining room; critics, though, do find prices unduly "hefty". / W1U 4RX; www.theprovidores.co.uk; 10.30 pm; set weekday L £46 (FP); SRA-60%.

**(Tapa Room)
The Providores W1** £52 ❷④❸
109 Marylebone High St 7935 6175 2–1A
Peter Gordon's Marylebone bar offers "deliciously crafted" Pacific-fusion tapas and "outstanding" Kiwi wines, which help to "make up for any unwanted cosiness" arising from its "cramped" lay-out; brunch is "fantastic", but the queues for it "get ever worse". / W1U 4RX; www.theprovidores.co.uk; @theprovidores; 10.30 pm, Sun 10 pm.

Prufrock Coffee EC1 £13 ❷❷❸
23-25 Leather Ln 224 3470 9–2A
"Off-the-scale good!" – it's not just the coffee which makes this Holborn spot of note, but also its "impressive" range of sandwiches and snacks – "perfect for a pick-me-up during the working day". / EC1N 7TE; www.prufrockcoffee.com; 6 pm, Sat 5 pm; L only, closed Sun; no Amex.

**The Punch Tavern
EC4** £37 ④❸❷
99 Fleet St 7353 6658 9–2A
"A real winner for value"; just off Ludgate Circus, this "busy" Victorian boozer offers a good selection of food at competitive prices. / EC4Y 1DE; www.punchtavern.com; 10.30 pm, Sat & Sun 6.30 pm.

Punjab WC2 £27 ❷❷④
80 Neal St 7836 9787 4–2C
"Dead in the centre of town", this "old-established", "traditional" and "solicitous" Indian fixture maintains a dedicated fan club. / WC2H 9PA; www.punjab.co.uk; 11 pm, Sun 10.30 pm.

Quaglino's SW1 £65 ⑤④④
16 Bury St 7930 6767 3–3D
"A dinosaur!"; the early '90s – when this St James's basement was a byword for glamour – are a bygone age, and this "tired" brasserie can strike today's reporters as having "absolutely nothing to commend it"; come on D&D – time for the revamp! / SW1Y 6AJ; www.quaglinos.co.uk; 10.30 pm, Fri & Sat 11 pm; closed Sun; no trainers; SRA-62%.

**The Quality Chop
House EC1** £40 ❷❷❷
94 Farringdon Rd 7278 1452 9–1A
"Off to a flying start"; the relaunch of this "vintage" Farringdon 'working class caterer' has "brought it back to life" with a bang, thanks not least to its "deceptively simple and simply delicious" British food, and its "fascinating" wine list. / EC1R 3EA;
www.thequalitychophouse.com; @QualityChop; 10.30 pm; closed Sun.

Quantus W4 £37 ❷0❷
38 Devonshire Rd 8994 0488 7–2A
"Leo, the owner, takes a personal interest in his customers", and his "charming" welcome is a huge plus for this "cosy" Chiswick venture; the South American-edged cuisine can sometimes seem a touch "eccentric", but it's often "excellent" too. / W4 2HD; www.quantus-london.com; 10 pm; closed Mon L, Tue L & Sun L.

Queen's Head W6 £38 ④❸❷
13 Brook Grn 7603 3174 7–1C
A "quaint" tavern on Brook Green, which "has charm in spite of its average food"; in particular, "you go here for the garden"… which is surprisingly vast. / W6 7BL; www.queensheadhammersmith.co.uk; 10 pm, Sun 9 pm.

**The Queens Arms
SW1** £42 ❸❸❷
11 Warwick Way 7834 3313 2–4B
In the Pimlico desert, this "friendly" and "consistent" boozer is establishing itself as a "popular" destination; "standard pub food, but well executed". / SW1V 1QT; www.thequeensarmspimlico.co.uk; @thequeensarms; 11 pm, Sun 10.30 pm.

Le Querce SE23 £39 0❷❸
66-68 Brockley Rise 8690 3761 1–4D
An "unexpectedly fine" family-run Sardinian in Brockley Park; fans cross town for its "truly fabulous" cooking, including "real and rare Italian specialities"; "the ice-cream and sorbet list is absolutely unbelievable". / SE23 1LN; 10 pm, Sun 8.30 pm; closed Mon & Tue L.

Quilon SW1 £65 0❷④
41 Buckingham Gate 7821 1899 2–4B
"Magnificent" Keralan cuisine ("fish is particularly good") and "courteous" service distinguish this "really impressive Indian", near Buckingham Palace; the businesslike décor, though, is "rather sterile". / SW1E 6AF; www.quilon.co.uk; 10.45 pm, Sun 10.15 pm; SRA-66%.

Quirinale SW1 £61 0❷④
North Ct, 1 Gt Peter St 7222 7080 2–4C
"Tucked-away" in a Westminster backstreet, a "very professional" (and arguably "under-rated") Italian, offering "superb" cooking and "impeccable" service; the slightly "sepulchral" basement setting is best when busy… typically with "lots of politicos pretending not to be lobbied". / SW1P 3LL; www.quirinale.co.uk; @quirinaleresto; 10.30 pm; closed Sat & Sun; set weekday L & pre-theatre £41 (FP).

Quo Vadis W1 £55 ❸❸❷
26-29 Dean St 7437 9585 4–2A
"Jeremy Lee has brought the fizz back to this elegant establishment", say fans of this "sophisticated" Soho favourite; such "lavish praise",

however, leaves other reporters "bemused", and – overall – the food is rated no better than "very competent". / W1D 3LL; www.quovadissoho.co.uk; 10.45 pm; closed Sun; set weekday L & pre-theatre £36 (FP).

Racine SW3 £66 ❸❸❸
239 Brompton Rd 7584 4477 5–2C
A reputation as "one of the best Gallic bistros in town" precedes Henry Harris's "traditional" Knightsbridge fixture, which, for many reporters, still offers a "special experience every time"; sadly, however, the survey confirms that standards are "slipping", and quite fast too. / SW3 2EP; www.racine-restaurant.com; 10.30 pm, Sun 10 pm; set weekday L £35 (FP).

Ragam W1 £27 ❶❸⑤
57 Cleveland St 7636 9098 2–1B
"Some of the best South Indian cuisine I've eaten… and I'm South Indian!" – this "terrific" café veteran, near the Telecom Tower, is "the real thing"; OK, "the decor sucks" ("and they've done it up!"), but the "fabulous" dishes come at "rock-bottom" prices; BYO. / W1T 4JN; www.ragam.co.uk; 10.45 pm; essential Fri & Sat.

Randall & Aubin W1 £52 ❷❷❶
16 Brewer St 7287 4447 3–2D
"A pretty much unique experience!"; offering "delicious" seafood, right in the sleazy heart of Soho, this "cosily perfect" (if "loud") champagne and seafood bar is "a real gem"; "get a window table to watch the goings-on outside". / W1F 0SG; www.randallandaubin.com; @edbaineschef; 11 pm, Sat midnight, Sun 10 pm; booking for L only; SRA-58%.

Rani N3 £27 ❸④④
7 Long Ln 8349 4386 1–1B
"Terrific and great value" – it's the buffet offer which makes this "homely" Indian veggie veteran, in Finchley, of more than local interest. / N3 2PR; www.raniuk.com; 10 pm.

Ranoush £46 ❸❸④
22 Brompton Rd, SW1 7584 6999 5–1D
338 King's Rd, SW3 7352 0044 5–3C
43 Edgware Rd, W2 7723 5929 6–1D
86 Kensington High St, W8 7938 2234 5–1A
"For a quick bite, you can't beat a salad and a chicken shawarma", at these "comfy" Lebanese pit stops – a less expensive part of the Maroush chain. / www.maroush.com; most branches close between 1 am-3 am.

Raoul's Café £45 ④❸❸
105-107 Talbot Rd, W11 7229 2400 6–1B
113-115 Hammersmith Grove, W6 8741 3692 7–1C
13 Clifton Rd, W9 7289 7313 8–4A
The "best eggs Benedict in town" are the highlight attraction for fans of these chillaxed Notting Hill, Hammersmith and Maida Vale hang-outs; "after

a disastrous start, W6 is much better now". / www.raoulsgourmet.com; 10.15 pm, W11 6.15 pm; booking after 5 pm only.

Rasa £37 ❷❷❸
6 Dering St, W1 7637 0222 3–2B
Holiday Inn Hotel, 1 Kings Cross, WC1 7833 9787 8–3D
55 Stoke Newington Church St, N16 7249 0344 1–1C
56 Stoke Newington Church St, N16 7249 1340 1–1C
"Outstanding" dishes – many of them veggie – have carved out a huge name for this small Keralan chain, with the original (55 S N Church St) still often voted one of London's best Indians; for some loyal fans, however, "it's still a favourite", but has seemed "less exciting and vibrant" of late. / www.rasarestaurants.com; 10.45 pm; WC1 & W1 closed Sun.

Rasoi SW3 £101 ❷❸❸
10 Lincoln St 7225 1881 5–2D
"Quite simply the best Indian food I've ever eaten!"; Vineet Bhattia is a "magician", whose "clever" cuisine enchants almost all visitors to this "classy and surprising" Chelsea townhouse; it's an "intimate" experience, and the setting is on the "quiet" side for some tastes. / SW3 2TS; www.rasoirestaurant.co.uk; 10.30 pm, Sun 10 pm; closed Mon & Sat L.

The Real Greek £39 ⑤④④
56 Paddington St, W1 7486 0466 2–1A
60-62 Long Acre, WC2 7240 2292 4–2D
Westfield, Ariel Way, W12 8743 9168 7–1C
1-2 Riverside Hs, Southwark Br Rd, SE1 7620 0162 9–3B
6 Horner Sq, E1 7375 1364 12–2B
This "noisy" small chain does have its fans, who praise its "good, solid meze", but critics just find it "so poor in every respect" – "like a bad '70s-themed Greek restaurant". / www.therealgreek.com; 10.45 pm; WC2 10.30 pm; EC1 closed Sun, N1 closed Sun-Mon; WC2 no booking.

Red Dog Saloon N1 £40 ❸❷❷
37 Hoxton Sq 3551 8014 12–1B
"It's always a giggle watching someone take on one of the ridiculous Man v Food challenges", at this "VERY hearty American BBQ" in Hoxton; the cooking's surprisingly "decent", though – the "devastator burger" rates special mention. / N1 6NN; www.reddogsaloon.co.uk; @reddogsaloonn1; 10.30 pm.

Red Fort W1 £65 ❸④④
77 Dean St 7437 2525 4–2A
This Soho stalwart – decorated nowadays "rather in international-hotel style" – no longer attracts the attention it once did; some loyalists still hail it as "London's best traditional Indian", but most assessments are more middle-of-the-road.

/ W1D 3SH; www.redfort.co.uk; 11.15 pm; closed
Sat L & Sun L; set weekday L & pre-theatre £38 (FP).

The Red Pepper W9　　£44　　❷❸④
8 Formosa St　7266 2708　8–4A
"Excellent pizzas... if you can get a seat" –
"cramped" and "noisy" it may be, but this Maida
Vale fixture has for many years been as "consistent"
a destination as you'll find. / W9 1EE;
theredpepper.net; Sat 11 pm, Sun 10.30 pm; closed
weekday L; no Amex.

Refettorio
The Crowne Plaza
Hotel EC4　　£55　　❸❸④
19 New Bridge St　7438 8052　9–3A
A "staple" for business types, this Italian dining
room, by Blackfriars Bridge, is "much better than
the other restaurants in the immediate locality" –
not, it should be noted, a particularly demanding
test! / EC4V 6DB; www.refettorio.com; 10.30 pm, Fri &
Sat 10 pm; closed Sat L & Sun.

Refuel
Soho Hotel W1　　£70　　④④❷
4 Richmond Mews　7559 3007　3–2D
"A beautiful boutique hotel hidden-away in the
middle of Soho", complete with "buzzing" bar,
provides the "scintillating" setting for this "cool"
dining room... where the food plays rather
a supporting role. / W1D 3DH; www.firmdale.com;
11 pm, Sun 10 pm; set always available £41 (FP).

Le Relais de Venise
L'Entrecôte　　£42　　❸④❸
120 Marylebone Ln, W1　7486 0878　2–1A
18-20 Mackenzie Walk, E14　3475 3331　11–1C
5 Throgmorton St, EC2　7638 6325　9–2C
"You know what you'll get", at these "cheek-by-jowl"
Gallic bistros, whose "simple but very well executed"
formula offers zero choice, just "classic steak/frites",
with secret sauce and salad (plus seconds); "fun"
too... aside from the "horrific" queues and
"impersonal" service. / www.relaisdevenise.com;
W1 11 pm, Sun 10.30 pm; EC2 10 pm; EC2 closed
Sat & Sun; no booking.

Le Rendezvous du
Café EC1　　£47　　❸❸❸
22 Charterhouse Sq　7336 8836　9–1B
Looking for dinner in "good solid French style"? –
you're unlikely to do much better than this long-
established Clerkenwell bistro, where "the entrecôte
is the star". / EC1M 6DX; www.cafedumarche.co.uk;
@cafedumarche; 10 pm; closed Mon, Tue D, Wed D,
Thu D, Fri D, Sat & Sun.

Retsina NW3　　£43　　④④❸
48-50 Belsize Ln　7431 5855　8–2A
A "friendly" family-run Belsize Park taverna, where
the cuisine is "reliable" (or better); "it can get a bit
squashed and noisy, especially at the end of the
week". / NW3 5AR; www.retsina-london.com; 11 pm;
closed Mon L; no Amex.

Reubens W1　　£50　　❸④④
79 Baker St　7486 0035　2–1A
Is increased kosher competition making this
Marylebone deli raise its game? – after years
of lacklustre feedback, it won consistent praise this
year for serving "the best" salt beef sandwiches
(if still at toppish prices). / W1M 1AJ;
www.reubensrestaurant.co.uk; 10 pm; closed Fri D & Sat;
no Amex.

The Rib Man N1　　£12　　❶❸–
KERB, King's Cross　no tel　8–3C
"Proof that street food need not be rubbish" –
Mark Gevaux vends "succulent and utterly
delicious" pork, topped with "legendary" hot sauces
at his Kerb Food stall, behind King's Cross. / N1;
www.theribman.co.uk; @theribman.

Rib Room
Jumeirah Carlton
Tower Hotel SW1　　£100　　❸❷④
Cadogan Pl　7858 7250　5–1D
"An old classic given new life after a makeover";
this "clubby" Belgravia dining room, renowned for
beef long before the current steakhouse trend,
remains as "abominably expensive" as ever,
but more reporters this year felt that "the food
matches up". / SW1X 9PY; www.jumeirah.com;
10.45 pm, Sun 10.15 pm.

RIBA Café
Royal Ass'n of Brit'
Architects W1　　£44　　④④❷
66 Portland Pl　7631 0467　2–1B
Looking for a "calm lunch location", not too far from
the West End? – this "spacious" high-ceilinged café,
inside the architects' Art Deco Marylebone HQ,
is hard to beat; service is "unpredictable", but the
food "reasonable"; star attraction – the hidden-away
summer terrace. / W1 4AD; www.riba-venues.com;
@riba; 6 pm, Tue 9 pm; closed Mon D, Wed D, Thu D,
Fri D, Sat D & Sun.

Riccardo's SW3　　£42　　⑤⑤④
126 Fulham Rd　7370 6656　5–3B
It's still "usually jammed", but this old-favourite
Chelsea Italian is "not what it used to be" –
it's "hit 'n' miss" nowadays, and some reports are
truly "terrible". / SW3 6HU; www.riccardos.it;
@riccardoslondon; 11.30 pm.

Riding House Café
W I £53 ④④❶
43-51 Great Titchfield St 7927 0840 3–1C
With its "straight-out-of-Brooklyn" vibe, this "buzzy" Fitzrovia brasserie has "perfected the recipe for casual dining" at any time of day (but particularly for brunch); no one seems to care that the food is "pretty average" (and service too, for that matter). / W1W 7PQ; www.ridinghousecafe.co.uk; 11 pm, Sun 10.30 pm.

Rising Sun NW7 £43 ❸❷❸
137 Marsh Ln, Highwood Hill 8959 1357 1–1B
An Italian landlord who's "a real character" adds interest to this "noisy" and sometimes "chaotic" Mill Hill gastropub; on a good day, the food can be "excellent" too. / NW7 4EY; www.therisingsunmillhill.co.uk; @therisingsunpub; 9.30 pm, Sun 8.30 pm; closed Mon L.

Il Ristorante Bulgari Hotel
SW7 [NEW] £85 ④❷④
171 Knightsbridge 7151 1025 5–1C
"What an anticlimax!"; this "ritzy" new Knightsbridge outpost of the Roman bling brand too often offers a "diabolical" parody of the design-hotel dining experience ("deafening" noise from the bar included); shame – sometimes the food is "surprisingly excellent". / SW7 1DW; 10.30 pm.

(Palm Court)
The Ritz W I £43 ❸❷❶
150 Piccadilly 7493 8181 3–4C
"One of those things to do before you die!"; "elegant and timeless", this bastion of tradition certainly deliver up a "sense of occasion", and its world-famous afternoon tea, is "very pricey, but worth it". / W1C 9BR; www.theritzlondon.com; 9.30 pm; jacket & tie.

The Ritz Restaurant
The Ritz W I £119 ④❸❶
150 Piccadilly 7493 8181 3–4C
"Unbeatable for sheer romance", "London's most beautiful dining room", in Louis XVI style, also "wows" some reporters with its food and service; as ever, though, critics find the cooking "competent, rather than memorable". / W1J 9BR; www.theritzlondon.com; 10 pm; jacket & tie.

Riva SW13 £59 ❷❷④
169 Church Rd 8748 0434 10–1A
With its "astonishingly good" cuisine and its "slick" service, Andreas Riva's Barnes Italian maintains its cult foodie following; even fans concede the interior's on the "drab" side, though, and – as usual – a small coterie of refuseniks dismisses the whole experience as "snooty" and "cold". / SW13 9HR; 10.30 pm, Sun 9 pm; closed Sat L.

THE RIVER CAFÉ W6 £90 ❸④❷
Thames Wharf, Rainville Rd 7386 4200 7–2C
Downturn or not, it's still "horrendously hard to get a table" at this "palpably buzzing" (and "crowded") Hammersmith Italian; even many ardent fans of its "elegant" and "intensely flavoured" Tuscan cuisine, however, feel bills are nothing short of "monstrous". / W6 9HA; www.rivercafe.co.uk; 9 pm, Sat 9.15 pm; closed Sun D.

The Riverfront
BFI Southbank SE1 £45 ④④❸
Southbank 7928 0808 2–3D
"Always busy" ... but "not quite as full or tourists as everywhere else nearby" – this attractive operation is one of the better budget options on the South Bank; arguably, though, "it's not very exciting, and not that cheap". / SE1 8XT; www.riverfrontbarandkitchen.com; @riverfront_bfi; 10.45 pm.

Rivington Grill £49 ④❸④
178 Greenwich High Rd, SE10 8293 9270 1–3D
28-30 Rivington St, EC2 7729 7053 12–1B
Despite backing by the glamorous Caprice group, these nowadays rather "tired" bar/brasseries, in Shoreditch and Greenwich, have never made waves; for "simple" British dishes in casual surroundings, though, they make an "OK" choice. / www.rivingtongrill.co.uk; 11 pm, Sun 10 pm; SE10 closed Mon, Tue L & Wed L.

Roast SE1 £70 ④④❸
Stoney St 0845 034 7300 9–4C
This first-floor English dining room certainly has a "beautiful" setting (especially on a sunny day), and it's "a great place for brunch after browsing the stalls of Borough Market"; lunch and dinner are "less of an attraction", though, and prices at any time are on the "grabby" side. / SE1 1TL; www.roast-restaurant.com; 10.30 pm; closed Sun D; SRA-71%.

Rocca Di Papa £42 ④④❸
73 Old Brompton Rd, SW7 7225 3413 5–2B
75-79 Dulwich Village, SE21 8299 6333 1–4D
"Classic" pizza joints; these "family-friendly" South Kensington and Dulwich Village spots may not be exciting, but they "make for an enjoyable all-round experience". / SW7 11.30 pm; SE21 11 pm.

Rocco SW5 £57 ④❷④
254-260 Old Brompton Rd 7259 2599 5–3A
On the site of of Langan's Coq D'Or (RIP), this Italian newcomer pleases fans with its "uncomplicated" but "serious" cooking, and "attentive" service; the "stripped back" decor is not to all tastes though, and "toppish" prices may explain why the place has not been more of a hit. / SW5 9HR; www.roccopoint.co.uk.

Rochelle Canteen E2 £40 ❷❷❷
Arnold Circus   7729 5677   12–1C
"A former bike-shed" provides the "works-canteen-like" setting for this "funky" Shoreditch outfit – a "great lunch venue" which attracts some "seriously trendy" punters with its "simple" but "excellent" daily-changing British dishes, "at really good prices"; BYO. / E2 7ES; www.arnoldandhenderson.com; L only, closed Sat & Sun; no Amex.

Rock & Rose TW9 £53 ❺❺❸
106-108 Kew Rd   8948 8008   1–4A
Supporters insist it offers "a good night out" (even if "the fun style doesn't quite compensate for the uninspiring food"), but critics are scathing about what they feel is a "pretentious" atmosphere at this Richmond party scene. / TW9 2PQ; www.rockandroserestaurant.co.uk; 10 pm, Fri & Sat 10.30 pm.

Rocket £45 ❸❸❸
2 Churchill Pl, E14   3200 2022   11–1C
201 Bishopsgate, EC2   7377 8863   12–2B
6 Adams Ct, EC2   7628 0808   9–2C
The E14 branch – with its "great views" – is the best-known of these "relaxed and fun" hang-outs, which serve an "interesting and creative" selection of pizzas and salads; for a cost-conscious Mayfair meal, however, the outlet tucked-away off Bond Street is also well worth knowing about. / 10.30 pm, Sun 9.30 pm; W1 closed Sun; EC2 closed Sat & Sun; SW15 Mon-Wed D only, Bishopsgate closed Sun D, E14.

The Roebuck W4 £41 ❹❸❸
122 Chiswick High Rd   8995 4392   7–2A
An "always-buzzy" Chiswick gastropub (with large garden); it has perhaps "slipped" a bit of late, but all reports are positive. / W4 1PU; www.theroebuckchiswick.co.uk; @the_roebuck; 11 pm, Sun 10.30 pm.

Roka £78 ❶❸❸
37 Charlotte St, W1   7580 6464   2–1C
Unit 4, Park Pavilion, 40 Canada Sq, E14   7636 5228   11–1C
"Extraordinary" Japanse-fusion dishes ("top-class" robata and "delectable" sushi) put the W1 original of this "slick" Asian duo ahead even of its famous sibling Zuma; does it need a revamp, though? – it has seemed a tad "impersonal" of late. / www.rokarestaurant.com; 11.15 pm, Sun 10.30 pm; booking: max 8.

Roots at N1 N1 £46 ❷❷❸
115 Hemingford Rd   7697 4488   8–3D
An out-of-the-way Islington pub-conversion provides the setting for this "hidden gem" – a "friendly and charming" outfit which offers, say fans, "all the excellence of London's top Indians, but without the crazy prices". / N1 1BZ; www.rootsatn1.com;

@rootsatn1 @Rootsatn1; 10 pm, Sun 9 pm; closed Mon, Tue–Sat D only, Sun open L & D.

Rosa's £37 ❸❷❸
23a, Ganton St, W1   7287 9617   3–2C
48 Dean St, W1   7494 1638   4–3A
12 Hanbury St, E1   7247 1093   12–2C
"Canteen-like, but offering very good and filling food" – these Brick Lane and Soho Thais are "lovely" little places, and often "very busy". / www.rosaslondon.com; 10.30 pm, Fri & Sat 11 pm, Ganton St Sun 10 pm; some booking restrictions apply.

Rossopomodoro £38 ❸❸❸
50-52 Monmouth St, WC2   7240 9095   4–3B
214 Fulham Rd, SW10   7352 7677   5–3B
184a Kensington Park Rd, W11   7229 9007   6–1A
1 Rufus St, N1   7739 1899   12–1B **NEW**
10 Jamestown Rd, NW1   7424 9900   8–3B **NEW**
46 Garrett Ln, SW18   07931 9 20377   10–2B **NEW**
"Full of homesick Italians", these outposts of a Neapolitan chain impress most reporters with their "bubbly" and "authentic" style. / www.rossopomodoro.co.uk; 11.30 pm; WC2 Sun 11.30 pm.

Roti Chai W1 £46 ❷❸❸
3 Portman Mews South   7408 0101   3–1A
"Lip-smacking" Indian street food – "at great prices" – wins a big fan club for this "fun" year-old operation, near Selfridges; in the "more formal" basement, the cooking's "a little more complex, but equally flavoursome". / W1H 6HS; www.rotichai.com; @rotichai; 10.30 pm.

Rotunda Bar & Restaurant
Kings Place N1 £50 ❹❹❸
90 York Way   7014 2840   8–3C
"Unbeatable when the weather is good"; this King's Cross office/arts centre café boasts fine views of the canal, and a large terrace, plus a menu well suited to "pre-concert dining". / N1 9AG; www.rotundabarandrestaurant.co.uk; @rotundalondon; 10.30 pm, Sun 6.30 pm.

Roux at Parliament Square
RICS SW1 £76 ❸❷❹
12 Great George St   7334 3737   2–3C
With a view of the Palace of Westminster from some seats, it's appropriate that this Gallic dining room has a "very discreet" style well-suited to a lobbying lunch; the experience is "good all-round", albeit in a mode which can ultimately seem "rather bland". / SW1P 3AD; www.rouxatparliamentsquare.co.uk; 10 pm; closed Sat & Sun.

Roux at the Landau
The Langham W1 £91 ❸❸❷
1c, Portland Pl   7965 0165   2–1B

"Beautiful" decor and "first-class" cuisine can make for "a splendid experience" at this "classically styled" chamber, near Broadcasting House; it's only the "excellent-value set lunch" which can really safely be recommended, though – the à la carte offering is sometimes "underwhelming". / W1B 1JA; www.thelandau.com; 10 pm; closed Sat L & Sun; no trainers.

Rowley's SW1 £69 ④④④
113 Jermyn St   7930 2707   3–3D
With its charming premises inherited from the original Wall's butcher's shop, this veteran St James's steakhouse has long been a popular, and sometimes "overcrowded", destination – with its "basic" and "overpriced" food, though, critics do feel it "trades on its reputation". / SW1Y 6HJ; www.rowleys.co.uk; @rowleys_steak; 11 pm.

Royal Academy W1 £53 ⑤④④
Burlington Hs, Piccadilly   7300 5608   3–3D
This civilised café in the bowels of the RA has long been a handy retreat from the Piccadilly mêlée, especially for afternoon tea; it's slipped notably under Peyton & Byrne's management, however – "slapdash", "pretentious" and "poor value". / W1J 0BD; www.royalacademy.org.uk; 9 pm; L only, ex Fri open L & D; no booking at L.

Royal China £46 ❷④④
24-26 Baker St, W1   7487 4688   2–1A
805 Fulham Rd, SW6   7731 0081   10–1B
13 Queensway, W2   7221 2535   6–2C
30 Westferry Circus, E14   7719 0888   11–1B
"Some of the best dim sum in the capital" – these "ever-reliable" Chinese benchmarks remain a "rushed" and "very crowded" weekend staple for legions of reporters; "service with a smile is an alien concept", though, and the "darkly shiny" decor is not to all tastes. / www.royalchinagroup.co.uk; 10.45 pm, Fri & Sat 11.15 pm, Sun 9.45 pm; no booking Sat & Sun L.

Royal China Club W1 £62 ❷❸④
40-42 Baker St   7486 3898   2–1A
"Sophisticated" cooking has made quite a name for this "pricey" (club-class) Marylebone Chinese; critics find service "inconsistent", though, and wonder if the premium over the tourist-class Royal Chinas is really justified. / W1U 7AJ; www.royalchinagroup.co.uk; 11 pm, Fri & Sat 11.30 pm, Sun 10.30 pm.

The Royal Exchange Grand Café
The Royal Exchange
EC3 £54 ④❸❷
The Royal Exchange Bank   7618 2480   9–2C
With its "beautiful" atrium setting (with "luxury boutiques all around"), this City seafood bar is some reporters' favourite business-lunch venue "by a Square Mile"; it's "pricey", though, and critics find the fare "pedestrian". / EC3V 3LR; www.royalexchange-grandcafe.co.uk; 9.30 pm; closed Sat & Sun; SRA-58%.

RSJ SE1 £45 ❸❸④
33 Coin St   7928 4554   9–4A
An "encyclopaedic" list of Loire vintages helps compensate for the "austere" atmosphere of this South Bank stalwart; its Gallic cooking is "absolutely reliable" too, and the location is "very convenient for the National Theatre". / SE1 9NR; www.rsj.uk.com; 11 pm; closed Sat L & Sun.

Rugoletta N2 £37 ❸❸④
59 Church Ln   8815 1743   1–1B
"Good, honest rustic Italian cooking, like your Mama made"; "very cramped and chaotic" it may be, but this neighbourhood BYO in East Finchley is a "fun" destination too, and it's "always busy". / N2 8DR; 10.30 pm; closed Sun.

Rules WC2 £74 ❸❷❶
35 Maiden Ln   7836 5314   4–3D
"Full of wealthy tourists", it may be, but London's oldest restaurant (1798) has a genuinely "lovely", "old school" ambience, and still strikes many (if not quite all) of the natives as "living up to its history" – the beef, in particular, is "excellent", and the game "the best in town". / WC2E 7LB; www.rules.co.uk; 11.30 pm, Sun 10.30 pm; no shorts.

Le Sacré-Coeur N1 £35 ④❸❸
18 Theberton St   7354 2618   8–3D
"A reliable stand-by"; the basic charms of this "very French" Islington side street bistro continue to please most of the reporters who comment on it. / N1 0QX; www.lesacrecoeur.co.uk; 11 pm, Sat 11.30 pm, Sun 10.30 pm; set weekday L £23 (FP).

Sacro Cuore NW10 £31 ❷❷❸
45 Chamberlayne Rd   8960 8558   1–2B
"Perfect ingredients" and "paper-thin" bases help inspire rave reviews for this tiny year-old Kensal Rise pizzeria, which "does the simple things really well". / NW10 3NB.

Sagar £37 ❸❸④
17a, Percy St, W1   7631 3319   3–2B
31 Catherine St, WC2   7836 6377   4–3D
157 King St, W6   8741 8563   7–2C
"Dosas to die for!"; these "basic" cafés (Hammersmith is the best-known) "could convert the most die-hard carnivore" with their "interesting" South Indian dishes; "good value too". / www.sagarveg.co.uk; Sun-Thu 10.45 pm, Fri & Sat 11.30 pm.

Sager & Wilde E2 NEW £22
193 Hackney Rd   no tel   12–1C
This Haggerston wine bar opened in the summer of 2013; we sadly didn't have have the opportunity to visit before this guide went to press, but the critical reaction has been very positive. / E2 8JP; www.sagerandwilde.com.

Saigon Saigon W6   £40   ③④❸
313-317 King St   8748 6887   7–2B
*"Low lighting" and characterful decor help create
a "warm" atmosphere, at this long-standing
Hammersmith Vietnamese, where "very tasty"
dishes come at "reasonable prices". / W6 9NH;
www.saigon-saigon.co.uk; @saigonsaigonuk; 11.30 pm,
Sun & Mon 10 pm.*

St John EC1   £57   ❷❷❷
26 St John St   7251 0848   9–1B
*"You can order anything, no matter how off-putting
it sounds, and it'll be really good", say devotees
of Fergus Henderson's infamously offal-friendly
Smithfield HQ – an "outstanding choice for
aficionados of unadulterated British food";
some fans are fretting though – "is the menu
becoming more mainstream?" / EC1M 4AY;
www.stjohngroup.uk.com; @SJRestaurant; 11 pm; closed
Sat L & Sun D.*

**St John Bread & Wine
E1**   £55   ❶❸❸
94-96 Commercial St   7251 0848   12–2C
*"The best of the St John stable"; with its "eclectic",
"simple" and "brilliant" British fare and its
"interesting" wines too, this "cramped" and "utterly
unpretentious" Shoreditch canteen is – for fans –
simply "the perfect restaurant". / E1 6LZ;
www.stjohngroup.uk.com/spitalfields; 10.30 pm,
Sun 9.30 pm.*

St Johns N19   £47   ❸❷❶
91 Junction Rd   7272 1587   8–1C
*The "wonderful dining room" – a former ballroom –
adds considerable pizzazz to this large and "lively"
Archway tavern; the food is "far better than you
might expect" too, but sliding ratings tend to confirm
recent concerns of "fallen" standards. / N19 5QU;
www.stjohnstavern.com; 11 pm, Sun 9.30 pm;
Mon-Thu D only, Fri-Sun open L & D; no Amex; booking:
max 12.*

St Moritz W1   £53   ③④❸
161 Wardour St   7734 3324   3–1D
*A "kitsch" Swiss-chalet-style Soho veteran,
long popular for its "friendly old-school" service and
"quality" fondues (plus "excellent game in season");
unusually, however, there were a couple of "really
disappointing" reports this year – hopefully a blip.
/ W1F 8WJ; www.stmoritz-restaurant.co.uk; 11.30 pm,
Sun 10.30 pm.*

**St Pancras Grand
St Pancras Int'l Station
NW1**   £51   ⑤⑤④
The Concourse   7870 9900   8–3C
*"A terrible waste of a good space"; this briefly-
glamorous brasserie, on the way to Paris, again put
in a "dismal" performance this year – the food
is "substandard", and "what on earth are the staff
actually doing?" / NW1 2QP; www.stpancrasgrand.com;
@SearcysBars; 10.30 pm.*

Sakana-tei W1   £34   ❷❷⑤
11 Maddox St   7629 3000   3–2C
*"The setting may be dingy, but the place has
a charm of its own!" – this Mayfair basement
Japanese offers "great value", and its menu includes
some items which are otherwise "hard to find".
/ W1S 2QF; 10 pm; closed Sun.*

Sake No Hana SW1   £69   ④❸④
23 St James's St   7925 8988   3–4C
*This style-conscious St James's Japanese deeply
divides opinions; fan hail it as a "great space" with
"terrific" fusion fare that "leaves other places
standing" – to critics, though, it's a "strange" place,
offering "westernised" food that's "deeply average".
/ SW1A 1HA; www.sakenohana.com; @sakenonhana;
11 pm, Fri-Sat 11.30 pm; closed Sun.*

Sakonis HA0   £20   ❷④⑤
127-129 Ealing Rd   8903 9601   1–1A
*A Wembley Gujarati, where "you don't go for the
ambience but for the tasty vegetarian food";
no booking – "push and shove to get a table,
just like in India!" / HA0 4BP; www.sakonis.co.uk;
@sakonis; 9.30 pm; no Amex.*

Sakura W1   £32   ❸❸④
23 Conduit St   7629 2961   3–2C
*A "no-frills" Japanese, well worth seeking out
in pricey Mayfair for its "authentic" dishes (including
sushi), "prompt" service and "great value for
money". / W1S 2XS; 10 pm.*

Salaam Namaste WC1 £34   ❷④④
68 Millman St   7405 3697   2–1D
*"Hard to find, but worth discovering";
this "contemporary" Indian, on a Bloomsbury
backstreet, serves up "a few unusual, regional
dishes", plus some "adventurous interpretations"
of more familiar classics. / WC1N 3EF;
www.salaam-namaste.co.uk; @SalaanNamasteUK;
11.30 pm, Sun 11 pm.*

Sale e Pepe SW1   £65   ④④❸
9-15 Pavilion Rd   7235 0098   5–1D
*"Very cramped and very noisy", "popular and
dependable" – that's how most reporters still see
this old-favourite trattoria, near Harrods; "it's got
a bit left behind" in recent years, however, and the
kitchen "needs a shake-up". / SW1X 0HD;
www.saleepepe.co.uk; 11.30 pm; no shorts; set weekday L
£43 (FP).*

Salloos SW1   £59   ❷❷④
62-64 Kinnerton St   7235 4444   5–1D
*"The best lamb chops anywhere" top the selection
of "subtly-spiced" dishes on offer at this "classy"
Pakistani, hidden-away in a Belgravia mews;
its rather '60s styling, however, can strike critics as a
touch "stale". / SW1X 8ER; www.salloos.co.uk; 11 pm;
closed Sun; need 5+ to book.*

Salt Yard W I £44 ❷❸❸
54 Goodge St 7637 0657 2–1B
"Seriously delicious" Mediterranean tapas and some
"outstanding" Italian/Spanish wines have carved out
a big name for Dehesa's older stablemate,
in Fitzrovia; it's a "buzzy" operation, but critics can
find its cramped quarters a touch "claustrophobic".
/ W1T 4NA; www.saltyard.co.uk; 11 pm; closed
Sat L & Sun; SRA-63%.

The Salusbury NW6 £44 ④④❸
50-52 Salusbury Rd 7328 3286 1–2B
An endearing Queen's Park hang-out, where the
food is "consistently decent", even if the
Mediterranean menu (including pizza) "doesn't
change much". / NW6 6NN; www.thesalusbury.co.uk;
10.30 pm; closed Mon L.

Sam's Brasserie W4 £49 ④❸❷
11 Barley Mow Pas 8987 0555 7–2A
"A trusty favourite"; this "relaxed" and "buzzy"
Chiswick haunt, in a former factory, is a particular
hit for weekend family brunches; "the food is never
bad… but rarely very good". / W4 4PH;
www.samsbrasserie.co.uk; @samsbrasserie; 10.30 pm,
Sun 10 pm; set weekday L £31 (FP); SRA-70%.

**San Carlo Cicchetti
W I** £46 ❸④④
215 Piccadilly 7494 9435 3–3D
Near Piccadilly Circus, a "buzzy" (and quite tightly-
packed) outpost of the glossy provincial Italian
restaurant chain – useful for a shopping or pre-
theatre bite. / W1J 9HN; www.sancarlo.co.uk;
@SanCarlo_Group; midnight.

**San Daniele del Friuli
N5** £42 ❸❷❸
72 Highbury Park 7226 1609 8–1D
A "high-quality local" that's long been a fixture
of Highbury Park, this "fun" Italian offers "lots of
menu variety". / N5 2XE;
www.sandanielehighbury.co.uk; 10.30 pm; closed Mon L,
Tue L, Wed L & Sun; no Amex.

San Lorenzo SW3 £66
22 Beauchamp Pl 7584 1074 5–1C
Once it was the epitome of an A-list haunt;
nowadays this Knightsbridge trattoria generates
so little feedback, we've felt it best to leave it un-
rated. / SW3 1NH; 11 pm.

**San Lorenzo Fuoriporta
SW19** £61 ⑤⑤④
38 Wimbledon Hill Rd 8946 8463 10–2B
The "trip-down-Memory-Lane" charms of this
Wimbledon trattoria ("last decorated in the 70s?")
still win over some reporters, and its "secret garden"
can still impress; the journey can be an "expensive"
one, though, and too often "doesn't measure up".
/ SW19 7PA; www.sanlorenzo.com; @fuoriporta;
10.40 pm.

The Sands End SW6 £50 ❸④❷
135 Stephendale Rd 7731 7823 10–1B
A "posh" but "friendly" Sands End boozer that
"manages to cater for all occasions"; "great bar
snacks" – which include legendary Scotch Eggs –
are a highlight. / SW6 2PR; www.thesandsend.co.uk;
@thesandsend; 11.30 pm, Thu-Sat midnight.

Santa Lucia SW10 £41 ❷❸❸
2 Hollywood Rd 7352 8484 5–3B
In a long-established 'restaurant row', in the Chelsea
backwoods, an outpost of the Made In Italy pizza
group – it attracts only a modest level
of commentary, but all positive. / SW10 9HY;
www.madeinitalygroup.co.uk; 11.30 pm, Sun 10.30 pm;
closed weekday L.

Santa Maria W5 £31 ❶❸❸
15 St Mary's Rd 8579 1462 1–3A
"A slice of heaven" – the pizzas at this "charming",
"no-frills" Neapolitan are arguably Ealing's
biggest contribution to London gastronomy (and are
sometimes claimed as the city's best); it's a "pokey"
place, though, with "awfully cramped" seating and
long queues. / W5 5RA; www.santamariapizzeria.com;
@SantaMariaPizza; 10.30 pm.

**Santa Maria del Sur
SW8** £50 ❸④❸
129 Queenstown Rd 7622 2088 10–1C
An Argentinian steakhouse that "has made its
mark", down Battersea way – "booking is essential";
even fans, though, may note that it's it's
"not cheap". / SW8 3RH; www.santamariadelsur.co.uk;
@StaMariadelSur; 10 pm; no Amex.

Santini SW I £68 ④④④
29 Ebury St 7730 4094 2–4B
A "spacious" Belgravia Italian, whose A-list status
is now a dim '80s memory; its still pretty pricey,
though, and even some reporters who tip it as
"very good for a business lunch" say they "wouldn't
spend their own money" there. / SW1W 0NZ;
www.santini-restaurant.com; 11 pm, Sun 10 pm; closed
Sat L & Sun L.

Santore EC I £42 ❷❷④
59 Exmouth Mkt 7812 1488 9–1A
"Authentic Neapolitan pizzas of the
highest calibre", served by the metre, inspire rave
reviews for this "friendly", "busy" and "noisy" joint,
in Exmouth Market. / EC1R 4QL;
www.santorerestaurant.co.uk; 11 pm.

Sapori Sardi SW6 £47 ❷❸④
786 Fulham Rd 7731 0755 10–1B
"Everyone wishes they had a family-run Italian like
this round the corner!" – this "lovely" small yearling
offers "fresh home cooking at extremely reasonable
prices". / SW6 5SL; www.saporisardi.co.uk; 11 pm;
closed Mon L; no Amex.

Sarastro WC2   £50   ⑤⑤❸
126 Drury Ln   7836 0101   2–2D
"Can't be beaten for entertainment value…" –
just as well, as the food and service at this OTT
operatic-themed Theatreland experience
(accompanied by live arias) can be very lacking.
/ WC2B 5SU; www.sarastro-restaurant.com; @SastroR;
10.30 pm, Fri & Sat 11.15 pm.

Sardo W1   £55   ❷❸④
45 Grafton Way   7387 2521   2–1B
"Top of the class for authenticity", this Fitzrovia
fixture, just off Tottenham Court Road, wins a
consistent thumbs-up for its "interesting Sardinian-
based menu" and "excellent" wines. / W1T 5DQ;
www.sardo-restaurant.com; 11 pm; closed Sat L & Sun.

Sarracino NW6   £41   ❷❸④
186 Broadhurst Gdns   7372 5889   1–1B
Neapolitan-style pizza by the metre is the main
deal at this raucous West Hampstead trattoria;
limited feedback this year, but all consistently
upbeat. / NW6 3AY; www.sarracinorestaurant.com;
11 pm; closed weekday L.

Sartoria W1   £58   ❸❸❸
20 Savile Row   7534 7000   3–2C
This "pleasantly laid out" D&D group establishment,
just off Regent Street, never sets the world on fire,
but it's often tipped for business, thanks to its
"smart Italian food", and its "discreet and
unobtrusive" service. / W1S 3PR;
www.sartoria-restaurant.co.uk; 10.45 pm; closed
Sat L & Sun; SRA-63%.

Satay House W2   £34   ❸④④
13 Sale Pl   7723 6763   6–1D
"Penang, minus the air travel!" – this Bayswater
veteran is, for fans, not just London's
oldest Malaysian, but also the "most authentic".
/ W2 1PX; www.satay-house.co.uk; 11 pm.

Sauterelle
Royal Exchange EC3   £70   ❸❸❸
Bank   7618 2483   9–2C
"Good for a business lunch or dinner"; the first-floor
D&D Group operation, looking into the atrium
of the Royal Exchange, has always been a "discreet"
sort of place; with its "improved" food of late,
some fans reckon it can now be hailed as a "proper
gastronomic destination" too! / EC3V 3LR;
www.sauterelle-restaurant.co.uk; 9.30 pm; closed
Sat & Sun; no trainers; set dinner £46 (FP); SRA-59%.

Savoir Faire WC1   £38   ❸❸④
42 New Oxford St   7436 0707   4–1C
A "quirky" and "good-value" bistro that makes
"a perfect choice after a visit to the British
Museum"; "useful pre-theatre" too. / WC1A 1EP;
www.savoir.co.uk; 11 pm.

(Savoy Grill)
The Savoy Hotel WC2 £79   ④❸❸
Strand   7592 1600   4–3D

Under the 'stewardship' of Gordon Ramsay,
this once-legendary Theatreland/power-dining
rendezvous has become "a pale shadow of its
former self"; it inspires wildly erratic commentary,
too much of it to the effect that it is now
"just another overpriced restaurant". / WC2R 0EU;
www.gordonramsay.com/thesavoygrill/; 10.45 pm,
Sun 10.15 pm; jacket required.

Scalini SW3   £75   ❸❷❷
1-3 Walton St   7225 2301   5–2C
Why is it "always mobbed"? – this "squashed-in"
Knightsbridge stalwart Italian is just "fantastico",
says fans of its "old-style" scoff, its "wonderfully
friendly" service, and its "electric" buzz. / SW3 2JD;
www.scalinionline.com; 11.30 pm, Sun 11 pm; no shorts.

Scandinavian Kitchen
W1   £16   ❷❷❸
61 Great Titchfield St   7580 7161   2–1B
"Abba nice day!"; "appealing" open sandwiches,
"delicious" pastries, "inventive" salads, "amazing"
cakes, and gorgeous cinnamon rolls … – is there
no end to the attractions of this "colourful and
healthy" Fitzrovia "oasis"? / W1W 7PP;
www.scandikitchen.co.uk; 7 pm, Sat 6 pm, Sun 4 pm;
L only; no Maestro; no Amex.

The Scarsdale W8   £39   ④❸❶
23a Edwardes Sq   7937 1811   7–1D
It's the "delightful location in a quiet Kensington
square" which makes this ancient hostelry (with a
"good terrace") really stand out, but its "good pub
food" usually hits the spot too. / W8 6HE; 10 pm,
Sun 9.30 pm.

SCOTT'S W1   £78   ❷❷❷
20 Mount St   7495 7309   3–3A
"Taking over where The Ivy left off" – Richard
Caring's "suave and sophisticated" Mayfair all-
rounder serves up "supreme" seafood (London's
best, say some) to an A-list crowd; is it starting
to coast, though? – ratings dipped a bit all-round
this year. / W1K 2HE; www.scotts-restaurant.com;
10.30 pm, Sun 10 pm; booking: max 6.

The Sea Cow SE22   £30   ❷❸❸
37 Lordship Ln   8693 3111   1–4D
"Delicious basic fish and chips, but also stunning
steamed and grilled options" – this "café-style"
East Dulwich chippy invariably pleases; "great value
when kids eat free at weekends" (before 4pm).
/ SE22 8EW; www.theseacow.co.uk; @seacowcrew;
11 pm, Sun-Mon 10 pm; closed Mon L, Tue L & Wed L;
no Amex.

Sea Pebbles HA5   £28   ❸④❸
348-352 Uxbridge Rd   8428 0203   1–1A
"A place to go, if you find yourself in Hatch End" –
a chippy that's "always full", thanks to its "excellent
fish", and its "great value for money". / HA5 4HR;
9.45 pm; closed Sun; debit cards only; need 8+ to book.

Seafresh SW1 £36 ③④⑤
80-81 Wilton Rd 7828 0747 2–4B
"Chips are never crisper, and the scampi tastes of the sea", say fans of this *"very reliable"* Pimlico fish 'n' chips veteran (which offers a menu of *"unusual range"*). / SW1V 1DL; www.seafresh-dining.com; 10.30 pm; closed Sun.

The Sea Shell NW1 £42 ❷❸④
49 Lisson Grove 7224 9000 8–4A
"Throw dietary caution to the wind", and have some *"excellent fish, chips 'n' mushy peas"* at this famous Marylebone chippy; *"now it's been redecorated"*, some regulars say, the interior's *"better"* too.
/ NW1 6UH; www.seashellrestaurant.co.uk; 10.30 pm; closed Sun; SRA-50%.

**Season Kitchen
N4** NEW £37 ❷❷❸
53 Stroud Green Rd 7263 5500 8–1D
"A very good addition to the north London scene"; this *"small but very cosy"* Finsbury Park spot offers some *"thoughtful"*, seasonal cooking, and local reporters find it *"really lovely on all levels"*. / N4 3EF; www.seasonkitchen.co.uk; 10.30 pm, Sun 9 pm; D only.

Sedap EC1 £28 ④④④
102 Old St 7490 0200 12–1A
"Not cutting-edge but reliably satisfying and reasonably-priced" – this Malaysian café, near Silicon Roundabout, makes a *"great cheap eat"*. / EC1V 9AY; www.sedap.co.uk; 10.30 pm, Sun 10 pm; closed Sat L & Sun L; no Amex.

Seven Park Place SW1 £91 ❸❸❸
7-8 Park Pl 7316 1600 3–4C
William Drabble's *"masterful"* cooking – with real *"artistry and substance"* – arguably deserves a wider audience than it finds in this *"niche"* St James's chamber; the *"opulent"* but *"odd"* parlour-style setting inspires mixed views, though – *"intimate"* to some tastes, but too *"staid"* for others.
/ SW1A 1LP; www.stjameshotelandclub.com; 10 pm; closed Mon & Sun; set weekday L £55 (FP).

Seven Stars WC2 £29 ❸④❷
53 Carey St 7242 8521 2–2D
People come to Roxy Beaujolais's tavern behind the Royal Courts of Justice *"for the quirkiness (the cat with the ruff and so on), and because it feels traditional"*; that said, *"the food, at pub prices, is above usual pub standards"*. / WC2A 2JB; 9.30 pm.

Seventeen W11 £47 ❸❸❸
17 Notting Hill Gate 7985 0006 6–2B
Somewhat marooned on busy Notting Hill Gate, this *"under-rated Chinese"* is worth seeking out; its styling, especially downstairs, is *"tasteful and modern"*, and the food *"always delivers on the classics, with some more exotic dishes too"*.
/ W11 3JQ; www.seventeen-london.co.uk; 11.15 pm.

Shake Shack WC2 NEW £23
23 The Mkt, Covent Garden 3598 1360 4–3D
Recently arrived in Covent Garden Market, an outpost of Danny Meyer's much-celebrated NYC-based burger bar chain; perhaps it's chauvinism, but the local press haven't been quite convinced that the burgers are so much better than the native offerings. / WC2E 8RD; www.shakeshack.com/location/london-covent-garden; @shakeshack; 11 pm, Sun 10.30 pm.

Shampers W1 £45 ❸❷❷
4 Kingly St 7437 1692 3–2D
An *"unfailing"* 80s wine bar, just off Regent Street; it's a *"lively"* but *"relaxed"* stalwart, offering *"good old-fashioned food"* plus *"one of the most comprehensive wine lists you'll find"*.
/ W1B 5PE; www.shampers.net; 10.45 pm; closed Sun.

Shanghai E8 £35 ❸④❸
41 Kingsland High St 7254 2878 1–1C
"My Chinese friend makes a big detour to come here!"; *"great dim sum"* is the highlight at *"Dalston's best Oriental"*, elegantly housed in a former pie 'n' eel shop – make sure you get a table at the front.
/ E8 2JS; www.shanghaidalston.co.uk; 11 pm; no Amex.

Shanghai Blues WC1 £66 ④⑤⑤
193-197 High Holborn 7404 1668 4–1D
Something seems to have gone awry at this once-admirable Holborn Chinese – formerly *"cool"* and *"intriguing"*, it now too often just appears *"cavernous"*, *"pretentious"* and *"disappointing"*.
/ WC1V 7BD; www.shanghaiblues.co.uk; 11.30 pm.

The Shed W8 NEW £38 ❸❷❶
122 Palace Gardens Ter 7229 4024 6–2B
"A brilliant new version of the old Ark"; this pint-sized, Notting Hill Gate landmark has been imaginatively re-born in *"casual"*, faux-*"rustic"* style – its *"delicious, British tapas-style"* dishes may be no bargain, but most reporters think they are *"wonderful"*, especially for a *"cool brunch"*.
/ W8 4RT; www.theshed-restaurant.com; @theshed_resto; 11 pm; closed Mon & Sun.

J SHEEKEY WC2 £70 ❷❶❶
28-34 St Martin's Ct 7240 2565 4–3B
"A class act" par excellence; Theatreland's *"elegant"* fish-legend (opened 1896) is once again London's most talked-about restaurant; *"superb fish pie"* is the exemplar of the *"utterly dependable"* menu, served in its *"clubby"* (if squashed) series of rooms. / WC2N 4AL; www.j-sheekey.co.uk; midnight, Sun 11 pm; booking: max 6.

**J Sheekey Oyster Bar
WC2** **£63** **❷⓿⓿**
32-34 St Martin's Ct 7240 2565 4–3B
It's "pure gastronomic theatre" to grab a high stool
in the Theatreland legend's "less formal" bar –
many reporters prefer its combination
of "real glamour" and "divine, simple but perfect
seafood" to the full -blown experience next door.
/ WC2N 4AL; www.j-sheekey.co.uk; midnight, Sun 11 pm;
booking: max 3.

Shilpa W6 **£30** **❷❸⑤**
206 King St 8741 3127 7–2B
"Excellently-spiced" Keralan food at "incredible"
prices inspires ardent praise for this "dull and
utilitarian" café, on Hammersmith's main drag;
"somehow its scruffiness makes it feel more
authentic!" / W6 0RA; www.shilparestaurant.co.uk;
11 pm, Thu-Sat midnight.

The Shiori W2 NEW **£84** **⓿❷④**
45 Moscow Rd 7221 9790 6–2C
"Exceptional kaiseki-style food" (including
"stunning" sushi) offers lovers of Japanese food
a "sublime" experiences at this Bayswater
newcomer; sadly, though, the setting is decidedly
"sterile". / W2 4AH; www.theshiori.com; 8.30 pm; closed
Mon & Sun.

The Ship SW18 **£47** **④④❸**
41 Jews Row 8870 9667 10–2B
Come summertime, this "understandably popular"
boozer, by Wandsworth Bridge, is rammed, thanks
to the attractions of its large Thames-side terrace
and dependable BBQ – "the food is nothing
special". / SW18 1TB; www.theship.co.uk;
@shipwandsworth; 10 pm; no booking, Sun L.

Shoryu Ramen **£27** **❷❸❸**
9 Regent St, SW1 no tel 3–3D NEW
3 Denman St, W1 no tel 3–2D NEW
"Getting very close to Tokyo chain standards!" –
this "cheap", "cheerful" and "tightly-packed" ramen
parlour is hailed by most reporters as a "superb" pit
stop… and just a few moments from Piccadilly
Circus too; now also in Soho. / Regent St 11.30 pm,
Sun 10.30 pm – Soho midnight, Sun 10.30 pm.

Shrimpy's N1 **£49** **④④❸**
King's Cross Filling Station, Good's Way 8880
6111 8–3C
A former petrol station, in redeveloping King's Cross,
that's become quite a "hipster heaven", despite its
"patchy" service, and its food which can "promise
a lot, and deliver little". / N1C 4UR;
www.shrimpys.co.uk; @shrimpysloves; 11 pm.

Siam Central W1 **£31** **④❸❸**
14 Charlotte St 7436 7460 2–1C
"Inexpensive, fresh, and speedy" – a Fitzrovia Thai
that's "ideal for a casual meal". / W1T 2LX;
10.45 pm, Sun 10.15 pm.

Sichuan Folk E1 **£43** **❷❸⑤**
32 Hanbury St 7247 4735 12–2C
A "superb gastronomic experience" ("if you like hot
and spicy Sichuan food") awaits those who seek out
this decidedly no-frills East Ender; "shame about the
cold atmosphere…" / E1 6QR; www.sichuan-folk.co.uk;
10.30 pm; no Amex; set weekday L £23 (FP).

The Sign of the Don EC4 NEW
21 St Swithin's Ln 7626 2606 9–3C
Opening in late-2013, a neighbouring offshoot
of City favourite The Don, offering a more casual
style, and the wine emphasis for which the parent
establishment is known; decor relates to the
Sandeman Port & Sherry heritage of the site.
/ EC4N 8AD; www.thesignofthedon.com.

Signor Sassi SW1 **£66** **④❸❸**
14 Knightsbridge Grn 7584 2277 5–1D
This "buzzy" ("noisy") old-time Knightsbridge Italian
is still a "favourite" for some reporters; it's the
"attentive" service which really makes the place,
but the food, if no bargain, is "always enjoyable".
/ SW1X 7QL; www.signorsassi.co.uk; 11.30 pm,
Sun 10.30 pm.

Simpson's Tavern EC3 **£37** **④❸⓿**
38 1/2 Ball Ct, Cornhill 7626 9985 9–2C
A "wonderful" hang-over from the time of Dickens –
an "ancient" chophouse delivering "old-school grub
at very fair prices", dispensed by matronly staff who
are "matter-of-fact and witty, to the point of being
cheeky and abrupt". / EC3V 9DR;
www.simpsonstavern.co.uk; @SimpsonsTavern; 3 pm;
L only, closed Sat & Sun.

**Simpsons-in-the-Strand
WC2** **£75** **④④❸**
100 Strand 7836 9112 4–3D
For fans, these grand and very English dining rooms,
on the fringe of Covent Garden, still offer "a great
trip down memory lane to the days of good old
roast beef" (and the breakfast is "super" too);
as ever, though, critics proclaim a "jaded" institution,
run "mainly for tourists". / WC2R 0EW;
www.simpsonsinthestrand.co.uk; 10.45 pm, Sun 9 pm;
no trainers.

**Singapore Garden
NW6** **£43** **❷❸④**
83a Fairfax Rd 7624 8233 8–2A
A "very dependable" Swiss Cottage fixture which
continues to please the locals with its "tasty,
well spiced dishes from a range of SE Asian
countries". / NW6 4DY; www.singaporegarden.co.uk;
11 pm, Fri & Sat 11.30 pm.

K10

Kaspars

Little Social Eating House

Flesh & Buns

(Gallery)
Sketch W1   **£75**   ④④④
9 Conduit St   7659 4500   3–2C
*This Mayfair fashionista favourite is "just amazing",
say those who feel this "eclectic" party scene is a
notably "fun" destination for "sociable dining";
for almost every fan, though, there's a foe who finds
the whole style "uncomfortably pretentious",
and with "prices to match". / W1S 2XG;
www.sketch.uk.com; 11 pm; D only; booking: max 10.*

(Lecture Room)
Sketch W1   **£119**   ④❸❶
9 Conduit St   7659 4500   3–2C
*A "quite extraordinary" Mayfair dining room offering
an experience which is "ostentatious" to an extent
rarely seen; its "terrific" cuisine – created by Parisian
über-chef Pierre Gagnaire – comes with "lots of
twists", but leaves some reporters unconvinced that
the "mega-buck" pricing is justified. / W1S 2XG;
www.sketch.uk.com; @sketchlondon; 10.30 pm; closed
Mon, Sat L & Sun; no trainers; booking: max 8.*

(The Parlour)
Sketch W1   **£62**   ④④❷
9 Conduit St   7659 4533   3–2C
*"Like Alice in Wonderland" – this "eternally quirky"
Mayfair parlour is, for fans, a "fun" experience,
and "recommended for afternoon tea" or a "chilled
breakfast"; to sceptics, though, it's just "massively
overpriced and ordinary". / W1S 2XG;
www.sketch.uk.com; 10 pm; no booking.*

Skipjacks HA3   **£39**   ❶❷④
268-270 Streatfield Rd   8204 7554   1–1A
*A "really down-to-earth" and "hectic but friendly"
Harrow chippy, acclaimed for its "brilliant fish 'n'
chips" in "huge portions". / HA3 9BY; 10.30 pm;
closed Sun.*

Skylon
South Bank Centre
SE1   **£59**   ④④❷
Belvedere Rd   7654 7800   2–3D
*If you can get a table by the massive windows,
this vast South Bank chamber offers "surely the
most romantic view in London"; other aspects of this
D&D group operation are very missable –
for the "distinctly so-so" food, the bills can
sometimes seem "unbelievable". / SE1 8XX;
www.skylonrestaurant.co.uk; 10.30 pm, Sun 10 pm;
no trainers; SRA-64%.*

Skylon Grill SE1   **£56**   ❸❸❷
Belvedere Rd   7654 7800   2–3D
*With its "gigantic windows for watching the sunset",
this "buzzy" cheaper section of the D&D group's
massive South Bank dining room is "better value
than the adjacent restaurant"; the grill fare
is "reliably good" and the view is just the same
as next door. / SE1 8XX; 11 pm.*

Smiths Brasserie
E1 NEW   **£51**   ❷❸❷
22 Wapping High St   7488 3456   11–1A
*"An excellent addition to the Wapping restaurant
scene" – this new outpost of a popular Essex
brasserie wins praise for its "wonderfully fresh fish";
"stunning views of Tower Bridge" too. / E1W 1NJ;
10 pm; closed Sun D.*

(Ground Floor)
Smiths of Smithfield
EC1   **£32**   ④④❸
67-77 Charterhouse St   7251 7950   9–1A
*"Sunday brunch at Smith's is a must", or at
least so say long-term fans of this "atmospheric"
hang-out, "slap bang in the middle of Smithfield";
of late, however, not all reporters have been that
impressed. / EC1M 6HJ; www.smithsofsmithfield.co.uk;
L only; no bookings.*

(Dining Room)
Smiths of Smithfield
EC1   **£53**   ④④④
67-77 Charterhouse St   7251 7950   9–1A
*"Reliable", "professional" and "no-nonsense" – that's
why most reporters like the "noisy" first floor of this
Smithfield warehouse-complex, where simple char-
grilled fare is the stock-in-trade; there's also
a feeling, however, that "for the price, nothing really
stands out". / EC1A 6HJ; www.smithsofsmithfield.co.uk;
10.45 pm; closed Sat L & Sun; booking: max 12.*

(Top Floor)
Smiths of Smithfield
EC1   **£72**   ⑤④④
67-77 Charterhouse St   7251 7950   9–1A
*A City-fringe rooftop steak venue, with an impressive
view; it's the vista you pay for, though – with its
"very standard" cooking and "aloof" service,
its standards are "not a patch on the modern
competition". / EC1M 6HJ;
www.smithsofsmithfield.co.uk; 10.45 pm; closed
Sat L & Sun D; booking: max 10.*

The Smokehouse Islington
N1 NEW   **£45**
63-69 Canonbury Rd   7354 1144   8–2D
*On the former Canonbury site of the House (RIP),
this large new gastropub opened just before this
guide went to press; we didn't have the opportunity
to visit, but there has been some very positive
commentary in the media. / N1 2RG;
www.smokehouseislington.co.uk.*

Social Eating House
W I NEW £55 ❸❸❸
58-59 Poland St 7993 3251 3–2D
*On most accounts, Jason Atherton's latest "buzzy"
baby is "a really great addition to the Soho scene",
offering "inventive" British fare that's both
"excellent" and "artistic"; the occasional report
of "bland" cuisine, however, slightly undercuts its
ratings. / W1F 7NR; www.socialeatinghouse.com; 10 pm;
closed Sun.*

Sofra £35 ❹❸❹
1 St Christopher's Pl, W1 7224 4080 3–1A
18 Shepherd St, W1 7493 3320 3–4B
36 Tavistock St, WC2 7240 3773 4–3D
*These "useful" Turkish "fall backs" are ideal for
"a quick, reliable" meal – "nothing's amazing but
meze are done well", and there are some "good-
value set-price deals". / www.sofra.co.uk;
11 pm-midnight.*

Soho Diner W I NEW £37 ❸❷❷
19 Old Compton St 7734 5656 4–2A
*Brooklyn comes to the heart of Soho; this fast-
service, small-menu diner (on the former site
of Bohème Kitchen RIP) really only offers simple
American 'bar' food, but it makes a good place
to watch the world go by. / W1D 5JJ; Rated on Editors'
visit; www.sohodiner.com; SohoDinerLDN.*

Soho Japan NW I £40 ❷❷❹
195 Baker St 7486 7000 2–1B
*Once an Irish pub – and little changed decor-wise –
this Japanese diner (north of Oxford Street) is well-
rated for "cheap 'n' cheerful" sushi. / NW1 6UY;
www.sohojapan.co.uk; @sohojapan; 10.30 pm; closed
Mon & Sun L; no Amex.*

Soif SW I I £46 ❹❹❹
27 Battersea Rise 7223 1112 10–2C
*Like its parent, Terroirs, this Battersea bistro
undoubtedly offers some "interesting biodynamic
wines"; otherwise, though, feedback on all aspects
of operations in this "awkwardly-shaped" room
is rather ambivalent. / SW11 1HG; 10 pm; closed
Mon L, Tue L, Wed L.*

Solly's NW I I £44 ❸❹❹
146-150 Golders Green Rd 8455 0004 1–1B
*A Golder's Green landmark – this "popular" Israeli
café/take-away (with upstairs restaurant) serves
"good-quality" wraps and meze, sometimes rather
brusquely. / NW11 8HE; 10.30 pm; closed
Fri D & Sat L; no Amex.*

Somerstown Coffee House
NW I £39 ❸❷❸
60 Chalton St 7387 7377 8–3C
*"A perfect meeting-place, between Euston and
St Pancras" – this "friendly and competent"
gastropub operates a "mainly tapas" formula that
generally satisfies. / NW1 1HS;
www.somerstowncoffeehouse.co.uk; 10 pm; no Amex.*

Sông Quê E2 £33 ❸⑤❹
134 Kingsland Rd 7613 3222 12–1B
*"Crazy menu, crazy choices, crazy green decor
sometimes crazy queues!" – this "authentic"
Shoreditch Vietnamese "marches to its own, no-frills
beat"; some long-term fans, though, think it's
"gone way downhill" in recent years. / E2 8DY;
www.sonque.co.uk; 11 pm; no Amex.*

Sonny's Kitchen SW I 3 £52 ❹❹❹
94 Church Rd 8748 0393 10–1A
*This Barnes linchpin (newly a 'Kitchen') has put
in an inconsistent performance since its 2012 relaunch – fans feel it has recaptured the "informal
and lively" mojo of old, with "stunning", "simple"
fare, whereas sceptics, just see a "noisy" place with
"disjointed" cooking and "slipshod" service.
/ SW13 0DQ; www.sonnyskitchen.co.uk; 10 pm, Fri-Sat
11 pm, Sun 9.30 pm; set weekday L £32 (FP), set Sun L
£39 (FP).*

La Sophia W I0 £46 ❷❸❹
46 Golborne Road 8968 2200 6–1A
*Still less commentary than we'd like on this North
Kensington two-year-old; such as it is, though,
suggests that this Middle Eastern/Mediterranean
spot is a notably "consistent" all-rounder. / W10 5PR;
www.lasophia.co.uk; Mon-Thu 10 pm, Fri & Sat
10.30 pm, Sun 9 pm; closed Mon L & Tue L.*

Sophie's Steakhouse £52 ❹❹❹
29-31 Wellington St, WC2 7836 8836 4–3D
311-313 Fulham Rd, SW10 7352 0088 5–3B
*Fans of these "straightforward" hang-outs applaud
their "fab cocktails", "succulent" steaks and
"buzzing atmosphere"; "with so many great
steakhouses around" nowadays, however,
the formula can seem rather "tired" in comparison.
/ www.sophiessteakhouse.com; SW10 11.45 pm,
Sun 11.15 pm; WC2 12.45 am, Sun 11 pm; no booking;
set weekday L £31 (FP).*

Sotheby's Café W I £57 ❹❷❷
34-35 New Bond St 7293 5077 3–2C
*For "a people-watching lunch", this café off the
foyer of the famous Mayfair auction house has its
attractions (particularly on sale or pre-sale days);
the lobster club-sandwich is a highlight of the rather
"limited" menu. / W1A 2AA; www.sothebys.com; L only,
closed Sat & Sun; booking: max 8.*

Spianata & Co £11 ❸❷❸
3 Hay Hill, W1 no tel 3–3C
Tooley St, SE1 8616 4662 9–4D
41 Brushfield St, E1 7655 4411 12–2B
20 Holborn Viaduct, EC1 7248 5947 9–2A
17 Blomfield St, EC2 7256 9103 9–2C
73 Watling St, EC4 7236 3666 9–2B
*A "friendly" Italian take-away (mainly) chain, where
the focus is on "authentic focaccia sandwiches" and
"the best coffee ever". / www.spianata.com; 3.30 pm;
EC3 11 pm; closed Sat & Sun; E1 closed Sat; no credit
cards; no booking.*

Spice Market
W Hotel London W1   £75   ④④④
10 Wardour St   7758 1088   4–3A
Very mixed (and remarkably few) reports on this
heart-of-the-West-End outpost of the empire of top
NYC chef Jean-Georges Vongerichten… which all
tends to support the view that it's "not a patch"
on the Manhattan Meatpacking District original.
/ W1D 6QF; www.spicemarketlondon.co.uk; 11 pm,
Thu-Sat 11.30 pm; set weekday L £46 (FP).

Spuntino W1   £40   ❷❸❷
61 Rupert St   no tel   3–2D
Russell Norman's "very hip" ("Brooklyn-style") bar,
in the sleazy heart of Soho, offers "great cocktails"
and a snack menu that includes "great sliders"
(mini-burgers) – "worth the queue!" / W1D 7PW;
www.spuntino.co.uk; 11.30 pm, Sun 10.30 pm.

THE SQUARE W1   £104   ❷⓿❸
6-10 Bruton St   7495 7100   3–2C
Phil Howard's "consistently assured" cuisine
"surprises even the most jaded palette", and the
appeal of his "calm" Mayfair HQ for some "serious
dining" – especially for expense accounters –
is completed by a wine list "to drain a sovereign
wealth fund"; fans insist the suit-heavy ambience
is "getting more lively" too. / W1J 6PU;
www.squarerestaurant.com; 9.45 pm, Sat 10.15 pm,
Sun 9.30 pm; closed Sun L; booking: max 8.

Sree Krishna SW17   £27   ❷❸④
192-194 Tooting High St   8672 4250   10–2C
"Unchanging, in a good way" – this 40-year-old
south Indian in Tooting is admittedly
"unatmospheric", but the food is "great, and very
good value"; BYO. / SW17 0SF; www.sreekrishna.co.uk;
@SreeKrishnaUk; 10.45 pm, Fri & Sat 11.45 pm;
set weekday L £13 (FP).

Star of India SW5   £51   ❷④④
154 Old Brompton Rd   7373 2901   5–2B
"No longer fashionable, but not forgotten!";
this "quirky" Earl's Court subcontinental, with its
'Sistine Chapel' interior, is still – for its many fans –
"one of the best"; service, though, is "up-and-down".
/ SW5 0BE; www.starofindia.eu; 11.45 pm,
Sun 11.15 pm.

Stick & Bowl W8   £22   ❷❷❸
31 Kensington High St   7937 2778   5–1A
"Real, honest Cantonese food" makes this "unique,
little noodle house", near Kensington Palace,
a mightily handy 'value' destination – "don't let the
scruffy, cramped, shared tables put you off!"
/ W8 5NP; 10.45 pm; no credit cards; no booking.

Sticks'n'Sushi   £47   ❸❸❷
11 Henrietta St, WC2   3141 8800   4–3D NEW
58 Wimbledon Hill Rd, SW19   3141 8800
10–2B
A "hugely popular" yearling, serving up "really
enjoyable Japanese fare with a Scandi twist", in a
setting that "looks like it should be somewhere
much trendier than Wimbledon" (and which even
fans can find "pricey" for what it is); a new branch
opens in Covent Garden in late-2013.
/ www.sticksnsushi.com; Sun - Tues 10 pm, Wed -Sat
11 pm.

Sticky Fingers W8   £42   ❸❸❸
1a Phillimore Gdns   7938 5338   5–1A
"Rolling Stones memorabilia drips from every wall,
staff are really helpful… and the burgers aren't bad
either" – this Kensington backstreet burger parlour
remains a "great" destination (especially
"with kids"). / W8 7QR; www.stickyfingers.co.uk;
10.45 pm.

STK Steakhouse
ME by Meliá London
WC2   £68   ④④❸
336-337 The Strand   7395 3450   4–3C
This "night-clubby and cool" new arrival, on the
fringe of Covent Garden gets mixed reports; to fans
it's "a sleek and sexy place, just like being back
in NYC", but foes (many) say it's "ridiculously
pricey" and "pretentious", and "so loud you can't
think". / WC2R 1HA; www.stkhouse.com.

Stock Pot   £27   ④❸❸
38 Panton St, SW1   7839 5142   4–4A
273 King's Rd, SW3   7823 3175   5–3C
"Get away from fancy meals, and get in touch with
the real world!" – these "friendly, noisy, busy and
fun" canteen-veterans offer "basic" fodder
at "fabulous" prices; they provide "a trip down
memory lane" too… if you're old enough to recall
the '60s! / SW1 11.30 pm, Wed-Sat midnight,
Sun 11 pm. SW3 10.15 pm, Sun 9.45 pm; no Amex.

Story SE1 NEW   £65   ⓿⓿❸
201 Tooley St   7183 2117   9–4D
Tom Sellers's "sensational" food with a "theatrical"
twist ("everyone will want to try the dripping
candle") has made his "NOMA-style" spot the
best of the 2013 newcomers – brave the "awful"
location, south of Tower Bridge, and you'll find
an "interesting" Scandi-style room where staff
simply "buzz with enthusiasm". / SE1 2UE;
www.restaurantstory.co.uk; 9.15 pm; closed Mon & Sun.

Story Deli E2   £42   ❷④❷
123 Bethnal Green Rd   819 7352   12–2B
"Get the East London vibe at this cool hangout" (still
near Brick Lane, but moved from the Truman
Brewery a couple of years ago), where thin-
crust pizza is the main event food-wise. / E2 7DG;
www.storydeli.com; 10.30 pm; no credit cards.

Strada £41 ④④④
Branches throughout London
A "patchy" performance by this pizza/pasta chain –
fans find it "reliable" and "family-friendly", but those
who remember its one-time culinary pre-eminence
feel it's "really gone downhill". / www.strada.co.uk;
10.30 pm-11 pm; some booking restrictions apply.

Street Kitchen EC2 £18 ❷❸–
Broadgate Circle no tel 12–2B
Proof positive that food vans are mainstream –
this silver Airstream, run by celeb chefs Mark Jankel
and Jun Tanaka, serves "great daily specials" from
their lunchtime perch at Broadgate Circle; other
locations (with other more dude-foodish menus) too.
/ EC2; www.streetkitchen.co.uk/home.shtml;
@Streetkitchen.

Suda WC2 £45 ❸❸❸
23 Slingsby Pl, St Martin's Ct 7240 8010 4–3C
OK, it has 'chain prototype' written all over it,
but this "handy" Covent Garden-fringe Thai still
impresses all who report on it with its "simple but
tasty" cuisine. / WC2E 9AB; www.suda-thai.com;
10.30 pm, Thu-Sat 11 pm.

Sufi W12 £30 ❸❷❸
70 Askew Rd 8834 4888 7–1B
"You won't find better bread" than the tandoori-
baked offering at this "ever-friendly and welcoming"
Persian spot, deep in Shepherd's Bush; dishes are
"fairly simple", but they offer "such good value".
/ W12 9BJ; www.sufirestaurant.com; 11 pm.

Suk Saran SW19 £51 ❸④⑤
29 Wimbledon Hill Rd 8947 9199 10–2B
"Very good" food ("amazing", say fans) makes this
Wimbledon Town Thai a handy local standby.
/ SW19 7NE; www.sukhogroup.com; 11 pm; booking:
max 20.

**Sukho Fine Thai Cuisine
SW6** £50 ❶❶④
855 Fulham Rd 7371 7600 10–1B
"The best Thai food in West London" – arguably the
whole capital – is to be had at this "wonderful" little
outfit, in deepest Fulham; staff are ultra-"charming"
too, leaving the "cramped" setting as the only real
downside. / SW6 5HJ; www.sukhogroup.co.uk; 11 pm.

**The Summerhouse
W9** £55 ④❸❷
60 Blomfield Rd 7286 6752 8–4A
"A lovely canalside setting" is the particular
attraction of this "great find" in Little Venice (which
is nowadays open all year) – the fish-centric cuisine
very much plays second fiddle. / W9 2PA;
www.thesummerhouse.co.uk; 10.30 pm, Sun 10 pm;
no Amex.

Sumosan W1 £76 ❷④④
26b Albemarle St 7495 5999 3–3C
"Wonderful" Japanese-fusion fare, including
"fabulous" sashimi and sushi, top the bill at this
style-conscious, and "outrageously expensive"
Mayfair Japanese; though it's sometimes "buzzy",
it never seems to have attracted the following of the
likes of Nobu and Zuma. / W1S 4HY;
www.sumosan.com; @sumosan_; 11.30 pm,
Sun 10.30 pm; closed Sat L & Sun L; set weekday L
£51 (FP).

The Surprise SW3 £45 ④❸❷
6 Christchurch Ter 7351 6954 5–3D
Hidden-away in Chelsea, this "lovely little pub"
is something of a "gem"; it serves a "simple but
imaginative" menu of British 'tapas'. / SW3 4AJ;
www.geronimo-inns.co.uk/thesurprise; 10 pm, Sun 9 pm;
SRA-60%.

Sushisamba EC2 £76 ❸④❷
Heron Tower, 110 Bishopsgate 3640 7330
9–2D
"Peerless" views and "the best terrace in town" have
certainly made this "showy" bar/restaurant complex,
on the 38th/39th floors of the City's Heron Tower,
an "exceptional" destination; although it's "wildly
expensive", the "sumptuous" Latino/Asian cuisine
is "surprisingly good" too. / EC2N 4AY; Sun-Thu
midnight, Fri & Sat 1 am.

Sushi Tetsu EC1 £54 ❶❶❸
12 Jerusalem Pas 3217 0090 9–1A
"Having lived in Tokyo for 5 years, this is the only
sushi bar in the UK that bears comparison!" –
this Clerkenwell hole-in-the-wall is "a labour of love"
which "redefines Japanese food in London";
"unfortunately the word is out and, as there are only
7 seats, it is impossible to get a booking".
/ EC1V 4JP; www.sushitetsu.co.uk.

Sushi-Say NW2 £43 ❶❷④
33b Walm Ln 8459 7512 1–1A
Don't let the unlikely Willesden Green location fool
you – this unassuming café is "definitely one
of London's best Japanese restaurants", and "proof
that authentic Japanese grub needn't leave you
hungry and bankrupt!" / NW2 5SH; 10 pm,
Sat 10.30 pm, Sun 9.30 pm; closed Mon, Tue, Wed L,
Thu L & Fri L; no Amex.

Sushinho £57 ❷❸❸
312-314 King's Rd, SW3 7349 7496 5–3C
9a, Devonshire Sq, EC2 7220 9490 9–2D
"Surprisingly fantastic" Japanese/Brazilian fusion
cuisine, and "excellent cocktails" too – this alluring
Chelsea bar/restaurant makes a good, if pricey,
destination for a night out; remarkably, though,
the new City branch has "no ambience".
/ www.sushinho.com; SW3 12 am, EC2 10.30 pm;
SW3 closed Sun-Fri L, EC2 closed Sat L.

The Swan W4 £44 ❷❷❶
119 Acton Ln 8994 8262 7–1A
The food shows impressive "attention to detail" and
the service is really "lovely", but it's the "fabulous"
atmosphere – and "the best pub garden" – which
primarily underpin the popularity of this
"traditional" Chiswick boozer. / W4 5HH;
www.theswanchiswick.co.uk; 10 pm, Fri & Sat 10.30 pm,
Sun 10 pm; closed weekday L.

Swan & Edgar NW1 £39 ❹❸❷
43 Linhope St 7724 6268 2–1A
"A nice hidden secret" – this "quirky" and "cosy"
bolt-hole, near Marylebone station, dishes up very
decent food, as well as "good wines by the glass".
/ NW1 6HL; www.swanandedgar.co.uk; 10 pm,
Sun 9 pm; D only, ex Sun open L & D.

**The Swan at the Globe
SE1** £54 ❹❹❷
21 New Globe Walk 7928 9444 9–3B
With its view of St Paul's, this "romantic" South
Bank first floor operation strikes fans as a "really
great dining room"; even they may concede that
"the food doesn't match the setting", though,
and harsher critics say "you might do better at the
local Pizza Express!" / SE1 9DT; www.loveswan.co.uk;
@swanabout; 9.45 pm, Sun 4.45 pm; closed Sun D.

**Sweet Thursday
N1** [NEW] £33 ❷❸❷
95 Southgate Rd 7226 1727 1–2C
In De Beauvoir, this "excellent" new pizzeria has
won instant local acclaim; the formula? – "huge"
thin crust pizza, with "interesting combos", "great
wine" (they do tastings) and "a wonderful homely
vibe". / N1 3JS; www.sweetthursday.co.uk;
@Pizza_and_Pizza; 10 pm, Sat 10.30 pm, Sun 9 pm.

Sweetings EC4 £58 ❸❸❷
39 Queen Victoria St 7248 3062 9–3B
If you're looking for "a real institution that never
changes", it would be hard to beat this "eccentric"
Victorian "national treasure" – "a classic City fish
bar" whose "enduring" nature is "part of its
appeal"; arrive early for a table, or have a sandwich
at the counter. / EC4N 4SA;
www.sweetingsrestaurant.com; 3.30 pm; L only, closed
Sat & Sun; no booking.

Taberna Etrusca EC4 £50 ❸❷❸
9 Bow Churchyard 7248 5552 9–2C
"Well-executed food in a charming location";
this long-established City Italian – which has some
particularly nice al fresco tables – has been dishing
up some unusually good meals of late. / EC4M 9DQ;
www.etruscarestaurants.com; 10 pm; closed Mon D,
Sat & Sun.

The Table SE1 £45 ❸❹❹
83 Southwark St 7401 2760 9–4B
A "fantastic" lunch or brunch-stop, particularly good
pre-Tate Modern – so claim fans of this "chilled"

canteen-like space, on the ground floor of a major
architectural practice; you can't book, though,
and prices can seem high, given the "basic" setting,
and sometimes "rushed" service. / SE1 0HX;
www.thetablecafe.com; @thetablecafe; 10.30 pm; closed
Mon D & Sun D; SRA-64%.

Taiwan Village SW6 £34 ❶❶❸
85 Lillie Rd 7381 2900 5–3A
"An extraordinary find for the area!";
this "welcoming" Chinese/Taiwanese, behind
an "unassuming shopfront" off the North End Road,
"deserves to be much better known"; the "leave-it-
to-the-chef" menu, in particular, is "an absolute
treat". / SW6 1UD; www.taiwanvillage.com; 11.30 pm,
Sun 10.30 pm; closed weekday L; booking: max 20.

Tajima Tei EC1 £35 ❷❸❸
9-11 Leather Ln 7404 9665 9–2A
Looking for "a quick Japanese lunch", in the heart
of legal-land? – this "authentic" fixture offers
an experience "like being back in Tokyo", offering
a "well-priced" menu that includes "consistently
excellent sushi". / EC1N 7ST; www.tajima-tei.co.uk;
10 pm; closed Sat & Sun; no booking, L.

Talad Thai SW15 £31 ❸❹❺
320 Upper Richmond Rd 8246 5791 10–2A
"It's canteen-like and functional to look at",
and service is "slightly haphazard", but this Putney
Thai wins acclaim for its "authentic and tasty" scoff
at "cheap" prices. / SW15 6TL;
www.taladthairestaurant.com; 10.30 pm, Sun 9.30 pm;
no Amex.

Tamarind W1 £72 ❷❸❹
20 Queen St 7629 3561 3–3B
This Mayfair veteran is still on top of its game,
and its "masterful" evolved Indian cuisine still
pleases most reporters; "the negatives are that
you're in a basement, and prices are high".
/ W1J 5PR; www.tamarindrestaurant.com; 10.45 pm,
Sun 10.30 pm; closed Sat L; set weekday L £41 (FP), set
pre-theatre £48 (FP).

Tandoori Nights SE22 £37 ❸❷❸
73 Lordship Ln 8299 4077 1–4D
"Lovely" owners make it worth seeking out this
"consistent" East Dulwich fixture, whose "ambiance
is pretty much what one would expect in a local
Indian", but where the curries are "very tasty".
/ SE22 8EP; www.tandoorinightsdulwich.co.uk; 11.30pm,
Fri & Sat midnight; closed weekday L & Sat L.

Tapas Brindisa £42 ❷❸❸
46 Broadwick St, W1 7534 1690 3–2D
18-20 Southwark St, SE1 7357 8880 9–4C
*"Iberico and olive oil alone justify the trip!";
this tapas bar duo, run by the Spanish food
importers, serve up "authentic" dishes from "high-
quality ingredients"; the always "rammed" Borough
Market original is much better known than the
more modern Soho spin-off. / 10.45 pm, Sun 10 pm;
W1 booking: max 10.*

Taqueria W11 £34 ❸❸④
139-143 Westbourne Grove 7229 4734 6–1B
*"Everything you could ask of a Mexican
restaurant!"; thanks to its small dishes with
"authentic" flavours, plus brilliant margaritas and
cocktails, this snug Notting Hill hang-out "feels
just like eating in a cantina in Mexico". / W11 2RS;
www.taqueria.co.uk; 11 pm, Fri & Sat 11.30 pm,
Sun 10.30 pm; no Amex; no booking Fri-Sun.*

Taro £34 ❸❸❸
10 Old Compton St, W1 7439 2275 4–2B
61 Brewer St, W1 7734 5826 3–2D
44a, Cannon St, EC4 7236 0399 9–3B
*Mr Taro's "no-frills" and usually "jam-packed" Soho
canteens are "straightforward and quick" for
a "filling, yummy and cheapish" Japanese snack.
/ www.tarorestaurants.co.uk; 10.30 pm, Sun 9.30 pm;
no Amex; Brewer St only small bookings.*

Tartufo SW3 NEW £50 ❶❶❸
11 Cadogan Gdns 7730 6383 5–2D
*"Hard to find, but worth it!"; Alexis Gauthier's new
establishment, in the "cosy" basement of a small
hotel near Sloane Square, has opened to huge
acclaim for its "first-class" cooking, and at
"reasonable prices" too! / SW3 2RJ;
www.tartufolondon.co.uk; 10 pm; closed Mon & Sun.*

Tas £36 ④❸❸
22 Bloomsbury St, WC1 7637 4555 2–1C
33 The Cut, SE1 7928 2111 9–4A
72 Borough High St, SE1 7403 7200 9–4C
76 Borough High St, SE1 7403 8557 9–4C
97-99 Isabella St, SE1 7620 6191 9–4A
37 Farringdon Rd, EC1 7430 9721 9–1A
*"Cheap", "cheerful" and "dependable", this Turkish
bistro chain is hailed by pretty much all reporters
as at least a "good stand-by", especially "for a late
meal". / www.tasrestaurant.com; 11.30 pm,
Sun 10.30 pm.*

Tas Pide SE1 £33 ④❸❸
20-22 New Globe Walk 7928 3300 9–3B
*"Stick to the signature Anatolian pizzas and the
Turkish desserts and you won't go wrong" – not bad
advice if you visit this "bustling" spot near
Shakespeare's Globe; it's still hailed as a "value-for-
money" destination, but critics do fear it's "not as
good as it used to be". / SE1 9DR;
www.tasrestaurant.com/tas_pide; 11.30 pm,
Sun 10.30 pm.*

**(Rex Whistler)
Tate Britain SW1** £53
Millbank 7887 8825 2–4C
*Re-opening in late-2013, this famous dining room
is being given a major refurb; its renowned Whistler
murals will survive, of course – we trust the
almost equally famous wine list will also be intact.
/ SW1 4RG; www.tate.org.uk; L & afternoon tea only.*

**(Restaurant, Level 7)
Tate Modern SE1** £48 ⑤④❸
Bankside 7887 8888 9–3B
*"Fabulous views across the river to St Paul's plus not
especially memorable food" – that's the 'middle
view' on the the top-floor restaurant of the world's
most-visited modern art gallery; reports, however,
span the whole range from "classy" to "shocking".
/ SE1 9TG; www.tate.org.uk; @TateFood; 9.30 pm;
Sun-Thu closed D, Fri & Sat open L & D; SRA-61%.*

Taylor St Baristas £15 ❷❸❸
22 Brooks Mews, W1 7629 3163 3–2B
Unit 3 Westminster Hs, Kew Rd, TW9
07969798650 1–4A
1 Harbour Exchange Sq, E14 3069 8833
11–2C
8 South Colonnade, E14 no tel 11–1C
110 Clifton St, EC2 7929 2207 12–2B
Unit 3, 125 Old Broad St, EC2 7256 6668
9–2C
2 Botolph Alley, EC3 7283 1835 9–3C
*"Beware too big a caffeine-hit!", when you visit this
"small chain out of Oz" – you may also avail
yourself of some of the "brilliant" cakes and snacks
to complement the "superb" coffee. / EC2M 4TP;
www.taylor-st.com; all branches 5 pm; Old Broad ST,
Clifton St, W1, E14 closed Sat & Sun; New St closed Sat;
TW9 closed Sun.*

Tayyabs E1 £28 ❶⑤❸
83 Fieldgate St 7247 9543 9–2D
*"Too popular, but otherwise perfect!"; this "seriously
addictive" East End Pakistani continues to dish
up "incredible" dishes (including "the best lamb
chops ever") at "bargain" prices, and it's a BYO too;
service can be "chaotic", but it's all part of the
experience. / E1 1JU; www.tayyabs.co.uk; 11.30 pm.*

Telegraph SW15 £39 ④④❸
Telegraph Rd 8788 2011 10–2A
*The sign at this Putney Heath boozer – 'A Country
Pub in London' – doesn't lie; service is "haphazard"
at busy weekends, but the food is decent, and it's all
very cosy (though "upstairs rather lacks
atmosphere"). / SW15 3TU;
www.thetelegraphputney.co.uk; 9 pm, Fri & Sat 9.30 pm.*

The 10 Cases WC2   **£55**   ④❶❷
16 Endell St   836 6801   4–2C
"Incredible" wines (from a short but ever-changing
list) have made a major hit of this "terrific",
if "cramped", Covent Garden yearling (which has
already expanded into the shop next door);
"the food's not bad either". / WC2H 9BD;
www.the10cases.co.uk; 11 pm; closed Sun.

10 Greek Street W1   **£46**   ❷❶❸
10 Greek St   7734 4677   4–2A
"Atmosphere, charm, style and originality" –
this "cramped" Soho yearling has them all,
plus "unshowy" but "wonderfully-flavoured" cooking
at "incredible-value" prices; no booking. / W1D 4DH;
www.10greekstreet.com; @10GreekStreet; 11.30 pm;
closed Sun.

Tendido Cero SW5   **£45**   ❷❷❷
174 Old Brompton Rd   7370 3685   5–2B
"Continues to impress on all fronts..."; Cambio
de Tercio's "buzzy" and "noisy" younger sibling
serves "designer" tapas to a "sleek thirty-something
clientele", at this "accommodating" Earl's Court
spot. / SW5 0BA; www.cambiodetercio.co.uk;
@CambiodTercio; 11 pm.

Tendido Cuatro SW6   **£41**   ❷❷❸
108-110 New King's Rd   7371 5147   10–1B
Cambio de Tercio's "buzzy", "friendly" and "slightly
cramped" Fulham outpost attracts consistent praise
for its "excellent tapas and very good wine".
/ SW6 4LY; www.cambiodetercio.co.uk; 11 pm,
Sun 10.30 pm.

Tentazioni SE1   **£51**   ❸❸❸
2 Mill St   7394 5248   11–2A
"The best-kept secret in Shad Thames!";
this "welcoming", "no-fuss" Italian has "quite
a reputation on the gourmet trail" for its "proper"
cooking (pasta in particular). / SE1 2BD;
www.tentazioni.co.uk; @TentazioniWorld; 10.45 pm;
closed Sat L & Sun.

Terroirs WC2   **£46**   ❸❸❸
5 William IV St   7036 0660   4–4C
"Hidden-away" near Charing Cross, this "stylishly
simple" Gallic bistro has won fame with its earthy,
"big-flavoured" dishes (often in small-plate format),
and its "almost perversely unusual" range of organic
wines; its ratings, however, continue to drift gently.
/ WC2N 4DW; www.terroirswinebar.com;
@terroirswinebar; 11 pm; closed Sun.

Texture W1   **£93**   ❷❷❸
34 Portman St   7224 0028   2–2A
Agnar Sverrisson's "incredible Noma-like food"
("marvellous subtleties of flavours"), with "superb
wine choices" too, are carving out an ever-bigger
reputation for this "eclectic" venture, near Selfridges
– a "vibrant" spot that's a little hard-edged and
"noisy" for some tastes. / W1H 7BY;
www.texture-restaurant.co.uk; 10.30 pm; closed
Mon & Sun.

Thai Corner Café
SE22   **£21**   ❸❸❸
44 North Cross Rd   8299 4041   1–4D
"A small corner Thai restaurant" in the depths
of East Dulwich; the food's "good" and "fresh",
but it's "the great bonus of BYO" which makes
locals seek it out. / SE22 9EU;
www.thaicornercafe.co.uk; 10.30 pm; closed
Mon L & Tue L; no credit cards.

Thai Garden SW11   **£31**   ❸❸④
58 Battersea Rise   7738 0380   10–2C
A low-profile neighbourhood Thai, near Clapham
Junction, that's proved very reliable over many years;
as a "cheap 'n' cheerful" option, it remains
a consistent local recommendation. / SW11 1EG;
www.thaigarden.co.uk; @thaigardenuk; 10.30 pm; D only,
closed Mon.

Thai Square   **£40**   ④④④
21-24 Cockspur St, SW1   7839 4000   2–3C
27-28 St Annes Ct, W1   7287 2000   3–1D
5 Princess St, W1   7499 3333   3–1C
148 The Strand, WC2   7497 0904   2–2D
166-170 Shaftesbury Ave, WC2   7836 7600
4–1B
229-230 Strand, WC2   7353 6980   2–2D
19 Exhibition Rd, SW7   7584 8359   5–2C
347-349 Upper St, N1   7704 2000   8–3D
2-4 Lower Richmond Rd, SW15   8780 1811
10–1A
563 Fulham Rd, SW6   7610 0055   5–4A
136-138 Minories, EC3   7680 1111   9–3D
1-7 Great St Thomas Apostle, EC4   7329 0001
9–3B
"Convenient", "solid", "nice" – such are the virtues
fans see in this Thai stand-by chain (and the SW15
branch has "great views" of the Thames too).
/ www.thaisquare.net; 10 pm-11.30 pm; SW1 Fri & Sat
1 am; EC3, EC4 & St Annes Ct closed Sat & Sun, Strand
branches and Princess St closed Sun.

Thali SW5   **£43**   ❷❸④
166 Old Brompton Rd   7373 2626   5–2B
"The owner's family recipes" are used as the basis
for some "fantastic" North Indian dishes,
with "clean and crisp flavours", at this "slightly
poncy" Earl's Court venture. / SW5 0BA;
www.thali.uk.com; 11.30 pm, Sun 10.30 pm.

The Thatched House
W6 £44 ❸④❸
115 Dalling Rd 8748 6174 7–1B
*"Improved since the relaunch", this "friendly"
Hammersmith gastroboozer offers an "awesome"
Sunday lunch, a "good choice of beers" and
a "lovely little garden". / W6 0ET;
www.thatchedhouse.com; @thethatched; Thu-Sat
midnight, Sun-Wed 11pm.*

Theo Randall
InterContinental Hotel
W1 £83 ❷❸④
1 Hamilton Pl 7318 8747 3–4A
*"Sublime" Italian dishes, "cooked with panache",
have won renown for this ex-River Café chef's
Mayfair HQ; gripes about "unspectacular" meals
and "incredible" prices rose this year, though,
and the windowless room is notoriously
"unatmospheric". / W1J 7QY; www.theorandall.com;
11 pm; closed Sat L & Sun; set weekday L & pre-theatre
£57 (FP).*

34 W1 £74 ④❸❸
34 Grosvenor Sq 3350 3434 3–2A
*Richard Caring's year-old grill-house "looks great",
say fans, and – with its "tender" steaks and
"awesome" burgers – it "never fails to impress";
those who find the cooking "not particularly
memorable", though, may be inclined to notice the
decidedly Mayfair prices. / W1K 2HD;
www.34-restaurant.co.uk; 10.30 pm.*

Thirty Six
Duke's Hotel SW1 £88 ❸⑤④
35-36 Saint James's Pl 7491 4840 3–4C
*Mixed feedback this year on this "quiet" St James's
basement; most reporters still say it's a "hidden
gem" with "well-executed" cuisine, but sceptics can
find it "rather dull", and the service is "rather flaky"
too often for comfort. / SW1A 1NY;
www.dukeshotel.com; @dukeshotel; 9.30 pm; closed
Mon L & Sun D; set weekday L £57 (FP), set pre-theatre
£61 (FP).*

The Thomas Cubitt
SW1 £60 ❸❸❷
44 Elizabeth St 7730 6060 2–4A
*This "always-buzzing" Belgravian rendezvous is,
say fans, "a pub in the same way a diamond is a
rock"; this said, the food – both on the ground floor
and in the restaurant above –
has "gone backwards" of late. / SW1W 9PA;
www.thethomascubitt.co.uk; 10 pm; closed
Sat L & Sun D; booking only in restaurant; SRA-75%.*

3 South Place
South Place Hotel
EC2 £60 ④❸④
3 South Pl 3503 0000 12–2A
*A "something-for-everyone" menu makes the
ground-floor dining room of this contemporary-style
D&D group hotel a handy City standby; for more
atmosphere, though, head for the top-floor Angler
(see also). / EC2M 2AF; www.southplacehotel.com.*

Tian Fu W12 £32 ❸⑤⑤
37 Bulwer St 8740 4546 7–1C
*"Spicy" and "unusual" Sichuan dishes at "low"
prices, and in an "unexpected" location by Westfield
too – the formula that's made a hit of this
Shepherd's Bush Chinese. / W12 8AR; 11 pm;
no Amex.*

tibits W1 £34 ❸❸❸
12-14 Heddon St 7758 4110 3–2C
*"Always fresh and interesting"; the veggie buffet
concept of this "cool" Swiss outlet, near Piccadilly
Circus, pleases all who report on it; it offers
an "impressive array" of dishes, for which "you pay
by weight at the check-out". / W1B 4DA;
www.tibits.co.uk; 11.30 pm, Sun 10 pm; no Amex;
Only bookings for 8+.*

Tierra Peru N1 £40 ④❸④
164 Essex Rd 7354 5586 8–3D
*This "closely-packed" Islington yearling offers
an "excellent take on Peruvian cooking"
(with ceviche rating particular mention); it doesn't
impress all reporters, though, and a disgruntled
minority say it's "a real let-down". / N1 8LY;
www.tierraperu.co.uk; @tierraperu; 11 pm; set weekday L
£26 (FP).*

Tinello SW1 £47 ❷❷❸
87 Pimlico Rd 7730 3663 5–2D
*"Meaty and hearty" Tuscan food "with a nice light
touch" combines with "very friendly and efficient"
service to make this "elegant", Locatelli-backed
Pimlico Italian a major hit; if there's a quibble it's
that it can feel a tad "subdued". / SW1W 8PH;
www.tinello.co.uk; 10.30 pm; closed Sun.*

Toasted SE22 NEW £45
38 Lordship Ln 8693 9021 1–4D
*A long way from Charing Cross, this East Dulwich
newcomer is the latest outpost of the Terroirs
empire, but in a style that's more 'classic wine bar'
than usual; it opened just as our survey for the year
was concluding – the first reporter was very
impressed! / SE22 8HJ; toastdulwich.co.uk; toastdulwich.*

Toff's N10 £39 ❷❷④
38 Muswell Hill Broadway 8883 8656 1–1B
*"The freshest fish, simply served" ("and not just the
usuals") – this "cramped" and "crowded" Muswell
Hill "institution" is hailed by many locals as "surely
the best chippy in town"; BYO. / N10 3RT;
www.toffsfish.co.uk; @toffsfish; 10 pm; closed Sun.*

Toku
Japan Centre SW1 **£40**
16 Regent St   3405 1246   3–3D
"It's pretty much a canteen" in style, but this café within Japan's West End cultural outpost serves a good range of "well-priced and authentic dishes"; a move to Shaftesbury Avenue is scheduled for late-2013. / SW1Y 4PH; 9.45 pm, Sun 8.45 pm; no Amex; no booking Sat.

Tokyo Diner WC2 **£26** ❸❷❸
2 Newport Pl   7287 8777   4–3B
"Unassuming, small and basic", this diner on the edge of Chinatown is well worth knowing about – "decent" sushi and noodles at "good prices", and "very fast and polite" service too. / WC2H 7JJ; www.tokyodiner.com; 11.30 pm; no Amex; no booking, Fri & Sat.

Tom Aikens SW3 **£91** ❷❸❸
43 Elystan St   7584 2003   5–2C
"Vastly improved since the refurbishment", Tom Aikens' "pared-down" but "stylish" HQ is back on true crowd-pleasing form; it's still very pricey, but offers "wonderfully creative" food from its "imaginative" small-plates menu, and "exciting" wines too. / SW3 3NT; www.tomaikens.co.uk; @TomAikensRest; 10.45 pm; closed Sat L & Sun; booking: max 8; set weekday L £55 (FP).

Tom's Deli W11 **£35** ❸❸❸
226 Westbourne Grove   7221 8818   6–1B
"Best eggs Benedict ever" – the sort of attraction that means "you may have to queue" for brunch at Tom Conran's ever-popular Notting Hill deli/diner. / W11 2RH; www.tomsdeli.co.uk; 5.30 pm; L only; no Amex; no booking.

Tom's Kitchen **£63** ④❸❸
Somerset House, 150 Strand, WC2   7845 4646   2–2D
27 Cale St, SW3   7349 0202   5–2C
11 Westferry Circus, E14   3011 1555   11–1C **NEW**
From the "buzzy" (if "squashed") Chelsea original to the "lovely" Somerset House outlet, Tom Aikens's branded spin-offs have plenty of "fun" hang-outs, especially for brunch; in truth, though, standards are pretty "ordinary". / 10 pm - 10.45 pm; WC2 closed Sun D.

Tommi's Burger Joint
W1 **NEW** **£18** ❷④④
30 Thayer St   awaiting tel   3–1A
For many reporters, this "too-cool-for-school" Marylebone ex-pop-up newcomer offers "truly great burgers", perhaps even "the best in town"; a few refuseniks, though, just can't see it. / W1U 2QP; www.burgerjoint.co.uk; @BurgerJointUk; 10.30 pm, Sun 9.30 pm.

Tonkotsu W1 **£31** ❸❸❸
63 Dean St   7437 0071   4–2A
"It took me back to Tokyo"; "ramen bars don't come better than this", say fans of this "hip" and somewhat "cramped" Soho noodle-spot, instantly "rammed with cool kids". / W1D 4QG; www.tonkotsu.co.uk; 10.30 pm, Sun 10 pm.

Tortilla **£18** ❸❸❸
6 Market Place, W1   7637 2800   3–1C
460 The Strand, WC2   7930 0269   4–3D
6a, King St, W6   8741 7959   7–2C
13 Islington High St, N1   7833 3103   8–3D
106 Southwark St, SE1   7620 0285   9–4B
22 The Broadway, SW19   8947 3589   10–2B
18 North Colonnade, E14   7719 9160   11–1C
213 The Balcony, Westfield Stratford City, E20   8555 3663   1–3D
28 Leadenhall Mkt, EC3   7929 7837   9–2D
Of the many burrito joints springing up around town, this "pleasant" chain is amongst the better options to "grab and go" – "portions are generous", and there's "a large choice of fillings". / www.tortilla.co.uk; W1 & N1 11 pm, Sun 9 pm, SE1 & E14 9 pm, EC3 7 pm, E14 Sun 7 pm; SE1 & EC3 closed Sat & Sun, N1 closed sun; no Amex; SRA-52%.

Tosa W6 **£41** ❷④④
332 King St   8748 0002   7–2B
A "friendly" Hammersmith café, offering "great yakitori and other grills" plus "some interesting Japanese dishes you don't often see". / W6 0RR; www.tosauk.com; 10.30 pm.

Tozi SW1 **NEW** **£40** ❷❷❷
8 Gillingham St   7769 9771   2–4B
"A great addition to Pimlico"; this "friendly" Venetian-influenced small-plates specialist is a big and bustling venture that manages to transcend the fact that it's attached to a hotel. / SW1V 1HN; www.tozirestaurant.co.uk; @ToziRestaurant; 10 pm.

Tramontana Brindisa
EC2 **£36** ❸④❸
152-154 Curtain Rd   7749 9961   12–1B
"A buzzy Shoreditch addition to the Brindisa stable"; it offers "a slight twist on your typical tapas, with more of a Catalan feel". / EC2A 3AT; Mon-Sat 11 pm, Sun 9 pm.

The Tramshed EC2 **£56** ④④❸
32 Rivington St   7749 0478   12–1B
"Eat under the watchful gaze of Damien Hurst's cow!"; Mark Hix's "enormous" grill house is certainly a "sensational transformation" of a Shoreditch industrial space, but the food – steak or chicken 'n' chips – is no more than "OK", and service can be a bit of a let-down too. / EC2A 3LX; www.chickenandsteak.co.uk.

Trinity SW4 £66 ❶❶❷
4 The Polygon 7622 1199 10–2D
*"How lucky are we to have this in our 'hood!";
with its "wonderful" cuisine that's "perfectly
balanced, fresh and delicious at every turn" and its
"polished" but "friendly" service, Adam Byatt's
"unassuming" foodie Mecca, in Clapham,
goes "from strength to strength". / SW4 0JG;
www.trinityrestaurant.co.uk; @TrinityLondon; 10.30 pm;
closed Mon L & Sun D; set weekday L £46 (FP).*

Trishna W1 £53 ❷❸❸
15-17 Blandford St 7935 5624 2–1A
*The "complex flavours" of "the finest, authentic
Indian cooking" – particularly from the tasting menu
with wine pairings – again win acclaim for this
Marylebone outpost of the famous Mumbai fish
restaurant; critics do feel, though, that the setting
is "not the most atmospheric". / W1U 3DG;
www.trishnalondon.com; @TrishnaLondon; 10.45 pm,
Sun 9.45 pm; set pre theatre £38 (FP).*

Les Trois Garçons E1 £70 ❸❶❶
1 Club Row 7613 1924 12–1C
*"Ravishing" decor that's "as camp as it comes"
makes this East End pub-conversion a "magical"
destination, which will "amaze any romantic date",
and the Gallic fare can be "superb" too… if at
a price. / E1 6JX; www.lestroisgarcons.com;
@lestroisgarcons; 9.30 pm, 10.30 pm; closed Mon L,
Tue L, Wed L, Sat L & Sun; need credit card to book £25
deposit; set weekday L £38 (FP).*

La Trompette W4 £65 ❷❷❸
5-7 Devonshire Rd 8747 1836 7–2A
*A revamp and expansion have divided opinion
on this "Chiswick star", which is historically one
of the survey's top performers; for fans it's still
"the best example of a fine dining neighbourhood
restaurant in town", but doubters say the cooking's
"lost wow factor" of late, with service seeming
"harassed" too. / W4 2EU; www.latrompette.co.uk;
10.30 pm, Sun 9.30 pm.*

Troubadour SW5 £42 ❹❹❶
263-267 Old Brompton Rd 7370 1434 5–3A
*"Bohemian, lively and loud, but still relaxed" –
this Earl's Court café/music venue is not a foodie
experience, but it's an "amusing" hang-out,
and "the ambience is always special". / SW5 9JA;
www.troubadour.co.uk; 11 pm.*

Trullo N1 £51 ❷❷❷
300-302 St Paul's Rd 7226 2733 8–2D
*Jordan Trullo's "skilful" Italian cuisine has helped this
Highbury two-year-old quickly become one of north
London's foodie hotspots; "a superb compendium
of Italian wines", "charming" service and a "lovely"
atmosphere add to the all-round appeal. / N1 2LH;
www.trullorestaurant.com; 10.30 pm; closed Sun D;
no Amex.*

Tsunami £48 ❷❹❹
93 Charlotte St, W1 7637 0050 2–1C
5-7 Voltaire Rd, SW4 7978 1610 10–1D
*"Sarf London's answer to Zuma!"; with its
"surprisingly complex" Japanese cuisine,
this Clapham fixture (with less interesting Fitzrovia
spin-off) is a "top-notch" destination; the "tacky"
dining room, however, is rather beginning to show its
age. / www.tsunamirestaurant.co.uk; @Tsunamirest;
SW4 10.30 pm, Fri & Sat 11 pm, Sun 9.30 pm;
W1 11 pm; SW4 closed Mon - Fri L; W1 closed Sat L
and Sun; SW4 no Amex.*

28-50 £52 ❸❷❸
15 Maddox St, W1 7495 1505 3–2C NEW
15-17 Marylebone Ln, W1 7486 7922 3–1A
140 Fetter Ln, EC4 7242 8877 9–2A
*"An unbelievable, affordable wine list" – an "ever-
changing selection, available by the glass" –
has made a big name for this "classy" chain
of "very metropolitan" modern wine bars (from the
Texture team); the food offer is "narrow", but the
"simple" dishes are "well cooked". / www.2850.co.uk;
EC4 9.30 pm; W1 Mon-Wed 10 pm, Thu-Sat 10.30 pm,
Sun 9.30 pm; EC4 closed Sat-Sun.*

2 Amici SW1 £46 ❹❸❹
48a Rochester Rw 7976 5660 2–4C
*A "relaxed", if somewhat unatmospheric, Italian –
handy for Westminster locals in a restaurant desert.
/ SW1P 1JU; www.2amici.org; 11 pm; closed Sat L & Sun.*

Two Brothers N3 £41 ❸❹❹
297-303 Regent's Park Rd 8346 0469 1–1B
*"Always long queues" for this famous Finchley
chippie (nowadays no longer owned by the two
founding brothers); on most accounts, the food
offers "incredible value", but a few doubters discern
"a lowering of standards" in the last year or so,
and say the chips "are no longer the best ever!"
/ N3 1DP; www.twobrothers.co.uk; 10 pm, Sun 8 pm;
closed Mon.*

2 Veneti W1 £46 ❹❷❹
10 Wigmore St 7637 0789 3–1B
*This "comfortable" Marylebone Venetian is "handy
for the Wigmore Hall", and serves "straightforward"
food that's "very consistent", if perhaps "expensive,
for what it is". / W1U 2RD; www.2veneti.com;
10.30 pm, Sat 11 pm; closed Sat L & Sun.*

Umu W1 £102 ❸❹❸
14-16 Bruton Pl 7499 8881 3–2C
*"The best kaiseki menu this side of Japan" delivers
"a startling array of flavours", say fans of Marlon
Abela's "classy" operation, hidden away in a Mayfair
mews; even they concede, though, that it might
be "cheaper to fly to Kyoto". / W1J 6LX;
www.umurestaurant.com; 11 pm; closed Sat L & Sun;
no trainers; booking: max 14.*

The Union Café W1   **£50**   ④④④
96 Marylebone Ln   7486 4860   3–1A
It my be "densely-packed" and sometimes rather
"noisy", but this Marylebone bistro retains its
impressive following; the food, though, is merely
"straightforward" – it's the good-value wine which
is "the main attraction". / W1U 2QA;
www.brinkleys.com; @BrinkleysR; 11 pm; closed Sun D.

Union Jacks   **£42**   ⑤④④
4 Central St Giles Piazza, WC2   3597 7888
4–1B
57 The Market, WC2   awaiting tel   4–3D
217-221 Chiswick High Rd, W4   3617 9988
7–2A
'English pizza' may be "laudable as a patriotic act",
but the execution at Jamie O's latest money-spinner
is notably "ramshackle" – "shocking to pay so much
for such astonishingly bad food", say critics.
/ www.unionjacksrestaurants.com; 11 pm, Sun 10.30 pm.

Union Street Café
SE1   **£48**
Harling Hs, Union St   7592 7977   9–4B
Gordon Ramsay's first London début for quite
a while belatedly opened its doors, in Southwark,
in late-2013, to a fairly middle-of-the-road reception
from the critics; David Beckham – much touted as a
co-proprietor – seems to have made his excuses
shortly before the launch. / SE1 0BS.

Upstairs SW2   **£52**   ❷❷❷
89b Acre Ln (door on Branksome Rd)   7733
8855   10–2D
"Behind an anonymous door", in Brixton, a "cool"
and "mysterious" find, seemingly reserved for those
"in the know"; "apart from the bill, it's like the best-
ever dinner party", with "inspired" and
"sophisticated" cooking, and "knowledgeable"
service too. / SW2 5TN; www.upstairslondon.com;
@Upstairslondon; 9.30 pm, Thu-Sat 10.30 pm; D only,
closed Mon & Sun.

Le Vacherin W4   **£57**   ❸❸❸
76-77 South Pde   8742 2121   7–1A
"A classic, traditional establishment", which wouldn't
look out of place in 'la France profonde', but which
seems quite a find opposite Acton Green; critics can
find the fare a touch "unexciting", though, and the
interior is "closely packed". / W4 5LF;
www.levacherin.co.uk; 9.45 pm, Fri & Sat 10.45 pm;
closed Mon L.

Vanilla Black EC4   **£55**   ❸❶❸
17-18 Tooks Ct   7242 2622   9–2A
"Outstanding" staff serve up some "unusual" and
"exquisite" veggie dishes at this smart legal-land
spot; if there is a criticism, it is that the cuisine can
sometimes seem a little "over-complicated".
/ EC4A 1LB; www.vanillablack.co.uk; @vanillablack1;
10 pm; closed Sat L & Sun.

Vapiano W1   **£25**   ❸❸❸
19-21 Great Portland St   7268 0080   3–1C
"Crazy busy" and sometimes "chaotic" it may be,
but – with its "fresh" fare (pizza, pasta, salads),
all "cooked in front of you" to order –
this Continental-style food court, near Oxford Circus,
makes a "great choice for a cheap and tasty meal".
/ W1W 8QB; www.vapiano.co.uk; 11 pm, Sun 10 pm.

Vasco & Piero's Pavilion
W1   **£58**   ❷❷❸
15 Poland St   7437 8774   3–1D
"Still going strong, and long may it continue";
this "delightful" (if "crowded") old-Soho fixture has
been in the same ownership for decades, and its
"chummy" staff still serve up Umbrian dishes which
are "simple" but "well-cooked". / W1F 8QE;
www.vascosfood.com; 10.15 pm; closed Sat L & Sun.

Veeraswamy W1   **£71**   ❷❷❷
Victory Hs, 99-101 Regent St   7734 1401
3–3D
"Maybe it is on the tourist route", but London's
longest-established Indian restaurant, handily located
near Piccadilly Circus, offers a "refined" and
"very modern" experience, including some "really
fine" cuisine. / W1B 4RS; www.realindianfood.com;
10.30 pm, Sun 10 pm; booking: max 12.

El Vergel SE1   **£32**   ❷❸❷
132 Webber St   7401 2308   9–4B
"The steak sandwiches are a winner", say fans
of this "airy" Borough canteen; more generally,
its menu comprises "simple" but "consistently very
good" Latino dishes. / SE1 0QL; www.elvergel.co.uk;
2.45pm, Sat-Sun 3.45 pm; closed D, closed Sun; no Amex.

Verru W1   **£51**   ❷❷❸
69 Marylebone Ln   7935 0858   2–1A
"Baltic cuisine merges with Nordic flavours"
to create some "fantastic" dishes at this "small,
quiet and professional" two-year-old, in Marylebone.
/ W1U 2PH; www.verru.co.uk; 10.30 pm; set weekday L
£33 (FP).

Vertigo 42
Tower 42 EC2   **£66**   ⑤④❷
25 Old Broad St   7877 7842   9–2C
Despite all the recent elevated competition,
this 42nd-floor City eyrie is "still a great place to see
the view and have a glass of fizz"; pity, though,
that the food is so "pretentious, pricey and
uninspired". / EC2N 1HQ; www.vertigo42.co.uk;
@vertigo42bar; 10.45 pm; closed Sat L & Sun; no shorts;
booking essential.

Viajante E2   £106   ❷❸❸
Patriot Sq   7871 0461   1–2D
"A real thrill", "unexpected delights", "gastronomic story-telling" – Nuno Mendes's "passionate" Bethnal Green venture inspires lyrical praise; its "quirky" setting may sometimes seem "a little sterile", and the bill can "shock"… but, for many reporters, this is "London's most interesting dining". / E2 9NF; www.viajante.co.uk; 9.30 pm; closed Mon, Tue, Wed L & Thu L; set weekday L £59 (FP).

Il Vicolo SW1   £49   ❸❷④
3-4 Crown Passage   7839 3960   3–4D
Hidden away in a pedestrian lane, this "good, local and friendly" Sicilian is an oddity in the heart of St James's; the worst anyone can say about it is that it makes a "decent fallback". / SW1Y 6PP; www.vicolo.co.uk; 10 pm; closed Sat L & Sun.

The Victoria SW14   £49   ❸❷❸
10 West Temple   8876 4238   10–2A
Handy for Richmond Park, a big and "friendly" East Sheen gastroboozer, where the "imaginative" and "very appealing" dishes are realised "with a sophistication worthy of pricier establishments". / SW14 7RT; www.thevictoria.net; @thevictoria_pub; 10 pm, Sat 10 pm; closed Sun D; no Amex; set weekday L £32 (FP).

Viet W1   £20   ❸④④
34 Greek St   7494 9888   4–3A
A "cheap 'n' cheerful" Soho café, offering "fresh and delicious" Vietnamese scoff, for which you may have to queue; BYO. / W1D 5DJ; 10.30 pm, Fri 11 pm; closed Sun; no Amex; no booking.

Viet Grill E2   £37   ❷④❸
58 Kingsland Rd   7739 6686   12–1B
"The best of the many restaurants in Little Vietnam"; this "lively" and "stylish" Shoreditch spot is "fast-paced, but un-rushed if you want to linger", and its fare is "authentic and of good quality". / E2 8DP; www.vietnamesekitchen.co.uk; 11 pm, Fri & Sat 11.30 pm, Sun 10.30 pm.

Viet Hoa E2   £32   ❷⑤④
70-72 Kingsland Rd   7729 8293   12–1B
"One of the best Vietnamese cafés along Kingsland Road"; this ever-"noisy" EastEnder is once again firing on all cylinders. / E2 8DP; www.viethoarestaurant.co.uk; 11.30 pm.

Vijay NW6   £30   ❸❷④
49 Willesden Ln   7328 1087   1–1B
A decidedly "un-posh" Kilburn survivor, where a "flavour adventure" is pretty much guaranteed, and "at prices so low you could almost be in southern India"; BYO. / NW6 7RF; www.vijayrestaurant.co.uk; 10.45 pm, Fri & Sat 11.45 pm.

Villa Bianca NW3   £60   ⑤④④
1 Perrins Ct   7435 3131   8–2A
In its mega-cute Hampstead sidestreet location, this Italian veteran has long got away with being on the cheesy side; of late, however, even fans have felt that it has become "excessively pricey", and seems to "lack soul". / NW3 1QS; www.villabiancanw3.com; 11.30 pm, Sun 10.30 pm; set weekday L £38 (FP).

Village East SE1   £55
171-173 Bermondsey St   7357 6082   9–4D
This large but "friendly" hang-out takes some credit for helping to make Bermondsey the "buzzy" place it is today; let's hope it emerges stronger than ever from the major refurb that closed it for a major part of 2013. / SE1 3UW; www.villageeast.co.uk; @villageeastse1; 10 pm, Sun 9.30 pm.

Villandry W1   £51   ④④④
170 Gt Portland St   7631 3131   2–1B
It's as a "good business lunch venue" that the dining room of this grand Marylebone deli often finds favour with reporters – foodies may simply bemoan the fact that "the wonderful groceries are not reflected in the dull menus!" / W1W 5QB; www.villandry.com; 10.30 pm; closed Sun D.

The Vincent Rooms
Westminster Kingsway
College SW1   £31   ❸❸❸
76 Vincent Sq   7802 8391   2–4C
"Service may depend on which year students are in", at this elegant dining room, which is part of a Westminster catering college; most reporters find playing guinea pig "a delightful experience", and it's not an expensive one. / SW1P 2PD; www.thevincentrooms.com; 7.15 pm; closed Mon D, Tue D, Fri D, Sat & Sun; no Amex.

VQ   £46   ④❸④
St Giles Hotel, Great Russell St, WC1   7300 3000   4–1A **NEW**
325 Fulham Rd, SW10   7376 7224   5–3B
A Chelsea fixture; London's original 24/7 restaurant is "pretty good" for somewhere that never sleeps, and breakfast, in particular, is "superb"; as we to go press, a new branch is set to open in Bloomsbury. / www.vingtquatre.co.uk; open 24 hours.

Vinoteca   £44   ④❸❷
15 Seymour Pl, W1   7724 7288   2–2A
55 Beak St, W1   3544 7411   3–2D
18 Devonshire Rd, W4   3701 8822   7–2A **NEW**
7 St John St, EC1   7253 8786   9–1B
"A stunning wine list with fair mark-ups" (and available by the glass too) is the mainstay of these "always packed" (rather "cramped") wine bars; their straightforward food is "a bit more variable" than in the early days, but usually "very decent". / www.vinoteca.co.uk; 11 pm, Seymour Pl Sun 5 pm; EC1 Sun; Seymour Pl Sun D.

Vivat Bacchus £52 ④④④
4 Hay's Ln, SE1 7234 0891 9–4C
47 Farringdon St, EC4 7353 2648 9–2A
*The menu may be quite "interesting" (kangaroo
anyone?), and there's an "inspirational" selection
of cheeses, but "you don't go for the food" to these
City-fringe and South Bank bars – it's all about the
dazzling array of South African wines.
/ www.vivatbacchus.co.uk; 9.30 pm; EC4 closed
Sat & Sun; SE1 closed Sat L & Sun.*

Vrisaki N22 £35 ④❸❸
73 Middleton Rd 8889 8760 1–1C
*An "old-favourite" Bounds Green taverna, renowned
for its "massive portions" (if, perhaps, favouring
"quantity over quality") and "good value" – "ignore
the fact that, from outside, it looks like a cheap
take-away". / N22 8LZ; 11.30 pm, Sun 9 pm; closed
Mon; no Amex.*

Wagamama £37 ④❸④
8 Norris St, SW1 7321 2755 4–4A
Harvey Nichols, Knightsbridge, SW1 7201
8000 5–1D
101a Wigmore St, W1 7409 0111 3–1A
10a Lexington St, W1 7292 0990 3–2D
4a Streatham St, WC1 7323 9223 2–1C
1 Tavistock St, WC2 7836 3330 4–3D
14a Irving St, WC2 7839 2323 4–4B
26a Kensington High St, W8 7376 1717 5–1A
N1 Centre, 37 Parkfield St, N1 7226 2664
8–3D
11 Jamestown Rd, NW1 7428 0800 8–3B
Royal Festival Hall, Southbank Centre, SE1
7021 0877 2–3D
50-54 Putney High St, SW15 8785 3636
10–2B
46-48 Wimbledon Hill Rd, SW19 8879 7280
10–2B
Jubilee Place, 45 Bank St, E14 7516 9009
11–1C
1a Ropemaker St, EC2 7588 2688 12–2A
22 Old Broad St, EC2 7256 9992 9–2C
Tower Pl, EC3 7283 5897 9–3D
109 Fleet St, EC4 7583 7889 9–2A
30 Queen St, EC4 7248 5766 9–3B
*With their "hustle and bustle", "speedy" service and
"large platefuls of freshly prepared Asian fare",
these ubiquitous and "cheap" canteens are,
for most reporters, "a formula that works"
(and "super-friendly to kids"); for some sceptics,
however the whole idea is a bit "past its sell-by
date". / www.wagamama.com; 10 pm-11 pm;
EC4 & EC2 closed Sat & Sun; no booking.*

Wahaca £32 ❸❸❷
19-23 Charlotte St, W1 7323 2342 2–1C
80-82 Wardour St, W1 7734 0195 3–2D
66 Chandos Pl, WC2 7240 1883 4–4C
Westfield, Ariel Way, W12 8749 4517 7–1C
68-69 Upper St, N1 3697 7990 8–3D
Southbank Centre, SE1 7928 1876 2–3D
Unit 4, Park Pavilion, 40 Canada Sq, E14
7516 9145 11–1C
6 Chestnut Plaza, Westfield Stratford City, E20
3288 1025 1–1D
*"It's an achievement in this country to make
Mexican food worth eating", and most reports are
full of praise for Thomasina Myers's "fun" and
"surprisingly funky" chain, and its array of "street
food with a twist"; a "menu update", though, might
not go amiss. / www.wahaca.com; WC2 & W1 & E14
11 pm, Sun 10.30 pm; W12 11 pm, Sun 10 pm;
no booking; SRA-73%.*

**The Wallace
The Wallace Collection
W1** £56 ④❺❶
Hertford Hs, Manchester Sq 7563 9505 3–1A
*A "surprising" modern atrium behind an 18th-
century palazzo provides a "stunning" setting for
this Marylebone venue; shame that – with its too
often "appalling" service – it can seem such
a "missed opportunity". / W1U 3BN;
www.thewallacerestaurant.com; Fri & Sat 9.15 pm;
Sun-Thu closed D; no Amex.*

**The Walmer Castle
W11** £39 ❸❸❷
58 Ledbury Rd 7229 4620 6–1B
*Perennially popular and trendy, this Notting Hill
boozer has a dining room "tucked-away" upstairs,
which has long served "great Thai food". / W11 2AJ;
www.walmercastle.co.uk; 11 pm, Fri & Sat midnight,
Sun 10.30 pm.*

Wapping Food E1 £51 ④④❶
Wapping Power Station, Wapping Wall 7680
2080 11–1A
*Surprisingly little feedback on this "amazing" post-
industrial Wapping restaurant and art-space –
"so unusual it makes a great place to take visitors";
the food can seem a touch "variable", but "lovely"
brunches are a highlight, and there are some
"good Australian wines" too. / E1W 3SG;
www.thewappingproject.com; 10.45 pm; Mon-Fri D only,
Sat open L & D, closed Sun D.*

**Waterloo Bar & Kitchen
SE1** £48 ④❸④
131 Waterloo Rd 7928 5086 9–4A
*"Useful for the Old Vic'"; this straightforward eatery
may be somewhat "hangar-like", but the food
it offers is "reliable" enough, and service is "helpful"
too. / SE1 8UR; www.barandkitchen.co.uk; 10.30 pm.*

The Waterway W9 £51 ④⑤❸
54 Formosa St 7266 3557 8–4A
The canalside terrace is undoubtedly "outstanding", but this "buzzy" Maida Vale hang-out otherwise inspires some irreconcilable reviews – all the way from "top-notch" to "disastrous and uncaring". / W9 2JU; www.thewaterway.co.uk; 10.30 pm, Sun 10 pm.

The Wells NW3 £47 ❸❸❷
30 Well Walk 7794 3785 8–1A
"A credit to Hampstead" – with a "cosy first-floor" restaurant, and "more bar-like" downstairs, this "very busy and buzzy" tavern makes a "lovely" destination; it offers a "high standard of cooking" too (even for your canine companion!). / NW3 1BX; www.thewellshampstead.co.uk; @WellsHampstead; 10 pm, Sun 9.30 pm; set Sun L £36 (FP).

The Wet Fish Cafe NW6 £46 ❸❷❷
242 West End Ln 7443 9222 1–1B
"In a street full of restaurants no one really wants to go to, this one shines out!" – this "friendly" West Hampstead "hide-away" (in a former fishmongers) is a "reliable" spot any time, but brunch is a particular highlight. / NW6 1LG; www.thewetfishcafe.co.uk; @thewetfishcafe; 10 pm; no Amex.

The Wharf TW11 £47 ④❸❷
22 Manor Rd 8977 6333 1–4A
"A lovely location, overlooking Teddington Lock" is the crown-jewel feature of this large, modern bar/brasserie – a "fun place", offering "good-value set meals". / TW11 8BG; www.thewharfteddington.com; 10 pm; closed Mon L & Tue L.

White Horse SW6 £51 ④④❸
1-3 Parsons Grn 7736 2115 10–1B
Fulham's most famous boozer, the 'Sloaney Pony', "can be very loud", and its "average" pub grub is arguably "too dear"; there's a "great selection of beers", though (plus excellent wines), and few would deny that this is a characterful destination. / SW6 4UL; www.whitehorsesw6.com; 10.30 pm.

White Rabbit N16 NEW £27 ❶❶❷
125 Stoke Newington Church St 3556 3350 1–1C
"A wonderfully refreshing take on the tapas revolution"; this "cool" Stoke Newington newcomer offers a "diverse and continually evolving menu of small plates designed for sharing" – just the trick, for most reporters. / N16 0UH; www.whiterabbitlondon.co.uk; 9.30 pm; D only, closed Mon.

The White Swan EC4 £53 ❸❸❸
108 Fetter Ln 7242 9696 9–2A
A bustling Fleet Street boozer, "transformed a few years ago from humdrum pub to gastronomic treat"; "very sound" cooking is served in the restaurant upstairs (which is completely insulated from the noisy bar below). / EC4A 1ES; www.thewhiteswanlondon.com; 10 pm; closed Sat & Sun.

Whitechapel Gallery Dining Room
Whitechapel Gallery
E1 £47 ❸❸❸
77-82 Whitechapel High St 7522 7896 12–2C
This "intimate" café, off the gallery's foyer, serves a "small menu that's well thought-out, and well priced"; "it's not quite the experience you might expect, given Angela Hartnett's involvement, but a welcome addition to the Whitechapel wasteland". / E1 7QX; www.whitechapelgallery.org/dine; 9.30 pm; closed Mon, Tue D & Sun D.

Whits W8 £47 ❷❶❷
21 Abingdon Rd 7938 1122 5–1A
"A warm and personal welcome" from the "wonderful owner" helps make this cute Gallic bistro one of Kensington's "hidden gems"; "come hungry, as portions are generous!" / W8 6AH; www.whits.co.uk; 10.30 pm; D only, closed Mon & Sun.

Whyte & Brown W1 NEW £36
Kingly Ct, Kingly St 3747 9820 3–2C
Chicken every which way – that's the deal at this new all-day restaurant, just off Carnaby Street; early-days press reviews are rather mixed. / W1B 5PW; www.whyteandbrown.com.

Wild Honey W1 £68 ❸④④
12 St George St 7758 9160 3–2C
Sad to record "a dive in quality" at this one-time Mayfair foodie hotspot; the food is still "perfectly enjoyable", but it "doesn't stand out from the crowd" any more, and service can be "hit 'n' miss". / W1S 2FB; www.wildhoneyrestaurant.co.uk; 11 pm, Fri & Sat 11.30 pm, Sun 10 pm.

William Curley £18 ❷❸❸
198 Ebury St, SW1 7730 5522 5–2D
10 Paved Ct, TW9 8332 3002 1–4A
"A truly dangerous place to enter!" – these deluxe chocolatiers, in Belgravia and Richmond, offer a wide choice of enticing treats from the "excellent dessert bar". / www.williamcurley.co.uk; 6.30 pm.

Wiltons SW1 £98 ❸④❷
55 Jermyn St 7629 9955 3–3C
"The best turbot", "excellent Dover sole", "seafood of superb quality" – such are the delicacies which still win a major following for this "civilised" but "absurdly overpriced" bastion of the St James's plutocracy – est 1742, and on this site since 1984. / SW1Y 6LX; www.wiltons.co.uk; 10.30 pm; closed Sat & Sun; jacket required; set pre-theatre £58 (FP), set weekday L £67 (FP).

The Windmill W1 £37 ❸④❸
6-8 Mill St 7491 8050 3–2C
"The best pies in the West End" are the big deal at this well-preserved ancient hostelry, on what's effectively the continuation of Savile Row.
/ W1S 2AZ; www.windmillmayfair.co.uk;
@tweetiepie_w1; 9.30 pm, Sat 4 pm; closed Sat & Sun; no Amex.

**The Windsor Castle
W8** £42 ④④❷
114 Campden Hill Rd 7243 8797 6–2B
Just off Notting Hill Gate, this ancient pub – named after the landmark once visible from the front door – boasts a snug interior and, as a star attraction, a "very pleasant" garden; the food is "competent", but not really the point. / W8 7AR;
www.thewindsorcastlekensington.co.uk;
@windsorcastlew8; 10 pm, Sun 9 pm.

Wine Gallery SW10 £46 ④❸❸
47 Hollywood Rd 7352 7572 5–3B
"Lovely" wines buoy the "lively" buzz at John Brinkley's deepest-Chelsea old favourite; not everyone's impressed by the scoff, but the overall package still seems "great value for money".
/ SW10 9HX; www.brinkleys.com; @BrinkleysR;
11.30 pm; booking: max 12.

The Wine Library EC3 £26 ⑤❷❶
43 Trinity Sq 7481 0415 9–3D
"A liquid lunch doesn't come any better" than at this "steadfast favourite" – ancient and "lovely" City cellars where the food (a buffet of pâté and cheese) is "entirely secondary" to "the best wine list in town", sold at "excellent prices"; book.
/ EC3N 4DJ; www.winelibrary.co.uk; 8 pm, Mon 6 pm; closed Mon D, Sat & Sun.

Wishbone SW9 £18 ⑤④④
Brixton Village, Coldharbour Ln 7274 0939 10–2D
This year-old Brixton "chicken shop", from the mega-trendy MEATshop team, is seen by many reporters as a "heinous hipster hang-out" – "loud", "soulless" and "overrated", and "expensive" too!
/ SW9 8PR; www.wishbonebrixton.co.uk.

Wolfe's WC2 £47 ❸④④
30 Gt Queen St 7831 4442 4–1D
This grand and comfortable Covent Garden diner may seem a bit dated, but fans insist it's still "a good place for a simple meal" – "delicious burgers" a highlight. / WC2B 5BB; www.wolfes-grill.net; @wolfesbargrill; 10 pm, Fri-Sat 10.30 pm, Sun 9 pm.

The Wolseley W1 £59 ❸❷❶
160 Piccadilly 7499 6996 3–3C
"Captains of industry rub shoulders with A-listers" at Corbin & King's perennially "exciting" grand café/brasserie, by the Ritz – its "old-school glamour" makes it "great for impressing people"; the "hit 'n' miss" food is not really the point, but absolutely everyone agrees this is the home of "the most glamorous breakfast in town".
/ W1J 9EB; www.thewolseley.com; midnight, Sun 11 pm; SRA-63%.

Wong Kei W1 £29 ④⑤⑤
41-43 Wardour St 7437 8408 4–3A
The waiters, sadly, are "not quite as rude as they used to be" at this vast and notorious Chinatown fixture; it still serves the same old "cheap 'n' cheerful" chow, though, at "very decent prices".
/ W1D 6PY; 11.30 pm, Fri & Sat 11.45 pm, Sun 10.30 pm; no credit cards; no booking.

Woodlands £40 ❸④④
37 Panton St, SW1 7839 7258 4–4A
77 Marylebone Ln, W1 7486 3862 2–1A
102 Heath St, NW3 7794 3080 8–1A
"Very reliable"; these low-key veggie stalwarts (part of an international chain) are worth seeking out for "a different take on a standard curry", including "a fine range" of "fresh and flavourful" dishes from South India.
/ www.woodlandsrestaurant.co.uk; 10 pm;
NW3 no L Mon.

**Workshop Coffee
EC1** £44 ❸❸❷
27 Clerkenwell Rd 7253 5754 9–1A
"Another winning Oz-style café"; with its "wonderful array of brunch and lunch dishes", as well as "incredible coffee", this "hip" Clerkenwell two-year-old has quickly won quite a following.
/ EC1M 5RN; www.workshopcoffee.com; 10 pm; closed Mon D, Sat D & Sun D.

Wright Brothers £52 ❷❸❷
13 Kingly St, W1 7434 3611 3–2D
11 Stoney St, SE1 7403 9554 9–4C
8 Lamb St, E1 awaiting tel 9–2D **NEW**
"Fabulous fresh oysters" and "perfect fish" have made a smash hit of this "casual", if "cramped", Borough Market bistro, which "oozes atmosphere"; "stick with SE1", however – the grander Soho offshoot is not nearly as well rated. / 10.30 pm, Sun 9 pm; booking: max 8.

XO NW3　　　　£47　　④④④
29 Belsize Ln　7433 0888　8–2A
*"A suburban staple where the menu could do with
some jazzing up" – this Belsize Park fusion
restaurant is "not as good as its siblings" (including
the ever-fashionable E&O), and it can seem "a little
over-priced" too. / NW3 5AS;
www.rickerrestaurants.com; 10.30 pm.*

Yalla Yalla　　　　£34　　❸④❸
1 Green's Ct, W1　7287 7663　3–2D
12 Winsley St, W1　7637 4748　3–1C
186 Shoreditch High St, E1　07725841372
8–3C
*"Brilliant flavours in dishes it's fun to share" still win
rave reviews for this Lebanese street food chain;
feedback was less enthusiastic this year, though,
with the "very small" original branch – "down a
Soho porn alley" – remaining reporters' favourite.
/ www.yalla-yalla.co.uk; Green's Court 11 pm, Sun 10 pm;
Winsley Street 11.30 pm, Sat 11 pm; W1 Sun.*

Yashin　　　　£82　　❶❸❸
117-119 Old Brompton Rd, SW7　awaiting tel
5–2B **NEW**
1a, Argyll Rd, W8　7938 1536　5–1A
*The "sensational" sushi and other "refined"
Japanese fare are "like works of modern art",
say fans of this Manhattan-esque (and quite un-
Japanese) Kensington two-year-old; the prices,
however, "will make your eyes water more than the
wasabi"; a new spin-off, 'Ocean House', opened
in late-2013. / www.yashinsushi.com; 11 pm.*

Yauatcha W1　　　　£68　　❶④❷
Broadwick Hs, 15-17 Broadwick St　7494 8888
3–2D
*"Exemplary" dim sum and "fabulous" cocktails
remain unchanging features at this "night-clubby"
Soho mainstay (as, sadly, does the "strict table
turning" policy); the "blingy", "oligarch-chic"
basement is generally preferred to the ground floor.
/ W1F 0DL; www.yauatcha.com; 11.15 pm,
Sun 10.30 pm.*

**The Yellow House
SE16**　　　　£43　　❷❷④
126 Lower Rd　7231 8777　11–2A
*A popular Rotherhithe local where the "passionate"
cooking "just keeps getting better"; highlights –
"brilliant" pizza from a wood-fired oven… and
"home-made fudge that's out of this world!"
/ SE16 2UE; www.theyellowhouse.eu;
@theyellowhousejazz; 10.30 pm, Sun 9.30 pm; closed
Mon, Tue–Sat closed L, Sun open L & D.*

Yi-Ban E16　　　　£44　　❸❸④
London Regatta Centre, Royal Albert Dock
7473 6699　11–1D
*The setting may feel a bit "tired" nowadays, but this
bizarrely-located Docklands Chinese can offer some
"great" food (including dim sum)… and you do get
to watch the planes taking off and landing
at London City Airport. / E16 2QT; www.yi-ban.co.uk;
10.45 pm.*

Yipin China N1　　　　£41　　❶❷⑤
70-72 Liverpool Rd　7354 3388　8–3D
*"The surroundings are very stark, but it doesn't
matter, as the focus is the food", at this "amazing"
Chinese yearling, in Islington, serving "wonderful and
different" Hunan/Sichuan cuisine at a fraction
of prices in the West End. / N1 0QD;
www.yipinchina.co.uk.*

Yming W1　　　　£44　　❷❷④
35-36 Greek St　7734 2721　4–2A
*"Always a star for 30 years" – Christine Yau's
"calm" and "rock-solid" Soho Chinese "marches
serenely on", and head waiter William "always has
a warm welcome"; main complaint about the
"consistently high-quality food"? – it's "too good
to be so cheap!" / W1D 5DL; www.yminglondon.com;
11.45 pm.*

Yo Sushi　　　　£28　　⑤⑤④
Branches throughout London
*"I only go because my children beg to see the
conveyor belt!" – this gimmicky chain is definitely
a hit with kids; but "gourmet it ain't", and too many
critics decry "shocking" food as part of a "grim"
overall experience. / www.yosushi.co.uk; 10.30 pm;
no booking.*

Yoisho W1　　　　£44　　❷④⑤
33 Goodge St　7323 0477　2–1C
*"Excellent" dishes come "thick and fast" at this
"utterly authentic" izakaya-style Fitzrovia Japanese
– just as well, as service is "so-so", and the décor
"appallingly shabby". / W1T 2PS; 10.30 pm; D only,
closed Sun; no Amex.*

York & Albany NW1　£57　　④④④
127-129 Parkway　7388 3344　8–3B
*A potentially "classy" operation, in an imposing
former boozer near Regent's Park; sadly, though,
it has "gone downhill", and is now just "another
example of overpriced and average food, riding
on the back of Gordon Ramsay's name". / NW1 7PS;
www.gordonramsay.com; 10.30 pm, Sun 8 pm.*

Yoshino W1　　　　£43　　❸❶⑤
3 Piccadilly Pl　7287 6622　3–3D
*Perhaps it's "not as good as in its distant heyday",
but this "austere" spot, hidden away in a Piccadilly
side-alley, still serves up a decidedly genuine
Japanese formula, including "tasty" fare
(with "delicious" sushi) at "reasonable prices".
/ W1J 0DB; www.yoshino.net; 10 pm; closed Sun.*

Young Turks at the Ten Bells
E I
£50 ❸❶❸
84 Commercial St   492986   12–2C
Above a Shoreditch pub, an "achingly cool" ex-pop-up, whose "smart and inventive" dishes are "consistently good and interesting"; "the front-of-house staff are great" too – "not so hip they can't be nice and friendly". / E1 6LY; www.tenbells.com; 11 pm; closed Mon & Sun D; no Amex.

Yum Yum N16
£39 ❷❸❷
187 Stoke Newington High St   7254 6751
1–1D
"A go-to destination when you need a good Thai" – this large Stoke Newington fixture still generates pretty consistent reports… but they have been surprisingly few in number of late. / N16 0LH; www.yumyum.co.uk; @yumyum; 10.30 pm, Fri & Sat 11.30 pm; set weekday L £24 (FP).

Zafferano SW1
£71 ❸❸④
15 Lowndes St   7235 5800   5–1D
This once-famous Belgravia Italian can still offer some "lovely" dishes, and is still a "favourite" for some reporters; in spite of the "eye-watering" bills, however, its no longer the culinary destination it once was, and the room, since its enlargement, has lost much of its former charm. / SW1X 9EY; www.zafferanorestaurant.com; 11 pm, Sun 10.30 pm.

Zaffrani N1
£44 ❷❷❷
47 Cross St   7226 5522   8–3D
A "charming" Islington Indian, "off the Upper Street beaten track", which all reports praise for its "sophisticated" cuisine – "it satisfies all five flavour centres, rather than carpet bombing them in cream or chilli". / N1 2BB; www.zaffrani-islington.co.uk; 10.30 pm.

Zaika W8
£66 ❷❸❸
1 Kensington High St   7795 6533   5–1A
"Sophisticated Indian fine dining" is to be found at this "spacious" former banking hall, in Kensington, (even if the odd "stumble" was not unknown this year); fans find the interior "magnificent", but it "helps the ambience considerably when it's full". / W8 5NP; www.zaika-restaurant.co.uk; 10.45 pm, Sun 9.45 pm; closed Mon L; set weekday L £43 (FP).

Zayna W1
£52 ❷❷④
25 New Quebec St   7723 2229   2–2A
"Not your usual curry!"; "great twists" on North Indian and Pakistani dishes win praise for this low-key outfit near Marble Arch; "make sure you sit upstairs". / W1H 7SF; www.zaynarestaurant.co.uk; 11.15 pm, Fri & Sat 11.45 pm.

Zero Degrees SE3
£42 ❸④④
29-31 Montpelier Vale   8852 5619   1–4D
"The food is better than you'd expect", at this buzzy (if slightly "clinical") Blackheath microbrewery, where "reliable" pizzas and moules-frites complement the "excellent" home brews. / SE3 0TJ; www.zerodegrees.co.uk; midnight, Sun 11.30 pm.

Ziani's SW3
£51 ❸❷❷
45 Radnor Walk   7351 5297   5–3C
"Tables are crowded, the food can be average, but you always have a good time!" – this "squashed" and "noisy" Chelsea Italian is a "long-standing local favourite"; prepare, though, for service that can be "almost too speedy"! / SW3 4BP; www.ziani.co.uk; 11 pm, Sun 10.30 pm.

Zizzi
£46 ④④④
Branches throughout London
"Generally OK, and you know what you will get" – this "decent, if unspectacular" pizza chain remains a useful stand-by for most reporters, especially those with kids in tow. / www.zizzi.co.uk; 11 pm.

Zoilo W1 `NEW`
£50 ❷❷④
9 Duke St   7486 9699   3–1A
Not far from Selfridges, a new Argentinian small-plates specialist, which includes "an interesting selection of wine" and "delightful" service among its attractions; some reporter, though, find conditions "overcrowded" and "awkward". / W1U 3EG; www.zoilo.co.uk; @Zoilo_London; 10.30 pm, Sun 9.30 pm.

Zucca SE1
£49 ❶❷❷
184 Bermondsey St   7378 6809   9–4D
"London's best Italian" – Sam Harris's "phenomenal" Bermondsey three-year-old is "on a par with the River Café" yet "at a fraction of the cost"; it's a surprisingly "civilised" experience too (for which you must book months ahead). / SE1 3TQ; www.zuccalondon.com; 10 pm; closed Mon & Sun D; no Amex.

Zuma SW7
£80 ❶❸❷
5 Raphael St   7584 1010   5–1C
"WAGs and men with mortgageable wrist watches" help power the "great vibe" at this "sexy" Mayfair canteen; "although the people-watching is enjoyable", though, it's "quickly forgotten" with the arrival of "divine" Japanese-fusion fare that's still amongst London's best. / SW7 1DL; www.zumarestaurant.com; 10.45 pm, Sun 10.15 pm; booking: max 8.

LONDON INDEXES

BREAKFAST
(with opening times)

Central
Abokado:WC2 (7.30)
Al Duca (9)
Amaranto (6.30, Sun 7)
Apsleys (7)
aqua nueva (Sun brunch 12 pm)
Asia de Cuba (7)
Athenaeum (7)
Aubaine:W1 (8, Sat 10)
Automat (Mon-Fri 7.30)
Baker & Spice:SW1 (7)
Balans: all central branches (8)
Bar Italia (6.30)
Bentley's (Mon-Fri 7.30)
Benugo: all central branches (7.30)
Bistro 1: Beak St W1 (9)
Black & Blue: Berners St W1 (9)
The Botanist (8, Sat & Sun 9)
La Bottega: Eccleston St SW1 (8, Sat 9);
    Lower Sloane St SW1 (8, Sat 9, Sun 9)
Boulevard (9)
Brasserie Max (7)
Browns (Albemarle) (7, Sun 7.30)
Browns:WC2 (9, 10 Sat & Sun)
Café Bohème (8, Sat & Sun 9)
Café in the Crypt (Mon-Sat 8)
Caffè Vergnano:WC1 (6.30 am,
    Sun 8.30 am);WC2 (8, Sun 11)
Canteen:W1 (8, Sat & Sun 9)
Cecconi's (7 am, Sat & Sun 8 am)
Christopher's (Sat & Sun 11.30)
The Cinnamon Club (Mon-Fri 7.30)
Comptoir Libanais:Wigmore
    St W1 (8.30); Broadwick St W1 (8 am)
Côte:W1 (8, Sat & Sun 10)
The Courtauld Gallery Café (10)
Cut (7am, Sat & Sun 7.30 am)
Daylesford Organic:SW1 (8, Sun 10)
Dean Street Townhouse (Mon-Fri
    7, Sat-Sun 8)
The Delaunay (7, Sat & Sun 11)
Diner:W1 (10, Sat & Sun 9);
    WC2 (9.30 am)
Dishoom:WC2 (8, Sat & Sun 10)
Dorchester Grill (7, Sat & Sun 8)
Ed's Easy Diner: Sedley Pl, 14 Woodstock
    St W1 (Sat 9.30 am)
Fernandez & Wells: Beak St W1 (7.30,
    sat& sun 9); Lexington St W1 (7 am);
    St Anne's Ct W1 (8, sat 10);
    WC2 (8am, sat-sun 9am)
Flat White (8, Sat & Sun 9)
Fleet River Bakery (7, Sat 9)
The Fountain (Fortnum's) (7.30,
    Sun 11)
Franco's (7, Sat 8)
La Fromagerie Café (8, Sat 9, Sun 10)
Fuzzy's Grub: SW1 (7)
Gelupo (Sat & Sun 12)
Giraffe:W1 (7.45, Sat & Sun 9)
The Goring Hotel (7, Sun 7.30)
Grazing Goat (7.30)
Hélène Darroze (Sat 11)
Homage (7)
Hush:WC1 (8 am)

Indigo (6.30)
Inn the Park (8, Sat & Sun 9)
JW Steakhouse (6.30, Sat & Sun 7)
Kaffeine (7.30, Sat 8.30, Sun 9.30)
Kaspar's Seafood and Grill (7)
Kazan (Cafe):Wilton Rd SW1 (8 am,
    Sun 9 am)
Konditor & Cook:WC1 (9.30);
    W1 (9.30, Sun 10.30)
Kopapa (8.30, Sat & Sun 10)
Ladurée:W1 (9); SW1 (Mon - Sat
    9, Sun noon - 1.30)
Lantana Café (8, Sat & Sun 9)
Leon:WC2 (7.30, Sat 9, Sun 10);
    Gt Marlborough St W1 (9.30, Sat & Sun
    10.30)
Maison Bertaux (8.30, Sun 9.15)
maze Grill (6.45)
Monmouth Coffee
    Company:WC2 (8)
The National Dining Rooms (10)
National Gallery Café (8, Sat
    & Sun 10)
Natural Kitchen:W1 (8, Sat 9, Sun 11)
Nopi (8, Sat & Sun 10)
Nordic Bakery: Dorset St W1 (8 am,
    Sat-Sun 9); Golden Sq W1 (Mon-Fri
    8, Sat 9, Sun 11)
The Northall (6, Sat & Sun 7)
Noura:William St SW1 (8)
One-O-One (7)
The Only Running Footman (7.30,
    Sat & Sun 9.30)
The Orange (8)
Oscar (7, Sun 8)
Ottolenghi: SW1 (8, Sun 9)
Ozer (7)
The Pantechnicon (Sat & Sun 9)
Paramount (8)
Paul:WC2 (7.30);W1 (7.30, Sat & Sun 8)
The Portrait (10)
Princi (8, Sun 8.30)
Providores (Tapa Room) (9, Sat
    & Sun 10)
Ranoush: SW1 (9)
Refuel (7, Sun 8)
Rib Room (7, Sun 8)
RIBA Café (8)
Riding House Café (7.30, Sat & Sun
    9)
The Ritz Restaurant (7, Sun 8)
Roux at the Landau (7)
Royal Academy (10)
Scandinavian Kitchen (8, Sat
    & Sun 10)
Simpsons-in-the-Strand (Mon-Fri
    7.30)
The Sketch (Parlour) (Mon-Fri
    8, Sat 10)
Sophie's Steakhouse: all
    branches (Sat & Sun 11)
Sotheby's Café (9.30)
Spice Market (7, Sat & Sun 8)
Stock Pot: SW1 (9.30)
Tate Britain (Rex Whistler) (Sat-
    Sun 10)
Taylor St Baristas:W1 (8 am)
Thirty Six (7)

tibits (9, Sun 11.30)
Tom's Kitchen:WC2 (Sat & Sun 10)
The Union Café (Sat & Sun 11)
Villandry (Sat 8 am, Sun 9 am)
The Wallace (10)
William Curley: all branches (9.30,
    Sun 10.30)
Wolfe's (9)
The Wolseley (7, Sat & Sun 8)
Yalla Yalla: Green's Ct W1 (Sat-Sun 10)

West
Adams Café (7.30 am)
Angelus (10)
Annie's:W4 (Tue - Thu 10, Fri & Sat
    10.30, Sun 10)
Aubaine: SW3 (8, Sun 9);W8 (Mon-Sat
    8 am, 9 am Sun)
Baker & Spice: all
    west branches (7, Sun 8)
Balans West: SW5,W4,W8 (8)
Bedlington Café (8.30)
Beirut Express:W2 (7)
Benugo:W12 (9)
Best Mangal: SW6 (10-12)
Bluebird Café (8)
La Brasserie (8)
Bumpkin: SW7 (11 am)
Bush Dining Hall (Tue-Fri 8.30 am)
The Cabin (Fri 12, Sat 11, Sun 10)
Chelsea Bun Diner (7, Sun 9)
The Chelsea Kitchen (7, Sun 8)
Comptoir Libanais: SW7 (8.30 am);
    W12 (9.30)
Daylesford Organic:W11 (8, Sun 11)
Ffiona's (Sat & Sun 10)
Gail's Bread:W11 (7, Sat & Sun 8)
Gallery Mess (Sat & Sun 10)
Geales Chelsea Green: SW3 (9 am
    Sat & Sun)
Giraffe:W4,W8 (7.45, Sat & Sun 9);
    W11 (8, Sat & Sun 9)
Granger & Co (7)
The Hampshire Hog (8, Sat& Sun 9)
The Henry Root (Sat & Sun 9)
High Road Brasserie (7, Sat & Sun 8)
Joe's Brasserie (Sat & Sun 11)
Julie's (10)
Kensington Square Kitchen (8, Sun
    9.30)
Lisboa Pâtisserie (7)
Lola & Simón (8, Sat & Sun 9.30)
Lucky Seven (Mon noon, Tue-Thu 10, Fri-
    Sun 9)
Mona Lisa (7)
Ottolenghi:W11 (8, Sun 8.30)
Pappa Ciccia: Fulham High
    St SW6 (7 am)
Pizza East Portobello:W10 (8)
PJ's Bar and Grill (Sat & Sun 10)
Ranoush:W8 (10);W2 (9); SW3 (noon)
Raoul's Café & Deli:W11 (8.30);
    W9 (8.30 am)
Il Ristorante (8)
Sam's Brasserie (9)
Sophie's Steakhouse: all
    branches (Sat & Sun 11)
Stock Pot: SW3 (8)

RIBA Café
Riding House Café
Scandinavian Kitchen
Tom's Kitchen: *all branches*
Villandry
The Wolseley

West
The Abingdon
Annie's: *all branches*
Aubaine: *all branches*
Baker & Spice: *all branches*
Balans West: *all branches*
Beach Blanket Babylon: *W11*
Bluebird
Bluebird Café
Bodean's: *SW6*
La Brasserie
The Builders Arms
Bumpkin: *SW7, W11*
The Cabin
Le Café Anglais
Chelsea Bun Diner
Cheyne Walk Brasserie
Daylesford Organic: *all branches*
The Enterprise
Ffiona's
First Floor
The Frontline Club
Gail's Bread: *W11*
Giraffe: *all branches*
Granger & Co
High Road Brasserie
Joe's Brasserie
Kensington Square Kitchen
Lola & Simón
Lucky Seven
Megan's Delicatessen
Mr Wing
The Oak: *W2*
Ottolenghi: *all branches*
PJ's Bar and Grill
Raoul's Café & Deli: *all branches*
Sam's Brasserie
The Shed
Sophie's Steakhouse: *SW10*
Taqueria
Tom's Deli
Tom's Kitchen: *all branches*
Troubadour
VQ: *SW10*
Zuma

North
Banners
Blue Legume: *all branches*
Caravan King's Cross: *all branches*
Diner: *N1*
The Engineer
Gail's Bread: *NW3*
Ginger & White: *all branches*
Giraffe: *all branches*
Kentish Canteen
Kenwood (Brew House)
Kipferl
Landmark (Winter Gdn)
Made In Camden

Ottolenghi: *all branches*
The Wet Fish Cafe

South
Annie's: *all branches*
Bellevue Rendez-Vous
Ben's Canteen
Butcher & Grill
Butlers Wharf Chop House
Canteen: *SE1*
Chapters
Frizzante Cafe
Garrison
Gastro
Giraffe: *all branches*
Harrison's
Hudsons
Inside
Joanna's
Lamberts
The Lido Cafe
Petersham Hotel
Rivington Grill: *all branches*
Roast
Sonny's Kitchen
The Table
El Vergel
Village East

East
Balans: *all branches*
Bistrotheque
Canteen: *E1*
Caravan: *all branches*
The Diner: *EC2*
Giraffe: *all branches*
Hawksmoor: *E1*
The Hoxton Grill
The Modern Pantry
Rivington Grill: *all branches*
St John Bread & Wine
Smiths (Ground Floor)
Tom's Kitchen: *all branches*
Wapping Food
Workshop Coffee

BUSINESS

Central
Al Duca
Alain Ducasse
Alloro
Alyn Williams
Amaya
Apsleys
Athenaeum
The Avenue
Axis
The Balcon
Bank Westminster
Bar Boulud
Bellamy's
Benares
Bentley's
Bob Bob Ricard
Boisdale

Boudin Blanc
Boulestin
Brasserie Blanc: *The Mkt WC2*
Brasserie Chavot
Browns (Albemarle)
Le Caprice
Cecconi's
China Tang
Christopher's
Le Cigalon
The Cinnamon Club
Clos Maggiore
Corrigan's Mayfair
Dean Street Townhouse
The Delaunay
Les Deux Salons
Le Deuxième
Dinner
Dorchester Grill
Elena's L'Etoile
L'Escargot
Fino
Franco's
Galvin at Windows
Galvin Bistrot de Luxe
Gaucho: *all branches*
Le Gavroche
La Genova
Goodman: *all branches*
The Goring Hotel
Green's
The Greenhouse
The Guinea Grill
Hakkasan: *Hanway Pl W1*
Hawksmoor: *all branches*
Hélène Darroze
Hibiscus
Homage
Hush: *all branches*
Indigo
The Ivy
JW Steakhouse
Kai Mayfair
Ken Lo's Memories
Koffmann's
Langan's Brasserie
Latium
Locanda Locatelli
Mango Tree: *Grosvenor Pl SW1*
Marcus Wareing
MASH Steakhouse
Massimo
Matsuri
maze Grill
Miyama
Mon Plaisir
Murano
Nobu
The Northall
One-O-One
Orrery
Oscar
Osteria Dell'Angolo
The Palm
The Pantechnicon
Paramount
Pétrus

Pied à Terre
Quilon
Quirinale
Quo Vadis
Refuel
Rib Room
RIBA Café
Roka: *all branches*
Roux at Parliament Square
Roux at the Landau
Rules
Santini
Sartoria
Savoy Grill
Scott's
J Sheekey
Simpsons-in-the-Strand
The Square
Tamarind
Theo Randall
Thirty Six
2 Veneti
Veeraswamy
Il Vicolo
The Wallace
Wild Honey
Wiltons
The Wolseley
Zafferano

West
Bibendum
The Frontline Club
Gaucho: *all branches*
Gordon Ramsay
The Ledbury
Manicomio: *all branches*
Outlaw's Seafood and Grill
Poissonnerie de l'Avenue
Racine
Sam's Brasserie
Tom Aikens
La Trompette
Zuma

North
Frederick's
Gaucho: *all branches*
Landmark (Winter Gdn)
Rotunda Bar & Restaurant
St Pancras Grand

South
Blueprint Café
Butlers Wharf Chop House
Gaucho: *all branches*
The Glasshouse
Hutong
Magdalen
Oblix
Oxo Tower (Brass')
Oxo Tower (Rest')
Le Pont de la Tour
Roast
Skylon
Vivat Bacchus: *all branches*
Zucca

East
Alba
L'Anima
Barbecoa
Bevis Marks
Bleeding Heart
Boisdale of Canary Wharf
Bonds
Café du Marché
Chamberlain's
The Chancery
Chinese Cricket Club
Chiswell Street Dining Rms
Cinnamon Kitchen
City Miyama
Club Gascon
Coq d'Argent
Dockmaster's House
The Don
Eyre Brothers
Fish Market
Forman's
The Fox and Anchor
Galvin La Chapelle
Gaucho: *all branches*
Goodman: *all branches*
Gow's
Hawksmoor: *all branches*
High Timber
The Hoxton Grill
Imperial City
Lutyens
Manicomio: *all branches*
The Mercer
Moro
New Street Grill
1901
One Canada Square
1 Lombard Street
Paternoster Chop House
Plateau
Portal
Refettorio
Roka: *all branches*
The Royal Exchange Grand Café
St John
Sauterelle
Smiths (Top Floor)
Smiths (Dining Rm)
Sweetings
Taberna Etrusca
28-50: *EC4*
Vertigo 42
Vivat Bacchus: *all branches*
The White Swan

BYO
*(Bring your own wine at no
or low – less than £3 – corkage.
Note for £5-£15 per bottle,
you can normally negotiate
to take your own wine
to many, if not most, places.)*

Central
Cyprus Mangal
Food for Thought
Fryer's Delight
Golden Hind
India Club
Patogh
Ragam
Viet

West
Adams Café
Alounak: *all branches*
Bedlington Café
Café 209
Chelsea Bun Diner
Faanoos: *all branches*
Fez Mangal
Fitou's Thai Restaurant
Miran Masala
Mirch Masala: *all branches*
Pappa Ciccia: *Munster Rd SW6*

North
Ali Baba
Chutneys
Diwana Bhel-Poori House
Huong-Viet
Jai Krishna
Rugoletta
Toff's
Vijay

South
Amaranth
Apollo Banana Leaf
Cah-Chi: *all branches*
Faanoos: *all branches*
Hot Stuff
Kaosarn: *SW9*
Lahore Karahi
Lahore Kebab House: *all branches*
Mien Tay: *all branches*
Mirch Masala: *all branches*
The Paddyfield
Sree Krishna
Thai Corner Café

East
Lahore Kebab House: *all branches*
Little Georgia Café: *E2*
Mangal 1
Mien Tay: *all branches*
Mirch Masala: *all branches*
Needoo
Rochelle Canteen
Tayyabs

CHILDREN

(h – high or special chairs
m – children's menu
p – children's portions
e – weekend entertainments
o – other facilities)

Central

A Wong *(h)*
Abeno:*WC2 (h);WC1 (hm)*
About Thyme *(hp)*
Al Duca *(hp)*
Al Hamra *(hp)*
Al Sultan *(hp)*
Albannach *(hmp)*
All Star Lanes: *all branches (hm)*
Alloro *(p)*
Alyn Williams *(hp)*
Amaranto *(hm)*
Ametsa with Arzak Instruction *(h)*
Apsleys *(hp)*
aqua nueva *(p)*
Arbutus *(h)*
Asadal *(h)*
Asia de Cuba *(hp)*
L'Atelier de Joel Robuchon *(hp)*
Athenaeum *(m)*
Aubaine: *all branches (h)*
Automat *(h)*
L'Autre Pied *(hp)*
Axis *(hmp)*
Babbo *(hp)*
Balans: *all central branches (hm)*
The Balcon *(hmp)*
Bank Westminster *(hm)*
Bar Boulud *(hp)*
Bar Italia *(hp)*
Il Baretto *(p)*
Barrica *(hp)*
Bar Shu *(h)*
Beiteddine *(p)*
Belgo Centraal: *Earlham*
   St WC2 (hm); Kingsway WC2 (m)
Bellamy's *(hp)*
Benares *(hm)*
Benihana:*W1 (hm)*
Benito's Hat: *Goodge St W1 (hp)*
Bentley's *(h)*
Bincho Yakitori *(hp)*
Bocca Di Lupo *(hp)*
Bodean's:*W1 (ehm)*
La Bodega Negra *(hp)*
Bonnie Gull *(hp)*
The Botanist *(h)*
Boudin Blanc *(hp)*
Boulevard *(hm)*
Brasserie Chavot *(hp)*
Brasserie Max *(hp)*
Brasserie Zédel *(hp)*
Briciole *(hp)*
Browns (Albemarle) *(hmp)*
Browns:*W1,WC2 (hp)*
Byron:*Wellington St WC2 (hm)*
C London *(hp)*
Café Bohème *(h)*
Café des Amis *(h)*

Café in the Crypt *(hp)*
Café Pacifico *(hm)*
Caffè Caldesi *(hp)*
Caffé Vergnano:*WC1 (hm);WC2 (p)*
Cantina Laredo *(hm)*
Cape Town Fish Market *(hp)*
Le Caprice *(hp)*
Caraffini *(h)*
Cecconi's *(hp)*
Le Cercle *(p)*
Ceviche *(h)*
China Tang *(h)*
Chipotle: *Charing Cross Rd WC2 (h)*
Chisou: *all branches (h)*
Chor Bizarre *(h)*
Christopher's *(hm)*
Chuen Cheng Ku *(h)*
Ciao Bella *(h)*
Cigala *(h)*
Le Cigalon *(hp)*
The Cinnamon Club *(h)*
Cinnamon Soho *(hp)*
Clos Maggiore *(hp)*
Como Lario *(hp)*
Comptoir Libanais: *Broadwick*
   St W1 (hm);Wigmore St W1 (m)
Côte: *all central branches (hm)*
Cotidie *(hm)*
The Courtauld Gallery Café *(h)*
Criterion *(hmp)*
Cyprus Mangal *(h)*
Dabbous *(hp)*
Daylesford Organic: *SW1 (hp)*
Dean Street Townhouse *(h)*
The Delaunay *(hp)*
Delfino *(hp)*
Les Deux Salons *(h)*
dim T:*W1 (hmo)*
Diner: *all central branches (hmp)*
Dinner *(hp)*
Dishoom:*WC2 (h)*
Donostia *(hp)*
Dorchester Grill *(hm)*
Downtown Mayfair *(hp)*
Ed's Easy Diner: *Rupert St W1, Moor*
   St W1 (ehm)
Elena's L'Etoile *(h)*
Empress of Sichuan *(h)*
L'Escargot *(p)*
Fairuz *(h)*
The Fifth Floor Restaurant *(hm)*
Fino *(hp)*
Fire & Stone:*WC2 (hm)*
Fishworks: *Marylebone High*
   St W1 (hmo)
Fleet River Bakery *(h)*
The Fountain (Fortnum's) *(hp)*
1707 *(hm)*
Franco's *(hp)*
La Fromagerie Café *(hp)*
Gaby's *(hp)*
Galvin at Windows *(hm)*
Galvin Bistrot de Luxe *(hp)*
Le Garrick *(h)*
Gaucho: *Swallow St W1,WC2 (h)*
Gauthier Soho *(hp)*
Gay Hussar *(hp)*

Gaylord *(hp)*
La Genova *(hp)*
Giraffe:*W1,WC1 (ehm)*
Golden Dragon *(h)*
Golden Hind *(hp)*
Goodman:*W1 (h)*
The Goring Hotel *(hm)*
Goya *(hp)*
Gran Paradiso *(hp)*
The Grand Imperial *(h)*
Grazing Goat *(hm)*
Great Queen Street *(h)*
Grumbles *(hp)*
The Guinea Grill *(p)*
Gustoso Ristorante & Enoteca *(h)*
Haozhan *(h)*
Harbour City *(hp)*
Hard Rock Café *(ehm)*
Hardy's Brasserie *(hm)*
Hare & Tortoise:*WC1 (h)*
Hawksmoor: *all branches (hp)*
Hélène Darroze *(hp)*
Hellenic *(hp)*
Hibiscus *(hp)*
Hix *(hp)*
Homage *(hpm)*
Hummus Bros:*WC1 (h)*
Hush: *all branches (hm)*
Ibérica: *all branches (p)*
Imli Street *(hmp)*
Imperial China *(h)*
Indali Lounge *(hp)*
Indigo *(ehm)*
Inn the Park *(hm)*
Ishbilia *(hp)*
Ishtar *(hp)*
The Ivy *(hp)*
Joe Allen *(hm)*
Joy King Lau *(h)*
JW Steakhouse *(ehmp)*
Kai Mayfair *(h)*
Kaspar's Seafood and Grill *(hm)*
Kazan:*Wilton Rd SW1 (hp)*
Ken Lo's Memories *(hp)*
Kettners *(hm)*
Kimchee *(hp)*
Koba *(hm)*
Koffmann's *(h)*
Kopapa *(h)*
Koya *(hp)*
Ladurée: *SW1 (h);WC2 (hp)*
Langan's Brasserie *(hp)*
Lantana Cafe *(p)*
Latium *(hp)*
Leong's Legends *(p)*
Levant *(hp)*
Locanda Locatelli *(hop)*
Loch Fyne:*WC2 (hp)*
The Lockhart *(hm)*
Lupita *(h)*
Made in Italy: *James St W1 (hp)*
Malabar Junction *(h)*
Mango Tree: *Grosvenor Pl SW1 (h)*
Marcus Wareing *(hp)*
Mari Vanna *(h)*
Maroush: *all branches (h)*
Masala Zone: *all branches (hm)*

Massimo *(hp)*
Matsuri *(hm)*
maze *(h)*
maze Grill *(hm)*
Mela *(hp)*
Mele e Pere *(hp)*
Mews of Mayfair *(hm)*
Carom at Meza *(h)*
Mildreds *(h)*
Mishkin's *(ho)*
Miyama *(h)*
Momo *(h)*
Mon Plaisir *(hmp)*
Motcombs *(hp)*
Moti Mahal *(hp)*
Mr Kong *(h)*
Murano *(hp)*
The National Dining Rooms *(hmp)*
National Gallery Café *(hm)*
Navarro's *(h)*
New Mayflower *(h)*
New World *(h)*
Nizuni *(h)*
Nobu *(h)*
Nobu Berkeley *(h)*
Nopi *(h)*
The Norfolk Arms *(hp)*
North Sea Fish *(hp)*
The Northall *(hmp)*
Noura: *Hobart Pl SW1, W1 (hp)*
Oliveto *(h)*
One-O-One *(hm)*
The Only Running Footman *(hp)*
Opera Tavern *(h)*
The Orange *(hp)*
Orrery *(hp)*
Orso *(hp)*
Oscar *(hp)*
Osteria Dell'Angolo *(hp)*
Ozer *(hmp)*
The Palm *(hm)*
The Pantechnicon *(hp)*
Paramount *(h)*
Paul: *WC2 (h); W1 (hp)*
Pescatori: *all branches (h)*
La Petite Maison *(h)*
Pétrus *(hp)*
Pho: *Great Titchfield St W1 (hp)*
Plum Valley *(h)*
Pollen Street Social *(hp)*
Polpo: *WC2 (hp); W1 (p)*
La Porchetta Pizzeria: *all branches (hp)*
La Porte des Indes *(eh)*
Porters English Restaurant *(hm)*
The Portrait *(hp)*
La Poule au Pot *(hp)*
Princess Garden *(h)*
Prix Fixe *(h)*
The Providores *(h)*
Providores (Tapa Room) *(h)*
Quaglino's *(hm)*
The Queens Arms *(hp)*
Quilon *(h)*
Quo Vadis *(h)*
Ranoush: *SW1 (hp)*
Rasa Maricham: *WC1 (h)*

Real Greek: *W1 (hm); WC2 (m)*
Refuel *(hmo)*
Le Relais de Venise
   L'Entrecôte: *W1 (hp)*
Reubens *(hmp)*
Rib Room *(hmp)*
RIBA Café *(hp)*
Riding House Café *(hmp)*
Ritz (Palm Court) *(h)*
The Ritz Restaurant *(hm)*
Roka: *W1 (h)*
Rossopomodoro: *WC2 (hp)*
Roti Chai *(h)*
Roux at the Landau *(hm)*
Rowley's *(hp)*
Royal Academy *(hp)*
Royal China: *all branches (h)*
Rules *(h)*
St Moritz *(hp)*
Sake No Hana *(p)*
Sakura *(h)*
Salaam Namaste *(hp)*
Sale e Pepe *(p)*
San Carlo Cicchetti *(hm)*
Sarastro *(h)*
Sardo *(p)*
Sartoria *(h)*
Savoir Faire *(hp)*
Savoy Grill *(h)*
Scandinavian Kitchen *(h)*
Scott's *(h)*
Seafresh *(h)*
Seven Park Place *(hp)*
Shampers *(p)*
Shanghai Blues *(h)*
J Sheekey *(h)*
J Sheekey Oyster Bar *(hp)*
Signor Sassi *(hp)*
Simpsons-in-the-Strand *(hmp)*
Sketch (Gallery) *(hm)*
Sketch (Lecture Rm) *(hm)*
The Sketch (Parlour) *(h)*
Sofra: *all branches (hp)*
Soho Diner *(hp)*
Sophie's Steakhouse: *all branches (hm)*
Spice Market *(h)*
Stock Pot: *SW1 (h)*
Suda *(h)*
Sumosan *(hp)*
Tamarind *(hp)*
Tapas Brindisa Soho: *W1 (h)*
Taro: *all central branches (h)*
Tate Britain (Rex Whistler) *(hm)*
Terroirs *(p)*
Texture *(hp)*
Theo Randall *(hm)*
34 *(hp)*
Thirty Six *(hm)*
The Thomas Cubitt *(hp)*
tibits *(hop)*
Tinello *(hp)*
Toku *(h)*
Tom's Kitchen: *WC2 (h)*
Trishna *(hm)*
28-50: *Marylebone Ln W1 (hp)*
2 Amici *(hp)*
2 Veneti *(p)*

Umu *(h)*
The Union Café *(hp)*
Union Jacks: *Central St Giles Piazza WC2 (hmp)*
Vapiano *(hm)*
Vasco & Piero's Pavilion *(p)*
Il Vicolo *(p)*
Villandry *(hm)*
The Vincent Rooms *(h)*
Vinoteca Seymour Place: *Seymour Pl W1 (hp)*
Wagamama: *all central branches (hm)*
Wahaca: *WC2 (h); Charlotte St W1 (hp)*
The Wallace *(ho)*
Wild Honey *(h)*
Wiltons *(p)*
Wolfe's *(hm)*
The Wolseley *(hp)*
Woodlands: *all branches (hp)*
Zafferano *(ehp)*
Zayna *(h)*

West

The Abingdon *(h)*
Abu Zaad *(h)*
Admiral Codrington *(hmp)*
Aglio e Olio *(hp)*
All Star Lanes: *all branches (hm)*
Alounak: *all branches (h)*
Anarkali *(h)*
Angelus *(h)*
The Anglesea Arms *(p)*
The Anglesea Arms *(hp)*
Annie's: *all branches (hm)*
L'Art du Fromage *(p)*
Assaggi *(hp)*
Atari-Ya: *W3 (hp)*
The Atlas *(hp)*
Aubaine: *all branches (h)*
Babylon *(hmp)*
Balans West: *SW5, W4, W8 (hm)*
Banana Tree Canteen: *W9 (hp)*
Bangkok *(h)*
Beach Blanket Babylon: *all branches (p)*
Bedlington Café *(hp)*
Belvedere *(hm)*
Benihana: *SW3 (h)*
Benugo: *Cromwell Rd SW7 (h)*
Best Mangal: *SW6, North End Rd W14 (h)*
Bibendum *(h)*
Bibendum Oyster Bar *(h)*
Big Easy: *SW3 (ehm)*
Bluebird *(h)*
Bluebird Café *(hm)*
Bodean's: *SW6 (ehm)*
Bombay Brasserie *(h)*
Bombay Palace *(hp)*
La Bouchée *(m)*
La Brasserie *(m)*
Brilliant *(hp)*
Brinkley's *(h)*
Brompton Bar & Grill *(hp)*
Bumpkin: *all west branches (hp)*
Bush Dining Hall *(hp)*
Butcher's Hook *(hp)*

155

VQ: *SW10 (hp)*
Wagamama: *W8 (hm)*
Wahaca: *W12 (hp)*
The Walmer Castle *(hm)*
The Waterway *(hp)*
White Horse *(hp)*
Wine Gallery *(hp)*
Yashin: *W8 (hp)*
Zaika *(hp)*
Zuma *(h)*

North

L'Absinthe *(hm)*
Afghan Kitchen *(h)*
The Albion *(hm)*
Ali Baba *(p)*
The Almeida *(hm)*
Anglo Asian Tandoori *(h)*
Antepliler: *all branches (hp)*
Artigiano *(hm)*
L'Artista *(hp)*
Assiette Anglaise *(hp)*
Les Associés *(hmp)*
Atari-Ya: *N12 (hp); NW4 (p)*
L'Aventure *(p)*
Il Bacio: *all branches (hmp)*
Bald Faced Stag *(hmp)*
The Banana Tree
    Canteen: *NW6 (hm)*
Banners *(ehmp)*
Belgo Noord: *NW1 (hm)*
Benito's Hat: *N1 (p)*
Beyoglu *(hp)*
Bistro Aix *(p)*
Blue Legume: *N1, N16 (hm)*
La Bota *(hp)*
Browns: *N1 (hm)*
Bull & Last *(hmp)*
Byron: *Upper St N1 (hm)*
La Cage Imaginaire *(hp)*
Camino *(hp)*
Carob Tree *(h)*
The Clissold Arms *(hm)*
La Collina *(hmp)*
dim T: *all north branches (hmo)*
The Drapers Arms *(h)*
The Duke of Cambridge *(hp)*
Eat Tokyo: *NW11 (hm)*
The Engineer *(hm)*
The Fellow *(h)*
Fifteen *(hp)*
The Fish & Chip Shop *(hm)*
500 *(hp)*
Frederick's *(hp)*
Freemasons Arms *(hmp)*
Gail's Bread: *NW3 (hmp)*
Gallipoli: *all branches (hp)*
Garufa *(hp)*
Gaucho: *NW3 (hp)*
Gem *(hp)*
Gilak *(hp)*
Gilbert Scott *(hp)*
Gilgamesh *(hp)*
Ginger & White: *England's
    Ln NW3 (hm); Perrins Ct NW3 (hmo)*
Giraffe: *N1, Rosslyn Hill NW3 (ehm)*
Good Earth: *NW7 (hp)*

Great Nepalese *(p)*
Gung-Ho *(h)*
Haché: *all branches (hmp)*
Harry Morgan's *(hmop)*
The Haven *(hm)*
The Horseshoe *(hp)*
Huong-Viet *(hp)*
Indian Rasoi *(hp)*
Izgara *(hp)*
Jin Kichi *(h)*
The Junction Tavern *(hp)*
Juniper Dining *(hm)*
Kaifeng *(h)*
Karpo *(hp)*
Kentish Canteen *(hm)*
Kenwood (Brew House) *(hm)*
Kipferl *(hp)*
Ladudu *(hp)*
Landmark (Winter Gdn) *(hmp)*
Lemonia *(p)*
The Little Bay: *all branches (hm)*
Made In Camden *(hp)*
Mangal II *(hm)*
Mango Room *(h)*
Manna *(hp)*
Marine Ices *(hp)*
Market *(hp)*
Masala Zone: *all branches (hm)*
Meat Mission *(hp)*
Mem & Laz *(hp)*
Le Mercury *(hp)*
Mestizo *(hp)*
Mill Lane Bistro *(hp)*
Mimmo la Bufala *(hp)*
Mosaica *(ehp)*
Nautilus *(hp)*
The North London Tavern *(hp)*
Odette's *(hp)*
The Old Bull & Bush *(h)*
The Old White Bear *(hp)*
Olympus Fish *(hm)*
One Blenheim Terrace *(hp)*
The Orange Tree *(hmp)*
Oslo Court *(hp)*
Ottolenghi: *N1 (h)*
Paradise Hampstead *(h)*
Petek *(hp)*
Phoenix Palace *(h)*
Pig & Butcher *(h)*
Pizzeria Oregano *(hp)*
Pizzeria Pappagone *(hm)*
Plum + Spilt Milk *(hp)*
La Porchetta Pizzeria: *all
    branches (hp)*
Rani *(hp)*
Rasa Travancore: *Stoke Newington
    Church St N16 (h); Stoke Newington
    Church St N16 (hp)*
Red Dog Saloon *(hp)*
Retsina *(hp)*
Rising Sun *(p)*
Roots at N1 *(hm)*
Rossopomodoro: *all north
    branches (hp)*
Rotunda Bar & Restaurant *(hm)*
Rugoletta *(hp)*
Le Sacré-Coeur *(hp)*

St Johns *(h)*
St Pancras Grand *(hmp)*
Sakonis *(hp)*
The Salusbury *(hp)*
San Daniele del Friuli *(hp)*
Sarracino *(h)*
Sea Pebbles *(hm)*
The Sea Shell *(hm)*
Season Kitchen *(hp)*
Shrimpy's *(p)*
Singapore Garden *(h)*
Skipjacks *(hp)*
Solly's *(h)*
Somerstown Coffee House *(hm)*
Sushi-Say *(h)*
Sweet Thursday *(hp)*
Toff's *(hm)*
Trullo *(hp)*
Two Brothers *(hm)*
Vijay *(hp)*
Villa Bianca *(p)*
Vrisaki *(hp)*
Wagamama: *all north branches (hm)*
The Wells *(hmp)*
Woodlands: *all branches (hp)*
XO *(hmo)*
York & Albany *(hm)*
Yum Yum *(h)*

South

A Cena *(hp)*
The Abbeville *(hmp)*
Abbeville Kitchen *(hp)*
Al Forno: *SW19 (hp)*
The Anchor & Hope *(h)*
Angels & Gypsies *(hp)*
Annie's: *all branches (hm)*
Antelope *(hp)*
Antico *(hp)*
Antipasto & Pasta *(hp)*
Avalon *(hm)*
Babur *(ho)*
Baltic *(hp)*
The Banana Tree
    Canteen: *SW11 (hmop)*
Bangalore Express: *SE1 (ehm)*
La Barca *(hp)*
Bayee Village *(h)*
Belgo: *SW4 (m)*
Bellevue Rendez-Vous *(hmp)*
Ben's Canteen *(hp)*
Bengal Clipper *(h)*
Benugo: *SE1 (hmp)*
Bianco43 *(hm)*
The Bingham *(hm)*
Bistro Union *(hmp)*
Blue Elephant *(eh)*
Blueprint Café *(hp)*
Al Boccon di'vino *(p)*
Bodean's: *SW4 (ehm)*
The Bolingbroke *(ehm)*
Boqueria *(hp)*
Brady's *(hp)*
Brasserie Toulouse-Lautrec *(hp)*
Brinkley's Kitchen *(hm)*
The Brown Dog *(hp)*
Browns: *SE1 (hm)*

157

Brula *(hp)*
Brunswick House Cafe *(p)*
Buenos Aires Café: *all branches (h)*
Buona Sera: *SW11 (hp)*
Butcher & Grill *(hm)*
Butlers Wharf Chop House *(hm)*
La Buvette *(m)*
Caffé Vergnano: *SE1 (hp)*
Cah-Chi: *SW18 (h)*
Cannizaro House *(hm)*
Canta Napoli: *all branches (hp)*
Canteen: *SE1 (hmp)*
Cantina Vinopolis *(h)*
Canton Arms *(h)*
Cattle Grid: *SW11 (hm)*
Champor-Champor *(h)*
Chapters *(hmp)*
Chez Bruce *(hp)*
Chutney *(h)*
Cocum *(h)*
Constancia *(h)*
Côte: *SW19 (hm)*
The Crooked Well *(m)*
Dalchini *(h)*
The Dartmouth Arms *(hop)*
The Depot *(hm)*
dim T: *SE1 (hmo)*
don Fernando's *(hmo)*
Donna Margherita *(hp)*
Dragon Castle *(h)*
Earl Spencer *(hp)*
Eco *(hmp)*
Elliot's Cafe *(p)*
Enoteca Turi *(hp)*
Everest Inn *(hp)*
Fat Boy's: *all south branches (h)*
The Fentiman Arms *(hp)*
Fish Club: *SW11 (hm); SW4 (hmp)*
Fish in a Tie *(hp)*
fish! *(hm)*
Florence *(hmo)*
40 Maltby Street *(p)*
Four Regions *(hp)*
Fox & Grapes *(hm)*
The Fox & Hounds *(hp)*
Franklins *(hp)*
Frizzante Cafe *(hm)*
Fujiyama *(hp)*
Fulham Wine Rooms *(hp)*
Ganapati *(p)*
Gandhi's *(m)*
Gastro *(m)*
Gazette: *SW11 (hm); SW12 (hmp)*
Giraffe: *SE1 (ehm)*
The Glasshouse *(hp)*
Gourmet Pizza Company *(h)*
The Gowlett *(hp)*
Haché: *all branches (hmp)*
Hare & Tortoise: *SW15 (h)*
Harrison's *(ehmp)*
Hashi *(hm)*
Hot Stuff *(hp)*
Hudsons *(hm)*
Indian Ocean *(h)*
Indian Zilla *(eh)*
Isola del Sole *(hm)*
Jam Tree: *SW4 (hm)*

Joanna's *(hmp)*
Kennington Tandoori *(h)*
Kew Grill *(hm)*
Lahore Karahi *(hmp)*
Lahore Kebab House: *SW16 (hmp)*
Lamberts *(hmp)*
The Lawn Bistro *(hm)*
The Lido Cafe *(hmp)*
The Light House *(hmp)*
Lobster Pot *(hmp)*
Lola Rojo *(h)*
The Lord Northbrook *(h)*
Ma Cuisine *(hmp)*
Ma Goa *(h)*
Magdalen *(p)*
Mango & Silk *(hmp)*
Mar I Terra *(hp)*
Masters Super Fish *(h)*
Matsuba *(h)*
Menier Chocolate Factory *(p)*
Mezzanine *(hp)*
Mien Tay: *all branches (h)*
Mirch Masala: *all south branches (h)*
Nazmins *(h)*
China Boulevard *(h)*
Numero Uno *(hp)*
The Old Brewery *(hp)*
Olley's *(ehm)*
Orange Pekoe *(h)*
Osteria Antica Bologna *(h)*
Oxo Tower (Brass') *(hm)*
Oxo Tower (Rest') *(hm)*
Le P'tit Normand *(hm)*
The Paddyfield *(h)*
The Palmerston *(hp)*
Palmyra *(hmp)*
Pantry *(hm)*
The Pepper Tree *(h)*
Petersham Hotel *(hmp)*
Petersham Nurseries *(hp)*
Pizarro *(h)*
Pizza Metro *(hp)*
Pizzeria Rustica *(hm)*
Plane Food *(hmp)*
Le Pont de la Tour *(hm)*
Le Querce *(hop)*
Real Greek: *SE1 (hm)*
Riva *(hp)*
The Riverfront *(hp)*
Rivington Grill: *SE10 (hmp)*
Roast *(hm)*
Rock & Rose *(hmp)*
Rossopomodoro: *SW18 (hp)*
RSJ *(p)*
San Lorenzo Fuoriporta *(hm)*
Santa Maria del Sur *(h)*
Sapori Sardi *(hm)*
The Sea Cow *(h)*
The Ship *(hmp)*
Skylon *(hmp)*
Skylon Grill *(hm)*
Sonny's Kitchen *(hmp)*
Sree Krishna *(h)*
Sticks'n'Sushi: *SW19 (hm)*
The Swan at the Globe *(hp)*
The Table *(hp)*
Talad Thai *(h)*

Tandoori Nights *(hp)*
Tas: *The Cut SE1, Borough High
   St SE1 (h); Isabella St SE1 (hp)*
Tas Pide *(hm)*
Tate Modern (Level 7) *(hm)*
Telegraph *(hm)*
Tentazioni *(hp)*
Trinity *(hp)*
Tsunami: *SW4 (h)*
Upstairs *(p)*
El Vergel *(hp)*
The Victoria *(ehm)*
Village East *(p)*
Wagamama: *SW15, SW19 (hm)*
Wahaca: *SE1 (hm)*
Waterloo Bar & Kitchen *(hm)*
The Wharf *(hm)*
The Yellow House *(hm)*
Zero Degrees *(hp)*
Zucca *(h)*

East

Alba *(hp)*
Albion: *E2 (hp)*
All Star Lanes: *all branches (hm)*
Amico Bio: *EC1 (hp)*
L'Anima *(h)*
Ark Fish *(hp)*
Balans: *E20 (hp)*
Banana Tree Canteen: *EC1 (hm)*
Bangalore Express: *EC3 (m)*
Barbecoa *(hp)*
Beach Blanket Babylon: *all branch-
   es (p)*
Bevis Marks *(hp)*
Bistrot Bruno Loubet *(hp)*
Bistrotheque *(h)*
Bodean's: *EC3 (hp)*
Bonds *(hm)*
Il Bordello *(h)*
Bouchon Fourchette *(hp)*
The Boundary *(h)*
Brasserie Blanc: *EC2 (h)*
Brasserie on St John Street *(hp)*
Brawn *(hp)*
Browns: *all east branches (hm)*
Buen Ayre *(h)*
Bumpkin: *E20 (hm)*
Café Below *(h)*
Café Spice Namaste *(hp)*
Canteen: *E1 (hmp)*
Caravan: *EC1 (h)*
The Chancery *(p)*
Chinese Cricket Club *(h)*
Chiswell Street Dining Rms *(hp)*
Cinnamon Kitchen *(hp)*
The Clove Club *(h)*
Club Gascon *(p)*
Comptoir Gascon *(h)*
Comptoir Libanais: *E20 (m)*
Coq d'Argent *(h)*
Dans le Noir *(m)*
The Diner: *EC2 (hmp)*
Dockmaster's House *(h)*
The Empress *(hp)*
Fabrizio *(hp)*
Faulkner's *(hm)*

ENTERTAINMENT
(Check times before you go)

Central

West

Nozomi
(DJ, nightly)
Okawari
(karaoke)
Old Parr's Head
(quiz night, Mon; poker, Tue)
Il Pagliaccio
(Elvis impersonator, opera nights monthly)
Paradise by Way of Kensal Green
(comedy, Wed; Jazz, Fri)
Ciro's (Pizza Pomodoro)
(live music, nightly)
Sam's Brasserie
(live music, first and third Sun of month)
La Sophia
(jazz, Fri D)
Sticky Fingers
(face painter, Sun)
Troubadour
(live music, most nights)
The Waterway
(live music, Thu)

North
Bull & Last
(quiz night, Sun)
Camino
(DJ, Thu-Sat)
The Fellow
(DJ, Fri)
Gilgamesh
(DJ, Fri & Sat)
Landmark (Winter Gdn)
(pianist & musicians, daily)
Mestizo
(DJ, Thu)
The North London Tavern
(jazz, Sun; quiz night, Mon; open mic, Tue; Every third Thu comedy)
Rotunda Bar & Restaurant
(jazz, Fri)
Thai Square: N1
(DJ, Thu-Sat)
Villa Bianca
(guitarist, Mon-Wed; pianist, Thu, Fri, Sat & Sun L)
The Wet Fish Cafe
(Spanish soul, occasionally)
White Rabbit
(DJ nights)
York & Albany
(live music, Tue D)

South
Al Forno: SW15
(live music, Sat)
Archduke Wine Bar
(jazz, Mon-Sun)
Avalon
(DJ, Fri & Sat)
Bayee Village
(pianist, Wed & Thu; karaoke)
Bengal Clipper
(pianist, Tue-Sun)
Brasserie Toulouse-Lautrec
(live music, nightly)
The Crooked Well
(jazz, Sun D)

Entrée
(jazz, Thu-Sat D)
The Fentiman Arms
(quiz night, Tue)
Florence
(play room)
Garrison
(cinema on Sun)
The Gowlett
(DJ, various nights)
Meson don Felipe
(guitarist, nightly)
China Boulevard
(live music)
Oxo Tower (Brass')
(jazz, Sat & Sun L, Sun-Mon D)
Le Pont de la Tour
(pianist, every evening; live jazz trio, Sun L)
Roast
(jazz, Sun)
Santa Maria del Sur
(live music, Mon)
The Ship
(live music, Sun; quiz, Wed)
Tas: The Cut SE1, Borough High St SE1
(guitarist, nightly)
Tas Pide
(live music, daily D)
Thai Square: SW15
(DJ, Fri & Sat)
The Wharf
(jazz, first Sun D of month; pianist, Wed & Thu)

East
All Star Lanes: all east branches
(bowling)
Beach Blanket Babylon: all branches
(DJ, Fri & Sat)
Bistrotheque
(regular drag shows and cabarets, piano brunch)
Boisdale of Canary Wharf
(live music, daily)
Café du Marché
(pianist & bass, Mon-Thu; pianist, Fri & Sat)
Cinnamon Kitchen
(DJ, Wed-Fri)
Elephant Royale
(live music, Thu-Sun)
The Gunmakers
(jazz, Mon)
The Hoxton Grill
(DJ, Thu-Sat)
Kenza
(belly dancers, Mon-Sat; tarot reader, Fri)
The Little Bay: EC1
(opera, Thu-Sat)
Mint Leaf: EC2
(Jazz, Fri D; DJ, weekends)
The Narrow
(quiz night, Mon; acoustic, Fri)
1 Lombard Street
(DJ, Fri)
Pizza East: E1
(DJ, live music, quiz nights, Tue, Thu, Sat)

The Punch Tavern
(poker nights, Mon; wine tasting, quiz & comedy nights, monthly)
Le Rendezvous du Café
(jazz, Mon-Sat)
Shanghai
(karaoke)
Smiths (Ground Floor)
(DJ, Wed-Sat (summer))
Tas: EC1
(guitarist, Tue-Sun)
Thai Square City: EC3
(DJ, Fri)
Vivat Bacchus: EC4
(jazz, Fri eves)
Yi-Ban
(live smooth jazz, Fri & Sat)

LATE
(open till midnight or later as shown; may be earlier Sunday)

Central
Al Sultan
All Star Lanes: WC1 *(Fri & Sat midnight)*
Asia de Cuba
L'Atelier de Joel Robuchon
Balans: *Old Compton St W1 (24 hours); Old Compton St W1 (5 am, Sun 1 am)*
Bam-Bou
Bar Italia *(open 24 hours, Sun 4 am)*
Beiteddine
Bistro 1: *Frith St W1, WC2*
La Bodega Negra *(1 am, not Sun)*
Bone Daddies *(Thu-Sat midnight)*
Brasserie Zédel
Café Bohème *(2.45 am, Sun midnight)*
Cantina Laredo *(Sat midnight)*
Le Caprice
Circus *(midnight, Fri & Sat 2 am)*
Côte: W1 *(Thu-Sat midnight)*
Dean Street Townhouse *(Fri & Sat midnight)*
The Delaunay
Le Deuxième
Diner: W1 *(12.30 am, Sun midnight)*
Dishoom: WC2 *(Fri & Sat midnight)*
Downtown Mayfair
Ed's Easy Diner: *Rupert St W1, Moor St W1 (midnight, Fri & Sat 1 am)*
Gaby's
Gelupo *(Thu-Sat 12.30 am)*
Hakkasan: *Hanway Pl W1 (12.30 am, not Sun)*
Harbour City *(Fri & Sat midnight)*
Hard Rock Café
Inamo: SW1 *(Fri & Sat 12.30 am)*
Indali Lounge
Joe Allen *(Fri & Sat 12.45 am)*
Levant *(Fri & Sat midnight)*
Maroush: W1 *(12.30 am)*
MEATLiquor *(Fri & Sat 1 am)*
Carom at Meza *(2 am, Thu-Sat 3 am)*
Mr Kong *(2.45 am, Sun 1.45 am)*
New Mayflower *(4 am)*
ping pong: *Gt Marlborough St W1,*

Paddington St W1
La Porchetta Pizzeria: WC1 *(Sat & Sun midnight)*
Princi
Ranoush: SW1
Refuel
Rossopomodoro: WC2
San Carlo Cicchetti
J Sheekey
J Sheekey Oyster Bar
Shoryu Ramen: W1
Sofra: *all branches*
Sophie's Steakhouse: *all branches (12.45 am, not Sun)*
VQ: *all branches (24 hours)*
The Wolseley

West
Anarkali
Balans: W8 ; SW5 *(2 am)*
Basilico: SW6
Beirut Express: SW7 ; W2 *(2 am)*
Best Mangal: SW6 ; North End Rd W14 *(midnight, Sat 1 am)*
Buona Sera: *all branches*
E l leven Park Walk
Gifto's *(Sat & Sun midnight)*
Halepi
Jam Tree: SW6 *(Fri & Sat 2 am)*
Khan's *(Sat & Sun midnight)*
Maroush: I) 21 Edgware Rd W2 *(1.45 am)*; VI) 68 Edgware Rd W2 *(12.30 am)*; SW3 *(3.30 am)*
Mirch Masala: *all branches*
Monty's: W5
Il Pagliaccio
ping pong: W2
Pizza East Portobello: W10 *(Fri & Sat midnight)*
Ciro's (Pizza Pomodoro) *(1 am)*
Ranoush: SW3 ; W8 *(1.30 am)*; W2 *(2.30 am)*
Rossopomodoro: *all west branches*
The Sands End *(Thu-Sat midnight)*
Shilpa *(Thu-Sat midnight)*
Sophie's Steakhouse: *all branches (12.45 am, not Sun)*
The Thatched House *(Thu-Sat midnight)*
VQ: *all branches (24 hours)*
The Walmer Castle *(Fri & Sat midnight)*

North
Ali Baba
Banners *(Fri & Sat midnight)*
Basilico: N1, NW3
Bistro Aix
Chilango: N1 *(Fri & Sat midnight)*
Diner: N1
Dirty Burger: NW5 *(Mon-Thu midnight, Fri & Sat 1 am)*
Gallipoli: *all branches (Fri & Sat midnight)*
Gem *(Fri & Sat midnight)*
Mangal II *(1 am)*
Meat Mission
Mem & Laz *(Fri & Sat midnight)*

Le Mercury *(12.30 am, not Sun)*
Pizzeria Pappagone
La Porchetta Pizzeria: NW1 *(Fri & Sat midnight)*; N4 *(Sat & Sun midnight)*; N1 *(weekends midnight)*
Yum Yum *(Fri & Sat midnight)*

South
The Balham Bowls Club *(Fri & Sat midnight)*
Basilico: *all south branches*
Belgo: SW4 *(midnight, Thu 1 am, Fri & Sat 2 am)*
Boqueria *(Fri & Sat midnight)*
Buona Sera: *all branches*
Caffé Vergnano: SE1
Cah-Chi: SW18 *(not Sat & Sun)*
Champor-Champor
Dirty Burger: SW8 *(Fri & Sat 2 am)*
Everest Inn
Fish in a Tie
Gastro
Indian Moment *(Fri & Sat midnight)*
Lahore Karahi
Lahore Kebab House: *all branches*
Mirch Masala: *all branches*
Nazmins
Tandoori Nights *(Fri & Sat midnight)*
Tsunami: SW4 *(Fri-Sun midnight)*
Zero Degrees

East
Brick Lane Beigel Bake *(24 hours)*
Cellar Gascon
The Diner: EC2 *(not Sun & Mon)*
Elephant Royale *(Fri & Sat midnight)*
The Jugged Hare *(Fri & Sat midnight)*
Lahore Kebab House: *all branches*
Mangal 1 *(midnight, Sat-Sun 1 am)*
Mirch Masala: *all branches*
Pizza East: E1 *(Thu midnight, Fri & Sat 1 am)*
La Porchetta Pizzeria: EC1 *(Sat & Sun midnight)*
Rocket: E14
Sushisamba *(midnight, Fri & Sat 1 am)*
Wapping Food

OUTSIDE TABLES
(* particularly recommended)

Central
A Wong
Abokado: WC2
Al Duca
Al Hamra
Al Sultan
Albannach
Amaranto
Andrew Edmunds
Antidote
aqua nueva
L'Artiste Musclé
Atari-Ya: W1
Aubaine: W1
Aurora
L'Autre Pied

Baker & Spice: SW1
Balans: Old Compton St W1
Bam-Bou
Bank Westminster
Bar Italia
Il Baretto
Barrafina: W1
Barrica
Benito's Hat: Goodge St W1
Bentley's
Benugo: *all central branches*
Bincho Yakitori
Bistro 1: Frith St W1, WC2
Bob Bob Ricard
Bonnie Gull
The Botanist
La Bottega: Lower Sloane St SW1, Eccleston St SW1
Boudin Blanc
The Bountiful Cow
Brasserie Blanc: The Mkt WC2*
Busaba Eathai: WC1
Café Bohème
Café des Amis
Caffè Caldesi
Il Calcio: W1
Cantina Laredo
Le Caprice
Caraffini
Cecconi's
Ceviche
Chisou: W1
Ciao Bella
Cigala
Comptoir Libanais: Wigmore St W1
Côte: WC2
The Courtauld Gallery Café
Da Mario
Daylesford Organic: *all branches*
Dean Street Townhouse
Dehesa
Delfino
dim T: W1
Diner: W1
Dishoom: WC2
Donostia
Downtown Mayfair
Ed's Easy Diner: Moor St W1
Fairuz
Flat White
Fleet River Bakery
Franco's
Fryer's Delight
Le Garrick
Gelupo
Giraffe: W1
Golden Hind
Goodman: W1
Gordon's Wine Bar*
Goya
Gran Paradiso
Grazing Goat
Great Queen Street
Grumbles
Hard Rock Café
Hardy's Brasserie
Hellenic

Hush: W1
Indali Lounge
Inn the Park
Ishbilia
Ishtar
Jenny Lo's Tea House
JW Steakhouse
Kaffeine
Kazan: all branches
The Keeper's House
Kopapa
Ladurée: SW1, W1
The Lady Ottoline
Lantana Cafe
Leon: Gt Marlborough St W1, WC2
The Lockhart
Maison Bertaux
Mildreds
Mishkin's
Momo
Motcombs
Nizuni
The Norfolk Arms
Noura: Hobart Pl SW1
Olivomare
The Only Running Footman
Opera Tavern
The Orange
Orrery
Oscar
Ozer
The Pantechnicon
Pescatori: Charlotte St W1
La Petite Maison
Piccolino: W1*
ping pong: Eastcastle St W1
El Pirata
Pizza Pilgrims
La Porchetta Pizzeria: WC1
La Poule au Pot
Prix Fixe
Providores (Tapa Room)
The Queens Arms
Quo Vadis
Le Relais de Venise L'Entrecôte: W1
Reubens
RIBA Café*
The Ritz Restaurant
Roka: W1
Royal Academy
Salaam Namaste
Salt Yard
Santini
Sardo
Savoir Faire
Scandinavian Kitchen
Scott's
Shampers
J Sheekey
J Sheekey Oyster Bar
Siam Central
Sofra: Shepherd St W1, WC2
Soho Diner
Suda
Tapas Brindisa Soho: W1
Taro: Brewer St W1
Tate Britain (Rex Whistler)

The Thomas Cubitt
tibits
Tinello
Toku
Tom's Kitchen: WC2
Trishna
Tsunami: W1
Union Jacks: Central St Giles Piazza WC2
Vapiano
Verru
Villandry
Vinoteca Seymour Place: Seymour Pl W1
The Wallace
William Curley: all branches
Wolfe's
Yalla Yalla: Green's Ct W1

West

The Abingdon
Admiral Codrington
Al-Waha
Anarkali
Angelus
The Anglesea Arms
The Anglesea Arms
Annie's: all branches
The Atlas*
Aubaine: SW3
Babylon
Baker & Spice: SW3
Balans: W12, W4
Beach Blanket Babylon: W11
Bedlington Café
Beirut Express: SW7
Belvedere
Benugo: Cromwell Rd SW7
Best Mangal: SW6, North End Rd W14
Bibendum Oyster Bar
Big Easy: SW3
Bird in Hand
Black & Blue: W8
Bluebird
Bluebird Café
Bombay Palace
La Bouchée
La Brasserie
Brinkley's
Bumpkin: SW3, SW7
Butcher's Hook
Byron: Gloucester Rd SW7, W8
The Cabin
Cambio de Tercio
Canta Napoli: W4
Capote Y Toros
The Carpenter's Arms*
Carvosso's
Casa Brindisa
Casa Malevo
Charlotte's Place
Chelsea Bun Diner
The Chelsea Ram
Cibo
Colchis
Le Colombier
Côte: W8
The Cow

Cumberland Arms
The Dartmouth Castle
Daylesford Organic: all branches
La Delizia Limbara
Duke of Sussex
Durbar
E&O
El I even Park Walk
Edera
The Enterprise
Essenza
La Famiglia*
Fat Boy's: all west branches
Fire & Stone: W12
First Floor
Foxtrot Oscar
Frantoio
Gail's Bread: W11
Galicia
Gallery Mess
The Gate: W6
Geales: W8
Giraffe: W4
Haché: SW10
The Hampshire Hog*
The Havelock Tavern
The Henry Root
Hereford Road
High Road Brasserie
Hole in the Wall*
Indian Zing
Jam Tree: SW6
Joe's Brasserie
Julie's
Karma
Kateh
Kensington Square Kitchen
Khan's
The Ladbroke Arms
Lola & Simón
Made in Italy: SW3
Madsen
The Mall Tavern
The Malt House
Manicomio: all branches
Maxela
Mazi
The Meat & Wine Co
Mediterraneo
Medlar
Megan's Delicatessen
Mona Lisa
Noor Jahan: W2
The Oak: W2
Old Parr's Head
Osteria Basilico
Osteria dell'Arancio
Otto Pizza
Il Pagliaccio
Pappa Ciccia: Fulham High St SW6
Paradise by Way of Kensal Green
Pellicano
Pentolina
Poissonnerie de l'Avenue
Polish Club
Il Portico
Portobello Ristorante*

Princess Victoria
Queen's Head*
Raoul's Café & Deli: W11*;W9
The Real Greek: W12
The Red Pepper
Riccardo's
The River Café
Rocca Di Papa: SW7
The Roebuck*
Rossopomodoro: W11
Royal China: SW6
Saigon Saigon
The Sands End
Santa Lucia
Santa Maria
The Scarsdale
The Shed
La Sophia
Sushinho: SW3
The Swan*
Tartufo
Tendido Cero
Tendido Cuatro
Thali
The Thatched House
Tom's Deli
Tosa
La Trompette
Troubadour
VQ: SW10
Wahaca: W12
The Walmer Castle
The Waterway*
White Horse
The Windsor Castle*
Wine Gallery

North
L'Absinthe
The Albion*
Ali Baba
The Almeida
Artigiano
Assiette Anglaise
Les Associés
L'Aventure
Bald Faced Stag
The Banana Tree Canteen: NW6
Blue Legume: N16
Bull & Last
Café del Parc
La Cage Imaginaire
Carob Tree
Charles Lamb
Chilango: N1
The Clissold Arms
La Collina
dim T: NW3
The Drapers Arms
The Duke of Cambridge
The Engineer*
The Fellow
The Flask
Frederick's
Freemasons Arms*
Gail's Bread: all north branches
Gallipoli: all branches

Gaucho: NW3
Gem
Ginger & White: Perrins Ct NW3
Giraffe: N1, Rosslyn Hill NW3
Haché: NW1
Harry Morgan's
The Haven
The Horseshoe
Indian Rasoi
Isarn
The Junction Tavern
Kentish Canteen
Kenwood (Brew House)*
Kipferl
Lemonia
Market
Masala Zone: N1
Mill Lane Bistro
Mimmo la Bufala
Mosaica
The North London Tavern
The Northgate
Odette's
The Old Bull & Bush
The Orange Tree*
Ottolenghi: N1
El Parador
Petek
Pig & Butcher
Pizzeria Pappagone
La Porchetta Pizzeria: NW1
Retsina
Rising Sun
Rotunda Bar & Restaurant*
Le Sacré-Coeur
St Johns
The Salusbury
Sea Pebbles
The Sea Shell
Singapore Garden
Soho Japan
Solly's
Somerstown Coffee House
Swan & Edgar
Sweet Thursday
Villa Bianca
The Wells
The Wet Fish Cafe
White Rabbit
York & Albany
Yum Yum

South
The Abbeville
Abbeville Kitchen
Al Forno: SW19
Alquimia
The Anchor & Hope
Annie's: all branches
Antelope
Antipasto & Pasta
Applebee's Cafe
Archduke Wine Bar
Avalon*
Baltic
Bangalore Express: SE1
La Barca

Bayee Village
Bellevue Rendez-Vous
The Bingham
Bistro Union
Black & Blue: SE1
Blueprint Café
Bodean's: SW4
The Bolingbroke
Boqueria
Brinkley's Kitchen
The Brown Dog*
Browns: SE1
Brula
Buenos Aires: SE3
Buona Sera: SW11
Butcher & Grill
Butlers Wharf Chop House
Caffé Vergnano: SE1
Cannizaro House
Canteen: SE1*
Canton Arms
Chapters
Chutney
Côte: SW19
The Crooked Well
The Dartmouth Arms
The Depot
dim T: SE1
don Fernando's
Donna Margherita
Earl Spencer
Eco
Elliot's Cafe
Everest Inn
Fat Boy's: SW14,TW1
The Fentiman Arms
fish!
Florence
40 Maltby Street
Four Regions
The Fox & Hounds
Franco Manca: SW9
Franklins
Frizzante Cafe
Fulham Wine Rooms
Ganapati
Gastro
Gaucho: TW10*
Gazette: SW11
Giraffe: SE1
Gourmet Pizza Company
The Gowlett
Harrison's
Hudsons
Indian Zilla
Joanna's
Kennington Tandoori
Lamberts
The Lido Cafe
Lola Rojo
Ma Cuisine
Mar I Terra
Numero Uno
Orange Pekoe
Osteria Antica Bologna
Oxo Tower (Brass')
Oxo Tower (Rest')

PRIVATE ROOMS

(for the most comprehensive listing of venues for functions – from palaces to pubs – visit www.hardens.com/party, or buy *Harden's London Party, Event & Conference Guide,* **available in all good bookshops)**
* particularly recommended

Downtown Mayfair *(40)*
Elena's L'Etoile *(10,14,16,34)*
Empress of Sichuan *(18)*
L'Escargot *(24,60,20)*
Fairuz *(22)*
Fire & Stone:WC2 *(23)*
Franco's *(16,55)*
La Fromagerie Café *(12)*
Galvin at Windows *(30)*
Galvin Bistrot de Luxe *(22)*
Gauthier Soho *(40,4,12,18,24)*
Gay Hussar *(12,25)*
The Giaconda Dining Rooms *(30)*
Golden Dragon *(14,14)*
Golden Hind *(30)*
Gopal's of Soho *(18)*
Gordon's Wine Bar *(8)*
The Goring Hotel *(18,14,50,6)*
Goya *(90)*
Gran Paradiso *(30,12)*
The Grand Imperial *(30)*
Grazing Goat *(50)*
Green's *(36)*
The Greenhouse *(12)*
Grumbles *(10)*
The Guinea Grill *(28)*
Gustoso Ristorante & Enoteca *(16)*
Haozhan *(40)*
Harbour City *(40)*
Hard Rock Café *(200)*
Hardy's Brasserie *(28,16,12,48)*
Hawksmoor:WC2 *(16)*
Hazuki *(25)*
Hélène Darroze *(20)*
Hellenic *(20)*
Hibiscus *(18)*
Hix *(10)*
Hush:WC1 *(45)*;W1 *(80)*
Ibérica: *all branches (50)*
Ikeda *(6)*
Imli Street *(45)*
Imperial China *(12,14,20,25,40,70)*
Inamo: *SW1 (16)*;W1 *(20)*
Indali Lounge *(15)*
India Club *(60)*
Indigo *(25,25,30)*
Ishbilia *(80,20,35)*
Ishtar *(8)*
The Ivy *(60)*
Joe Allen *(50)*
Joy King Lau *(50)*
JW Steakhouse *(10)*
Kai Mayfair *(10)*
Kaspar's Seafood and Grill *(14)*
Kazan:Wilton Rd SW1 *(40,80)*
Ken Lo's Memories *(10,15)*
Kettners *(10,12,40,85,55,24,18)*
Kiku *(8)*
Koba *(20)*
Koffmann's *(14)*
The Lady Ottoline *(18)*
Levant *(10,12)*
Locanda Locatelli *(50)*
Loch Fyne:WC2 *(50)*
The Lockhart *(40)*
Lupita *(15)*
Maison Bertaux *(18)*

Marcus Wareing *(16,8)*
Mari Vanna *(35)*
MASH Steakhouse *(18)*
Massimo *(18)*
Matsuri *(6,18,18)*
maze *(40,40,10,150)*
maze Grill *(14)*
Mela *(35)*
Mews of Mayfair *(28,16)*
Carom at Meza *(44)*
Mildreds *(12)*
Mint Leaf: *all branches (60)*
Mon Plaisir *(25)*
Motcombs *(18,32)*
Moti Mahal *(35)*
Mr Chow *(10,60,70)*
Murano *(12)*
National Gallery Café *(30)*
New World *(200)*
Nobu *(50)*
Nopi *(28)*
The Norfolk Arms *(20,10)*
The Northall *(24,30)*
Noura: *Hobart Pl SW1 (15,30,10);*
  W1 (55)
Novikov (Asian restaurant) *(20,28)*
Novikov (Italian restaurant) *(18,18)*
One-O-One *(10)*
The Only Running Footman *(40,18)*
The Orange *(40,30,70)*
Orrery *(18)*
Oscar *(32,14,10)*
Osteria Dell'Angolo *(22)*
The Palm *(50,50,30)*
The Pantechnicon *(14,20,32)*
Paramount *(30)*
Patara: *Greek St W1 (30)*
Pescatori: *Dover St W1 (16); Charlotte*
  St W1 (50)
Pied à Terre *(14)*
El Pirata *(6,7)*
Pizza Pilgrims *(16)*
Pollen Street Social *(14)*
Polpo:WC2 *(20)*
La Porte des Indes *(10,14)*
La Poule au Pot *(16)*
Princess Garden *(15,15,50)*
Prix Fixe *(25)*
The Providores *(42)*
Quaglino's *(43,16)*
The Queens Arms *(30)*
Quilon *(18)*
Quo Vadis *(32,12)*
Refuel *(12)*
Reubens *(50)*
Rib Room *(14)*
Riding House Café *(18)*
Ritz (Palm Court) *(23,40)*
The Ritz Restaurant *(20,50)*
Roux at Parliament Square *(10,18)*
Roux at the Landau *(16)*
Royal China:W1 *(12,24,36)*
Royal China Club *(11,24)*
Rules *(8,16)*
St Moritz *(30)*
Salt Yard *(44)*
Santini *(30)*

Sartoria *(20,20)*
Savoy Grill *(50)*
Scott's *(40)*
Seven Park Place *(40,16,10)*
Shampers *(45)*
Shanghai Blues *(30)*
Signor Sassi *(15,30)*
Simpsons-in-the-Strand *(50,120)*
Sketch (Gallery) *(150)*
Sketch (Lecture Rm) *(24,130)*
Sofra:WC2 *(90)*
Spice Market *(40)*
The Square *(18)*
Sumosan *(120)*
Taro: *Old Compton St W1 (30)*
The 10 Cases *(16)*
10 Greek Street *(12)*
Texture *(16)*
Thai Square: *SW1 (8)*
Theo Randall *(25)*
Thirty Six *(40)*
The Thomas Cubitt *(20,30,12,20)*
tibits *(70)*
Tinello *(28)*
Tom's Kitchen:WC2 *(30)*
Trishna *(12)*
28-50: *Marylebone Ln W1 (18)*
2 Amici *(30)*
Umu *(12)*
Union Jacks: *Central St Giles Piazza*
  WC2 (65)
Vasco & Piero's Pavilion *(36)*
Veeraswamy *(24)*
Verru *(8)*
Il Vicolo *(45)*
Villandry *(12,18)*
The Vincent Rooms *(35)*
Vinoteca Seymour Place: *Seymour*
  Pl W1 (35)
Wiltons *(20)*
The Windmill *(32)*
Wolfe's *(14)*
The Wolseley *(14)*
Yming *(12,18)*
Zafferano *(28)*
Zayna *(18)*

West
Abu Zaad *(100)*
Adams Café *(24)*
Admiral Codrington *(30)*
Aglio e Olio *(55)*
Albertine *(28)*
Anarkali *(16)*
Angelus *(22,6)*
The Anglesea Arms *(35)*
Annie's:W4 *(30)*
L'Art du Fromage *(20)*
The Atlas *(45)*
Babylon *(12,28)*
Beach Blanket Babylon:W11 *(60)*
Belvedere *(20)*
Benihana: *all branches (10)*
Bird in Hand *(18)*
Bluebird *(30,30,30,70)*
Bombay Brasserie *(16)*
Bombay Palace *(30)*

165

Villa Bianca *(40)*
Vrisaki *(15)*
The Wells *(12,22,16)*
White Rabbit *(100)*
XO *(22)*
York & Albany *(40)*
Yum Yum *(100)*

South
Al Forno: *SW15 (85)*
Amaranth *(25)*
Annie's: *SW13 (35)*
Antelope *(120)*
Antico *(100)*
Antipasto & Pasta *(35)*
Avalon *(20)*
The Balham Bowls Club *(200,100)*
Baltic *(30)*
Bayee Village *(26)*
Ben's Canteen *(50)*
The Bingham *(99)*
Blue Elephant *(16)*
The Bolingbroke *(35)*
Boqueria *(10-50)*
Brasserie Toulouse-Lautrec *(14)*
Brinkley's Kitchen *(30)*
Browns: *SE1 (40,30)*
Brula *(24,10,10)*
Brunswick House Cafe *(12)*
Cah-Chi: *SW18 (22)*
Champor-Champor *(8)*
Chapters *(50)*
Chez Bruce *(16)*
Chutney *(15)*
The Crooked Well *(40)*
Dalchini *(40)*
The Dartmouth Arms *(60,40)*
dim T: *SE1 (16)*
Dragon Castle *(50)*
Earl Spencer *(70)*
Emile's *(35,45)*
Enoteca Turi *(18)*
Entrée *(45)*
Everest Inn *(100)*
The Fentiman Arms *(35)*
Four Regions *(30,40)*
The Fox & Hounds *(30)*
Franklins *(35)*
Frizzante Cafe *(40)*
Fujiyama *(90)*
Fulham Wine Rooms *(20)*
Gandhi's *(14)*
Garrison *(25)*
Gazette: *SW11 (14,14); SW12 (40)*
Harrison's *(14)*
Hashi *(10)*
Hudsons *(100)*
Indian Zilla *(30)*
Joanna's *(6)*
Kennington Tandoori *(16)*
Lahore Karahi *(70,60)*
The Lawn Bistro *(22)*
The Light House *(12)*
Lobster Pot *(20,28)*
Lola Rojo *(20)*
Magdalen *(30,30)*

Mar I Terra *(45)*
Mezzanine *(12,12)*
Mien Tay: *SW11 (20)*
Nazmins *(16)*
China Boulevard *(25)*
Le P'tit Normand *(20)*
Palmyra *(30)*
Petersham Hotel *(28,16)*
Pizarro *(10)*
Pizzeria Rustica *(30)*
Le Pont de la Tour *(20,24)*
Le Querce *(24)*
Rock & Rose *(14)*
RSJ *(24,30)*
San Lorenzo
    Fuoriporta *(25,52,32,20)*
Sapori Sardi *(12,26)*
The Sea Cow *(15)*
The Ship *(14,26)*
Skylon *(33)*
Sonny's Kitchen *(15)*
Sree Krishna *(50,60)*
The Swan at the Globe *(16,120,450)*
Talad Thai *(40)*
Telegraph *(50,120)*
Tentazioni *(35,15)*
Trinity *(12)*
Upstairs *(26,22)*
The Victoria *(50)*
Village East *(20)*
Waterloo Bar & Kitchen *(30)*
The Wharf *(60)*

East
Alba *(12,35)*
Amico Bio: *EC1 (25)*
L'Anima *(12,15)*
Barbecoa *(35)*
Beach Blanket Babylon: *E1 (120)*
Bird of Smithfield *(26)*
Bistrot Bruno Loubet *(50,10,12,30)*
Bistrotheque *(50,96)*
Bleeding Heart *(18,35,40,44,120)*
Boisdale of Canary
    Wharf *(12,12,25,40)*
Bonds *(8,10,16)*
Brasserie Blanc: *EC2 (50)*
Brasserie on St John
    Street *(40,35,38)*
Busaba Eathai: *E20 (12+)*
Café du Marché *(30,60)*
Café Spice Namaste *(40)*
Caravan: *EC1 (12)*
Chamberlain's *(70,15)*
The Chancery *(25,30,18)*
Chiswell Street Dining Rms *(12)*
Cinnamon Kitchen *(18)*
City Miyama *(4,4,8,10)*
Corner Room *(16)*
Dans le Noir *(30)*
Dockmaster's House *(70,22,54)*
The Don *(18,24,45,45)*
Fabrizio *(18)*
Faulkner's *(20)*
Fish Central *(100)*
Forman's *(10,20)*
Galvin La Chapelle *(12)*

George & Vulture *(24)*
Goodman City : *EC2 (10)*
Green Papaya *(35)*
The Gun *(16,22)*
The Gunmakers *(15)*
Hawksmoor: *E1 (14); EC2 (22)*
Hazev *(24)*
High Timber *(18,10)*
HKK *(10)*
The Hoxton Grill *(22,22,16,14,12)*
Ibérica: *all branches (50)*
Imperial City *(12)*
Kenza *(50,14)*
Lahore Kebab House: *E1 (50)*
Little Georgia Café: *E2 (50)*
Lutyens *(20,8,6,12)*
Manicomio: *all branches (30)*
The Mercer *(4,10,20,40,40,120)*
Mien Tay: *E2 (40)*
Mint Leaf: *all branches (60)*
The Modern Pantry *(12,22)*
Morgan M *(40)*
Mugen *(10)*
My Old Place *(30)*
The Narrow *(18,40)*
Needoo *(45)*
Northbank *(30)*
1 Lombard Street *(45)*
Orpheus *(18)*
The Oyster Shed *(28,40)*
Paternoster Chop House *(13)*
The Peasant *(18)*
Piccolino: *EC2 (24)*
Pizza East: *E1 (18)*
Plateau *(20,30)*
Portal *(9,14)*
The Punch Tavern *(20,110)*
Refettorio *(30)*
Le Rendezvous du Café *(30,60)*
Rivington Grill: *EC2 (25)*
Rocket: *Adams Ct EC2 (25)*
Rosa's: *E1 (40)*
Royal China: *E14 (12,12,12)*
The Royal Exchange Grand
    Café *(26)*
St John *(18)*
Sauterelle *(26)*
Sedap *(14)*
Shanghai *(40,50)*
Sichuan Folk *(15)*
Simpson's Tavern *(40-100)*
Smiths (Dining Rm) *(36)*
Sushisamba *(63,160,230)*
Taberna Etrusca *(30)*
Tajima Tei *(16,6,4)*
Tas: *EC1 (50)*
Tayyabs *(35)*
Les Trois Garçons *(10)*
28-50: *EC4 (14,6)*
Viajante *(16)*
Viet Grill *(100)*
Vinoteca: *EC1 (30)*
Vivat Bacchus: *EC4 (25)*
Whitechapel Gallery *(14)*
Workshop Coffee *(45)*
Yi-Ban *(30)*
Young Turks at the Ten Bells *(14)*

ROMANTIC

Central
Andrew Edmunds
Archipelago
L'Artiste Musclé
L'Atelier de Joel Robuchon
Aurora
Bam-Bou
The Berners Tavern
Bob Bob Ricard
Boudin Blanc
Café Bohème
Le Caprice
Cecconi's
Le Cercle
Chor Bizarre
Clos Maggiore
Corrigan's Mayfair
Coya
Crazy Bear
Dean Street Townhouse
The Delaunay
Les Deux Salons
Elena's L'Etoile
L'Escargot
Galvin at Windows
Gauthier Soho
Le Gavroche
Gay Hussar
Gordon's Wine Bar
Hakkasan: *Hanway Pl W1*
Honey & Co
Hush: *W1*
The Ivy
Kettners
Langan's Brasserie
Levant
Locanda Locatelli
Marcus Wareing
Momo
Mon Plaisir
Orrery
La Petite Maison
Pied à Terre
Polpo: *W1*
La Porte des Indes
La Poule au Pot
Refuel
Ritz (Palm Court)
The Ritz Restaurant
Roux at the Landau
Rules
St Moritz
Sarastro
Scott's
J Sheekey
J Sheekey Oyster Bar
The Wolseley
Zafferano

West
Albertine
Angelus
Annie's: *all branches*
Assaggi
Babylon

Beach Blanket Babylon: *all branches*
Belvedere
Bibendum
La Bouchée
Brinkley's
Charlotte's Place
Cheyne Walk Brasserie
Clarke's
Le Colombier
Daphne's
The Dock Kitchen
E&O
Eight Over Eight
La Famiglia
Ffiona's
First Floor
The Five Fields
Julie's
Launceston Place
The Ledbury
Maggie Jones's
Mediterraneo
Mr Wing
Osteria Basilico
Paradise by Way of Kensal Green
Patio
Pissarro
Polish Club
Portobello Ristorante
Racine
The River Café
La Sophia
Star of India
The Summerhouse
La Trompette
Troubadour
Le Vacherin
The Walmer Castle
Zuma

North
L'Absinthe
Anglo Asian Tandoori
Les Associés
L'Aventure
Bistro Aix
La Cage Imaginaire
The Engineer
The Flask
Frederick's
The Little Bay: *all branches*
Mango Room
Le Mercury
Odette's
Oslo Court
Villa Bianca

South
A Cena
Annie's: *all branches*
Bellevue Rendez-Vous
The Bingham
Blue Elephant
Blueprint Café
Al Boccon di'vino
Brula
La Buvette

Cannizaro House
Champor-Champor
Chez Bruce
The Depot
Emile's
Enoteca Turi
Gastro
The Glasshouse
Hutong
Joanna's
Lobster Pot
Oblix
Oxo Tower (Brass')
Petersham Hotel
Petersham Nurseries
Le Pont de la Tour
Rock & Rose
Skylon
The Swan at the Globe
Trinity
Upstairs
The Wharf

East
Beach Blanket Babylon: *all branches*
Bleeding Heart
Café du Marché
Club Gascon
Comptoir Gascon
Galvin La Chapelle
The Little Bay: *all branches*
LMNT
Moro
Pizza East: *E1*
Les Trois Garçons
Vertigo 42
Wapping Food

ROOMS WITH A VIEW

Central
Dinner
Galvin at Windows
Inn the Park
Kaspar's Seafood and Grill
The National Dining Rooms
Orrery
Paramount
The Portrait

West
Babylon
Belvedere
Cheyne Walk Brasserie
Min Jiang
Pissarro
The Summerhouse
The Waterway

North
Rotunda Bar & Restaurant

South
Alquimia
The Bingham
Blueprint Café
Butlers Wharf Chop House

The Depot
dim T: *SE1*
Gourmet Pizza Company
Hutong
Joanna's
China Boulevard
Oblix
Oxo Tower (Brass')
Oxo Tower (Rest')
Petersham Hotel
Le Pont de la Tour
Roast
The Ship
Skylon
Skylon Grill
The Swan at the Globe
Tate Modern (Level 7)
Thai Square: *SW15*
Upstairs
The Wharf

East
Barbecoa
Boisdale of Canary Wharf
Coq d'Argent
Duck & Waffle
Elephant Royale
Forman's
The Grapes
The Gun
High Timber
Lotus Chinese Floating Restaurant
The Narrow
Northbank
The Oyster Shed
Plateau
Smiths (Top Floor)
Sushisamba
Vertigo 42
Yi-Ban

NOTABLE WINE LISTS

Central
Alyn Williams
Andrew Edmunds
Antidote
Apsleys
Arbutus
Barrica
Bedford & Strand
Boisdale
Café des Amis
Le Cercle
Cigala
Clos Maggiore
Copita
Cork & Bottle
Dehesa
Ebury Rest' & Wine Bar
L'Escargot
The Fifth Floor Restaurant
Fino
The Fountain (Fortnum's)
1707
La Fromagerie Café
Galvin Bistrot de Luxe

Le Gavroche
Gordon's Wine Bar
Green Man & French Horn
The Greenhouse
Hardy's Brasserie
Hibiscus
The Ivy
Kai Mayfair
Latium
Locanda Locatelli
Marcus Wareing
Olivo
Olivomare
Opera Tavern
Orrery
Otto's
Pétrus
Pied à Terre
The Providores
Providores (Tapa Room)
Quo Vadis
The Ritz Restaurant
St Moritz
Salt Yard
Sardo
Savoy Grill
Shampers
Sotheby's Café
The Square
Tate Britain (Rex Whistler)
The 10 Cases
10 Greek Street
Terroirs
Texture
28-50: *all branches*
The Union Café
Vinoteca Seymour Place: *all branches*
Wild Honey
Zafferano

West
Albertine
Angelus
Bibendum
Brinkley's
Brompton Bar & Grill
Cambio de Tercio
Clarke's
Le Colombier
L'Etranger
The Frontline Club
Gordon Ramsay
The Kensington Wine Rooms
The Ledbury
Locanda Ottomezzo
Osteria dell'Arancio
Popeseye: *all branches*
Princess Victoria
Racine
The River Café
Tendido Cuatro
Tom Aikens
La Trompette
Vinoteca: *all branches*
White Horse
Wine Gallery

North
La Collina
Swan & Edgar
Trullo

South
Brinkley's Kitchen
Brula
Cantina Vinopolis
Chez Bruce
Emile's
Enoteca Turi
40 Maltby Street
Fulham Wine Rooms
The Glasshouse
José
Magdalen
Pizarro
Le Pont de la Tour
Popeseye: *all branches*
Riva
RSJ
Soif
Tentazioni
Toasted
Vivat Bacchus: *all branches*

East
Alba
Bleeding Heart
Brawn
Cellar Gascon
Club Gascon
Comptoir Gascon
Coq d'Argent
The Don
Eyre Brothers
High Timber
The Jugged Hare
Moro
Portal
The Quality Chop House
Sager & Wilde
St John Bread & Wine
The Sign of the Don
Smiths (Top Floor)
28-50: *all branches*
Vinoteca: *all branches*
Vivat Bacchus: *all branches*
Wapping Food
The Wine Library

Plum & Spilt Milk

Sager & Wilde

Story

Tom's Kitchen

An asterisk (*) after an entry indicates exceptional or very good cooking

AMERICAN
Central
All Star Lanes (WC1)
Automat (W1)
Big Easy (WC2)
Bodean's (W1)
Bubbledogs (W1)
Christopher's (WC2)
Hard Rock Café (W1)
Jackson & Whyte (W1)
Joe Allen (WC2)
The Lockhart (W1)
Mishkin's (WC2)
The Palm (SW1)
Pitt Cue Co (W1)*
Soho Diner (W1)
Spuntino (W1)*

West
All Star Lanes (W2)
Big Easy (SW3)
Bodean's (SW6)
Lucky Seven (W2)
Sticky Fingers (W8)

North
Chicken Shop (NW5)
John Salt (N1)
Karpo (NW1)
Red Dog Saloon (N1)
Shrimpy's (N1)

South
Bodean's (SW4)
Oblix (SE1)
Wishbone (SW9)

East
All Star Lanes (E1, E20)
Beard to Tail (EC2)
Bodean's (EC3)
The Hoxton Grill (EC2)

AUSTRALIAN
Central
Lantana Cafe (W1)

West
Granger & Co (W11)

BELGIAN
Central
Belgo (WC2)

North
Belgo Noord (NW1)

South
Belgo (SW4)

BRITISH, MODERN
Central
Alyn Williams (W1)*
Andrew Edmunds (W1)
The Angel & Crown (WC2)

Arbutus (W1)
Athenaeum (W1)*
Aurora (W1)
The Avenue (SW1)
Axis (WC2)
Balthazar (WC2)
Bank Westminster (SW1)
Bellamy's (W1)
The Berners Tavern (W1)
Bob Bob Ricard (W1)
The Botanist (SW1)
Brasserie Max (WC2)
Le Caprice (SW1)
Coopers Restaurant & Bar (WC2)
Criterion (W1)
Daylesford Organic (SW1)
Dean Street Townhouse (W1)
Le Deuxième (WC2)
Dorchester Grill (W1)
Ducksoup (W1)
Ebury Rest' & Wine Bar (SW1)
The Fifth Floor Restaurant (SW1)
Gordon's Wine Bar (WC2)
The Goring Hotel (SW1)
Grazing Goat (W1)
Hardy's Brasserie (W1)
Hix (W1)
Homage (WC2)
Hush (W1, WC1)
Indigo (WC2)
Inn the Park (SW1)
The Ivy (WC2)
Kettners (W1)
Langan's Brasserie (W1)
Little Social (W1)*
Mews of Mayfair (W1)
Newman Street Tavern (W1)
No 11 Pimlico Road (SW1)
The Norfolk Arms (WC1)
The Northall (WC2)
The Only Running Footman (W1)
The Orange (SW1)
Oscar (W1)
Ozer (W1)
The Pantechnicon (SW1)
Paramount (WC1)
Picture (W1)*
Pollen Street Social (W1)*
The Portrait (WC2)
Quaglino's (SW1)
The Queens Arms (SW1)
Quo Vadis (W1)
Randall & Aubin (W1)*
Refuel (W1)
RIBA Café (W1)
Roux at Parliament Square (SW1)
Roux at the Landau (W1)
Seven Park Place (SW1)
Seven Stars (WC2)
1707 (W1)
Shampers (W1)
Social Eating House (W1)
Sotheby's Café (W1)
Tate Britain (Rex Whistler) (SW1)
10 Greek Street (W1)*
Thirty Six (SW1)
The Thomas Cubitt (SW1)
Tom's Kitchen (WC2)
The Union Café (W1)
Union Jacks (WC2)
Villandry (W1)

The Vincent Rooms (SW1)
Vinoteca (W1)
VQ (WC1)
Whyte & Brown (W1)
Wild Honey (W1)
The Wolseley (W1)

West
The Abingdon (W8)
The Anglesea Arms (W6)*
The Anglesea Arms (SW7)
Babylon (W8)
Beach Blanket Babylon (W11)
Belvedere (W8)
Bluebird (SW3)
Brinkley's (SW10)
Brompton Bar & Grill (SW3)
The Builders Arms (SW3)
Bush Dining Hall (W12)
Butcher's Hook (SW6)
The Cadogan Arms (SW3)
The Carpenter's Arms (W6)
Carvosso's (W4)
The Chelsea Ram (SW10)
Clarke's (W8)
The Cow (W2)
The Dartmouth Castle (W6)
Daylesford Organic (W11)
The Dock Kitchen (W10)
Duke of Sussex (W4)
The Enterprise (SW3)
First Floor (W11)
The Five Fields (SW3)*
Formosa Dining Room (W9)
The Frontline Club (W2)
Harwood Arms (SW6)*
The Havelock Tavern (W14)*
Hedone (W4)*
The Henry Root (SW10)
High Road Brasserie (W4)
Hole in the Wall (W4)
Jam Tree (SW6)
Joe's Brasserie (SW6)
Julie's (W11)
Kensington Place (W8)
Kensington Square Kitchen (W8)
Kitchen W8 (W8)*
The Ladbroke Arms (W11)*
Launceston Place (W8)*
The Ledbury (W11)*
The Magazine Restaurant (W2)
The Mall Tavern (W8)
Marianne (W2)
Medlar (SW10)*
Megan's Delicatessen (SW6)
Paradise by Way of Kensal Green (W10)
Pissarro (W4)
Princess Victoria (W12)
Queen's Head (W6)
The Roebuck (W4)
Sam's Brasserie (W4)
The Sands End (SW6)
The Shed (W8)
The Thatched House (W6)
Tom Aikens (SW3)*
Tom's Deli (W11)
Tom's Kitchen (SW3)
Union Jacks (W4)
VQ (SW10)
Vinoteca (W4)

The Waterway (W9)
White Horse (SW6)
Whits (W8)*

North
The Albion (N1)
Bald Faced Stag (N2)
Bradley's (NW3)
Caravan King's Cross (N1)
Charles Lamb (N1)
The Clissold Arms (N2)
Le Coq (N1)
The Drapers Arms (N1)
The Duke of Cambridge (N1)
The Engineer (NW1)
The Fellow (N1)
Frederick's (N1)
Freemasons Arms (NW3)
Grain Store (N1)*
The Haven (N20)
The Horseshoe (NW3)
The Junction Tavern (NW5)
Juniper Dining (N5)*
Landmark (Winter Gdn) (NW1)
Made In Camden (NW1)
Mango Room (NW1)
Market (NW1)
Mosaica (N22)
The North London Tavern (NW6)
The Northgate (N1)*
Odette's (NW1)
The Old Bull & Bush (NW3)
Pig & Butcher (N1)*
Plum + Spilt Milk (N1)
Rising Sun (NW7)
Rotunda Bar & Restaurant (N1)
St Pancras Grand (NW1)
Season Kitchen (N4)*
Somerstown Coffee House (NW1)
The Wells (NW3)
The Wet Fish Cafe (NW6)

South
The Abbeville (SW4)
Abbeville Kitchen (SW4)*
Albion (SE1)
Antelope (SW17)
Avalon (SW12)
The Balham Bowls Club (SW12)
Ben's Canteen (SW11)
The Bingham (TW10)*
Bistro Union (SW4)
Blueprint Café (SE1)
The Bolingbroke (SW11)
The Brown Dog (SW13)
Brunswick House Cafe (SW8)
Cannizaro House (SW19)
Cantina Vinopolis (SE1)
Chapters (SE3)
Chez Bruce (SW17)*
The Crooked Well (SE5)*
The Dairy (SW4)
The Dartmouth Arms (SE23)
The Depot (SW14)
Earl Spencer (SW18)
Elliot's Cafe (SE1)
Emile's (SW15)
Entrée (SW11)
The Fentiman Arms (SW8)
Florence (SE24)
40 Maltby Street (SE1)*

Franklins (SE22)
Garrison (SE1)
The Glasshouse (TW9)*
Harrison's (SW12)
Inside (SE10)*
Jam Tree (SW4)
Lamberts (SW12)*
The Lido Cafe (SE24)
Magdalen (SE1)*
Menier Chocolate Factory (SE1)
Mezzanine (SE1)
The Old Brewery (SE10)
Oxo Tower (Rest') (SE1)
The Palmerston (SE22)
Petersham Hotel (TW10)
Petersham Nurseries (TW10)
Plane Food (TW6)
Le Pont de la Tour (SE1)
Rivington Grill (SE10)
Rock & Rose (TW9)
RSJ (SE1)
Skylon (SE1)
Skylon Grill (SE1)
Sonny's Kitchen (SW13)
Story (SE1)*
The Swan at the Globe (SE1)
The Table (SE1)
Tate Modern (Level 7) (SE1)
Trinity (SW4)*
Union Street Café (SE1)
The Victoria (SW14)
Waterloo Bar & Kitchen (SE1)
The Wharf (TW11)

East
The Anthologist (EC2)
Balans (E20)
Beach Blanket Babylon (E1)
Bevis Marks (E1)
Bird of Smithfield (EC1)
Bistrotheque (E2)
The Boundary (E2)*
Brasserie on St John Street (EC1)
Bread Street Kitchen (EC4)
Café Below (EC2)
Caravan (EC1)
The Chancery (EC4)
Chiswell Street Dining Rms (EC1)
The Clove Club (EC1)*
The Don (EC4)
Duck & Waffle (EC2)
The Empress (E9)*
Foxlow (EC1)
Gin Joint (EC2)
Gow's (EC2)
The Gun (E14)
The Gunmakers (EC1)*
High Timber (EC4)
Hilliard (EC4)*
Hoi Polloi (E1)
The Jugged Hare (EC1Y)
The Mercer (EC2)
The Modern Pantry (EC1)
The Morgan Arms (E3)
The Narrow (E14)
1901 (EC2)
Northbank (EC4)
One Canada Square (E14)
1 Lombard Street (EC3)
The Peasant (EC1)
Princess of Shoreditch (EC2)

The Punch Tavern (EC4)
Rivington Grill (EC2)
Rochelle Canteen (E2)*
Sager & Wilde (E2)
The Sign of the Don (EC4)
Smiths Brasserie (E1)*
Smiths (Ground Floor) (EC1)
Street Kitchen (EC2)*
3 South Place (EC2)
Tom's Kitchen (E14)
Vertigo 42 (EC2)
Vinoteca (EC1)
Wapping Food (E1)
The White Swan (EC4)
Whitechapel Gallery (E1)
Young Turks at the Ten Bells (E1)

BRITISH, TRADITIONAL
Central
Boisdale (SW1)
Browns (Albemarle) (W1)
Canteen (W1)
Corrigan's Mayfair (W1)
Dinner (SW1)
The Fountain (Fortnum's) (W1)
Fuzzy's Grub (SW1)
Great Queen Street (WC2)*
Green's (SW1)
The Guinea Grill (W1)
Hardy's Brasserie (W1)
The Keeper's House (W1)
The Lady Ottoline (WC1)
The National Dining Rooms (WC2)
Porters English Restaurant (WC2)
Rib Room (SW1)
Rules (WC2)
Savoy Grill (WC2)
Scott's (W1)*
Simpsons-in-the-Strand (WC2)
Wiltons (SW1)
The Windmill (W1)

West
The Brown Cow (SW6)
Bumpkin (SW3, SW7, W11)
Ffiona's (W8)
The Hampshire Hog (W6)
Hereford Road (W2)*
Maggie Jones's (W8)
The Malt House (SW6)*
The Surprise (SW3)

North
Bull & Last (NW5)*
Gilbert Scott (NW1)
Greenberry Cafe (NW1)
Kentish Canteen (NW5)
The Old White Bear (NW3)
St Johns (N19)

South
The Anchor & Hope (SE1)*
Butlers Wharf Chop House (SE1)
Canteen (SE1)
Canton Arms (SW8)*
Fox & Grapes (SW19)
The Lord Northbrook (SE12)
The Manor Arms (SW16)*
The Riverfront (SE1)
Roast (SE1)

East
Albion *(E2)*
Bumpkin *(E20)*
Canteen *(E1, E14)*
The Fox and Anchor *(EC1)**
Fuzzy's Grub *(EC4)*
George & Vulture *(EC3)*
Hix Oyster & Chop House *(EC1)*
The Oyster Shed *(EC4)*
Paternoster Chop House *(EC4)*
E Pellicci *(E2)*
The Quality Chop House *(EC1)**
St John *(EC1)**
St John Bread & Wine *(E1)**
Simpson's Tavern *(EC3)*
Sweetings *(EC4)*

EAST & CENT. EUROPEAN
Central
The Delaunay *(WC2)*
Gay Hussar *(W1)*
The Wolseley *(W1)*

North
Kipferl *(N1)*

FISH & SEAFOOD
Central
Belgo Centraal *(WC2)*
Bellamy's *(W1)*
Bentley's *(W1)**
Bonnie Gull *(W1)**
Burger & Lobster *(W1)**
Cape Town Fish Market *(W1)*
Fishworks *(W1)*
Green's *(SW1)*
Kaspar's Seafood and Grill *(WC2)*
Loch Fyne *(WC2)*
Olivomare *(SW1)**
One-O-One *(SW1)*
The Pantechnicon *(SW1)*
Pescatori *(W1)*
Quaglino's *(SW1)*
Randall & Aubin *(W1)**
Rib Room *(SW1)*
Royal China Club *(W1)**
Scott's *(W1)**
J Sheekey *(WC2)**
J Sheekey Oyster Bar *(WC2)**
Wiltons *(SW1)*
Wright Brothers *(W1)**

West
Bibendum Oyster Bar *(SW3)**
Big Easy *(SW3)*
Le Café Anglais *(W2)*
Chez Patrick *(W8)*
The Cow *(W2)*
Geales *(W8)*
Kensington Place *(W8)*
Mandarin Kitchen *(W2)**
Outlaw's Seafood and Grill *(SW3)**
Poissonnerie de l'Avenue *(SW3)**
The Summerhouse *(W9)*

North
Belgo Noord *(NW1)*
Bradley's *(NW3)*
Carob Tree *(NW5)*
Olympus Fish *(N3)**

Prawn On The Lawn *(N1)*
Sea Pebbles *(HA5)*
Toff's *(N10)**

South
Applebee's Cafe *(SE1)*
fish! *(SE1)*
Gastro *(SW4)*
Lobster Pot *(SE11)**
Le Querce *(SE23)**
Wright Brothers *(SE1)**

East
Angler *(EC2)*
Burger & Lobster *(EC1)**
Chamberlain's *(EC3)*
Fish Central *(EC1)*
Fish Market *(EC2)*
Forman's *(E3)**
Gow's *(EC2)*
The Grapes *(E14)*
Hix Oyster & Chop House *(EC1)*
Loch Fyne *(EC3)*
Orpheus *(EC3)**
The Royal Exchange Grand
  Café *(EC3)*
Sweetings *(EC4)*
Wright Brothers *(E1)**

FRENCH
Central
Alain Ducasse *(W1)*
Antidote *(W1)*
L'Artiste Musclé *(W1)*
L'Atelier de Joel Robuchon *(WC2)**
Aubaine *(W1)*
L'Autre Pied *(W1)**
The Balcon *(SW1)*
Bar Boulud *(SW1)*
Bellamy's *(W1)*
Boudin Blanc *(W1)*
Boulestin *(SW1)*
Boulevard *(WC2)*
Brasserie Blanc *(W1, WC2)*
Brasserie Chavot *(W1)**
Brasserie Zédel *(W1)*
Café Bohème *(W1)*
Café des Amis *(WC2)*
Le Cercle *(SW1)*
Chabrot Bistrot d'Amis *(SW1)*
Le Cigalon *(WC2)*
Clos Maggiore *(WC2)**
Colbert *(SW1)*
Côte *(W1, WC2)*
Les Deux Salons *(WC2)*
Elena's L'Etoile *(W1)*
L'Escargot *(W1)*
Galvin at Windows *(W1)*
Galvin Bistrot de Luxe *(W1)**
Le Garrick *(WC2)*
Gauthier Soho *(W1)**
Le Gavroche *(W1)**
The Giaconda Dining
  Rooms *(WC2)*
Green Man & French Horn *(WC2)*
The Greenhouse *(W1)**
Hélène Darroze *(W1)*
Hibiscus *(W1)*
Koffmann's *(SW1)**
Marcus Wareing *(SW1)*

maze *(W1)*
Mon Plaisir *(WC2)*
Orrery *(W1)*
Otto's *(WC1)**
La Petite Maison *(W1)**
Pétrus *(SW1)**
Pied à Terre *(W1)**
La Poule au Pot *(SW1)*
Prix Fixe *(W1)*
Randall & Aubin *(W1)**
Le Relais de Venise
  L'Entrecôte *(W1)*
The Ritz Restaurant *(W1)*
Savoir Faire *(WC1)*
Savoy Grill *(WC2)*
Sketch (Lecture Rm) *(W1)*
Sketch (Gallery) *(W1)*
The Square *(W1)**
Terroirs *(WC2)*
28-50 *(W1)*
Verru *(W1)**
Villandry *(W1)*
The Wallace *(W1)*

West
Albertine *(W12)*
Angelus *(W2)*
L'Art du Fromage *(SW10)**
Aubaine *(SW3, W8)*
Belvedere *(W8)*
Bibendum *(SW3)*
La Bouchée *(SW7)*
La Brasserie *(SW3)*
Le Café Anglais *(W2)*
Charlotte's Bistro *(W4)**
Charlotte's Place *(W5)*
Cheyne Walk Brasserie *(SW3)*
Chez Patrick *(W8)*
Le Colombier *(SW3)*
Côte *(SW6, W2, W4, W8)*
L'Etranger *(SW7)*
Garnier *(SW5)*
Goode & Wright *(W11)*
Gordon Ramsay *(SW3)*
The Pig's Ear *(SW3)*
Poissonnerie de l'Avenue *(SW3)**
Quantus *(W4)**
Racine *(SW3)*
La Sophia *(W10)**
La Trompette *(W4)*
Le Vacherin *(W4)*
Whits *(W8)**

North
L'Absinthe *(NW1)*
The Almeida *(N1)*
Assiette Anglaise *(N7)**
Les Associés *(N8)*
L'Aventure *(NW8)**
Bistro Aix *(N8)**
Blue Legume *(N1, N16, N8)*
Bradley's *(NW3)*
La Cage Imaginaire *(NW3)*
Charles Lamb *(N1)*
Le Mercury *(N1)*
Michael Nadra *(NW1)**
Mill Lane Bistro *(NW6)*
One Blenheim Terrace *(NW8)*
Oslo Court *(NW8)**
Le Sacré-Coeur *(N1)*
The Wells *(NW3)*

South
Bellevue Rendez-Vous *(SW17)*
Brasserie Blanc *(SE1)*
Brasserie Toulouse-Lautrec *(SE11)*
Brula *(TW1)**
La Buvette *(TW9)*
Casse-Croute *(SE1)*
Côte *(SE1, SW19)*
Gastro *(SW4)*
Gazette *(SW11, SW12)*
The Lawn Bistro *(SW19)*
Lobster Pot *(SE11)**
Ma Cuisine *(TW9)*
Le P'tit Normand *(SW18)*
Soif *(SW11)*
Toasted *(SE22)*
Upstairs *(SW2)**

East
Bistrot Bruno Loubet *(EC1)*
Bleeding Heart *(EC1)*
Bouchon Fourchette *(E8)**
Brasserie Blanc *(EC2, EC3, EC4)*
Brawn *(E2)**
Café du Marché *(EC1)**
Cellar Gascon *(EC1)**
Chabrot Bistrot des Halles *(EC1)**
Club Gascon *(EC1)**
Comptoir Gascon *(EC1)*
Coq d'Argent *(EC2)*
Côte *(EC4)*
The Don *(EC4)*
Galvin La Chapelle *(E1)**
Lutyens *(EC4)*
Morgan M *(EC1)**
Plateau *(E14)*
Relais de Venise L'Entrecôte *(E14, EC2)*
Le Rendezvous du Café *(EC1)*
The Royal Exchange Grand Café *(EC3)*
Sauterelle *(EC3)*
Les Trois Garçons *(E1)*
28-50 *(EC4)*

FUSION
Central
Archipelago *(W1)*
Asia de Cuba *(WC2)*
Bubbledogs (Kitchen Table @) *(W1)**
Kopapa *(WC2)*
Providores (Tapa Room) *(W1)**

West
E&O *(W11)**
Eight Over Eight *(SW3)*
L'Étranger *(SW7)*
Sushinho *(SW3)**

North
XO *(NW3)*

South
Champor-Champor *(SE1)**
Tsunami *(SW4)**
Village East *(SE1)*

East
Caravan *(EC1)*

Sushinho *(EC2)**
Viajante *(E2)**

GAME
Central
Boisdale *(SW1)*
Rules *(WC2)*
Wiltons *(SW1)*

West
Harwood Arms *(SW6)**

North
San Daniele del Friuli *(N5)*

GREEK
Central
Hellenic *(W1)*
Real Greek *(W1, WC2)*

West
Halepi *(W2)*
Mazi *(W8)*
The Real Greek *(W12)*

North
Carob Tree *(NW5)*
Lemonia *(NW1)*
Retsina *(NW3)*
Vrisaki *(N22)*

South
Real Greek *(SE1)*

East
Kolossi Grill *(EC1)*
Real Greek *(E1)*

HUNGARIAN
Central
Gay Hussar *(W1)*

INTERNATIONAL
Central
Balans *(W1)*
Bedford & Strand *(WC2)*
Boulevard *(WC2)*
Browns *(SW1, W1, WC2)*
Café in the Crypt *(WC2)*
Cork & Bottle *(WC2)*
Giraffe *(SW1, W1, WC1)*
Gordon's Wine Bar *(WC2)*
Grumbles *(SW1)*
Carom at Meza *(W1)**
Motcombs *(SW1)*
National Gallery Café *(WC2)*
The Providores *(W1)**
Sarastro *(WC2)*
Stock Pot *(SW1)*
The 10 Cases *(WC2)*
Terroirs *(WC2)*

West
Annie's *(W4)*
Balans West *(SW5, W12, W4, W8)*
Chelsea Bun Diner *(SW10)*
The Chelsea Kitchen *(SW10)*
Foxtrot Oscar *(SW3)*
Gallery Mess *(SW3)*

Giraffe *(W11, W4, W8)*
The Kensington Wine Rooms *(W8)*
Michael Nadra *(W4)**
Mona Lisa *(SW10)*
The Scarsdale *(W8)*
Stock Pot *(SW3)*
Troubadour *(SW5)*
The Windsor Castle *(W8)*
Wine Gallery *(SW10)*

North
Banners *(N8)*
Browns *(N1)*
The Flask *(N6)*
Giraffe *(N1, NW3)*
The Haven *(N20)*
The Old Bull & Bush *(NW3)*
The Orange Tree *(N20)*
Petek *(N4)*
Swan & Edgar *(NW1)*

South
Annie's *(SW13)*
Brinkley's Kitchen *(SW17)*
Browns *(SE1)*
Giraffe *(SE1)*
Hudsons *(SW15)*
Joanna's *(SE19)*
The Light House *(SW19)*
The Riverfront *(SE1)*
The Ship *(SW18)*
Telegraph *(SW15)*
Vivat Bacchus *(SE1)*
The Wharf *(TW11)*
The Yellow House *(SE16)**

East
Browns *(E14, EC2)*
Dans le Noir *(EC1)*
Giraffe *(E1)*
LMNT *(E8)*
Les Trois Garçons *(E1)*
Vivat Bacchus *(EC4)*
The Wine Library *(EC3)*

IRISH
East
Lutyens *(EC4)*

ITALIAN
Central
Al Duca *(SW1)*
Alloro *(W1)*
Amaranto *(W1)*
Amico Bio *(WC1)*
Apsleys *(SW1)*
Babbo *(W1)*
Il Baretto *(W1)*
Bocca Di Lupo *(W1)**
La Bottega *(SW1)*
Briciole *(W1)*
C London *(W1)*
Caffè Caldesi *(W1)*
Caffè Vergnano *(WC2)*
Il Calcio *(W1)*
Caraffini *(SW1)*
Cecconi's *(W1)*
Ciao Bella *(WC1)*
Como Lario *(SW1)*
Il Convivio *(SW1)**

Cotidie (W1)
Da Mario (WC2)
Polpo (WC2)
Dehesa (W1)*
Delfino (W1)*
Downtown Mayfair (W1)
Franco's (SW1)
La Genova (W1)
Gran Paradiso (SW1)
Gustoso Ristorante &
  Enoteca (SW1)
Jamie's Italian (WC2)
Latium (W1)*
Locanda Locatelli (W1)
Made in Italy (W1)
Mele e Pere (W1)
Murano (W1)
Novikov (Italian restaurant) (W1)
Obika (W1)
Oliveto (SW1)*
Olivo (SW1)*
Olivocarne (SW1)
Olivomare (SW1)*
Opera Tavern (WC2)*
Orso (WC2)
Osteria Dell'Angolo (SW1)
Ottolenghi (SW1)*
Pescatori (W1)
Piccolino (W1)
Polpo (W1)
La Porchetta Pizzeria (WC1)
Princi (W1)
Quirinale (SW1)*
Rossopomodoro (WC2)
Sale e Pepe (SW1)
Salt Yard (W1)*
San Carlo Cicchetti (W1)
Santini (SW1)
Sardo (W1)*
Sartoria (W1)
Signor Sassi (SW1)
Theo Randall (W1)*
Tinello (SW1)*
Tozi (SW1)*
2 Amici (SW1)
2 Veneti (W1)
Vapiano (W1)
Vasco & Piero's Pavilion (W1)*
Il Vicolo (SW1)
Zafferano (SW1)

West
Oak (W12)*
Aglio e Olio (SW10)
Assaggi (W2)*
Bird in Hand (W14)
La Bottega (SW7)
Buona Sera (SW3)
Calcio (SW5)
Canta Napoli (W4)
Cibo (W14)*
Da Mario (SW7)
Daphne's (SW3)
La Delizia Limbara (SW3)
E l I even Park Walk (SW10)
Edera (W11)*
Essenza (W11)
La Famiglia (SW10)
Frantoio (SW10)
Jamie's Italian (W12)
Locanda Ottomezzo (W8)

Lucio (SW3)
Made in Italy (SW3)
Manicomio (SW3)
Mediterraneo (W11)
Mona Lisa (SW10)
Napulé (SW6)
Nuovi Sapori (SW6)
The Oak (W2)*
Obika (SW3)
Osteria Basilico (W11)
Osteria dell'Arancio (SW10)
Ottolenghi (W11,W8)*
Il Pagliaccio (SW6)
Pappa Ciccia (SW6)
Pellicano (SW3)
Pentolina (W14)*
Il Portico (W8)
Portobello Ristorante (W11)*
The Red Pepper (W9)*
Riccardo's (SW3)
Il Ristorante (SW7)
The River Café (W6)
Rocco (SW5)
Rossopomodoro (SW10,W11)
San Lorenzo (SW3)
Santa Lucia (SW10)*
Scalini (SW3)
Tartufo (SW3)*
Ziani's (SW3)

North
Artigiano (NW3)
L'Artista (NW11)
Il Bacio (N16, N5)
La Collina (NW1)
Fabrizio (N19)
Fifteen (N1)
500 (N19)
Marine Ices (NW3)
Mimmo la Bufala (NW3)
Ostuni (NW6)
Ottolenghi (N1)*
Pizzeria Oregano (N1)*
Pizzeria Pappagone (N4)
La Porchetta Pizzeria (N1, N4, NW1)
Rugoletta (N2)
The Salusbury (NW6)
San Daniele del Friuli (N5)
Sarracino (NW6)*
Trullo (N1)*
Villa Bianca (NW3)
York & Albany (NW1)

South
A Cena (TW1)
Al Forno (SW15, SW19)
Antico (SE1)
Antipasto & Pasta (SW11)
La Barca (SE1)
Al Boccon di'vino (TW9)*
Buona Sera (SW11)
Canta Napoli (TW11)
Donna Margherita (SW11)*
Enoteca Turi (SW15)*
Frizzante Cafe (SE16)
Isola del Sole (SW15)
Lorenzo (SE19)
Numero Uno (SW11)
Osteria Antica Bologna (SW11)
Pizza Metro (SW11)*
Le Querce (SE23)*

Riva (SW13)*
San Lorenzo Fuoriporta (SW19)
Sapori Sardi (SW6)*
The Table (SE1)
Tentazioni (SE1)
Zucca (SE1)*

East
Alba (EC1)
Amico Bio (EC1)
L'Anima (EC2)*
Il Bordello (E1)*
Fabrizio (EC1)*
La Figa (E14)
Frizzante at City Farm (E2)*
Jamie's Italian (E14)
Lardo (E8)
Manicomio (EC2)
Obika (E14)
E Pellicci (E2)
Piccolino (EC2)
Polpo (EC1)
La Porchetta Pizzeria (EC1)
Refettorio (EC4)
Santore (EC1)*
Taberna Etrusca (EC4)

MEDITERRANEAN
Central
About Thyme (SW1)*
Bistro 1 (W1,WC2)
Dabbous (W1)*
Hummus Bros (W1,WC1)
Massimo (SW1)
Nopi (W1)*
The Norfolk Arms (WC1)
Riding House Café (W1)

West
The Atlas (SW6)*
Cumberland Arms (W14)*
Locanda Ottomezzo (W8)
Made in Italy (SW3)
Mediterraneo (W11)
Raoul's Cafe (W9)
Raoul's Café & Deli (W11,W6)
La Sophia (W10)*
The Swan (W4)*
Tom's Deli (W11)
Troubadour (SW5)

North
Blue Legume (N16)
The Little Bay (NW6)
Mem & Laz (N1)
Petek (N4)

South
Cantina Vinopolis (SE1)
Fish in a Tie (SW11)
The Fox & Hounds (SW11)*
Oxo Tower (Brass') (SE1)
The Wharf (TW11)

East
Bonds (EC2)
The Eagle (EC1)
Hummus Bros (EC1, EC2)
The Little Bay (EC1)
Morito (EC1)*

Portal *(EC1)*
Rocket *(E14, EC2)*
Vinoteca *(EC1)*

ORGANIC
Central
Daylesford Organic *(SW1)*

West
Daylesford Organic *(W11)*

North
The Duke of Cambridge *(N1)*

East
Smiths (Dining Rm) *(EC1)*

POLISH
West
Daquise *(SW7)*
Polish Club *(SW7)*
Patio *(W12)*

South
Baltic *(SE1)*

PORTUGUESE
West
Lisboa Pâtisserie *(W10)*

East
Corner Room *(E2)*
Eyre Brothers *(EC2)*
The Gun *(E14)*
Portal *(EC1)*

RUSSIAN
Central
Bob Bob Ricard *(W1)*
Mari Vanna *(SW1)*

SCANDINAVIAN
Central
Nordic Bakery *(W1)*
Scandinavian Kitchen *(W1)*
Texture *(W1)*
Verru *(W1)*

West
Madsen *(SW7)*

SCOTTISH
Central
Albannach *(WC2)*
Boisdale *(SW1)*

East
Boisdale of Canary Wharf *(E14)*

SPANISH
Central
Ametsa with Arzak
   Instruction *(SW1)*
aqua nueva *(W1)*
Barrafina *(W1,WC2)*
Barrica *(W1)*
Cigala *(WC1)*
Copita *(W1)*

Dehesa *(W1)*
Donostia *(W1)*
Fino *(W1)*
Goya *(SW1)*
Ibérica *(W1)*
Navarro's *(W1)*
Opera Tavern *(WC2)*
El Pirata *(W1)*
Salt Yard *(W1)*
Tapas Brindisa Soho *(W1)*

West
Cambio de Tercio *(SW5)*
Capote Y Toros *(SW5)*
Casa Brindisa *(SW7)*
Duke of Sussex *(W4)*
Galicia *(W10)*
Notting Hill Kitchen *(W11)*
El Pirata de Tapas *(W2)*
Tendido Cero *(SW5)*
Tendido Cuatro *(SW6)*

North
La Bota *(N8)*
Café del Parc *(N19)*
Camino *(N1)*
El Parador *(NW1)*

South
Alquimia *(SW15)*
Angels & Gypsies *(SE5)*
Boqueria *(SW2)*
don Fernando's *(TW9)*
José *(SE1)*
Lola Rojo *(SW11)*
Mar I Terra *(SE1)*
Meson don Felipe *(SE1)*
Pizarro *(SE1)*
Tapas Brindisa *(SE1)*

East
Eyre Brothers *(EC2)*
Ibérica *(E14)*
Morito *(EC1)*
Moro *(EC1)*
Tramontana Brindisa *(EC2)*

STEAKS & GRILLS
Central
Black & Blue *(W1)*
Bodean's *(W1)*
The Bountiful Cow *(WC1)*
Chop Shop *(SW1)*
Christopher's *(WC2)*
Cut *(W1)*
Flat Iron *(W1)*
Garufin *(WC1)*
Gaucho *(W1,WC2)*
Goodman *(W1)*
Grillshack *(W1)*
The Guinea Grill *(W1)*
Hawksmoor *(W1,WC2)*
JW Steakhouse *(W1)*
MASH Steakhouse *(W1)*
maze Grill *(W1)*
Carom at Meza *(W1)*
The Palm *(W1)*
Le Relais de Venise
   L'Entrecôte *(W1)*
Rib Room *(SW1)*

Rowley's *(SW1)*
Sophie's Steakhouse *(WC2)*
STK Steakhouse *(WC2)*
34 *(W1)*
Wolfe's *(WC2)*

West
Admiral Codrington *(SW3)*
Black & Blue *(W8)*
Bodean's *(SW6)*
The Cabin *(W4)*
Casa Malevo *(W2)*
Gaucho *(SW3)*
Haché *(SW3)*
Kings Road Steakhouse *(SW3)*
Lola & Simón *(W6)*
Maxela *(SW7)*
The Meat & Wine Co *(W12)*
PJ's Bar and Grill *(SW3)*
Popeseye *(W14)*
Sophie's Steakhouse *(SW10)*

North
Garufa *(N5)*
Gaucho *(NW3)*
Haché *(NW1)*
The Smokehouse Islington *(N1)*

South
Archduke Wine Bar *(SE1)*
Black & Blue *(SE1)*
Bodean's *(SW4)*
Buenos Aires Café *(SE10, SE3)*
Butcher & Grill *(SW11)*
Cattle Grid *(SW11, SW12)*
Constancia *(SE1)*
Gaucho *(SE1, SE10,TW10)*
Kew Grill *(TW9)*
Popeseye *(SW15)*
Santa Maria del Sur *(SW8)*

East
Barbecoa *(EC4)*
Buen Ayre *(E8)*
Gaucho *(E14, EC1, EC2, EC3)*
Goodman *(E14)*
Goodman City *(EC2)*
Hawksmoor *(E1, EC2)*
Hix Oyster & Chop House *(EC1)*
New Street Grill *(EC2)*
Relais de Venise L'Entrecôte *(E14, EC2)*
Simpson's Tavern *(EC3)*
Smiths (Top Floor) *(EC1)*
Smiths (Dining Rm) *(EC1)*
Smiths (Ground Floor) *(EC1)*
The Tramshed *(EC2)*

SWISS
Central
St Moritz *(W1)*

VEGETARIAN
Central
Amico Bio *(WC1)*
Chettinad *(W1)*
Food for Thought *(WC2)*
Hummus Bros *(W1,WC1)*
Malabar Junction *(WC1)*
Masala Zone *(W1)*

177

Mildreds *(W1)**
Orchard *(WC1)*
Ragam *(W1)**
Rasa Maricham *(WC1)**
Sagar *(W1)*
tibits *(W1)*
Woodlands *(SW1,W1)*

West
The Gate *(W6)*
Masala Zone *(SW5, SW6,W2)*
Sagar *(W6)*

North
Chutneys *(NW1)*
Diwana Bhel-Poori House *(NW1)*
Jai Krishna *(N4)**
Manna *(NW3)*
Masala Zone *(N1)*
Rani *(N3)*
Rasa Travancore *(N16)**
Sakonis *(HA0)**
Vijay *(NW6)*
Woodlands *(NW3)*

South
Blue Elephant *(SW6)*
Cocum *(SW20)**
Ganapati *(SE15)**
Le Pont de la Tour *(SE1)*
Sree Krishna *(SW17)**

East
Amico Bio *(EC1)*
The Gate *(EC1)*
Hummus Bros *(EC2)*
Vanilla Black *(EC4)*

AFTERNOON TEA
Central
Athenaeum *(W1)*
The Diamond Jub' Salon
   (Fortnum's) *(W1)*
The Fountain (Fortnum's) *(W1)*
La Fromagerie Café *(W1)**
Ladurée *(SW1,W1,WC2)*
Maison Bertaux *(W1)**
Notes *(WC2)*
Oscar *(W1)*
Ritz (Palm Court) *(W1)*
Royal Academy *(W1)*
The Sketch (Parlour) *(W1)*
Villandry *(W1)*
The Wallace *(W1)*
William Curley *(SW1)**
The Wolseley *(W1)*
Yauatcha *(W1)**

North
Kenwood (Brew House) *(NW3)*
Landmark (Winter Gdn) *(NW1)*

South
Cannizaro House *(SW19)*
San Lorenzo Fuoriporta *(SW19)*
William Curley *(TW9)**

East
Ladurée *(EC3)**

BURGERS, ETC
Central
Automat *(W1)*
Bar Boulud *(SW1)*
Black & Blue *(W1)*
The Bountiful Cow *(WC1)*
Burger & Lobster *(SW1,W1)**
Byron *(SW1,W1,WC2)*
Diner *(W1,WC2)*
Ed's Easy Diner *(W1)*
Five Guys *(WC2)*
Goodman *(W1)**
Hard Rock Café *(W1)*
Hawksmoor *(W1,WC2)**
Honest Burgers *(W1)**
Joe Allen *(WC2)*
Kettners *(W1)*
MEATLiquor *(W1)**
MEATmarket *(WC2)*
Opera Tavern *(WC2)*
Patty and Bun *(W1)**
Shake Shack *(WC2)*
Tommi's Burger Joint *(W1)**
Wolfe's *(WC2)*

West
Admiral Codrington *(SW3)*
Big Easy *(SW3)*
Black & Blue *(W8)*
Byron *(SW3, SW5, SW7,W12,W8)*
The Chelsea Ram *(SW10)*
Diner *(SW7)*
Haché *(SW10)*
Honest Burgers *(W11)**
Lucky Seven *(W2)*
Sticky Fingers *(W8)*
Troubadour *(SW5)*

North
Byron *(N1)*
Diner *(N1, NW1, NW10)*
Dirty Burger *(NW5)**
Duke's Brew & Que *(N1)**
Haché *(NW1)*
Harry Morgan's *(NW8)*
Honest Burgers *(NW1)**
Meat Mission *(N1)**
Red Dog Saloon *(N1)*
The Rib Man *(N1)**

South
Ben's Canteen *(SW11)*
Black & Blue *(SE1)*
Byron *(SW15)*
Cattle Grid *(SW11, SW12)*
Dirty Burger *(SW8)**
Haché *(SW4)*
Honest Burgers *(SW9)**
The Old Brewery *(SE10)*
Village East *(SE1)*

East
Big Apple Hot Dogs *(EC1)**
Burger & Lobster *(EC1, EC4)**
Byron *(E14, EC2)*
Comptoir Gascon *(EC1)*
The Diner *(EC2)*
Goodman *(E14)**
Goodman City *(EC2)**
Haché *(EC2)*

Hawksmoor *(E1, EC2)**
Smiths (Dining Rm) *(EC1)*

FISH & CHIPS
Central
Fryer's Delight *(WC1)*
Golden Hind *(W1)*
North Sea Fish *(WC1)*
Seafresh *(SW1)*

West
Geales *(W8)*
Geales Chelsea Green *(SW3)*
Kerbisher & Malt *(W5,W6)*

North
The Fish & Chip Shop *(N1)**
Nautilus *(NW6)**
The Sea Shell *(NW1)**
Skipjacks *(HA3)**
Toff's *(N10)**
Two Brothers *(N3)*

South
Brady's *(SW18)**
Fish Club *(SW11, SW4)**
Masters Super Fish *(SE1)**
Moxon's Fish Bar *(SW12)**
Olley's *(SE24)**
The Sea Cow *(SE22)**

East
Ark Fish *(E18)**
Faulkner's *(E8)**

ICE CREAM
Central
Gelupo *(W1)**

North
Marine Ices *(NW3)*

PIZZA
Central
Il Baretto *(W1)*
Delfino *(W1)**
Fire & Stone *(WC2)*
Kettners *(W1)*
Made in Italy *(W1)*
Oliveto *(SW1)**
The Orange *(SW1)*
Piccolino *(W1)*
Pizza Pilgrims *(W1)*
La Porchetta Pizzeria *(WC1)*
Princi *(W1)*
Rossopomodoro *(WC2)*
Union Jacks *(WC2)*

West
Oak *(W12)**
Basilico *(SW6)*
Bird in Hand *(W14)*
Buona Sera *(SW3)*
Canta Napoli *(W4)*
Da Mario *(SW7)*
La Delizia Limbara *(SW3)*
Fire & Stone *(W12)*
Franco Manca *(W4)**
Made in Italy *(SW3)*

The Oak (W2)*
Osteria Basilico (W11)
Otto Pizza (W2)*
Il Pagliaccio (SW6)
Pappa Ciccia (SW6)
Pizza East Portobello (W10)*
Ciro's (Pizza Pomodoro) (SW3)
Portobello Ristorante (W11)*
The Red Pepper (W9)*
Rocca Di Papa (SW7)
Rossopomodoro (SW10,W11)
Santa Lucia (SW10)*
Santa Maria (W5)*
Union Jacks (W4)

North
Il Bacio (N16, N5)
Basilico (N1, N8, NW3)
Fabrizio (N19)
Marine Ices (NW3)
Mimmo la Bufala (NW3)
Pizza East (NW5)*
Pizzeria Oregano (N1)
Pizzeria Pappagone (N4)
La Porchetta Pizzeria (N1, N4, NW1)
Rossopomodoro (N1, NW1)
Sacro Cuore (NW10)*
The Salusbury (NW6)
Sweet Thursday (N1)*
White Rabbit (N16)*

South
Al Forno (SW15, SW19)
Basilico (SW11, SW14)
Bianco43 (SE10)
Buona Sera (SW11)
Donna Margherita (SW11)*
Eco (SW4)*
Franco Manca (SW11, SW9)*
Gourmet Pizza Company (SE1)
The Gowlett (SE15)*
Lorenzo (SE19)
Pizza Metro (SW11)*
Pizzeria Rustica (TW9)
Rocca Di Papa (SE21)
Rossopomodoro (SW18)
San Lorenzo Fuoriporta (SW19)
The Yellow House (SE16)*
Zero Degrees (SE3)

East
Il Bordello (E1)*
La Figa (E14)
Fire & Stone (E1)
Franco Manca (E20)*
Piccolino (EC2)
Pizza East (E1)*
La Porchetta Pizzeria (EC1)
Rocket (E14, EC2)
Story Deli (E2)*

SANDWICHES, CAKES, ETC
Central
Abokado (W1)
Baker & Spice (SW1)
Bar Italia (W1)
Benugo (W1)
Caffè Vergnano (WC1)
The Courtauld Gallery Café (WC2)

Fernandez & Wells (W1,WC2)
Flat White (W1)*
Fleet River Bakery (WC2)*
La Fromagerie Café (W1)*
Fuzzy's Grub (SW1)
Kaffeine (W1)
Konditor & Cook (W1,WC1)
Ladurée (SW1,W1)*
Leon (W1,WC2)
Maison Bertaux (W1)*
Monmouth Coffee
    Company (WC2)
Natural Kitchen (W1)
Nordic Bakery (W1)
Notes (WC2)
Paul (W1,WC2)
Pod (WC1)
Royal Academy (W1)
Scandinavian Kitchen (W1)*
The Sketch (Parlour) (W1)
Spianata & Co (W1)
Taylor St Baristas (W1)*
William Curley (SW1)*

West
Baker & Spice (SW3,W9)
Benugo (SW7,W12)
Bluebird Café (SW3)
Gail's Bakery (W4)
Gail's Bread (W11)
Lisboa Pâtisserie (W10)
Tom's Deli (W11)

North
Benugo (NW1)
Euphorium Bakery (N1)
Gail's Bread (NW3, NW8)
Ginger & White (NW3)
Kenwood (Brew House) (NW3)
Notes (N7)

South
Benugo (SE1)
Caffè Vergnano (SE1)
Fulham Wine Rooms (SW6)
Gail's Bread (SW11)
Konditor & Cook (SE1)
Leon (SE1)
Monmouth Coffee Company (SE1,
    SE16)*
Orange Pekoe (SW13)*
Pantry (SW18)
Pod (SE1)
Spianata & Co (SE1)
Taylor St Baristas (TW9)*
William Curley (TW9)*

East
Abokado (EC1, EC4)
Benugo (E2, EC1)
Brick Lane Beigel Bake (E1)*
Caffè Vergnano (EC4)
Department of Coffee (EC1)
Dose (EC1)*
Fuzzy's Grub (EC1)
Gail's Bakery (EC1)
Konditor & Cook (EC3)
Leon (E1, E14, EC4)
Look Mum No Hands! (EC1)
Natural Kitchen (EC4)

Nusa Kitchen (EC1, EC2)*
Pod (EC1, EC2, EC3, EC4)
Prufrock Coffee (EC1)*
Spianata & Co (E1, EC1, EC2, EC4)
Taylor St Baristas (E14, EC2, EC3)*
Workshop Coffee (EC1)

SALADS
Central
Kaffeine (W1)
Natural Kitchen (W1)

West
Beirut Express (SW7,W2)*

East
Natural Kitchen (EC3, EC4)

ARGENTINIAN
Central
Gaucho (W1,WC2)
Zoilo (W1)*

West
Casa Malevo (W2)
Gaucho (SW3)
Lola & Simón (W6)
Quantus (W4)*

North
Garufa (N5)*
Gaucho (NW3)

South
Buenos Aires Café (SE10, SE3)
Constancia (SE1)
Gaucho (SE1, SE10,TW10)
Santa Maria del Sur (SW8)

East
Buen Ayre (E8)*
Gaucho (E14, EC1, EC2, EC3)

BRAZILIAN
West
Sushinho (SW3)*

East
Sushisamba (EC2)

MEXICAN/TEXMEX
Central
Benito's Hat (W1,WC2)
La Bodega Negra (W1)
Café Pacifico (WC2)
Cantina Laredo (WC2)
Chilango (WC2)*
Chipotle (W1,WC2)
Lupita (WC2)
Tortilla (W1,WC2)
Wahaca (W1,WC2)

West
Taqueria (W11)
Tortilla (W6)
Wahaca (W12)

North
Benito's Hat (N1)

Chilango *(N1)**
Chipotle *(N1)*
Mestizo *(NW1)*
Tortilla *(N1)*
Wahaca *(N1)*

South
Chipotle *(SW19)*
Tortilla *(SE1, SW19)*
Wahaca *(SE1)*

East
Chilango *(E1, EC2, EC4)**
Daddy Donkey *(EC1)**
Tortilla *(E14, E20, EC3)*
Wahaca *(E14, E20)*

PERUVIAN
Central
Ceviche *(W1)*
Coya *(W1)**
Lima *(W1)*

North
Tierra Peru *(N1)*

East
Sushisamba *(EC2)*

SOUTH AMERICAN
West
Quantus *(W4)**

South
El Vergel *(SE1)**

AFRO-CARIBBEAN
North
Mango Room *(NW1)*

MOROCCAN
West
Adams Café *(W12)*

East
Kenza *(EC2)*

NORTH AFRICAN
Central
Momo *(W1)*

West
Azou *(W6)*

East
Kenza *(EC2)*

TUNISIAN
West
Adams Café *(W12)*

EGYPTIAN
North
Ali Baba *(NW1)*

ISRAELI
Central
Gaby's *(WC2)*

North
Solly's *(NW11)*

KOSHER
Central
Reubens *(W1)*

North
Kaifeng *(NW4)**
Solly's *(NW11)*

East
Bevis Marks *(E1)*
Brick Lane Beigel Bake *(E1)**

LEBANESE
Central
Al Hamra *(W1)*
Al Sultan *(W1)*
Beiteddine *(SW1)*
Comptoir Libanais *(W1)*
Fairuz *(W1)*
Ishbilia *(SW1)*
Levant *(W1)*
Maroush *(W1)**
Noura *(SW1,W1)*
Ranoush *(SW1)*
Yalla Yalla *(W1)*

West
Al-Waha *(W2)**
Beirut Express *(SW7,W2)**
Chez Marcelle *(W14)**
Comptoir Libanais *(SW7,W12)*
Maroush *(W2)**
Maroush *(SW3)**
Ranoush *(SW3,W2,W8)*

South
Meza *(SW17)**
Palmyra *(TW9)**

East
Comptoir Libanais *(E20)*
Kenza *(EC2)*
Yalla Yalla *(E1)*

MIDDLE EASTERN
Central
Honey & Co *(W1)**
Patogh *(W1)**

North
Solly's *(NW11)*

East
Morito *(EC1)**
Pilpel *(E1, EC4)**

PERSIAN
West
Alounak *(W14,W2)*
Colbeh *(W2)**
Faanoos *(W4)*
Kateh *(W9)**
Sufi *(W12)*

North
Gilak *(N19)*

South
Faanoos *(SW14)*

SYRIAN
West
Abu Zaad *(W12)*

TURKISH
Central
Cyprus Mangal *(SW1)**
Ishtar *(W1)*
Kazan *(SW1)*
Sofra *(W1,WC2)*
Tas *(WC1)*

West
Best Mangal *(SW6,W14)**
Fez Mangal *(W11)**

North
Antepliler *(N1, N4)*
Beyoglu *(NW3)*
Gallipoli *(N1)*
Gem *(N1)*
Izgara *(N3)*
Mangal II *(N16)*
Petek *(N4)*

South
Tas (Cafe) *(SE1)*
Tas Pide *(SE1)*

East
Haz *(E1, EC2, EC3)*
Hazev *(E14)*
Mangal I *(E8)**
Tas *(EC1)*

AFGHANI
North
Afghan Kitchen *(N1)**

BURMESE
West
Mandalay *(W2)*

CHINESE
Central
A Wong *(SW1)*
Ba Shan *(W1)**
Baozi Inn *(WC2)*
Bar Shu *(W1)**
Bo London *(W1)*
The Bright Courtyard *(W1)*
Chilli Cool *(WC1)*
China Tang *(W1)*
Chuen Cheng Ku *(W1)*
Empress of Sichuan *(WC2)**
The Four Seasons *(W1)**
Golden Dragon *(W1)*
The Grand Imperial *(SW1)*
Hakkasan *(W1)*
Haozhan *(W1)**
Harbour City *(W1)*
Hunan *(SW1)**
Imperial China *(WC2)*
Jenny Lo's Tea House *(SW1)*
Joy King Lau *(WC2)*
Kai Mayfair *(W1)*

Ken Lo's Memories *(SWI)*
Mr Chow *(SWI)*
Mr Kong *(WC2)*
New Mayflower *(WI)*
New World *(WI)*
Plum Valley *(WI)*
Princess Garden *(WI)*
Royal China *(WI)*
Royal China Club *(WI)*
Shanghai Blues *(WCI)*
Wong Kei *(WI)*
Yauatcha *(WI)*
Yming *(WI)*

West
Choys *(SW3)*
Fortune Cookie *(W2)*
The Four Seasons *(W2)*
Gold Mine *(W2)*
Good Earth *(SW3)*
Ken Lo's Memories of China *(W8)*
Mandarin Kitchen *(W2)*
Maxim *(W13)*
Min Jiang *(W8)*
Mr Wing *(SW5)*
North China *(W3)*
Pearl Liang *(W2)*
Royal China *(SW6,W2)*
Seventeen *(W11)*
Stick & Bowl *(W8)*
Taiwan Village *(SW6)*
Tian Fu *(W12)*

North
Good Earth *(NW7)*
Green Cottage *(NW3)*
Gung-Ho *(NW6)*
Kaifeng *(NW4)*
Phoenix Palace *(NWI)*
Sakonis *(HA0)*
Singapore Garden *(NW6)*
Yipin China *(NI)*

South
Bayee Village *(SW19)*
Dalchini *(SW19)*
Dragon Castle *(SE17)*
Four Regions *(TW9)*
Hutong *(SE1)*
China Boulevard *(SW18)*

East
Chinese Cricket Club *(EC4)*
Gourmet San *(E2)*
HKK *(EC2)*
Imperial City *(EC3)*
Lotus Chinese Floating
    Restaurant *(E14)*
My Old Place *(EI)*
Royal China *(E14)*
Sedap *(EC1)*
Shanghai *(E8)*
Sichuan Folk *(EI)*
Yi-Ban *(E16)*

CHINESE, DIM SUM
Central
The Bright Courtyard *(WI)*
Chuen Cheng Ku *(WI)*
dim T *(WI)*

Golden Dragon *(WI)*
The Grand Imperial *(SWI)*
Hakkasan *(WI)*
Harbour City *(WI)*
Imperial China *(WC2)*
Joy King Lau *(WC2)*
Leong's Legends *(WI)*
New World *(WI)*
ping pong *(WI)*
Princess Garden *(WI)*
Royal China *(WI)*
Royal China Club *(WI)*
Shanghai Blues *(WCI)*
Yauatcha *(WI)*

West
Min Jiang *(W8)*
Pearl Liang *(W2)*
ping pong *(W2)*
Royal China *(SW6,W2)*

North
dim T *(N6, NW3)*
Phoenix Palace *(NWI)*

South
dim T *(SE1)*
Dragon Castle *(SE17)*
China Boulevard *(SW18)*
ping pong *(SE1)*

East
Lotus Chinese Floating
    Restaurant *(E14)*
ping pong *(E1, EC4)*
Royal China *(E14)*
Shanghai *(E8)*
Yi-Ban *(E16)*

GEORGIAN
West
Colchis *(W2)*

North
Little Georgia Café *(NI)*

East
Little Georgia Café *(E2)*

INDIAN
Central
Amaya *(SWI)*
Benares *(WI)*
Chettinad *(WI)*
Chor Bizarre *(WI)*
The Cinnamon Club *(SWI)*
Cinnamon Soho *(WI)*
Dishoom *(WC2)*
Gaylord *(WI)*
Gopal's of Soho *(WI)*
Gymkhana *(WI)*
Imli Street *(WI)*
Indali Lounge *(WI)*
India Club *(WC2)*
Malabar Junction *(WCI)*
Masala Zone *(WI,WC2)*
Mela *(WC2)*
Mint Leaf *(SWI)*
Moti Mahal *(WC2)*
La Porte des Indes *(WI)*

Punjab *(WC2)*
Ragam *(WI)*
Red Fort *(WI)*
Roti Chai *(WI)*
Sagar *(WI,WC2)*
Salaam Namaste *(WCI)*
Salloos *(SWI)*
Tamarind *(WI)*
Trishna *(WI)*
Veeraswamy *(WI)*
Woodlands *(SWI,WI)*
Zayna *(WI)*

West
Anarkali *(W6)*
Bombay Brasserie *(SW7)*
Bombay Palace *(W2)*
Brilliant *(UB2)*
Chakra *(W11)*
Chutney Mary *(SW10)*
Durbar *(W2)*
Gifto's *(UB1)*
The Greedy Buddha *(SW6)*
Indian Zing *(W6)*
Karma *(W14)*
Khan's *(W2)*
Khan's of Kensington *(SW7)*
Madhu's *(UB1)*
Malabar *(W8)*
Masala Zone *(SW5, SW6,W2)*
Miran Masala *(W14)*
Mirch Masala *(UB1)*
Monty's *(SW6,W13,W5)*
Noor Jahan *(SW5,W2)*
The Painted Heron *(SW10)*
Potli *(W6)*
Rasoi *(SW3)*
Sagar *(W6)*
Star of India *(SW5)*
Thali *(SW5)*
Zaika *(W8)*

North
Anglo Asian Tandoori *(N16)*
Chutneys *(NWI)*
Delhi Grill *(NI)*
Diwana Bhel-Poori House *(NWI)*
Eriki *(NW3)*
Great Nepalese *(NWI)*
Guglee *(NW3, NW6)*
Indian Rasoi *(N2)*
Jai Krishna *(N4)*
Masala Zone *(NI, NWI)*
Paradise Hampstead *(NW3)*
Rani *(N3)*
Roots at N1 *(NI)*
Sakonis *(HA0)*
Vijay *(NW6)*
Woodlands *(NW3)*
Zaffrani *(NI)*

South
Apollo Banana Leaf *(SW17)*
Babur *(SE23)*
Bangalore Express *(SE1)*
Bengal Clipper *(SE1)*
Chutney *(SW18)*
Cocum *(SW20)*
Dalchini *(SW19)*
Everest Inn *(SE3)*

Ganapati (SE15)*
Gandhi's (SE11)
Holy Cow (SW11)*
Hot Stuff (SW8)*
Indian Moment (SW11)
Indian Ocean (SW17)*
Indian Zilla (SW13)*
Kennington Tandoori (SE11)*
Lahore Karahi (SW17)*
Lahore Kebab House (SW16)*
Ma Goa (SW15)*
Mango & Silk (SW14)*
Mango Food of India (SE1)
Mirch Masala (SW16, SW17)*
Nazmins (SW18)
Sree Krishna (SW17)*
Tandoori Nights (SE22)

East
Bangalore Express (EC3)
Café Spice Namaste (E1)*
Cinnamon Kitchen (EC2)*
Dishoom (E2)
Dockmaster's House (E14)*
Lahore Kebab House (E1)*
Mint Leaf (EC2)*
Mirch Masala (E1)*
Needoo (E1)*
Tayyabs (E1)*

INDIAN, SOUTHERN
Central
India Club (WC2)
Malabar Junction (WC1)
Quilon (SW1)*
Ragam (W1)*
Rasa Maricham (WC1)*
Rasa Samudra (W1)*
Sagar (W1, WC2)
Woodlands (SW1, W1)

West
Sagar (W6)
Shilpa (W6)*

North
Chutneys (NW1)
Rani (N3)
Rasa Travancore (N16)*
Vijay (NW6)
Woodlands (NW3)

South
Cocum (SW20)*
Ganapati (SE15)*
Sree Krishna (SW17)*

JAPANESE
Central
Abeno (WC1, WC2)
Abokado (W1, WC2)
aqua kyoto (W1)
Atari-Ya (W1)*
Benihana (W1)
Bincho Yakitori (W1)*
Bone Daddies (W1)*
Chisou (W1)*
Chotto Matte (W1)
Defune (W1)*
Dinings (W1)*

Eat Tokyo (WC1, WC2)
Flesh and Buns (WC2)
Hazuki (WC2)
Ikeda (W1)
Kiku (W1)*
Kikuchi (W1)*
Kirazu (W1)*
Koya (W1)*
Koya-Ko (W1)
Kulu Kulu (W1, WC2)
Matsuri (SW1)
Miyama (W1)*
Nizuni (W1)*
Nobu (W1)*
Nobu Berkeley (W1)
Roka (W1)*
Sakana-tei (W1)*
Sake No Hana (SW1)
Sakura (W1)
Shoryu Ramen (SW1, W1)*
Sticks'n'Sushi (WC2)
Sumosan (W1)*
Taro (W1)
Toku (SW1)
Tokyo Diner (WC2)
Tonkotsu (W1)
Tsunami (W1)*
Umu (W1)
Wagamama (SW1, W1, WC1, WC2)
Yoisho (W1)*
Yoshino (W1)

West
Atari-Ya (W3, W5)*
Benihana (SW3)
Chisou (SW3, W4)*
Eat Tokyo (W6, W8)
Inaho (W2)*
Itsu (SW3, W11)
Kiraku (W5)*
Kulu Kulu (SW7)
Maguro (W9)*
Nozomi (SW3)
Okawari (W5)
The Shiori (W2)*
Sushinho (SW3)*
Tosa (W6)*
Wagamama (W8)
Yashin (SW7, W8)*
Zuma (SW7)*

North
Akari (N1)*
Asakusa (NW1)*
Atari-Ya (N12, NW4, NW6)*
Bento Cafe (NW1)*
Café Japan (NW11)*
Dotori (N4)*
Eat Tokyo (NW11)
Jin Kichi (NW3)*
Soho Japan (NW1)*
Sushi-Say (NW2)*
Wagamama (N1, NW1)

South
Cho-San (SW15)*
Fujiyama (SW9)
Hashi (SW20)*
Matsuba (TW9)*
Sticks'n'Sushi (SW19)

Tsunami (SW4)*
Wagamama (SE1, SW15, SW19)

East
Abokado (EC1, EC4)
City Miyama (EC4)
Itsu (E14)
K10 (EC2)*
Kurumaya (EC4)
Mugen (EC4)
Pham Sushi (EC1)*
Roka (EC4)
Sushisamba (EC2)
Sushi Tetsu (EC1)*
Tajima Tei (EC1)*
Taro (EC4)
Wagamama (E14, EC2, EC3, EC4)

KOREAN
Central
Asadal (WC1)
Bibimbap Soho (W1)
Kimchee (WC1)
Koba (W1)

North
Dotori (N4)*

South
Cah-Chi (SW18, SW20)*

East
Jubo (EC2)

MALAYSIAN
Central
C&R Cafe (W1)
Spice Market (W1)

West
Satay House (W2)

North
Singapore Garden (NW6)*

South
Champor-Champor (SE1)*

East
Sedap (EC1)

PAKISTANI
Central
Salloos (SW1)*

West
Miran Masala (W14)*
Mirch Masala (UB1)*

South
Lahore Karahi (SW17)*
Lahore Kebab House (SW16)*
Mirch Masala (SW16, SW17)*

East
Lahore Kebab House (E1)*
Mirch Masala (E1)*
Needoo (E1)*
Tayyabs (E1)*

PAN-ASIAN
Central
Banana Tree Canteen (W1)
Circus (WC2)
dim T (SW1, W1)
Haozhan (W1)*
Hare & Tortoise (WC1)
Inamo (SW1, W1)
Novikov (Asian restaurant) (W1)
Spice Market (W1)

West
Banana Tree Canteen (W2, W9)
E&O (W11)*
Eight Over Eight (SW3)
Hare & Tortoise (W14, W5)
Mao Tai (SW6)*

North
The Banana Tree Canteen (NW6)
dim T (N6, NW3)
Gilgamesh (NW1)
XO (NW3)

South
The Banana Tree Canteen (SW11)
dim T (SE1)
Hare & Tortoise (SW15)

East
Banana Tree Canteen (EC1)
Hare & Tortoise (EC4)

THAI
Central
Busaba Eathai (SW1, W1, WC1, WC2)
C&R Cafe (W1)
Crazy Bear (W1)
Mango Tree (SW1)
Patara (W1)*
Rosa's Soho (W1)
Siam Central (W1)
Spice Market (W1)
Suda (WC2)
Thai Square (SW1, W1, WC2)

West
Addie's Thai Café (SW5)*
Bangkok (SW7)*
Bedlington Café (W4)*
Busaba Eathai (SW3, W12)
C&R Cafe (W2)
Café 209 (SW6)
Churchill Arms (W8)
Esarn Kheaw (W12)*
Fat Boy's (W4, W5)
Fitou's Thai Restaurant (W10)*
Old Parr's Head (W14)
101 Thai Kitchen (W6)*
Patara (SW3)*
Sukho Fine Thai Cuisine (SW6)*
Thai Square (SW7)
The Walmer Castle (W11)

North
Isarn (N1)*
Thai Square (N1)
Yum Yum (N16)*

South
Amaranth (SW18)*
The Begging Bowl (SE15)*
Blue Elephant (SW6)
Fat Boy's (SW14, TW1, TW8)
Kaosarn (SW11, SW9)*
The Paddyfield (SW12)*
The Pepper Tree (SW4)
Suk Saran (SW19)
Talad Thai (SW15)
Thai Corner Café (SE22)
Thai Garden (SW11)
Thai Square (SW15)
Thai Square City (SW6)

East
Busaba Eathai (E20, EC1)
Elephant Royale (E14)
Naamyaa Café (EC1)
Rosa's (E1)
Thai Square (EC4)
Thai Square City (EC3)

VIETNAMESE
Central
Bam-Bou (W1)
Cây Tre (W1)
Pho (W1)*
Viet (W1)

West
Pho (W12)*
Saigon Saigon (W6)

North
Huong-Viet (N1)
Ladudu (NW6)

South
Cafe East (SE16)*
Mien Tay (SW11)*
The Paddyfield (SW12)*

East
Cây Tre (EC1)
City Càphê (EC2)*
Green Papaya (E8)*
Mien Tay (E2)*
Pho (E1, EC1)*
Sông Quê (E2)
Viet Grill (E2)*
Viet Hoa (E2)*

JOIN *LOVE FOOD GIVE FOOD* IN SUPPORT OF ACTION AGAINST HUNGER.

Our experienced team can support your establishment's charity partnership by offering:

- Employee engagement
- Customer satisfaction
- Brand differentiation

For more information please contact

Emma Cullingford
020 8853 7560
e.cullingford@
actionagainsthunger.org.uk
lovefoodgivefood.org

Find us: lovefoodgivefood.org @ACF_UK #lovefoodgivefood

CENTRAL

Soho, Covent Garden & Bloomsbury
(Parts of W1, all WC2 and WC1)

£80+			
L'Atelier de Joel Robuchon	French		2 2 2
Asia de Cuba	Fusion		4 5 4

£70+			
Christopher's	American		3 3 2
Brasserie Max	British, Modern		4 4 3
Homage	"		4 4 3
The Ivy	"		4 3 2
Refuel	"		4 4 2
Rules	British, Traditional		3 2 0
Savoy Grill	"		4 3 3
Simpsons-in-the-Strand	"		4 4 3
Kaspar's Seafood and Grill	Fish & seafood		3 2 3
J Sheekey	"		2 0 0
Gaucho	Steaks & grills		3 4 4
MASH Steakhouse	"		3 3 3
aqua kyoto	Japanese		4 4 3
Spice Market	Pan-Asian		4 4 4

£60+			
Axis	British, Modern		4 4 4
Balthazar	"		5 4 3
Bob Bob Ricard	"		3 2 0
Hix	"		4 4 5
Indigo	"		4 3 4
Paramount	"		4 4 2
Tom's Kitchen	"		4 3 3
The Delaunay	East & Cent. European		3 2 0
J Sheekey Oyster Bar	Fish & seafood		2 0 0
Gauthier Soho	French		0 0 2
aqua nueva	Spanish		5 5 4
Hawksmoor	Steaks & grills		2 2 3
STK Steakhouse	"		4 4 3
Ladurée	Afternoon tea		2 4 3
Shanghai Blues	Chinese		4 5 5
Yauatcha	"		0 4 2
Red Fort	Indian		3 4 4
Circus	Pan-Asian		4 4 2

£50+			
Big Easy	American		3 3 2
Joe Allen	"		5 4 2
Dean Street Townhouse	British, Modern		4 4 2
Le Deuxième	"		4 4 5
Ducksoup	"		4 4 4
Hush	"		4 5 4
Kettners	"		4 3 3
The Northall	"		3 2 2
The Portrait	"		4 4 0
Quo Vadis	"		3 3 2
Social Eating House	"		3 3 3
The National Dining Rms	British, Traditional		5 5 4

	Wright Brothers	Fish & seafood	③③②
	Antidote	French	③④③
	Brasserie Blanc	"	④④④
	Café des Amis	"	④④④
	Clos Maggiore	"	②④①
	Les Deux Salons	"	④④③
	L'Escargot	"	③②②
	The Giaconda	"	③②④
	Mon Plaisir	"	④③③
	Otto's	"	②②③
	Randall & Aubin	"	②②①
	Kopapa	Fusion	③④④
	Sarastro	International	⑤⑤③
	The 10 Cases	"	④①②
	Bocca Di Lupo	Italian	①②②
	Orso	"	④③④
	Vasco & Piero's Pavilion	"	②②③
	Nopi	Mediterranean	②②③
	Albannach	Scottish	④④③
	The Bountiful Cow	Steaks & grills	④④④
	Sophie's Steakhouse	"	④④④
	St Moritz	Swiss	③④③
	Cantina Laredo	Mexican/TexMex	③②⑤
	Bar Shu	Chinese	②⑤④
	Moti Mahal	Indian	②②④
	Chotto Matte	Japanese	– – –
	Flesh and Buns	"	– – –
	Haozhan	Pan-Asian	②④⑤
	Patara	Thai	②③③
£40+	All Star Lanes	American	④③③
	Bodean's	"	③④③
	Mishkin's	"	⑤④③
	Spuntino	"	②③②
	Belgo	Belgian	④④④
	Andrew Edmunds	British, Modern	③②①
	The Angel & Crown	"	③④④
	Arbutus	"	③③④
	Aurora	"	③②①
	Coopers	"	③③④
	The Norfolk Arms	"	③④④
	Shampers	"	③②②
	10 Greek Street	"	②①③
	Union Jacks	"	⑤④④
	Vinoteca	"	④③②
	VQ	"	④③④
	Great Queen Street	British, Traditional	②③③
	The Lady Ottoline	"	④④③
	Porters	"	④③③
	Cape Town Fish Market	Fish & seafood	④④③
	Loch Fyne	"	④③④
	Café Bohème	French	③③②
	Le Cigalon	"	③②②
	Côte	"	④③④

			Rating		
	Le Garrick	"	④	④	❸
	Green Man & French Horn	"	❸	❷	❸
	Terroirs	"	❸	❸	❸
	Gay Hussar	*Hungarian*	④	❸	❷
	Balans	*International*	⑤	④	④
	Bedford & Strand	"	④	④	❸
	Boulevard	"	④	④	❸
	Browns	"	⑤	④	④
	Cork & Bottle	"	④	④	❷
	Giraffe	"	⑤	⑤	⑤
	National Gallery Café	"	❸	④	❸
	Ciao Bella	*Italian*	④	❷	❷
	Da Mario	"	❸	❷	❸
	Dehesa	"	❶	❷	❷
	Jamie's Italian	"	⑤	⑤	④
	Made in Italy	"	❸	④	❸
	Mele e Pere	"	❸	❸	④
	San Carlo Cicchetti	"	❸	④	④
	Barrafina	*Spanish*	❶	❶	❷
	Cigala	"	❸	❸	④
	Copita	"	❸	④	❸
	Opera Tavern	"	❷	❸	❸
	Tapas Brindisa Soho	"	❷	❸	❸
	Garufin	*Steaks & grills*	❸	❷	❸
	Mildreds	*Vegetarian*	❷	④	❸
	Orchard	"	❸	❸	❸
	Burger & Lobster	*Burgers, etc*	❷	❸	❸
	Wolfe's	"	❸	④	④
	Fire & Stone	*Pizza*	④	④	④
	La Bodega Negra	*Mexican/TexMex*	④	❸	❷
	Café Pacifico	"	④	④	❷
	Ceviche	*Peruvian*	❸	❸	❷
	Ba Shan	*Chinese*	❷	④	④
	Imperial China	"	④	④	④
	Plum Valley	"	❷	❸	❷
	Yming	"	❷	❷	④
	Cinnamon Soho	*Indian*	④	④	④
	Dishoom	"	❸	❸	❶
	Malabar Junction	"	❸	④	❸
	Mela	"	❸	④	④
	Abeno	*Japanese*	❸	❸	❸
	Hazuki	"	❸	④	④
	Sticks'n'Sushi	"	❸	❸	❷
	Inamo	*Pan-Asian*	④	④	④
	Suda	*Thai*	❸	❸	❸
	Thai Square	"	④	④	④
£35+	Soho Diner	*American*	❸	❷	❷
	Whyte & Brown	*British, Modern*	–	–	–
	Brasserie Zédel	*French*	⑤	❸	❶
	Prix Fixe	"	❸	❷	❸
	Savoir Faire	"	❸	❸	④
	Real Greek	*Greek*	⑤	④	④
	Polpo	*Italian*	④	❸	❶

	Amico Bio	*Vegetarian*	③④❸
	Byron	*Burgers, etc*	❸❸❸
	Honest Burgers	*"*	❶❷❸
	North Sea Fish	*Fish & chips*	❸❸④
	Rossopomodoro	*Pizza*	❸❸❸
	Lupita	*Mexican/TexMex*	④④❸
	Sofra	*Turkish*	④❸④
	Tas	*"*	④❸❸
	Chuen Cheng Ku	*Chinese*	❸④④
	Empress of Sichuan	*"*	❷❸❷
	Harbour City	*"*	❸④⑤
	New Mayflower	*"*	❷❷④
	New World	*"*	④④❸
	Leong's Legends	*Chinese, Dim sum*	❸④❸
	Imli Street	*Indian*	❸❷❷
	Sagar	*"*	❸❸④
	Rasa Maricham	*Indian, Southern*	❷❷❸
	Bincho Yakitori	*Japanese*	❸❸❸
	Kirazu	*"*	– – –
	Wagamama	*"*	④❸④
	Asadal	*Korean*	❸④④
	Kimchee	*"*	④④❸
	Busaba Eathai	*Thai*	❸❸❷
	Rosa's Soho	*"*	❸❷❸
	Cây Tre	*Vietnamese*	❸④❸
	Pho	*"*	❷❷❷
£30+	Café in the Crypt	*International*	④④④
	Gordon's Wine Bar	*"*	⑤④❶
	Carom at Meza	*"*	❷❷❸
	Caffè Vergnano	*Italian*	④❸❷
	La Porchetta Pizzeria	*"*	❸❸❸
	Princi	*"*	❸④❷
	Diner	*Burgers, etc*	④❸❷
	Ed's Easy Diner	*"*	④④❸
	MEATmarket	*"*	❸④④
	Caffè Vergnano	*Sandwiches, cakes, etc*	④❸❷
	The Courtauld (Café)	*"*	④❸❸
	Fernandez & Wells	*"*	❸❸❷
	Wahaca	*Mexican/TexMex*	❸❸❷
	Gaby's	*Israeli*	❸❸④
	Yalla Yalla	*Lebanese*	❸④❸
	Chilli Cool	*Chinese*	❸⑤⑤
	The Four Seasons	*"*	❷⑤⑤
	Golden Dragon	*"*	❸④❸
	Joy King Lau	*"*	❸④④
	Mr Kong	*"*	④❸④
	ping pong	*Chinese, Dim sum*	④❷❸
	Gopal's of Soho	*Indian*	❸❸④
	Masala Zone	*"*	❸❷❷
	Salaam Namaste	*"*	❷④④
	Koya	*Japanese*	❷❸❸
	Koya-Ko	*"*	– – –
	Kulu Kulu	*"*	④⑤④

189

	Taro	"	❸❸❸
	Tonkotsu	"	❸❸❸
	Banana Tree Canteen	Pan-Asian	❹❹❸
£25+	Pitt Cue Co	American	❶❸❸
	Seven Stars	British, Modern	❸❹❷
	Bar Italia	Sandwiches, cakes, etc	❹❷❶
	Konditor & Cook	"	❸❹❹
	Leon	"	❹❸❸
	Paul	"	❹❺❹
	Benito's Hat	Mexican/TexMex	❸❸❹
	Comptoir Libanais	Lebanese	❹❹❸
	Wong Kei	Chinese	❹❺❺
	India Club	Indian	❸❸❺
	Punjab	"	❷❷❹
	Shoryu Ramen	Japanese	❷❸❸
	Tokyo Diner	"	❸❷❸
	Bibimbap Soho	Korean	❸❸❹
	Hare & Tortoise	Pan-Asian	❸❸❸
	C&R Cafe	Thai	❸❹❹
£20+	Bistro 1	Mediterranean	❹❷❸
	Flat Iron	Steaks & grills	❸❷❷
	Grillshack	"	❸❷❹
	Food for Thought	Vegetarian	❸❸❹
	Shake Shack	Burgers, etc	– – –
	Pizza Pilgrims	Pizza	– – –
	Fleet River Bakery	Sandwiches, cakes, etc	❷❹❸
	Bone Daddies	Japanese	❷❹❸
	Eat Tokyo	"	❸❸❹
	Viet	Vietnamese	❸❹❹
£15+	Hummus Bros	Mediterranean	❸❸❹
	Nordic Bakery	Scandinavian	❸❹❸
	Maison Bertaux	Afternoon tea	❷❸❶
	Notes	Sandwiches, cakes, etc	❹❷❷
	Chilango	Mexican/TexMex	❷❷❸
	Chipotle	"	❸❸❹
	Tortilla	"	❸❸❸
	Baozi Inn	Chinese	❸❹❹
	Abokado	Japanese	❹❹❹
£10+	Five Guys	Burgers, etc	– – –
	Fryer's Delight	Fish & chips	❸❹❺
	Gelupo	Ice cream	❶❷❸
	Flat White	Sandwiches, cakes, etc	❷❷❷
	Monmouth Coffee Co	"	❶❶❷
	Pod	"	❸❸❹

Mayfair & St James's (Parts of W1 and SW1)

£130+	Le Gavroche	French	❶❶❷

Price	Name	Cuisine	Rating
£120+	Alain Ducasse	*French*	④❸④
	Hélène Darroze	*"*	❸❸❷
	Hibiscus	*"*	④④④
£110+	The Ritz Restaurant	*French*	④❸❶
	Sketch (Lecture Rm)	*"*	④❸❶
£100+	The Greenhouse	*French*	❷❶❷
	The Square	*"*	❷❶❸
	Umu	*Japanese*	❸④❸
£90+	Dorchester Grill	*British, Modern*	❸❷④
	Seven Park Place	*"*	❸❸❸
	Wiltons	*British, Traditional*	❸④❷
	Galvin at Windows	*French*	④❸❶
	C London	*Italian*	⑤⑤④
	Downtown Mayfair	*"*	④④④
	Murano	*"*	❸❷❸
	Cut	*Steaks & grills*	⑤⑤⑤
	Kai Mayfair	*Chinese*	④④④
£80+	Pollen Street Social	*British, Modern*	❷❷❸
	Thirty Six	*"*	❸⑤④
	Corrigan's Mayfair	*British, Traditional*	④④④
	maze	*French*	④④④
	La Petite Maison	*"*	❷❸❷
	Amaranto	*Italian*	④④⑤
	Theo Randall	*"*	❷❸④
	Bo London	*Chinese*	❸❷④
	Hakkasan	*"*	❸⑤❷
	Benares	*Indian*	❷❷❸
	Matsuri	*Japanese*	❸❷⑤
	Nobu, Park Ln	*"*	❷④④
	Nobu, Berkeley St	*"*	❸④④
£70+	Alyn Williams	*British, Modern*	❷❶④
	Athenaeum	*"*	❷❶❸
	Le Caprice	*"*	❸❷❷
	Browns (Albemarle)	*British, Traditional*	④❸❸
	Bentley's	*Fish & seafood*	❷❸❷
	Scott's	*"*	❷❷❷
	Brasserie Chavot	*French*	❷❸❸
	Sketch (Gallery)	*"*	④④④
	Babbo	*Italian*	⑤④④
	Cecconi's	*"*	④④❷
	Franco's	*"*	❸❸❸
	Novikov (Italian restaurant)	*"*	⑤⑤④
	Gaucho	*Steaks & grills*	❸④④
	JW Steakhouse	*"*	④④❸
	maze Grill	*"*	④④④
	34	*"*	④❸❸
	Coya	*Peruvian*	❷❷❶
	China Tang	*Chinese*	④④❸
	Tamarind	*Indian*	❷❸④

	Veeraswamy	"	❷❷❷
	Sumosan	Japanese	❷④④
	Novikov (Asian restaurant)	Pan-Asian	❸④❸
£60+	Automat	American	④④④
	Bellamy's	British, Modern	❸❷❷
	The Berners Tavern	"	– – –
	Criterion	"	④④❶
	Langan's Brasserie	"	④❷❷
	Little Social	"	❷❷❷
	Mews of Mayfair	"	④❸❷
	Quaglino's	"	⑤④④
	Wild Honey	"	❸④④
	The Fountain (Fortnum's)	British, Traditional	④❸❸
	Green's	"	❸❸④
	The Keeper's House	"	– – –
	Boudin Blanc	French	④④❷
	Boulestin	"	❸❷❸
	Goodman	Steaks & grills	❷❷❸
	The Guinea Grill	"	❸❷❷
	Hawksmoor	"	❷❷❸
	Rowley's	"	④④④
	Ladurée	Afternoon tea	❷④❸
	The Sketch (Parlour)	Sandwiches, cakes, etc	④④❷
	Momo	North African	④④❶
	Gymkhana	Indian	– – –
	Benihana	Japanese	④④④
	Ikeda	"	❷❷⑤
	Sake No Hana	"	④❸④
£50+	The Avenue	British, Modern	❸❸❸
	Hush	"	④⑤④
	Sotheby's Café	"	④❷❷
	The Wolseley	"	❸❷❶
	Fishworks	Fish & seafood	❸④④
	Pescatori	"	❸❸④
	Aubaine	French	⑤⑤④
	Brasserie Blanc	"	④❸④
	28-50	"	❸❷❸
	Alloro	Italian	❸❸④
	Il Calcio	"	– – –
	La Genova	"	④④④
	Piccolino	"	④❸④
	Sartoria	"	❸❸❸
	Diamond Jub' (Fortnum's)	Afternoon tea	❸❶❶
	Delfino	Pizza	❷❸④
	Royal Academy	Sandwiches, cakes, etc	⑤④④
	Al Hamra	Lebanese	④④④
	Noura	"	❸④❸
	Princess Garden	Chinese	❶❷❸
	Chor Bizarre	Indian	❷❷❷
	Mint Leaf	"	❷❸❸
	Chisou	Japanese	❷❸④
	Kiku	"	❷❷⑤

	Miyama	"	②②⑤
	Patara	Thai	②❸❸
£40+	Hard Rock Café	American	❸❸❷
	Inn the Park	British, Modern	④❸❷
	The Only Running Footman	"	❸④❷
	1707	"	❸②❸
	L'Artiste Musclé	French	④④❸
	Browns	International	⑤④④
	Al Duca	Italian	④④⑤
	Il Vicolo	"	❸②④
	Chop Shop	Steaks & grills	❸❸④
	Ritz (Palm Court)	Afternoon tea	❸②❶
	Burger & Lobster	Burgers, etc	②❸❸
	Al Sultan	Lebanese	❸②④
	Woodlands	Indian	❸④④
	Toku	Japanese	– – –
	Yoshino	"	❸⓪⑤
	Inamo	Pan-Asian	④④④
	Thai Square	Thai	④④④
£35+	The Windmill	British, Traditional	❸④❸
	El Pirata	Spanish	④②❶
	Byron	Burgers, etc	❸❸❸
	Benugo	Sandwiches, cakes, etc	④④❷
	Sofra	Turkish	④❸④
	Rasa Samudra	Indian, Southern	②②❸
	Wagamama	Japanese	④❸④
	Busaba Eathai	Thai	❸❸❷
£30+	tibits	Vegetarian	❸❸❸
	Ed's Easy Diner	Burgers, etc	④④❸
	Sakana-tei	Japanese	②②⑤
	Sakura	"	❸❸④
£25+	Stock Pot	International	④❸❸
	Shoryu Ramen	Japanese	②❸❸
£15+	La Bottega	Italian	❸❸❷
	Taylor St Baristas	Sandwiches, cakes, etc	②❸❸
£10+	Fuzzy's Grub	Sandwiches, cakes, etc	❸④④
	Spianata & Co	"	❸②❸

Fitzrovia & Marylebone (Part of W1)

£100+	Pied à Terre	French	⓪⓪❸
£90+	Roux at the Landau	British, Modern	❸❸❷
	Bubbledogs (Kitchen Table@)	Fusion	❶②②
	Texture	Scandinavian	②②❸
£80+	Hakkasan	Chinese	❸⑤❷

			Rating
£70+	L'Autre Pied	French	2 2 4
	Orrery	"	3 2 2
	The Providores	International	2 4 5
	Cotidie	Italian	– – –
	Locanda Locatelli	"	3 3 4
	Gaucho	Steaks & grills	3 4 4
	Roka	Japanese	1 3 3
£60+	Oscar	British, Modern	4 4 2
	Galvin Bistrot de Luxe	French	2 2 2
	Il Baretto	Italian	– – –
	Dabbous	Mediterranean	1 1 3
	Royal China Club	Chinese	2 3 4
	La Porte des Indes	Indian	3 2 2
	Defune	Japanese	2 3 5
	Crazy Bear	Thai	3 4 2
£50+	The Lockhart	American	– – –
	Grazing Goat	British, Modern	3 4 3
	The Union Café	"	4 4 4
	Fishworks	Fish & seafood	3 4 4
	Pescatori	"	3 3 4
	Elena's L'Etoile	French	4 4 4
	28-50	"	3 2 3
	Villandry	"	4 4 4
	The Wallace	"	4 5 1
	Archipelago	Fusion	4 4 3
	Providores (Tapa Room)	"	2 4 3
	Caffè Caldesi	Italian	3 3 3
	Sardo	"	2 3 4
	Riding House Café	Mediterranean	4 4 1
	Verru	Scandinavian	2 2 3
	Black & Blue	Steaks & grills	3 3 4
	Zoilo	Argentinian	2 2 4
	Lima	Peruvian	3 4 4
	Reubens	Kosher	3 4 4
	Levant	Lebanese	4 3 2
	The Bright Courtyard	Chinese	4 4 4
	Gaylord	Indian	3 3 4
	Trishna	"	2 3 3
	Zayna	"	2 2 4
	Dinings	Japanese	1 2 5
	Bam-Bou	Vietnamese	3 3 2
£40+	Hardy's Brasserie	British, Modern	3 4 3
	Newman Street Tavern	"	4 4 3
	Ozer	"	4 2 4
	RIBA Café	"	4 4 2
	Vinoteca Seymour Place	"	4 3 2
	Canteen	British, Traditional	5 5 5
	Bonnie Gull	Fish & seafood	2 3 2
	Hellenic	Greek	– – –
	Giraffe	International	5 5 5
	Latium	Italian	2 0 3

	Made in Italy	"	❸④❸
	Obika	"	❸❸❸
	2 Veneti	"	④❷④
	Donostia	Spanish	❸❷❷
	Fino	"	❸❸❸
	Ibérica	"	❸❸❸
	Navarro's	"	❸④❸
	Salt Yard	"	❷❸❸
	Le Relais de Venise	Steaks & grills	❸④❸
	Fairuz	Lebanese	❸❷❸
	Maroush	"	❷❸④
	Ishtar	Turkish	❸❷❸
	Royal China	Chinese	❷④④
	Indali Lounge	Indian	❷❷④
	Roti Chai	"	❷❸❸
	Woodlands	"	❸④④
	Kikuchi	Japanese	❶④⑤
	Nizuni	"	❷❷④
	Tsunami	"	❷④④
	Yoisho	"	❷④⑤
	Koba	Korean	❸❸④
£35+	Real Greek	Greek	⑤④④
	Briciole	Italian	❸❸❸
	Barrica	Spanish	❷❷❶
	MEATLiquor	Burgers, etc	❷④❸
	Benugo	Sandwiches, cakes, etc	④④❷
	La Fromagerie Café	"	❷④❷
	Natural Kitchen	Salads	❸④❸
	Sofra	Turkish	④❸④
	Sagar	Indian	❸❸④
	Wagamama	Japanese	④❸④
	Pho	Vietnamese	❷❷❷
£30+	Bubbledogs	American	④❸❷
	Lantana Cafe	Australian	❸❸❷
	Picture	British, Modern	❷❷④
	Wahaca	Mexican/TexMex	❸❸❷
	Yalla Yalla	Lebanese	❸④❸
	Honey & Co	Middle Eastern	❷❷④
	ping pong	Chinese, Dim sum	④❷❸
	Chettinad	Indian	❸❸④
	Atari-Ya	Japanese	❶④⑤
	dim T	Pan-Asian	④④④
	Siam Central	Thai	④❸❸
£25+	Vapiano	Italian	❸❸❸
	Golden Hind	Fish & chips	❸❶❸
	Leon	Sandwiches, cakes, etc	④❸❸
	Paul	"	④⑤④
	Benito's Hat	Mexican/TexMex	❸❸④
	Comptoir Libanais	Lebanese	④④❸
	Ragam	Indian	❶❸⑤

| £20+ | Patty and Bun | *Burgers, etc* | ❶❸❸ |
| | Patogh | *Middle Eastern* | ❷❷④ |

£15+	Nordic Bakery	*Scandinavian*	❸④❸
	Scandinavian Kitchen	*"*	❷❷❸
	Tommi's Burger Joint	*Burgers, etc*	❷④④
	Nordic Bakery	*Sandwiches, cakes, etc*	❸④❸
	Chipotle	*Mexican/TexMex*	❸❸④
	Tortilla	*"*	❸❸❸
	Abokado	*Japanese*	④④④

| £10+ | Kaffeine | *Sandwiches, cakes, etc* | ❸❷⓪ |

Belgravia, Pimlico, Victoria & Westminster (SW1, except St James's)

| £110+ | Marcus Wareing | *French* | ❸❷❷ |

| £100+ | Apsleys | *Italian* | ④④❸ |
| | Rib Room | *Steaks & grills* | ❸❷④ |

£90+	Dinner	*British, Traditional*	❸❸❸
	One-O-One	*Fish & seafood*	❶❸⑤
	Pétrus	*French*	❷⓪❸

£80+	Koffmann's	*French*	❷⓪❸
	Massimo	*Mediterranean*	⑤⑤④
	Ametsa	*Spanish*	⑤④⑤
	The Palm	*Steaks & grills*	④⑤④
	Mr Chow	*Chinese*	④④④

£70+	The Goring Hotel	*British, Modern*	❸⓪⓪
	Roux at Parliament Square	*"*	❸❷④
	Zafferano	*Italian*	❸❸④
	Amaya	*Indian*	❶❸❷

£60+	Bank Westminster	*British, Modern*	④④④
	The Botanist	*"*	⑤⑤⑤
	The Thomas Cubitt	*"*	❸❸❷
	Olivomare	*Fish & seafood*	❶❸❸
	The Balcon	*French*	❸❸❸
	Bar Boulud	*"*	❸❷❸
	Colbert	*"*	④④❸
	Motcombs	*International*	④❸❷
	Quirinale	*Italian*	❶❷④
	Sale e Pepe	*"*	④④❸
	Santini	*"*	④④④
	Signor Sassi	*"*	④❸❸
	Mari Vanna	*Russian*	④⑤❷
	Ladurée	*Afternoon tea*	❷④❸
	Hunan	*Chinese*	❶❸④
	Ken Lo's Memories	*"*	❸❸④
	The Cinnamon Club	*Indian*	❷❸❷
	Quilon	*Indian, Southern*	❶❷④

			Ratings
£50+	Ebury Rest' & Wine Bar	British, Modern	④④④
	The Fifth Floor Restaurant	"	❸❸❸
	The Orange	"	❸❸❷
	The Pantechnicon	"	❸❸❷
	Tate Britain (Rex Whistler)	"	– – –
	Le Cercle	French	❸❷❸
	Chabrot Bistrot d'Amis	"	❸❷❸
	La Poule au Pot	"	❸❸❶
	Caraffini	Italian	❸❶❷
	Il Convivio	"	❷❷❸
	Olivo	"	❷❷④
	Olivocarne	"	❸❷④
	Osteria Dell'Angolo	"	❸❷④
	About Thyme	Mediterranean	❷❶❸
	Boisdale	Scottish	❸❸❷
	Oliveto	Pizza	❷④④
	Beiteddine	Lebanese	❸❷④
	Ishbilia	"	❸❷⑤
	Noura	"	❸④❸
	The Grand Imperial	Chinese	❸❷❷
	Salloos	Pakistani	❷❷④
	Mango Tree	Thai	❸④④
£40+	Daylesford Organic	British, Modern	④⑤④
	No 11 Pimlico Road	"	④⑤④
	The Queens Arms	"	❸❸❷
	Browns	International	⑤④④
	Giraffe	"	⑤⑤⑤
	Grumbles	"	④❸❸
	Como Lario	Italian	④④❸
	Gran Paradiso	"	④❸④
	Gustoso	"	❸❶❸
	Ottolenghi	"	❶❷❸
	Tinello	"	❷❷❸
	Tozi	"	❷❷❷
	2 Amici	"	④❸④
	Goya	Spanish	❷❸❸
	Burger & Lobster	Burgers, etc	④④④
	Baker & Spice	Sandwiches, cakes, etc	④④④
	Ranoush	Lebanese	❸❸④
	Kazan (Cafe)	Turkish	❸❸④
£35+	Seafresh	Fish & chips	❸④⑤
	Wagamama	Japanese	④❸④
£30+	The Vincent Rooms	British, Modern	❸❸❸
	Cyprus Mangal	Turkish	❷❸④
	A Wong	Chinese	❸❸❸
	Jenny Lo's	"	❸❷④
	dim T	Pan-Asian	④④④
£15+	La Bottega	Italian	❸❸❷
	William Curley	Afternoon tea	❷❸❸

WEST

Chelsea, South Kensington, Kensington, Earl's Court & Fulham (SW3, SW5, SW6, SW7, SW10 & W8)

£120+	Gordon Ramsay	French	④④④
£100+	Rasoi	Indian	❷❸❸
£90+	Tom Aikens	British, Modern	❷❸❸
£80+	Outlaw's Seafood and Grill	Fish & seafood	❷⓪❸
	Il Ristorante	Italian	④❷④
	Nozomi	Japanese	④④⑤
	Yashin	"	⓪❸❸
	Zuma	"	⓪❸❷
£70+	Babylon	British, Modern	④④❷
	The Five Fields	"	❷⓪❷
	Launceston Place	"	❷❷❷
	Bibendum	French	❸❷⓪
	Scalini	Italian	❸❷❷
	Gaucho	Steaks & grills	❸④④
	Min Jiang	Chinese	❷❷⓪
£60+	Bluebird	British, Modern	⑤④④
	Clarke's	"	❸❷ –
	Kitchen W8	"	⓪❷❸
	Medlar	"	❷❷④
	Tom's Kitchen	"	④❸❸
	Poissonnerie de l'Av.	Fish & seafood	❷❷④
	Belvedere	French	④④❷
	Cheyne Walk Bras'	"	④④❸
	L'Etranger	"	❸④❸
	Racine	"	❸❸❸
	Daphne's	Italian	④❷❷
	La Famiglia	"	④④❸
	Lucio	"	❸④④
	San Lorenzo	"	– – –
	Locanda Ottomezzo	Mediterranean	④④④
	Cambio de Tercio	Spanish	❷❷❷
	Zaika	Indian	❷❸❸
	Benihana	Japanese	④④④
	Mao Tai	Pan-Asian	❷❷❷
£50+	Big Easy	American	❸❸❷
	The Abingdon	British, Modern	❸❸❷
	Brinkley's	"	⑤④❸
	Brompton Bar & Grill	"	❸❷❸
	The Enterprise	"	④❸❷
	Harwood Arms	"	⓪❷❸
	The Henry Root	"	④④❸
	Kensington Place	"	❸❸④
	The Sands End	"	❸④❷

	White Horse	"	4 4 3
	Bumpkin	British, Traditional	5 5 4
	Ffiona's	"	4 3 3
	Maggie Jones's	"	4 4 1
	The Malt House	"	2 3 3
	Bibendum Oyster Bar	Fish & seafood	2 3 3
	Aubaine	French	5 5 4
	La Brasserie	"	3 4 2
	Le Colombier	"	3 2 2
	Garnier	"	3 2 4
	The Pig's Ear	"	4 4 3
	Sushinho	Fusion	2 3 3
	Mazi	Greek	3 4 4
	Foxtrot Oscar	International	4 4 5
	Gallery Mess	"	4 4 4
	The Kensington Wine Rms	"	4 3 3
	Calcio	Italian	– – –
	El I even Park Walk	"	3 3 4
	Frantoio	"	4 2 2
	Manicomio	"	3 4 3
	Osteria dell'Arancio	"	3 3 3
	Pellicano	"	4 1 4
	Rocco	"	4 2 4
	Tartufo	"	1 1 3
	Ziani's	"	3 2 2
	Polish Club	Polish	4 4 2
	Admiral Codrington	Steaks & grills	3 4 4
	Black & Blue	"	3 3 4
	Kings Road Steakhouse	"	4 4 5
	PJ's Bar and Grill	"	4 2 2
	Sophie's Steakhouse	"	4 4 4
	Good Earth	Chinese	2 3 3
	Ken Lo's Memories	"	3 4 4
	Bombay Brasserie	Indian	2 1 2
	Chutney Mary	"	1 2 3
	The Painted Heron	"	2 4 4
	Star of India	"	2 3 4
	Chisou	Japanese	3 2 3
	Eight Over Eight	Pan-Asian	3 2 3
	Patara	Thai	2 3 3
	Sukho Fine Thai Cuisine	"	1 1 4
£40+	Bodean's	American	3 4 3
	Sticky Fingers	"	3 3 3
	The Anglesea Arms	British, Modern	4 4 2
	The Builders Arms	"	4 3 3
	Butcher's Hook	"	3 2 3
	The Cadogan Arms	"	3 4 3
	The Chelsea Ram	"	4 3 2
	Jam Tree	"	3 3 2
	Joe's Brasserie	"	3 2 3
	The Mall Tavern	"	3 3 3
	Megan's Delicatessen	"	3 3 2
	VQ	"	4 3 4

Name	Cuisine	Ratings
Whits	"	② ⓪ ②
The Brown Cow	British, Traditional	③ ③ ②
The Surprise	"	④ ③ ②
L'Art du Fromage	French	② ③ ③
La Bouchée	"	④ ④ ③
Chez Patrick	"	③ ⓪ ③
Côte	"	④ ③ ④
Balans West	International	⑤ ④ ④
Giraffe	"	⑤ ⑤ ⑤
Troubadour	"	④ ④ ⓪
The Windsor Castle	"	④ ④ ②
Wine Gallery	"	④ ③ ③
Aglio e Olio	Italian	③ ③ ④
Da Mario	"	③ ③ ③
Made in Italy	"	③ ④ ③
Nuovi Sapori	"	③ ⓪ ③
Obika	"	③ ③ ③
Ottolenghi	"	⓪ ② ③
Il Portico	"	④ ③ ③
Riccardo's	"	⑤ ⑤ ④
The Atlas	Mediterranean	② ② ②
Daquise	Polish	④ ③ ④
Madsen	Scandinavian	③ ④ ⑤
Capote Y Toros	Spanish	② ③ ③
Casa Brindisa	"	④ ④ ④
Tendido Cero	"	② ② ②
Tendido Cuatro	"	② ② ③
Maxela	Steaks & grills	⓪ ③ ④
Geales Chelsea Green	Fish & chips	④ ④ ④
Ciro's (Pizza Pomodoro)	Pizza	③ ④ ②
Rocca Di Papa	"	④ ④ ③
Santa Lucia	"	② ③ ③
Baker & Spice	Sandwiches, cakes, etc	④ ④ ④
Bluebird Café	"	⑤ ⑤ ④
Beirut Express	Lebanese	② ④ ④
Maroush	"	② ③ ④
Ranoush	"	③ ③ ④
Choys	Chinese	④ ③ ④
Mr Wing	"	④ ④ ②
Royal China	"	② ④ ④
Khan's of Kensington	Indian	③ ③ ④
Malabar	"	② ② ③
Thali	"	② ③ ④
Thai Square	Thai	④ ④ ④
£35+ The Shed	British, Modern	③ ② ⓪
The Scarsdale	International	④ ③ ⓪
Buona Sera	Italian	④ ③ ③
Napulé	"	③ ③ ③
Il Pagliaccio	"	③ ② ③
Pappa Ciccia	"	③ ③ ③
Haché	Steaks & grills	③ ③ ②
Byron	Burgers, etc	③ ③ ③
Basilico	Pizza	③ ② ④

	La Delizia Limbara	"	❸④④
	Rossopomodoro	"	❸❸❸
	Benugo	Sandwiches, cakes, etc	④④❷
	Best Mangal	Turkish	❷❸❸
	Noor Jahan	Indian	❷❷❸
	Wagamama	Japanese	④❸④
	Bangkok	Thai	❷❷❸
	Busaba Eathai	"	❸❸❷
£30+	Kensington Square Kitchen	British, Modern	❸❶❷
	Diner	Burgers, etc	④❸❷
	Taiwan Village	Chinese	❶❶❸
	The Greedy Buddha	Indian	❸④④
	Masala Zone	"	❸❷❷
	Monty's	"	❸❸❸
	Itsu	Japanese	④❸④
	Kulu Kulu	"	④⑤④
	Addie's Thai Café	Thai	❷❸❸
	Churchill Arms	"	❸❷❶
£25+	Chelsea Bun Diner	International	❸④④
	The Chelsea Kitchen	"	④④❸
	Mona Lisa	"	❸❷❷
	Stock Pot	"	④❸❸
	Comptoir Libanais	Lebanese	④④❸
£20+	Stick & Bowl	Chinese	❷❷❸
	Eat Tokyo	Japanese	❸❸④
	Café 209	Thai	④❸❶
£15+	La Bottega	Italian	❸❸❷

Notting Hill, Holland Park, Bayswater, North Kensington & Maida Vale (W2, W9, W10, W11)

£110+	The Ledbury	British, Modern	❶❶❷
£80+	Marianne	British, Modern	– – –
	The Shiori	Japanese	❶❷④
£70+	Angelus	French	❸❷❸
	Assaggi	Italian	❶❶❸
£60+	Beach Blanket Babylon	British, Modern	⑤④❸
	Julie's	"	④④❶
	Edera	Italian	❷❶④
	Chakra	Indian	❸④④
£50+	The Cow	British, Modern	❸❸❶
	The Dock Kitchen	"	❸❸❶
	The Frontline Club	"	❸④❸
	The Waterway	"	④⑤❸
	Bumpkin	British, Traditional	⑤⑤④

	The Summerhouse	*Fish & seafood*	④	❸	❷
	Le Café Anglais	*French*	❸	④	❷
	Goode & Wright	*"*	❸	④	④
	Essenza	*Italian*	❸	❸	④
	Mediterraneo	*"*	❸	❸	❸
	The Oak	*"*	❷	❸	❶
	Osteria Basilico	*"*	❸	❸	❷
	Casa Malevo	*Argentinian*	❸	❸	❸
	Colchis	*Georgian*	❷	❸	❸
	Bombay Palace	*Indian*	❶	❶	❸
	E&O	*Pan-Asian*	❷	❸	❶
£40+	All Star Lanes	*American*	④	❸	❸
	Granger & Co	*Australian*	④	⑤	❸
	Daylesford Organic	*British, Modern*	④	⑤	④
	First Floor	*"*	❸	④	❶
	Formosa Dining Room	*"*	④	④	❸
	The Ladbroke Arms	*"*	❷	❸	❷
	Paradise, Kensal Green	*"*	❸	❸	❷
	Hereford Road	*British, Traditional*	❷	❸	❸
	Côte	*French*	④	❸	④
	La Sophia	*"*	❷	❸	④
	Halepi	*Greek*	❸	❶	❸
	Giraffe	*International*	⑤	⑤	⑤
	Ottolenghi	*Italian*	❶	❷	❸
	Portobello Ristorante	*"*	❷	❷	❷
	Raoul's Cafe	*Mediterranean*	④	❸	❸
	El Pirata de Tapas	*Spanish*	❸	❸	❷
	Pizza East Portobello	*Pizza*	❷	❸	❶
	The Red Pepper	*"*	❷	❸	④
	Baker & Spice	*Sandwiches, cakes, etc*	④	④	④
	Al-Waha	*Lebanese*	❷	④	④
	Beirut Express	*"*	❷	④	④
	Maroush	*"*	❷	❸	④
	Ranoush	*"*	❸	❸	④
	Kateh	*Persian*	❷	❷	❷
	Mandarin Kitchen	*Chinese*	❷	④	⑤
	Pearl Liang	*"*	❷	❸	❸
	Royal China	*"*	❷	④	④
	Seventeen	*"*	❸	❸	❸
£35+	Lucky Seven	*American*	❸	❸	❷
	Galicia	*Spanish*	❸	❸	❷
	Honest Burgers	*Burgers, etc*	❶	❷	❸
	Rossopomodoro	*Pizza*	❸	❸	❸
	Tom's Deli	*Sandwiches, cakes, etc*	❸	❸	❸
	Noor Jahan	*Indian*	❷	❷	❸
	Inaho	*Japanese*	❶	⑤	⑤
	Maguro	*"*	❶	❷	❸
	The Walmer Castle	*Thai*	❸	❸	❷
£30+	Notting Hill Kitchen	*Spanish*	❷	❸	❷
	Taqueria	*Mexican/TexMex*	❸	❸	④
	The Four Seasons	*Chinese*	❷	⑤	⑤

	Gold Mine	"	③④⑤
	ping pong	Chinese, Dim sum	④❷❸
	Durbar	Indian	❷❷❷
	Masala Zone	"	❸❷❷
	Itsu	Japanese	④❸④
	Satay House	Malaysian	❸④④
	Banana Tree Canteen	Pan-Asian	④④❸
£25+	Otto Pizza	Pizza	❷❷❷
	Gail's Bread	Sandwiches, cakes, etc	④④❸
	Alounak	Persian	❸④❸
	Colbeh	"	❷④④
	Mandalay	Burmese	❸❷⑤
	Fortune Cookie	Chinese	❷④⑤
	C&R Cafe	Thai	❸④④
	Fitou's Thai Restaurant	"	❷❸④
£20+	Fez Mangal	Turkish	❶❷❸
	Khan's	Indian	❸④❸
£5+	Lisboa Pâtisserie	Sandwiches, cakes, etc	❸❸④

Hammersmith, Shepherd's Bush, Olympia, Chiswick, Brentford & Ealing (W4, W5, W6, W12, W13, W14, TW8)

£90+	The River Café	Italian	❸④❷
£70+	Hedone	British, Modern	❷❸❸
£60+	La Trompette	French	❷❷❸
£50+	The Anglesea Arms	British, Modern	❷❸❷
	Le Vacherin	French	❸❸❸
	Michael Nadra	International	❶❸④
	Oak	Italian	❷❸❶
	Cibo	"	❷❶❸
	The Meat & Wine Co	Steaks & grills	④❸④
	Popeseye	"	④④⑤
	Chisou	Japanese	❷❸④
£40+	Bush Dining Hall	British, Modern	❸④❸
	The Carpenter's Arms	"	❸❸❸
	Carvosso's	"	④❸❷
	The Dartmouth Castle	"	④❸❸
	Duke of Sussex	"	❸④❷
	The Havelock Tavern	"	❷④❷
	High Road Brasserie	"	④④❸
	Hole in the Wall	"	④❸❸
	Pissaro	"	④④❶
	Princess Victoria	"	④❷❷
	The Roebuck	"	④❸❸
	Sam's Brasserie	"	④❸❷
	The Thatched House	"	❸④❸

	Union Jacks	"	⑤④④
	Vinoteca	"	④❸❷
	The Hampshire Hog	British, Traditional	④❸❸
	Charlotte's Bistro	French	❷❷❷
	Charlotte's Place	"	❸❷❸
	Côte	"	④❸④
	Annie's	International	④❷❷
	Balans	"	⑤④④
	Giraffe	"	⑤⑤⑤
	Jamie's Italian	Italian	⑤⑤④
	Pentolina	"	❷❷❸
	Cumberland Arms	Mediterranean	❷❷❸
	Raoul's Café & Deli	"	④❸❸
	The Swan	"	❷❷❶
	The Cabin	Steaks & grills	④④④
	The Gate	Vegetarian	❸④④
	Bird in Hand	Pizza	❸❸❸
	Fire & Stone	"	④④④
	Lola & Simón	Argentinian	❸❷❸
	Azou	North African	❸❷❷
	North China	Chinese	❷❷❷
	Indian Zing	Indian	❶❷❸
	Tosa	Japanese	❷④④
	Saigon Saigon	Vietnamese	❸④❸
£35+	Queen's Head	British, Modern	④❸❷
	The Real Greek	Greek	⑤④④
	Canta Napoli	Italian	❸❸④
	Patio	Polish	④❷❶
	Byron	Burgers, etc	❸❸❸
	Benugo	Sandwiches, cakes, etc	④④❷
	Quantus	South American	❷❶❷
	Best Mangal	Turkish	❷❸❸
	Maxim	Chinese	❸④❸
	Brilliant	Indian	❷❷❸
	Karma	"	❷❶④
	Potli	"	❷④④
	Sagar	"	❸❸④
	Okawari	Japanese	❸④❸
	Busaba Eathai	Thai	❸❸❷
	Pho	Vietnamese	❷❷❷
£30+	Albertine	French	④❷❷
	Santa Maria	Pizza	❶❸❸
	Wahaca	Mexican/TexMex	❸❸❷
	Adams Café	Moroccan	❸❶❷
	Chez Marcelle	Lebanese	❶⑤④
	Sufi	Persian	❸❷❸
	Tian Fu	Chinese	❸⑤⑤
	Anarkali	Indian	❸❸④
	Madhu's	"	❸❸❸
	Monty's	"	❸❸❸
	Shilpa	Indian, Southern	❷❸⑤
	Atari-Ya	Japanese	❶④⑤

	Kiraku	"	❶❷❸
	Bedlington Café	Thai	❷❸④
	Esarn Kheaw	"	❷❸⑤
	Fat Boy's	"	④④❸
	101 Thai Kitchen	"	❷❸⑤
£25+	Gail's Bakery	Sandwiches, cakes, etc	④④❸
	Comptoir Libanais	Lebanese	④④❸
	Alounak	Persian	❸④❸
	Faanoos	"	❸④❸
	Hare & Tortoise	Pan-Asian	❸❸❸
£20+	Franco Manca	Pizza	❷❸❸
	Abu Zaad	Syrian	❸❸④
	Eat Tokyo	Japanese	❸❸④
	Miran Masala	Pakistani	❶❷❸
	Mirch Masala	"	❷④⑤
	Old Parr's Head	Thai	❸❸④
£15+	Kerbisher & Malt	Fish & chips	❸❸④
	Tortilla	Mexican/TexMex	❸❸❸
	Gifto's	Indian	❷❸④

NORTH

Hampstead, West Hampstead, St John's Wood, Regent's Park, Kilburn & Camden Town (NW postcodes)

£80+	Landmark (Winter Gdn)	*British, Modern*	❸②❶
£70+	Gaucho	*Steaks & grills*	❸④④
	Gilgamesh	*Pan-Asian*	❸❸②
£60+	Bull & Last	*British, Traditional*	②❸❸
	Gilbert Scott	"	④④❷
	One Blenheim Terrace	*French*	⑤④④
	Oslo Court	"	❷❶❶
	Villa Bianca	*Italian*	⑤④④
£50+	Bradley's	*British, Modern*	④❸④
	The Engineer	"	④④❸
	Odette's	"	❸④❸
	St Pancras Grand	"	⑤⑤④
	L'Aventure	*French*	❷❶❶
	Michael Nadra	"	❶❸④
	La Collina	*Italian*	❸❸❷
	Mimmo la Bufala	"	④❸④
	York & Albany	"	④④④
	Manna	*Vegetarian*	④④④
	Good Earth	*Chinese*	❷❸❸
	Kaifeng	"	❷❷❸
	Phoenix Palace	"	❸④④
£40+	Karpo	*American*	❸④④
	Belgo Noord	*Belgian*	④④④
	Freemasons Arms	*British, Modern*	⑤⑤④
	The Horseshoe	"	❸❸❸
	The Junction Tavern	"	❸❶❷
	Market	"	❸④④
	The North London Tavern	"	④④❸
	The Old Bull & Bush	"	④④④
	Rising Sun	"	❸❷❸
	The Wells	"	❸❸❷
	The Wet Fish Cafe	"	❸❷❷
	Greenberry Cafe	*British, Traditional*	❸❸④
	Kentish Canteen	"	④❸❸
	The Old White Bear	"	❸❷❸
	L'Absinthe	*French*	④❷❸
	La Cage Imaginaire	"	④④❸
	Mill Lane Bistro	"	❸❷❷
	Lemonia	*Greek*	④❷❶
	Retsina	"	④④❸
	Giraffe	*International*	⑤⑤⑤
	Artigiano	*Italian*	❸④❸
	Ostuni	"	– – –
	The Salusbury	"	④④❸
	Sarracino	"	❷❸④

			Rating
	Nautilus	Fish & chips	①②⑤
	The Sea Shell	"	②③④
	Pizza East	Pizza	②③①
	Mestizo	Mexican/TexMex	④④③
	Mango Room	Afro-Caribbean	③③③
	Solly's	Israeli	③④④
	Green Cottage	Chinese	③④⑤
	Woodlands	Indian	③④④
	Café Japan	Japanese	②④④
	Jin Kichi	"	①②④
	Soho Japan	"	②②④
	Sushi-Say	"	①②④
	Singapore Garden	Malaysian	②③④
	XO	Pan-Asian	④④④
£35+	Made In Camden	British, Modern	③③③
	Somerstown Coffee House	"	③②③
	Swan & Edgar	International	④③②
	Marine Ices	Italian	– – –
	El Parador	Spanish	②②②
	Haché	Steaks & grills	③③②
	Harry Morgan's	Burgers, etc	③③④
	Honest Burgers		①②③
	Skipjacks	Fish & chips	①②④
	Basilico	Pizza	③②④
	Rossopomodoro	"	③③③
	Benugo	Sandwiches, cakes, etc	④④②
	Beyoglu	Turkish	③③④
	Gung-Ho	Chinese	③②③
	Eriki	Indian	②③④
	Asakusa	Japanese	①④④
	Bento Cafe	"	②②④
	Wagamama	"	④③④
	Ladudu	Vietnamese	③③④
£30+	Chicken Shop	American	③②②
	Carob Tree	Greek	③②②
	L'Artista	Italian	④③③
	La Porchetta Pizzeria	"	③③③
	The Little Bay	Mediterranean	④②①
	Diner	Burgers, etc	④③②
	Sacro Cuore	Pizza	②②③
	Kenwood (Brew House)	Sandwiches, cakes, etc	④③①
	Chutneys	Indian	④③④
	Diwana B-P House	"	④④⑤
	Great Nepalese	"	③②⑤
	Guglee	"	③③④
	Masala Zone	"	③②②
	Paradise Hampstead	"	①②③
	Vijay	"	③②④
	Atari-Ya	Japanese	①④⑤
	The Banana Tree Canteen	Pan-Asian	④④③
	dim T	"	④④④

207

| £25+ | Sea Pebbles | Fish & seafood | ③④③ |
| | Gail's Bread | Sandwiches, cakes, etc | ④④③ |

£20+	Ali Baba	Egyptian	③②④
	Sakonis	Indian	②④⑤
	Eat Tokyo	Japanese	③③④

| £15+ | Ginger & White | Sandwiches, cakes, etc | ③②② |

| £10+ | Dirty Burger | Burgers, etc | ②③③ |

Hoxton, Islington, Highgate, Crouch End, Stoke Newington, Finsbury Park, Muswell Hill & Finchley (N postcodes)

| £60+ | Frederick's | British, Modern | ③②② |
| | Fifteen Restaurant | Italian | – – – |

£50+	The Duke of Cambridge	British, Modern	③③②
	Grain Store	"	②②⓪
	Rotunda Bar & Restaurant	"	④④③
	The Almeida	French	③④④
	Bistro Aix	"	②⓪②
	Trullo	Italian	②②②
	Isarn	Thai	②②④

£40+	Red Dog Saloon	American	③②②
	Shrimpy's	"	④④③
	The Albion	British, Modern	③③⓪
	Bald Faced Stag	"	③④③
	Caravan King's Cross	"	③③②
	Charles Lamb	"	③③⓪
	The Clissold Arms	"	④③③
	The Drapers Arms	"	③③③
	The Fellow	"	③④④
	The Haven	"	④④⑤
	Juniper Dining	"	②③③
	Mosaica	"	④④③
	The Northgate	"	②②③
	Pig & Butcher	"	②②②
	Plum + Spilt Milk	"	③③②
	St Johns	British, Traditional	③②⓪
	Kipferl	East & Cent. European	③④③
	Assiette Anglaise	French	②③③
	Les Associés	"	③②④
	Blue Legume	"	④②②
	Banners	International	③③⓪
	Browns	"	⑤④④
	The Flask	"	④④②
	Giraffe	"	⑤⑤⑤
	The Orange Tree	"	④⑤③
	500	Italian	③③④
	Ottolenghi	"	⓪②③
	Pizzeria Oregano	"	②②③

			Rating
	San Daniele	"	3 2 3
	Camino	Spanish	3 2 2
	Garufa	Steaks & grills	2 4 3
	The Smokehouse Islington	"	– – –
	Duke's Brew & Que	Burgers, etc	2 3 4
	The Fish & Chip Shop	Fish & chips	1 2 2
	Two Brothers	"	3 4 4
	Il Bacio	Pizza	3 3 3
	Tierra Peru	Peruvian	4 3 4
	Yipin China	Chinese	1 2 5
	Roots at N1	Indian	2 2 3
	Zaffrani	"	2 2 2
	Thai Square	Thai	4 4 4
£35+	John Salt	American	4 4 3
	Le Coq	British, Modern	– – –
	Season Kitchen	"	2 2 3
	Le Sacré-Coeur	French	4 3 3
	Vrisaki	Greek	4 3 3
	Pizzeria Pappagone	Italian	3 2 2
	Rugoletta	"	3 3 4
	Café del Parc	Spanish	2 1 2
	Byron	Burgers, etc	3 3 3
	Toff's	Fish & chips	2 2 4
	Basilico	Pizza	3 2 4
	Rossopomodoro	"	3 3 3
	Gilak	Persian	3 2 4
	Gallipoli	Turkish	4 2 3
	Mangal II	"	3 3 4
	Little Georgia Café	Georgian	3 4 3
	Anglo Asian Tandoori	Indian	3 2 3
	Indian Rasoi	"	2 2 3
	Rasa	Indian, Southern	2 2 3
	Akari	Japanese	2 3 3
	Wagamama	"	4 3 4
	Yum Yum	Thai	2 3 2
£30+	Olympus Fish	Fish & seafood	2 3 4
	La Porchetta Pizzeria	Italian	3 3 3
	La Bota	Spanish	3 4 4
	Diner	Burgers, etc	4 3 2
	Meat Mission	"	2 4 3
	Fabrizio	Pizza	3 2 4
	Sweet Thursday	"	2 3 2
	Wahaca	Mexican/TexMex	3 3 2
	Antepliler	Turkish	3 4 3
	Gem	"	3 2 3
	Izgara	"	3 4 5
	Petek	"	3 2 2
	Delhi Grill	Indian	2 2 3
	Masala Zone	"	3 2 2
	Atari-Ya	Japanese	1 4 5
	dim T	Pan-Asian	4 4 4
	Huong-Viet	Vietnamese	3 4 4

£25+	Prawn On The Lawn	*Fish & seafood*	– – –
	Le Mercury	*French*	④④❸
	Mem & Laz	*Mediterranean*	④❸❸
	White Rabbit	*Pizza*	❶❶❷
	Benito's Hat	*Mexican/TexMex*	❸❸④
	Afghan Kitchen	*Afghani*	❷④④
	Rani	*Indian*	❸④④
	Dotori	*Korean*	❷④④
£15+	Notes	*Sandwiches, cakes, etc*	④❷❷
	Chilango	*Mexican/TexMex*	❷❷❸
	Chipotle	*"*	❸❸④
	Tortilla	*"*	❸❸❸
	Jai Krishna	*Indian*	❷④④
£10+	The Rib Man	*Burgers, etc*	❶❸ –
	Euphorium Bakery	*Sandwiches, cakes, etc*	❸④❸

SOUTH

South Bank (SE1)

£80+	Oxo Tower (Rest')	British, Modern	5 5 4
£70+	Le Pont de la Tour	British, Modern	4 4 2
	Roast	British, Traditional	4 4 3
	Oxo Tower (Brass')	Mediterranean	5 5 4
	Gaucho	Steaks & grills	3 4 4
	Hutong	Chinese	3 4 1
£60+	Story	British, Modern	1 1 3
	Butlers W'f Chop-house	British, Traditional	4 4 4
£50+	Oblix	American	4 3 1
	Cantina Vinopolis	British, Modern	4 4 3
	Elliot's Cafe	"	3 4 4
	Magdalen	"	2 3 3
	Mezzanine	"	4 4 4
	Skylon	"	4 4 2
	Skylon Grill	"	3 3 2
	The Swan at the Globe	"	4 4 2
	fish!	Fish & seafood	4 4 3
	Wright Brothers	"	2 3 2
	Brasserie Blanc	French	4 3 4
	Village East	Fusion	– – –
	Vivat Bacchus	International	4 4 4
	La Barca	Italian	4 2 2
	Tentazioni	"	3 3 3
	Baltic	Polish	3 3 2
	Archduke Wine Bar	Steaks & grills	5 5 4
	Black & Blue	"	3 3 4
	Mango Food of India	Indian	3 3 4
£40+	Albion	British, Modern	4 4 3
	Blueprint Café	"	4 4 1
	40 Maltby Street	"	2 3 3
	Garrison	"	3 3 2
	Menier Chocolate Factory	"	5 4 3
	RSJ	"	3 3 4
	The Table	"	3 4 4
	Tate Modern (Level 7)	"	5 4 3
	Union Street Café	"	– – –
	Waterloo Bar & Kitchen	"	4 3 4
	The Anchor & Hope	British, Traditional	1 1 3
	Canteen	"	5 5 5
	The Riverfront	"	4 4 3
	Applebee's Cafe	Fish & seafood	3 3 4
	Côte	French	4 3 4
	Champor-Champor	Fusion	2 3 1
	Browns	International	5 4 4
	Giraffe	"	5 5 5
	Antico	Italian	3 3 4

			Rating
	Zucca	"	1 2 2
	José	Spanish	1 2 1
	Pizarro	"	2 2 1
	Tapas Brindisa	"	2 3 3
	Constancia	Argentinian	3 3 3
	Bengal Clipper	Indian	3 3 2
£35+	Casse-Croute	French	– – –
	Real Greek	Greek	5 4 4
	Meson don Felipe	Spanish	4 4 3
	Benugo	Sandwiches, cakes, etc	4 4 2
	Tas (Cafe)	Turkish	4 3 3
	Bangalore Express	Indian	4 4 3
	Wagamama	Japanese	4 3 4
£30+	Mar I Terra	Spanish	3 3 2
	Gourmet Pizza Co.	Pizza	4 4 3
	Caffé Vergnano	Sandwiches, cakes, etc	4 3 2
	Wahaca	Mexican/TexMex	3 3 2
	El Vergel	South American	2 3 2
	Tas Pide	Turkish	4 3 3
	ping pong	Chinese, Dim sum	4 2 3
	dim T	Pan-Asian	4 4 4
£25+	Masters Super Fish	Fish & chips	2 4 5
	Konditor & Cook	Sandwiches, cakes, etc	3 4 4
	Leon	"	4 3 3
£15+	Tortilla	Mexican/TexMex	3 3 3
£10+	Monmouth Coffee Co	Sandwiches, cakes, etc	1 1 2
	Pod	"	3 3 4
	Spianata & Co	"	3 2 3

Greenwich, Lewisham, Dulwich & Blackheath
(All SE postcodes, except SE1)

			Rating
£70+	Gaucho	Steaks & grills	3 4 4
£60+	Lobster Pot	Fish & seafood	2 3 4
£50+	The Palmerston	British, Modern	3 4 4
	Buenos Aires Café	Argentinian	3 4 3
	Babur	Indian	1 1 2
£40+	Chapters	British, Modern	4 3 4
	The Crooked Well	"	2 2 2
	Florence	"	4 4 2
	Franklins	"	3 4 3
	Inside	"	2 2 5
	The Lido Cafe	"	3 3 2
	The Old Brewery	"	4 4 2
	Rivington Grill	"	4 3 4

Toasted	French	– – –
Joanna's	International	3 2 2
The Yellow House	"	2 2 4
Lorenzo	Italian	4 2 3
Angels & Gypsies	Spanish	2 3 2
Bianco43	Pizza	3 3 4
Rocca Di Papa	"	4 4 3
Zero Degrees	"	3 4 4
Ganapati	Indian	1 1 2
Kennington Tandoori	"	2 2 2
£35+	The Dartmouth Arms	British, Modern	4 3 3
	The Lord Northbrook	British, Traditional	3 2 2
	Brasserie Toulouse-Lautrec	French	3 2 2
	Le Querce	Italian	1 2 3
	Olley's	Fish & chips	2 3 3
	Dragon Castle	Chinese	2 3 4
	Tandoori Nights	Indian	3 2 3
	The Begging Bowl	Thai	1 2 3
£30+	Frizzante Cafe	Italian	3 2 3
	The Sea Cow	Fish & chips	2 3 3
	The Gowlett	Pizza	2 3 2
	Everest Inn	Indian	2 2 3
£25+	Gandhi's	Indian	3 4 3
£20+	Thai Corner Café	Thai	3 3 3
	Cafe East	Vietnamese	2 4 4
£10+	Monmouth Coffee Company	Sandwiches, cakes, etc	1 1 2

Battersea, Brixton, Clapham, Wandsworth, Barnes, Putney & Wimbledon (All SW postcodes south of the river)

£60+	Cannizaro House	British, Modern	4 4 2
	Chez Bruce	"	1 1 2
	Trinity	"	1 1 2
	San Lorenzo Fuoriporta	Italian	5 5 4
£50+	Entrée	British, Modern	3 2 2
	Sonny's Kitchen	"	4 4 4
	Fox & Grapes	British, Traditional	4 4 3
	The Lawn Bistro	French	4 2 4
	Upstairs	"	2 2 2
	Brinkley's Kitchen	International	4 4 3
	Enoteca Turi	Italian	2 1 3
	Numero Uno	"	3 2 2
	Riva	"	2 2 4
	Alquimia	Spanish	2 2 2
	Popeseye	Steaks & grills	4 4 5
	Fulham Wine Rooms	Sandwiches, cakes, etc	3 3 3
	Santa Maria del Sur	Argentinian	3 4 3

	Suk Saran	Thai	3 4 5
£40+	Bodean's	American	3 4 3
	Belgo	Belgian	4 4 4
	The Abbeville	British, Modern	4 3 2
	Abbeville Kitchen	"	2 2 3
	Antelope	"	3 2 2
	Avalon	"	4 4 3
	The Balham Bowls Club	"	3 3 2
	Ben's Canteen	"	4 4 4
	Bistro Union	"	3 2 3
	The Bolingbroke	"	4 3 3
	The Brown Dog	"	3 3 2
	Brunswick House Cafe	"	3 4 2
	The Depot	"	3 2 2
	Earl Spencer	"	3 4 3
	Emile's	"	3 2 4
	The Fentiman Arms	"	3 3 2
	Harrison's	"	4 4 3
	Jam Tree	"	3 3 2
	Lamberts	"	0 0 2
	The Victoria	"	3 2 3
	Canton Arms	British, Traditional	2 2 2
	Bellevue Rendez-Vous	French	3 2 2
	Côte	"	4 3 4
	Gastro	"	4 4 2
	Le P'tit Normand	"	3 2 3
	Soif	"	4 4 4
	Annie's	International	4 2 2
	Hudsons	"	4 4 3
	The Light House	"	4 3 3
	The Ship	"	4 4 3
	Antipasto & Pasta	Italian	3 2 4
	Donna Margherita	"	2 3 4
	Isola del Sole	"	4 4 4
	Ost. Antica Bologna	"	3 3 3
	Pizza Metro	"	2 4 4
	Sapori Sardi	"	2 3 4
	The Fox & Hounds	Mediterranean	2 2 2
	Lola Rojo	Spanish	3 4 4
	Butcher & Grill	Steaks & grills	4 3 3
	Cattle Grid	"	3 4 4
	Bayee Village	Chinese	3 4 4
	China Boulevard	"	3 4 3
	Indian Zilla	Indian	0 0 3
	Cho-San	Japanese	2 2 3
	Sticks'n'Sushi	"	3 3 2
	Tsunami	"	2 4 4
	Blue Elephant	Thai	3 3 2
	Thai Square	"	4 4 4
£35+	The Dairy	British, Modern	– – –
	The Manor Arms	British, Traditional	2 3 4
	Gazette	French	4 4 2

	Telegraph	*International*	④④❸
	Buona Sera	*Italian*	④❸❸
	Fish in a Tie	*Mediterranean*	④❷❷
	Byron	*Burgers, etc*	❸❸❸
	Haché	*"*	❸❸❷
	Honest Burgers	*"*	❶❷❸
	Fish Club	*Fish & chips*	❷❷④
	Al Forno	*Pizza*	④❸❷
	Basilico	*"*	❸❷④
	Rossopomodoro	*"*	❸❸❸
	Dalchini	*Chinese*	④❸④
	Ma Goa	*Indian*	❷❶❷
	Nazmins	*"*	❸❸❸
	Hashi	*Japanese*	❷❷❸
	Wagamama	*"*	④❸④
	Cah-Chi	*Korean*	❷❷❸
£30+	Boqueria	*Spanish*	❷❷❷
	Brady's	*Fish & chips*	❷❷❷
	Eco	*Pizza*	❷❸❷
	Pantry	*Sandwiches, cakes, etc*	❸❸❸
	Chutney	*Indian*	❷❷❸
	Cocum	*"*	❷❷❸
	Indian Moment	*"*	❸④④
	Mango & Silk	*"*	❷❷❸
	The Banana Tree Canteen	*Pan-Asian*	④④❸
	Amaranth	*Thai*	❷❸❷
	Fat Boy's	*"*	④④❸
	Talad Thai	*"*	❸④⑤
	Thai Garden	*"*	❸❸④
	Mien Tay	*Vietnamese*	❷④④
£25+	Moxon's Fish Bar	*Fish & chips*	❶❸⑤
	Gail's Bread	*Sandwiches, cakes, etc*	④④❸
	Orange Pekoe	*"*	❷❷❷
	Faanoos	*Persian*	❸④❸
	Holy Cow	*Indian*	❷④❸
	Indian Ocean	*"*	❷❷❸
	Sree Krishna	*"*	❷❸④
	Fujiyama	*Japanese*	❸④④
	Lahore Kebab House	*Pakistani*	❶④④
	Hare & Tortoise	*Pan-Asian*	❸❸❸
	Kaosarn	*Thai*	❷❷❷
	The Pepper Tree	*"*	❸❷④
	The Paddyfield	*Vietnamese*	❷❷❸
£20+	Franco Manca	*Pizza*	❷❸❸
	Apollo Banana Leaf	*Indian*	❶❷⑤
	Hot Stuff	*"*	❷❷❸
	Lahore Karahi	*Pakistani*	❷④④
	Mirch Masala SW17	*"*	❷④⑤
£15+	Wishbone	*American*	⑤④④
	Chipotle	*Mexican/TexMex*	❸❸④

	Tortilla	"	❸❸❸
	Meza	*Lebanese*	❷❸❸
£10+	Dirty Burger	*Burgers, etc*	❷❸❸

Outer western suburbs
Kew, Richmond, Twickenham, Teddington

£70+	The Bingham	*British, Modern*	❷❷❶
	Petersham Nurseries	"	❸❺❸
	Gaucho	*Steaks & grills*	❸④④
£60+	The Glasshouse	*British, Modern*	❷❷❸
	Petersham Hotel	"	④❸❷
	Al Boccon di'vino	*Italian*	❶❷❷
£50+	Plane Food	*British, Modern*	④④④
	Rock & Rose	"	❺❺❸
	Brula	*French*	❷❶❷
	A Cena	*Italian*	❸❷❸
	Kew Grill	*Steaks & grills*	❸❷❸
£40+	The Wharf	*British, Modern*	④❸❷
	La Buvette	*French*	❸❷❷
	Ma Cuisine	"	❸❸❸
	don Fernando's	*Spanish*	④❷④
	Palmyra	*Lebanese*	❷❷④
	Four Regions	*Chinese*	❸❷④
	Matsuba	*Japanese*	❷④④
£35+	Canta Napoli	*Italian*	❸❸④
	Pizzeria Rustica	*Pizza*	❸❸④
£30+	Fat Boy's	*Thai*	④④❸
£15+	William Curley	*Afternoon tea*	❷❸❸
	Taylor St Baristas	*Sandwiches, cakes, etc*	❷❸❸

EAST

Smithfield & Farringdon (EC1)

£70+			
Club Gascon	French		❷❸❸
Dans le Noir	International		④④④
Gaucho	Steaks & grills		❸④④
Smiths (Top Floor)	"		⑤④④

£60+			
Chiswell Street Dining Rms	British, Modern		④❸④
The Clove Club	"		❷⓪❷
Bleeding Heart	French		❸❷⓪
Morgan M	"		❷❸⑤

£50+			
Bird of Smithfield	British, Modern		④④❸
The Modern Pantry	"		④④④
St John	British, Traditional		❷❷❷
Bistrot Bruno Loubet	French		❸❸❸
Café du Marché	"		❷❷⓪
Fabrizio	Italian		❷⓪⑤
Portal	Portuguese		④④❸
Moro	Spanish		⓪❷❷
Hix	Steaks & grills		④❸❸
Smiths (Dining Rm)	"		④④④
Sushi Tetsu	Japanese		⓪⓪❸

£40+			
Brasserie on St John Street	British, Modern		❸④④
Caravan	"		❸❸❷
Foxlow	"		– – –
The Gunmakers	"		❷❷❸
The Peasant	"		❸❷❸
Vinoteca	"		④❸❷
The Fox and Anchor	British, Traditional		❷❷⓪
The Quality Chop House	"		❷❷❷
Chabrot Bistrot des Halles	French		❷❷❸
Comptoir Gascon	"		❸④❸
Le Rendezvous du Café	"		❸❸❸
Alba	Italian		❸❷④
Santore	"		❷❷④
The Gate	Vegetarian		❸④④
Burger & Lobster	Burgers, etc		❷❸❸
Workshop Coffee	Sandwiches, cakes, etc		❸❸❷

£35+			
Cellar Gascon	French		❷❸❷
Polpo	Italian		④❸⓪
Morito	Spanish		❷❷❸
Amico Bio	Vegetarian		❸④❸
Benugo	Sandwiches, cakes, etc		④④❷
Tas	Turkish		④❸❸
Pham Sushi	Japanese		⓪④⑤
Tajima Tei	"		❷❸❸
Busaba Eathai	Thai		❸❸❷
Naamyaa Café	"		④④❸
Cây Tre	Vietnamese		❸④❸

	Pho	*"*	**2 2 2**

£30+			
	Smiths (Ground Floor)	*British, Modern*	4 4 **3**
	Kolossi Grill	*Greek*	4 **2 2**
	La Porchetta Pizzeria	*Italian*	**3 3 3**
	The Eagle	*Mediterranean*	**3** 4 **2**
	The Little Bay	*"*	4 **2 1**
	Banana Tree Canteen	*Pan-Asian*	4 4 **3**

£25+			
	Fish Central	*Fish & seafood*	**3 2** 4
	Gail's Bakery	*Sandwiches, cakes, etc*	4 4 **3**
	Look Mum No Hands!	*"*	**3 3 2**
	Sedap	*Malaysian*	4 4 4

£15+			
	Hummus Bros	*Mediterranean*	**3 3** 4
	Department of Coffee	*Sandwiches, cakes, etc*	**3 2 2**
	Daddy Donkey	*Mexican/TexMex*	**2 3** –
	Abokado	*Japanese*	4 4 4

£10+			
	Big Apple Hot Dogs	*Burgers, etc*	**2 2** –
	Dose	*Sandwiches, cakes, etc*	**2 3** 4
	Nusa Kitchen	*"*	**2 3** 4
	Pod	*"*	**3 3** 4
	Prufrock Coffee	*"*	**2 2 3**
	Spianata & Co	*"*	**3 2 3**

The City (EC2, EC3, EC4)

£120+	HKK	*Chinese*	**2 2** 4

£70+			
	Chamberlain's	*Fish & seafood*	**3** 4 4
	Lutyens	*French*	4 4 4
	Sauterelle	*"*	**3 3 3**
	L'Anima	*Italian*	**2 2 3**
	Gaucho	*Steaks & grills*	**3** 4 4
	Sushisamba	*Japanese*	**3** 4 **2**

£60+			
	Bread Street Kitchen	*British, Modern*	4 4 4
	The Don	*"*	**3 2 3**
	Duck & Waffle	*"*	4 4 **1**
	1901	*"*	4 4 **3**
	1 Lombard Street	*"*	4 4 **3**
	3 South Place	*"*	4 **3** 4
	Vertigo 42	*"*	5 4 **2**
	Angler	*Fish & seafood*	**3 2 2**
	Coq d'Argent	*French*	4 4 **3**
	Bonds	*Mediterranean*	4 4 **3**
	Barbecoa	*Steaks & grills*	4 4 4
	Goodman City	*"*	**2 2 3**
	Hawksmoor	*"*	**2 2 3**
	New Street Grill	*"*	4 **2 2**
	Ladurée	*Afternoon tea*	**2** 4 **3**

£50+			
The Hoxton Grill	American		④④❷
The Chancery	British, Modern		❸❸④
Gin Joint	"		– – –
High Timber	"		④❸❸
The Jugged Hare	"		④④❸
The Mercer	"		❸❸❸
Northbank	"		❸④❸
The White Swan	"		❸❸❸
Paternoster Chop House	British, Traditional		⑤⑤⑤
Fish Market	Fish & seafood		❸❷❸
Gow's	"		❸❸④
Sweetings	"		❸❸❷
Brasserie Blanc	French		④❸④
The Royal Exchange	"		④❸❷
28-50	"		❸❷❸
Sushinho	Fusion		❷❸❸
Vivat Bacchus	International		④④④
Manicomio	Italian		❸④❸
Piccolino	"		④❸④
Refettorio	"		❸❸④
Taberna Etrusca	"		❸❷❸
Eyre Brothers	Spanish		❸❸❸
The Tramshed	Steaks & grills		④④❸
Vanilla Black	Vegetarian		❸❶❸
Kenza	Lebanese		④④❸
Chinese Cricket Club	Chinese		④④⑤
Cinnamon Kitchen	Indian		❷❷❸
Mint Leaf	"		❷❸❸
City Miyama	Japanese		❸④⑤

£40+			
Beard to Tail	American		④❸④
Bodean's	"		❸④❸
The Anthologist	British, Modern		❸❸❷
Princess of Shoreditch	"		❸④❸
Rivington Grill	"		④❸④
George & Vulture	British, Traditional		④❸❷
The Oyster Shed	"		④④❸
Loch Fyne	Fish & seafood		④❸④
Orpheus	"		❷❷④
Côte	French		④❸④
Browns	International		⑤④④
Rocket	Mediterranean		❸❸❸
Relais de Venise L'Entrecôte	Steaks & grills		❸④❸
Burger & Lobster	Burgers, etc		❷❸❸
Imperial City	Chinese		④④④
Kurumaya	Japanese		❸❸④
Mugen	"		❸❸④
Thai Square	Thai		④④④

£35+			
The Punch Tavern	British, Modern		④❸❷
Simpson's Tavern	British, Traditional		④❸❶
Tramontana Brindisa	Spanish		❸④❸
Byron	Burgers, etc		❸❸❸
Haché	"		❸❸❷

219

			Rating
	Natural Kitchen	*Salads*	③④③
	Haz	*Turkish*	④④③
	Bangalore Express	*Indian*	④④③
	K10	*Japanese*	②②④
	Wagamama	*"*	④③④
£30+	Café Below	*British, Modern*	④④③
	The Diner	*Burgers, etc*	④③②
	Caffé Vergnano	*Sandwiches, cakes, etc*	④③②
	ping pong	*Chinese, Dim sum*	④②③
	Taro	*Japanese*	③③③
£25+	Hilliard	*British, Modern*	②②③
	The Wine Library	*International*	⑤②⓪
	Konditor & Cook	*Sandwiches, cakes, etc*	③④④
	Leon	*"*	④③③
	Hare & Tortoise	*Pan-Asian*	③③③
£15+	Street Kitchen	*British, Modern*	②③ –
	Hummus Bros	*Mediterranean*	③③④
	Taylor St Baristas	*Sandwiches, cakes, etc*	②③③
	Chilango	*Mexican/TexMex*	②②③
	Tortilla	*"*	③③③
	Abokado	*Japanese*	④④④
	Jubo	*Korean*	– – –
£10+	Fuzzy's Grub	*Sandwiches, cakes, etc*	③④④
	Nusa Kitchen	*"*	②③④
	Pod	*"*	③③④
	Spianata & Co	*"*	③②③
	City Càphê	*Vietnamese*	①③⑤
£5+	Pilpel	*Middle Eastern*	②②④

East End & Docklands (All E postcodes)

			Rating
£100+	Viajante	*Fusion*	②③③
£70+	Galvin La Chapelle	*French*	②②⓪
	Les Trois Garçons	*"*	③⓪⓪
	Gaucho	*Steaks & grills*	③④④
	Roka	*Japanese*	①③③
£60+	Beach Blanket Babylon	*British, Modern*	⑤④③
	The Boundary	*"*	②②②
	Tom's Kitchen	*"*	④③③
	Boisdale of Canary Wharf	*Scottish*	④④③
	Goodman	*Steaks & grills*	②②③
	Hawksmoor	*"*	②②③
	Bevis Marks	*Kosher*	④④④
£50+	Bistrotheque	*British, Modern*	③③②
	The Gun	*"*	③③②

Hoi Polloi	"	- - -
One Canada Square	"	- - -
Smiths Brasserie	"	❷❸❷
Wapping Food	"	④④❶
Young Turk at the Ten Bells	"	❸❶❸
Bumpkin	British, Traditional	⑤⑤④
St John Bread & Wine	"	❶❸❸
Forman's	Fish & seafood	❷❸④
Wright Brothers	"	❷❸❷
Plateau	French	⑤④⑤
Buen Ayre	Argentinian	❶④④
Café Spice Namaste	Indian	❷❷❸
Dockmaster's House	"	❷❸④

£40+

All Star Lanes	American	④❸❸
Balans	British, Modern	⑤④④
The Empress	"	❷❸❷
The Morgan Arms	"	❸❸❷
The Narrow	"	⑤④④
Rochelle Canteen	"	❷❷❷
Whitechapel Gallery	"	❸❸❸
Albion	British, Traditional	④④❸
Canteen	"	⑤⑤⑤
The Grapes	Fish & seafood	④④❷
Brawn	French	❷❷❸
Browns	International	⑤④④
Giraffe	"	⑤⑤⑤
Il Bordello	Italian	❷❶❷
La Figa	"	❸❷④
Jamie's Italian	"	⑤⑤④
Obika	"	❸❸❸
Rocket	Mediterranean	❸❸❸
Corner Room	Portuguese	❶❷❸
Ibérica	Spanish	❸❸❸
Relais de Venise L'Entrecôte	Steaks & grills	❸④❸
Ark Fish	Fish & chips	❶❷④
Fire & Stone	Pizza	④④④
Pizza East	"	❷❸❶
Story Deli	"	❷④❷
Lotus	Chinese	④④❸
Royal China	"	❷④④
Sichuan Folk	"	❷❸⑤
Yi-Ban	"	❸❸④
Dishoom	Indian	❸❸❶
Elephant Royale	Thai	❸④❸

£35+

Bouchon Fourchette	French	❷❷❸
Real Greek	Greek	⑤④④
LMNT	International	④❸❶
Lardo	Italian	❸④❸
Byron	Burgers, etc	❸❸❸
Benugo	Sandwiches, cakes, etc	④④❷
Haz	Turkish	④④❸
My Old Place	Chinese	❷⑤④

Shanghai	"	❸❹❸
Little Georgia Café	Georgian	❸❹❸
Wagamama	Japanese	❹❸❹
Busaba Eathai	Thai	❸❸❷
Rosa's	"	❸❷❸
Pho	Vietnamese	❷❷❷
Viet Grill	"	❷❹❸
£30+		
Frizzante at City Farm	Italian	❷❹❹
Wahaca	Mexican/TexMex	❸❸❷
Yalla Yalla	Lebanese	❸❹❸
Hazev	Turkish	❹❸❸
Mangal I	"	❶❹❹
ping pong	Chinese, Dim sum	❹❷❸
Itsu	Japanese	❹❸❹
Green Papaya	Vietnamese	❷❸❹
Mien Tay	"	❷❹❹
Sông Quê	"	❸❺❹
Viet Hoa	"	❷❺❹
£25+		
Faulkner's	Fish & chips	❷❹❹
Leon	Sandwiches, cakes, etc	❹❸❸
Comptoir Libanais	Lebanese	❹❹❸
Gourmet San	Chinese	❷❺❺
Lahore Kebab House	Pakistani	❶❹❹
Needoo	"	❷❹❹
Tayyabs	"	❶❺❸
£20+		
Sager & WIlde	British, Modern	– – –
E Pellicci	Italian	❹❷❶
Franco Manca	Pizza	❷❸❸
Mirch Masala	Pakistani	❷❹❺
£15+		
Taylor St Baristas	Sandwiches, cakes, etc	❷❸❸
Chilango	Mexican/TexMex	❷❷❸
Tortilla	"	❸❸❸
£10+		
Spianata & Co	Sandwiches, cakes, etc	❸❷❸
£5+		
Brick Lane Beigel Bake	Sandwiches, cakes, etc	❶❷❹
Pilpel	Middle Eastern	❷❷❹

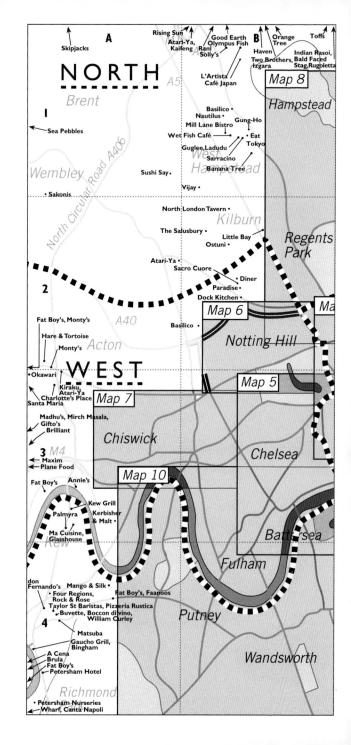

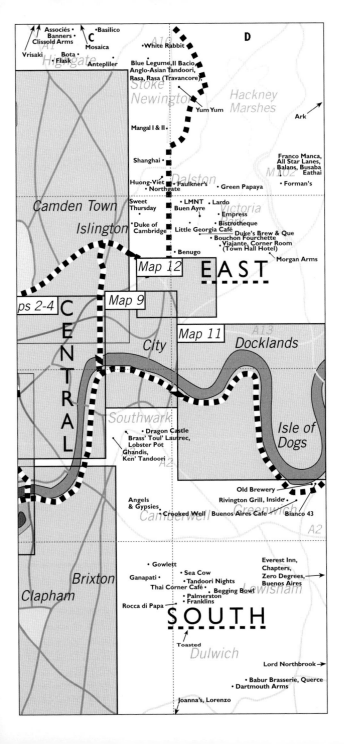

C

Associés •
Banners •
Clissold Arms •
Vrisaki •
Bota •
Flask •
Mosaica •
Antepliler •
•Basilico

Highgate

D

A10

•White Rabbit

Blue Legume, Il Bacio,
Anglo-Asian Tandoori,
Rasa, Rasa (Travancore),

*Stoke
Newington*

*Hackney
Marshes*

Yum Yum

Ark →

Mangal I & II •

Shanghai •

Dalston

Huong-Viet • Faulkner's
• Northgate

• Green Papaya

Franco Manca,
All Star Lanes,
Balans, Busaba
Eathai

M102

• Forman's

Camden Town

Islington

Sweet
Thursday

Duke of
Cambridge •

• LMNT
Buen Ayre

Little Georgia Café

• Lardo

Victoria

• Empress

• Bistrotheque

Duke's Brew & Que

• Bouchon Fourchette
• Viajante, Corner Room
(Town Hall Hotel)

Morgan Arms

• Benugo

Map 12

E A S T

ps 2-4

C

Map 9

E

City

Map 11

N
T
R
A
L

Southwark

Docklands

*Isle of
Dogs*

• Dragon Castle
Brass' Toul' Lautrec,
Lobster Pot
Ghandis,
Ken' Tandoori

A2

Old Brewery

Rivington Grill, Inside •

Angels
& Gypsies •

Camberwell

• Crooked Well

Buenos Aires Cafe

Bianco 43

A2

Greenwich

• Gowlett

Ganapati •

• Sea Cow

• Tandoori Nights
Thai Corner Café •

• Begging Bowl

• Palmerston
• Franklins

Rocca di Papa •

Everest Inn,
Chapters,
Zero Degrees,
Buenos Aires →

Lewisham

Brixton

Clapham

S O U T H

Toasted

Dulwich

Lord Northbrook →

• Babur Brasserie, Querce
• Dartmouth Arms

Joanna's, Lorenzo

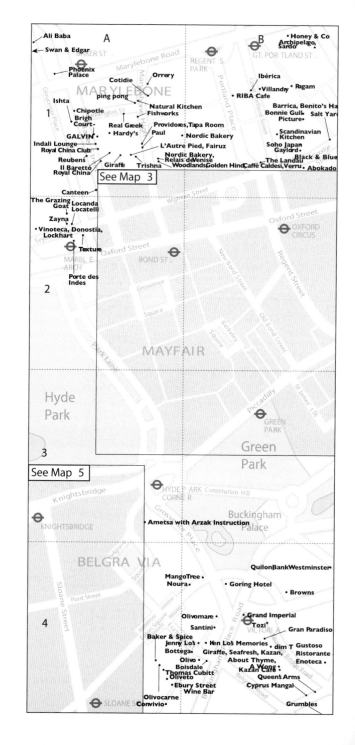

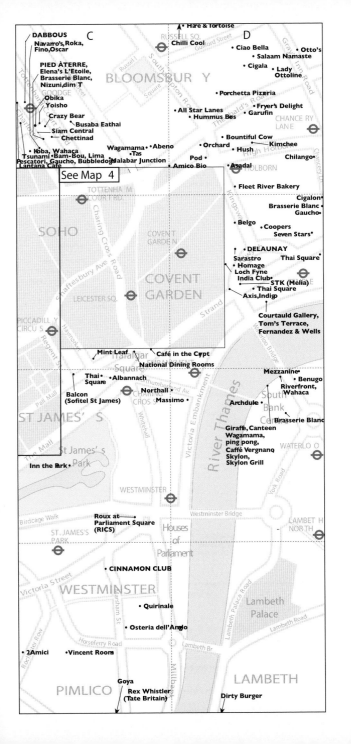

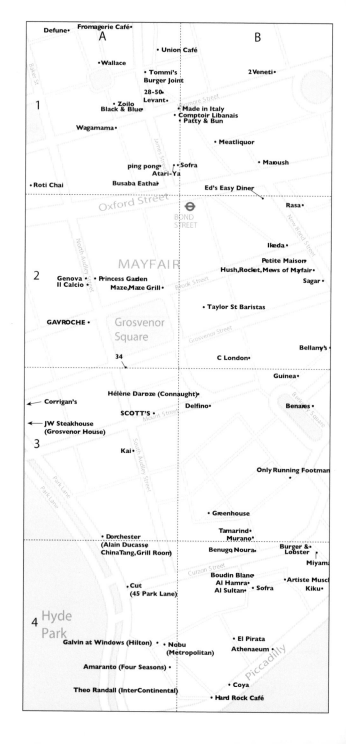

MAP **3** – MAYFAIR, ST. JAMES'S & WEST SOHO

Defune•   Fromagerie Café•
A
B

• Union Café

•Wallace
2 Veneti•

• Tommi's
Burger Joint

28-50•
Levant•
1   • Zoilo   • Made in Italy
Black & Blue   • Comptoir Libanais
• Patty & Bun

Wagamama•
• Meatliquor

ping pong•   •• Sofra   • Maoush
Atari-Ya
• Roti Chai   Busaba Eathai
Ed's Easy Diner

Oxford Street
Rasa•

BOND
STREET

Ikeda •

MAYFAIR   Petite Maison•
Hush, Rocket, Mews of Mayfair•
2   Genova • • Princess Garden
Il Calcio •   Maze, Maze Grill •   Sagar •

• Taylor St Baristas

GAVROCHE •   Grosvenor
Square
Bellany's •

34   C London•

Guinea•

Hélène Darroze (Connaught)•
• Corrigan's   Delfino•   Benares •
SCOTT'S •
• JW Steakhouse
(Grosvenor House)
3
Kai •

Only Running Footman
•

• Greenhouse

Tamarind•
• Dorchester   Murano•
(Alain Ducasse   Burger &
ChinaTang, Grill Room)   Benugo Noura•   Lobster
Miyam

Boudin Blanc
• Cut   Al Hamra•   •Artiste Musc
(45 Park Lane)   Al Sultan• • Sofra   Kiku•

4 Hyde
Park
Galvin at Windows (Hilton) • • Nobu   • El Pirata
(Metropolitan)   Athenaeum •

Amaranto (Four Seasons) •   Piccadilly

Theo Randall (InterContinental)   • Coya
• Hard Rock Café

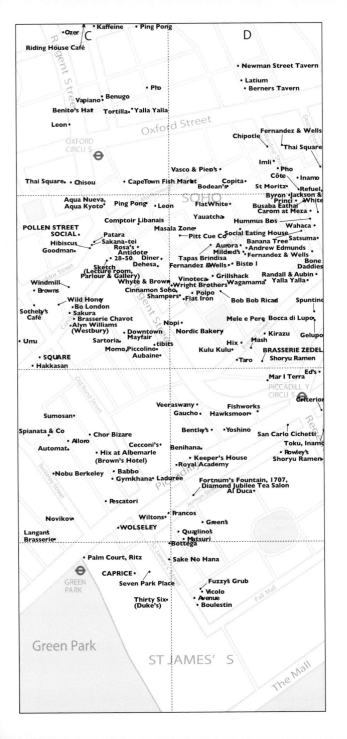

MAP 4 – EAST SOHO, CHINATOWN & COVENT GARDEN

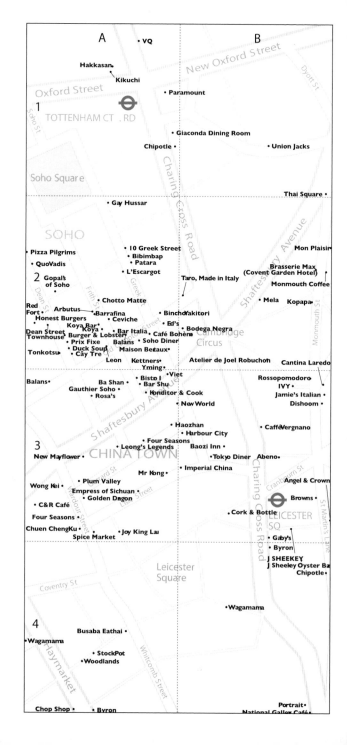

A · VQ

B

New Oxford Street

Dyott St

Hakkasan.
· Kikuchi

· Paramount

Oxford Street

1 TOTTENHAM CT . RD

Soho St

· Giaconda Dining Room

Chipotle · · Union Jacks

Soho Square

Charing Cross Road

Thai Square ·

Shaftesbury Avenue

· Gay Hussar

SOHO

· Pizza Pilgrims

· 10 Greek Street
· Bibimbap
· Patara

· QuoVadis

Mon Plaisir

2 Gopal's
of Soho

Dean St

· L'Escargot

Taro, Made in Italy

Brasserie Max
(Covent Garden Hotel) ·

Monmouth Coffee

Frith St

Greek Street

Red
Fort·

· Chotto Matte

· Mela   Kopapa·

Monmouth St

Arbutus
Honest Burgers

·Barrafina
· Ceviche

· Binchoyakitori

Koya Bar·
Dean Street   Koya
Townhouse Burger & Lobster
· Prix Fixe
· Duck Soup
Tonkotsu·   · Cây Tre

· Bar Italia · Café Bohème
Balans · Soho Diner
Maison Bertaux·

· Ed's
· Bodega Negra

Cambridge
Circus

Leon   Kettners·
Yming·

Atelier de Joel Robuchon   Cantina Laredo

Balans·

Ba Shan ·
Gauthier Soho ·
· Rosa's

· Bisto I ·Viet
· Bar Shu
· Konditor & Cook
· New World

Rossopomodoro·
IVY ·
Jamie's Italian ·
Dishoom ·

Shaftesbury Avenue

· Haozhan
· Harbour City

· Caffè Vergnano

3 New Mayflower ·

Wardour St

CHINATOWN

· Four Seasons
· Leong's Legends

Baozi Inn ·

·Tokyo Diner Abeno·

Charing Cross Road

Cranbourn St

Mr Kong ·

· Imperial China

Angel & Crown

Wong Kei ·

· Plum Valley
Empress of Sichuan ·
· Golden Dragon

· Browns ·

St Martin's Lane

· C&R Café

Wardour St

· Cork & Bottle LEICESTER

Four Seasons ·

SQ

Chuen ChengKu·
Spice Market

· Joy King Lau

· Gaby's

· Byron

J SHEEKEY
J Sheeley Oyster Bar
Chipotle·

Leicester
Square

Coventry St

·Wagamama

4   Busaba Eathai ·

·Wagamama

Haymarket

· StockPot
·Woodlands

Whitcomb Street

Chop Shop ·   · Byron

Portrait·
National Gallery Café·

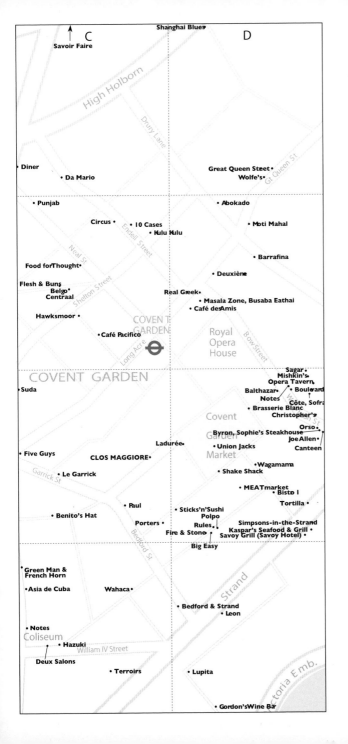

Shanghai Blues

C

D

↑ Savoir Faire

High Holborn

Drury Lane

Gt Queen St.

• Diner

• Da Mario

Great Queen Steet •
Wolfe's •

• Punjab

• Abokado

Circus •

• 10 Cases
• Kulu Kulu

• Moti Mahal

Endell Street

Neal St

• Barrafina

Food for Thought •

• Deuxième

Flesh & Buns
Belgo •
Centraal

Shelton Street

Shelton Street

Real Greek •

• Masala Zone, Busaba Eathai
• Café des Amis

Hawksmoor •

COVENT
GARDEN

Royal
Opera
House

• Café Pacifico

Long Acre

Bow Street

COVENT GARDEN

• Suda

Sagar •
Mishkin's
Opera Tavern
Balthazar •   • Boulevard
Notes
Côte, Sofra
• Brasserie Blanc
Christopher's

Covent

Byron, Sophie's Steakhouse
Ladurée •   • Union Jacks

Orso •
Joe Allen •

• Five Guys

CLOS MAGGIORE •

Garden
Market

Canteen

Garrick St

• Le Garrick

• Wagamama
• Shake Shack

• MEATmarket
• Bistro 1
Tortilla •

• Paul

• Benito's Hat

Porters •

Bedford St

• Sticks'n'Sushi
Polpo
Rules •
Fire & Stone •

Simpsons-in-the-Strand
Kaspar's Seafood & Grill •
Savoy Grill (Savoy Hotel) •

Big Easy

• Green Man &
French Horn

• Asia de Cuba

Wahaca •

Strand

• Bedford & Strand
• Leon

• Notes

Coliseum

• Hazuki

William IV Street

Deux Salons

• Terroirs

• Lupita

Victoria Emb.

• Gordon's Wine Bar

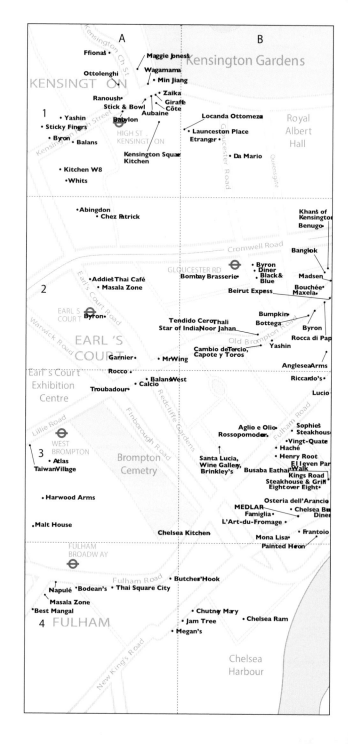

A

B

Kensington Gardens

Ffionas •

Maggie Jones •
Wagamama •
• Min Jiang

Ottolenghi •

KENSINGTON

Ranoush •
• Zaika
• Girafe
Stick & Bowl
• Côte
Aubaine

1
• Yashin
• Sticky Fingers
Babylon
Locanda Ottomezzo
• Byron
• Launceston Place
HIGH ST
• Balans
KENSINGTON
Etranger •

Royal
Albert
Hall

• Da Mario
Kensington Square
Kitchen

• Kitchen W8
•Whits

•Abingdon
• Chez Patrick

Khans of
Kensington
Benugo•

Cromwell Road

Banglok

GLOUCESTER RD
• Byron
• Diner
Bombay Brasserie•
• Black &
Blue

Madsen

•Addies Thai Café
• Masala Zone

2

Beirut Express

Bouchée•
Maxela•

EARL S
COURT
Byron•

Bumpkin•
Bottega

Tendido Cero
Thali
Star of India
Noor Jahan

Byron

EARL'S
COURT

Old Brompton
Yashin •
Rocca di Pap

Cambio deTercio,
Capote y Toros

• Garnier •
• MrWing
AngleseaArms

Rocco •

Earl's Court
Exhibition
Centre
Troubadour•
• Balans West
• Calcio

Riccardo's•

Lucio

Lillie Road
WEST
BROMPTON

Aglio e Olio•
Rossopomodor•

Sophies
• Steakhouse

3
• Atlas
TaiwanVillage

Brompton
Cemetery

•Vingt-Quatr
• Haché
• Henry Root
Santa Lucia,
Wine Gallery,
Brinkley's
Busaba Eathai
Eleven Par
Walk
Kings Road
Steakhouse & Grill
Eight over Eight•

• Harwood Arms

Osteria dell'Arancio

MEDLAR
• Chelsea Bu
Famiglia•
Diner
L'Art-du-Fromage •

•Malt House

Chelsea Kitchen
• Frantoio
Mona Lisa•
Painted Heron

FULHAM
BROADWAY

Fulham Road
• Butchers Hook

Napulé •Bodean's
• Thai Square City

Masala Zone
•Best Mangal

4 FULHAM

• Chutney Mary
• Jam Tree
• Megan's

• Chelsea Ram

Chelsea
Harbour

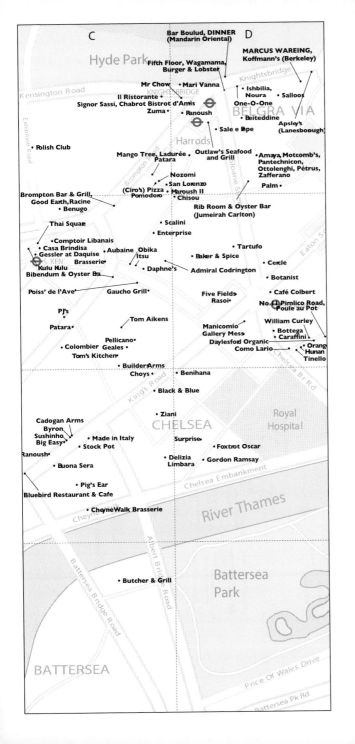

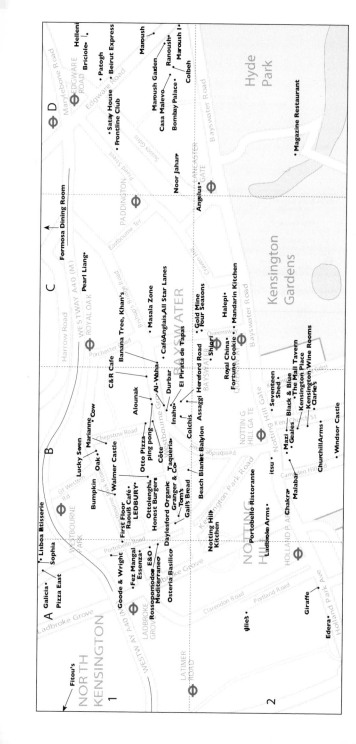

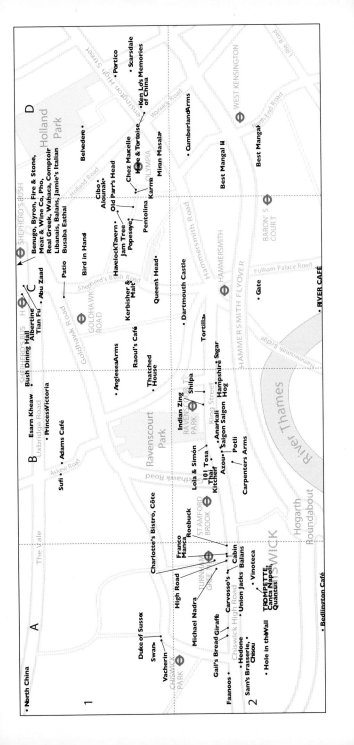

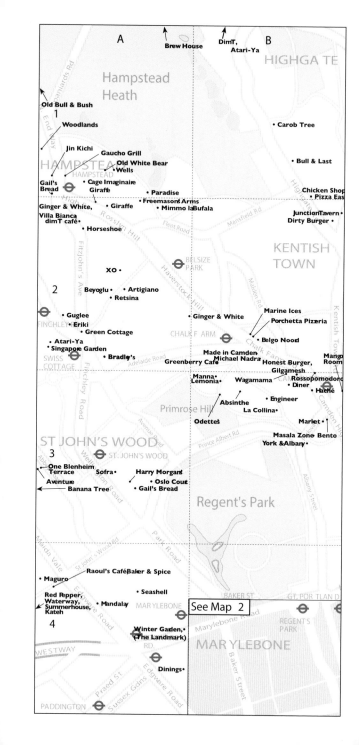

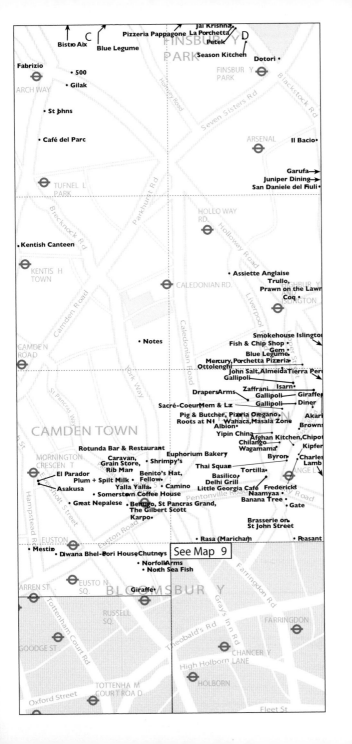

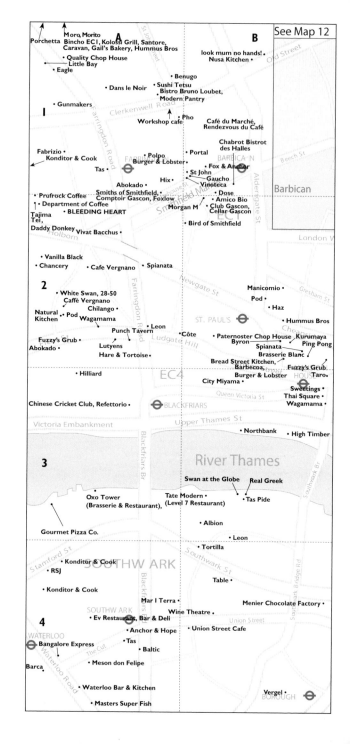

MAP **9** – THE CITY

See Map 12

A

B

Porchetta
Moro, Morito
Bincho EC1, Kolossi Grill, Santore,
Caravan, Gail's Bakery, Hummus Bros
Quality Chop House
Little Bay
Eagle

look mum no hands!
Nusa Kitchen

Benugo

Dans le Noir
Sushi Tetsu
Bistro Bruno Loubet,
Modern Pantry

Gunmakers

Pho

Café du Marché,
Rendezvous du Café

Workshop cafe

1

Clerkenwell Road

St John St

Old Street

Beech St

Chabrot Bistrot
des Halles

Fabrizio
Konditor & Cook

Polpo
Burger & Lobster

Portal

Tas

Abokado

Hix

St John
Fox & Anchor
Gaucho
Vinoteca

Prufrock Coffee
Department of Coffee
Tajima
Tei,
Daddy Donkey

Smiths of Smithfield,
Comptoir Gascon, Foxlow

Dose
Amico Bio
Club Gascon,
Cellar Gascon

BLEEDING HEART

Morgan M

Vivat Bacchus

Bird of Smithfield

Aldersgate St

Barbican

London W

Holborn

Vanilla Black
Chancery

Cafe Vergnano

Spianata

Newgate St

Gresham St

2

White Swan, 28-50
Caffè Vergnano
Chilango
Pod
Wagamama

Manicomio
Pod
Haz

Natural
Kitchen

ST. PAUL'S

Hummus Bros

Leon
Punch Tavern

Côte

Paternoster Chop House
Byron

Kurumaya
Ping Pong

Fuzzy's Grub
Abokado

Lutyens
Hare & Tortoise

Ludgate Hill

Spianata
Brasserie Blanc

Bread Street Kitchen,
Barbecoa,

Fuzzy's Grub
Taro.

Hilliard

EC4

City Miyama

Burger & Lobster

Sweetings
Thai Square
Wagamama

Chinese Cricket Club, Refettorio

BLACKFRIARS

Queen Victoria St

Victoria Embankment

Upper Thames St

Northbank

High Timber

Blackfriars Br

River Thames

Southwark Br

3

Swan at the Globe

Real Greek

Oxo Tower
(Brasserie & Restaurant),

Tate Modern
(Level 7 Restaurant)

Tas Pide

Gourmet Pizza Co.

Albion

Leon

Tortilla

Stamford St

Konditor & Cook
RSJ

SOUTHWARK

Southwark St

Konditor & Cook

Table

Mar I Terra

Menier Chocolate Factory

Southwark Bridge Rd

SOUTHWARK

Wine Theatre

4

Ev Restaurant, Bar & Deli

WATERLOO

Bangalore Express

Anchor & Hope
Tas

Union Street Cafe

Union Street

Barca

Baltic

Meson don Felipe

Waterloo Bar & Kitchen

Vergel

BOROUGH

Masters Super Fish

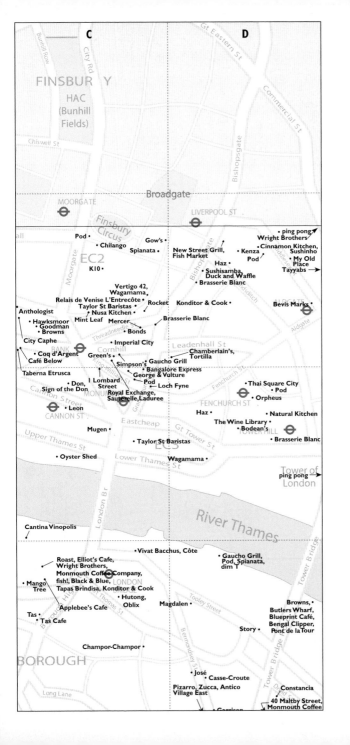

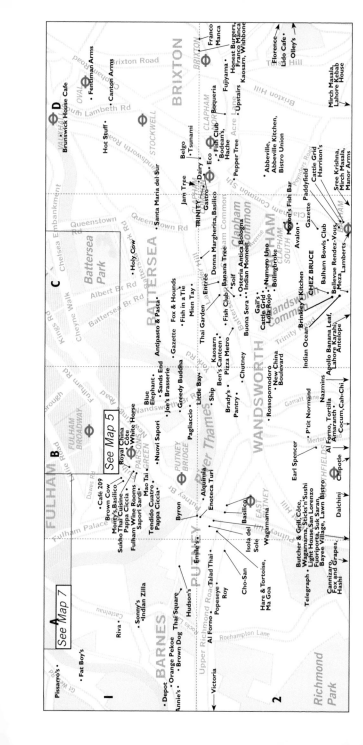

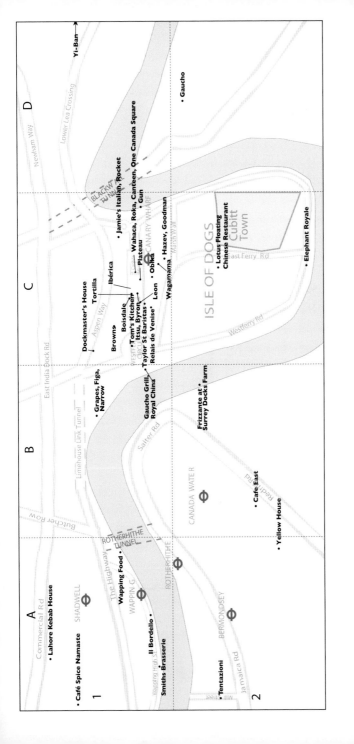

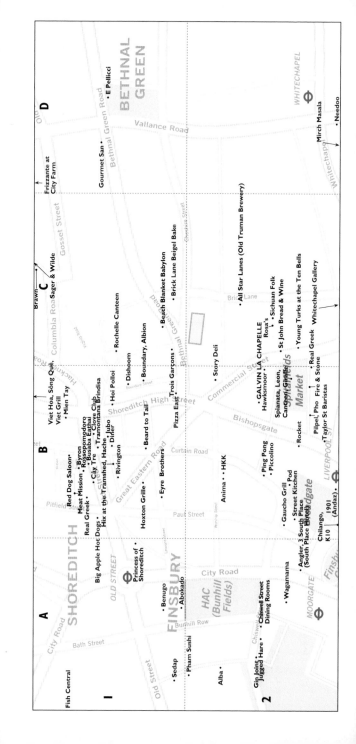

PLACES PEOPLE TALK ABOUT

These are the restaurants outside London that were mentioned most frequently by reporters (last year's position is shown in brackets). For the list of London's most mentioned restaurants, see page 16.

1 **Manoir aux Quat' Saisons** (1)
   Great Milton, Oxon
2 **Fat Duck** (2)
   Bray, Berks
3 **Waterside Inn** (3)
   Bray, Berks
4 **Hand & Flowers** (4)
   Marlow, Bucks
5 **L'Enclume** (9)
   Cartmel, Cumbriax

Manoir aux Quat' Saisons

6 **Seafood Restaurant** (5)
   Padstow, Cornwall
7 **Sportsman** (13)
   Whitstable, Kent
8 **Hind's Head** (6)
   Bray, Berks
9 **Chapter One** (8)
   Locksbottom, Kent
10 **Northcote** (7)
   Langho, Lancs

Waterside Inn

11 **Gidleigh Park** (10)
   Chagford, Devon
12 **Midsummer House** (-)
   Cambridge, Cambs
13= **Restaurant Sat Bains** (-)
   Nottingham, Notts
13= **Great House** (-)
   Lavenham, Suffolk
15 **The Kitchin** (11)
   Edinburgh

Seafood Restaurant

16 **Vineyard at Stockcross** (20)
   Stockcross, Berks
17 **Rocksalt** (-)
   Folkestone, Kent
18 **Artichoke** (-)
   Amersham, Bucks
19 **Walnut Tree** (-)
   Llandewi Skirrid, Monmouthshire
20 **Restaurant Nathan Outlaw** (-)
   Rock, Cornwall

Northcote

TOP SCORERS

All restaurants whose food rating is ❶; plus restaurants whose price is £50+ with a food rating of ❷.

£230+	The Fat Duck *(Bray)*	❶❷④
£200+	Waterside Inn *(Bray)*	❶❶❷
£170+	Le Manoir aux Quat' Saisons *(Great Milton)*	❶❶❷
£130+	Andrew Fairlie *(Auchterarder)*	❶❶❷
	Gidleigh Park *(Chagford)*	❶❶❷
	Midsummer House *(Cambridge)*	❶❶❷
£120+	Restaurant Nathan Outlaw *(Rock)*	❶❶❷
£110+	L'Enclume *(Cartmel)*	❶❷❸
£100+	Restaurant Sat Bains *(Nottingham)*	❶❶❸
	Lucknam Park *(Colerne)*	❷❶❷
	The Latymer *(Bagshot)*	❷❶❷
	Winteringham Fields *(Winteringham)*	❷❸❷
	Dining Room *(Easton Gray)*	❷❷④
£90+	Restaurant Martin Wishart *(Edinburgh)*	❶❶❷
	Number One *(Edinburgh)*	❶❶❸
	Casamia *(Bristol)*	❶❷❸
	Boath House Hotel *(Nairn)*	❷❶❶
	Holbeck Ghyll *(Windermere)*	❷❷❶
	Lords of the Manor *(Upper Slaughter)*	❷❷❶
	Amberley Castle *(Amberley)*	❷❸❶
	Simon Radley *(Chester)*	❷❶❷
	Kinloch Lodge *(Sleat)*	❷❷❷
	Martin Wishart *(Loch Lomond)*	❷❷❷
	21212 *(Edinburgh)*	❷❷❸
	Paris House *(Woburn)*	❷❷❸
	The Dower House *(Bath)*	❷❷❸
	Adam Simmonds *(Marlow)*	❷④❸
£80+	The Albannach *(Lochinver)*	❶❷❶
	The Three Chimneys *(Dunvegan)*	❶❷❶
	Bohemia *(Jersey)*	❶❶❷
	Fraiche *(Oxton)*	❶❶❷
	Mr Underhill's *(Ludlow)*	❶❶❷
	Seafood Restaurant *(Padstow)*	❶❶❷
	Simpsons *(Birmingham)*	❶❶❷
	The Kitchin *(Edinburgh)*	❶❶❷

	Yorke Arms *(Ramsgill-in-Nidderdale)*	❶❶❷
	Hambleton Hall *(Hambleton)*	❶❷❷
	Harry's Place *(Great Gonerby)*	❶❶❸
	Read's *(Faversham)*	❶❷❸
	Drakes *(Ripley)*	❶❶④
	Bybrook Restaurant *(Castle Combe)*	❶❷④
	Burgh Island Hotel *(Bigbury-on-Sea)*	❷❶❶
	The French Horn *(Sonning-on-Thames)*	❷❶❶
	Ocean Restaurant *(Jersey)*	❷❶❷
	Gilpin Lodge *(Windermere)*	❷❷❷
	Strathearn Restaurant *(Auchterarder)*	❷❷❷
	The Hambrough *(Ventnor)*	❷❷❷
	The Pompadour by Galvin *(Edinburgh)*	❷❷❷
	Mallory Court *(Bishops Tachbrook)*	❷❸❷
	Morston Hall *(Morston)*	❷❸❷
	Fischers at Baslow Hall *(Baslow)*	❷❷❸
	The Pass Restaurant *(Horsham)*	❷❷❸
£70+	Cotto *(Cambridge)*	❶❶❷
	Northcote *(Langho)*	❶❶❷
	The Castle Terrace *(Edinburgh)*	❶❶❷
	The Harrow at Little Bedwyn *(Marlborough)*	❶❶❷
	The Peacock *(Rowsley)*	❶❶❷
	Driftwood Hotel *(Rosevine)*	❶❷❷
	Raby Hunt *(Summerhouses)*	❶❷❷
	Tyddyn Llan *(Llandrillo)*	❶❷❷
	Monachyle Mhor *(Balquhidder)*	❶④❷
	Purnells *(Birmingham)*	❶❶❸
	The French Restaurant *(Manchester)*	❶❶❸
	Airds Hotel *(Port Appin)*	❶❷❸
	Black Swan *(Oldstead)*	❶❷❸
	Le Champignon Sauvage *(Cheltenham)*	❶❷④
	Gravetye Manor *(East Grinstead)*	❷❶❶
	The Oak Room *(Egham)*	❷❶❶
	Bailiffscourt Hotel *(Climping)*	❷❷❶
	Combe House *(Honiton)*	❷❷❶
	Ormer *(Jersey)*	❷❶❷
	The Dining Room *(Ashbourne)*	❷❶❷
	Aubergine *(Marlow)*	❷❷❷
	Hipping Hall *(Kirkby Lonsdale)*	❷❷❷
	Michael Caines *(Chester)*	❷❷❷
	Samuel's *(Masham)*	❷❷❷
	Elephant Restaurant & Brasserie *(Torquay)*	❷❷❸
	Lasan *(Birmingham)*	❷❷❸
	The Box Tree *(Ilkley)*	❷❷❸

Gaucho *(Manchester)*		❷❹❸
Van Zeller *(Harrogate)*		❷❷❹
Hand & Flowers *(Marlow)*		❷❸❹
JSW *(Petersfield)*		❷❸❹
Alimentum *(Cambridge)*		❷❸⑤
£60+	Artichoke *(Amersham)*	❶❶❷
	Braidwoods *(Dalry)*	❶❶❷
	Caldesi in Campagna *(Bray)*	❶❶❷
	Little Barwick House *(Barwick)*	❶❶❷
	The Neptune *(Old Hunstanton)*	❶❶❷
	The Peat Inn *(Cupar)*	❶❶❷
	Checkers *(Montgomery)*	❶❷❷
	Paul Ainsworth at Number 6 *(Padstow)*	❶❷❷
	Tanners Restaurant *(Plymouth)*	❶❷❷
	The Old Inn *(Drewsteignton)*	❶❷❷
	The Royal Hotel *(Ventnor)*	❶❷❷
	The Star Inn *(Harome)*	❶❷❷
	Loves *(Birmingham)*	❶❶❸
	Menu Gordon Jones *(Bath)*	❶❶❸
	Ramsons *(Ramsbottom)*	❶❶❸
	5 North Street *(Winchcombe)*	❶❷❸
	Gamba *(Glasgow)*	❶❷❸
	Lavender House *(Brundall)*	❶❷❸
	The Vanilla Pod *(Marlow)*	❶❷❸
	The West House *(Biddenden)*	❶❷❸
	Sienna *(Dorchester)*	❶❶④
	Lumière *(Cheltenham)*	❶❷④
	Hotel Tresanton *(St Mawes)*	❷❶❶
	Bodysgallen Hall *(Llandudno)*	❷❷❶
	Craig Millar @ 16 West End *(St Monans)*	❷❷❶
	Hassop Hall *(Hassop)*	❷❷❶
	Plas Bodegroes *(Pwllheli)*	❷❷❶
	Silver Darling *(Aberdeen)*	❷❷❶
	The Kings Head *(Leighton Buzzard)*	❷❷❶
	The Merchant Hotel *(Belfast)*	❷❷❶
	Ubiquitous Chip *(Glasgow)*	❷❷❶
	Bluebells *(Sunningdale)*	❷❶❷
	Marcliffe Hotel *(Aberdeen)*	❷❶❷
	Brockencote Hall *(Chaddesley Corbett)*	❷❷❷
	Café 21 *(Newcastle upon Tyne)*	❷❷❷
	Calcot Manor *(Tetbury)*	❷❷❷
	Castellamare *(Swansea)*	❷❷❷
	La Parmigiana *(Glasgow)*	❷❷❷
	Rogano *(Glasgow)*	❷❷❷

TOP SCORERS

The Dysart Arms (Richmond)	❷❷❷
The Feathered Nest Inn (Nether Westcote)	❷❷❷
The Mirabelle (Eastbourne)	❷❷❷
The Restaurant at Drakes (Brighton)	❷❷❷
Berwick Lodge (Bristol)	❷❸❷
Crab & Lobster (Asenby)	❷❸❷
The Hind's Head (Bray)	❷❸❷
Seafood Restaurant (St Andrews)	❷④❷
Aumbry (Manchester)	❷⓿❸
Kinloch House (Blairgowrie)	❷⓿❸
The Alderley (Alderley Edge)	❷⓿❸
Jesses Bistro (Cirencester)	❷❷❸
Restaurant 23 (Leamington Spa)	❷❷❸
Roger Hickman's (Norwich)	❷❷❸
The Cross (Kingussie)	❷❷❸
The Old Plow (Speen)	❷❷❸
The Three Lions (Stuckton)	❷❷❸
The Walnut Tree (Llandewi Skirrid)	❷❷❸
The Marquis (Alkham)	❷❸❸
The Seahorse (Dartmouth)	❷❸❸
Michael Caines (Manchester)	❷❷④
The Olive Tree (Bath)	❷❸④

£50+	The Pipe & Glass Inn (Beverley)	⓿❷⓿
	Chapter One (Locksbottom)	⓿⓿❷
	Great House (Lavenham)	⓿⓿❷
	Hart's (Nottingham)	⓿⓿❷
	Maison Bleue (Bury St Edmunds)	⓿⓿❷
	Queans Restaurant (Leamington Spa)	⓿⓿❷
	The Butcher's Arms (Eldersfield)	⓿⓿❷
	The Creel (Orkney Islands)	⓿⓿❷
	The Crooked Billet (Stoke Row)	⓿⓿❷
	Alfresco (St Ives)	⓿❷❷
	Chez Roux (Inverness)	⓿❷❷
	Crabshakk (Glasgow)	⓿❷❷
	Freemasons at Wiswell (Wiswell)	⓿❷❷
	Mithas (Edinburgh)	⓿❷❷
	Restaurant Tristan (Horsham)	⓿❷❷
	The Oyster Shack (Bigbury-on-Sea)	⓿❷❷
	The Pig (Brockenhurst)	⓿❷❷
	The Q Restaurant (Fowey)	⓿❷❷
	The Wellington Arms (Baughurst)	⓿❷❷
	The Mason's Arms (Knowstone)	⓿❸❷
	Bosquet (Kenilworth)	⓿⓿❸
	Gingerman (Brighton)	⓿⓿❸

TOP SCORERS

	Tailors (Warwick)	❸❸❸
	Terravina (Woodlands)	❸❸❸
	The Nut Tree Inn (Murcott)	❸❸❸
	The Old Passage Inn (Arlingham)	❸❸❸
	Wedgwood (Edinburgh)	❸❸❸
	Wilks (Bristol)	❸❸❸
	Bilash (Wolverhampton)	❸❷❸
	Dining Room (Rock)	❸❷❸
	The Honours (Edinburgh)	❸❷❸
	Terre à Terre (Brighton)	❸❷④
	The French Table (Surbiton)	❸❷④
	The Sir Charles Napier (Chinnor)	❷❷❶
	Timberyard (Edinburgh)	❷❷❶
	Carters (Birmingham)	❷❷❷
	Chez Roux (Gullane)	❷❷❷
	Estbek House (Sandsend)	❷❷❷
	The Jetty (Christchurch)	❷❷❷
	The Pheasant Hotel (Harome)	❷❷❷
	The Wensleydale Heifer (West Witton)	❷❷❷
	Two Fat Ladies at The Buttery (Glasgow)	❷❷❷
	Alec's (Brentwood)	❷❸❷
	Ondine (Edinburgh)	❷❸❷
	The Crab at Chieveley (Newbury)	❷❸❷
	Ode (Shaldon)	❷❶❸
	Damson (Salford)	❷❷❸
	Greyhound (Stockbridge)	❷❷❸
	Restaurant 27 (Portsmouth)	❷❷❸
	The Curlew (Bodiam)	❷❷❸
	The Oystercatcher (Portmahomack)	❷❷❸
	Wesley House (Winchcombe)	❷❷❸
	63 Tay Street (Perth)	❷❸❸
	Chino Latino (Nottingham)	❷❸❸
	La Chouette (Dinton)	❷❸❸
	Lucknam Park (Brasserie) (Colerne)	❷❸❸
	Orwells (Shiplake)	❷❸❸
	Sebastian's (Oswestry)	❷❸❸
	The Black Rat (Winchester)	❷❸❸
	Rogan & Co (Cartmel)	❷④❸
	Apicius (Cranbrook)	❷❷④
	Goodfellows (Wells)	❷❸④
£40+	Ethicurean (Wrington)	❶❷❶
	Gurnards Head (Treen)	❶❷❶
	Seafood Temple (Oban)	❶❷❶
	Stravaigin (Glasgow)	❶❷❶

Wheelers Oyster Bar *(Whitstable)*	❶❷❶
Adam's *(Birmingham)*	❶❶❷
Austells *(St Austell)*	❶❶❷
Prithvi *(Cheltenham)*	❶❶❷
Retro *(Teddington)*	❶❶❷
Stagg Inn *(Titley)*	❶❶❷
The Sportsman *(Whitstable)*	❶❶❷
The Timble Inn *(Timble)*	❶❶❷
Yalbury Cottage *(Lower Bockhampton, Dorchester)*	❶❶❷
Café Fish *(Tobermory, Isle of Mull)*	❶❷❷
Cail Bruich *(Glasgow)*	❶❷❷
El Gato Negro Tapas *(Ripponden)*	❶❷❷
Gardener's Cottage *(Edinburgh)*	❶❷❷
Loch Fyne Oyster Bar *(Clachan)*	❶❷❷
Margot's *(Padstow)*	❶❷❷
Primrose Café *(Bristol)*	❶❷❷
The Grassington House Hotel *(Grassington)*	❶❷❷
The Parkers Arms *(Newton-in-Bowland)*	❶❷❷
Mourne Seafood Bar *(Belfast)*	❶❸❷
Fat Olives *(Emsworth)*	❶❶❸
Anokaa *(Salisbury)*	❶❷❸
Anoki *(Derby)*	❶❷❸
Les Mirabelles *(Nomansland)*	❶❷❸
Maliks *(Cookham)*	❶❷❸
Mint and Mustard *(Cardiff)*	❶❷❸
Purple Poppadom *(Cardiff)*	❶❷❸
Riverford Field Kitchen *(Buckfastleigh)*	❶❷❸
Rose Garden *(Manchester)*	❶❷❸
Scran & Scallie *(Edinburgh)*	❶❷❸
The Ambrette *(Margate)*	❶❷❸
The Apron Stage *(Stanley)*	❶❷❸
The Wild Mushroom *(Westfield)*	❶❷❸
Vujon *(Newcastle upon Tyne)*	❶❷❸
Wild Thyme *(Chipping Norton)*	❶❷❸
Albert's Table *(Croydon)*	❶❸❸
The Chilli Pickle *(Brighton)*	❶❸❸
Le Langhe *(York)*	❶④❸
Sojo *(Oxford)*	❶❶④
Magpie Café *(Whitby)*	❶❷④
Sutor Creek *(Cromarty)*	❶❷④
Yang Sing *(Manchester)*	❶❷④
The Feathers Inn *(Hedley On The Hill)*	❶❸④
The Ambrette at Rye *(Rye)*	❶④④
Maliks *(Gerrards Cross)*	❶⑤④

TOP SCORERS

Ethicurean

Bar 44

The White Horse

ABERAERON, CEREDIGION   4–3C

Harbourmaster   **£ 47** ❹❹❸
Quay Pde SA46 0BT   (01545) 570755
*"A fantastic location overlooking the harbour"
underpins the popularity of this "busy and fun"
seafront restaurant-with-rooms; it's inspired some
"erratic" reports of late, however, on both the food
and service fronts.
/ Details: www.harbour-master.com; @hmaberaeron;
9 pm; no Amex.* **Accommodation:** *13 rooms,
from £110.*

The Hive On The Quay   **£ 43** ❶
Cadwgan Pl SA46 0BU   (01545) 570445
*A "lively, bustling little place", on the water, tipped
for its "good seafood" ("sometimes Cardigan Bay
lobster"); "delicious honey ice cream" too!
/ Details: www.thehiveaberaeron.com; 9 pm; closed
Mon & Sun D; no Amex.*

ABERDEEN, ABERDEENSHIRE   9–2D

Marcliffe Hotel   **£ 63** ❷❶❷
North Deeside Rd AB15 9YA   (01224) 861000
*"Quality food in 5-star surroundings" – to dine at
this grand Victorian house, just outside the city, is to
enjoy a "very upmarket" experience which, all
reporters agree, is realised to a very high and
consistent level. / Details: www.marcliffe.com;
8.30pm.*

Silver Darling   **£ 64** ❷❷❶
Pocra Quay, North Pier AB11 5DQ
(01224) 576229
*"The best view ever over the water" (from the
former harbour control building) rewards visitors to
this accomplished all-rounder, where fish is the
speciality; all the oil money, though, pushes prices to
"London levels". / Details: www.thesilverdarling.co.uk;
9 pm; closed Sat L & Sun; children: +16 after 8 pm.*

ABERGAVENNY, MONMOUTHSHIRE   2–1A

The Angel Hotel   **£ 49** ❶
15 Cross St NP7 5EN   (01873) 857121
*Afternoon tea is often tipped as the highlight of
reporters' visits to this "delightful" (but often "busy")
former coaching inn, and breakfast is "very good
value" too… as are lunch and dinner for that
matter. / Details: www.angelhotelabergavenny.com;
@lovetheangel; 10 pm.* **Accommodation:** *35 rooms,
from £101.*

The Hardwick   **£ 59** ❸❹❹
Old Raglan Rd NP7 9AA   (01873) 854220
*Fans of Stephen Terry's renowned gastropub (with
rooms) laud the "fine ingredients, beautifully
cooked" as befitting his "classical culinary training";
it is now "quite expensive though", and there are a
growing number of reports of "average meals,
poorly served". / Details: www.thehardwick.co.uk;*

10 pm, Sun 9 pm; no Amex. **Accommodation:** *8
rooms, from £150.*

ABERSOCH, GWYNEDD   4–2B

Venetia   **£ 38** ❷❷❸
Lon Sarn Beach LL53 7EB   (01758) 713354
*A good find in this popular seaside village – a "lively
and modern" dining room inside a boutique-ified
Victorian villa; chef Marco "knows his fish" and
results can be outstanding.
/ Details: www.venetiawales.com.*
Accommodation: *5 rooms, from £80.*

ABERYSTWYTH, POWYS   4–3C

Gwesty Cymru   **£ 43** ❶
19 Marine Ter SY23 2AZ   (01970) 612252
*"An oasis in a vast desert", this seafront hotel is
tipped for its use of "fresh local produce"; the dining
room is "too small", so on summer nights it's best to
"eat in the garden, and watch the sun go down".
/ Details: www.gwestycymru.com; @gwestyc; 9 pm;
closed Tue L; no Amex; children: 5+.*
Accommodation: *8 rooms, from £85.*

Ultracomida   **£ 31** ❶
31 Pier St SY23 2LN   (01970) 630686
*"Behind a (great) Spanish delicatessen lurks this
wonderful tapas bar", with "sociable" (communal
table) dining, particularly tipped as a lunchtime
destination; "super wines" and "reasonable prices"
too. / Details: www.ultracomida.com; 9 pm;
Mon-Thu & Sat L only, Fri open L & D, closed Sun.*

ACHILTIBUIE, ROSSSHIRE   9–1B

Summer Isles Hotel   **£ 75** ❸❹❷
IV26 2YG   (01854) 622282
*Rather up-and-down reports in recent years on this
remote and "stunningly located" hotel (overlooking
the islands it's named for); most praise the "variety
and quality" of the food, but more than one regular
feels that, of late, it has been somewhat "riding on
the coat tails of its former reputation".
/ Details: www.summerisleshotel.com;
@SummerIslesHot; 25m N of Ullapool on A835; 8 pm;
Closed from 1st Nov - 1st Apr; no Amex; no jeans;
children: 8+.* **Accommodation:** *13 rooms, from £155.*

ADDINGHAM, WEST YORKSHIRE   5–1C

Fleece   **£ 41** ❷❸❹
152-4 Main St LS29 0LY   (01943) 830491
*A "very busy" inn, which "goes from strength to
strength" – "highly recommended" for its "delicious
pub food" and "fantastic views".
/ Details: www.fleeceinnaddingham.co.uk; 9.15 pm,
Sun 8pm; no Amex.*

ALBOURNE, WEST SUSSEX	3–4B

The Ginger Fox £ 46 ❷❷❸
Muddleswood Road BN6 9EA
(01273) 857 888
"A gem of a restaurant in rural Sussex"; this
"understated" outpost of Brighton's Gingerman
group is "well worth the ride out" from the city
thanks to some "good gastropub grub"; "best on a
weekday, when it is more of a gastronomic
experience".
/ **Details:** www.gingermanrestaurants.com;
@gingerfox; 10 pm, Sun 9 pm.

ALDEBURGH, SUFFOLK	3–1D

**Aldeburgh Fish And
Chips** £ 15 ❶❷④
225 High St IP15 5DB (01728) 454685
"The tastiest of fish 'n' chips", served by a "great
team" at "excellent" prices, make it "worth the wait
in the queue" at this seaside chippy – "the tangy
sea smell just completes the experience!"
/ **Details:** 8 pm; no credit cards.

The Lighthouse £ 42 ❸❷❸
77 High St IP15 5AU (01728) 453377
Considered by many the "best restaurant in
Alderburgh" (and certainly the most popular) – this
"charming" staple "continues to deliver year after
year" with its "fun" style, "hospitable" host and
"reliable" cooking; on the downside, it can get "a bit
overcrowded".
/ **Details:** www.lighthouserestaurant.co.uk; 10 pm.

Regatta £ 42 ❸❷④
171-173 High St IP15 5AN (01728) 452011
"Fish is always spanking fresh and carefully cooked"
at this popular spot; its approach, though, strikes
some reporters as "too safe", leading to a feeling
that the cooking "doesn't quite live up to the chef's
outstanding credentials".
/ **Details:** www.regattaaldeburgh.com; @AldeburghR;
10 pm.

The Wentworth Hotel £ 40 ④❸❸
Wentworth Rd IP15 5BD (01728) 452312
This "lovely, old-fashioned family-run hotel" is "solid
rather than exciting" when it comes to food, but it's
"comfortable", "sensibly priced" and the kind of
place that's perfect for a "first-class Sunday lunch".
/ **Details:** www.wentworth-aldeburgh.com; 9 pm;
no jeans or trainers. **Accommodation:** 35 rooms,
from £170.

ALDERLEY EDGE, CHESHIRE	5–2B

**The Alderley
Alderley Edge Hotel** £ 62 ❷❶❸
Macclesfield Rd SK9 7BJ (01625) 583033
Deep in the 'Footballer Belt', a "comfortable" and
"very professional" hotel dining room where Chris
Holland's cooking (including a 5-course tasting
menu) is "very impressive".
/ **Details:** www.alderleyedgehotel.com; @AlderleyHotel;
9.45 pm; closed Sun D.

ALDFORD, CHESHIRE	5–3A

The Grosvenor Arms £ 39 ❸❸❶
Chester Rd CH3 6HJ (01244) 620228
"Best of the Brunning & Price outlets"; this grand
ducal estate village inn is an outpost of the leading
local gastropub operator; in their classic "family-
friendly" style, it's a notably "comfortable and very
characterful" place, where the food is "always
good". / **Details:** www.grosvenorarms-aldford.co.uk;
6m S of Chester on B5130; 10 pm, Sun 9 pm.

ALKHAM, KENT	3–3D

The Marquis £ 69 ❷❸❸
Alkham Valley Rd CT15 7DF (01304) 873410
This "lovely restaurant-with-rooms" (a former pub)
pleases practically all reporters with its "beautifully
constructed menu sourced from local producers",
and "exceptionally good wines".
/ **Details:** www.themarquisatalkham.co.uk; 9.30 pm,
Sun 8.30 pm; closed Mon L; children: 8+ D; SRA-64%.
Accommodation: 10 rooms, from £95.

ALLOSTOCK, CHESHIRE	5–2B

Three Greyhounds £ 33 ❸❷❷
Holmes Chapel Rd WA16 9JY
(01565) 723455
A "busy" Georgian freehouse, with a nice garden,
that attracts consistently positive reports; the only
complaint – "the portions are too large to leave
space for the excellent desserts!"
/ **Details:** www.thethreegreyhoundsinn.co.uk; 9.15 pm,
Fri & Sat 9.45 pm, Sun 8.45 pm.

ALNWICK, NORTHUMBERLAND	8–1B

**Treehouse
Alnwick Castle** £ 42 ❸❷❶
Denwick Ln NE66 1YU (01665) 511350
The "spectacular" setting – suspended from trees
next to the Duchess's stunning garden – makes this
(real) treehouse a "magical" destination; the food is
"not remarkable", but "everything is very fresh and
of good quality"; shame the "Harry Potter-ish"
chairs are rather "hard".
/ **Details:** www.alnwickgarden.com; 9.15pm; closed
Mon D, Tue D & Wed D.

ALRESFORD, HAMPSHIRE	2–3D

Caracoli £ 29 ❸❷❷
15 Broad St SO24 9AR (01962) 738730
Atop a cookware shop in a super-modern town-
centre building, this "always busy" café (one of three
branches locally) is often "overflowing", thanks to its
"superb coffee and sandwiches".
/ **Details:** www.caracoli.co.uk; 2.30 pm; L only;
no Amex; no booking.

ALVESTON, WARWICKSHIRE   2–1C

Baraset Barn   **£ 45** ❸❷❷
I Pimlico Lane CV37 7RJ   (01789) 295510
This large and "buzzing" modern gastroboozer is a "glamorous" and "relaxed" sort of place ("ideal for a ladies' lunch"); its fare – "hearty or light" – continues to please almost all who report on it.
/ Details: www.barasetbarn.co.uk; @TheBarasetBarn; 9.30 pm, Sat 10 pm; closed Sun D; no Amex.

AMBERLEY, WEST SUSSEX   3–4A

Amberley Castle   **£ 93** ❷❸❶
BN18 9LT   (01798) 831992
"A star is born" – new chef Robby Jenks (formerly of the Brownsword Group's sister venue Gidleigh Park) has "transformed the kitchen" at this "enchanting" medieval castle, which re-opened after refurbishment in March 2013; it's "excellent" in every way, "except for the prices" (obviously).
/ Details: www.amberleycastle.co.uk; N of Arundel on B2139; 9 pm; no jeans or trainers; booking: max 6; children: 12+. Accommodation: 19 rooms, from £315.

AMBLESIDE, CUMBRIA   7–3D

Drunken Duck   **£ 56** ❸❹❷
Barngates LA22 0NG   (01539) 436347
"A really cosy pub with well-constructed food" that – unlike many such ventures in the Lake District – isn't aimed at people in their retirement"; it's particularly noted for "locally sourced dishes" and "exceptional beers" (brewed on site).
/ Details: www.drunkenduckinn.co.uk; 3m from Ambleside, towards Hawkshead; 9 pm; no Amex; booking: max 10 (D only). Accommodation: 17 rooms, from £105.

Fellini's   **£ 38** ❷❸❸
Church St LA22 0BT   (01539) 432487
"An excellent veggie restaurant, attached to a boutique cinema" – this "attractive" dining room inspires only positive commentary, not least for its "innovative" cuisine; "for top value, get a film and dinner combo". / Details: www.fellinisambleside.com; 10 pm; no Amex; Strongly recommended.

Lucy's on a Plate   **£ 43** ❶
Church St LA22 0BU   (01539) 431191
A real Lakeland "institution", this intimate bistro is tipped for the "huge selection of puddings" which are its trademark; (on the first Wednesday of the month "Up The Duff" pudding nights allow diners to "gorge on six desserts instead of a meal and not feel embarrassed"!).
/ Details: www.lucysofambleside.co.uk; 9 pm.

Zeffirelli's   **£ 33** ❸❷❷
Compston Rd LA22 9AD   (01539) 433845
'The Lake District's premier cinema, restaurant and jazz bar experience', so they say; this "creative"

(veggie) pizza 'n' pasta stop is more than a restaurant, it's a whole night out, and one which is "always enjoyable" – for top value, get an all-in-one ticket. / Details: www.zeffirellis.com; 10 pm; no Amex.

AMERSHAM, BUCKINGHAMSHIRE   3–2A

Artichoke   **£ 68** ❶❶❷
9 Market Sq HP7 0DF   (01494) 726611
Two 17th-century cottages knocked together, with a kitchen on view, provide the setting for this "beautiful little spot in a lovely town"; Laurie Gear's cooking is "going from strength to strength", delivering "amazing flavour combinations with subtlety". / Details: www.theartichokerestaurant.co.uk; 9.15 pm, Fri & Sat 9.30 pm; closed Mon & Sun; no shorts.

Gilbey's   **£ 48** ❸❷❸
I Market Sq HP7 0DF   (01494) 727242
This "cramped" local fixture, part of a small chain linked to the gin dynasty, has been "consistently good for many years now"; OK, it's "not in the excellent class", but wins impressively consistent commendations for "competent food at a not unreasonable price". / Details: www.gilbeygroup.com; @GilbeysAmersham; 9.30 pm, Sat 9.45 pm, Sun 8.45 pm.

ANSTRUTHER, FIFE   9–4D

Anstruther Fish Bar   **£ 25** ❶❷❷
42-44 Shore St KY10 3AQ   (01333) 310518
"The freshest fish", "tasty batter" and "crispy chips" make for potent satisfaction with the Smith family's well-known institution, in a "delightful setting" near the harbour. / Details: www.anstrutherfishbar.co.uk; 10 pm; no Amex; no booking.

APPLECROSS, HIGHLAND   9–2B

Applecross Inn   **£ 38** ❷❸❸
Shore St IV54 8LT   (01520) 744262
Remotely located it may be, but this famous inn is worth seeking out for its "locally sourced and delicious home-made food", with "fresh seafood", naturally, the highlight; "lovely gardens" too.
/ Details: www.applecross.uk.com; off A896, S of Shieldaig; 9 pm; no Amex; need 6+ to book. Accommodation: 7 rooms, from £90.

ARGYLL, ARGYLL AND BUTE   9–3B

Kilberry Inn   **£ 51** ❶
Nr Tarbert PA29 6YD   (01880) 770223
It may be "remote" (and therefore sparse on the report-generation front), but this restaurant–with-rooms is once again strongly tipped as "worth the trip"; previous reports have praised its vibrant cooking and its eclectic range of wines.
/ Details: www.kilberryinn.com; @Kilberryinn; 9 pm; closed Mon; no Amex. Accommodation: 5 rooms, from £210.

ARLINGHAM, GLOUCESTERSHIRE 2–2B

The Old Passage Inn **£ 58** ❶❹❸
Passage Rd GL2 7JR (01452) 740547
"The freshest fish and very friendly people, in a scenic, if hard-to-find location" – one reporter neatly summarises the pluspoints of this "very pleasant" seafood specialist, on the banks of the Severn; "eat on the terrace if weather permits".
/ Details: www.theoldpassage.com; 9 pm; closed Mon & Sun D. Accommodation: 3 rooms, from £80.

ARUNDEL, WEST SUSSEX 3–4A

Sage Of Arundel **£ 63** ❶
2-8 Castle Mews BN18 9DG (01903) 883477
"Jonas Tester is a very talented chef and Claire Masson a great host, and together they offer a real treat, always with something new and interesting", at this "tucked-away" spot, that comes strongly tipped. / Details: www.sageofarundel.com.

The Town House **£ 48** ❸❷❸
65 High St BN18 9AJ (01903) 883847
A "friendly" restaurant-with-rooms, with a "great location overlooking the castle", and also "one of the most unexpected and stunning ceilings" (from 16th-century Florence); it serves "good cooking at a good price". / Details: www.thetownhouse.co.uk; 9.30 pm; closed Mon & Sun. Accommodation: 4 rooms, from £95.

ASCOT, BERKSHIRE 3–3A

Ascot Oriental **£ 53** ❷❷❷
London Rd SL5 0PU (01344) 621877
High praise for Konrad Liu's "very special" rural pan-Asian "favourite"; you get a "perfect meal" here, say fans, and with an upmarket wine list to match. / Details: www.ascotoriental.com; 10.15 pm.

Restaurant Coworth Park
Coworth Park **£ 90** ❸❷❷
Blacknest Rd SL5 7SE (01344) 876 600
Fans find the "fancy" dining room of this "slick" country house hotel ("the Dorchester's country cousin") an "all-round stunner" with "really attentive" service an undoubted highlight; the "brilliant lunch experience" aside however, "it's not exactly cheap" and provokes the odd disappointment. / Details: www.coworthpark.com; 9.45 pm; closed Mon & Sun D.

ASENBY, NORTH YORKSHIRE 8–4C

Crab & Lobster **£ 68** ❷❸❷
Dishforth Rd YO7 3QL (01845) 577286
With its "rich assortment of bric-à-brac", and line in "superbly executed fish dishes", this "quirky" thatched pub offers an "experience to remember"… not to mention "the most romantic supper in the North"; the attached bedrooms, "based on famous hotels", are likewise
"outstanding". / Details: www.crabandlobster.co.uk; at junction of Asenby Rd & Topcliffe Rd; 9 pm, 9.30 pm Sat. Accommodation: 17 rooms, from £160.

ASHBOURNE, DERBYSHIRE 5–3C

The Dining Room **£ 70** ❷❶❷
33 St. John's St DE6 1GP (01335) 300666
In a "charming ancient building", this "unashamedly ambitious" eight-table restaurant run by a husband-and-wife duo "beats the pants off Derbyshire's duller grand country hotels"; on Thursdays and Fridays there is a more affordable, "shorter menu".
/ Details: www.thediningroomashbourne.co.uk; 7 pm; D only, closed Mon–Wed & Sun; no Amex; booking essential; children: 12+. Accommodation: 1 room, at about £120.

ASHBURTON, DEVON 1–3D

Agaric **£ 60** ❶
30 North St TQ13 7QD (01364) 654478
"Every Devon town should have a restaurant like this", say fans of this "reliable" restaurant-with-rooms, tipped for the "interplay of flavours" offered by its cuisine, and the "warmth" of its service.
/ Details: www.agaricrestaurant.co.uk; 9.30 pm; closed Mon, Tue, Sat L & Sun; no Amex. Accommodation: 5 rooms, from £110.

ASTON TIRROLD, OXFORDSHIRE 2–2D

The Sweet Olive **£ 49** ❷❸❸
Baker St OX11 9DD (01235) 851272
A gastropub "worth driving from London for"; "standards never seem to drop" at this "very French" establishment, where – on most reports – the food is "always excellent".
/ Details: www.sweet-olive.com; half a mile off the A417 between Streatley & Wantage; 9 pm; closed Feb.

AUCHTERARDER, PERTH AND KINROSS 9–3C

Andrew Fairlie
Gleneagles Hotel **£ 131** ❶❶❷
PH3 1NF (01764) 694267
"The best place to eat in Scotland" (and, for some reporters, "in the UK" too) – a visit to Andrew Fairlie's "dark" dining room, within the famous Edwardian golfing hotel, is summarised in almost all reports as an experience that can only be described as "phenomenal". / Details: www.andrewfairlie.com; 10 pm; L only, closed Sun; children: 12+; SRA-74%. Accommodation: 273 rooms, from £320.

Jon & Fernanda's **£ 48** ❶
34 High St PH3 1DB (01764) 662442
Fancy a change from the grandeur of Gleneagles? – this high street veteran (run by refugees from the big house) is again tipped for its "good food and value". / Details: www.jonandfernandas.co.uk; 9 pm; D only, closed Mon & Sun; no Amex; children: 10 years.

Strathearn Restaurant　£ 86　❷❷❷
PH3 1NF　(01764) 662231
Perhaps as perfect a 'classic' hotel dining room as you'll find, this large and gracious chamber, recently refurbished, offers a "lovely" setting for an experience acclaimed by all reporters as simply "first-class" all round. / Details: 10 pm; D only, ex Sun open L & D.

AXMINSTER, DEVON　2–4A

River Cottage Canteen　£ 39　❷❷❸
Trinity Sq EX13 5AN　(01297) 630 300
The most popular of Hugh Fearnley-Whittingstall's outposts, this "lovely" informal restaurant (behind a deli) inspires consistent praise with food that's "very fresh, local and wholesome"; beware, though – daytimes can be a bit of a "pushchair paradise". / Details: www.rivercottage.net; 8.30 pm; closed Mon D & Sun D; SRA-87%.

AYLESBURY, BUCKINGHAMSHIRE　3–2A

Hartwell House　£ 77　❸❷❷
Oxford Rd HP17 8NR　(01296) 747444
Surroundings don't come much more "magnificent" than the "quirky" country house that once served as home to Louis XVIII in exile; the food is never rated less than good. / Details: www.hartwell-house.com; 2m W of Aylesbury on A418; 9.45 pm; no jeans or trainers; children: 4+. Accommodation: 49 rooms, from £260.

AYLESFORD, KENT　3–3C

Hengist　£ 50　❷❸❸
7-9 High St ME20 7AX　(01622) 719273
"First choice for a romantic meal" thanks to its chic setting, "very good (albeit rather "safe") food" and "exemplary service"; reporters feel that, of late, it's also "notably more consistent" too. / Details: www.hengistrestaurant.co.uk; @hengistrestaura; 10 pm; closed Mon, Tue L, Wed L, Thu L & Sun D.

BABINGTON, SOMERSET　2–3B

Babington House　£ 50　❶
BA11 3RW　(01373) 812266
Hang out with the Notting Hill set, in this media-club-cum-country house (where you have to stay to dine, if not a member) – a supremely "relaxed" destination, offering simple food of consistent "good quality". / Details: www.babingtonhouse.co.uk; 11 pm; open to residents & members only; children: 16+ in the Orangery. Accommodation: 33 rooms, from £260.

BAGSHOT, SURREY　3–3A

The Latymer
Pennyhill Park Hotel　£ 109　❷❶❷
London Rd GU19 5EU　(01276) 471774
Michael Wignall's "phenomenal" food (with "inventive combinations" and "superlative attention

to detail") is beginning to put this "professional" and "friendly" country house hotel dining room very firmly on the map; the experience? – "not too stuffy... but formal enough to feel special!" / **Details:** www.pennyhillpark.co.uk; 9.15 pm, Fri & Sat 9.30 pm; closed Mon, Tue L, Sat L & Sun; booking: max 8; children: 11. **Accommodation:** 123 rooms, from £315.

BAKEWELL, DERBYSHIRE　5–2C

The Monsal Head Hotel　£ 40　❷❸❷
DE45 1NL　(01629) 640250
"One of those out-of-the-way places that's worth seeking out"; in the Peak District National Park, a hotel restaurant tipped for its "stunning view over Monsal Dale", and its "well-cooked and presented" food; "go into the bar at the rear – same menu, but bags of atmosphere". / Details: www.monsalhead.com; 9.30 pm, Sun 9 pm; no Amex. Accommodation: 7 rooms, from £90.

Piedaniels　£ 48　❸❸④
Bath St DE45 1BX　(01629) 812687
It's perhaps for the "excellent-value lunch menu" that this "very traditional" somewhat "upmarket" Gallic bistro – a comfy barn conversion in an "under-provided tourist town" – is of most particular note, but all aspects of the operation are solidly rated. / Details: www.piedaniels-restaurant.com; 10.30 pm, open on Sun only 2 weekends per month; closed Mon & Sun D.

BALLANTRAE, SOUTH AYRSHIRE　7–2A

Glenapp Castle　£ 99　❶
KA26 0NZ　(01465) 831212
A Scottish Baronial country house hotel, tipped for its "stunning" setting, and often "great" food too; service, though, can seem "in need of greater direction". / Details: www.glenappcastle.com; 9.30 pm; D only; children: 5+ after 7 pm. Accommodation: 17 rooms, from £445.

BALLATER, ABERDEENSHIRE　9–3C

Darroch Learg　£ 63　❶
56 Braemar Rd AB35 5UX　(01339) 755443
This "lovely" country house hotel is still tipped for its "good-quality" cooking, and its "unstuffy" service too; there's also a counter-view, though, that it's a rather "expensive" sort of place that's "living on its reputation". / Details: www.darrochlearg.co.uk; on A93 W of Ballater; 9 pm; D only, ex Sun open L & D; no Amex. Accommodation: 12 rooms, from £140.

Green Inn　£ 64　❶
9 Victoria Rd AB35 5QQ　(01339) 755701
Few reports on this friendly family-run restaurant-with-rooms; it's still tipped, however, as a venue that "never disappoints". / Details: www.green-inn.com; 9 pm; D only, closed Mon & Sun; no Amex; no shorts. Accommodation: 3 rooms, from £60.

BALQUHIDDER,
PERTH AND KINROSS   9–3C

Monachyle Mhor   **£ 73**   **❶④❷**
FK19 8PQ   (01877) 384622
"Really brilliant food" features in all feedback on the
Lewis family's "very remote" restaurant-with-rooms,
which enjoys a "fantastic location and views" in the
Trossachs National Park; service, though, sometimes
seems to be a weak link. / **Details:** www.mhor.net;
take the Kings House turning off the A84; 8.45 pm.
Accommodation: 14 rooms, from £185.

BARNET, HERTFORDSHIRE   3–2B

Savoro   **£ 41**   **❷❷❸**
206 High St EN5 5SZ   (020) 8449 9888
"Amazing food at suburban prices" – this "lovely,
honest restaurant", in a small hotel, is acclaimed as
the "best in the area by some distance".
/ **Details:** www.savoro.co.uk; 9.45 pm; closed Sun D.
Accommodation: 9 rooms, from £75.

BARNSLEY, GLOUCESTERSHIRE   2–2C

Barnsley House   **£ 58**   **④④④**
GL7 5EE   (01285) 740000
Some "very enjoyable" meals are reported at this
contemporary-style country house hotel; it also has
its critics, though, who find the whole style "strange"
and "pretentious", and service a tad "amateurish".
/ **Details:** www.barnsleyhouse.com; 9 pm, Sat & Sun
9.45 pm; children: 14+ after 7.30 pm.
Accommodation: 18 rooms, from £280.

The Village Pub   **£ 45**   **❷❶❶**
GL7 5EF   (01285) 740421
Uniform praise from reporters for the "top-of-the-
range grub" at this village pub, linked to nearby
Barnsley House; it has a "lovely, cosy atmosphere"
too. / **Details:** www.thevillagepub.co.uk;
@The_Village_Pub; 9.30 pm, Sun 9 pm.
Accommodation: 6 rooms, from £130.

BARRASFORD, NORTHUMBERLAND   8–2A

Barrasford Arms   **£ 40**   **❷❷❸**
NE48 4AA   (01434) 681237
"Consistently good food at a pub which punches
above its weight in gastronomic terms"; it is
particularly tipped for "Sunday lunches of superb
value and quality".
/ **Details:** www.barrasfordarms.co.uk; 9 pm; closed
Mon L & Sun D; no Amex; children: 18 + in bar after
9.30pm. **Accommodation:** 7 rooms, from £85.

BARTON-ON-SEA, HAMPSHIRE   2–4C

Pebble Beach   **£ 54**   **❷❷❷**
Marine Drive BH25 7DZ   (01425) 627777
Not only "spectacular views across the Solent" make
this "consistently good" cliff-top spot a major hit
with reporters (especially those who dine al fresco);
head chef Pierre Chevillard is "simply superb with

fish", and prices are relatively "affordable" too; a
downside? – the interior is too '80s for some tastes.
/ **Details:** www.pebblebeach-uk.com; 9 pm, Fri & Sat
9.30 pm; booking advisable. **Accommodation:** 4
rooms, from £90.

BARWICK, SOMERSET   2–3B

Little Barwick House   **£ 65**   **❶❶❷**
BA22 9TD   (01935) 423902
"Quite simply wonderful!" – the general verdict on
Tim and Emma Ford's "cosy" restaurant-with-rooms
in a Georgian dower house, where the cooking is
"always delicious and seasonal", and comes
accompanied by top fine wines; "do stay – breakfast
is worth it!" / **Details:** www.littlebarwickhouse.co.uk;
take the A37 Yeovil to Dorchester road, turn left at the
brown sign for Little Barwick House; Tue-Fri 9 pm, Sat
9.30 pm; closed Mon, Tue L & Sun; children: 5+ .
Accommodation: 6 rooms, from £69 pp.

BASLOW, DERBYSHIRE   5–2C

Fischers at Baslow Hall   **£ 80**   **❷❷❸**
Calver Rd DE45 IRR   (01246) 583259
"A lovely venue for a romantic meal or a family
gathering" – Max & Susan Fischer's Peak District
country house hotel near Chatsworth is, for most
reporters, a "classy" and "charming" all-rounder; for
a small minority, however, its approach is "too
formal". / **Details:** www.fischers-baslowhall.co.uk; on
the A623; Sun-Fri 8.30 pm, Sat 9 pm; no jeans or
trainers; children: 12+ at D, 8+ L .
Accommodation: 11 rooms, from £155.

Rowley's   **£ 48**   **❸❷❸**
Church Ln DE45 IRY   (01246) 583880
A "modern pub-conversion" run by the Fischers of
Baslow Hall, praised for its "reliably good", "bistro-
style" cooking and "friendly" service.
/ **Details:** www.rowleysrestaurant.co.uk;
@RowleysBaslow; 9 pm, Fri & Sat 10 pm; closed Sun D;
no Amex.

BATH, SOMERSET   2–2B

Bath Priory Hotel   **£ 105** **❸❷❸**
Weston Rd BA1 2XT   (01225) 331922
Sam Moody's "meticulous" and "beautifully
presented" cooking wins many plaudits for this
country house hotel and dining room, and service is
"impeccable" too; prices are "eye-watering", though,
and a dining room (with garden views) that, for fans,
is "so beautiful" can be too "sterile" for other
tastes. / **Details:** www.thebathpriory.co.uk; 9.30 pm;
no jeans or trainers; children: 12+ D; SRA-65%.
Accommodation: 33 rooms, from £210.

Bistro La Barrique   **£ 39**   **❷❷❸**
31 Barton St BA1 IHG   (01225) 463861
"A little taste of France"; most reporters are
charmed by this "innovative" bistro, near the
Theatre Royal, which offers a pre-show-friendly

"small plates" menu; good selection of wines too.
/ **Details:** www.bistrolabarrique.co.uk; 10pm, Fri-Sat
10.30 pm; closed Sun; no Amex.

Casanis   **£ 50**   ❷❷❷
4 Saville Row BA1 2QP   (01225) 780055
*"It's rare when the meal is better than expected
and the bill smaller"... such can be the case,
however, at this "lovely, genuine" Fresh bistro, which
enjoys a "very pretty setting" too; it delivers "honest
food done well", with "personal" service from the
husband-and-wife proprietors.*
/ **Details:** www.casanis.co.uk; @CasanisBistro; 10 pm;
closed Mon & Sun; no Amex.

The Circus   **£ 43**   ❷❷❷
34 Brock St BA1 2LN   (01225) 466020
*A "friendly" and "atmospheric" bistro near the Royal
Crescent, praised in all reports for "really enjoyable"
dishes from a monthly-changing menu.*
/ **Details:** www.thecircuscafeandrestaurant.co.uk;
@CircusBath; 10 pm; closed Sun; no Amex; children: 7+
at D.

Colonna & Smalls   **£ 17**   ❶
6 Chapel Row BA1 1HN   (07766) 808067
*A top city-centre tip for caffeine connoisseurs – a
bright and airy café that's "intense about the quality
of its coffee"; good cakes too.*
/ **Details:** www.colonnaandsmalls.co.uk; 5.30 pm, Sun
4 pm; no Amex; max. table size 6.

Demuths   **£ 46**   ❷❸⑤
2 North Parade Pas BA1 1NX
(01225) 446059
*Offering an "interesting menu" of seasonal meat-
free cooking, this small spot near the abbey gets
"full marks for continuing to provide Bath's veggies
with some excellent food"; given the prices, though,
the setting can seem a bit of a letdown.*
/ **Details:** www.demuths.co.uk; @demuths; 9.30 pm;
no Amex; booking: max 10.

**The Dower House
Royal Crescent Hotel**   **£ 90**   ❷❷❸
16 Royal Cr BA1 2LS   (01225) 823333
*This famously grand townhouse "classic" offers a
marvellously "stylish", "comfortable" and "romantic"
dining experience (set amidst gorgeous gardens)
that's "excellent on all levels"; no surprises about
the catch – it's "expensive".*
/ **Details:** www.royalcrescent.co.uk; @royalcrescent;
9.30 pm, Fri & Sat 10 pm; no jeans or trainers; booking:
max 8. **Accommodation:** 45 rooms, from £249.

The Eastern Eye   **£ 39**   ❸❷❶
8a Quiet St BA1 2JS   (01225) 422323
*"An awesome room, so not like an Indian
restaurant!" – this "stunning" Georgian ballroom is
most definitely a "one-off", and serves "good, honest
subcontinental food at reasonable prices".*
/ **Details:** www.easterneye.co.uk; 11.30 pm.

Gascoyne Place   **£ 41**   ❷❷❸
1 Sawclose BA1 1EY   (01225) 445854
*"Doesn't look anything special but wow!"; this
Georgian inn is tipped for food that's "almost always
a cut above"; it makes a "good place just for a
drink" too.* / **Details:** www.gascoyneplace.co.uk;
9.30 pm, Fri-Sun 10 pm; no Amex.

The Hare and Hounds   **£ 42**   ❷❸❷
Lansdown Rd BA1 5TJ   (01225) 482682
*This city fringe gastropub is a really popular all-
rounder, where "good traditional pub food and local
beers are not outdone by the amazing view"; non-
parents may prefer to avoid early Saturday
evenings, when "sprog suppertime" rules!*
/ **Details:** www.hareandhoundsbath.com; 9.30 pm, sun
9 pm; no Amex.

Hon Fusion   **£ 31**   ❷❸④
25 Claverton Buildings BA2 4LD
(01225) 446020
*"Easily the best Chinese in Bath"; this restaurant in
"up-and-coming Widcombe" – which is to say
behind Bath Spa railway station – is run by a family
from Hong Kong, and inspires consistent praise for
its "very good food, great value and efficient
service".* / **Details:** www.honfusion.com; 11 pm;
no Amex.

The Hudson Bar & Grill   **£ 56**   ❶
14 London St BA1 5BU   (01225) 332323
*This "low-key", first-floor operation inspires
impressively consistent tips as a destination for
"terrific" steak.* / **Details:** www.hudsonbars.co.uk;
@hudsonsteakbath; 10.30 pm; D only, closed Sun.

Menu Gordon Jones   **£ 62**   ❶❶❸
2 Wellsway BA2 3AQ   (01225) 480871
*"The most imaginative food to land in the West
Country for a very long time!" – this "lovely little
restaurant", which serves a single 6-course menu
nightly, inspires the highest praise for its cuisine, and
has an "amazing wine list" too; no wonder it's
"booked up on Saturdays for months ahead".*
/ **Details:** www.menugordonjones.co.uk; 9 pm; closed
Mon & Sun; no Amex.

**The Olive Tree
Queensberry Hotel**   **£ 64**   ❷❸④
Russell St BA1 2QF   (01225) 447928
*The basement setting can seem "awkward", but this
well-established hotel dining room is going from
strength to strength under new chef Chris Cleghorn
(a protégé of Michael Caines and Heston
Blumenthal), and the food is often hailed as
"superb" nowadays.*
/ **Details:** www.thequeensberry.co.uk; @olivetreebath;
9.45 pm; closed Mon L. **Accommodation:** 29 rooms,
from £125.

The Pump Room   **£ 46**   ❶
Stall St BA1 1LZ   (01225) 444477
Bath's top tip for a "very special" experience is of

course to visit this famous and "beautiful" Georgian chamber; safest to stick to breakfast or tea, though – more serious culinary endeavours can be "woeful". / **Details:** www.searcys.co.uk; @searcysbars; L only; no booking, Sat & Sun.

Rajpoot   **£ 39**   ❼
4 Argyle St BA2 4BA   (01225) 466833
An "atmospheric traditional Indian" tipped for its impressive setting in a Georgian cellar, and offering food that's "good, but not memorably so"; prices can seem high, so remember that "portions are substantial". / **Details:** www.rajpoot.com; 11 pm.

Raphael   **£ 40**   ❼
Upper Borough Walls BA1 1RN
(01225) 480042
A bistro tipped for "good-value food served with speed, charm and efficiency" – "the perfect choice for a meal before a play at the nearby Theatre Royal". / **Details:** www.raphaelrestaurant.co.uk; 10.15 pm; closed Sun.

The Wheatsheaf   **£ 51**   ❷❸❷
Combe Hay BA2 7EG   (01225) 833504
A "superb" village location adds to the "smashing atmosphere" ("terrace in summer, cosy log fire in winter") at this "perfect pub-with-rooms", whose appeal is rounded off by its "fab food and friendly welcome". / **Details:** www.wheatsheafcombehay.com; 9.30 pm; closed Mon & Sun D; no Amex.
Accommodation: 4 rooms, from £120.

Yen Sushi   **£ 33**   ❷❸④
11-12 Bartlett St BA1 2QZ   (01225) 333313
"When I crave sushi, I come here"; this handily-sited kaiten (conveyor belt) operation is an all-round crowd-pleaser; obviously, though, "the ambience is more suited to lunch than to dinner".
/ **Details:** www.yensushi.co.uk; 10.30 pm.

BAUGHURST, HAMPSHIRE   2–3D

The Wellington Arms   **£ 52**   ❶❷❷
Baughurst Rd RG26 5LP   (0118) 982 0110
Jason King & Simon Page's gastropub "oasis" inspires many eulogies; boons include "hugely charming owners", "terrific food", and "lovely rooms"... and, "having added an extension, they are now able to serve more customers" too.
/ **Details:** www.thewellingtonarms.com; @WellingtonArms; 9.30 pm; closed Sun D; no Amex.
Accommodation: 2 rooms, from £130.

BAWTRY, SOUTH YORKSHIRE   5–2D

The Dower House   **£ 35**   ❷❸❸
Market Pl DN10 6JL   (0130) 271 9696
"If you're looking for a great curry in these parts, this is the business" – "always consistent" cooking, with "quality ingredients" and "efficient" service.
/ **Details:** www.dower-house.com; 10.30 pm; children: 5+.

BEACONSFIELD,
BUCKINGHAMSHIRE   3–3A

The Cape Etc.   **£ 52**   ❼
Station Rd HP9 1NN   (01494) 681137
"Superb food" (plus good wines) make this South African-themed fixture a top local tip "at any time of the day". / **Details:** www.thecapeonline.com; 9.30 pm; closed Sun-Tue D; no Amex.

Crazy Bear   **£ 64**   ④④❶
75 Wycombe End HP9 1LX   (01494) 673086
A "weird and wacky environment" can mean this "eclectic" Anglo-Thai haunt is "brilliant for a celebratory night out"; even fans find it "pricey for what it is", though, while critics feel that the prices "don't reflect anything other than the expensive decor".
/ **Details:** www.crazybeargroup.co.uk/beaconsfield; 10 pm; children: bar, not after 6pm.
Accommodation: 17 rooms, from £290.

The Royal Standard of England   **£ 39**   ❷❷❶
Brindle Ln HP9 1XS   (01494) 673382
In addition to its "lovely" ancient setting – the backdrop to more than one film – the "oldest freehouse in England" has been acclaimed for some "very good" traditional pub cooking of late.
/ **Details:** www.rsoe.co.uk; 10 pm, Sun 9 pm; no Amex.

Spice Merchant   **£ 49**   ❷❸④
33 London End HP9 2HW   (01494) 675474
"Always top-class"; a contemporary Indian offering "delicious and interesting" dishes.
/ **Details:** www.spicemerchantgroup.com; 11 pm, Sun 9.30 pm; no Amex.

BEARSTED, KENT   3–3C

Fish On The Green   **£ 53**   ❷❷❸
Church Ln ME14 4EJ   (01622) 738 300
"A delight to find a good restaurant around Maidstone"; this fish specialist with a "small but pleasant dining area" garners plenty of positive feedback – particularly for its "very good-value" set lunch. – / **Details:** www.fishonthegreen.com; 9.30 pm, Fri & Sat 10 pm; closed Mon & Sun D; no Amex.

BEAULIEU, HAMPSHIRE   2–4D

The Terrace
Montagu Arms Hotel   **£ 100**   ❸❷④
SO42 7ZL   (01590) 612324
"Surprising proper French cooking, at quite an old-fashioned inn" – that's the majority view on this long-established four-star; its ratings, however, were dragged down by a couple of indifferent reports.
/ **Details:** www.montaguarmshotel.co.uk; @themontaguarms; 9 pm; closed Mon & Tue L; no jeans or trainers; children: 12+ D.
Accommodation: 22 rooms, from £143.

BEAUMARIS, ISLE OF ANGLESEY   4–1C

The Loft Restaurant
Ye Olde Bull's Head   **£ 64**   🇹
Castle St LL58 8AP   (01248) 810329
Tipped as an "expensive but pleasant surprise on Anglesea" – the upstairs dining room at this ancient coaching inn; a number of reporters prefer the modern (and cheaper) brasserie downstairs instead.
/ **Details:** *www.bullsheadinn.co.uk; @bullsheadinn; on the High Street; 9.30 pm; D only, closed Mon & Sun; no jeans; children: 7+ at D.* **Accommodation:** *26 rooms, from £105.*

BEELEY, DERBYSHIRE   5–2C

Devonshire Arms   **£ 41**   ❸❹❸
Devonshire Sq DE4 2NR   (01629) 733259
Near Chatsworth, an Estate inn where the food is generally "well done", and comes with the occasional "unusual twist"; critics say that the cooking tends to be "unremarkable", though, and "the new extension is out of keeping with the rest of the building". / **Details:** *www.devonshirebeeley.co.uk; 9.30 pm; bookings for breakfast.*
Accommodation: *14 rooms, from £125.*

BELFAST, COUNTY ANTRIM   10–1D

The Bar & Grill At James Street
South   **£ 49**   ❷❷❷
21 James Street South BT2 7GA
(028) 9560 0700
Already (significantly) eclipsing its sibling James Street South, a self-explanatory establishment where "lovely" staff dish up "great steaks and burgers".
/ **Details:** *www.belfastbargrill.co.uk; 10.15 pm; no Amex.*

Deanes   **£ 60**   🇹
36-40 Howard St BT1 6PF   (028) 9056 0000
Michael Deane is something of a household name in Ulster, and the food at this large city-centre restaurant is tipped as "usually very good"; it can be "inconsistent", though, and critics find the ambience "too business-y for a friendly night out".
/ **Details:** *www.michaeldeane.co.uk; 10 pm; closed Sun.*

Deanes At Queens   **£ 50**   🇹
1 College Gdns BT9 6BQ   (028) 9038 2111
Near the university, a relaxed outpost of the Michael Deane empire, tipped by most (if not quite all) reporters as a venue which "never disappoints".
/ **Details:** *www.michaeldeane.co.uk; 10 pm, Mon & Tue 9 pm; closed Sun D.*

Ginger   **£ 44**   ❷❷❷
7-8 Hope St BT2 5EE   (0871) 426 7885
Fare that's "most enjoyable" and "good value" too ensures that Simon McCance's bohemian bistro, near the Europa Hotel, is "popular for both lunch and dinner"; just a pity, says one fan, that the "lunch

menu doesn't change as much as we'd like".
/ **Details:** *www.gingerbistro.com; 9.30 pm, Mon 9 pm, Fri & Sat 10 pm; closed Mon L & Sun; no Amex.*

James Street South   **£ 53**   ❷❸❸
21 James Street South BT2 7GA
(028) 9043 4310
It's a mystery why Niall McKenna's city-centre fine dining venture doesn't elicit more feedback... those who do comment on it are full of praise for "dining as it used to be – good service, good food, good wines – and a restful, even quiet setting".
/ **Details:** *www.jamesstreetsouth.co.uk; @jamesstsouth; 10.45 pm; closed Sun.*

The Merchant Hotel   **£ 69**   ❷❷❶
16 Skipper Street BT1 2DZ   (028) 90234888
This "sophisticated" hotel dining room, in a former bank, is a "seriously good place to eat" amid "wonderful" decor; for some fans, though, it's "more about the cocktails" served in the adjoining jazz bar. / **Details:** *www.themerchanthotel.com; @MerchantHotel; 9.45 pm, Sun 8.30 pm.*
Accommodation: *62 rooms, from £220.*

Mourne Seafood Bar   **£ 41**   ❶❸❷
34-36 Bank St BT1 1HL   (028) 9024 8544
"Superb fresh seafood", "courteous" service and "sensible prices" – "what more could you want?"; "watch out for the queues"; there's a seaside branch in Dundrum. / **Details:** *www.mourneseafood.com; Mon 5 pm, Tue & Wed 9.30 pm, Thu, Fri & Sat 10.30 pm, Sun 6 pm; closed Mon D & Sun D; no booking at L.*

Nick's Warehouse   **£ 36**   🇹
35 Hill St BT1 2LB   (028) 9043 9690
Still "understandably popular", this long-time resident of the Cathedral Quarter is perennially tipped as "one of the best places in Belfast for lunch".
/ **Details:** *www.nickswarehouse.co.uk; behind St Anne's Cathedral; 9.30 pm; closed Mon & Sun; children: 18+ after 9 pm.*

Il Pirata   **£ 32**   🇹
279-281 Upper Newtownards Rd BT4 3JF
(028) 9067 3421
Not the upsurge of reviews we'd hoped for on this year-old Italian; it's still tipped though as an "enjoyable", "lively" and "relaxed" all-rounder.
/ **Details:** *www.facebook.com/ilPirataBelfast; @ilpiratabelfast; 10 pm; no Amex.*

Shu   **£ 47**   🇹
253 Lisburn Rd BT9 7EN   (028) 9038 1655
Wish we had more reports on this modern Gallic operation, near Adelaide station, which is strongly tipped for its "top-class" Gallic-based cuisine.
/ **Details:** *www.shu-restaurant.com; by Windsor Park; 10 pm; closed Sun.*

Tedfords Restaurant   **£ 51**   ❷❷❹
5 Donegall Quay BT1 3EA   (028) 90434000
"One of the few places in Belfast to have survived

the credit crunch in its original form!" – this large operation, near the Waterfront Hall, offers some "exquisite" dishes, and the service often "matches up"; "if your surroundings matter to you", though, "always ask for a table upstairs".
/ **Details:** www.tedfordsrestaurant.com; 9.30 pm; closed Mon, Tue L, Sat L & Sun.

BENDERLOCH, NR. OBAN, ARGYLL AND BUTE   9–3B

Hawthorn Restaurant   **£ 39**   **❼**
5 Keil Crofts PA37 1QS   (01631) 720 777
The location may be "very remote", but this crofter's house, opened as a restaurant only in 2012, wins praise, if from limited feedback, for "breathtakingly special food, with thought and love in each dish".
/ **Details:** www.thehawthornrestaurant.co.uk; 9 pm; closed Mon, Tue L, Wed L & Thu L.

BERKHAMSTED, HERTFORDSHIRE   3–2A

The Gatsby   **£ 54**   **❼**
97 High St HP4 2DG   (01442) 870403
"Cool but stylish", this monument to Art Deco (the foyer of a 1930s cinema) is mainly tipped for its architectural and atmospheric charms ("especially when there's jazz"); the food is "competent but pricey". / **Details:** www.thegatsby.net; 10.30 pm, Sun 9.30 pm; no Amex; booking: max 10.

BEVERLEY, EAST YORKSHIRE   6–2A

The Pipe & Glass Inn   **£ 56**   **❷❷❶**
West End HU17 7PN   (01430) 810246
"What an amazing place in the Yorkshire countryside" – James & Kate Mackenzie's "cracking" rustic pub is a large operation that's become one of the UK's best known on account of its "faultless" food, "delicious" wines, "effortlessly natural" service and its "lovely welcoming feel".
/ **Details:** www.pipeandglass.co.uk; @pipeandglass; 9.30 pm; closed Mon & Sun D.

Westwood Bar & Grill   **£ 51**   **❸❸❸**
4 New Walk HU17 7AE   (01482) 881999
"A great place that gets better every year"; this casual eatery is a "consistent" performer par excellence, not least as regards the "interesting" food from its "regularly changing" menu.
/ **Details:** www.thewestwood.co.uk; 9.30 pm; closed Mon & Sun L; no Amex.

Whites   **£ 52**   **❷❸❸**
12-12a North Bar Without HU17 7AB
(01482) 866121
The chef-patron's "real devotion to fine dining" pleases practically all who report on this "intimate" restaurant in a lovely town; "the tasting menu is outstanding in quality and value", say fans, though portions can sometimes seem a little on the small side. / **Details:** www.whitesrestaurant.co.uk; 9 pm;

closed Mon & Sun; no Amex; booking essential.
Accommodation: 4 rooms, from £85.

BIBURY, GLOUCESTERSHIRE   2–2C

Bibury Court
Bibury Court Hotel   **£ 54**
GL7 5NT   (01285) 740337
"Tucked away from the tourist hoards of the classic nearby Cotswolds village", this "magnificent" hotel is something of an "oasis"; reports in this year's survey were mixed, but in mid-2013 things have looked set to perk up with the arrival of James Graham (until recently chef-patron of Fairford's Allium, RIP).
/ **Details:** www.biburycourt.co.uk; 9 pm.
Accommodation: 18 rooms, from £170.

BIDDENDEN, KENT   3–4C

The Three Chimneys   **£ 51**   **❸❹❷**
Hareplain Rd TN27 8LW   (01580) 291472
A "delightful" pub all-rounder, offering "reliable" food in "generous" portions, and a "good choice" of beers, ciders and ales too; it can seem "overpriced", though. / **Details:** www.thethreechimneys.co.uk; A262 between Biddenden and Sissinghurst; 9 pm, Fri & Sat 9.30 pm; no Amex.

The West House   **£ 60**   **❶❷❸**
28 High St TN27 8AH   (01580) 291341
Graham Garrett's "superb combinations, and flavours to tingle your tastebuds" win high culinary praise for this "cosy and friendly" venture – "not slick, but charming" – in a "beautiful" village, also lauded for its "very quirky wine list".
/ **Details:** www.thewesthouserestaurant.co.uk; @grahamgarrett; Tue-Fri 9 pm, Sat 10pm; closed Mon, Sat L & Sun D; no Amex.

BIDFORD ON AVON, WARWICKSHIRE   2–1C

The Bridge   **£ 44**   **❷❸❶**
High St B50 4BG   (01789) 773700
"The location on a riverbank adds to the enjoyment" of a visit to this modern brasserie (complete with "decking area overlooking the picturesque stretch of water"); fish dishes are "especially good".
/ **Details:** www.thebridgeatbidford.com/; 9 pm, Fri & Sat 9.30 pm; closed Sun D; no Amex.

BIGBURY-ON-SEA, DEVON   1–4C

Burgh Island Hotel   **£ 81**   **❷❶❶**
TQ7 4BG   (01548) 810514
"There's no other place like it!"; reporters aren't just blown away by the "wonderful setting" of this Agatha Christie-style hotel (which "takes the diner back to the 1920s") – the new chef's locally sourced cuisine is widely hailed as "faultless" too.
/ **Details:** www.burghisland.com; 8.30 pm; D only, ex Sun open L & D; no Amex; jacket & tie; children: 12+ at D. **Accommodation:** 25 rooms, from £400.

The Oyster Shack   **£ 52   ❶❷❷**
Millburn Orchard Farm, Stakes Hills TQ7 4BE
(01548) 810876
*A simple joint, whose "plastic chairs and vinyl
tablecloths epitomise the beach shack-feel";
"shellfish to die for" and "great local craft beers"
mean it's "definitely worth the drive".
/ Details: www.oystershack.co.uk; 9 pm.*

BILDESTON, SUFFOLK   3–1C

The Bildeston Crown
The Crown Hotel   **£ 62   ❸④④**
High St IP7 7EB   (01449) 740510
*Most reports agree it's "worth seeking out" this
"pleasant" inn, not least for its sometimes
"excellent" food; even positive feedback can come
with a 'catch' though – "hit-and-miss service" and
"London prices" being prominent amongst them.
/ Details: www.thebildestoncrown.com; from the A14,
take the B115 to Bildeston; 9.45 pm, Sun 9 pm.
Accommodation: 13 rooms, from £100.*

BILLERICAY, ESSEX   3–2C

The Magic Mushroom   **£ 50   ❸❷❸**
Barleyland Rd CM11 2UD   (01268) 289963
*"Gets better and better", say local fans of Darren
Bennet's "welcoming", well-established bistro, which
is "quite an oasis" for the locale.
/ Details: www.magicmushroomrestaurant.co.uk; next
to "Barleylands Farm"; midnight; closed Mon & Sun D.*

BIRCHANGER, ESSEX   3–2B

The Three Willows   **£ 39   ❶**
Birchanger Ln CM23 5QR   (01279) 815913
*A handy tip "just off the M11" – an unpretentious
village inn that's "good for fish". / Details: one mile
from Birchanger Green service station on M11; 9 pm;
closed Sun D; no Amex.*

BIRCHINGTON, KENT   3–

The Minnis   **£ 45   ❸❷❸**
The Parade CT7 9QP   (01843) 841844
*Overlooking the beach at Minnis Bay, within a '70s-
designed building, this "reasonably priced" venture is
praised by fans for its "very decent" cooking
("fantastic '70s-inspired puds"); the view taken by
sceptics diverges by 180° – they say it's
"overpriced" and "a lot of fuss about nothing".
/ Details: www.theminnis.co.uk; 9 pm, Sun 8 pm.*

BIRMINGHAM, WEST MIDLANDS   5–4C

Adam's   **£ 48   ❶❶❷**
21a Bennetts Hill B2 5QP   (01216) 433745
*"The new kid on the block of Birmingham's
gastronomic line-up"; this city-centre operation, run
by a husband-and-wife team, is an "intimate"
venture, where the ambitious range of tasting
menus (up to 9 courses) are realised to an
"incredibly high standard".*

*/ Details: www.adamsrestaurant.co.uk;
@RestaurantAdams; 9.30 pm; closed Mon & Sun;
Booking advised; children: 8+ D.*

Asha's Indian Bar
and Restaurant   **£ 45   ❷❷❷**
12-22 Newhall St B3 3LX   (0121) 200 2767
*In the city-centre, this "excellent and very authentic
Indian" – the only English branch of a Gulf States
chain – is "worth serious attention"; fans praise its
"amazing staff and amazing food", and a
particularly "fab quality fixed-price lunch"; "wish we
had one of these in London!"
/ Details: www.ashasuk.co.uk; 10.30 pm, Thu-Sun
11 pm; closed Sat L & Sun L.*

Carters   **£ 55   ❷❷❷**
2C Wake Green Rd B13 9EZ   (0121) 449
8885
*This "relative newcomer" in Moseley is an "excellent
neighbourhood restaurant"; "you really can't beat
this sort of innovative cooking and fantastic service
– not at the price of a local bistro!"
/ Details: www.cartersofmoseley.co.uk; 9.30 pm; closed
Mon & Tue; children: Min 8+.*

Cielo   **£ 51   ❶**
6 Oozells Sq B1 2JB   (0121) 632 6882
*"A bit of a find in a rather soulless area" – this
Brindleyplace Italian is particularly tipped as a "very
useful" pre-theatre venue.
/ Details: www.cielobirmingham.com; @Cielo_Italian;
11 pm, Sun 10 pm; Max booking: 20, Sat & Sun D.*

Edmunds   **£ 65**
6 Central Sq B1 2JB   (0121) 633 4944
*Up-and-down feedback again on this ambitious
Brindleyplace spot; let's hope, however, that reports
that it has been "revitalised" or "much improved" by
the new chef (who arrived towards the end of our
survey year) turn out to be correct.
/ Details: www.edmundsrestaurant.co.uk; 10 pm;
closed Mon L, Sat L & Sun.*

Hotel du Vin et Bistro   **£ 53   ④④❸**
25 Church St B3 2NR   (0121) 200 0600
*For a "casual" meal, this better-than-average
outpost of the once-celebrated hotel/bistro chain
does have its fans; unfortunately, true to the general
group performance, it can also seem "very average"
and "uninspiring". / Details: www.hotelduvin.com;
@HdV_Birmingham; 10 pm, Fri & Sat 10.30 pm;
booking: max 12. Accommodation: 66 rooms,
from £160.*

Itihaas   **£ 41   ❶**
18 Fleet St B3 1JL   (0121) 212 3383
*Fewer reports than we'd like on this smart city-
centre Indian, but it's very strongly tipped for its
"wonderful, authentic and well-spiced food", and its
"friendly" service too. / Details: www.itihaas.co.uk;
@itihaasindian; 10 pm; closed Sat L & Sun L.*

Adam's

Opus Restaurant

Purnells

Jyoti   **£ 23**   ❷❸⑤
105 Stratford Rd B28 8AS (0121) 77855501
*"Forget the surroundings", the "flavoursome" dishes
at this Formica-topped Gujarati restaurant are "all
individual labours of love", and at "cheap, cheap
prices" too.* / **Details:** *www.jyotis.co.uk; 10 pm; closed
Mon, Tue-Thu D only; no Amex.*

Lasan   **£ 74**   ❷❷❸
3-4 Dakota Buildings, James St B3 1SD
(0121) 212 3664
*"Indian food, but not as you know it"; that's the
deal, – complete with "stunning presentation" and
"amazing attention to detail" – that makes this
"innovative" city-centre "benchmark" a
"memorable" destination for almost all who
comment on it; it has a café-offshoot in Hall Green.*
/ **Details:** *www.lasan.co.uk; 11 pm; closed Sat L;
no trainers.*

Loves
The Glasshouse   **£ 65**   ❶❶❸
B16 8FL (0121) 454 5151
*Steve Love "is a perfectionist and it shows", at this
waterside city-centre venue, which offers a "top
gastronomic experience" (including an "inventive
vegetarian tasting menu"); "efficient but not stuffy"
service too.* / **Details:** *www.loves-restaurant.co.uk;
@lovesrestaurant; 9 pm, Fri-Sat 9.30 pm; closed Mon,
Tue, Wed L, Thu L & Sun; no Amex; children: 8+.*

MPW Steakhouse
Birmingham   **£ 50**   ④④❷
200 Wharfside St, The Cube B1 1PR
(01216) 435948
*"Fantastic views (even if they are only of
Birmingham!)" underpin the popularity of this city-
centre steakhouse; most reporters approve its "high
end chain" experience, but they acknowledge its
"amateurish" service, and critics find it "very
average all-round".*
/ **Details:** *www.mpwsteakhousebirmingham.com.*

Opus Restaurant   **£ 60**   ❸❷❸
54 Cornwall St B3 2DE (0121) 200 2323
*A handy city-centre spot fans say is "the most
consistent high-class restaurant in town"; for critics
though, popularity with the business world rather
inflates prices.* / **Details:** *www.opusrestaurant.co.uk;
@opuscornwallst; 9.30 pm; closed Sat L & Sun;
no Amex; SRA-75%.*

Purnells   **£ 75**   ❶❶❸
55 Cornwall St B3 2DH (0121) 212 9799
*"Amazing, the best food and service I have ever
had!" – the "sharp" and "businesslike" ambience of
Glynn P's city-centre beacon may not be
remarkable, but the "flawless" cuisine and the
"superb" service certainly are.*
/ **Details:** *www.purnellsrestaurant.com; 9.15 pm;
closed Mon, Sat L & Sun; children: 6+.*

Saffron   **£ 36**   ❷❷❸
126 Colmore Row B3 3AP (0121) 212 0599
*"A real experience of subcontinental food at its
best" – this "very unusual and innovative" modern
Indian is praised for "accomplished" cooking by a
"talented" chef; more reports please!*
/ **Details:** *www.saffronbirmingham.co.uk.*

San Carlo   **£ 51**   ❸❶❷
4 Temple St B2 5BN (0121) 633 0251
*One of the best outlets of the glitzy chain, a "buzzy
and amusing" city-centre spot, where the cuisine
almost invariably satisfies (even if it can be a little
"rich" for some tastes); locally "some people
patently don't like it", but most reporters are fans.*
/ **Details:** *www.sancarlo.co.uk; @SanCarlo_Group;
11 pm.*

Simpsons   **£ 81**   ❶❶❷
20 Highfield Rd B15 3DU (0121) 454 3434
*"The best restaurant in Birmingham" occupies a fine
Georgian villa in leafy Edgbaston; its "brilliant but
unostentatious" cuisine and "attentive" and
"efficient" service combine to deliver an experience
that's "unstuffy but luxurious".*
/ **Details:** *www.simpsonsrestaurant.co.uk;
@simpsons_rest; 9 pm, Fri & Sat 9.30 pm; closed
Sun D.* **Accommodation:** *4 rooms, from £160.*

Turners   **£ 81**   ❶
69 High St B17 9NS (0121) 426 4440
*Wish we had more reports on Richard Turner's
Harborne dining room; supporters say the food is
"fantastic", but it attracts too little feedback for
more than tip status.*
/ **Details:** *www.turnersrestaurantbirmingham.co.uk;
@TurnersRestBrum; 9.30 pm; closed Mon, Tue L,
Wed L, Thu L & Sun; no Amex.*

BISHOPS STORTFORD,
HERTFORDSHIRE   3–2B

Baan Thitiya   **£ 36**   ❷❶❸
102 London Rd CM23 3DS (01279) 658575
*A "reliable" suburban restaurant, formerly a 1930s
pub, with a "nice garden attached", where the
"hearty Thai food, garnished to the max" almost
invariably satisfies.* / **Details:** *www.baan-thitiya.com;
10.30 pm, Sun 9.30 pm.*

BISHOPS TACHBROOK,
WARWICKSHIRE   5–4C

Mallory Court   **£ 80**   ❷❸❷
Harbury Ln CV33 9QB (01926) 330214
*"Magic!"; for most reporters, the dining room of this
Lutyens-style country house hotel is a "perfect"
destination all-round, with "superb" haute cuisine; for
a small minority, though, it can strike the wrong
note, however, and appear "stodgy" and
"unimaginative".* / **Details:** *www.mallory.co.uk;
@mallorycourt; 2m S of Leamington Spa, off B4087;*

8.30 pm; closed Sat L; no trainers; SRA-53%.
Accommodation: *31 rooms, from £159.*

BLAIRGOWRIE,
PERTH AND KINROSS   9–3C

Kinloch House   **£ 69   ❷❶❸**
PH10 6SG   (01250) 884237
*Few (and slightly mixed) reports this year on this remote but "pleasantly located" Georgian country house; even the reporter who had a disappointing visit, though, concedes standards are "very professional". / **Details:** www.kinlochhouse.com; past the Cottage Hospital, turn L, procede 3m along A923, (signposted Dunkeld Road); 8.30 pm; no Amex; jacket required; children: 6 for dinner.* **Accommodation:** *15 rooms, from £230.*

BLAKENEY, NORFOLK   6–3C

The White Horse Hotel   £ 44   ❷❸❸
4 High St   NR25 7AL   (01263) 740574
*"Our first stop on every visit to Norfolk!" – this old coaching inn is a popular gastropub nowadays, with fish dishes often winning special mention. / **Details:** www.blakeneywhitehorse.co.uk; off the A149; 9 pm, Fri & Sat 9.30 pm; no Amex.* **Accommodation:** *9 rooms, from £70.*

BODIAM, EAST SUSSEX   3–4C

The Curlew   **£ 56   ❷❷❸**
Junction Rd   TN32 5UY   (01580) 861 394
*"A surprise find in deepest Sussex"; most reporters feel that the "brilliant and serious" menu at this former coaching inn has "improved from an already high standard" since the appointment of a new chef, Andrew Scott, in late-2012. / **Details:** www.thecurlewrestaurant.co.uk; @thecurlewbodiam; 9.30 pm, Sun 9 pm.*

BODSHAM, KENT   3–3C

**Froggies at The Timber
Batts**   **£ 51   ❷❷❷**
School Ln   TN25 5JQ   (01233) 750237
*"Joel Gros continues to produce beautiful food" – spanning "lovely French dishes" and "traditional British pub fare" – at this secluded 15th-century inn, plus a "pretty impressive" selection of Loire Valley wines. / **Details:** www.thetimberbatts.co.uk; 9 pm; closed Mon, Tue L & Sun D; no Amex; booking essential.*

BOLLINGTON, CHESHIRE   5–2B

Lord Clyde   **£ 43   ❶**
Kerridge   SK10 5AH   (01625) 562123
*Fewer reports than we'd like on this well-located inn, but it is tipped for its "consistently high standards". / **Details:** www.thelordclyde.co.uk; 9 pm; closed Mon & Sun D.*

BOLNHURST, BEDFORDSHIRE   3–1A

The Plough at Bolnhurst £ 48   ❷❷❷
MK44 2EX   (01234) 376274
*Martin Lee's "no-pretensions" gastroboozer is a great all-rounder – a "lovely" country pub, with a "wonderful atmosphere", "friendly" staff and "terrific" cooking. / **Details:** www.bolnhurst.com; 9.30 pm; closed Mon & Sun D; no Amex.*

BOLTON ABBEY, NORTH YORKSHIRE   5–1B

**Burlington
The Devonshire Arms   £ 91   ❸❶❷**
BD23 6AJ   (01756) 718 111
*With its "truly excellent cuisine, made from the highest quality luxury ingredients", "immense" wine list, "precise" service and a setting that's "all class", the Duke of Devonshire's luxurious rural hotel has a lot going for it; there is catch – "now don't get me wrong, we had a lovely meal, but it was extremely expensive". / **Details:** www.thedevonshirearms.co.uk; 9.30 pm, Sat & Sun 10 pm; closed Mon; jacket at D; children: 7+.* **Accommodation:** *40 rooms, from £250.*

**The Devonshire Brasserie
The Devonshire Arms   £ 50   ❷❷❸**
BD23 6AJ   (01756) 710710
*The "buzzing" brasserie of this "beautiful" hotel pleases most reporters with its "well-cooked" fare; there's the occasional hint, though, that "the cost of the helipad upkeep" perhaps inflates the prices! / **Details:** www.devonshirehotels.co.uk; on A59, 5m NE of Skipton; 9.30 pm, Sun 9 pm.* **Accommodation:** *40 rooms, from £200.*

BOREHAM, ESSEX   3–2C

The Lion Inn   **£ 40   ❸❸❸**
Main Rd   CM3 3JA   (01245) 394900
*A "popular" gastropub with a "refreshing" menu (featuring "plenty of fish options"), as well one for kids – if there's an issue, it's that it can be "over-busy", and rather "noisy". / **Details:** www.lioninnhotel.co.uk; 9 pm, Sun 8 pm; no Amex.* **Accommodation:** *15 rooms, from £105.*

BOUGHTON LEES, KENT   3–3C

**The Manor Restaurant
Eastwell Manor**   **£ 46   ❸❷❶**
Eastwell Pk   TN25 4HR   (01233) 213000
*This Elizabethan manor provides a "superb" and extremely "romantic" setting for a meal (with an "excellent pianist", and "beautiful gardens" too); and while the food isn't the main event, it generally "does not disappoint". / **Details:** www.eastwellmanor.co.uk; 3m N of Ashford on A251; 9.30 pm; no jeans or shorts; booking: max 8.* **Accommodation:** *62 rooms, from £180.*

BOUGHTON MONCHELSEA, KENT 3–3C

The Mulberry Tree £ 50 ❷❸❸
Hermitage Ln ME17 4DA (01622) 749082
This smart-looking 'country restaurant and bar' has
a "lovely setting", and is hailed by most reporters as
a "very pleasant place to eat"; the dining room can
be "noisy", though, and off days on the service front
are not unknown.
/ **Details:** www.themulberrytreekent.co.uk; 9 pm, Fri &
Sat 9.30 pm; closed Mon & Sun D; no Amex.

BOURNEMOUTH, DORSET 2–4C

Chez Fred £ 26 ❶❷④
10 Seamoor Rd BH4 9AN (01202) 761023
Fred Capel's famous, upscale chippy serves "perfect
fish 'n' chips every time!"; "it needs bigger premises
now though" – "we had to queue from outside the
door". / **Details:** www.chezfred.co.uk; 9.45 pm, 9 Sun;
closed Sun L; no Amex; no booking.

Edge £ 55 ❶
2 Studland Rd BH4 8JA (01202) 757 007
A top-floor restaurant tipped for its "majestic sea
views" and its "cool" modern interior; the food has
its fans too, but critics say "the location is what it's
all about". / **Details:** www.edgerestaurant.co.uk;
9.30 pm; closed Mon.

Ocean Palace £ 33 ❷❷④
8 Priory Rd BH2 5DG (01202) 559127
A "good selection" and "friendly" service are
hallmarks of this well-established, traditional Chinese
near the pier; shame "it's incredibly echoey".
/ **Details:** www.oceanpalace.co.uk; 11 pm.

WestBeach £ 52 ❷❸❷
Pier Approach BH2 5AA (01202) 587785
"Honest", "well-prepared" fish and seafood "cooked
to order straight from the local catch" – the winning
formula at this restaurant "virtually on the beach
beside the pier" (and with a "fabulous view" of the
harbour); it's "able to make a meal a really adult
experience whilst catering for children too".
/ **Details:** www.west-beach.co.uk; 10 pm.

BOURTON ON HILL, GLOUCESTERSHIRE 2–1C

Horse & Groom £ 41 ❷❸❸
GL56 9AQ (01386) 700413
Will and Tom Greenstock's "really buzzy" Cotswold
inn is of note for the "consistently good" results from
its "interesting" and "varied" menu – "it changes
through the night as dishes run out and new ones
are added!" / **Details:** www.horseandgroom.info;
9 pm, Fri & Sat 9.30 pm; closed Sun D; no Amex.
Accommodation: 5 rooms, from £120.

BOWNESS-ON-WINDERMERE, CUMBRIA 7–3D

**Miller Howe Restaurant
& Hotel** £ 69 ❸❸❸
Rayrigg Rd LA23 1EY (01539) 442536
"Views don't come much better than this", says a
fan of the dining room at this classic Lakeland
country house hotel; the food is often "very good"
too, but "when it's bad it's quite average" and not
cheap either. / **Details:** www.millerhowe.com; on
A592 between Windermere & Bowness; 8.45 pm;
no Amex. **Accommodation:** 15 rooms, from £150.

BRADFORD, WEST YORKSHIRE 5–1C

Akbar's £ 33 ❶❷❸
1276 Leeds Rd BD3 8LF (01274) 773311
Cradle to quite a Northern empire – this "very busy
and large" Indian is always popular with "Asian
families out celebrating"; expect "tasty curries",
"excellent" starters, and "naans the size of a
tablecloth!" / **Details:** www.akbars.co.uk; midnight,
Sun 11.30 pm; D only; I.

Karachi £ 25 ❶❸④
15-17 Neal St BD5 0BX (01274) 732015
A "wonderful, basic Formica-tabled curry house",
serving "superbly flavoured" food at decent prices;
"no cutlery, but plenty of chapatis". / **Details:** 1 am,
2 am Fri & Sat; no credit cards.

Mumtaz £ 27 ❷❸❸
Great Horton Rd BD7 3HS (01274) 571861
"One of the country's best curry houses"; this
"colourful" landmark manages to remain "different
from the herd", and offers "excellent food at very
good northern prices!"; the only downside? – no
licence. / **Details:** www.mumtaz.com; midnight.

Prashad £ 36 ❷❸❸
86 Horton Grange Rd BD7 2DW
(01274) 575893
Now in a new Drighlington location, this long
standing Gujarati continues to elicit the highest
praise for its "accomplished and imaginative"
vegetarian fare ("even my carnivore son thinks its
fantastic"), and "enthusiastic and knowledgeable"
service. / **Details:** www.prashad.co.uk; 10.30 pm;
closed Mon; no Amex.

Zouk £ 33 ❶
1312 Leeds Rd BD3 8LF (01274) 258 025
This café-style Indian restaurant attracts praise from
all who comment on it, and it is particularly tipped
for its "sublime" balanced spicing, and for fish
starters which are "a wonder to behold".
/ **Details:** www.zoukteabar.co.uk; 10.30 pm; no Amex;
no shorts.

BRAMPTON, DERBYSHIRE   5–2C

Nonsolovino   **£ 53**   **☉**
417 Chatsworth Rd S40 3AD   (01246) 276760
This town centre wine bar is attached to an Italian wine merchant, and is strongly tipped for its "imaginative" cuisine – my "best meal outside France", claims one reporter!
/ Details: www.nonsolovino.co.uk; 9 pm; closed Mon L.

BRANCASTER STAITHE, NORFOLK   6–3B

The White Horse   **£ 48**   **❸❸❷**
Main Rd PE31 8BY   (01485) 210262
"Wide-ranging views over the salt marshes" from the "lovely conservatory dining room", and an "imaginative local menu" too – what's not to like about this coastal inn?; it also boasts a "great deck to enjoy the sun".
/ Details: www.whitehorsebrancaster.co.uk; @whitehorsebranc; 9 pm; no Amex.
Accommodation: *15 rooms, from £94.*

BRAY, BERKSHIRE   3–3A

Caldesi in Campagna   **£ 67**   **❸❷❷**
Old Mill Ln SL6 2BG   (01628) 788500
"Amazing, amazing, amazing… take yourself off on a journey to Italy!" – Giancarlo Caldesi's "elegant" venture offers "fabulous" food in a "gorgeous" riverfront setting; it might be "overshadowed locally by the big guns", but it's "so much better value".
/ Details: www.caldesi.com; @KatieCaldesi; 10 pm; closed Mon & Sun L.

Crown Inn   **£ 53**   **❸④④**
High St SL6 2AH   (01628) 621936
Heston may own it, but don't expect fireworks at this "quaint" old pub; its "limited" menu of "comfort food" is fine, but is rated no better than thousands of other such places, and reporters with high hopes found it "not as good as we were expecting".
/ Details: www.crownatbray.com; @thecrownatbray; 9.30 pm, Fri & Sat 10 pm; booking advised at weekends.

The Fat Duck   **£ 237**   **❸❷④**
High St SL6 2AQ   (01628) 580333
"The most memorable meal ever!" – Heston Blumenthal's world-famous HQ delivers a "brilliantly choreographed" experience, featuring his wilfully bonkers culinary inventions ("you really feel you've fallen down that rabbit hole"); nowadays, however, prices are at risk of seeming "seriously excessive" (especially as the interior is "very plain").
/ Details: www.thefatduck.co.uk; 9 pm; closed Mon & Sun.

The Hind's Head   **£ 61**   **❷❸❷**
High St SL6 2AB   (01628) 626151
"Heston's 'other' place in this picturesque village" is one of the UK's most popular gastropubs; "deluxe" pub grub served in "proper pub surroundings"

makes for a straightforward but "epic" formula that impresses a massive fan club, even if prices are "steep". / Details: www.hindsheadbray.com; 9.30 pm; closed Sun D.

Riverside Brasserie   **£ 57**   **☉**
Monkey Island Ln, Bray Marina SL6 2EB (01628) 780553
Top tip for "a treat on a sunny day"; it may be "hard to find", but those who truffle out this Bray Marina restaurant are rewarded with some "very well-executed dishes", and "right by the river" too.
/ Details: www.riversidebrasserie.co.uk; 9.30 pm; closed Mon, Tue & Sun D.

Waterside Inn   **£ 201**   **❷❷❷**
Ferry Rd SL6 2AT   (01628) 620691
"Deservedly a legend"; for reporters of a more traditional bent, "nothing can beat" the Roux family's "perfect" Thames-side haven; "shocking" prices notwithstanding, it's the ideal destination to mark a major birthday or anniversary… or "one's investiture at Windsor Castle".
/ Details: www.waterside-inn.co.uk; off A308 between Windsor & Maidenhead; 10 pm; closed Mon & Tue; no jeans or trainers; booking: max 10.
Accommodation: *11 rooms, from £225.*

BREARTON, NORTH YORKSHIRE   8–4B

The Malt Shovel   **£ 48**   **❸❷❷**
HG3 3BX   (01423) 862929
A "wonderful" rural pub, praised in most reports for its "very tasty" cooking ("German-inspired", which is a rarity) and staff who "couldn't do more to help"; it inspired a couple of uncharacteristically poor reviews this year however – hopefully just a blip.
/ Details: www.themaltshovelbrearton.co.uk; off A61, 6m N of Harrogate; 9.30 pm; closed Mon & Sun D; no Amex.

BRECON, POWYS   2–1A

The Felin Fach Griffin   **£ 48**   **❸❸❷**
Felin Fach LD3 0UB   (01874) 620111
A "charming, charming inn" at the foot of the Brecon Beacons which has made a big name for itself thanks to "superlative cooking with interesting twists"; overall, though, reports this year are definitely a fraction less enthusiastic than in the past. / Details: www.eatdrinksleep.ltd.uk; @felifachgriff; 20 mins NW of Abergavenny on A470; 9 pm, Fri & Sat 9.30 pm; no Amex.
Accommodation: *7 rooms, from £115.*

BRENTWOOD, ESSEX   3–2B

Alec's   **£ 58**   **❷❸❷**
Navestock Side CM14 5SD   (01277) 375 696
"The new best place to eat in Essex", say fans of this expansive "London-style" pub conversion – a "busy" spot, where the menu ("mostly fish") is realised to a standard "as good as you'll find in

these parts"; critics, though, think prices are "outrageous". / **Details:** www.alecsrestaurant.co.uk; 10 pm, Sun 4.30 pm; closed Mon, Tue L, Wed L & Sun D; no Amex; children: 12+.

BRIDPORT, DORSET   2–4B

The Bull Hotel   £ 46   ❶
34 East St DT6 3LF   (01308) 422878
Tipped locally for those in search of a "family-friendly gastropub", with "reliable" fare; there's the odd concern though as to whether former standards are now being maintained.
/ **Details:** www.thebullhotel.co.uk; 9.30 pm.
Accommodation: 19 rooms, from £85.

Hive Beach Cafe   £ 43   ❷❹❸
Beach Rd DT6 4RF   (01308) 897070
"No more than a tent on a cliff-top, so don't expect luxury" – do, however, expect "gloriously fresh seafood" at this "perennially popular" café, with its "incredible" location by the sea; it's "always heaving when it's sunny". / **Details:** www.hivebeachcafe.co.uk; no bookings. **Accommodation:** 2 rooms, from £95.

Riverside   £ 52   ❷❷❷
West Bay DT6 4EZ   (01308) 422011
"Unassuming, but a real destination"; "wonderful" fish dishes are the highlight of Arthur Watson's harbour-side veteran, and they are "served by people who obviously care about providing an unforgettable experience"; it has a "terrific" waterside location too.
/ **Details:** www.thefishrestaurant-westbay.co.uk; 9 pm; closed Mon & Sun D.

BRIGHTON, EAST SUSSEX   3–4B

Arch 139   £ 46   ❸❹❸
139 King's Road Arches BN1 2FN
(01273) 821218
"Sit upstairs at the front", or even better al fresco ("the other areas inside are a bit gloomy"), if you visit this beachside restaurant, below the Grand, where "good, if straightforward" fish is the menu highlight. / **Details:** www.arch139.com; 9.45 pm.

Basketmakers Arms   £ 39   ❷❷❷
12 Gloucester Rd BN1 4AD   (01273) 689006
The "best proper pub food in Brighton"; no wonder this old-fashioned North Laine boozer gets "very busy" – "time it right, though, and a visit can be a true joy". / **Details:** www.basketmakersarms.co.uk; 8.30 pm; no booking.

Bill's at the Depot   £ 40   ❹❸❷
100 North Rd, The Depot BN1 1YE
(01273) 692894
"It's a pity Bill's has been taken over by the big boys", but the chain's "busy and bustling" North Laine diner is still proving a hit thanks to its "reasonably priced nosh" ("great brekkie" in

particular) and an appealing "bare-brick interior".
/ **Details:** www.bills-website.co.uk; 10 pm; no Amex.

Casa Don Carlos   £ 31   ❸❸❸
5 Union St BN1 1HA   (01273) 327177
"We love this place!", exclaim fans of this "heaving" Lanes tapas joint who claim it's "worth the squeeze" for "varied and seasonal" dishes that are "not too expensive either!"; book for peak times.
/ **Details:** 11 pm, Thu 9 pm, Fri-Sun 10 pm; closed Thu L.

The Chilli Pickle   £ 41   ❶❸❸
17 Jubilee St BN1 1GE   (01273) 900 383
"The sort of zip, zing and authenticity you only otherwise get at the top London places!" – the food at "Brighton's best Indian by far" goes "from strength to strength" in its new premises.
/ **Details:** www.thechillipickle.com; 10.30pm, Sun 10.15pm; closed Tue.

The Coal Shed   £ 51   ❷❸❸
8 Boyces St BN1 1AN   (01273) 322998
"Taking great pride in their ingredients", this new grill-house near Churchill Square is "a very welcome addition to the Brighton scene", and "not just for its meat", either.
/ **Details:** www.coalshed-restaurant.co.uk; @thecoalshed1; 10 pm, Fri & Sat 10.30 pm.

Donatello   £ 30   ❸❸❷
1-3 Brighton Pl BN1 1HJ   (01273) 775477
A "cheap and cheerful" Lanes Italian that's always "bustling and busy in a good way"; "you won't feel embarrassed with your noisy toddler!"
/ **Details:** www.donatello.co.uk; 11.30 pm.

The Restaurant at Drakes
Drakes Hotel   £ 60   ❷❷❷
44 Marine Pde BN2 1PE   (01273) 696934
Very positive reviews of late for the "divine" food at this fine dining restaurant below a Kemptown boutique hotel, whose "very small basement" setting strikes most reporters as "very private" and "romantic".
/ **Details:** www.therestaurantatdrakes.co.uk; @drakeshotel; 9.30 pm. **Accommodation:** 20 rooms, from £115.

English's   £ 50   ❹❹❸
29-31 East St BN1 1HL   (01273) 327980
With its "tightly packed rooms", this very "old-fashioned" Lanes fish veteran (of over 150 years standing) can provide "a trip down memory lane"; prices are "quite frightening" however, and even the odd fan concedes "it's possibly a tourist trap".
/ **Details:** www.englishs.co.uk; @englishsofbrighton; 10 pm, Sun 9.30 pm.

Fishy Fishy   £ 45   ❷❷❸
36 East St BN1 1HL   (01273) 723750
"Always fresh and varied" – the fish dishes on offer at this "friendly" but "cramped" Lanes townhouse-bistro help make it an almost invariable crowd-

Food for Friends

Gingerman

pleaser. / **Details:** www.fishyfishy.co.uk;
@fishybrasserie; 9.30 pm, Fri & Sat 10 pm.

Food for Friends **£ 41** **❷❷❸**
17-18 Prince Albert St BN1 1HF
(01273) 202310
"A fabulous veggie with a regularly changing
menu!"; some regulars perennially insist that this
Lanes institution is "resting on its laurels a bit", but
more striking is the ardent praise for its
"imaginative" but "un-faddy" cuisine, with "real
depth of taste". / **Details:** www.foodforfriends.com;
10 pm, Fri & Sat 10.30 pm; no booking, Sat L & Sun L.

Giggling Squid **£ 26** **❸❸❸**
129 Church Rd BN3 2AE (01273) 771991
"A really enjoyable no-fuss Thai" (part of a growing
and creditable small chain), offering tapas-style
dishes as well as the traditional offerings – it's
"always full". / **Details:** www.gigglingsquid.com;
Mon-Sat 10.45pm Sun 9.45pm.

The Ginger Dog **£ 44** **❷❷❸**
12 College Pl BN2 1HN (01273) 620 990
Part of what's arguably the leading local
restaurant/pub empire, this intimate Kemptown
corner spot offers "rich and hearty gastropub
cooking", and from an "interesting" menu too, which
includes "lots of seasonal choices".
/ **Details:** www.gingermanrestaurants.com;
@gingerdogdish; off Eastern Road near Brighton
College; 10 pm.

The Ginger Pig **£ 47** **❷❷❸**
3 Hove St BN3 2TR (01273) 736123
This "scrubbed-up boozer" gets plenty of positive
reports for "consistently great" food – especially
"wonderful puddings" and Sunday roasts that "lift it
above pub levels"; it can be a "noisy" place, though,
and the occasional critic does wonder if it might
become a victim of its own success.
/ **Details:** www.gingermanrestaurant.com;
@gingerpigdish; 10 pm, Sun 9pm; no trainers.

Gingerman **£ 50** **❶❶❸**
21a Norfolk Sq BN1 2PD (01273) 326688
"Small but perfectly formed" – Ben McKellar's
"intimate" ("cramped") dining room, "tucked-away
down a side street", remains Brighton's best; the
food is "not flashy" and "not cutting edge", but
"excellently cooked", and service is "attentive
without being smothering".
/ **Details:** www.gingermanrestaurant.com;
@thegingerchef; 9.45 pm; closed Mon.

Graze **£ 50** **❸❸④**
42 Western Rd BN3 1JD (01273) 823707
Oddly mixed reports on this Hove small plates
outfit; according to fans, it's "still the best place in
town", but critics find the style "fussy" and
"insubstantial"… "almost as if they can't decide if
this is a serious restaurant or just a trendy eatery".
/ **Details:** www.graze-restaurant.co.uk; 9.30 pm.

Indian Summer **£ 44** **❷❷❸**
69 East St BN1 1HQ (01273) 711001
"Leading the way" with its "really creative" cuisine,
this Lanes fixture is the "best Indian in Brighton" on
most accounts; the lunch menu, in particular, is "an
absolute bargain".
/ **Details:** www.indian-summer.org.uk;
@indiansummer108; 10.30 pm, Sun 10 pm; closed
Mon L.

Iydea **£ 19** **❷❷❸**
17 Kensington Gdns BN1 4AL
(01273) 667 992
"Superlative and healthy", this veggie café in the
Lanes serves a "good selection" of hot mains and
"the yummiest salads"; the "communal eating" can
"lead to some great conversations" too.
/ **Details:** www.iydea.co.uk; 5 pm; no Amex or Maestro.

Plateau **£ 43** **❷❷❷**
1 Bartholomews BN1 1HG (01273) 733085
"Classic French food, but with innovative
presentation" – handily located opposite the Town
Hall, a "scrubbed tables and candles" wine bar
where "everything is spot on"; they even do
"fabulous cocktails"!
/ **Details:** www.plateaubrighton.co.uk; 10 pm, Thu 10.
30 pm, Fri & Sat 11 pm.

The Regency **£ 30** **❸❸❸**
131 Kings Rd BN1 2HH (01273) 325014
"The best fish 'n' chips in town" (plus "a wide
selection of other fish dishes") – and in "substantial
portions" – help create "astonishing value" at this
family-friendly institution, overlooking the sea.
/ **Details:** www.theregencyrestaurant.co.uk; 10 pm.
Accommodation: 30 rooms, from £50.

Riddle & Finns **£ 48** **❷❷❸**
12a Meeting House Ln BN1 1HB
(01273) 323008
"The only decent high-end seafood restaurant in
town!"; this "hidden gem", in the Lanes, dishes up
"delicious fish by candlelight, washed down with
some excellent wines"; "shared tables may not seem
ideal, but actually it's all part of the atmosphere".
/ **Details:** www.riddleandfinns.co.uk;
@RiddleandFinns1; 10 pm, Fri & Sat 11 pm;
no reservations.

Small Batch Coffee **£ 15** **❶**
17 Jubilee St BN1 1GE (01273) 697597
Looking for "the best coffee in Brighton"? – the
"cheerful" branches of this fast-growing chain of
"excellent coffee bars" are strong contenders; the
branch listed is the group's 'flagship'.
/ **Details:** smallbatchcoffee.co.uk; 7 pm, Sun 6 pm.

Terre à Terre **£ 51** **❶❷④**
71 East St BN1 1HQ (01273) 729051
"Still the best vegetarian restaurant in the UK"; this
Lanes phenomenon's menu may "read like the
worst of MasterChef", but its "ludicrously

ambitious" and "entertaining" dishes are supremely enjoyable, even for carnivores.
/ **Details:** www.terreaterre.co.uk; @TerreaTerre; 10.30 pm; booking: max 8 at weekends.

Warung Tujuh　　　　**£ 35**　**❷❸④**
7 Pool Valley BN1 1NJ　(01273) 720 784
"A bit of a find" in "the insalubrious area around the bus station", this "small" Indonesian impresses everyone with its "fine", "fresh and spicy" flavours; "good value for money" too.
/ **Details:** www.warungtujuh.com; 11 pm.

BRIGHTWELL BALDWIN, OXFORDSHIRE	5–2D

Lord Nelson　　　　　**£ 46**　**❸❶❷**
OX49 5NP　(01491) 612497
"The epitome of a cosy country pub/restaurant!" in an "idyllic village" particularly praised for its "exemplary" service, but on most accounts hailed for its "first-class" food too.
/ **Details:** www.lordnelson-inn.co.uk; Mon-Sat 10 pm, Sun 9.30 pm; no Amex.

BRISTOL, CITY OF BRISTOL	2–2B

The Albion　　　　　**£ 46**　**❸④❸**
Boyces Ave BS8 4AA　(0117) 973 3522
Cutely located "in a quiet back street of busy Clifton Village", this "lovely gastropub with rustic dining room above a bustling bar" serves "really tasty and unpretentious" scoff.
/ **Details:** www.thealbionclifton.co.uk; 10 pm; closed Mon L & Sun D.

Bell's Diner　　　　　**£ 53**　**❼**
1 York Rd BS6 5QB　(0117) 924 0357
Chris Wicks's bohemian bistro in Montpelier has long been a well-known neighbourhood fixture, with an "unpretentious" and "cosy" style all of its own; reports are less numerous and more mixed than they once were however – fans still love its "originality", but foes say it's "just average" nowadays.
/ **Details:** www.bellsdinerandbarrooms.co.uk; 9.30 pm, Fri & Sat 10 pm; closed Mon, Sat L & Sun.

Berwick Lodge　　　　**£ 61**　**❷❸❷**
Berwick Drive BS10 7TD　(0117) 9581590
"Handy for the city, but hard-to-find"; the dining room Chris Wicks (of Bell's Diner fame) runs at this Arts & Crafts country house hotel offers a "short, but well thought-out" menu, on which some dishes are "outstanding". / **Details:** www.berwicklodge.co.uk; 10 pm; no Amex. **Accommodation:** 10 rooms, from £90.

Bordeaux Quay　　　　**£ 48**　**④④④**
Canons Way BS1 5UH　(0117) 943 1200
"An excellent location by the waterfront" underpins the popularity of this eco-friendly establishment, in particular its relaxed downstairs brasserie; but there's also a lot of lukewarm comments about food

"not as good as you want it to be", and service "which often lets the place down".
/ **Details:** www.bordeaux-quay.co.uk; @bordeauxquay; 10.30 pm; closed Mon, Tue-Sat D only, closed Sun D; SRA-77%.

Casamia　　　　　　**£ 90**　**❶❷❸**
38 High St BS9 3DZ　(0117) 959 2884
There's "no doubting the creativity and brilliance" at the Sanchez-Iglesias family's "exemplary" venue in Westbury-on-Trym – cooking that's "playful" and "light on its feet" is part of a "spot-on" overall experience; even some fans don't like the prices, though – "ouch!"
/ **Details:** www.casamiarestaurant.co.uk; 10 pm; closed Mon & Sun; no Amex.

The Cowshed　　　　　**£ 48**　**❷❸④**
46 Whiteladies Rd BS8 2NH　(0117) 973 3550
"Cracking" – "as the name suggests, they take a particular pride in their beef" at this Clifton spot, although "other dishes are also impressive"; on the downside, it's "not exactly romantic", and all that bare wood can make it "very noisy".
/ **Details:** www.thecowshedbristol.com; 11.30 pm.

Fishers　　　　　　**£ 42**　**❼**
35 Princess Victoria St BS8 4BX
(0117) 974 7044
"Perfect after a morning's shopping in Clifton"; this "very creditable" venture is tipped for its "innovative cooking" (including the "interesting fish dishes" you might hope for), and its "good-value lunchtime specials". / **Details:** www.fishers-restaurant.com; 10.30 pm, Sun 10 pm.

Flinty Red　　　　　**£ 42**　**❷❸⑤**
34 Cotham Hill BS6 6LA　(0117) 923 8755
"Superb and innovative" small plates and an "outstanding" range of wines by the glass earn high praise for this Cotham bistro (which is owned by a wine merchant); this is a small place, though, and the ambience is "very dependent on the other diners" (can be "cold and clackety").
/ **Details:** www.flintyred.co.uk; @flintyred; 10 pm; closed Mon L & Sun; booking essential.

The Glass Boat　　　　**£ 41**　**④❸❷**
Welsh Back BS1 4SB　(0117) 929 0704
"You could be in Amsterdam or Prague", say fans of this "beautifully located" and "romantic" floating restaurant; the food, in contrast, is rather "predictable", making lunchtime and pre-theatre offers all the more worth seeking out.
/ **Details:** www.glassboat.co.uk; @GlassboatRest; below Bristol Bridge; 10.30 pm, Mon 10 pm; closed Mon L, Sat L & Sun D.

Greens' Dining Room　　　**£ 42**　**❷❷❷**
25 Zetland Rd BS6 7AH　(0117) 924 6437
Under its new régime, this "modest-looking" Redlands bistro newcomer has got off to a cracking start – "a great neighbourhood restaurant that

punches above its weight on quality and service".
/ Details: www.greensbristol.co.uk; @greensbristol;
10 pm; closed Mon & Sun D; no Amex.

Hotel du Vin et Bistro   **£ 51**   ❸④❷
Sugar Hs, Narrow Lewins Mead BS1 2NU
(0117) 925 5577
"One of the better HdVs!" – indeed, reporters
confirm that this is one of the few outlets of the
wine-led hotel-bistro chain where "the food is worth
waiting for"… as, unfortunately, you may well have
to! / Details: www.hotelduvin.com; @HdV_Bristol;
10.30 pm; booking: max 10. **Accommodation:** *40*
rooms, from £119.

Juniper   **£ 38**   ❷⓿❸
21 Cotham Road South BS6 5TZ
(0117) 9421744
"Inventive yet unpretentious" cooking, combined with
"superb" service and a "relaxing" and "informal"
style inspires very consistent upbeat feedback on
this "good-humoured" Cotham venture.
/ Details: www.juniperrestaurant.co.uk.

Lido   **£ 50**   ❷❸⓿
Oakfield Pl BS8 2BJ   (0117) 933 9533
It's not just the "one-off ambience" of this
"gorgeous" café/restaurant overlooking the pool of
Clifton's revamped lido that wows reporters... the
ex-Moro chef's "tapas-style" food is "reliably good,
and sometimes truly excellent" too; "ice cream is a
speciality, and really worth it".
/ Details: www.lidobristol.com; @lidobristol; 10 pm;
closed Sun D; no Amex.

Maitreya Social   **£ 38**   ⓿
89 St Marks Rd BS5 6HY   (0117) 951 0100
Under new ownership in recent times, an
"imaginative veggie" offering "unusual and
complex" (if, at times, "rich and heavy") dishes.
/ Details: www.maitreyasocial.co.uk; 9.45pm; closed
Mon, Tue L, Wed L, Thu L & Sun D; no Amex.

Primrose Café   **£ 45**   ⓿❷❷
1 Clifton Arcade, 6 Boyces Ave BS8 4AA
(0117) 946 6577
A cute Clifton Village café, under the same
ownership for twenty years; it comes highly
recommended as a "wonderful place for lunch", and
also by night when it serves some "beautifully
judged" more ambitious cooking.
/ Details: www.primrosecafe.co.uk; @theprimrosecafe;
10 pm; Sun D; no booking at L.

Prosecco   **£ 38**   ❷❸④
25 The Mall BS8 4JG   (0117) 973 4499
A Clifton "hidden gem" that's "a cut above the
standard trattoria", offering an "authentic" menu
that's "not the most extensive", "but what they do,
they do well"; service is "friendly and efficient" too.
/ Details: www.proseccoclifton.com; 11 pm; closed
Mon & Sun, Tue-Thu L ; no Amex.

riverstation   **£ 48**   ❸❸⓿
The Grove BS1 4RB   (0117) 914 4434
"Wonderful views of the docks" are the highpoint at
this "harbour-side gem" – a stylishly converted, river
police station; food-wise, it's "normally good to very
good" both in the downstairs bar/café, and the airy
first floor restaurant.
/ Details: www.riverstation.co.uk; 10.30 pm, Fri & Sat
11 pm; closed Sun D; no Amex.

Rockfish   **£ 54**   ❸❷❸
128-130 Whiteladies Road BS8 2RS
(0117) 9737384
"Sublime seafood, expertly prepared" wins much
praise for Mitch Tonks's fishmonger-cum-restaurant,
where "ironed linen tablecloths" and "cosseting
banquettes" help "make the best of an unpromising
site"; not everyone was impressed, however, with
"silly" prices a prime complaint.
/ Details: www.rockfishgrill.co.uk; 10 pm, Fri & Sat
10.30 pm; closed Mon & Sun.

San Carlo   **£ 39**   ❷❸④
44 Corn St BS1 1HQ   (0117) 922 6586
This seafood-centric Italian in the city-centre is a
particularly good outpost of the San Carlo brand,
acclaimed for its "superb quality food"; critics can
find it a touch "pretentious" and "pricey", however.
/ Details: www.sancarlo.co.uk; 11 pm.

The Thali Café   **£ 30**   ❸❷❸
12 York Rd BS6 5QE   (0117) 942 6687
This "Bristol favourite" offers "simple" but
"terrifically tasty" tiffin boxes to eat in or take away;
the address listed is the "fun" Montpelier HQ – a
fourth offshoot has recently opened in Southville's
trendy Tobacco Factory.
/ Details: www.thethalicafe.co.uk; 10.30 pm; closed
weekday L; no Amex; SRA-75%.

Wilks   **£ 55**   ⓿⓿❸
1 Chandos Rd BS6 6PG   (0117) 9737 999
"The excellent successor to Culinaria"; James
Wilkins's "modern" Redland bistro is already touted
as "the best restaurant in Bristol" thanks to his
"delectable" and "stylish" cooking; what's more,
"Madame, the front of house is brilliant – crisp and
efficient in the classic French manner, but with
charm and humour".
/ Details: www.wilksrestaurant.co.uk/; 10 pm, sun
9 pm; closed Mon & Tue; no Amex.

BRIXHAM, DEVON   1–3D

Poopdeck   **£ 46**   ❷❷❸
14 The Quay TQ5 8AW   (01803) 858 681
"A lovely little restaurant overlooking Brixham
harbour", praised for its "great fresh fish" (and a
chef who is "prepared to cook off-piste on
request"); "it's a popular choice, so book ahead".
/ Details: www.poopdeckrestaurant.com.

Wilks

Maitreya Social

Berwick Lodge

BROAD HAVEN, PEMBROKESHIRE	4–4B

Druidstone Hotel   £ 44   ④④❶
SA62 3NE   (01437) 781221
"Stupendous views of the sea and coastline" (with
beautiful gardens too) will always make this
"quirky" and "family-friendly" cliff-top hotel a special
destination; "the food has a struggle to keep up",
but on a good day is "excellent" too.
/ **Details:** www.druidstone.co.uk; from B4341 at Broad
Haven turn right, then left after 1.5m; 9.30 pm.
Accommodation: 11 rooms, from £80.

BROADWAY, WORCESTERSHIRE	2–1C

Buckland Manor   £ 92   ❼
WR12 7LY   (01386) 852626
An impressive country house hotel tipped for "well-
sourced dishes, well cooked"; let's hope the odd hint
of a "drop in standards" under new owner, the
Brownsword Group, is just 'early days'.
/ **Details:** www.bucklandmanor.co.uk; 2m SW of
Broadway on B4632; 9 pm; jacket & tie at D; booking:
max 8; children: 12+. **Accommodation:** 13 rooms,
from £305.

Russell's   £ 50   ❼
20 High St   WR12 7DT   (01386) 853555
This restaurant-with-rooms in the heart of an idyllic
Cotswolds village is tipped for its "relaxed"
atmosphere and "good food"; the new upmarket
chippy, behind, has also been well received.
/ **Details:** www.russellsofbroadway.co.uk;
@russelsRandR; 9.30 pm; closed Sun D.
Accommodation: 7 rooms, from £110.

BROCKENHURST, HAMPSHIRE	2–4D

The Pig   £ 52   ❶❷❷
Beaulieu Rd   SO42 7QL   (01590) 622354
"Idiosyncratic food in a great location"; this "New
Forest gem" – the dining room of an "always
buzzing", stylishly "distressed" country house hotel –
seduces reporters with its "robust" and
"unpretentious" cuisine (much of it sourced hyper-
locally). / **Details:** www.thepighotel.com; 9.30 pm;
SRA-87%. **Accommodation:** 26 rooms, from £135.

BROCKHAM, SURREY	3–3A

The Grumpy Mole   £ 42   ❼
RH3 7JS   (01737) 845 101
"Perfect for suburban Surrey", this "classic British
bistro-pub" – part of a small chain – is tipped for its
"wholesome home cooking" (that "neither
challenges nor disappoints"), accompanied by a
"basic" wine list.
/ **Details:** www.thegrumpymole.co.uk; 9.30 pm;
no Amex.

BROMESWELL, SUFFOLK	3–1D

British Larder   £ 49   ❷❸❸
Oxford Rd   IP12 2PU   (01394) 460 310
"A haven of good food in east Suffolk"; this former
inn, run by a South African couple, is quite a "find"
thanks to its "inventive" use of "excellent"
ingredients "presented with flair"; parents may also
be attracted by the "kids' play area".
/ **Details:** www.britishlardersuffolk.co.uk; 9 pm, Fri-Sat
9.30 pm; no Amex.

BROMLEY, GREATER LONDON	3–3B

Cinnamon Culture   £ 50   ❷❷❸
46 Plaistow Ln   BR1 3PA   (020) 8289 0322
"What a rare find in suburbia!" – offering a "great
modern twist on Indian cuisine", this "large"
operation "tucked away at the station" wins
impressively consistent ratings across-the-board.
/ **Details:** www.cinnamonculture.com.

BROMLEY, KENT	3–3B

Tamasha   £ 50   ❼
131 Widmore Rd   BR1 3AX   (020) 8460 3240
"Excellent food and service in a mock-colonial
setting"; this suburban Indian may be "expensive",
but it is still tipped by its local fans as "an
experience worth doing a couple of times a year".
/ **Details:** www.tamasha.co.uk; 10.30 pm; no shorts.
Accommodation: 7 rooms, from £75.

BROUGHTON GIFFORD, WILTSHIRE	2–

Fox   £ 44   ❸④❸
The St   SN12 8PN   (01225) 782949
Ten miles from Bath, a "quaint old inn, turned into a
dining pub with a bar, and very nice food"; "quite
adventurous" cooking is part of the formula that's
made it "very popular".
/ **Details:** @thefoxbroughton; 9.30 pm; closed Mon L.

BROUGHTON, NORTH YORKSHIRE	8–4B

Bull at Broughton   £ 40   ❼
BD23 3AE   (01756) 792065
The Yorkshire outpost of the Northcote-inspired
Ribble Valley Inns group, tipped as a "reliable"
destination for "good food, well-served".
/ **Details:** www.thebullatbroughton.com; 8.30 pm, Fri &
Sat 9 pm.

BRUNDALL, NORFOLK	6–4D

Lavender House   £ 63   ❶❷❸
39 The St   NR13 5AA   (01603) 712215
The food is "better than ever", say fans of Richard
Hughes's "fabulous" restaurant (and cookery
school), which offers not just "super food" but
"fantastic value-for-money" too; only criticism? – "for
such excellent eating, the space is rather limited" for
some tastes. / **Details:** www.thelavenderhouse.co.uk;
9.30 pm; D only, closed Sun & Mon; no Amex.

BRUTON, SOMERSET   2–3B

At The Chapel   **£ 50** ❸❷❶
28 High St BA10 0AE   (01749) 814070
In an "attractive little town", this former
congregational chapel with a "luminous" interior is
"working on so many levels"; "you could spend all or
any part of the day" enjoying fare that's always
"delicious" – "especially pizzas from the wood-fired
oven". / **Details:** www.atthechapel.co.uk;
@at_the_chapel; 9.30 pm. **Accommodation:** 8
rooms, from £100.

BUCKFASTLEIGH, DEVON   1–3D

Riverford Field Kitchen   **£ 41** ❶❷❸
Wash Barn, Buckfast Leigh TQ11 0JU
(01803) 762074
"Drive past sheds and pallets" or "walk through the
fields where your food is grown" to reach this
"casual" venue, where you "eat communally from
big platters" at long trestle tables; the "wholesome"
food is "unbeatable", "especially the veg" – "my only
complaint is it's so delicious I eat too much!"
/ **Details:** www.riverford.co.uk; 8 pm; closed Sun D;
no Amex.

BUCKHORN WESTON, DORSET   2–3B

The Stapleton Arms   **£ 40** ❶
Church Hill SP8 5HS   (01963) 370396
This stylish rural inn recently came under new
management, but fans report that the change
"hasn't affected the quality at all"; no great
excitements, but it's tipped as a "friendly" all-
rounder nonetheless.
/ **Details:** www.thestapletonarms.com; 10 pm.
Accommodation: 4 rooms, from £100.

BUCKLAND MARSH, OXFORDSHIRE   2–2C

The Trout Inn   **£ 47** ❸❹❸
Tadpole Bridge SN7 8RF   (01367) 870382
"A fabulous location near the Thames", with "a
garden going down to the river" is a highpoint at
this "gorgeous" looking pub; its "traditional" fare can
be "excellent" too, but standards, including of
service, can dip on occasion.
/ **Details:** www.trout-inn.co.uk; 11 pm, sun 10.30 pm;
no Amex. **Accommodation:** 6 rooms, from £130.

BUNBURY, CHESHIRE   5–3B

The Dysart Arms   **£ 42** ❸❸❷
Bowes Gate Rd CW6 9PH   (01829) 260183
"Consistently good pub food in a lovely Cheshire
inn" – this "welcoming" member of the Brunning &
Price empire pleases almost all of the many
reporters who comment on it.
/ **Details:** www.dysartarms-bunbury.co.uk; 9.30 pm,
Sun 9 pm.

BUNNY, NOTTINGHAMSHIRE   5–3D

Rancliffe Arms   **£ 40** ❶
139 Loughborough Rd NG11 6QT
(0115) 98447276
"The best carvery around"; and it doesn't only
please carnivores – the range of veg' on offer is
"formidable"! / **Details:** www.rancliffearms.co.uk;
9 pm; no Amex.

BURFORD, OXFORDSHIRE   2–2C

The Bull at Burford   **£ 54** ❷❶❷
105 High St OX18 4RG   (01993) 822 220
Reporters "continue to be impressed with the whole
experience" of eating at this historic town-centre inn
– in particular the "fantastic service instigated by
the wonderfully gregarious patron Jean-Marie
Lauzier". / **Details:** www.bullatburford.co.uk; 9 pm.
Accommodation: 15 rooms, from £80.

BURNHAM MARKET, NORFOLK   6–3B

Hoste Arms   **£ 53** ❹❹❹
The Grn PE31 8HD   (01328) 738777
The new regime at this picturesque inn inspires
mixed reports; fans still speak of "excellent locally
sourced dishes" and "friendly" service, but there's an
emphatic band of critics for whom this once-famous
establishment is "not what it was".
/ **Details:** www.thehoste.com; 6m W of Wells;
9.15 pm. **Accommodation:** 62 rooms, from £112.

BURNHAM ON CROUCH, ESSEX   3–2C

Contented Sole   **£ 41** ❶
80 High St CM0 8AA   (01621) 786900
Isolated it may be (and generating few reports), but
this "lovely" little restaurant is again tipped for its
"excellent" fish dishes, and "wonderful" steak too.
/ **Details:** www.contentedsole.co.uk; 10 pm; closed
Tue & Sun D.

BURTON-ON-TRENT,
STAFFORDSHIRE   5–

99 Station Street   **£ 45** ❶
99 Station St DE14 1BT   (01283) 516859
Any rail traveller would be blessed to stumble upon
this "wonderful" local restaurant, near the station,
which is tipped for "fantastic" food from a menu on
which "everything is home-made".
/ **Details:** www.99stationstreet.com; 9 pm; closed Mon,
Tue, Wed L & Sun D; no Amex.

BURY ST EDMUNDS, SUFFOLK   3–1C

Benson Blakes   **£ 21** ❷❸❸
88-89 St. Johns St IP33 1SQ   (01284) 755188
"Phenomenal burgers" (and "amazing cocktails")
top the bill at this popular bar and grill, which also
offers a range of "top beers from the USA, UK and
Europe". / **Details:** www.bensonblakes.co.uk;
@BensonBlakes; 9 pm, Fri & Sat 9.30 pm.

Maison Bleue £ 51 ❶❷❷
30-31 Churchgate St IP33 IRG
(01284) 760623
"Better than ever"; run by the Crépy family (of
Great House, Lavenham fame), this restaurant elicits
a wealth of superlatives for its "excellent fish",
"lovely waiting staff" and "delightfully romantic"
ambience; there's even a "top-notch cheese trolley".
/ **Details:** www.maisonbleue.co.uk; @Maison_Bleue;
9 pm, Sat 9 pm; closed Mon & Sun; no Amex.

Pea Porridge £ 47 ❷❸❸
28-29 Cannon St IP33 IJR (01284) 700200
"A true gem"; Justin Sharp's "great little bistro" is a
"cosy and homely but rather crowded" former
bakery, in a backstreet outside the town centre – a
"friendly" sort of place, where the "quirky" and
"eclectic" cuisine is absolutely "spon on", and "good
value" too. / **Details:** www.peaporridge.co.uk; 10 pm;
closed Mon, Tue L & Sun; no Amex.

Valley Connection £ 42 ❸❷❸
42 Churchgate St IP33 IRG (01284) 753161
This "welcoming" town-centre Indian is still tipped,
as "the best in the area" – staff are "so friendly"
and the food is well-rated by nearly all those who
report on it. / **Details:** www.valley-connection.com;
11.30 pm.

BUSHEY HEATH, HERTFORDSHIRE 3–2A

The Alpine £ 49 ❶
135 High Rd WD23 IJA (020) 8950 2024
A "great Italian", tipped as a destination where "all
generations are superbly looked after", and at a
reasonable price; "it's recommended to eat at
ground floor level".
/ **Details:** www.thealpinerestaurant.co.uk;
@The_Alpine; 10.30 pm; closed Mon.

BUSHEY, HERTFORDSHIRE 3–2A

St James £ 45 ❸❸❹
30 High St WD23 3HL (020) 8950 2480
"A gem of a place in a culinary desert"; "OK, it
wouldn't turn heads in the West End", but this
"totally reliable" spot has "upped its game in terms
of presentation and adventure" of late, and is "very
reasonably priced" to boot.
/ **Details:** www.stjamesrestaurant.co.uk; opp St James
Church; 9.30 pm; closed Sun D; booking essential.

CAMBER, EAST SUSSEX 3–4C

**The Beach Bistro
Gallivant Hotel** £ 51 ❷❷❸
New Lydd Rd TN31 7RB (01797) 225 057
"Fine dining by any standard"; with "its stunningly
fresh" fish from a "marvellous menu", this "lovely
seaside spot", in a New England-style hotel, is
"highly recommended" by all who comment on it.
/ **Details:** www.thegallivanthotel.com; @thegallivant;
9 pm, Fri-Sat 9.30 pm.

CAMBRIDGE, CAMBRIDGESHIRE 3–1B

Alimentum £ 71 ❷❸⑤
152-154 Hills Rd CB2 8PB (01223) 413000
"Technically very clever" cuisine that can be
"astonishingly wonderful" has won a major culinary
reputation for Mark Poynton's foodie mecca; "it's an
odd place" though – a "stark" room "not in the
most salubrious bit of town" – and the overall
experience can seem "cold".
/ **Details:** www.restaurantalimentum.co.uk;
@alimentum1; 9.30 pm; closed Sun; booking essential.

Bill's £ 40 ❹❹❸
34-35 Green St CB2 3JX (01223) 329638
OK, it's a chain, but this "fun and buzzy" café is "a
welcome addition to Cambridge", and is most
popular for its "luscious" brunch.
/ **Details:** www.bills-website.co.uk; 11 pm, Sun
10.30 pm.

**The Cambridge Chop
House** £ 47 ❹❸❸
1 Kings Pde CB2 1SJ (01223) 359506
All reporters recommend this self-explanatory
operation even if it "neither surprises nor
disappoints" – "given the general lack of affordable
quality eating in Cambridge, it's honest and
unpretentious", and handily located (opposite
King's). / **Details:** www.cambridgechophouse.co.uk;
@cambscuisine; 10.30 pm, Sat 11 pm, Sun 9.30 pm.

Cotto £ 73 ❶❶❷
183 East Rd CB1 1BG (01223) 302010
"Just lovely every time we go"; despite its "strange
location" (you enter through a café), this fine dining
venture "never disappoints", thanks to its
"spectacularly good" cuisine, from a "thoughtful
menu making the most of local and seasonal
produce". / **Details:** www.cottocambridge.co.uk;
9.15 pm; D only, Wed-Sat; no Amex.

d'Arry's £ 45 ❶
2-4 King St CB1 1LN (01223) 505015
Handily located behind Christ's College, this
"friendly" gastropub is generally tipped for high
standards across the board; however, the former
chef left during the survey year (to establish a new
venture, Great Northern).
/ **Details:** www.darrys.co.uk; 10 pm; no Amex; need 8+
to book.

Dojo £ 30 ❶
1-2 Millers Yd, Mill Ln CB2 1RQ
(01223) 363471
"For a quick and tasty fill-up", a town-centre
"student hang-out" tipped for "large portions" of
"good-value" pan-Asian noodles and broths.
/ **Details:** www.dojonoodlebar.co.uk; 10.30 pm;
no Amex; no booking.

Fitzbillies **£ 36** ❸④④
52 Trumpington St CB2 1RG (01223) 352500
Locals remain "delighted with this reopening of
what is a Cambridge institution", renowned for its
"superb Chelsea buns" (and other cakes); now
thanks to Tim Hayward it also operates a dining
area offering "big gutsy flavours and interesting
dishes" too, although this space is "a tad sparse",
and "service can slip". / **Details:** www.fitzbillies.com;
8pm, Fri & Sat 9.45 pm; closed Sun D.

Hotel du Vin et Bistro **£ 55** ❸❸❸
15-19 Trumpington St CB2 1QA
(01223) 227330
This "atmospheric" outpost of the wine-led bistro
and hotel chain, a poor performer in former years, is
now hailed in most reports as a "reliable" standby
(where the "great steak 'n' chips" makes a
particularly dependable choice); even fans, though,
note that it's "not cheap".
/ **Details:** www.hotelduvin.com; 9.45 pm, Fri & Sat
10.30 pm. **Accommodation:** 41 rooms, from £180.

Midsummer House **£ 133** ❶❶❷
Midsummer Common CB4 1HA
(01223) 369299
"Awesome", "adventurous", "truly wonderful" – fans
find Daniel Clifford's Cam-side restaurant is a
destination "on which it would be hard to improve";
there's no denying, however, that there's a small
minority of punters for whom the style of the place
will just never 'click'.
/ **Details:** www.midsummerhouse.co.uk; 9.30 pm;
closed Mon, Tue L & Sun.

Oak Bistro **£ 44** ❸❸④
6 Lensfield Rd CB2 1EG (01223) 323361
"Better than most places in Cambridge, though
there should still be more competition!"; this little
spot, "halfway between the station and the city-
centre", is "often booked up" thanks to its "solid
British bistro fare". / **Details:** www.theoakbistro.co.uk;
10 pm; closed Sun.

Pipasha Restaurant **£ 32** ❼
529c, Newmarket Rd CB5 8PA
(01223) 577786
The "location isn't great" ("not in the town on what
looks like a housing estate"), but if you're looking for
a "fantastic Indian meal", this is a top tip locally.
/ **Details:** www.pipasha-restaurant.co.uk; 11 pm;
D only.

Rainbow Café **£ 31** ❼
9a King's Pde CB2 1SJ (01223) 321551
Handily located near King's College, this basement
veggie is tipped by fans for its "wonderfully
interesting and varied" fare; it has to be admitted,
though, that there is a minority for whom it's
"overhyped". / **Details:** www.rainbowcafe.co.uk;
9.30 pm; closed Mon & Sun D; no Amex; no booking.

Sea Tree **£ 31** ❸❸④
13 The Broadway CB1 3AH (01223) 414349
A "great take-away chippy", tipped for "excellent-
quality fish". / **Details:** www.theseatree.co.uk; 10 pm,
Sun 9 pm; closed Mon L & Sun L.

**The St John's Chop
House** **£ 50** ❸❸❸
21-24 Northampton St CB3 0AD
(01223) 353 110
"Far enough from the tourist track to be delightful",
this sibling to the Cambridge Chophouse delivers
"very British, carnivorous fare" in a "cosy", if no-
nonsense setting.
/ **Details:** www.stjohnschophouse.co.uk; 10.30 pm, Sat
10 pm, Sun 9.30 pm.

Restaurant 22 **£ 51** ❸❸❸
22 Chesterton Rd CB4 3AX (01223) 351880
This cosy riverside villa outside the city centre
continues to be a romantic and gastronomic choice
for some reporters; overall, however, the realisation
of the "exciting" menu is judged "good not great",
and the interior can seem a mite "provincial and
'80s". / **Details:** www.restaurant22.co.uk; 9.30 pm;
D only, closed Mon & Sun; children: 12+.

CANTERBURY, KENT 3–3D

Apeksha **£ 32** ❼
24 St Peters St CT1 2BQ (01227) 780079
"Not your usual curry restaurant"; near the
Westgate Tower, an establishment tipped for a
"more interesting" menu than usual, with a "good
choice for fish-eaters and vegetarians"; the daily
lunchtime buffet is "amazingly good value".
/ **Details:** www.apeksha.co.uk; 11 pm.

Café des Amis **£ 40** ❸❸❷
95 St Dunstan's St CT2 8AD (01227) 464390
"Still as good as it ever was" – this "long-standing
favourite", by the Westgate, is a "very cheerful" sort
of spot that offers "excellent Mexican food" (and
"heavenly" puds to boot).
/ **Details:** www.cafedez.com; 10 pm, Fri & Sat
10.30 pm, Sun 9.30 pm; booking: max 6 at D Fri-Sat.

Cafe du Soleil **£ 40** ❼
4-5 Pound Lane CT1 2BZ (01227) 479999
An old riverside building tipped for its "good pizzas,
lovely staff and beautiful décor"; reports are still
relatively few, though, and not 100% consistent.
/ **Details:** www.cafedusoleil.co.uk; 10 pm.

Cafe Mauresque **£ 38** ❷❸❷
8 Butchery Ln CT1 2JR (01227) 464300
Just off the main drag, a "dark and atmospheric
basement decorated and lit in Moorish style",
serving "very good" Moroccan small plates.
/ **Details:** www.cafemauresque.com; 10 pm, Fri & Sat
10.30 pm.

Deeson's British Restaurant £ 50 ❷⓿❷
25-27 Sun St CT1 2HX (01227) 767854
All the more remarkable for being "just a few steps from the cathedral", this "lovely" spot offers "seasonal dishes with flair and flavour" and "exemplary" service; "for a leisurely lunch with friends or a special dinner, you can't fault this place". / Details: www.deesonsrestaurant.co.uk; @deesonsbritish; 10 pm.

Goods Shed £ 49 ❷❹❸
Station Road West CT2 8AN (01227) 459153
Set in the permanent farmers' market just by Canterbury West, this "intriguing and eccentric" venue sources its ingredients from the "excellent" produce stalls below; it's particularly recommended as the ideal location for a "perfect fry-up". / Details: www.thegoodsshed.co.uk; 9.30 pm; closed Mon & Sun D.

Michael Caines ABode Canterbury £ 71 ❸❹❹
High St CT1 2RX (01227) 766266
"Can be very good indeed, but, oh dear, the menus are rather strange sometimes" – reports on this city-centre outpost of the Gidleigh Park chef remain somewhat mixed; and "when lightly populated, the room lacks atmosphere." / Details: www.michaelcaines.com; @michaelcaines; 10 pm; closed Sun D. Accommodation: 73 rooms, from £105.

La Trappiste £ 39 ❸❺❷
1-2 Sun St CT1 2HX (01227) 479111
An "amazing beer menu" is the 'crown jewel' feature at these "quirky" premises near the Cathedral (once a gents' outfitters), but the food (from coffee and cakes, to more substantial fare) is "really good" too; at peak-times though, service can be "very slow". / Details: www.latrappiste.com; 10.30 pm; no Amex.

CARDIFF, CARDIFF 2–2A

Casanova £ 39 ❷❸❹
13 Quay St CF10 1EA (029) 2034 4044
"Despite the uninspiring exterior", this "tiny, authentic Italian" shines in a city of "all-too-common pizza and pasta places"; all reporters praise the "very good" food, and it is complemented by a "well-chosen" wine list. / Details: www.casanovacardiff.com; 10 pm; closed Sun.

Fish at 85 £ 25 ❷❷❷
85 Pontcanna St CF11 9HS (02920) 020212
"A unique concept, grouping fish wholesaler, retailer and restaurant" – if you're looking for "the sort of food you might find in a harbour-side establishment in France or Italy", this "small", "fishmonger-style" venture (with fish on display) is emphatically the top

tip locally. / **Details:** www.fishat85.co.uk; @Fishat85; 9 pm; closed Mon & Sun; no Amex.

Happy Gathering £ 32 ❷❸❸
233 Cowbridge Road East CF11 9AL (029) 2039 7531
This Cantonese quarter-centenarian located appropriately enough in Canton, is say fans "the best Chinese in South Wales"; for top results from the "vast menu", "go off piste and ask to be recommended dishes." / Details: www.happygatheringcardiff.co.uk; 10.30 pm; Sun 9 pm.

Mint and Mustard £ 41 ❶❷❸
134 Whitchurch Rd CF14 3LZ (02920) 620333
"Proving that Indian food can be a gourmet experience"; this "extremely accommodating" Gabalfa spot comes "highly recommended" for a meal that's "brilliant and different, while still quintessentially Indian". / Details: www.mintandmustard.com; 11 pm; D only; no shorts.

The Potted Pig £ 53 ❸❷❸
27 High St CF10 1PU (029) 2022 4817
This "semi-subterranean venue" – a former bank vault, with some feel of a "dark and crowded dungeon" – is "clearly one of Cardiff's 'in' places", offering some "mouth-watering original dishes" (if "not a lot of pig"!). / Details: www.thepottedpig.com; 9 pm; closed Mon & Sun D.

Purple Poppadom £ 47 ❶❷❸
185a, Cowbridge Road East CF11 9AJ (029) 2022 0026
A former Mint & Mustard chef has now taken his "creative" skills – plus a good few of his customers – to this "high-class" (but "noisy") two-year-old Indian in Canton; fans claim that the results here are "even better" (but the food score still lags its rival). / Details: purplepoppadom.com; Mon-Sat 11pm; Sun 9pm.

Vegetarian Food Studio £ 26 ❶❷❹
115-117 Penarth Rd CF11 6JU (029) 2023 8222
"A grand spot that is soon to be grander as they are moving to double the size of place!" – success has brought expansion for this brilliant Gujarati outfit (previously at 109), serving outstanding veggie fare at bargain prices; BYO (£1 corkage). / Details: www.vegetarianfoodstudio.co.uk; 9.30 pm; closed Mon; no Amex.

Woods Brasserie £ 47 ❸❸❸
Pilotage Building, Stuart St CF10 5BW (029) 2049 2400
This "attractively located" waterfront restaurant is "highly thought-of locally" on account of its quite stylish design and "good, simple bistro food".

/ *Details: www.woods-brasserie.com; 10 pm; closed Sun D; no Amex.*

CARLISLE, CUMBRIA   7–2D

Alexandros   **£ 40** ❸❷❸
68 Warwick Rd CA1 1DR (01228) 592227
"Very well cooked, no-frills Greek food"; this "friendly family restaurant", run by its attentive owner, serves authentic specialities like "whole grilled sea bream, skewered lamb and kleftiko".
/ *Details: www.thegreek.co.uk; 9.30 pm; closed Mon L & Sun.*

CARTMEL FELL, CUMBRIA   7–4D

The Masons Arms   **£ 43** ❸❸❷
Strawberry Bank LA11 6NW (01539) 568486
"A must for lunch, if you are walking in the area", this "traditional Lakeland pub" remains a "longtime favourite" for all the reporters who comment on it; attractions include a "great choice of beers", and "open fires" too. / Details: www.strawberrybank.com; W from Bowland Bridge, off A5074; 9 pm.
Accommodation: *7 rooms, from £75.*

CARTMEL, CUMBRIA   7–4D

L'Enclume   **£ 118** ❶❷❸
Cavendish St LA11 6PZ (01539) 536362
Simon Rogan's sheer "artistry" – "mixing innovation, tradition and local produce" in an "astonishing range" of dishes, delivered by "passionate" staff – produces one of the UK's most "divine" culinary experiences, at this "beautiful and remote" former Lakeland smithy. / Details: www.lenclume.co.uk; J36 from M6, down A590 towards Cartmel; 9 pm; closed Mon L & Tue L; children: 12+. **Accommodation:** *17 rooms, from £99.*

Rogan & Co   **£ 55** ❷❹❸
Devonshire Sq LA11 6QD (01539) 535917
L'Enclume's adjacent bistro-style spin-off offers "a more straightforward menu than its prestigious parent", but fans say it's "just as exceptional" in its way; weak service is a bugbear though – "occasionally you feel a visit to charm school wouldn't go amiss".
/ *Details: www.roganandcompany.co.uk; @simon_rogan; 9 pm; closed Mon & Tue; no Amex.*

CASTLE COMBE, WILTSHIRE   2–2B

**Bybrook Restaurant
Manor House Hotel**   **£ 87** ❶❷❹
Manor House Hotel and Golf Course SN14 7HR (01249) 782206
It's not just the "picture-perfect setting" which sets this country house dining room apart – Richard Davies's cuisine impresses all reporters with its great "attention to detail"; the space itself, however, can seem "a bit soulless".
/ *Details: www.exclusivehotels.co.uk; @themanorhouse; 9.30 pm; closed Mon L; no jeans or*

trainers; children: 11+. **Accommodation:** *48 rooms, from £205.*

CAVENDISH, SUFFOLK   3–1C

The George   **£ 46** ❷❷❷
The Green CO1 8BA (01787) 280248
In a "great setting overlooking the Green", a "stylish and popular" 16th-century restaurant-with-rooms offering consistently "good-value" fare; dining possibilities range from an "enormous dining table that can take several generations" to a "more intimate bistro and bar area to the rear".
/ *Details: www.thecavendishgeorge.co.uk; 9.30 pm; closed Sun D.* **Accommodation:** *5 rooms, from £60.*

CHADDESLEY CORBETT, WORCESTERSHIRE   5–4B

Brockencote Hall   **£ 62** ❷❷❷
DY10 4PY (01562) 777876
Corporate ownership seems to have done no harm at all to standards at this "fabulous" and "romantic" country house hotel; it's "getting better each season as the new regime beds in", not least insofar as the "superb service and wonderful food" are concerned.
/ *Details: www.brockencotehall.com; on A448, outside village; 9 pm; no trainers.* **Accommodation:** *21 rooms, from £135.*

CHAGFORD, DEVON   1–3C

Gidleigh Park   **£ 135** ❶❶❷
TQ13 8HH (01647) 432367
"An extraordinary experience in all respects!"; this culinary Shangri-La – again, the UK's foodie No. 1 – occupies a plush Tudorbethan mansion, set in "glorious" scenery (and gardens), on a remote fringe of Dartmoor; Michael Caines's "beautifully crafted" cuisine is "unbelievably excellent", and matched with a "vast selection" of unusual wines.
/ *Details: www.gidleigh.com; from village, right at Lloyds TSB, take right fork to end of lane; 9.30 pm; no jeans or trainers; children: 8+ at L + D.* **Accommodation:** *24 rooms, from £345.*

22 Mill Street   **£ 61** ❶
22 Mill St TQ13 8AW (01647) 432244
"An unexpected find"; this small restaurant-with-rooms is a handy tip if you're in search of something a little less grand and pricey than the famous establishment up the road; reports, though, have been less numerous since the former chef departed in 2012. / Details: www.22millst.com; @22millst; 9.30 pm; closed Mon, Tue & Sun; no trainers; children: 12+. **Accommodation:** *2 rooms, from £99.*

CHANDLER'S CROSS, HERTFORDSHIRE   3–2A

The Clarendon   **£ 55** ❹❹❸
Redhall Ln WD3 4LU (01923) 270009
There's a lot of survey feedback on this "modernised country pub", but it's mixed – fans say

it's a "fantastic local" with good "straightforward" cuisine, foes that it's "nothing particularly memorable, and perhaps a little expensive for what it is". / **Details:** www.theclarendon.co.uk; Mon-Sat 10 pm, Sun 9.30 pm.

Colette's
The Grove　　　　**£ 91**　④④④
WD17 3NL　(01923) 296015
With its "very talented" chef, the main restaurant of this contemporary country house hotel is, for some reporters, a "delight"; it inspires every shade of opinion, though, and critics dismiss it as a "cold dining room… and very expensive!"
/ **Details:** www.thegrove.co.uk; 9.30 pm; D only, closed Mon & Sun; children: 16+. **Accommodation:** 227 rooms, from £310.

The Glasshouse
The Grove　　　　**£ 58**　❼
WD3 4TG　(01923) 296015
A top tip for those who like "lots of choice" – "all you can eat, in more luxury than usual", at the generously stocked buffet, at the heart of this "smart" modern country house hotel complex.
/ **Details:** www.thegrove.co.uk; 9.30 pm, Sat 10 pm. **Accommodation:** 227 rooms, from £310.

The Stables at The Grove £ 55　④❸❸
WD3 4TG　(01923) 296015
In the "glorious" grounds of a 'groovy-grand' country house (where Stubbs painted, apparently), this "bright" and luxurious venue near the golf tees wins praise for its attractive style; on the downside, it's predictably "expensive". / **Details:** 9.30 pm.

CHELTENHAM, GLOUCESTERSHIRE　　2–1C

Le Champignon Sauvage £ 76　❶❷④
24-28 Suffolk Rd　GL50 2AQ　(01242) 573449
"Astonishingly good" cooking that's "both exciting and innovative", a wine list that's "both interesting and affordable", and "friendly" service too – for most, if not quite all, reporters, the Everitt-Mathieus' town-centre legend remains a "delightful" destination, somewhat "subdued" ambience notwithstanding.
/ **Details:** www.lechampignonsauvage.co.uk; @lechampsauvage; 8.30 pm; closed Mon & Sun.

The Curry Corner　　**£ 45**　❷❸④
133 Fairview Rd　GL52 2EX　(01242) 528449
A Bangladeshi gem, where the "subtly spiced" food is "not only always of a high standard, but more varied than the ubiquitous curry house fare" too.
/ **Details:** www.thecurrycorner.com; @thecurrycorner; 11 pm; closed Mon & Fri L.

The Daffodil　　　**£ 52**　❷❸❶
18-20 Suffolk Pde　GL50 2AE　(01242) 700055
Set "in an old Art Deco Cinema" (with the kitchen where the screen would have been), this "quirky" venue has a "wonderful" ambience, especially when hosting its regular jazz nights; its cooking nowadays is "reliably good" (not always the case in past years). / **Details:** www.thedaffodil.com; @thedaffodil; 10 pm, Sat 10.30 pm; closed Sun.

Lumière　　　　　**£ 67**　❶❷④
Clarence Pde　GL50 3PA　(01242) 222200
Higher ranking than the celebrated Champignon Sauvage, Jon Howe & Helen Aubrey's "plain, neat dining room in a side-street" belies it's slightly "dull" appearance with its "exquisite" cooking – which "allows great ingredients to be tasted in very imaginative combinations" – and its "delightful" service. / **Details:** www.lumiere.cc; 9 pm; closed Mon & Sun, Tue L; children: 8+ D.

Prithvi　　　　　**£ 44**　❶❶❷
37 Bath Rd　GL53 7HG　(01242) 226229
"Definitely one of the best Indian meals I've had outside India!"; all reports confirm that this "not particularly fancy-looking" Indian "outclasses all the local competition" with its "very unusual" and "remarkably good" cooking.
/ **Details:** www.prithvirestaurant.com; @37Prithvi; 10.30 pm; closed Mon & Tue L; no Amex.

Purslane　　　　**£ 48**　❷❸④
16 Rodney Rd　GL50 1JJ　(01242) 321639
"A welcome newcomer to the town that's one to watch" – this "small central bistro" ("tucked away so you won't stumble upon it") wins high ratings for its "imaginative" menu "with the focus on fresh fish and local produce"; service is "not polished, but willing". / **Details:** www.purslane-restaurant.co.uk; 9.30pm; closed Mon & Sun.

The Royal Well Tavern　　**£ 44**　❼
5 Royal Well Pl　GL50 3DN　(01242) 221212
"No shocks, no surprises", just a town-centre gastropub, offering "a really warm welcome" – a venue tipped not only for its "fixed-price lunch menu" but also "for a date".
/ **Details:** www.theroyalwelltavern.com; Mon-Wed 9.30 pm, Thu 10 pm, Fri & Sat 10.30 pm, Sun 9 pm.

CHESTER, CHESHIRE　　　　5–2A

Architect　　　　**£ 46**　❸❸❷
54 Nicholas St　CH1 2NX　(01244) 353070
Pre-eminent local pub chain Brunning & Price recently opened this "nicely situated" gastropub, by the racecourse; fans of the brand feel they "know what to expect", and its "good, reliable food" and "attentive service" do not disappoint.
/ **Details:** www.brunningandprice.co.uk/architect; 10 pm, Sun 9.30 pm; no Amex.

La Brasserie
Chester Grosvenor　　**£ 60**　❸❸❷
Eastgate　CH1 1LT　(01244) 324024
Views differ on the recent refurb, but this "expensive but very splendid" Gallic brasserie, off the foyer of the city's grand hotel pleases most, if not quite all, of

the reporters who comment on it, with its comfortable style and "compact" menu.
/ **Details:** www.chestergrosvenor.com; 10 pm, Sun 9 pm. **Accommodation:** 80 rooms, from £230.

1539 £ 53 ○
The Racecourse CH1 2LY (01244) 304 611
An impressive position overlooking the city's racecourse helps makes this modern restaurant a top "special occasion" tip for some reporters; it's perhaps best sampled for the good-value lunchtime menu, though – those paying full prices may feel the food tastes "more like outside catering".
/ **Details:** www.restaurant1539.co.uk; 10 pm; closed Sun D; special booking rules apply on race days.

Joseph Benjamin £ 45 ❷❷❷
140 Northgate St CH1 2HT (01244) 344295
"A deli-cum-restaurant almost under the city walls", offering a "varied and well thought-out menu catering for all tastes", and at "reasonable prices" too; its new tapas offshoot, Porta, also attracts praise for its "freshly-cooked" fare.
/ **Details:** www.josephbenjamin.co.uk; 9.30 pm; closed Mon, Tue D, Wed D & Sun D.

Michael Caines
ABode Hotels £ 73 ❷❷❷
Grosvener Rd CH1 2DJ (01244) 347 000
"Overlooking the racecourse, with views down to the River Dee", a top-floor restaurant in a modern hotel development, offering dishes of often "excellent" quality (albeit in rather "small" portions); look out for some "really great promotional offers".
/ **Details:** www.michaelcaines.com; @michaelcaines; 9 pm, Sat 10 pm; closed Sun L; no jeans or trainers.
Accommodation: 85 rooms, from £.

Moules A Go Go £ 40 ○
39 Watergate Row CH1 2LE (01244) 348818
Up on the city's unique medieval 'rows', a "reliable" informal eatery, tipped in particular as "good value for lunch". / **Details:** www.moulesagogo.co.uk; @MoulesaGoGo; 10 pm, Sun 9 pm.

The Old Harkers Arms £ 45 ○
Russell St CH3 5AL (01244) 344525
Near the canal, and handy for the railway station, an outpost of the Brunning & Price gastropub empire; by night it can get "rammed", so it's really tipped as a location for a (more tranquil) lunch.
/ **Details:** www.brunningandprice.co.uk; 9.30 pm; no Amex.

Simon Radley
The Chester Grosvenor £ 97 ❷○❷
Eastgate CH1 1LT (01244) 324024
For a "luxurious experience" full of "old-fashioned graciousness", this "comfy" (if windowless) dining room – in an unusually grand hotel, next to the city's iconic Eastgate clock – makes a fine destination; service is "immaculate" and the cuisine "consistently first class" (with a "massive" wine list to go with it).

/ **Details:** www.chestergrosvenor.com; @TheGrosvenor; 9 pm; D only, closed Mon & Sun; no trainers; children: 12+. **Accommodation:** 80 rooms, from £230.

Sticky Walnut £ 45 ❷❷❷
11 Charles St CH2 3AZ (01244) 400400
Tucked away in Hoole, a short cab ride from the town's picturesque centre, this "intimate and friendly neighbourhood bistro" wins high praise for its "very-well prepared cuisine"; there is the odd critic, however, for whom it's become "very average".
/ **Details:** www.stickywalnut.com; @stickywalnut; 10 pm, Sun 3 pm; closed Sun D.

Upstairs at the Grill £ 50 ❷❷❸
70 Watergate St CH1 2LA (01244) 344883
"A top place for a treat!" – this self-proclaimed 'Manhattan-style' steakhouse is a "professional" sort of operation, that's "pricey, but worth it for the whole experience".
/ **Details:** www.upstairsatthegrill.co.uk; 11 pm; Mon-Thu D only, Fri-Sun open L & D.

CHESTERFIELD, DERBYSHIRE 5–2C

Nonna's £ 45 ○
131 Chatsworth Rd S40 2AH (01246) 380035
A "sleek", "upmarket" and "deservedly popular" (slightly "noisy") Italian, tipped as a reliable destination in this poorly-served town.
/ **Details:** @NonnasCucina; 11 pm; closed Mon.

CHICHESTER, WEST SUSSEX 3–4A

The Kennels £ 61 ❸❷○
Goodwood Hs PO18 0PX (01243) 755000
With its "fabulous setting" on the Goodwood Estate, and its "perfect" cooking, this "relaxing" restaurant gives no cause for complaint… apart, of course, from the fact that it can seem rather "pricey".
/ **Details:** www.goodwood.co.uk/thekennels; Tue-Fri 9.15pm, Sun 3pm; closed Mon & Sun D.

Lemongrass £ 38 ○
5-6 Saint Pancras PO19 7SJ (01243) 533280
Top tip locally for "consistently tasty Thai" cooking; this slick establishment near the town centre is "very reasonably priced" too.
/ **Details:** www.lemongrasssussex.co.uk; 10.45 pm; no Amex.

CHIDDINGFOLD, SURREY 3–3A

The Swan Inn £ 48 ❷❷❷
Petworth Rd GU8 4TY (01428) 684 688
The former proprietors of Knightsbridge pub the Swag 'n' Tails now run this "classy" and "stylish" boutique hotel-cum-gastropub, where – all reporters agree – the food is "consistently very good".
/ **Details:** www.theswaninnchiddingfold.com; 10 pm, Sun 9 pm. **Accommodation:** 10 rooms, from £100.

CHINNOR, OXFORDSHIRE   2–2D

The Sir Charles Napier   £ 56   ❷❷❶
Spriggs Alley OX39 4BX   (01494) 483011
With its "beautiful" Chilterns location, "lovely
sculpture garden" and "cosy and welcoming
interior", Julie Griffiths's well-known posh pub would
be a big hit even without its "enticing menu of well-
executed cuisine" and "brilliantly conceived wine
list"; "you'll have trouble finding it" though, and
when you do it's "expensive".
/ **Details:** www.sircharlesnapier.co.uk; Tue-Fri 9.30 pm,
Sat 10 pm; closed Mon & Sun D.

CHIPPING CAMPDEN,
GLOUCESTERSHIRE   2–1C

The Ebrington Arms   £ 44   ❸❸❷
GL55 6NH   (01386) 593 223
A favourite family-run inn, serving up "imaginative"
food (with some "good-value specials"), in a "lovely"
location. / **Details:** www.theebringtonarms.co.uk;
@theebrington; 9 pm; SRA-51%.

CHIPPING NORTON, OXFORDSHIRE   2–1C

Wild Thyme   £ 49   ❶❷❸
10 New St OX7 5LJ   (01608) 645060
"Memorable", "quite outstanding in every way",
"can't fault it" – this family-run restaurant serves
"wonderful food" to the "highest standard"; the
occasional critic, though, can find portions rather
"small". / **Details:** www.wildthymerestaurant.co.uk;
@wtrestaurant; 9 pm; closed Mon & Sun.
Accommodation: 3 rooms, from £75.

CHIPSTEAD, KENT   3–3B

The George & Dragon   £ 42   ❷❸❸
39 High St TN13 2RW   (01732) 779 019
"The best gourmet pub in the area", say fans,
making "excellent use of seasonal and local
ingredients"; the ambience is "hard to beat" too,
especially "in front of the massive fireplace".
/ **Details:** www.georgeanddragonchipstead.com;
@georgechipstead; 9.30 pm, Sun 8.30 pm; no Amex.

CHOBHAM, SURREY   3–3A

Stovell's   £ 53   ❷❷❷
125 Windsor Rd GU24 8QS   (01276) 858000
"Recently opened, and already a destination", this
"beautifully refurbished" 16th-century building
boasts "not one skilled chef-proprietor, but two!";
"portions are small, and prices high, but the quality
is superb". / **Details:** www.stovells.com; 9.30 pm;
closed Mon, Sat L & Sun D.

CHRISTCHURCH, DORSET   2–4C

The Jetty   £ 56   ❷❷❷
95 Mudeford BH23 3NT   (01202) 400950
"A beautiful view of Christchurch harbour" is just
one of the attractions of this glam and "very

enjoyable" waterside spot, where Alex Aitken
"maintains excellent culinary standards", and which
"always offers a good choice of fish fresh from the
catch". / **Details:** www.thejetty.co.uk; 9.45 pm, Sun
7.45 pm; SRA-71%.

CHURCHILL, OXFORDSHIRE   2–1C

Chequers   £ 52   ❷❷❷
Church Ln OX7 6NJ   (01608) 659393
"Quirky, hip and offering a sophistication which
eludes so many country pubs", this "little gem"
delights all reporters with its "properly
accomplished" cuisine (with the "main focus on
steak"), and its "friendly" service.
/ **Details:** 9.30 pm, sun 9 pm.

CIRENCESTER, GLOUCESTERSHIRE 2–2C

Jesses Bistro   £ 60   ❷❷❸
Black Jack St GL7 2AA   (01285) 641497
"A hidden gem"; externally, it may look "like a
shed", but this cutely hidden-away town centre
bistro is praised by all who comment on it for its
"home-made" and "very tasty" cuisine, which
includes lots of fish. / **Details:** www.jessesbistro.co.uk;
@jessesbistro; 9.15 pm; closed Mon D & Sun.

Made By Bob   £ 44   ❷❸④
The Cornhall 26 Market Pl GL7 2NY
(01285) 641818
"Probably the best kept secret in the West!"; in a
poorly-served city, this handy bistro scores high
praise for its "perfectly executed dishes" (including
"excellent breakfasts"), plus "delicious deli items" to
take home too. / **Details:** www.foodmadebybob.com;
9.30 pm; closed Mon D, Tue D, Wed D, Sat D & Sun D.

CLACHAN, ARGYLL AND BUTE   9–3B

Loch Fyne Oyster Bar   £ 49   ❶❷❷
PA26 8BL   (01499) 600236
No longer part of the chain it spawned – a famous,
if remote lochside destination that's still of note for
its "wonderfully fresh seafood"; staff are "cheery"
and "welcoming" too. / **Details:** www.loch-fyne.com;
10m E of Inveraray on A83; 8 pm.

CLAVERING, ESSEX   3–2B

The Cricketers   £ 44   ❸❸❸
Wicken Rd CB11 4QT   (01799) 550442
"Jamie Oliver's dad's pub" sits by a "beautiful"
village green in north Essex, and "cheery and
helpful service (despite being very busy)" adds to its
"comfy" charms; the food is "well-sourced and well-
cooked", but some long term fans feel "the
standard's gone down" in recent years.
/ **Details:** www.thecricketers.co.uk; @CricketersThe; on
B1038 between Newport & Buntingford; 9.30 pm;
no Amex. **Accommodation:** 14 rooms, from £95.

CLIFTON, CUMBRIA   8–3A

George & Dragon   **£ 46**   ❸❸❸
CA10 2ER   (01768) 865381
A "well-chosen menu of pub classics using locally sourced ingredients" and "surprisingly handy for the M6 too" – this is a useful gastropub to know about, so let's hope the occasional "off-day" reported of late is not the start of a trend.
/ **Details:** www.georgeanddragonclifton.co.uk; on the A6 in the village of Clifton; 9 pm.
Accommodation: 12 rooms, from £95.

CLIMPING, WEST SUSSEX   3–4A

Bailiffscourt Hotel   **£ 71**   ❷❷❶
BN17 5RW   (01903) 723511
This "faux-medieval" country house (and spa) is a "beautiful hideaway", and most reports confirm that its dining room offers an "outstanding" culinary experience too. / **Details:** www.hshotels.co.uk; 9.30 pm; booking: max 8; children: 7+.
Accommodation: 39 rooms, from £205.

CLIPSHAM, RUTLAND   6–4A

The Olive Branch   **£ 50**   ❷❸❸
Main St LE15 7SH   (01780) 410355
This "beautiful old pub", not far from the A1, has carved a formidable reputation for its "superior food" and "great wines to try by the glass"; those who experienced it a few years ago, however, feel it's "still lovely, still always interesting, but has lots its 'edge'". / **Details:** www.theolivebranchpub.com; @theolivebranch; 2m E from A1 on B664; 9.30 pm, Sun 9 pm; no Amex. **Accommodation:** 6 rooms, from £135.

CLITHEROE, LANCASHIRE   5–1B

The Assheton Arms   **£ 41**   ❷❷❸
BB7 4BJ   (01200) 441227
A "friendly" new operation from the fishing family who also own The Oyster and Otter (Feniscowles); it offers a "great menu", with – rather unsurprisingly – "fish a speciality"! and results can be "stunning".

Inn at Whitewell   **£ 49**   ❷❸❶
Forest of Bowland BB7 3AT   (01200) 448222
This celebrated inn ("seamlessly" expanded in recent years) is, for many, "the perfect pub" thanks to its "unfailing" cuisine, and "wonderful" location with "views to die for" of the Trough of Bowland; "it's a pity it gets so crowded, particularly at weekends". / **Details:** www.innatwhitewell.com; 9.30 pm; bar open L & D, restaurant D only; no Amex.
Accommodation: 23 rooms, from £120.

CLYST HYDON, DEVON   1–3D

The Five Bells Inn   **£ 45**   ❷❷❶
EX15 2NT   (01844) 277288
This "friendly" 16th-century village inn is not only of

note for its "great atmosphere" – it also offers a "fantastic" range of "delicious" locally-sourced dishes that please all who comment on them.

CLYTHA, MONMOUTHSHIRE   2–1A

Clytha Arms   **£ 48**   ❷❷❸
NP7 9BW   (01873) 840206
"Excellent, locally-sourced produce" (with "high-quality shellfish" a highlight) is served in "monster portions" at this rural inn, long in the ownership of the same family. / **Details:** www.clytha-arms.com; on Old Abergavenny to Raglan road; 9.30 pm; closed Mon L & Sun D. **Accommodation:** 4 rooms, from £80.

COBHAM, SURREY   3–3A

La Capanna   **£ 63**   ❸❷❸
48 High St KT11 3EF   (01932) 862121
In "an historic and picturesque building, with a minstrels' gallery for secluded dining", this is the sort of place "where everyone locally seems to go for a special occasion"; the food – Italian – doesn't get much of a mention, but it never seems to disappoint. / **Details:** www.lacapanna.co.uk; 11 pm.

COGGESHALL, ESSEX   3–2C

Baumann's Brasserie   **£ 54**   ④④❸
4-6 Stoneham St CO6 1TT   (01376) 561453
Established in 1986, this "accommodating" brasserie is hailed by its fans as "the perfect local"; some former supporters are unimpressed nowadays however, citing, for example, that it has become "pricier". / **Details:** www.baumannsbrasserie.co.uk; 9.30 pm, Fri & Sat 10 pm, Sun 9 pm; closed Mon & Tue.

COLERNE, WILTSHIRE   2–2B

Lucknam Park   **£ 107**   ❷❶❷
SN14 8AZ   (01225) 742777
This "ravishing" Palladian country house hotel offers a "fantastic experience, starting from the second you walk through the door"; Hywel Jones's cooking is "top class" – "just what an award winning restaurant should be about".
/ **Details:** www.lucknampark.co.uk; 6m NE of Bath; 10 pm; closed Mon, Tue–Sat D only, closed Sun D; jacket and/or tie; children: 5+ D & Sun L.
Accommodation: 42 rooms, from £345.

Lucknam Park (Brasserie)   **£ 56**   ❷❸❸
SN14 8AZ   (01225) 742777
"More relaxing", and "lacking the culinary embellishment of the Park Restaurant" – this country house hotel's No. 2 destination is an "upmarket" brasserie, with "sharp" cooking, "excellent" cocktails and staff who "look after you very well"; "beautiful terrace" too.

/ **Details:** *www.lucknampark.co.uk; 6m NE of Bath; 10 pm.*

COLNE, LANCASHIRE   5–1B

Banny's Restaurant   **£ 29**   ❷❸④
I Vivary Way BB8 9NW   (01282) 856220
*"In the culinary desert of east Lancashire, a welcome find" – a "modern", "bright" and "comfortable", "marine-themed" operation serving up "excellent traditional fish 'n chips" (it's part of, but not attached to the Boundary Mill Outlet). / **Details:** www.bannys.co.uk; 8.45 pm; no Amex.*

CONGLETON, CHESHIRE   5–2B

Pecks   **£ 55**   ❸❸❸
Newcastle Rd CW12 4SB   (01260) 275161
*With its "unique" no-choice, one-sitting, 7-course 'dinner at 8' formula, this "theatrical" family-run fixture remains, for most reporters, a destination that "never fails to impress"; lunches are more conventional, but also "good value". / **Details:** www.pecksrest.co.uk; off A34; 8 pm; closed Mon & Sun D; booking essential.*

COOKHAM, BERKSHIRE   3–3A

Bel & The Dragon   **£ 52**   ❸❸❷
High St SL6 9SQ   (01628) 521263
*By the Stanley Spencer Museum, a "very large" gastroboozer (part of a local chain), whose attractions are a "fun" atmosphere, "nice" (if sometimes "slow") service and a pleasant terrace; the "vivid" food is good too, so the place is "rammed at weekends". / **Details:** www.belandthedragon-cookham.co.uk; @BelDragon_R; 10 pm, Sun 9.30 pm.*

Maliks   **£ 40**   ❶❷❸
High St SL6 9SF   (01628) 520085
*"First-rate food is served with charm and efficiently" at this renowned Indian, which occupies a "beautiful timbered building" in the "pretty village of Cookham". / **Details:** www.maliks.co.uk; from the M4, Junction 7 for A4 for Maidenhead; 11.30 pm, Sun 10.30 pm.*

Luke's Dining Room
Sanctum on The Green
Hotel   **£ 51**   ❼
The Old Cricket Common SL6 9NZ
(01628) 482638
*The eponymous Luke may be barely out of his teens, but the dining room at this "informal" restaurant-with-rooms is tipped for a cuisine that's "simple but well-prepared". / **Details:** www.lukesdiningroom.com; @cheflukethomas; 9 pm; closed Mon D & Sun D; booking: max 6 on Sat. **Accommodation:** 9 rooms, from £120.*

The White Oak   **£ 40**   ④④④
The Pound SL6 9QE   (01628) 523043
*Mixed views this year on this well-known village pub; to most reporters it remains a "charming" venue whose quality is "a big surprise", but a number of critics complain of "disappointing" food and "absent" service. / **Details:** www.thewhiteoak.co.uk; 9.30 pm, Sun 8.30 pm.*

COPSTER GREEN, LANCASHIRE   5–1B

Yu And You   **£ 43**   ❷❷❸
500 Longsight Rd BB1 9EU   (01254) 247111
*Under "incredibly hospitable" owners, this "award-winning Chinese" (of Ramsay TV fame) is going from strength to strength, thanks to its "amazing" Cantonese dishes from "properly sourced ingredients" – "not cheap but worth it". / **Details:** www.yuandyou.com; @yuandyou; off the A59 7 miles towards Clitheroe; 11 pm, Fri & Sat 2 am; D only, closed Mon; no Amex.*

CORSE LAWN, GLOUCESTERSHIRE   2–1B

Corse Lawn Hotel   **£ 51**   ❸❸④
GL19 4LZ   (01452) 780771
*After nearly 40 years under the same ownership, it's perhaps no surprise that the Hine family's restaurant-with-rooms can strike critics as "stuck in the era of Constance Spry"; the cuisine is still pretty "reliable", though, with "local game" a highlight; the bistro is sometimes preferred to the main restaurant. / **Details:** www.corselawnhotel.co.uk; 5m SW of Tewkesbury on B4211; 9.30 pm. **Accommodation:** 18 rooms, from £160.*

CORSHAM, WILTSHIRE   2–2B

Methuen Arms   **£ 50**   ❸④④
2 High St SN13 0HB   (01249) 717060
*"A town-centre inn, where the food is of restaurant quality" – given its rather "old-fashioned" appearance, its standards can come as a "pleasant surprise". / **Details:** www.themethuenarms.com; 10pm.*

COWBRIDGE, VALE OF GLAMORGAN   1–1D

Bar 44   **£ 13**   ❷❸❸
44c High St CF71 7AG   (01446) 776488
*"It keeps improving, and now on a par with London-based tapas operations" – this "relaxed" bar makes "a good first floor retreat from shopping", and is a top tip in these parts on account of its "very good tapas". / **Details:** www.bar44.co.uk; @Bar44tapas; 9 pm, Fri - Sun 10 pm; closed Mon D; no Amex.*

COWLEY, GLOUCESTERSHIRE   2–1C

Cowley Manor   **£ 51**   ❼
GL53 9NL   (01242) 870900
Surprisingly few reports on what is sometimes tipped as "the best-located country house dining

room in England" – contemporary in style, and "ideal for a laid-back lunch, followed by a roam around afterwards".
/ **Details:** www.cowleymanor.com; 10 pm, Fri & Sat 11 pm; SRA-54%. **Accommodation:** 30 rooms, from £245.

CRANBROOK, KENT   3–4C

Apicius   **£ 56**   **❷❷**④
23 Stone St TN17 3HF   (01580) 714666
"Sensational!"; fans are vociferous in their praise for the "fascinatingly intricate" dishes on offer at Faith Hawkins & Timothy Johnson's out-of-the-way village restaurant… but "oh for a bit more atmosphere"!
/ **Details:** www.restaurant-apicius.co.uk; 9 pm; closed Mon, Tue, Sat L & Sun D; no Amex; children: 8+.

CRASTER, NORTHUMBERLAND   8–1B

Jolly Fisherman   **£ 37**   **❷**④**❷**
NE66 3TR   (01665) 576461
"Amazing seafood, especially the kipper paté and the crab sandwiches", and "sea views to die for" – no wonder this waterside inn remains an ever-popular destination; fans say it's "worth a huge detour". / **Details:** near Dunstanburgh Castle; 9 pm; no Amex; no booking.

CRAYKE, NORTH YORKSHIRE   5–1D

Durham Ox   **£ 49**   **❸❷❷**
Westway YO61 4TE   (01347) 821506
With its "impressive views over the Vale of York", this village pub is a "special place", serving "fantastic home-cooked food" in a "cosy" atmosphere; be advised, though, "portions are so large they seem aimed at those who have been on a seven-mile hike!" / **Details:** www.thedurhamox.com; 9.30 pm, Sun 8.30 pm. **Accommodation:** 5 rooms, from £100.

CREIGIAU, CARDIFF   2–2A

Caesars Arms   **£ 48**   **❸❷❸**
Cardiff Rd CF15 9NN   (029) 2089 0486
"Choose your ingredients (meat/fish) from the fridge, sit back and enjoy" – the "simple formula" which makes this "bustling and friendly" (if somewhat "old-school") inn "a useful place to know about"; it's a very popular destination locally.
/ **Details:** www.caesarsarms.co.uk; beyond Creigiau, past the golf club; 10 pm; closed Sun D.

CRICKHOWELL, POWYS   2–1A

The Bear   **£ 39**   ④**❸**④
High St NP8 1BW   (01873) 810408
A famous "traditional" coaching inn which generates a lot of reports; but is it relying on its reputation? – fans do praise its "great range of pub food" cooked "to a pretty high standard", but to critics it's just "really unimaginative".
/ **Details:** www.bearhotel.co.uk; 9.30 pm; D only, ex

Sun open L only, closed Mon; children: 10+.
Accommodation: 36 rooms, from £95.

CROMARTY, HIGHLAND   9–2C

Sutor Creek   **£ 43**   **❶❷**④
21 Bank St IV11 8YE   (01381) 600855
"This tiny little café produced a crab tart topped with a Hollandaise sauce that ranks as the best dish I have eaten!" – this may be 'just' a pizzeria-cum-seafood joint, but all reports sing its praises as a "great value" destination that's "hard to beat" – "a real treat!" / **Details:** www.sutorcreek.co.uk; 9 pm; closed Mon & Tue; no Amex.

CROSTHWAITE, CUMBRIA   7–4D

The Punch Bowl   **£ 49**   **❷❸❷**
LA8 8HR   (01539) 568237
"The Lakes' best pub for food", claim fans of this very well-known inn (with rooms), which wins very steady praise with its "idyllic" location, "fine" cooking, "great indoor and outdoor spaces", and "well-curated" list of wines and beers.
/ **Details:** www.the-punchbowl.co.uk; off A5074 towards Bowness, turn right after Lyth Hotel; 9.30 pm.
Accommodation: 9 rooms, from £105.

CROYDON, SURREY   3–3B

Albert's Table   **£ 48**   **❶❸❸**
49c South End CR0 1BF   (020) 8680 2010
"A jewel in south Croydon"; Joby Wells's restaurant "continues to excel in a dull suburban setting" with its "unexpected fine dining" for which "fresh British seasonal ingredients" are "imaginatively combined and beautifully presented".
/ **Details:** www.albertstable.co.uk; @albertstable; 10.30 pm; closed Mon & Sun D.

McDermotts Fish & Chips   **£ 28**   **❶❷**④
5-7 The Forestdale Shopping Centre Featherbed Ln CR0 9AS   (020) 8651 1440
Fans acclaim Tony McDermott's venture as the "best fish and chip shop in the UK", combining "excellent" fare with "speed, style and service"; the decor, on the other hand, is not to all tastes.
/ **Details:** www.mcdermottsfishandchips.co.uk; 9.30 pm, Sat 9 pm; closed Mon & Sun.

CRUDWELL, WILTSHIRE   2–2C

The Potting Shed   **£ 44**   **❸❷❷**
The St SN16 9EW   (01666) 577833
"A great find" – this "very popular gastropub", in a scenic Cotswolds location, offers "good seasonal food" ("not flash but fab") and "caring service".
/ **Details:** www.thepottingshedpub.com; @pottingshedpub; 9.30 pm, Sun 9 pm; no Amex.
Accommodation: 12 rooms, from £95.

CUCKFIELD, WEST SUSSEX 3–4B

Ockenden Manor **£ 78** ❸④④
Ockenden Ln RH17 5LD (01444) 416111
"Only fair to good, despite the Michelin star"; fans do find it a "lovely" location with "superb" cuisine, but some reports suggest that this country house hotel "is competent but lacks the wow factor", with service, in particular, too often seeming "quite amateur". / Details: www.hshotels.co.uk; 8.30 pm; no jeans or trainers. Accommodation: 28 rooms, from £190.

CUPAR, FIFE 9–3D

The Peat Inn **£ 69** ❶❶❷
KY15 5LH (01334) 840206
There a certain "magic" to visiting Geoffrey and Katherine Smeddle's famous country inn – a "cosseting" haven of "fine dining in an isolated rural location"; the cuisine is "clean, fresh, innovative and well-presented", and the wine list "heavenly". / Details: www.thepeatinn.co.uk; @thepeatinn; at junction of B940 & B941, SW of St Andrews; 9 pm; closed Mon & Sun. Accommodation: 8 rooms, from £180.

DALRY, NORTH AYRSHIRE 9–4B

Braidwoods **£ 64** ❶❶❷
Drumastle Mill Cottage KA24 4LN
(01294) 833544
"Still the finest dining experience to be had in Scotland", say fans; Keith and Nicola Braidwood's cosily converted croft inspires enthusiastic praise for its "marvellous" cooking and "always welcoming" style – "a remarkable achievement for such a tiny team". / Details: www.braidwoods.co.uk; 9 pm; closed Mon, Tue L & Sun; children: 12+ at D.

DANEHILL, EAST SUSSEX 3–4B

Coach And Horses **£ 54** ❷❸❷
School Ln RH17 7JF (01825) 740369
"Locally sourced ingredients, well cooked", plus a "warm welcome, and great beers and wines" are the making of this atmospheric rural boozer. / Details: www.coachandhorses.co; off A275; 9 pm, Fri-Sat 9.30 pm, Sun 3 pm; closed Sun D.

DARTMOUTH, DEVON 1–4D

RockFish Seafood and Chips **£ 34** ❷❸④
8 South Embankment TQ6 9BH
(01803) 832800
Mitch Tonks's "relaxed" riverside fish 'n' chip joint (with "boats passing close by and the smell of the sea") certainly "sells on location", and child-friendliness too ("amazing kids packs"); everyone says the scoff is "excellent", too; (now in Plymouth also). / Details: www.rockfishdevon.co.uk/index.php; 9.30pm.

The Seahorse **£ 65** ❷❸❸
5 South Embankment TQ6 9BH
(01803) 835147
"Dartmouth's jewel" – Mitch Tonks's understated dining room near the river "straddles the smart/casual line perfectly" and serves "outstanding fresh fish", cooked in a "beautifully simple" (perhaps slightly unadventurous) fashion. / Details: www.seahorserestaurant.co.uk; @SeahorseDevon; 9.30 pm; closed Mon, Tue L & Sun D.

DATCHWORTH, HERTFORDSHIRE 3–2B

The Tilbury **£ 48** ❸④❸
Watton Rd SG3 6TB (01438) 815 550
"Skillful cooking" at "fair prices", wins many plaudits for this "warm and comfortable" dining room, annexed to a pub; there's an "excellent wine list" too, with "good availability by the glass and the carafe". / Details: www.thetilbury.co.uk; 9 pm, Fri & Sat 9.30 pm; closed Mon & Sun.

DEAL, KENT 3–3D

81 Beach Street **£ 42** ❼
81 Beach St CT14 6JB (01304) 368136
An "exceptional view" rewards visitors to this sea-view restaurant, tipped for food of a "very good standard" (including a "fantastic-value" lunch). / Details: www.81beachstreet.co.uk; @81beachstreet; 10 pm; closed Sun D.

DEDHAM, ESSEX 3–2C

The Sun Inn **£ 45** ④❺❸
High St CO7 6DF (01206) 323351
This Constable country pub elicits many reports, but they remain rather mixed; fans praise the "unusual but excellent menu" and "very good and reasonably-priced wine list", but critics feel that it "trades on its location", with service in particular "very hit and miss". / Details: www.thesuninndedham.com; Fri & Sat 10 pm, 9.30 pm; no Amex. Accommodation: 7 rooms, from £110.

Le Talbooth **£ 67** ❸❷❶
Gun Hill CO7 6HP (01206) 323150
This vintage Constable country hotel offers a "first-class", ultra-"romantic" experience that's "even better" since its recent (60th anniversary) refurbishment; let's hope the new chef (recruited from the spiritually similar Auberge du Lac) keeps up the good work. / Details: www.milsomhotels.com; 5m N of Colchester on A12, take B1029; 9 pm; closed Sun D; no jeans or trainers.

DERBY, DERBYSHIRE 5–3C

Anoki **£ 42** ❶❷❸
First Floor, 129 London Rd DE1 2QN
(01332) 292888

"Beautifully-presented food that's full of flavour", and served by *"fantastic" staff* makes it well worth discovering this city-centre Indian occupying a former Art Deco cinema; likewise the *"authentic"* fare at its nearby Burton spin-off makes it *"an incredible find just off the A38".* / **Details:** www.anokiderby.co.uk; 11.30 pm, Sun 9.30; D only.

Darleys £ 54 ❷❸❷
Darley Abbey Mill DE22 1DZ (01332) 364987
"Consistently a very good option that others in Derby should strive to match!"; this restaurant with *"a lovely modern setting overlooking the river"* garners very positive reports (not least for its *"exceptional-value" lunch);* the *"vegetarian menu is a bonus".* / **Details:** www.darleys.com; 9 pm; closed Sun D; no Amex; children: 10+ Sat eve.

Ebi Sushi £ 37 ❶❷④
Abbey St DE22 3SJ (01332) 265656
Thanks to the "Toyota factory literally just down the road", this café in an un-lovely bit of town is without doubt *"the best Japanese in the East Midlands"!* – reporters are wowed by the *"truly authentic" cuisine* at *"astonishingly reasonable prices"* (and the absence of *"tourist kitsch"* too). / **Details:** 10.30 pm; D only, closed Mon & Sun; no Amex.

DINTON, BUCKINGHAMSHIRE 2–3C

La Chouette £ 56 ❷❸❸
Westlington Grn HP17 8UW (01296) 747422
The *"mercurial"/"charismatic"* Belgian chef-patron adds *"quirky"* interest to this dining room styled *"to look (intentionally) like someone's front room";* assuming you like *"heavily sauced, traditional French fare",* it's *"a great place to go if you can stand the insults"* (most of them well-meant!) / **Details:** off A418 between Aylesbury & Thame; 9 pm; closed Sat L & Sun; no Amex.

DODDISCOMBSLEIGH, DEVON 1–3D

The NoBody Inn £ 47 ④❸❶
EX6 7PS (01647) 252394
"Wow, what a setting!" – this *"old-fashioned inn in the middle of nowhere"* pleases all reporters with its *"unpretentious but stellar" cooking* and *"excellent wine list";* the cheese board is *"particularly worth trying".* / **Details:** www.nobodyinn.co.uk; off A38 at Haldon Hill (signed Dunchidrock); 9 pm, Fri & Sat 9.30 pm; no Amex. **Accommodation:** 5 rooms, from £60.

DONHEAD ST ANDREW, WILTSHIRE 2–3C

The Forester £ 42 ❷❸❸
Lower St SP7 9EE (01747) 828038
"Maintaining excellent standards", this village gastroboozer serves *"high-class"* cuisine, with fish the speciality.

/ **Details:** www.theforesterdonheadstandrew.co.uk; off A30; 9 pm; closed Sun D.

DORCHESTER, DORSET 2–4B

Sienna £ 63 ❶❶④
36 High West St DT1 1UP (01305) 250022
Russell & Elena Brown's decade-old town centre restaurant continues to wow reporters with dishes *"cooked to perfection"* and *"warm and friendly"* service too; the premises are *"very small"* – fans find them *"cosy",* but others feel the atmosphere *"could be improved".* / **Details:** www.siennarestaurant.co.uk; @siennadorset; 9 pm; closed Mon, Tue L & Sun; no Amex; children: 12+.

DORKING, SURREY 3–3A

Restaurant Two To Four £ 49 ❸❷❷
2-4 West St RH4 1BL (01306) 889923
"A real bonus for Dorking!"; this *"charming"* beamed building on the edge of the town is not just a destination for the local *"ladies who lunch"* – on most accounts it offers *"excellent food at reasonable prices".* / **Details:** www.2to4.co.uk; @Two_FourDorking; 10 pm; closed Mon & Sun D.

DOUGLAS, ISLE OF MAN 7–4B

Tanroagan £ 54 ❷❷❸
9 Ridgeway St IM1 1EW (01624) 612 355
"One of the better places to eat on the Isle of Man" wins culinary praise for its *"lovely seafood menu";* the only problem is that the *"friendly little dining room"* is *"really too crowded"* for comfort. / **Details:** www.tanroagan.co.uk; @Tanroagan_Rest; 9.30 pm; closed Sat L & Sun; no Amex.

DREWSTEIGNTON, DEVON 1–3C

The Old Inn £ 61 ❶❷❷
EX6 6QR (01647) 281 276
Unanimous praise for the *"super-friendly"* reception (not least from the *"lovely dogs"*) at this *"homely inn"* manned by former 22 Mill Street chef Duncan Walker, whose *"great soufflés"* rate particular mention. / **Details:** www.old-inn.co.uk; 9 pm; closed Sun-Tue, Wed L, Thu L; no Amex; children: 12 or over. **Accommodation:** 3 rooms, from £90.

DUNBAR, EAST LOTHIAN 9–4D

The Rocks £ 38 ❷❶❷
Marine Rd EH42 1AR (01368) 862287
"Nothing is too much trouble" for staff at this characterful (*"slightly old-fashioned"*) waterside inn, which enjoys fine coastal views; *"make sure you go hungry"* to get the most out of its *"hearty portions of excellent shellfish".* / **Details:** www.therocksdunbar.co.uk; 9 pm; no Amex. **Accommodation:** 11 rooms, from £75.

DUNVEGAN, HIGHLAND 9–2A

The Three Chimneys £ 88 ❷❷❶
Colbost IV55 8ZT (01470) 511258
*"An oasis of pleasure in a faraway place"; from its
"magical location" in a former crofter's cottage by
Loch Dunvegan, to its "superb fresh fish and
shellfish", Eddie and Shirley Spear's remote venture
really is "outstanding all round"; if there's a quibble,
it's that its style can seem "a bit hushed".*
/ **Details:** www.threechimneys.co.uk; 5m from
Dunvegan Castle on B884 to Glendale; 9.45 pm; closed
Sun L; children: 8+. **Accommodation:** 6 rooms,
from £295.

DURHAM, COUNTY DURHAM 8–3B

Bistro 21 £ 48 ❸❸❸
Aykley Heads Hs DH1 5TS (0191) 384 4354
*A "splendid restaurant all round, even though you
need a car to get there"; this well-established
outpost of Terry Laybourne's Newcastle-based
empire offers "reliable bistro cooking, with
interesting choices and specials" in a "relaxed"
setting a little out of the centre.*
/ **Details:** www.bistrotwentyone.co.uk; @bistro_21;
10 pm; closed Sun D.

Finbarr's £ 46 ❶
Flass Vale DH1 4BG (0191) 370 9999
*Only a modest number of reports on this "smart"
restaurant, sometimes tipped as "the best dining
experience in Durham"; the occasional critic,
though, thinks prices are "crazy".*
/ **Details:** www.finbarrsrestaurant.co.uk; 9.30 pm, Sun
9 pm.

Gourmet Spot
Farnley Tower Hotel £ 59 ❶
The Avenue DH1 4DX (0191) 384 6655
*An out-of-the-way basement restaurant, tipped for
"excellent food and service"* / **Details:**
www.gourmet-spot.co.uk; 9 pm; D only, closed Mon &
Sun. **Accommodation:** 13 rooms, from £95.

Oldfields £ 46 ❹❸❹
18 Claypath DH1 1RH (0191) 370 9595
*A handily located all-day brasserie whose "quality
locally sourced food" and reasonable prices make it
"a regular stop off" for many reporters; there are
critics, though, who find its standards too "ordinary".*
/ **Details:** www.oldfieldsrealfood.co.uk; @eatoldfields;
10 pm, Sun 9 pm.

EAST CHILTINGTON, EAST SUSSEX 3–4B

Jolly Sportsman £ 49 ❷❸❸
Chapel Ln BN7 3BA (01273) 890400
*A "lovely spot just off the South Downs"; fans praise
Bruce Wass's inn for "great food" an "interesting
atmosphere" and a formidable list of wines and
whiskies, while even critics admit that "despite any
blips, it's always enjoyable".*
/ **Details:** www.thejollysportsman.com;
@JollySportsman1; NW of Lewes; 10 pm; closed
Mon & Sun D; no Amex.

EAST CHISENBURY, WILTSHIRE 2–3C

Red Lion £ 51 ❷❷❸
SN9 6AQ (01980) 671124
*"Top-notch food in a tiny old inn in the middle of
nowhere", from an "ex-Chez Bruce team"; it's "not
cheap, for a pub", but worth it for the "excellent
British cooking".*
/ **Details:** www.redlionfreehouse.com; 8.45 pm;
no Amex.

EAST CLANDON, SURREY 3–3A

Queen's Head £ 40 ❷❷❷
The Street GU4 7RY (01483) 222332
*"Brilliant pub food, and dog-friendly too!" – this
smartly modernised village inn, in the Surrey Hills, is
a notably consistent all-round crowd-pleaser.*
/ **Details:** www.queensheadeastclandon.co.uk.

EAST GRINSTEAD, WEST SUSSEX 3–4B

Gravetye Manor £ 79 ❷❶❶
Vowels Ln RH19 4LJ (01342) 810567
*The new regime finally seems to be getting to grips
with this "lovely" Elizabethan country house hotel
(set amid famously "wonderful" gardens); "it's hard
not to be seduced on all fronts", including "superb"
cooking that increasingly lives up to the location.*
/ **Details:** www.gravetyemanor.co.uk; 2m outside
Turner's Hill; 9.30 pm, Sun 9 pm; booking: max 8;
children: 7+. **Accommodation:** 17 rooms, from £240.

EAST HADDON, NORTHAMPTONSHIRE 5–4D

The Red Lion £ 46 ❷❸❸
Main St NN6 8BU (01604) 770223
*"A popular pub/restaurant in a pretty village",
offering "inventive" cooking, "beautifully served";
(the rooms are "extremely comfortable" too).*
/ **Details:** www.redlioneasthaddon.co.uk; 9.30 pm,
Sat & Sun 10 pm; no Amex. **Accommodation:** 5
rooms, from £75.

EAST HENDRED, OXFORDSHIRE 2–2D

The Eyston Arms £ 48 ❷❷❷
High St OX12 8JY (01235) 833320
*The style may be "informal", but the ambitious
dishes at this out-of-the-way inn, near the Ridgeway,
are often realised to simply "excellent" standards.*
/ **Details:** www.eystons.co.uk; 9 pm; closed Sun D.

EAST LAVANT, WEST SUSSEX 2–4D

The Royal Oak £ 50 ❸❷❷
Pook Ln PO18 0AX (01243) 527 434
*This "lovely country pub" (with rooms) – "over-run
during events at Goodwood" – is a "real find" for*

most reporters, serving pub grub that's *"always good"*. / **Details:** www.royaloakeastlavant.co.uk; 9 pm, Sat 9.30 pm; no shorts. **Accommodation:** 10 rooms, from £125.

EAST LOOE, CORNWALL   1–4C

Trawlers   **£ 50**   ❶
On The Quay PL13 1AH   (01503) 263593
"In a part of the world knee-deep in good fish places", an establishment tipped as standing out from the crowd with the *"creative"* presentation of its *"first-class"* ingredients, and a list boasting some *"decent Cornish wines"*.
/ **Details:** www.trawlersrestaurant.co.uk; 9.30 pm.

EAST MOLESEY, SURREY   3–3A

Mezzet   **£ 32**   ❷❷❸
43 Bridge Rd KT8 9ER   (020) 89794088
"The meze are memorable" at this *"smart"* and *"pleasant"* Lebanese operation, which inspires only positive reports; *"main courses from the BBQ"* come well recommended too. / **Details:** www.mezzet.co.uk; 10 pm; closed Sun D.

EAST WITTON, NORTH YORKSHIRE   8–4B

Blue Lion   **£ 48**   ❸❹❸
DL8 4SN   (01969) 624273
In a *"delightful"* coaching inn, this *"longstanding favourite"* serves up food with *"a local accent"* (including *"some of the best game in the region"*); it's also recommended as a prime place to stay.
/ **Details:** www.thebluelion.co.uk; @blueloninn; between Masham & Leyburn on A6108; 9.15 pm; no Amex. **Accommodation:** 15 rooms, from £94.

EASTBOURNE, EAST SUSSEX   3–4B

The Mirabelle
The Grand Hotel   **£ 65**   ❷❷❷
King Edwards Pde BN21 4EQ   (01323) 412345
"Fine dining in a truly grand hotel"; now back on top form, this is one of those rare seaside dining rooms which is *"rather continental in its high standards"*.
/ **Details:** www.grandeastbourne.com; 9.45 pm; closed Mon & Sun; jacket or tie required at D.
Accommodation: 152 rooms, from £199.

EASTON GRAY, WILTSHIRE   2–2C

Dining Room
Whatley Manor   **£ 102**   ❷❷❹
SN16 0RB   (01666) 822888
In this *"truly luxurious and relaxing"* country house hotel, Martin Bruge delivers some *"outstanding dishes"* (and others that are *"just extremely good"*); the styling, though, does strike some reporters as overly dated. / **Details:** www.whatleymanor.com; 8 miles from J17 on the M4, follow A429 towards Cirencester to Malmesbury on the B4040; 9.30 pm; D only, closed Mon-Tue; no jeans or trainers; children: 12+. **Accommodation:** 23 rooms, from £305.

Angels With Bagpipes   **£ 50**   ❸❹❹
343 High St, Royal Mile EH1 1PW
(0131) 2201111
"Don't be put off by the exterior – inside there's a warm welcome" say fans of this outpost of the Valvona & Crolla empire, which has *"a great location on the Royal Mile"*; for its critics, however, its Scottish cuisine remains *"outrageously pricey"*.
/ **Details:** www.angelswithbagpipes.co.uk; @angelsfood; 9.45 pm.

Bell's Diner   **£ 29**   ❸❸❸
7 St Stephen St EH3 5EN   (0131) 225 8116
"Generation after generation love this entirely unpretentious, fairly scruffy place" – *"quality hamburgers, with the usual sides, plus old-fashioned American desserts"* are *"cheerfully served"*, in a *"fun"* space that's *"now acquired a definite air of retro chic!"* / **Details:** 10 pm; closed weekday L & Sun L; no Amex.

Cafe Andaluz   **£ 39**   ❷❸❷
77B, George St EH2 3EE   (0131) 220 9980
"Best for tapas"; this large New Town outpost of a small Weegie group is not just a *"fun"* sort of place – all reports say the food's excellent too.
/ **Details:** www.cafeandaluz.com; 10.30 pm, Sun 10 pm; no Amex.

Café Fish   **£ 50**   ❷❸❹
15 North West Circus Pl EH3 6SX
(0131) 2254431
On the fringe of the New Town, these former bank premises can be *"buzzy"* but can also seem *"a bit big and empty"*; the food generally hits the spot though – *"excellent fish of every description, in a variety of styles"*. / **Details:** www.cafefish.net; @cafefishedin; 9.30 pm, Sun 4 pm; closed Mon & Sun D.

Café Marlayne   **£ 41**   ❸❷❸
1 Thistle St EH2 1EN   (0131) 226 2230
"Cramped and busy, but the food is worth it" – almost all reports on this *"classic"* New Town bistro concur that it's *"a favourite to keep going back to"* (especially for lunch).
/ **Details:** www.cafemarlayne.com; 10 pm; no Amex.

Le Café St-Honoré   **£ 46**   ❷❷❷
34 NW Thistle Street Ln EH2 1EA
(0131) 226 2211
"Gallic charm and no pretensions" mean that this *"crisp"* and *"oh-so-French"* bistro *"hidden away down a side street"* in New Town *"never fails to delight"*, not least with its *"classic"* cooking.
/ **Details:** www.cafesthonore.com; 10 pm; SRA-80%.

Calistoga Central   **£ 42**   ❸❸❹
70 Rose St EH2 3DX   (01312) 251233
"Hidden in the most obscure location, you venture into the back alleys of Edinburgh to find this little

gem"; the pay off? – "interesting wines from California" at "a fixed mark-up of £5/bottle", and food that does it reasonable justice. / **Details:** www.calistoga.co.uk; 10 pm.

The Castle Terrace　**£ 75**　❶❷❸
33/35 Castle Ter　EH1 2EL　(0131) 229 1222
"A better setting than Kitchin, and more accessible"; by the castle, Tom K's "wonderful" restaurant it hailed for its often "amazing" cuisine; even in the face of this "excellence all round", there's the odd hint in reports that prices are getting "silly". / **Details:** www.castleterracerestaurant.com; 10 pm; closed Mon & Sun.

Centotre　**£ 48**　④⑤❸
103 George St　EH2 3ES　(0131) 225 1550
"A buzzing place to eat or drink", this former New Town banking hall undoubtedly has a "fantastic" setting; the "standard Italian fare" often pleases too, but, like the service, it can also be a bit "hit and miss". / **Details:** www.centotre.com; @centotre; 10 pm, Fri & Sat 11 pm, Sun 8 pm.

Chaophraya　**£ 49**　❷❷❸
33 Castle St　EH2 3DN　(01312) 267614
"A beautiful location for this chain that doesn't feel like a chain"; the former site of Oloroso (RIP) – with its "superb" castle-views – now offers a "great range" of Thai fare, realised to a standard somewhere between "good" and "excellent". / **Details:** www.chaophraya.co.uk; @ChaophrayaThai; On the 4th Floor; 10 pm.

David Bann　**£ 40**　④④④
56-58 St Marys St　EH1 1SX　(0131) 556 5888
This well-established Old Town veggie still inspires a fair amount of feedback; even some fans acknowledge that results are "hit or miss", however, and although the "hits are really good", the misses can "sound delicious but end up tasteless". / **Details:** www.davidbann.com; 10 pm, Fri & Sat 10.30 pm.

Divino Enoteca　**£ 49**　❸❷❷
5 Merchant St　EH1 2QD　(0131) 225 1770
An "excellent" Old Town Italian all-rounder, situated in a cellar just off the Royal Mile; it attracts plaudits not just for its "authentic" food but for its "great wine selection by the glass" too.
/ **Details:** www.vittoriagroup.co.uk; midnight, Fri & Sat 1 am; closed Sun.

The Dogs　**£ 38**　❷④❷
110 Hanover St　EH2 1DR　(0131) 220 1208
This "shabby chic" New Town gastroboozer offers "rustic" and "hearty" dishes that are "a great modern twist on traditional Scottish fare" (with a particularly "affordable" lunchtime menu); service, though, has its ups and downs.
/ **Details:** www.thedogsonline.co.uk; 10 pm.

The Dome　**£ 46**　❶
14 George St　EH2 2PF　(0131) 624 8624
"Timeless, elegant and wonderful", this former bank is a "stunning" building of an opulence rarely seen, even in the New Town; it's especially tipped as a "great place for afternoon tea", but it makes a handy rendezvous at any time.
/ **Details:** www.thedomeedinburgh.com; 10 pm.

Dusit　**£ 50**　❷❷④
49a Thistle St　EH2 1DY　(0131) 220 6846
"Great food, could be a bit cosier" – a neat summary of the many reports on this Thai restaurant, "tucked away" in the New Town.
/ **Details:** www.dusit.co.uk; 11 pm.

L' Escargot Blanc　**£ 35**　❶
17 Queensferry St　EH2 4QW　(0131) 226 1890
A New Town "gem" which "retains the feel of a true French bistrot", and which is tipped for its "decent cooking and friendly staff"; "steep" entry steps, though. / **Details:** www.lescargotblanc.co.uk; 10 pm, Fri & Sat 10.30 pm; closed Sun.

L'Escargot Bleu　**£ 41**　❷❷❷
56 Broughton St　EH1 3SA　(0131) 557 1600
"Just like being in France in every respect" – this "Edinburgh favourite" in the New Town is an "excellent value" bistro – the sort of place serving "fantastic côte de beouf".
/ **Details:** www.lescargotblanc.co.uk; 10 pm, Fri & Sat 10.30 pm; closed Sun; no Amex.

Favorita　**£ 44**　❷❷❸
325 Leith Walk　EH6 8SA　(0131) 554 2430
"That wood-fired oven makes all the difference!", say fans of this bustling Morningside Italian – "a family favourite, with superb pizza".
/ **Details:** www.la-favorita.com; 11 pm.

Field　**£ 34**　❷❸❸
41 West Nicolson St　EH8 9DB　(01316) 677010
"A tiny place, punching above its weight!" – this "new kid on the block in Southside" (on the side of Home Bistro, RIP) wins a big thumbs up for its "modern British/Scottish" fare "with interesting twists". / **Details:** www.fieldrestaurant.co.uk; @Field_Edinburgh.

Fishers Bistro　**£ 43**　❷❷❸
1 The Shore　EH6 6QW　(0131) 554 5666
This "popular", "friendly", and "well-run" fish restaurant, with a super location on the Leith waterfront, is a real all-round crowd-pleaser; "in case fish is not your thing, they even offer very good steaks!" / **Details:** www.fishersrestaurantgroup.co.uk; 10.30 pm.

Fishers in the City　**£ 45**　❸❸❸
58 Thistle St　EH2 1EN　(0131) 225 5109
"Always reliable" – this cramped New Town bistro

Field

Pompadour

Timberyard

serves *"great oysters, fish 'n' chips, and many other fish dishes"*, and is often noted for the *"even"* quality of its cooking and *"good value"*. / **Details:** *www.fishersbistros.co.uk; 10.30 pm.*

Forth Floor
Harvey Nichols £ 58 🕐
30-34 St Andrew Sq EH2 2AD
(0131) 524 8350
Not many, but consistent, reports on this elevated department store dining room, tipped for *"clever dishes, discreet service, and great views of the castle"*. / **Details:** *www.harveynichols.com; @hn_forthfloor; 10 pm; closed Mon D & Sun D; SRA-65%.*

Galvin Brasserie de Luxe
The Caledonian £ 51 🕐
Princes St EH1 2AB (0131) 222 8988
Still early days, but reports on the Galvin brothers' grandly-housed brasserie operation are unexpectedly middling (*"we expected great things, but…"*); on balance, though, it's still said to be a *"pretty good"* performer. / **Details:** 10 pm. **Accommodation:** 245 rooms, from £.

Gardener's Cottage £ 41 ❶❷❷
Royal Ter EH7 5DX (0131) 558 1221
"You can't be fussy – you get six courses, and no choice", all served at communal tables, at this *"quirky"* yearling, near the A1; it's been a smash hit though – service is *"passionate"*, the style is *"sociable"*, the food – from the *"finest produce"* – is *"earthy"* and all-in-all it's a *"genuinely new and interesting"* venture. / **Details:** 10 pm; closed Tue & Wed.

La Garrigue £ 46 ❸❸❸
31 Jeffrey St EH1 1DH (0131) 557 3032
"Becoming an institution!" – *"a very French bistro"* in the Old Town, whose *"friendly"* style makes it *"a popular choice for family meals"*; the focus is south west France, with a *"superb wine list and good solid fare to boot"*. / **Details:** *www.lagarrigue.co.uk; @lagarrigue; 9.30 pm.*

Grain Store £ 59 🕐
30 Victoria St EH1 2JW (0131) 225 7635
A *"lovely"* former warehouse in the Old Town, tipped for its *"intimate"* ambience; for the menu on offer, however, critics can find prices *"slightly ambitious"*. / **Details:** *www.grainstore-restaurant.co.uk; 10 pm.*

Henderson's £ 33 ④④❸
94 Hanover St EH2 1DR (0131) 225 2131
"About to celebrate 50 years and still serving interesting, high-quality veggie fare"; this characterful New Town basement – *"a real Edinburgh Institution"* – is still for fans *"a place of pilgrimage"*; they also say it *"rarely disappoints"*, but there was also the odd off report this year. / **Details:** *www.hendersonsofedinburgh.co.uk; 10 pm; closed Sun D; no Amex.*

The Honours £ 54 ❶❷❸
58a, North Castle St EH2 3LU (0131) 220 2513
Martin Wishart's *"classy"* New Town yearling *"ticks all the boxes"* for a *"memorable"* meal; the setting is *"buzzy yet intimate"*, service *"thoughtful"*, and the *"faultless"* kitchen delivers *"elegant"* brasserie cuisine at *"reasonable prices"*. / **Details:** *www.thehonours.co.uk; 10 pm; closed Mon & Sun.*

Indian Cavalry Club £ 44 ❷❷❷
22 Coates Cr EH3 7AF (0131) 220 0138
"More expensive than your average Indian, but good for business or pleasure" – this grand and atmospheric New Town spot is a consistent recommendation from reporters. / **Details:** *www.indiancavalryclub.co.uk; 10.45 pm.*

Karen's Unicorn £ 31 🕐
8b Abercomby Pl EH3 6LB (01315) 566333
One of a brace of restaurants of this name; they don't inspire a huge amount of feedback, but fans tip them as *"busy and fun with great food"*. / **Details:** *www.karensunicorn.com; 11 pm.*

Khushi's £ 30 ❷❸④
10 Antigua St EH1 3NH (0131) 558 1947
"Cheerful and helpful staff serve large portions of Asian/Indian food promptly and efficiently" at this Leith Walk veteran (est. 1947, if on a different site); it's *"always busy – a testament to its popularity!"* / **Details:** *www.khushis.com; Fri & Sat 11 pm, Sun 10 pm.*

The Kitchin £ 88 ❶❶❷
78 Commercial Quay EH6 6LX (0131) 555 1755
"One of the best, and most genuine restaurants in the UK" – Tom Kitchin's Leith flagship *"marries French cuisine with the finest Scottish produce"*, to *"exciting"* effect; *"despite his ever-busier TV schedule, the great man is usually there"*. / **Details:** *www.thekitchin.com; @TomKitchin; 9.30 pm; closed Mon & Sun; children: 5 +.*

Malvarosa £ 37 ❷❷❸
262 Portobello High St EH15 2AT (01316) 697711
"Excellent tapas" plus *"service that turns a pleasure into a delight"* – if you should find yourself anywhere near the (distant) suburb of Portobello, this *"authentic"* and *"welcoming"* spot is well worth seeking out. / **Details:** *www.malvarosa.co.uk; 10 pm, Sun 9 pm; closed Tue; no Amex.*

Mithas £ 53 ❶❷❷
7 Dock Pl EH6 6LU (0131) 554 0008
"A great upmarket Indian from the Khushi family"; the *"delicately spiced"* food at this *"posh"* Leith spot is acclaimed in all reports as absolutely *"cracking"*; *"and it's BYO, so you can choose a decent bottle"*.

/ **Details:** www.mithas.co.uk; @MithasEdinburgh;
10 pm; closed Mon; children: 8.

Mother India's Cafe   **£ 32**   ❷❸❸
3-5 Infirmary St EH1 1LT   (0131) 524 9801
"Nearly as good as the Weegie original, and a great
addition to Edinburgh!" – this Old Town spin off
serves "small tapas-like helpings" of "fresh and
spicy" dishes that "are the stuff of dreams", and
"astonishingly good for the price".
/ **Details:** www.motherindiaglasgow.co.uk; Sun 10 pm,
10.30 pm, Fri & Sat 11 pm; no Amex.

Mussel Inn   **£ 42**   ❶
61-65 Rose St EH2 2NH   (0131) 225 5979
"Fish heaven"; this New Town mussel veteran
impresses all reporters with its "reasonably-priced"
and "well cooked" seafood, served in "simple
surroundings". / **Details:** www.mussel-inn.com;
9.50 pm.

Number One
Balmoral Hotel   **£ 91**   ❶❶❸
1 Princes St EH2 2EQ   (0131) 557 6727
"Not be missed when Edinburgh!"; this basement
dining room transcends its subterranean location
(albeit in the grandest hotel in town) to offer an
experience which, almost all reports agree, is
"wonderful, from start to finish"; Jeff Bland's cuisine
is "beautifully presented, but not over fussy, or too
complicated". / **Details:** www.thebalmoralhotel.com;
10 pm; D only; no jeans or trainers; booking essential.
Accommodation: 188 rooms, from £360.

Ondine   **£ 58**   ❷❸❷
2 George IV Bridge EH1 1AD   (0131) 2261888
"Edinburgh's top seafood"; just off the Royal Mile,
this "light"-filled (if perhaps "slightly clinical") dining
room is a leading destination for "fish that's as fresh
as you can get".
/ **Details:** www.ondinerestaurant.co.uk; 10 pm; closed
Sun; booking: max 8.

The Outsider   **£ 44**   ❷❸❷
15-16 George IV Bridge EH1 1EE
(0131) 226 3131
With its "tried and tested formula", this "eclectic",
"fun", and "buzzing" spot (with castle views) is a
real crowd-pleaser; it's "open later than most
places" too. / **Details:** 11 pm; no Amex; booking:
max 12.

Plumed Horse   **£ 78**   ❸④④
50-54 Henderson St EH6 6DE
(0131) 554 5556
Often hyped as the holder of one of you-know-who's
stars, this Leith pub conversion continues to inspire
surprisingly limited and mixed feedback; although
fans do see evidence of a "genius" in the kitchen,
there are also critics who leave distinctly
underwhelmed. / **Details:** www.plumedhorse.co.uk;
9 pm; closed Mon & Sun; children: 5+.

The Pompadour by Galvin
The Caledonian   **£ 83**   ❷❷❷
Princes St EH1 2AB   (0131) 222 8975
"Full-scale posh, with superb food and charming
service" – the Galvin brothers deliver the "full
works" in this wonderful "old school" and
"romantic" dining room, where the cuisine is of the
"serious French" variety, and which reporters hail as
"a staggeringly good addition to the city".
/ **Details:** www.galvinrestaurants.com; 10 pm; closed
Mon & Sun.

Purslane   **£ 45**   ❷❸❸
33A St Stephen Street EH3 5AH
(01312) 263500
An "intimate" Stockbridge restaurant offering
"casual dining at its finest"; its "wonderful seasonal
food" is praised by all who comment on it.

Restaurant Martin
Wishart   **£ 97**   ❶❶❷
54 The Shore EH6 6RA   (0131) 553 3557
"Competes with the cooking you can find in any
capital of the world!" – "every course presents
beautiful combinations of flavour and design", says
one of the almost uniformly ecstatic reports on
Martin W's "very smart" and "professional" Leith
landmark. / **Details:** www.martin-wishart.co.uk;
9.30 pm; closed Mon & Sun; no trainers.

Rhubarb
Prestonfield Hotel   **£ 76**   ❶
Priestfield Rd EH16 5UT   (0131) 225 1333
Tipped for its "obscenely opulent and romantic"
interior, and its "dark and dangerously sexy dining
room", a country house not far from the city; some,
if not quite all, reporters are very impressed by the
food too. / **Details:** www.prestonfield.com; 10 pm,
Fri & Sat 11 pm; children: 12+ at D, none after 7pm.
Accommodation: 23 rooms, from £295.

Scran & Scallie   **£ 47**   ❶❷❸
1 Comely Bank Rd EH4 1DT   (0131) 332
6281
"A great addition to Stockbridge"; Tom Kitchin's new
gastroboozer has opened to rave reviews and is
already "bursting at the seams" – our least positive
report reads: "may not really be the pub it would
like to be… but the food is lovely".
/ **Details:** scranandscallie.com/; 10 pm.

The Shore   **£ 42**   ❷❸❶
3-4 The Shore EH6 6QW   (0131) 553 5080
"A real gem"; this "tiny, cosy and welcoming"
bar/restaurant near Leith's waterfront continues to
impress with its "mega-fresh" and "beautifully
prepared" fish and seafood.
/ **Details:** www.fishersbistros.co.uk; 10.30 pm.

Sweet Melindas   **£ 45**   ❷❸❸
11 Roseneath St EH9 1JH   (0131) 229 7953
"An excellent, intimate neighbourhood restaurant" –
almost all reports on this "very friendly and reliable"

Marchmont spot are to pretty much the same effect. / **Details:** www.sweetmelindas.co.uk; 10 pm; closed Mon & Sun; children: 5+.

Timberyard £ 59 ❷❷⓪
10 Lady Lawson St EH3 9DS (01312) 211222
This converted warehouse – built as a prop and costume store – near the Traverse Theatre, has been "beautifully renovated" by the Radford family; it's now a "trendy" hang out ("just the right side of pretentious"), with "exceptional" cocktails, and where the food's "very interesting" too.
/ **Details:** www.timberyard.co; @timberyard10; 9.30 pm; closed Mon & Sun; no Amex.

The Tower
Museum of Scotland £ 64 ❸❷❸
Chambers St EH1 1JF (0131) 225 3003
The "stunning location" is the USP of this "relaxed but smart" room with dramatic castle views; most reports say the food (seafood in particular) is also a highlight, but as ever it takes flak for being noticeably "overpriced".
/ **Details:** www.tower-restaurant.com; 11 pm.

21212 £ 93 ❷❷❸
3 Royal Ter EH7 5AB (0845) 222 1212
"Loved every minute!"; Paul Kitching's "magnificently odd" cuisine – "nothing is as it seems" and "every mouthful is a new, and newly complex experience" – inspires notably consistent praise nowadays for his Calton townhouse venture.
/ **Details:** www.21212restaurant.co.uk; @paulk21212; 9.30 pm; closed Mon & Sun; children: 5 +. **Accommodation:** 4 rooms, from £95.

Valvona & Crolla £ 37 ⓪
19 Elm Row EH7 4AA (0131) 556 6066
Limited feedback of late on this well-known café annex to the famous Italian deli and wine importer, on the way to Leith; all suggest it's "good value for a pleasant lunch", but given its foodie renown, raves are notable by their absence.
/ **Details:** www.valvonacrolla.com; 11.30 pm, Sun 6 pm.

Wedgwood £ 56 ⓪⓪❸
267 Canongate EH8 8BQ (0131) 558 8737
"A real find" just off the Royal Mile; Paul Wedgwood's "intimate" venture wins pretty much universal acclaim for "creative" and "interesting" cooking alongside "lovely" and "informed" service.
/ **Details:** www.wedgwoodtherestaurant.co.uk; 10 pm.

The Witchery by the
Castle £ 74 ④❸⓪
Castlehill, The Royal Mile EH1 2NF (0131) 225 5613
It's "so so sexy" – "no girl would fail to be wowed" – at this well-known Gothic stalwart, right by the Castle, whose "fabulous" wine list adds to its seductive allure; there is a catch – the food is too often "nowhere near the standard you'd expect",

and "hopelessly overpriced" to boot.
/ **Details:** www.thewitchery.com; @thewitchery; 11.30 pm. **Accommodation:** 8 rooms, from £325.

EGHAM, SURREY 3–3A

The Oak Room
Great Fosters Hotel £ 79 ❷⓪⓪
Stroude Rd TW20 9UR (01784) 433822
"Truly magical surroundings" underpin the all-round satisfaction with this "lovely", Elizabethan country house hotel, whose "improving" cuisine is ever-more living up to the "perfect romantic setting"; "do leave time for a walk around the garden".
/ **Details:** www.greatfosters.co.uk; 9.30 pm; no jeans or trainers; booking: max 12. **Accommodation:** 43 rooms, from £155.

ELDERSFIELD, GLOUCESTERSHIRE 2–1B

The Butcher's Arms £ 58 ⓪⓪❷
Lime St GL19 4NX (01452) 840 381
"Fantastic food in a pub with charm and character in abundance"; the "inspired" and "accurate" cooking at James & Elizabeth Winter's rural inn seems so far to have survived being honoured by the tyre men (but fans do note it's "becoming more expensive"); NB limited service hours, and no children under 10.
/ **Details:** www.thebutchersarms.net.

ELIE, FIFE 9–4D

Sangster's £ 59 ⓪
51 High St KY9 1BZ (01333) 331001
As usual, this intimate village-restaurant inspires only a small volume of reports; as ever, though, it is tipped for its "real family feel" and its "huge commitment to producing excellent food".
/ **Details:** www.sangsters.co.uk; 8.30 pm; closed Mon, Tue–Sat D only, closed Sun D; no jeans or shorts; children: 12+ at D.

ELLAND, WEST YORKSHIRE 5–1C

La Cachette £ 48 ❷❷❷
31 Huddersfield Rd HX5 9AH (01422) 378833
"Excellent food and classy service" are to be had at Jonathan Nichols's "great" Gallic all-rounder; "unusual and great-value wines" too.
/ **Details:** www.lacachette-elland.com; 9.30 pm, Fri & Sat 10 pm; closed Sun; no Amex.

ELLEL, LANCASTER, LANCASHIRE 5–1A

The Bay Horse £ 44 ❷④④
Bay Horse Ln LA2 0HR (01524) 791204
Craig Wilkinson's "very good" (and sometimes "excellent") "classically-based" cuisine is the particular reason to seek out this "cramped" rural inn; it deserves better than the sometimes "amateurish" service.

/ *Details: www.bayhorseinn.com; 9 pm, Sun 8 pm; closed Mon; no Amex.*

ELSLACK, NORTH YORKSHIRE   5–1B

The Tempest Arms   **£ 41** ❷❷❷
BD23 3AY   (01282) 842 450
"Always very busy, and reliably good in every way" – this quietly-located, rural watering hole is tipped for its *"hot and delicious"* dishes, and *"excellent, prompt service"* too. / *Details: www.tempestarms.co.uk; 9 pm, Fri & Sat 9.30 pm, Sun 7.30 pm.*
Accommodation: 21 rooms, from £89.95.

ELY, CAMBRIDGESHIRE   3–1B

The Boathouse   **£ 46** ❹❹❸
5-5A, Annesdale CB7 4BN   (01353) 664388
No one doubts it has a "lovely location overlooking the water", but this "huge" venture otherwise inspires rather mixed reviews – what is "dependable" and "accommodating" to fans is to sceptics just "mediocre".
/ *Details: www.cambscuisine.com/theboathouse; @cambscuisine; 9 pm, Fri-Sat 9.30 pm.*

Old Fire Engine House   **£ 42** ❼
25 St Mary's St CB7 4ER   (01353) 662582
Fans of this '60s survivor, near the Cathedral, say it's "always a pleasure to eat here" – a "feel-good" experience (with free seconds as standard); there's also a disgruntled minority, however, for whom it's "average, expensive and tired".
/ *Details: www.theoldfireenginehouse.co.uk; 9 pm; closed Sun D; no Amex.*

EMSWORTH, HAMPSHIRE   2–4D

Fat Olives   **£ 48** ❶❶❸
30 South St PO10 7EH   (01243) 377914
"A tremendous dining experience"; the Murphys' "small" fixture, in an old fisherman's house on the hill leading to the harbour, has a disproportionately huge fan club thanks to its "beautiful" cooking (particularly fish), "intimate" style and "lovely" service. / Details: www.fatolives.co.uk; @fat_olives; 9.15 pm; closed Mon & Sun; no Amex; children: 8+ D & L, unless Sat L.

36 on the Quay   **£ 81** ❸❸❸
47 South St PO10 7EG   (01243) 375592
"Ramon Farthing's cooking never disappoints", say fans of this "amazing", well-established gastronomic destination on the harbour; there are also quite a few doubters, though, who find it "a bit underwhelming" and are "surprised it has a Michelin star". / Details: www.36onthequay.co.uk; off A27 between Portsmouth & Chichester; 9 pm; closed Mon & Sun; no Amex. Accommodation: 5 (plus cottage) rooms, from £100.

EPSOM, SURREY   3–3B

Field to Fork Restaurant £ 39   ❼
6 South Street KT18 7PF   (01372) 744130
A proudly 'British brasserie' showcasing local, seasonal food – this "friendly" contemporarily styled operation consistently attracts very positive reports.
/ *Details: 10 pm; no Amex.*

Le Raj   **£ 32** ❷❷❸
211 Fir Tree Rd KT17 3LB   (01737) 371371
With its "innovative menu", this "smart" and long-established suburban curry house "takes Indian cuisine to a new level"… even if it can seem a little "expensive" for what it is.
/ *Details: www.lerajrestaurant.co.uk; 11 pm; no jeans or trainers.*

ESHER, SURREY   3–3A

Good Earth   **£ 49** ❷❷❸
14-18 High St KT10 9RT   (01372) 462489
"The quality of ingredients puts it head and shoulders above its competitors"; this Chinese "stalwart" may charge "Knightsbridge prices" (funny, they have a branch there too), but few reporters seem to begrudge the cost.
/ *Details: www.goodearthgroup.co.uk; 11.15 pm, Sun 10.45 pm; booking: max 12, Fri & Sat.*

ETON, BERKSHIRE   3–3A

Gilbey's   **£ 42** ❼
82-83 High St SL4 6AF   (01753) 854921
"A nice conservatory at the back" is a highpoint at this "attractive" stalwart, near the foot bridge to Windsor (owned by the family of distillers); its "traditional" fare "looks better than it tastes", but there's an "excellent wine list".
/ *Details: www.gilbeygroup.com; 5 min walk from Windsor Castle; 9.45 pm, Fri & Sat 10 pm.*

EVERSHOT, DORSET   2–4B

Summer Lodge   **£ 86** ❸❸❷
DT2 0JR   (01935) 482000
"If you like formal cosiness" then this chintzy country house hotel "deep in lovely Dorset countryside" can offer a "delightful" dining experience, aided and abetted by a "treasure trove" of a wine list; "in some respects it's twee, it's not cool, but so welcoming, so put cynicism aside!"
/ *Details: www.summerlodgehotel.co.uk; 12m NW of Dorchester on A37; 9.30 pm; no jeans or trainers; SRA-77%. Accommodation: 24 rooms, from £235.*

EVESHAM, WORCESTERSHIRE   2–1C

Evesham Hotel   **£ 48** ❹❷❷
Coopers Ln WR11 1DA   (01386) 765566
"Quirky" – the word invariably used to describe "bonkers" host John Jenkinson's "wonderful" hotel dining room; the food is "solid" but beside the point

– it's all about the "eccentric and clever" welcome, and "wacky wine list", which runs to several giant photo albums, and "refuses to include French vintages". / **Details:** www.eveshamhotel.com; 9.30 pm; Max 16. **Accommodation:** 40 rooms, from £133.

EXETER, DEVON   1–3D

The Hour Glass Inn   **£ 35   ❷❸❷**
21 Melbourne St. EX2 4AU   (01392) 258722
This "individual" and "lovely" boozer is off the beaten track, but worth discovering; fans say the food's "always good" too, and even sceptics report "more hits than misses".

Michael Caines
Royal Clarence Hotel   **£ 73   ❸❹❸**
Cathedral Yd EX1 1HD   (01392) 223 638
Not too far distant from MC's Gidleigh Park HQ, this cathedral-view dining room is credited by most reporters with the "wow" cuisine you might hope for; not everyone's convinced, however, and its ratings overall are good to middling.
/ **Details:** www.michaelcaines.com; @michaelcaines; 9.45 pm; closed Sun; booking essential.
Accommodation: 53 rooms, from £79.

EXTON, HAMPSHIRE   2–3D

Shoe Inn   **£ 40   ❶**
Shoe Ln SO32 3NT   (01489) 877526
In the Meon Valley, a "popular and worthwhile pub" tipped for "unpretentious" food that's "always of a high standard"; "quiet garden" too.
/ **Details:** www.theshoeinn.moonfruit.com.

FALMOUTH, CORNWALL   1–4B

The Flying Fish Restaurant
St Michael's Hotel & Spa £ 44   ❸❷❷
Gyllyngvase Beach TR11 4NB   (01326) 312707
This family hotel has a "spacious" and attractive modern dining room that makes "a romantic spot to gaze across the bay", and serves well-prepared fish and seafood "with warmth and enthusiasm".
/ **Details:** www.stmichaelshotel.co.uk; 9 pm, 9.30 pm Sat & Sun. **Accommodation:** 62 rooms, from £82.

Oliver's   **£ 41   ❷❷❸**
33 High St TR11 2AD   (01326) 218138
"The range, inventiveness and quality of dishes surprises", says a fan of this town-centre restaurant; it's "hugely popular locally", not least for the "excellent value for money" offered by its lunch menu. / **Details:** www.oliversfalmouth.com; @oliversfalmouth; 9 pm; closed Mon & Sun; no Amex.

Rick Stein's Fish & Chips £ 36   ❸❹❹
Discovery Quay TR11 3XA   (01841) 532700
"Worth braving the 2-metre waves on the ferry from St Mawes to Falmouth" for the "best fish 'n' chips ever", says a typically enthusiastic fan of the TV chef's chippy (and upstairs seafood bar) by the

---

National Maritime Museum; it can seem pricey though. / **Details:** www.rickstein.com; @TheSeafood; 9 pm; no Amex; no booking.

Wheelhouse   **£ 37   ❷❷❷**
Upton Slip TR11 3DQ   (01326) 318050
This "hidden gem of a restaurant" may be "reminiscent of someone's front room", but praise from reporters for its "superb simple cooking" (with seafood, of course, the highlight) is rock-solid; "only open four evenings a week", so "book ahead".
/ **Details:** 9 pm; D only, closed Sun-Tue; no credit cards.

FARNBOROUGH, HAMPSHIRE   3–3A

Aviator   **£ 44   ❷❸❷**
55 Farnborough Rd GU14 6EL
(01252) 555890
"High-quality food in a lovely setting" – it may be a bit "pricey", but the dining facilities as this smartly-styled ("unique") hotel impress all who comment on them; "make sure you go for a cocktail, as the bar is amazing". / **Details:** www.aviatorbytag.com.

FAVERSHAM, KENT   3–3C

Read's   **£ 81   ❷❷❸**
Macknade Manor, Canterbury Rd ME13 8XE
(01795) 535344
"A little bit of chintz and old-fashioned good manners" never go amiss, and the Pitchford family's "delightful" long-running venture (est. 1977) put in a "fabulous" showing this year, winning enthusiastic praise for its "memorable" cooking and its "thoughtful" service. / **Details:** www.reads.com; 9.30 pm; closed Mon & Sun. **Accommodation:** 6 rooms, from £165.

FENCE, LANCASHIRE   5–1B

Fence Gate Inn   **£ 42   ❶**
Wheatley Lane Rd BB12 9EE   (01282) 618101
A "reliable" inn that's a top tip locally; "slightly old-fashioned cooking, but well-executed… and, round Burnley, you're just grateful that a place like this exists!" / **Details:** www.fencegate.co.uk; @fencegateinn; 9 pm, Fri 9.30 pm, Sat 10 pm, Sun 8 pm; no Amex.

FERRENSBY, NORTH YORKSHIRE   8–4B

General Tarleton   **£ 49   ❷❷❷**
Boroughbridge Rd HG5 0PZ   (01423) 340284
"A top spot"; this "sophisticated" gastropub-with-rooms, just off the A1, elicits high praise from reporters for some "excellent" dishes from its "enterprising" menu, and "nothing is too much trouble" for the "friendly" and "efficient" staff.
/ **Details:** www.generaltarleton.co.uk; @generaltarleton; 2m from A1, J48 towards Knaresborough; 9.15 pm. **Accommodation:** 14 rooms, from £129.

FLAUNDEN, HERTFORDSHIRE   3–2A

The Bricklayers Arms   **£ 53**   ❸❸❸
Hogpits Bottom HP3 0PH   (01442) 833322
Fans of this successful operation "in the middle of
nowhere" say it's "simply the best" – "a little
cramped at busy times" but with an "appetising"
("short") menu and "friendly" service; it also
inspired a couple of 'off' reports this year –
hopefully just a one off.
/ **Details:** www.bricklayersarms.com; @bricklayerspub;
J18 off the M25, past Chorleywood; 9.30 pm, Sun
8.30 pm.

FLETCHING, EAST SUSSEX   3–4B

The Griffin Inn   **£ 46**   ❸❸❷
TN22 3SS   (01825) 722890
A "nostalgic reminder of what English pubs are
supposed to be like", and where the food is
"generally very good"; "occasionally there's a let
down", but the "lovely atmosphere" and garden are
steady attractions. / **Details:** www.thegriffininn.co.uk;
off A272; 9.30 pm, Sun 9 pm. **Accommodation:** 13
rooms, from £85.

FOLKESTONE, KENT   3–4D

Rocksalt   **£ 44**   ❸❸❶
4-5 Fishmarket CT19 6AA   (01303) 212 070
"A sumptuous glazed wall overlooking Folkestone's
fishing harbour" exemplifies the "sleek" style and
"stunning setting" of Mark Sergeant's "airy"
yearling; most reports say it's "a real surprise – and
a pleasant one" thanks to the "fantastic" food, but a
few find the cuisine rather "up-and-down".
/ **Details:** www.rocksaltfolkestone.co.uk;
@rocksalt_kent; 10 pm; closed Sun D.
Accommodation: 4 rooms, from £75.

FONTHILL GIFFORD, WILTSHIRE   2–3C

Beckford Arms   **£ 44**   ❸❸❷
SP3 6PX   (01747) 870 385
"The best place to stop on the way to the West
Country"; this "classy" gastropub-with-rooms is run
by an ex-Soho House team, "and it shows" – from
the "quirky decor" to the "gorgeous food"; the flip-
side is that it's "just a touch pretentious", too.
/ **Details:** www.thebeckfordarms.co.uk;
@beckfordarms; 9.30 pm, Sun 9 pm; no Amex.
Accommodation: 10 rooms, from £95.

FOREST GREEN, SURREY   3–3A

The Parrot Inn   **£ 41**   ❸❸❷
RH5 5RZ   (01306) 621339
In a "quiet but pleasant location", the Gotto family's
"wonderful country pub" offers a "good range of
real ales" and "top-quality meat sourced from the
owners' own farm"; there's also a farm shop next
door. / **Details:** www.theparrot.co.uk; 10 pm; closed
Sun D; no Amex.

FORT WILLIAM, HIGHLAND   9–3B

Crannog   **£ 57**   ❼
Town Pier PH33 6DB   (01397) 705589
"Nothing too fancy or cutting edge, but a nice spot
for dinner" – a restaurant which is tipped for its
"good quality seafood", and its "great views down
Loch Linhe" too. / **Details:** www.crannog.net;
9.30 pm; no Amex.

FOWEY, CORNWALL   1–4B

Food For Thought   **£ 28**   ❼
4 Town Quay PL23 1AT   (01726) 832221
A quayside restaurant, with al fresco tables, tipped
for its use of "fabulous fresh local produce", and
complemented with a "value-for-money" wine list
too. / **Details:** www.foodforthought.com; 9 pm;
no Amex; children: 10+ at D.

**The Q Restaurant
The Old Quay House**   **£ 53**   ❶❷❷
28 Fore St PL23 1AQ   (01726) 833302
An award-winning boutique hotel with "lovely views
of the River Fowey" and a "top-notch" restaurant to
match; now under chef Ashley Wright, it's praised
for "staggeringly good" food (especially the "brilliant
combinations of fruit and vegetables") and "first-
class value for money".
/ **Details:** www.theoldquayhouse.com;
@theoldquayhouse; 9 pm; closed Tue L; children: 8+ at
D. **Accommodation:** 11 rooms, from £180.

Sam's   **£ 42**   ❸❷❷
20 Fore St PL23 1AQ   (01726) 832273
"Amazing burgers, great drinks, great service, great
tunes" – every town should have a place like this
"buzzy", "high quality burger/cocktail joint"; visits
"need to be well timed to avoid a wait".
/ **Details:** www.samsfowey.co.uk; @samscornwall;
9.30 pm; no Amex; no booking.

FRESSINGFIELD, SUFFOLK   3–1D

The Fox & Goose   **£ 47**   ④❷❸
Church Rd IP21 5PB   (01379) 586247
Reports on this big country pub are a little mixed;
most insist it's a "gorgeous" venue offering "top
notch" food "with military efficiency"… but there's
also quite a strong critical current which insists that
the grub is somewhere between "adequate" and
"uninspiring". / **Details:** www.foxandgoose.net; off
A143; 8.45 pm, Fri & Sat 9 pm, Sun 8.15 pm; closed
Mon; no Amex; children: 9+ for D.

FRILSHAM, BERKSHIRE   2–2D

The Pot Kiln   **£ 50**   ❷❷❷
RG18 0XX   (01635) 201366
"Delicious venison-burgers and, in summer, the best
pizzas too!" are served in the garden and tiny bar
of this "excellent", and scenically located pub,
whereas its dining room is famously "great for

game"; service is "very friendly" and "attentive" too.
/ **Details:** www.potkiln.org; between J12 and J13 of the
M4; 9 pm, Sun 8.30 pm; closed Tue.

FRITHSDEN, HERTFORDSHIRE   3–2A

The Alford Arms   £ 48   ❸❷❶
HP1 3DD   (01442) 864480
"Nestled in a lovely part of the county", this
"beautiful" "tucked away" hostelry is "the best for
miles around", and has a huge fan club, thanks to
its "enthusiastic" service, "solidly reliable" food, and
"decent beer".
/ **Details:** www.alfordarmsfrithsden.co.uk;
@alfordarmshp1; near Ashridge College and vineyard;
9.30 pm, Fri & Sat 10 pm; booking: max 12.

FROXFIELD, WILTSHIRE   2–2C

The Palm   £ 36   ❶
Bath Rd SN8 3HT   (01672) 871 818
Just off the M4, an Indian "hidden gem", tipped for
its delicious cuisine and opulent décor.
/ **Details:** www.thepalmindian.com.

GATESHEAD, TYNE AND WEAR   8–2B

Raval   £ 45   ❷❷❸
Church St, Gateshead Quays   NE8 2AT
(0191) 4771700
The "best on Tyneside, especially for seafood curry!"
– fans of this popular Indian rate say its fare is
"never dull", and that the views are "great" too.
/ **Details:** www.ravalrestaurant.com; @ravalrestaurant;
11 pm; D only, closed Sun; no shorts.

GERRARDS CROSS,
BUCKINGHAMSHIRE   3–3A

Apple Tree   £ 45   ❶
Oxford Rd SL9 7AH   (01753) 887335
"Friendly" and "reasonably priced", a "popular"
gastropub, tipped for its "reliable" standards.
/ **Details:** www.appletreegerrardscross.co.uk; 10 pm.

Maliks   £ 43   ❶⑤④
14 Oak End Way   SL9 8BR   (01753) 880888
This spin-off of the celebrated Cookham restaurant
is a "consistently top-notch Indian" whose culinary
results – "mostly classics with some more
interesting dishes" – "lives up to its reputation".
/ **Details:** www.maliks.co.uk; 10.45 pm.

Three Oaks   £ 46   ❶
Austenwood Ln SL9 8NL   (01753) 899 016
A "fine gastropub" tipped as a "pleasant destination
overall" – feedback is not extensive, but it is notably
consistent. / **Details:** www.thethreeoaksgx.co.uk;
9.15 pm.

GLASGOW, CITY OF GLASGOW   9–4C

Café Gandolfi   £ 43   ❷❶❷
64 Albion St   G1 1NY   (0141) 552 6813
All reporters find something to admire about this

characterful Merchant City institution, be it the "real
local feel" of the space, the "excellent" cooking, or
front-of-house staff "who actually seem to like their
customers!"; it's so adaptable too – "great for
business, coffee, breakfast, lunch…".
/ **Details:** www.cafegandolfi.com; 11 pm; no booking,
Sat.

Cail Bruich   £ 48   ❶❷❷
725 Great Western Road   G12 8QX
(01413) 346265
"A family-run restaurant full of character, in the
heart of the West End" ("not on the most
prepossessing strip of road") hailed by fans as
"possibly the best food in Glasgow at the moment";
Chris Charalambous's cooking is "Scottish-
flavoured", "extremely able" and has some
"interesting" ideas. / **Details:** 9 pm; closed Mon.

Crabshakk   £ 51   ❶❷❷
Finnestone   G3 8TD   (0141) 334 6127
"Definitely the place to eat in Glasgow"; with its
"first-rate" fish "done honestly and very well", this
"cramped" but atmospheric joint is "a winner every
time"; book ahead. / **Details:** www.crabshakk.com;
12 am; closed Mon; no Amex.

Gamba   £ 67   ❶❷❸
225a West George St   G2 2ND
(0141) 572 0899
"The best fish soup in town" and "superbly
prepared seafood" help evidence the "very serious
cooking" at Derek Marshall's city-centre basement –
a "cosy" (if "rather dim") destination, that has long
been one of the Glasgow's culinary standard
bearers. / **Details:** www.gamba.co.uk; 10 pm; closed
Sun L; SRA-77%.

Gandolfi Fish   £ 51   ❸④④
64 Albion St   G1 1NY   (0141) 552 9475
Looking for "a good fish restaurant in the Merchant
City"? – with its "super-fresh" dishes, this "relaxed",
modern operation next to the mothership is
generally hailed as a "worthy addition" to the
Gandolfi brand. / **Details:** www.cafegandolfi.com;
10.30 pm, Sun 9 pm.

Mother India   £ 36   ❶❸❸
28 Westminster Ter   G3 7RU   (0141) 221 1663
"Always different from the run-of-the-mill Indians",
this atmospheric and well-known West End corner
fixture serves "particularly interesting" dishes in
"tapas-sized" portions, "so you get to try lots of
different things"; "it's crowded, but rightly so".
/ **Details:** www.motherindiaglasgow.co.uk; 10.30 pm,
Fri & Sat 11 pm, Sun 10 pm; Mon-Thu D only, Fri-Sun
open L & D.

La Parmigiana   £ 61   ❷❷❷
447 Great Western Rd   G12 8HH
(0141) 334 0686
"A tiny restaurant offering authentic, beautifully
prepared dishes" – this Italian classic on the borders

Café Gandolfi

Rogano

Ubiquitous Chip

of the West End is well into its fourth decade, and very highly rated by its small fan club.
/ **Details:** www.laparmigiana.co.uk; 10 pm, Sun 6 pm.

Rogano £ 64 ❷❷❷
11 Exchange Pl G1 3AN   (0141) 248 4055
A "traditional winner, steeped in history" – this "glorious" and "romantic" Art Deco restaurant has been on stronger form of late, winning praise for its "stylish and well-presented food", and its "unbeatable" service.
/ **Details:** www.roganoglasgow.com; @roganoglagow; 10.30 pm.

Shish Mahal £ 39 ❷❸④
66-68 Park Rd G4 9JF   (0141) 334 7899
"Possibly the best curry west of Delhi!" (well nearly); approaching 50 years in business (and claimed as the home of chicken tikka masala), this "friendly" subcontinental, near Kelvinbridge Underground, continues to dish up "consistently excellent" dishes.
/ **Details:** www.shishmahal.co.uk; 11 pm; closed Sun L.

Stravaigin £ 49 ❶❷❶
28 Gibson St G12 8NX   (0141) 334 2665
Perennially one of Glasgow's favourite eateries – Colin Clydesdale & Carol Wright's casual bar (upstairs) and more formal (basement) dining room has long been renowned locally for its "inventive, world-wide and daring menu", served at "seriously cheap" prices. / **Details:** www.stravaigin.co.uk; @straivaiging12; 11 pm; closed weekday L; no Amex.

Two Fat Ladies £ 51 ❷❸❸
118a, Blythswood St G2 4EG   (0141) 847 0088
"The seafood is particularly good" at these Glaswegian institutions, both in this "busy and popular" city-centre outpost, and the "delightfully small and relaxed" original, at 88 Dumbarton Road G11, tel 0141 339 1944; see also 'Two Fat Ladies at the Buttery'.
/ **Details:** www.twofatladiesrestaurant.com; 10 pm, Fri & Sat 11 pm, Sun 9 pm.

Two Fat Ladies at The Buttery £ 57 ❷❷❷
652 Argyle St G3 8UF   (0141) 221 8188
Despite a down-at-heel location by the SECC, this characterful old Victorian veteran is a "smart", "buzzy" place, where "beautiful" food (predominantly fish) is twinned with "impeccable" service; several reporters call it their "favourite branch" of the local seafood mini-chain.
/ **Details:** www.twofatladiesrestaurant.com; 10 pm, Sun 9 pm.

Ubiquitous Chip £ 60 ❷❷❶
12 Ashton Ln G12 8SJ   (0141) 334 5007
"'The Chip' as its known locally" has long been Glasgow's best-known destination (est. 1971); "the courtyard is a great setting", but the whole enterprise has a "jolly" and "quirky" charm, bolstered by "solid" Scottish food, and "a wine list

the size of the old Glasgow telephone directory".
/ **Details:** www.ubiquitouschip.co.uk; 11 pm; no Amex.

La Luna £ 48 ❷❷❸
10-14 Wharf St GU7 1NN   (01483) 414155
"Busy and buzzy – an unexpected find in boring Godalming!"; with its "surprisingly spot-on Italian food" and "tremendous wine list", this is the best restaurant in town "by a mile"; the "only downside is the price, but the lunch menu helps on that front".
/ **Details:** www.lalunarestaurant.co.uk; 10 pm; no Amex.

The Taverners £ 37 ❶
High St PO38 3HZ   (01983) 840 707
A homely pub, on the tourist trail, tipped for its use of fantastically local produce in general – "we're harvesting your asparagus now!" – and a "well above average" ploughman's lunch in particular.
/ **Details:** www.thetavernersgodshill.co.uk; 9 pm, Fri & Sat 9.30 pm; closed Sun D.

The Fox And Hounds Inn £ 53 ❶
YO21 3RX   (01947) 893372
We wish we had more reports on chef Jason Davies's hidden-away country inn, which is strongly tipped by fans as offering "some of the best food in North Yorkshire".
/ **Details:** www.foxandhoundsgoldsborough.co.uk; 8.30 pm; D only, closed Sun-Tue; no Amex.

Leatherne Bottel £ 59 ④⑤❶
Bridleway RG8 0HS   (01491) 872667
"If you haven't had a long, lazy alfresco lunch on the Thames here, you haven't lived" – so say fans of this "magically located" Thames-side venture; it changed hands last year, however, and too many visits of late have encountered "amateurish" service and "uninspiring" cooking.
/ **Details:** www.leathernebottel.co.uk; 9 pm; closed Sun D; children: 10+ for D.

The Jumble Room £ 46 ❷❷❷
Langdale Rd LA22 9SU   (01539) 435188
"Quirky as ever", this tiny and wackily-decorated Lakeland venture continues to offer "high standards all round"; the modern cuisine makes "innovative" use of "much local produce".
/ **Details:** www.thejumbleroom.co.uk; 9.30 pm; closed Mon, Tue, Wed L & Thu L. **Accommodation:** 3 rooms, from £180.

GRASSINGTON, NORTH YORKSHIRE   8–4B

The Grassington House Hotel   **£ 41   ❶❷❷**
5 The Sq BD23 5AQ   (01756) 752406
"What a gem!", and "at such reasonable prices"
too!; Sue & John Rudden's "well-appointed
restaurant in a smart Dales hotel" makes good use
of "unusual cuts of meat" as the basis for dishes
which are "a work of art"; also "cookery classes and
themed weekends".
/ **Details:** www.grassingtonhousehotel.co.uk; 9.30 pm,
Sun 7.30pm. **Accommodation:** 9 rooms, from £110.

GREAT GONERBY, LINCOLNSHIRE   5–3D

Harry's Place   **£ 80   ❶❶❸**
17 High St NG31 8JS   (01476) 561780
"The sureness of touch and the warmth of the
welcome fully justify the price", at Harry and
Caroline Hallam's 10-seater one-off, where – though
choice is limited – the cooking is "brilliant"; "it's
about the only place this expensive where we come
away every time working out how soon we can
afford to go again…" / **Details:** on B1174 1m N of
Grantham; 8.30 pm; closed Mon & Sun; no Amex;
booking essential; children: 5+.

GREAT MILTON, OXFORDSHIRE   2–2D

Le Manoir aux Quat' Saisons   **£ 171 ❶❶❷**
Church Rd OX44 7PD   (01844) 278881
"Absolutely perfect, not cheap but worth it" – the
cost issue may be ever-present, but Raymond
Blanc's "fabulous" manor house hotel and
restaurant remains THE destination for those in
search of a "fantastic all-round experience"; make
sure you leave time for "wandering round the
garden". / **Details:** www.manoir.com; from M40, J7
take A329 towards Wallingford; 9.15 pm; booking:
max 12; SRA-84%. **Accommodation:** 32 rooms,
from £550.

GREAT MISSENDEN, BUCKINGHAMSHIRE   3–2A

The Nags Head   **£ 50   ④④❸**
London Rd HP16 0DG   (01494) 862200
Lots of feedback of late on this "charming" pub, but
it is mixed – fans say it's "more expensive than
average, but worth it", whereas critics speak more in
terms of "odd" combinations that are "not always
successful". / **Details:** www.nagsheadbucks.com; off
the A413; 9.30 pm, Sun 8.30 pm.
Accommodation: 5 rooms, from £95.

GREETHAM, RUTLAND   5–

The Wheatsheaf   **£ 39   ❷❷❸**
Stretton Rd LE15 7NP   (01572) 812325
"What a surprise… doesn't look anything special
but WOW!"; "a young couple who learned their

trade in top London places" run this "village pub
with a small restaurant", which delivers "superb
food from chef Carol", plus a wine list with some
"terrific and inspired choices". / **Details:** 9pm; closed
Sun D.

GRESFORD, WREXHAM   5–3A

Pant-yr-Ochain   **£ 45   ❸❸❶**
Old Wrexham Rd LL12 8TY   (01978) 853525
"Like having your own country club!"; this "very
comfortable" former manor house (with lake!) is
now a Brunning & Price operation, praised for its
"ever-changing" gastropub fare and "attentive"
service.
/ **Details:** www.brunningandprice.co.uk/pantyrochain;
1m N of Wrexham; 9.30 pm, Sun 9 pm.

GRINDLETON, LANCASHIRE   5–1B

The Duke Of York Inn   **£ 46   ❷❸④**
Clitheroe BB7 4QR   (01200) 441266
"Not to be missed" – the verdict of all reporters on
this "excellent gastropub", which is noted for "classy
cooking" which "makes the most of the local
produce the Ribble Valley has to offer".
/ **Details:** www.dukeofyorkgrindleton.com; 9 pm, Sun
7.30 pm; closed Mon; no Amex.

GRINSHILL, SHROPSHIRE   5–3A

The Inn at Grinshill   **£ 50   ❼**
The High St SY4 3BL   (01939) 220410
An attractive village inn tipped for "consistently
good" food; the atmosphere, though, doesn't always
live up. / **Details:** www.theinnatgrinshill.co.uk;
@Innatgrinshill; 9.30 pm; closed Mon, Tue & Sun D;
no Amex. **Accommodation:** 6 rooms, from £90.

GUERNSEY, CHANNEL ISLANDS

Da Nello   **£ 45   ❸❷❸**
46 Lower Pollet St GY1 1WF   (01481) 721552
"Still going strong after so many years" – this St
Peter Port "institution" continues to satisfy a loyal
clientele with its "traditional" Italian cuisine, its
"reasonable prices" and its "amazing views".
/ **Details:** www.danello.gg; 10 pm.

Le Petit Bistro   **£ 52   ❷④❷**
56 Le Pollet GY1 1WF   (01481) 725055
Currently on quite a high, this "intimate and
comfortable" ("if occasionally cramped") St Peter
Port fixture offers "great classic French cooking" in
"large and hearty portions".
/ **Details:** www.petitbistro.co.uk; 10 pm, 10.30 pm
Fri & Sat; closed Sun.

GUILDFORD, SURREY   3–3A

Cau   **£ 47   ❷④④**
274 High St GU1 3JL   (01483) 459777
"Feels like a chain in the making", says one report
on this "good steakhouse" (now with Cambridge

sibling); this "no-nonsense" formula, with an Argentinian twist, is generally hailed as "better value than most such places". / **Details:** www.caurestaurants.com; @CAUrestaurants; 11 pm, Sun 10.30 pm.

Rumwong   £ 37   ❷❸❸
18-20 London Rd GU1 2AF   (01483) 536092
"A star still shining"; this "traditional and authentic" Thai restaurant has been in business since 1978, and the food it offers is still "fresh, delicious and very tasty" – no surprise it's "always busy". / **Details:** www.rumwong.co.uk; 10.30 pm; closed Mon; no Amex.

The Thai Terrace   £ 40   ❷❷❷
Castle Car Pk, Sydenham Rd GU1 3RW
(01483) 503350
Perched "on top of a multi-storey car park", it's no particular surprise that this "modern Thai" boasts "great views over Guildford" (and has "a huge terrace for summer drinks"); more surprising is the fact that it serves food that's consistently "excellent". / **Details:** 10.30 pm; closed Sun; no Amex.

GULLANE, EAST LOTHIAN   9–4D

Chez Roux
Greywalls Hotel   £ 56   ❷❷❷
EH31 2EG   (01620) 842144
A "very comfortable" Lutyens house provides the "beautiful" setting for this "luxurious" outpost of the Roux empire, where (nearly) all reports say the food "is up to the quality the name would suggest". / **Details:** www.greywalls.co.uk; 10 pm; jacket at D. **Accommodation:** 23 rooms, from £260.

La Potinière   £ 51   ❷④④
Main St EH31 2AA   (01620) 843214
"Excellent food as usual", at this "very small operation", run for the past decade by Keith Marley and Mary Runciman; "service can be slow", but there's "always something to enjoy" on the "good-value lunch menu"; more reports please. / **Details:** www.la-potiniere.co.uk; 20m E of Edinburgh, off A198; 8.30 pm; closed Mon, Tue & Sun D; no Amex; no jeans or trainers; booking essential.

HALE, CHESHIRE   5–2B

Earle   £ 51   ❶
4 Cecil Rd WA15 9PA   (0161) 929 8869
A popular local brasserie that attracts rather mixed commentary as a serious culinary option; it makes a handy standby though, and is particularly tipped as a destination for a "decent-value lunch". / **Details:** www.earlerestaurant.co.uk; @EarleHale; 9.30 pm, Sun 8 pm; closed Mon L.

HALIFAX, WEST YORKSHIRE   5–1C

Ricci's Place   £ 32   ❷❷❸
4 Crossley Hs, Crossley St HX1 1UG
(01422) 410203
"You'd be mad to go anywhere else!" – this grandly-housed all-day Mediterranean operation, by the Town Hall has "brilliant" cooking that's "the best value for money", and consequently is "always packed". / **Details:** www.riccis-place.co.uk; @riccisplaceltd; 9 pm; closed Sun; no Amex; Strongly recommended.

Shibden Mill Inn   £ 51   ❸❷❷
Shibden Mill Fold HX3 7UL   (01422) 365840
"One of the stars of Halifax's up-and-coming dining scene", say fans, this "homely" inn offers "high-quality food in great surroundings". / **Details:** www.shibdenmillinn.com; @ShibdenMill; off the A58, Leeds/Bradford road; 9 pm, Fri & Sat 9.30 pm, Sun 7.30 pm. **Accommodation:** 11 rooms, from £111.

HAMBLETON, RUTLAND   5–4D

Finch's Arms   £ 43   ❸④❷
Oakham Rd LE15 8TL   (01572) 756575
The food at this rustic inn, with a "charming interior" and "fine views of Rutland Water" from the terrace and garden, can be "very good"; it gets "very busy in season", though, and critics take issue with the "patchy" service, and "greedy" pricing. / **Details:** www.finchsarms.co.uk; 9.30 pm, Sun 8 pm. **Accommodation:** 10 rooms, from £100.

Hambleton Hall   £ 89   ❶❷❷
LE15 8TH   (01572) 756991
A "beautiful location on a peninsular jutting into Rutland Water" sets the scene for Tim Hart's "impeccable" (and slightly "stiff") country house hotel, where Aaron Patterson's "complex" and "wonderfully confident" cooking achieves an "utterly consistent" standard. / **Details:** www.hambletonhall.com; near Rutland Water; 9.30 pm. **Accommodation:** 17 rooms, from £265.

HARDWICK, CAMBRIDGESHIRE   3–1B

The Blue Lion   £ 51   ❸❷❸
74 Main St CB23 7QU   (01954) 210328
A "lovely", "olde-worlde" inn without pretensions, which elicits high praise from reporters (not least for its "excellent fish finger sarnies and corned beef hash"!); "gluten-free options abound". / **Details:** www.bluelionhardwick.co.uk; 9 pm, Sun 8 pm; no Amex.

HAROME, NORTH YORKSHIRE   8–4C

The Pheasant Hotel   £ 55   ❷❷❷
YO62 5JG   (01439) 771241
This "elegant" inn rivals its more famous parent, the

Star, in recent feedback (if, on many fewer reports); indeed the only difference some reporters can see is that this "romantic" location is "classier" and "more spacious"! / Details: www.thepheasanthotel.com; 9 pm; no Amex; Essential for weekends.
Accommodation: *15 rooms, from £150.*

The Star Inn　　　　　**£ 62**　**❶❷❷**
YO62 5JE　(01439) 770397
"Andrew Pern was an early exponent of making the most of his local larder and has refined that approach to perfection" at this "ne plus ultra of pubs", serving "gold standard" British "classics with a twist"; "that it still has locals in the bar creates real atmosphere".
/ Details: www.thestaratharome.co.uk; 3m SE of Helmsley off A170; 9.30 pm, Sun 6 pm; closed Mon L & Sun; no Amex. **Accommodation:** *8 rooms, from £150.*

HARROGATE, NORTH YORKSHIRE　　　5–1C

Bettys　　　　　**£ 45**　**❷❷❶**
1 Parliament St　HG1 2QU　(01423) 814070
"I doubt anyone will ever be able to beat Betty's!"; this famous "haven of civility" always "feels like a treat"… whether for breakfast or the "full works" afternoon tea; expect to queue.
/ Details: www.bettysandtaylors.co.uk; 9 pm; no Amex; no booking.

Drum & Monkey　　　　　**£ 44**　**❷❷❸**
5 Montpellier Gdns　HG1 2TF　(01423) 502650
"Back to the way it used to be" – this locally famous institution is winning renewed praise for its "brilliant selection of fish dishes" at "very good prices for these austere times"; the elegance may seem a touch "faded", but "the food makes up for it".
/ Details: www.drumandmonkey.co.uk; 10 pm; closed Sun; no Amex; booking: max 10.

Graveley's Fish & Chip Restaurant　　　　　**£ 39**　**❶❷④**
8-12 Cheltenham Pde　HG1 1DB (01423) 507093
"More so than Betty's… this is THE must-visit eatery on any trip to Harrogate!"; this notably superior chippy is hailed for offering "some of the very best fish and chips" in the region (plus "more sophisticated" options too).
/ Details: www.graveleysofharrogate.com; 9 pm, Fri & Sat 10 pm, Sun 8 pm.

Mirabelles　　　　　**£ 47**　**❷❶❷**
28a, Swan Rd　HG1 2SE　(01423) 565551
This "comfortable and attractive restaurant", run by Alsacien chef-patron Lionel Strub, continues to elicit enthusiastic reports with its "well priced", "imaginative" and "very French" cuisine … although "they are always pleased to offer a simple alternative for the fussy eater"!
/ Details: www.mirabellerestaurant.co.uk; @mirabellesHG1; 9.30 pm; closed Mon L & Sun.

Orchid　　　　　**£ 42**　**❷❷❸**
28 Swan Rd　HG1 2SE　(01423) 560425
"Always a winner!"; "fantastic" pan-Asian cuisine with "very clean and fresh" flavours and a "buzzy atmosphere" make this hotel restaurant a "consistently good" bet in the eyes of its many fans; the "superb-value" Sunday buffet attracts particular praise. / Details: www.orchidrestaurant.co.uk; 10 pm; closed Sat L. **Accommodation:** *28 rooms, from £115.*

Quantro　　　　　**£ 46**　**❸❷❷**
3 Royal Pde　HG1 2SZ　(01423) 503034
This "stylish" venture near Valley Gardens has a "great choice on the menu", with good vegetarian and gluten-free options; service is noted for being "unobtrusive", yet "helpful", with "a definite feeling that the customer is all important".
/ Details: www.quantro.co.uk; 10 pm, Sat 10 pm; closed Sun; children: no under 4's in evening.

Sasso　　　　　**£ 43**　**❶**
8-10 Princes Sq　HG1 1LX　(01423) 508 838
A family-friendly restaurant tipped for its "good Italian feel" (and also for its "very imaginative treatment of humdrum dishes like fish 'n' chips!").
/ Details: www.sassorestaurant.co.uk.

Van Zeller　　　　　**£ 71**　**❷❷④**
8 Montpellier St　HG1 2TQ　(01423) 508762
"Outstanding and inventive" food (with a "good and reasonably priced" wine list to go with it) makes Tom Van Zeller's ambitious venture one of the most accomplished in this wealthy town; when it's quiet, though, atmosphere can seem decidedly "lacking".
/ Details: www.vanzellerrestaurants.co.uk; 9.30 pm; closed Mon & Sun; booking advised.

William & Victoria　　　　　**£ 36**　**❸❷❷**
6 Cold Bath Rd　HG2 0NA　(01423) 521510
A basement wine bar, very consistently praised for its "hearty food", "good choice of wines" and "bustling atmosphere".
/ Details: www.williamandvictoria.com; 10 pm; no Amex.

HARROW, GREATER LONDON　　　3–3A

Incanto
The Old Post Office　　　　　**£ 50**　**❸④④**
41 High St, Harrow On The Hill　HA1 3HT (020) 8426 6767
"Trying very hard and generally succeeding" – this Italian veteran would, say fans, "not be out of place in the West End"; it does have its detractors, though, who find it a "boring" locale where "the quality is too inconsistent for the high prices".
/ Details: www.incanto.co.uk; @incantoharrow; 10.30 pm; closed Mon & Sun D.

HARTSHEAD, WEST YORKSHIRE   5–1C

The Gray Ox Inn   **£ 42**   ❷❷❷
15 Hartshead Ln WF15 8AL   (01274) 872845
"A delight to have as our 'local'" – this olde-worlde
venue charms all reporters with "classic pub food
cooked superbly", a "good range of beers", and
"fantastic Yorkshire hospitality"; "good value" too!
/ **Details:** www.grayoxinn.co.uk; Mon-Fri 8.45pm, Sat
9.15pm, Sun 6.45 pm; closed Sun D.

HARWICH, ESSEX   3–2D

The Pier at Harwich   **£ 54**   ❶
The Quay CO12 3HH   (01255) 241212
Though it is a top tip "pre-ferry", the Milson family's
hotel attracts rather mixed reports; it's perhaps
worth knowing that "upstairs has the view, but
downstairs is more fun".
/ **Details:** www.milsonhotels.com; 9.30 pm, Sat
10 pm; closed Mon & Tue; no jeans.
Accommodation: 14 rooms, from £117.

HASSOP, DERBYSHIRE   5–2C

Hassop Hall   **£ 66**   ❷❷❶
DE45 1NS   (01629) 640488
"Still cannot fault this beautiful place" – the general
verdict on the Chapman family's "elegant" and
"wonderfully located" country house hotel; the
cuisine may be in a bit of a "time warp", but fans
"love the chateaubriand trolley and all that
silverware". / **Details:** www.hassophall.co.uk; on the
B6001 Bakewell - Hathersage Road, Junction 29 of M1;
9 pm; closed Mon L, Sat L & Sun D.
Accommodation: 13 rooms, from £100.

HASTINGS, EAST SUSSEX   3–4C

Maggie's   **£ 21**   ❷❶❸
Rock-a-Nore Rd TN34 3DW   (01424) 430
205
"Fish and chips don't come fresher or better", says
one of the fans of this famous chippy, "right on the
working fishing beach" – "not your usual seaside
fayre at all!" / **Details:** 1.45 pm; L only, closed Sun;
no credit cards.

Webbe's Rock-a-Nore   **£ 47**   ❸④④
1 Rock-a-Nore Rd TN34 3DW
(01424) 721650
"Less formal" than other venues in Paul Webbe's
local chain; some reporters are "not impressed" by
his "busy" seafront venture, but feedback says its
"good for all kinds of local fish and shellfish", and
the open kitchen "adds a touch of drama".
/ **Details:** www.webbesrestaurants.co.uk; 9.30 pm.

HATFIELD PEVEREL, ESSEX   3–2C

The Blue Strawberry   **£ 47**   ❷❷❷
The St CM3 2DW   (01245) 381333
This long-running village "staple" is generally

considered "the best Chelmsford has to offer for a
special evening"; it's praised for a "good variety of
options" on the menu, and an "intimate setting".
/ **Details:** www.bluestrawberrybistro.co.uk;
@thebluestrawb; 3m E of Chelmsford; 10 pm; closed
Sun D.

HAWKHURST, KENT   3–4C

The Great House   **£ 45**   ❶
Gills Grn TN18 5EJ   (01580) 753119
In an old Wealden house, a gastropub tipped for a
"good choice" of grub, plus "excellent and changing
guest beers".
/ **Details:** www.elitepubs.com/the_greathouse;
9.30 pm; no Amex.

HAY-ON-WYE, HEREFORDSHIRE   2–1A

Three Tuns   **£ 42**   ❸❸❸
4 Broad St HR3 5DB   (01497) 821855
"A haven during the Festival, not cheap but
excellent!" – this elegant 16th-century gastropub is
a real all-rounder, and the food is never rated less
than "decent". / **Details:** 9 pm; no Amex.

HAYWARDS HEATH, WEST SUSSEX   3–4B

Jeremy's at Borde Hill   **£ 52**   ❷❷❷
Balcombe Rd RH16 1XP   (01444) 441102
Jeremy Ashpool's "brilliant" cuisine "should perhaps
have received more accolades than it has", and fans
extol this "delightful", "informal" venture; it's
adjacent to a "beautiful walled garden" (which its
terrace overlooks), and "dining here al fresco is one
of life's pleasures".
/ **Details:** www.jeremysrestaurant.com; Exit 10A from
the A23; 10 pm; closed Mon & Sun D.

**HEDLEY ON THE HILL,
NORTHUMBERLAND**   8–2B

The Feathers Inn   **£ 42**   ❶❸④
Hedley-on-the-Hill NE43 7SW
(01661) 843607
"Probably the best pub in Northumberland!" – this
old village inn gets an enthusiastic thumbs-up from
all who comment on it thanks to its "excellent-
quality local food"; the interior, however, is "rather
squashed". / **Details:** www.thefeathers.net;
@thefeathersinn; 8.30 pm; closed Mon & Sun D;
no Amex.

HELMSLEY, NORTH YORKSHIRE   8–4C

Black Swan   **£ 60**   ❸④❸
Market Pl YO62 5BJ   (01439) 770466
This "traditional market town inn" (now boutique-
ified) is a commercial art gallery by day, and a
canvas for chef Paul Peters's "imaginative" food
(including a "very good" tasting menu) by night;
there's the odd gripe, however, about "not very
generous portions".

/ *Details:* www.blackswan-helmsley.co.uk; 9.30 pm.
Accommodation: 45 rooms, from £130.

Feversham Arms **£ 72** ❼
1-8 High St Y062 5AG (01439) 770766
A luxurious inn (complete with open-air swimming pool), tipped for food which is "exquisitely prepared and tasty"; especially by Yorkshire standards, though, portions can seem rather "on the nouvelle cuisine side". / Details: www.fevershamarmshotel.com; *9.30 pm; no trainers; children: 12+ after 8 pm.*
Accommodation: 33 rooms, from £260.

HEMINGFORD GREY, CAMBRIDGESHIRE	3–1B

The Cock **£ 48** ❷❷❷
47 High St PE28 9BJ (01480) 463609
This "simply converted pub restaurant in an attractive riverside village" (near the A1) is a "haven" known to many reporters, thanks to its "well presented" fare; the wine list is also "worthy of mention". / Details: www.thecockhemingford.co.uk; *@cambscuisine; off the A14; follow signs to the river; 9 pm, Fri & Sat 9.30 pm, Sun 8.30 pm; children: 5+ at D.*

HENLEY ON THAMES, OXFORDSHIRE	3–3A

Giggling Squid **£ 26** ❷④❸
40 Hart St RG9 2AU (01491) 411044
"Some of the best Thai food this side of the Andaman sea" (well nearly!) wins praise for this new outpost of a growing south eastern chain; locals judge its success by "the number of chauffeur driven Bentleys and Rollers waiting outside". / Details: www.gigglingsquid.com; @GigglingSquid; *10 pm.*

Hotel du Vin et Bistro **£ 51** ❼
New St RG9 2BP (01491) 848400
A nicely situated outpost of the wine-led bistro/hotel format, tipped for "superb food in a great bistro environment". / Details: www.hotelduvin.com; *10 pm, Sat 10.30 pm, Sun 9.30 pm.* **Accommodation:** 43 rooms, from £110.

The Little Angel **£ 44** ❼
Remenham Ln RG9 2LS (01491) 411 008
Handily situated for visitors, near the bridge, an atmospheric large boozer with an "attractive conservatory", generally tipped for its "interesting" menu and its "friendly" service.
/ *Details:* www.thelittleangel.co.uk; *10 pm, Sun 9 pm.*

Luscombes at the Golden Ball **£ 59** ❸❸④
Lower Assendon RG9 6AH (01491) 574157
A "good local" (more restaurant than pub) with a "great garden for when the weather allows"; it's judged a "consistent performer" by most reporters, although it can appear "quite pricey".
/ *Details:* www.luscombes.co.uk; *10.30 pm, Sun 9 pm; no Amex.*

Spice Merchant **£ 40** ❷❸❸
Thameside RG9 2LJ (01491) 636118
An "elegant and tasteful" riverside restaurant, offering "wonderfully inventive" Indian cooking (with "superb breads" a highlight); service is typically "excellent" too.
/ *Details:* www.spicemerchantgroup.com; *11 pm; no Amex.*

Villa Marina **£ 38** ❷❷❸
18 Thameside RG9 1BH (01491) 575262
"Genuine Italian food, served with Italian charm" makes this well-established venture "one of the few places in Henley you can be sure of a good meal with service to match". / Details: opp Angel pub, nr Bridge; *10.30 pm.*

HENLEY, WEST SUSSEX	3–4A

The Duke Of Cumberland **£ 50** ❸❷❷
GU27 3HQ (01428) 652280
An "out-of-the-way, destination pub", in an "idyllic" location (with "lots of outside tables" and "breathtaking views"), offering "inventive" cooking that's often rated as "top-class"; however, the occasional critic can find the food "uninspired".
/ *Details:* @theduke_Henley; *9 pm; closed Mon D & Sun D.*

HEREFORD, HEREFORDSHIRE	2–1B

Café at All Saints **£ 25** ❼
All Saints Church, High St HR4 9AA
(01432) 370415
"A fabulously unique café in a church", tipped not just for "the best cappuccino in Herefordshire", but also an "imaginative" range of dishes – "a useful destination for tourists and locals alike".
/ *Details:* www.cafeatallsaints.co.uk; *5 pm; closed Sun; no Amex; no booking.*

Castle House Restaurant
Castle House Hotel **£ 51** ❸❸❸
Castle St HR1 2NW (01432) 356321
"Sophisticated" cooking in a "lovely central location" – almost all reporters agree on the attractions of "Hereford's best restaurant by far", occupying the dining room of a townhouse hotel.
/ *Details:* www.castlehse.co.uk; *9.30 pm, Sun 9 pm.*
Accommodation: 24 rooms, from £150.

HERNE BAY, KENT	3–3D

Le Petit Poisson **£ 40** ❷❷❸
Pier Approach, Central Parade CT6 5JN
(01227) 361199
"Beautifully cooked fish" is indeed the highlight at this restaurant "just a few feet from the waves"; "charming" staff, "quirky" atmosphere and "reasonable" prices help make it "a rare find".
/ *Details:* www.lepetitpoisson.co.uk; *9.30 pm, Sun 15.30 pm; closed Mon & Sun D; no Amex.*

HETHE, OXFORDSHIRE   2–

The Muddy Duck   **£ 44** ❸❷❷
Main St OX27 8ES   (01869) 278099
A newish gastropub-offshoot of a popular local deli, hailed by its fans as offering "the perfect balance of guaranteed good food and informality", and "in the middle of nowhere" too. / Details: 9 pm.

HETTON, NORTH YORKSHIRE   5–1B

The Angel Inn   **£ 50** ❷❷❷
BD23 6LT   (01756) 730263
It may feel "isolated", but this renowned inn remains well "worth the journey" for its "brilliantly judged" cooking (particularly "incredibly fine seafood"), "extensive" wine list and "cosy, comfortable surroundings"; there is still the odd report, though, of a performance that's "patchy". / Details: www.angelhetton.co.uk; 5m N of Skipton off B6265 at Rylstone; 9 pm; D only, ex Sun open L only. Accommodation: 9 rooms, from £150.

HEXHAM, NORTHUMBERLAND   8–2A

Bouchon Bistrot   **£ 44** ❸❹❸
4-6 Gilesgate NE46 3NJ   (01434) 609943
*"As close as we can get to France up here"; this Gallic bistro generally pleases reporters with "good food" and a "good wine list"; service is "sometimes slow", though, and there is the occasional hint that it is "resting on its laurels".
/ Details: www.bouchonbistrot.co.uk; 9.30 pm; closed Sun; no Amex.*

HIGH WYCOMBE,
BUCKINGHAMSHIRE   3–2A

The Old Queens Head   **£ 48** ❶
Hammersley Ln HP10 8EY   (01494) 813371
In an underserved area, this "well-run", large and rambling Tudor inn is tipped for its "convivial" atmosphere and "competent" food; "service is slow during busy times" though, and some regulars caution that "standards are not what they were". / Details: www.oldqueensheadpenn.co.uk; 9.30 pm, Fri & Sat 10 pm.

HINDON, WILTSHIRE   2–3C

The Lamb Inn   **£ 38** ❶
High St SP3 6DP   (01747) 820573
Tipped as an "ideal place to stop for lunch on the way to the West Country" – an "attractive country inn" that's an outpost of London's Boisdale empire. / Details: www.lambathindon.co.uk; 2 minutes from the A350, 5 minutes from the A303; 9.30 pm, Sun 9 pm. Accommodation: 19 rooms, from £75.

HINTLESHAM, SUFFOLK   3–1D

Hintlesham Hall   **£ 68** ❸❸❷
Duke St IP8 3NS   (01473) 652334
The new management is "trying hard", say friends of this "beautiful" and "romantic" country house hotel, set "in glorious ground"; the word "expensive" does keep cropping up in reports, but most reporters say the cooking is "very good". / Details: www.hintleshamhall.com; 4m W of Ipswich on A1071; 9.30 pm; jacket at D; children: 12. Accommodation: 33 rooms, from £99.

HINTON ST GEORGE, SOMERSET   2–3A

Lord Poulett Arms   **£ 46** ❷❸❷
TA17 8SE   (01460) 73149
"A real find in this quiet Somerset village"; with "roaring fires", and "very good food", reporters find "little to dislike" at this "beautiful old pub". / Details: www.lordpoulettarms.com; 9 pm; no Amex. Accommodation: 4 rooms, from £85.

HITCHIN, HERTFORDSHIRE   3–2B

Hermitage Rd   **£ 40** ❹❹❷
20-21 Hermitage Rd SG5 1BT
(01462) 433603
Looking for "a New York style bar, dropped into a suburban Hertfordshire town, which rocks every night"? – not all reporters are wowed by the results from the open kitchen at this "very buzzy" converted night club, but most feel it offers "good casual dining". / Details: www.hermitagerd.co.uk; 10 pm; no Amex.

HOLT, NORFOLK   6–3C

The Pigs   **£ 43** ❸❷❸
Norwich Rd NR24 2RL   (01263) 587634
This "pleasant foodie country pub" is "a great place to eat inventive and quirky dishes" (especially the puddings), with "locally-brewed beer only adding to the general happiness"; thanks to various play areas, it's also judged a "top option for kids". / Details: www.thepigs.org.uk; @PigsPubNorfolk; 9 pm. Accommodation: 10 rooms, from £110.

HONITON, DEVON   2–4A

Combe House   **£ 79** ❷❷❶
Gittisham EX14 3AD   (01404) 540400
This "beautiful Elizabethan country house" in "rolling countryside" has the romantic "wow factor" in spades, and offers food which "ranges from outstanding to merely delicious" – "just wish it wasn't quite so expensive so we could go more often". / Details: www.combehousedevon.com; on the outskirts of Honiton; not far from the A30, A375, 303; 9.30 pm; no Amex. Accommodation: 15+ rooms, from £215.

The Holt   **£ 42** ❷❷❸
178 High St EX14 1LA   (01404) 47707
This family-run pub attracts consistent praise for its "frequently changing menu" and "reasonable prices"; perhaps a few more soft furnishings wouldn't go amiss, though – some reporters find it

rather "echoey". / Details: www.theholt-honiton.com; 11 pm; closed Mon & Sun.

HOOK, HAMPSHIRE 2–3D

Old House at Home £ 47 ❶
Newham Grn RG27 9AH (01256) 762222
Most reporters still tip this "enjoyable" pub for the "excellent fresh food" served in the bar and restaurant; this year's reports also included a major 'off-day', though – hopefully just a one-off. / Details: @oldhousenewnham; 9 pm; closed Sun D.

HORNDON ON THE HILL, ESSEX 3–3C

The Bell Inn £ 48 ❷❷❷
High Rd SS17 8LD (01375) 642463
"The daddy of all gastropubs"; now in its fourth decade, John and Christine Vereker's inn is a "fantastic oasis" that's "well worth the dreary drive from London"; it offers "top-notch creative cooking", a "great-value wine list", and a "true Essex" atmosphere ("with an amusing smattering of footballers' wives!") / Details: www.bell-inn.co.uk; signposted off B1007, off A13; 9.45 pm; booking: max 12. Accommodation: 15 rooms, from £50.

HORSHAM, WEST SUSSEX 3–4A

Camellia Restaurant
South Lodge Hotel £ 66 ❶
Brighton Rd RH13 6PS (01403) 891711
Looking for "solid hotel dining" in the grand country house style? – this rather "old-fashioned" room remains a top tip; weather permitting, you can lunch on the impressive terrace, which has splendid views. / Details: www.southlodgehotel.co.uk; 9.30 pm. Accommodation: 85 rooms, from £195.

The Pass Restaurant
South Lodge Hotel £ 87 ❷❷❸
Brighton Rd RH13 6PS (01403) 891711
"It's a delight to watch the experts at work", and to sample Matthew Gillan's "divine" and "inspiring" 7-course menu, say fans of a dining room which seems "very modern" in the setting of this 19th-century country house hotel – Lord Grantham would certainly not approve of the way the chefs pass dishes directly to diners! / Details: www.southlodgehotel.co.uk; 8.30 pm; closed Mon & Tue; booking essential. Accommodation: 89 rooms, from £235.

Restaurant Tristan £ 56 ❶❷❷
3 Stans Way, East St RH12 1HU
(01403) 255688
Terms like "brave", "ambitious" and "brilliant" fly around in the many reports on Tristan Mason's "confident" cooking, in this attractive 16th-century building; what's more service is "delightful" and prices "very reasonable". / Details: www.restauranttristan.co.uk; 9.30 pm; closed Mon & Sun.

WABI £ 52 ❷❹❸
38 East St RH12 1HL (01403) 788140
It's been a turbulent year for this upmarket Japanese, as the chef and co-founder left to open a London sister (which soon closed); now under a new young cook, the original HQ still attracts plaudits for "fantastic food" and a "great range of cocktails". / Details: www.wabi.co.uk; @WabiHorsham; 10.45 pm; closed Mon & Sun.

HOUGH ON THE HILL, LINCOLNSHIRE 6–3A

Brownlow Arms £ 48 ❸❷❷
NG32 2AZ (01400) 250234
There's little disagreement among reporters about this gastropub with a "lovely village atmosphere"; it delivers "consistently good" food, albeit "at a price". / Details: www.brownlowarms.com; on the Grantham Road; 9.15 pm; closed Mon, Tue–Sat D only, closed Sun D; no Amex; children: 10+. Accommodation: 5 rooms, from £98.

HOVE, EAST SUSSEX 3–4B

The Foragers £ 39 ❷❷❷
3 Stirling Pl BN3 3YU (01273) 733134
Befitting the name, the owners of this "excellent gastropub" serve "foraged food they collect themselves", plus locally-sourced meat and fish, creating dishes that are "very different from standard restaurant fare". / Details: www.theforagerpub.co.uk; 10 pm; closed Sun D; no Amex; children: 12+ after 8 pm.

HUDDERSFIELD, WEST YORKSHIRE 5–1C

Bradley's £ 45 ❶
84 Fitzwilliam St HD1 5BB (01484) 516773
In business for over twenty years, a "friendly" bistro that's still tipped for its "consistently high standards at low prices". / Details: www.bradleyscatering.co.uk; 10 pm; closed Mon, Sat L & Sun; no Amex.

Eric's £ 50 ❷❷❸
73-75 Lidget St HD3 3JP (01484) 646416
"Unusual combinations of food, served well" make this Lindley restaurant well worth seeking out; when it's full, though, it can be "a little noisy". / Details: www.ericsrestaurant.co.uk; 10 pm; closed Mon, Sat L & Sun D; no Amex.

Med One £ 40 ❷❷❸
10-12 West Gate HD1 1NN (01484) 511100
"Great Middle Eastern food at reasonable prices" – the gist of all reports on this "basic" but "enthusiastic" town-centre spot. / Details: www.med-one.co.uk.

HUNSDON, HERTFORDSHIRE 3–2B

The Fox And Hounds £ 42 ❷❷❷
2 High St SG12 8NH (01279) 843999
"A real good old-fashioned family-run pub" offering

"a very good menu of fresh local produce", *"superb" cask beers and a "reasonable" wine list too* – *for almost all reporters, it is "always a treat".* / **Details:** www.foxandhounds-hunsdon.co.uk; @thefoxhunsdon; off the A414, 10 min from Hertford; 10 pm; no Amex.

HUNTINGDON, CAMBRIDGESHIRE 3–1B

Old Bridge Hotel £ 53 ❷❷❸
1 High St PE29 3TQ (01480) 424300
It's not the food (although it can be "terrific") which makes this ivy-clad townhouse hotel stand out – the real gem is the "sensational" wine list, available to pre-taste in the adjoining shop; the rooms are also noted as "good for romance". / **Details:** www.huntsbridge.com; @oldbridgehotel; off A1, off A14; 10 pm. **Accommodation:** 24 rooms, from £160.

HURWORTH, COUNTY DURHAM 8–3B

The Bay Horse £ 50 ❷❸❷
45 The Grn DL2 2AA (01325) 720 663
Jonathan Hall and Marcus Bennett's village inn is a hit with almost all who comment on it, even if – the "great value-for-money" prix-fixe menu notwithstanding – it's "quite pricey for what is essentially a pub restaurant". / **Details:** www.thebayhorsehurworth.com; @thebayhorse_; 9.30 pm, Sun 8.30 pm.

HUTTON MAGNA, NORTH YORKSHIRE 8–3B

The Oak Tree Inn £ 46 ❷❷❷
DL11 7HH (01833) 627371
"A tiny pub in a small village worth seeking out for really fine cooking"; "it's consistently amazing, I hate to share it with anyone…" / **Details:** www.theoaktreeinn.co.uk; Tue-Sat 11pm Sun 10.30pm; closed Mon.

HYTHE, KENT 3–4D

Hythe Bay £ 44 ❷❷❸
Marine Pde CT21 6AW (01303) 267024
You get fine views over Dover Harbour and the Channel from this "small and delightful" restaurant, unanimously praised in reports for its "very good fish, most of it locally caught". / **Details:** www.thehythebay.co.uk; 9.30 pm.

ILKLEY, WEST YORKSHIRE 5–1C

Bettys £ 46 ❷❷❶
32-34 The Grove LS29 9EE (01943) 608029
"You don't go to Betty's for lunch or dinner, though those are decent enough – you go for the fabulous cakes and coffee"; and while fans may fret that this famous grand café chain is "getting too commercial", this particular branch "still manages to maintain its traditional atmosphere".

/ **Details:** www.bettysandtaylors.com; 5.30 pm; no Amex; no booking.

The Box Tree £ 73 ❷❷❸
35-37 Church St LS29 9DR (01943) 608484
Simon Gueller is currently chef at this cottage-y bastion of provincial fine dining (est 1962), which most reporters deem a "gem", with "consistent" standards harking "back to the good old days"; no denying, though, that the occasional refusenik finds the style too "unadventurous" for comfort. / **Details:** www.theboxtree.co.uk; on A65 near town centre; 9.30 pm; closed Mon & Sun D; no jeans or trainers.

The Far Syde £ 43 ❷❷❷
1-3 New Brook St LS29 8DQ (01943) 602030
"Ilkley is lucky to have it!", is the general view on Gavin Beedhan's town-centre bistro – "a winner very time", with "consistently good" food, and "they really know their wine" too. / **Details:** www.thefarsyde.co.uk; @farsyde; 10 pm; closed Mon & Sun; no Amex.

Ilkley Moor Vaults £ 42 ❷❸❸
Stockeld Rd LS29 9HD (01943) 607012
A "reliable" well-established spot, serving "inexpensive" but "tasty" home-made food (inspired by the Slow Food movement) in "very hearty" portions; unsurprisingly, weekends in particular are often "busy". / **Details:** www.ilkleymoorvaults.co.uk; 9 pm, Sun 7 pm; closed Mon.

ILMINGTON, WARWICKSHIRE 2–1C

The Howard Arms £ 44 ❸❷❷
Lower Grn CV36 4LT (01608) 682226
"Much more than another gastropub", this "lovely old Cotswolds inn" (with "spacious" rooms) wins high praise for its "varied and unpretentious menu"; even a reporter who says quality "blows hot and cold" says "when they get it right it's hard to fault". / **Details:** www.howardarms.com; 8m SW of Stratford-upon-Avon off A4300; 9 pm, Sat & Sun 9.30 pm; no Amex. **Accommodation:** 8 rooms, from £110.

INVERNESS, HIGHLAND 9–2C

Chez Roux
Rocpool Reserve £ 54 ❶❷❷
Culduthel Rd IV2 4AG (01463) 240089
"Immaculate lobster, superb soufflé Suissesse, great wines, unimprovable views and surprisingly good service too…" – these are the sorts of attractions which inspire only extremely positive reports on this outpost of the Roux empire, by the river Ness. / **Details:** www.rocpool.com; @ICMI_UK; 10 pm. **Accommodation:** 11 rooms, from £210.

The Mustard Seed £ 43 ❸❸❷
16 Fraser St IV1 1DW (01463) 220220
"A room with great atmosphere" – a Georgian church building on the banks of the River Ness –

helps create a "wonderful" experience, at this well-established venture, also praised for its "well-executed" cuisine, including "super value" lunch and early-evening menus.
/ **Details:** www.themustardseedrestaurant.co.uk; 10 pm.

Rocpool　　　　　**£ 52**　**❷❷❷**
1 Ness Walk IV3 5NE　(01463) 717274
This "well-run" riverside brasserie is the most-mentioned in town, and likewise "stands out in the sea of mediocrity which is Inverness", with its "interesting and varied menu", and an atmosphere that's "always busy and buzzy".
/ **Details:** www.rocpoolrestaurant.com; 10 pm; closed Sun L , open Sun evenings June-Sept only..

IPSWICH, SUFFOLK	3–1D

Baipo　　　　　**£ 36**　**❸❸⑤**
63 Upper Orwell St IP4 1HP　(01473) 218402
"Still retaining its standards as our finest local Thai" – this "utterly reliable" spot offers some dishes which aficionados claim are "rare even in Thailand"; ambience, though, "is not a strength".
/ **Details:** www.baipo.co.uk; 10.45 pm; closed Mon L & Sun; no Amex.

Mariners at Il Punto　　**£ 42**　**❷❷❷**
Neptune Quay IP4 1AX　(01473) 289748
"One of the better Ipswich restaurants"; the Crépy family's restored naval vessel, in the marina certainly has a "wonderful ambience" and, as one reporter notes: "the chef must be a magician to make such superb food from such a small kitchen!".
/ **Details:** www.marinersipswich.co.uk; 9.30 pm; closed Mon & Sun; no Amex.

Trongs　　　　　**£ 34**　**❷❶④**
23 St Nicholas St IP1 1TW　(01473) 256833
"One of the better Chinese restaurants in the countryside" even "after so many years"; the food at this Vietnamese-run venture "never disappoints" – particularly the "vast" and "extraordinary value-for-money" set menus; it has "the nicest staff ever" too!
/ **Details:** 10.30 pm; closed Sun; booking essential.

IRBY, MERSEYSIDE	5–2A

Da Piero　　　　　**£ 52**　**❷❶④**
5-7 Mill Hill Rd CH61 4UB　(0151) 648 7373
A family-run venture that's "what all neighbourhood restaurants should be like"; recently expanded, it offers "proper", "rustic" Sicilian cooking, and "charming" service too. / **Details:** www.dapiero.co.uk; 9 pm; D only, closed Mon & Sun; no Amex.

JERSEY, CHANNEL ISLANDS

Bohemia
The Club Hotel & Spa　　**£ 84**　**❶❶❷**
Green St, St Helier JE2 4UH　(01534) 876500
Early days for new chef Steven Smith at this contemporary style St Helier dining room; initial

reports do tend to suggest, though, that "he has really hit the ground running" – "his five different tasting menus are out of this world!"
/ **Details:** www.bohemiajersey.com; 10 pm; closed Sun; no trainers. **Accommodation:** 46 rooms, from £185.

Green Island Restaurant £ 54　**❷❷❷**
St Clement JE2 6LS　(01534) 857787
"A small beachside terrace restaurant providing excellent seafood and the freshest fish right from the bay"; the only recurrent complaint? – it's "not cheap!". / **Details:** www.greenisland.je; 9.30 pm; closed Mon & Sun D; no Amex.

Longueville Manor　　　**£ 84**　**❸❶❷**
Longueville Rd, St Saviour JE2 7WF (01534) 725501
A famously traditional country house hotel-style dining experience, on the outskirts of St Helier; "back to its best" in recent times, it offers not just general "cosseting", but some "very good food" too.
/ **Details:** www.longuevillemanor.com; @longuevillemanor; head from St. Helier on the A3 towards Gorey; less than 1 mile from St. Helier; 10 pm; no jeans or trainers. **Accommodation:** 31 rooms, from £170.

Mark Jordan at the
Beach　　　　　**£ 49**　**❶**
La Plage, La Route de la Haule, St Peter JE3 7YD　((0)1534) 780180
Tipped for its "wonderful beach location" (St Aubin's Bay), this seaside seafood-specialist is also praised in most (if not quite all) reports for its "super-fresh" seafood and its "attentive" service.
/ **Details:** www.theatlantichotel.com/dining/mark-jorda n-at-the-beach; 9.30 pm; closed Mon.

Ocean Restaurant
Atlantic Hotel　　　　**£ 80**　**❷❷❷**
Le Mont de la Pulente, St Brelade JE3 8HE (01534) 744101
"A wonderful location" in an ocean liner-style dining room, with sea views sets the scene at this highly rated operation, which wins acclaim with Mark Jordan's "skillful" cooking and service that's "beyond compare". / **Details:** www.theatlantichotel.com; 10 pm; no jeans or trainers. **Accommodation:** 50 rooms, from £150 - 250.

Ormer　　　　　**£ 74**　**❷❷❷**
7-11 Don St, St Helier JE2 4TQ　(015) 3472 5100
Shaun Rankin, formerly of Bohemia, has recently set up on his own at this new site in the heart of St Helier; still early days, but one fan reports standards "just as before"… which is to say very high indeed.
/ **Details:** www.ormerjersey.com; 10pm; closed Sun.

The Oyster Box　　　　**£ 52**　**❷❷❶**
St Brelade's Bay JE3 8EF　(01534) 743311
"Beats the South of France any day!"; with its "brilliant" fish (and crustacea), and its "lovely" St

Brelade's Bay location, this "spectacular" beachside all-rounder pleases all who comment on it; the adjacent Crab Shack (same owners) is also good, but cheaper. / **Details:** www.oysterbox.co.uk; 9 pm; closed Mon L; no Amex.

KENILWORTH, WARWICKSHIRE   5–4C

Bosquet   **£ 54**   ❶❶❸
97a Warwick Rd CV8 1HP (01926) 852463
Locally "nowhere else competes", say fans of the "real" ("rich and generously portioned") south-western French cooking "served with passion" by Bernard Lignier and his family at this "charming if somewhat dated" establishment for over three decades now; the wine list is "worth highlighting" too. / **Details:** www.restaurantbosquet.co.uk; 9.15 pm; closed Mon, Sat L & Sun; closed 2 weeks in Aug.

KENTON, GREATER LONDON   3–2A

Blue Ginger   **£ 37**   ❷❷❸
383 Kenton Rd HA3 0XS (020) 8909 0100
This modern operation is tipped for an "excellent range" of Indian (and Asian) food; its "great value" ("especially the fixed price option") makes it "a good choice for large groups", and "those with large appetites" too! / **Details:** www.bgrestaurant.com/contact.html; 11.15 pm; closed Mon L; no Amex.

KESTON, KENT   3–3B

Lujon   **£ 50**   ❷❸❸
6 Commonside BR2 6BP (01689) 855501
With a "lovely setting overlooking the village green", this "very welcoming" local is of particular note for its "exceptional fish dishes", and "nice wines by the glass" too. / **Details:** www.lujon.co.uk; @lujonkeston; midnight; closed Mon, Tue & Sun D.

KESWICK, CUMBRIA   7–3D

Lyzzick Hall Country House Hotel   **£ 50**   ❸❷❷
CA12 4PY (017687) 72277
"Fantastic (Mediterranean) food served with a personal touch" – and the "interesting and wide-ranging" wine list – reflects the Spanish heritage of the family behind this well-established country house hotel; it has a "great location", offering excellent views from the terrace. / **Details:** www.lyzzickhall.co.uk; 9 pm.

KETTLESHULME, CHESHIRE   5–2B

The Swan Inn   **£ 45**   ❷❸❸
Macclesfield Rd SK23 7QU (01663) 732943
A "top-class" boozer in "traditional" style, where "fabulous seafood, sourced daily" is a highlight; the setting is a little "cramped" for some tastes, but "plenty of locals calling in for a drink" add to the atmosphere.

/ **Details:** www.verynicepubs.co.uk/swankettleshulme/; 8.30 pm, Thu-Fri 7 pm, Sat 9 pm, Sun 4 pm; closed Mon; no Amex.

KEYSTON, CAMBRIDGESHIRE   3–1A

The Pheasant at Keyston £ 50   ❸❸❸
Loop Rd PE28 0RE (01832) 710241
"Much improved under new ownership", this "small village pub" attracts praise for its "capable" cuisine in "cosy" surroundings; only quibble – the menu is "perhaps now too similar to that of its (Huntsbridge Group) sibling, The Old Bridge in Huntingdon". / **Details:** www.thepheasant-keyston.co.uk; 1m S of A14 between Huntingdon & Kettering, J15; 9.30 pm; closed Mon & Sun D; no Amex.

KIBWORTH BEAUCHAMP, LEICESTERSHIRE   5–4D

The Lighthouse   **£ 46**   ❷❷❷
9 Station St LE8 0LN (0116) 279 6260
"It was a brave decision for the Bobolis to close their very successful 'Firenze' Italian and re-open as a fish restaurant"; it's paid off, though – the "breezy and informal" service remains, and "although the menu's dumbed down slightly everything is still of a high standard". / **Details:** www.lighthousekibworth.co.uk; @ourlighthouse; 9.30 pm; D only, closed Mon & Sun; no Amex.

KILLIECRANKIE, PERTH AND KINROSS   9–3C

Killiecrankie House Hotel   **£ 57**   ❶
PH16 5LG (01796) 473220
"A good hotel, but the restaurant is better" – a top tip hereabouts, if you're looking for food that's "tasty" and "freshly cooked". / **Details:** www.killiecrankiehotel.co.uk; 8.30 pm; no Amex; no shorts. **Accommodation:** 10 rooms, from £150.

KINGHAM, GLOUCESTERSHIRE   2–1C

Daylesford Café   **£ 42**   ❸❺❷
GL56 0YG (01608) 731700
A hit with the 4x4 set – this converted barn (with deli and kitchen shop attached) is "a really useful contemporary and stylish venue of a type sadly lacking in the countryside"; "when it's good, it's very, very good, but when it's bad, it's rubbish" (service in particular). / **Details:** www.daylesfordorganic.com; Mon-Wed 5 pm, Thu-Sat 6 pm, Sun 4pm; L only.

KINGHAM, OXFORDSHIRE   2–1C

The Kingham Plough   **£ 48**   ❷❸❷
The Green OX7 6YD (01608) 658327
OK, it "gets flack for being the favoured haunt of the Chipping Norton Set", but Emily Watkins's "congenial" inn is well-praised for its "top-quality restaurant food", "thoughtful service", and – for

those who stay – "the best breakfast ever"!
/ **Details:** www.thekinghamplough.co.uk; 8.30 pm,
Fri & Sat 8.45 pm, Sun 8 pm; no Amex.
Accommodation: 7 rooms, from £95.

KINGSTON UPON THAMES, SURREY   3–3A

The Canbury Arms   £ 44   ❸❸④
49 Canbury Park Rd KT2 6LQ   (020) 8255
9129
This "justly popular gastropub" continues to win
much local praise for "homemade" pub grub that's
"always good"; but try not to get "relegated to the
rather cold conservatory".
/ **Details:** www.thecanburyarms.com;
@thecanburyarms; 9 pm, Fri & Sat 10 pm.

fish! Kitchen   £ 46   ❷❸⑤
56-58 Coombe Rd KT2 7AF   (020) 8546 2886
OK, it's "not really the place for an occasion", but if
you're just looking for "fresh fish simply cooked", this
"basic" and "cramped" canteen may be just the
spot. / **Details:** www.fishkitchen.com; 10 pm; closed
Mon & Sun.

Roz ana   £ 46   ❷❸④
4-8 Kingston Hill KT2 7NH   (020) 8546 6388
"Not your regular curry house by a long way" – this
Norbiton favourite wins a hymn of praise for its
"very interesting interpretation of Indian food" –
"fresh, healthy, but still authentically flavoursome".
/ **Details:** www.roz-ana.com; 10.30 pm, Fri & Sat
11 pm, Sun 10 pm; no Amex.

KINGUSSIE, HIGHLAND   9–2C

The Cross   £ 68   ❷❸❸
Tweed Mill Brae, Ardbroilach Rd PH21 1LB
(01540) 661166
"A divine restaurant with rooms", where a young
chef is tipped for consistently "excellent" cuisine;
stay the night, and breakfasts are "wonderful" too.
/ **Details:** www.thecross.co.uk; 8.30 pm; children: 9+.
Accommodation: 8 rooms, from £100.

KIRKBY LONSDALE, CUMBRIA   7–4D

Hipping Hall   £ 72   ❷❷❷
Cowan Bridge LA6 2JJ   (01524) 271187
This 15th-century hall offers some notably
"excellent" cuisine, and in a "lovely rural setting" too;
there is the very occasional misfire, but most reports
are full of praise. / **Details:** www.hippinghall.com;
9 pm; closed weekday L; no Amex; no trainers; booking
essential; children: 10+. **Accommodation:** 9 rooms,
from £219.

KNOWSTONE, DEVON   1–2D

The Mason's Arms   £ 59   ❶❸❷
EX36 4RY (01398) 341231
"A rare gem in this part of the world"; this "quaint
pub" – run by the former head chef of the
Waterside Inn at Bray – offers "a quality of cooking

which would cost three times as much in the
metropolis"! / **Details:** www.masonsarmsdevon.co.uk;
9 pm; closed Mon & Sun D; children: 5+ after 6pm.

KNUTSFORD, CHESHIRE   5–2B

Belle Époque   £ 50   ❸❸❷
60 King St WA16 6DT   (01565) 633060
"A stunning restaurant within an original Art
Nouveau building"; most reports are also highly
upbeat about the cooking too, but there's also a
view that it's "ordinary and not up to the prices".
/ **Details:** www.thebelleepoque.com;
@TheBelleEpoque; 1.5m from M6, J19; 9.30 pm; closed
Sun D; booking: max 6, Sat. **Accommodation:** 7
rooms, from £110.

LALEHAM, MIDDLESEX   3–3A

Three Horsehoes   £ 39   ❷❷❷
25 Shepperton St TW18 1SE   (01784) 455014
"The exterior isn't the greatest", but this "excellent"
venture is "everything else you'd want in a
gastropub" and features in a number of reports as
the ideal venue for impressing foreigners ("our
American friends groaned in delight!").
/ **Details:** www.3horseshoeslaleham.co.uk; 9.45 pm.

LAMPETER, CEREDIGION   4–4C

Falcondale Hotel   £ 49   ❶
Falcondale Drive SA48 7RX   (01570) 422910
Tipped as "hard to better at the price", a country
house hotel where, on most reports, "well-executed"
dishes are twinned with a "good-value wine list"; the
setting is "superb" too, with magnificent views of
beautiful countryside.
/ **Details:** www.thefalcondale.co.uk; 8.30 pm.
Accommodation: 19 rooms, from £149.

LANCASTER, LANCASHIRE   5–1A

Quite Simply French   £ 84   ❶
27a St Georges Quay LA1 1RD
(01524) 843199
Tipped for "unexpectedly imaginative" food and
"reasonably priced" too, this long-established bistro
"can be busy even on the foulest of nights";
"charming" and "attentive" service too.
/ **Details:** www.quitesimplyfrench.co.uk; 9.30 pm,
Sun & Mon 9 pm; D only, ex Sun open L & D; no Amex.

LANGAR, NOTTINGHAMSHIRE   5–3D

Langar Hall   £ 54   ❸❸❷
Church Ln NG13 9HG   (01949) 860559
"Standards are maintained" at "wonderful, if
eccentric" hostess, Imogen Skirving's "quirky and
fun" country house hotel – a "beautiful" and
romantic location; "prices are relatively high for the
area", but the food is "first class".
/ **Details:** www.langarhall.com; off A52 between
Nottingham & Grantham; 9.30 pm; no Amex;
no trainers. **Accommodation:** 12 rooms, from £100.

LANGHO, LANCASHIRE   5–1B

Northcote   **£72** **❶❷❸**
Northcote Rd BB6 8BE (01254) 240555
"Maintaining the highest standards in all respects",
this long-established manor house restaurant-with-
rooms Messrs Bancroft and Haworth's "flagship"
impresses almost all who report on it with its
"superbly executed" menu, its "old-fashioned
customer service" and its "extensive" selection of
wines. / **Details:** www.northcote.com; M6, J31 then
A59; 9.30 pm; no trainers; SRA-60%.
Accommodation: 14 rooms, from £230.

LANGSHOTT, SURREY   3–3B

Langshott Manor   **£68** **❶**
Ladbroke Rd RH6 8PB (01293) 786680
Handy for Gatwick, a "beautiful little country house
hotel", tipped for its "really good" cooking… and
"good value too, if you seek out the set menus".
/ **Details:** www.langshottmanor.com; just off the A23,
in Horley; 9.30 pm; no trainers. **Accommodation:** 22
rooms, from £190.

LAPWORTH, WARWICKSHIRE   5–4C

The Boot   **£42** **❶**
Old Warwick Rd B94 6JU (01564) 782464
A "very busy South Birmingham pub", tipped for its
"reasonable" food, but perhaps rather more for the
attractions of its "great beer garden".
/ **Details:** www.lovelypubs.co.uk; 10 pm, Sun 9 pm;
no Amex.

LAVANT, WEST SUSSEX   3–4A

The Earl of March   **£49** **❷❸❸**
Lavant Rd PO18 0BQ (01243) 533993
Offering "stunning" fish and good "seasonal
specialities", this "excellent country pub/restaurant"
is, by almost all accounts, a "great find"; prices,
though, can occasionally strike reporters as "very
high". / **Details:** www.theearlofmarch.com; 9.30 pm.

LAVENHAM, SUFFOLK   3–1C

**Marco Pierre White's
Angel Hotel**   **£55** **⑤⑤④**
Market Pl CO10 9QZ (01787) 247388
Even some fans concede "teething problems", but
say "things have settled down and the food is great"
at what's nowadays an outpost of the Wheeler's
empire; for too many reporters, however, it's become
"a terrible let down" – "such a shame MPW cannot
make a better show of things".
/ **Details:** www.marcopierrewhite.org; on A1141 6m
NE of Sudbury; 9.30 pm. **Accommodation:** 9 rooms,
from £110.

Great House   **£54** **❶❶❷**
Market Pl CO10 9QZ (01787) 247431
"One of the best restaurants in England, but still
relatively affordable"; almost all reports confirm that

its patrons for three decades, the Crépy family,
"maintain top standards" in this "beautiful medieval
house" – a "little piece of France", on the market
square; lunchtime menus offer particularly "great
value". / **Details:** www.greathouse.co.uk;
@GreatHouseHotel; follow directions to Guildhall;
9.30 pm; closed Mon & Sun D; closed Jan; no Amex.
Accommodation: 5 rooms, from £95.

Swan Hotel   **£53** **❷❷❷**
High St CO10 9QA (01787) 247477
It's not just the "beautiful" and "impressive" half-
timbered building that makes this well-known hotel
quite a culinary "favourite" with all who comment
on it; both its brasserie and its restaurant are
consistently highly rated across the board.
/ **Details:** www.theswanatlavenham.co.uk; 9.30 pm;
no jeans or trainers; children: 12+ at D.
Accommodation: 45 rooms, from £195.

LEAMINGTON SPA, WARWICKSHIRE   5–4C

La Coppola   **£51** **❷❷❷**
86 Regent St CV32 4NS (01926) 888 873
Consistently cited as "the best Italian restaurant in
town", serving an "extensive" menu including
"outstanding fish and seafood"; it may be "pricey"
but is "always very full" with many recommending
that you "book in advance".
/ **Details:** www.lacoppola.co.uk; 10 pm, Sun 9 pm.

Oscars French Bistro   **£43** **❷❷❸**
39 Chandos St CV32 4RL (01926) 452807
"French fare stylishly served" – the very "authentic"
formula for consistent satisfaction at this "cosy" and
"charming" spot; Auberge Night (Tuesday) is "an
incredible deal".
/ **Details:** www.oscarsfrenchbistro.co.uk; 9.30 pm;
closed Mon & Sun.

Queans Restaurant   **£50** **❶❶❷**
15 Dormer Pl CV32 5AA (01926) 315522
"Great food, great ethos" – chef-patronne Laura
Hamilton's basement restaurant beneath a
Georgian townhouse "thrives on her personal
attention", and offers some "really fine" dining, all at
bargain prices.
/ **Details:** www.queans-restaurant.co.uk; 9.30 pm;
closed Mon, Tue L, Sat L & Sun.

Restaurant 23   **£64** **❷❷❸**
34 Hamilton Ter CV32 4LY (01926) 422422
"A nice change from the pretentious restaurants in
which Warwickshire seems to specialise!" – this
"stylish" (if admittedly "slightly hushed") operation
wins nothing but praise for its "amazing" standards;
it moved in February 2012 to its "splendid" new
quarters, in a listed Victorian house.
/ **Details:** www.restaurant23.com; Mon-Sat 9.30pm;
closed Mon L & Sun D.

LECHLADE, GLOUCESTERSHIRE   3–2C

The Five Alls   **£ 41**   ❷④❸
Filkins GL7 3JQ   (01367) 860875
"The Snows, formerly of the über-groovy Swan at
Southrop, have proved 'fairy landlords' to the pub in
the next village", and the food at the relaunched
establishment can be "terrific"; neither service nor
ambience are as highly rated.
/ **Details:** www.thefiveallsfilkins.co.uk; 9.30 pm, Fri &
Sat 10 pm; closed Sun D; no Amex.

LEEDS, WEST YORKSHIRE   5–1C

Aagrah   **£ 37**   ❷❸❸
Aberford Rd LS25 2HF   (0113) 287 6606
"Beats any curry we've found in London and the
South"; this "very consistent" city-centre outpost of
the leading local chain remains more than one fan's
"favourite branch", thanks to its "balance between
spiciness and refinement" and "easy-going" service.
/ **Details:** www.aagrah.com; from A1 take A642
Aberford Rd to Garforth; 11.30 pm, Sun 10.30 pm;
D only.

Akbar's   **£ 31**   ❷④④
16 Greek St LS1 5RU   (0113) 242 5426
"The gargantuan family naan breads could be used
as a duvet for a small child!" – a highpoint at the
"large, always busy and lively" Leeds spin-off from
the Bradford original servicing "very tasty" and
"reasonably priced" curries.
/ **Details:** www.akbars.co.uk; midnight; D only.

Art's   **£ 41**   ❸④❸
42 Call Ln LS1 6DT   (0113) 243 8243
"A good place for a working lunch or catch-up in
the city-centre" – this ever-popular spot, near the
Corn Exchange, was the city's original trendy
restaurant ("it's named for the modern art on the
walls"), and the "hearty" cooking is "still good".
/ **Details:** www.artscafebar.com; 10 pm.

Bibis Italianissimo   **£ 41**   ⑤⑤❸
Criterion Pl, Swinegate LS1 4AG   (0113) 243
0905
Fans acclaim this ritzy Art Deco-style Italian near
the station for "fantastic" calzones and pizzas
which "still take some beating"; equal amounts of
reporters "cannot see what the hype is about",
though, and feel that the joint "fancies itself rotten".
/ **Details:** www.bibisrestaurant.com; @bibisrestaurant;
11 pm; closed Mon; no shorts; no booking, Sat.

Flying Pizza   **£ 37**   ❸❷❷
60 Street Ln LS8 2DQ   (0113) 266 6501
"Going from strength to strength as part of the San
Carlo empire", this well-known Headingley pizzeria
"has had a new lease on life since the take-over";
"it's rather pricey" still, but "good across the board".
/ **Details:** www.theflyingpizza.co.uk; 11 pm, Sun
10 pm; no shorts.

Fuji Hiro   **£ 25**   ❸④④
45 Wade Ln LS2 8NJ   (0113) 243 9184
"Noodles don't come better than this", say fans of
this "quick" and "friendly" city-centre Japanese.
/ **Details:** 10 pm, Fri & Sat 11 pm; need 5+ to book.

La Grillade   **£ 49**   ❷❷❷
Wellington St LS1 4HJ   (0113) 245 9707
"Despite the proliferation of steakhouses and grill
restaurants in Leeds in recent times, this remains
THE go-to for steak frites"; from the "lovely
atmosphere", to the "excellent-value authentic
French food", this Gallic spot is still a real all-round
hit, especially with the business set.
/ **Details:** www.lagrillade.co.uk; 10 pm, Sat 10.30 pm;
closed Sat L & Sun.

Hansa's   **£ 30**   ❶❶❸
72-74 North St LS2 7PN   (0113) 244 4408
The "best veggie Indian just about anywhere!"; Mrs
Hansa Dabhi's "brilliantly authentic", long-
established city-centre Gujarati continues to please
its many fans with "light, varied and elegant"
cuisine… and "at very good prices" too.
/ **Details:** www.hansasrestaurant.com; 10 pm, Fri &
Sat 11 pm; D only, ex Sun L only.

Kendells Bistro   **£ 44**   ❸❸❷
St Peters square LS9 8AH   (0113) 243 6553
"Candelight, blackboards full of delightful classic
French dishes, and a decent wine list too" – Mr
Kendell's "small" and "busy" bistro is an excellent
option in the city-centre.
/ **Details:** www.kendellsbistro.co.uk; @KendellsBistro;
9 pm, Fri & Sat 10 pm; D only, closed Mon & Sun;
no Amex; booking essential.

Red Chilli   **£ 39**   ❸❸❸
6 Great George St LS1 3DW   (01132) 429688
"Top-notch Sichuan cooking" is a highlight of the
"huge choice of fabulous Chinese food" on offer – at
"modest prices" but in "hefty portions" – at this city-
centre basement spot; "helpful and involved service"
too. / **Details:** www.redchillirestaurant.co.uk;
10.30 pm, Fri & Sat 11.30 pm.

The Reliance   **£ 37**   ❷❷❷
76-78 North St LS2 7PN   (0113) 295 6060
"A bit of a hidden treasure"; this "beautiful" boozer
has quite a fan club thanks to its "lovely, relaxed"
atmosphere, "imaginative" cooking and "friendly"
service. / **Details:** www.the-reliance.co.uk; 10 pm,
Thu-Sat 10.30 pm, Sun 9.30 pm; no booking.

Salvo's   **£ 46**   ❷❷❷
115 Otley Rd LS6 3PX   (0113) 275 5017
"A real local favourite"; from the "authentic pizzas"
to the "real Italian feel", there's a "good all-round
experience" to be had at this Headingley fixture,
and it's even better after a recent refit.
/ **Details:** www.salvos.co.uk; @salvosleeds; 10.30 pm,
Fri & Sat 11 pm, Sun 9 pm; no booking at D.

Sous le Nez en Ville **£ 45** **❸❷❷**
Quebec Hs, Quebec St LS1 2HA
(0113) 244 0108
Despite all the new openings in Leeds... this "cosy" Gallic perennial "is still the standard by which others are judged", and there are some "exceptional" choices on the wine list, too; beware, though – this large, low-ceilinged city-centre basement can get very noisy with groups on the "incredible-value" Early Bird deals. / Details: www.souslenez.com; @souslenez; 10 pm, Sat 11 pm; closed Sun.

Sukhothai **£ 40** **❷❶❸**
8 Regent St LS7 4PE (0113) 237 0141
"A jewel in the crown of Thai dining" – the "unwaveringly friendly" Chapel Allerton original of what's now a group of four restaurants in the Leeds area; "it's always packed even after the recent refurb and enlargement" thanks to its "elegant" interior and "consistently excellent" cooking. / Details: www.sukhothai.co.uk; 11 pm; Mon-Thu D only, Fri-Sun open L & D; no Amex.

Whitelocks Luncheon Bar **£ 23** **❶**
Turk's Head Yd, off Briggate LS1 6HB
(0113) 245 3950
"Under new ownership, and back on song"; this fascinating city-centre boozer is once again "an institution in the best tradition", and tipped for "the best pub food in Leeds". / Details: www.whitelocks.co.uk; 9 pm, Sun 5pm; no Amex.

LEICESTER, LEICESTERSHIRE 5–4D

Bobby's **£ 24** **❷❸④**
154-156 Belgrave Rd LE4 5AT
(0116) 266 0106
A landmark of the Golden Mile since 1976, this well-known Keralan dive offers "a myriad of food choices" including "sweets to die for"; the buffet is a particularly good deal – "can there be better-value veggie Indian grub anywhere in Britain?" / Details: www.eatatbobbys.com; 10 pm; closed Tue; no Amex.

Hotel Maiyango **£ 45** **❷❷❷**
13-21 St Nicholas Pl LE1 4LD
(0116) 251 8898
A "top quality" town-centre boutique hotel and restaurant offering "excellent cuisine with a north African influence", and "now with a deli just around the corner"; could it be more though? – "it's easily the best in the city-centre, excellent, locally sourced, but not yet with the edge to move up a league". / Details: www.maiyango.com; 9 pm; closed Mon L, Tue L & Sun L. Accommodation: 14 rooms, from £90.

Kayal **£ 35** **❷❷❸**
153 Granby St LE1 6FE (0116) 255 4667
There are dozens of competitors, but the survey is clear that this unprepossessing but comfortable outfit, near the railway station, is "the best Indian restaurant in town"; the cuisine is Keralan, so expect a "particular emphasis on seafood". / Details: www.kayalrestaurant.com; 11 pm, Sun 10 pm.

LEIGH-ON-SEA, ESSEX 3–3C

Sandbank **£ 38** **❸❷❸**
1470 London Rd SS9 2UR (01702) 719 000
"An oasis"; even a critic, who finds the culinary style "fussy" and the room rather "austere" agrees that this well-established restaurant undoubtedly offers "the best fine food locally". / Details: www.sandbankrestaurant.co.uk; @sandbankdining; 10.30 pm; closed Mon, Sat L & Sun D.

LEIGHTON BUZZARD, BEDFORDSHIRE 3–2A

The Kings Head **£ 61** **❷❷❶**
Ivinghoe LU7 9EB (01296) 668388
Unstinting praise of late for the "excellent food and silver service" at this "atmospheric" 17th-century inn, long known for its Aylesbury duck; celebrating something? – "cakes can be made and served to your requirements". / Details: www.kingsheadivinghoe.co.uk; 3m N of Tring on B489 to Dunstable; 9.15 pm; closed Sun D; jacket & tie required at D; SRA-60%.

LEINTWARDINE, SHROPSHIRE 5–4A

Jolly Frog **£ 47** **❶**
The Todden SY7 0LX (01547) 540298
Under new owners, this rural gastropub, near Ludlow Castle, is tipped for its "young and enthusiastic staff" and "quirky menu". / Details: www.jollyfrogpub.co.uk; 9.30 pm; closed Mon; no Amex.

LEWDOWN, DEVON 1–3C

Lewtrenchard Manor **£ 58** **❸❸❷**
EX20 4PN (01566) 783256
"Quiet, quaint and a bit faded around the edges", this "wonderful" Elizabethan country house hotel, in a large estate, certainly offers a retreat from the 21st century; generally, the cooking is "solid", but make sure you stay for breakfast – a "true gastronomic treat". / Details: www.lewtrenchard.co.uk; off A30 between Okehampton & Launceston; 9 pm; no jeans or trainers; children: 8+ at D. Accommodation: 14 rooms, from £155.

LEWES, EAST SUSSEX   3–4B

Bill's Produce Store   **£ 40**   ❸❷❸
56 Cliffe High St BN7 2AN (01273) 476918
The base of what's now a national chain, "the original Bill's in Lewes is still a favourite", especially for a "really lovely" breakfast – indeed, the main problem seems to be that this "buzzy" location sometimes just gets too "crowded".
/ Details: www.bills-website.co.uk; 10.30 pm, Fri-Sat 11.30 pm; no Amex.

Pelham House   **£ 41**   ❷❷⓿
BN7 1UW (01273) 488600
"Unexpectedly fine dining at this hotel in the town's old centre"; pretty much all reporters agree that this is a "beautiful" place to eat ("especially in the historic wood-panelled room"), and offering "sophisticated" cooking too.
/ Details: www.pelhamhouse.com; @pelhamlewes; off the High Street in Lewes; 9 pm, Sun 8.30 pm.
Accommodation: 31 rooms, from £130.

LINCOLN, LINCOLNSHIRE   6–3A

Browns Pie Shop   **£ 44**   ❶
33 Steep Hill LN2 1LU (01522) 527330
A handy tip for a meal that's "always reliable and enjoyable" (and especially good value if you seek out the Early Bird deal); its ancient cellar location is "very romantic" – "shame about the red paper napkins", though.
/ Details: www.brownspieshop.co.uk; 9.30 pm, Sun 8 pm; no Amex.

Jew's House Restaurant   **£ 48**   ❷❷❷
15 The Strait LN2 1JD (01522) 524851
"A gem" – this "friendly" spot, atmospherically located in one of Lincoln's oldest buildings, is praised by all who comment on it for "well cooked food" and "lovely" ambience.
/ Details: www.jewshouserestaurant.co.uk; 9.30 pm; closed Mon, Tue L & Sun; no Amex.

The Old Bakery   **£ 48**   ④④④
26-28 Burton Rd LN1 3LB (01522) 576057
It's a "godsend for Lincoln", say fans of this restaurant-with-rooms, lauding its "delightful" style ("olde worlde at the front, and with an airy conservatory at the back") and with "rustic" cooking; not everyone's impressed though, and critics find so so service and "too many tastes on the plate".
/ Details: www.theold-bakery.co.uk; @theoldbakeryrestaurant; 9 pm; closed Mon; no jeans.
Accommodation: 4 rooms, from £65.

The Wig & Mitre   **£ 41**   ❸❷④
30-32 Steep Hill LN2 1TL (01522) 535190
A big, well-known pub/restaurant, near the Cathedral, where "food is served all-day, every day"; even if it's not quite back to its glory days, it's tipped as "well worth a visit" (under recently installed management who are "doing great things").

/ Details: www.wigandmitre.com; 10 pm, Fri & Sat 10.30 pm, Sun 10 pm.

LINLITHGOW, WEST LOTHIAN   9–4C

Champany Inn   **£ 75**   ❶
EH49 7LU (01506) 834532
This famous steakhouse-inn is still the sort of place tipped for an "amazing châteaubriand", and "chips to die for" (plus a wine list of great repute); it's certainly no bargain, though, and the style is "rather old-fashioned" for some tastes.
/ Details: www.champany.com; 2m NE of Linlithgow on junction of A904 & A803; 10 pm; closed Sat L & Sun; no jeans or trainers; children: 8+.
Accommodation: 16 rooms, from £125.

LISS, HAMPSHIRE   2–3C

Madhuban   **£ 30**   ❶
94 Station Rd GU33 7AQ (01730) 893363
Strongly tipped for its "outstanding" cooking, this contemporary-style Bangladeshi village-restaurant offers the "best subcontinental food in the area".
/ Details: www.madhubanrestaurant.co.uk; 10 pm; closed Fri L.

LITTLE ECCLESTON, LANCASHIRE   5–1A

The Cartford Inn   **£ 41**   ❷④④
Cartford Ln PR3 0YP (01995) 670 166
Now boasting a river-view dining room, this "welcoming", "spruced-up" Gallic-owned inn, by the Carford Toll Bridge, is "well worth seeking out"; the decor is a little "individual", and service erratic, but "stick to the simpler dishes, and you'll eat well".
/ Details: www.thecartfordinn.co.uk; 9 pm, Fri & Sat 10 pm, Sun 8.30 pm; closed Mon L.

LITTLE WILBRAHAM,
CAMBRIDGESHIRE   3–1B

The Hole In The Wall   **£ 46**   ④❸④
2 High St CB21 5JY (01223) 812282
Former MasterChef winner Alex Rushmer's inn is, on some accounts, a "gem of a place", offering "eclectic" food to an "excellent" standard, and at "reasonable" prices too; no denying, though, that there's a strongly dissident camp, which feels the venture has been "heavily talked up".
/ Details: www.holeinthewallcambridge.com; @hitwcambridge; 9 pm; closed Mon & Sun D; no Amex.

LITTLEHAMPTON, WEST SUSSEX   3–4A

East Beach Cafe   **£ 43**   ④④❷
Sea Rd, The Promenade BN17 5GB
(01903) 731903
"What a sea view" – "a delightful setting right on the beach" helps win fans for this "lovely" café, in a striking modern building; it can be "let down by its service" however. / Details: www.eastbeachcafe.co.uk;

8.30 pm; closed Mon D, Tue D, Wed D, Thu D & Sun D.

LIVERPOOL, MERSEYSIDE   5–2A

Chaophraya   £ 46 ❸❸❷
5-6 Kenyon Steps L1 3DF (0151) 7076323
This Liverpool ONE branch of a Northern Thai chain strikes some as "a little artificial", but it's "definitely competent all round"; a recent make-over has added a "cosy downstairs room, excellent on a cold winter's day". / Details: www.chaophraya.co.uk; 10.30 pm.

Delifonseca   £ 40 ❸❷④
12 Stanley St L1 6AF (0151) 255 0808
The setting may be "a bit café-like" for some tastes, but a "good choice" of "eclectic" and "flavoursome" dishes from the blackboard commend these all-day deli/dining rooms to most reporters who comment on them; service is "super" too.
/ Details: www.delifonseca.co.uk; 9 pm, Fri & Sat 9.30 pm; closed Sun D.

Host   £ 38 ❸❷❸
31 Hope St L1 9XH (0151) 708 5831
A "really good pre-concert venue near the Phil"; this "minimalist" offshoot of 60 Hope Street serves a crowd-pleasing mix of "Asian and other" food ("suitable for vegetarians").
/ Details: www.ho-st.co.uk; 11 pm, Sun 10 pm.

The Italian Club Fish   £ 45 ❼
128 Bold St L1 4JA (0151) 707 2110
A "cheeky Italo-Scottish" bistro, near Central Station, tipped for its "buzzy" ambience ("like you're in a café in Milan"!) "friendly" service, and "good food" too. / Details: www.theitalianclubfish.co.uk; @italianclubnews; 10 pm, Sun 9 pm; no Amex.

The London Carriage Works
Hope Street Hotel   £ 54 ❸❸❸
40 Hope St L1 9DA (0151) 705 2222
"Recovering after a dip", say fans, this once oh-so-fashionable design hotel and dining room still inspires somewhat muted praise, but most reports suggest it's "worth a visit".
/ Details: www.thelondoncarriageworks.co.uk; 10 pm, Sun 9 pm; no shorts. **Accommodation:** 89 rooms, from £150.

Lunya   £ 44 ❸❸④
18-20 College Ln L1 3DS (0151) 706 9770
"Excellent city-centre tapas"; this "friendly" fixture can sometimes be "a bit loud and clubby", but it pleases all reporters with its "enjoyable" food, and its "extensive" wine list too.
/ Details: www.lunya.co.uk; @Lunya; 11 pm, Sun 10 pm.

The Monro   £ 41 ❸❸❸
92-94 Duke St L1 5AG (0151) 707 9933
A "great little gastropub" with "a traditional feel" – it's recommended by most reporters for its

"excellent" real ales, "fantastic Sunday roasts" and some "very interesting theme nights and set menus". / Details: www.themonro.com; 9.30 pm, Sun 7.30 pm; no Amex; no trainers.

Panoramic
Beetham West Tower   £ 56 ⑤❶❶
Brook St L3 9PJ (0151) 236 5534
"The food is a huge letdown... but everything else is top class!"; fortunately, this "overpriced" 34th-floor dining room has "lovely" staff, and is "worth it for the view". / Details: www.panoramicliverpool.com; @Panoramic34; 9.30 pm, Sun 8 pm; closed Mon; no trainers.

Puschka   £ 49 ❸④❸
16 Rodney St L1 2TE (0151) 708 8698
This "buzzy little place", in the city's Georgian Quarters, tontines to win praise for its "well-crafted" cooking, although more sceptical reporters feel "it's more interesting on the menu than it is on the plate..." / Details: www.puschka.co.uk; 10 pm, Sun 9 pm; D only.

The Quarter   £ 34 ❸❸❷
7-15 Falkner St L8 7PU (0151) 707 1965
A "decent" and "consistently reliable" eatery, with an Italian twist that's often "very busy", especially in summer, when al fresco diners enjoy cathedral views; great brunch spot.
/ Details: www.thequarteruk.com; 11 pm, Sun 10.30 pm.

Salthouse   £ 33 ❷❸④
Hanover St L1 3DW (0151) 706 0092
"A lively mix of all ages" pack into this city-centre two-year-old, handy for Liverpool One – the ambience is "bustling" ("noisy") and there's a "wide selection" of dishes done to an "impressive" standard, which "go a step beyond a typical tapas bar". / Details: www.salthousetapas.co.uk; @salthousetapas; 10.30 pm.

San Carlo   £ 46 ❸❷❶
41 Castle St L2 9SH (0151) 236 0073
"Still the place to be seen, but the food doesn't suffer!"; this glam and buzzy city-centre outpost of the glitzy national chain is "probably the city's best Italian", with fish and seafood a highlight; "staff are great characters, which always makes it fun".
/ Details: www.sancarlo.co.uk; @SanCarlo_Group; 11 pm.

60 Hope Street   £ 57 ❸❸❸
60 Hope St L1 9BZ (0151) 707 6060
Near the Anglican Cathedral, this townhouse fixture – the city's original modern British venture – is "still setting the standard locally" with its "interesting" cuisine; a slight feeling of unrealised potential, however, won't entirely go away.
/ Details: www.60hopestreet.com; 10.30 pm, Sun 8 pm.

Spire £ 45 ❷❸❸
1 Church Rd L15 9EA (0151) 734 5040
"Wonderful flavours" and "good-quality" dishes
(especially the fish 'n' chips) make this "cramped"
Wavertree restaurant "Liverpool's No. 1" for some
reporters; others judge its performance more
middling, however – "very well cooked, but not very
inspired". / **Details:** www.spirerestaurant.co.uk;
@spirerestaurant; Mon-Thu 9 pm, Fri & Sat 9.30 pm;
closed Mon L, Sat L & Sun.

Tai Pan £ 35 ❶
WH Lung Bdg, Great Howard St L5 9TZ
(0151) 207 3888
Not far from the city centre, a "hangar-sized"
operation, above an oriental supermarket, tipped for
its "great dim sum"; weekends can be very busy.
/ **Details:** 11.30 pm, Sun 9.30 pm.

LLANARMON DC, DENBIGHSHIRE 5–3A

The Hand at Llanarmonn £ 44 ❶
Ceiriog Valley LL20 7LD (01691) 600666
"A welcome stop in an area where there's little
culinary excellence" – this "cheerful pub-cum-
restaurant" is a top tip hereabouts; service, though,
can be "slow". / **Details:** www.thehandhotel.co.uk;
8.45 pm; no Amex. **Accommodation:** 13 rooms,
from £105.

The West Arms Hotel £ 46 ❶
LL20 7LD (01691) 600665
In an area not replete with competing attractions,
an "isolated" hotel, tipped for its "real character",
and its "modern Welsh cuisine, based on local
ingredients". / **Details:** www.thewestarms.co.uk; 9 pm;
no Amex. **Accommodation:** 15 rooms, from £65.

LLANDENNY, MONMOUTHSHIRE 2–2A

Raglan Arms £ 45 ❶
NP15 1DL (01291) 690800
A smart rural gastropub, tipped for its "regularly
changing" menu of dishes that are "always fresh".
/ **Details:** www.raglanarms.com; 9 pm; closed Mon &
Sun D.

LLANDEWI SKIRRID,
MONMOUTHSHIRE 2–1A

The Walnut Tree £ 66 ❷❷❸
NP7 8AW (01873) 852797
"Probably the best restaurant in Wales"; "Shaun Hill
has resurrected the reputation of this famous
destination" with his "outstanding", "robust" and
"honest" cuisine; it's style is "between rustic and
formal, between restaurant and pub, in a lovely rural
location down a winding lane".
/ **Details:** www.thewalnuttreeinn.com; 3m NE of
Abergavenny on B4521; 10 pm; closed Mon & Sun.
Accommodation: 5 rooms, from £180.

LLANDRILLO, DENBIGHSHIRE 4–2D

Tyddyn Llan £ 78 ❶❷❷
LL21 0ST (01490) 440264
"A true find" with food "really to shout about";
Bryan & Susan Webb's "super-comfortable"
("traditional" and quite "low key") rural bolthole
wins acclaim for the "inspired simplicity" of its
cooking (served in "comforting-sized portions") and
"excellent wine list". / **Details:** www.tyddynllan.co.uk;
@bryanwweb; on B4401 between Corwen and Bala;
9 pm; (Mon-Thu L by prior arrangement only); no Amex;
booking essential breakfast & weekday L.
Accommodation: 12 rooms, from £180.

LLANDUDNO, CONWY 4–1D

Bodysgallen Hall £ 67 ❷❷❶
LL30 1RS (01492) 584466
This long-established Elizabethan manor house
hotel combines "fantastic surroundings" (just outside
the town, with beautiful gardens) with a dining room
achieving "impeccable standards"; the only real
complaint is that the menu can sometimes seem
rather "static". / **Details:** www.bodysgallen.com; 2m
off A55 on A470; 9.15 pm, Fri & Sat 9.30 pm; closed
Mon; no jeans or trainers; children: 6+.
Accommodation: 31 rooms, from £179.

Jaya £ 36 ❶
36 Church Walks LL30 2HN (01492) 818 198
"Interesting Indian food, sometimes with an African
influence" – that's the rare appeal of this strongly-
tipped dining room (with B&B attached); house
sport? – "watching the staff dealing, tactfully, with
punters who come in and ask for a vindaloo
(which, of course, is not on the menu)".
/ **Details:** www.jayarestaurant.co.uk; 9.15 pm; closed
Mon, Tue, Wed L, Thu L, Fri L, Sat L & Sun L; no Amex.

**Terrace Restaurant
St Tudno Hotel** £ 48 ❶
Promenade LL30 2LP (01492) 874411
A (heavily) Victorian-style hotel, by the pier, tipped
for its "secluded tables" and "huge choice" of dishes
(from "cheap to very expensive").
/ **Details:** www.st-tudno.co.uk; @sttudnohotel;
9.30 pm; no shorts; children: 6+ after 6.30 pm.
Accommodation: 18 rooms, from £100.

LLANFRYNACH, POWYS 2–1A

White Swan £ 46 ❶
Brecon LD3 7BZ (01874) 665276
With a "superb location", minutes from Brecon, this
17th-century coaching inn is tipped as a "quiet" and
"relaxed" sort of place, offering "very good locally-
sourced food".
/ **Details:** www.white-swan-brecon.co.uk; 9 pm; closed
Mon & Tue; booking essential.

LLANGOLLEN, DENBIGHSHIRE 5–3A

Corn Mill **£ 43** ✪
Dee Ln LL20 8PN (01978) 869555
Tipped for its "spectacular" location ("overhanging
the River Dee and with its own working water
wheel"), this intriguing town-centre venue may have
no great culinary aspirations, but it does generally
offer "good value-for-money".
/ **Details:** www.cornmill-llangollen.co.uk; 9.30 pm, Sun
9 pm.

LLANWRTYD WELLS, POWYS 4–4D

Carlton Riverside **£ 53** ✪
Irfon Cr LD5 4SP (01591) 610248
A traditional-style restaurant-with-rooms still tipped
as "an oasis in an otherwise under-served part of
mid-Wales"; there is a slight sense is some quarters,
though, of an establishment that's "going through
the motions". / **Details:** www.carltonriverside.com;
8.30 pm; D only, closed Sun; no Amex.
Accommodation: 4 rooms, from £60.

LOCH LOMOND, DUNBARTONSHIRE 9–4B

Martin Wishart
Cameron House **£ 93** ✪✪✪
G83 8QZ (01389) 722504
"Everything about this restaurant is faultless", say
fans of Martin Wishart's "beautiful" dining room,
overlooking Loch Lomand (which feels "far nicer
than the heavily tartan'd, rather dour" country house
hotel it sits within); although pricey, the food is
"superb".
/ **Details:** www.martinwishartlochlomond.co.uk; over
Erskine Bridge to A82, follow signs to Loch Lomond;
9.45 pm. **Accommodation:** 129 rooms, from £215.

LOCHINVER, HIGHLAND 9–1B

The Albannach **£ 81** ✪✪✪
IV27 4LP (01571) 844407
A "luxurious" restaurant-with-rooms, in a "fantastic
scenic setting", which wows all who comment on it –
"from the pre-dinner nibbles (often including an
oyster) to the petit fours, the food is all expertly
sourced and cooked".
/ **Details:** www.thealbannach.co.uk; one sitting; D only,
closed Mon; no Amex; children: 12+.
Accommodation: 5 rooms, from £295.

LOCKSBOTTOM, KENT 3–3B

Chapter One **£ 56** ✪✪✪
Farnborough Common BR6 8NF
(01689) 854848
"A lonely beacon, of a type rare in the 'burbs"; this
"uncompromisingly high-quality" fixture, "in a small
village outside Bromley", delights "locals and those
from farther afield" with Andrew McLeish's
"technically excellent" cuisine, served by "extremely
friendly and helpful" staff.

/ **Details:** www.chaptersrestaurants.com; Sun-Thu
9.15 pm, Fri & Sat 9.45 pm; no trainers; booking:
max 12.

LONG CRENDON, BUCKINGHAMSHIRE 2–2D

The Angel **£ 51** ✪✪✪
47 Bicester Rd HP18 9EE (01844) 208268
"A delightful gastropub in a picturesque village"
remains the general view on this popular spot; one
or two reports suggest it's "slipped of late" –
hopefully just a blip.
/ **Details:** www.angelrestaurant.co.uk; 2m NW of
Thames, off B4011; 9.30 pm; closed Sun D; no Amex.
Accommodation: 4 rooms, from £110.

The Mole & Chicken **£ 50** ✪✪✪
Easington HP18 9EY (01844) 208387
"Wonderful views from the terrace" distinguish this
"gem" of a pub, whose culinary attractions range
from some "unusual" dishes to "Sunday lunch with
all the trimmings"; there's a "great garden for the
younger ones too".
/ **Details:** www.themoleandchicken.co.uk;
@moleandchicken; follow signs from B4011 at Long
Crendon; 9.30 pm, Sun 9 pm. **Accommodation:** 5
rooms, from £110.

LONG MELFORD, ESSEX 3–2C

Melford Valley Tandoori £ 27 ✪✪✪
Hall St CO10 9JT (01787) 311 518
"London curries in the country!" – fans agree the
Indian cuisine at this smartly modern subcontinental
is "by far the best in Suffolk".
/ **Details:** www.melfordvalley.com; 11.30 pm.

Swan **£ 47** ✪✪✪
Hall St CO10 9JQ (01787) 464545
"A great find"; this "delightful" and "welcoming"
village gastropub run by a brother and sister pleases
all who comment on it with its "enterprising" and
"innovative" menu.
/ **Details:** www.longmelfordswan.co.uk; Mon-Thu 9pm,
Fri/Sat 10pm; closed Sun D.

LONG WHITTENHAM, OXFORDSHIRE 2–2D

The Vine and Spice **£ 41** ✪✪✪
High St OX14 4QH (01865) 409 900
"In an old pub in a pretty village", an "unusually
good" Indian, serving "very fresh" dishes "from all
over the subcontinent".
/ **Details:** www.thevineandspice.co.uk; 10.30 pm.

LOUGHBOROUGH, LEICESTERSHIRE 5–3D

The Hammer and Pincers £ 50 ✪✪✪
5 East Rd LE12 6ST (01509) 880735
In the village of Wymeswold, a popular beamed
restaurant, offering "a good mix of gastropub-style
food and fine dining", which is "not always as good
as it can be, but when on form is really very good".

/ **Details:** www.hammerandpincers.co.uk; 9.30 pm, Sun 6 pm; closed Mon & Sun D; no Amex.

LOWER BOCKHAMPTON, DORCHESTER, DORSET   2–4B

Yalbury Cottage   **£ 49**   ❶❶❷
DT2 8PZ   (01305) 262382
"More than excellent all-round", "to die for", "worth the 100 mile trip" ... – Ariane & Jamie Jones's "off-the-beaten-track" thatched, restaurant-with-rooms inspires only adulatory reviews, not least for food that's "so imaginative, and beautifully presented, with real flavour in everything from the humblest soups". / **Details:** www.yalburycottage.com; 9 pm; closed Mon, Tue–Sat D only, closed Sun D; no Amex. **Accommodation:** 8 rooms, from £95.

LOWER FROYLE, ALTON, HAMPSHIRE   2–3D

The Anchor Inn   **£ 49**   ❸❹❸
GU34 4NA   (01420) 23261
"An upmarket pub, well-regarded locally and further afield"; although there's a sense that it's "perhaps not cooking to the standard set a few years ago", it still offers "consistently good food" (with "unusual game dishes a highlight"). / **Details:** www.anchorinnatlowerfroyle.co.uk; 9.30 pm, Sun 9 pm. **Accommodation:** 5 rooms, from £120.

LOWER HARDRES, KENT   3–3D

The Granville   **£ 43**   ❷❷❸
Street End CT4 7AL   (01227) 700402
"Unashamedly a pub", but whose kitchen "leans towards restaurant levels of quality and finery", serving "locally-sourced" and "well-cooked" fare; "open log fires" add to the winter ambience. / **Details:** 9 pm; closed Mon & Sun D.

LOWER ODDINGTON, GLOUCESTERSHIRE   2–1C

The Fox Inn   **£ 45**   ❸❸❸
GL56 0UR   (01451) 870555
"A very sound all-rounder", this "lovely pub", in bucolic surroundings, is "now similar to The Old Butchers in Stow" (which recently took it over); with log fires in winter and open-air dining in summer, it remains a "year-round favourite", though it does seem a little less atmospheric under the new regime. / **Details:** www.foxinn.net; on A436 near Stow-on-the-Wold; 9.30 pm, Sun 9.30 pm; no Amex. **Accommodation:** 3 rooms, from £85.

LOWER SLAUGHTER, GLOUCESTERSHIRE   2–1C

Lower Slaughter Manor Von Essen   **£ 49**   ❷❷❶
GL54 2HP   (01451) 820456
"Simply divine!"; very consistent reports on this luxurious Cotswolds country house hotel, whose "attention to detail" and "imaginative" cooking form part of a seamless and very "romantic" overall performance. / **Details:** www.lowerslaughter.co.uk; 2m from Burton-on-the-Water on A429; 9 pm; no jeans or trainers. **Accommodation:** 19 rooms, from £310.

LUDLOW, SHROPSHIRE   5–4A

La Bécasse   **£ 86**   ❸❹❸
17 Corve St SY8 1DA   (01584) 872325
"Outstanding food, but sadly the front-of-house didn't match up" – too common a report, of late, on this famous outpost of the star-hungry '10-in-8' empire, in a "lovely" building in the centre of the town; a new chef took over in late-2013. / **Details:** www.labecasse.co.uk; 9 pm, Sat 9.30 pm; closed Mon, Tue L & Sun D; no Amex; no trainers.

Green Café Ludlow Mill On The Green   **£ 35**   ❶❷❷
Dinham Millennium Grn SY8 1EG (01584) 879872
With its "amazing location on the river next to a weir and below a castle", this "great little café" is "a hit with all generations", and Clive David prepares "simple and delicious fare, seasoned to perfection" – and "where else do you get a hot water bottle if you sit outside?!" / **Details:** www.ludlowmillonthegreen.co.uk; closed Mon, L only Tue-Sun; no Amex.

Mr Underhill's   **£ 87**   ❶❶❷
Dinham Weir SY8 1EH   (01584) 874431
"A wonderful riverside setting, a relaxed yet discreetly attentive atmosphere and food that takes eating to an altogether different plane" – the many reports on Chris & Judy Bradley's "fantastic" restaurant-with-rooms remain quite remarkable in their consistency. / **Details:** www.mr-underhills.co.uk; 8.15 pm; D only, closed Mon & Tue; no Amex; children: 8+. **Accommodation:** 6 rooms, from £140.

LUPTON, CUMBRIA   7–4D

The Plough Inn   **£ 43**   ❷❷❸
Cow Brow LA6 1PJ   (01539) 567 700
"A real treat" – this recently refurbished inn (sister of the Punch Bowl in Crossthwaite) is a "great all-rounder", say fans, offering "adventurous" specials; sceptics, though, would say it's "more of a reliable stopping point" (and just off the M6 too). / **Details:** www.theploughatlupton.co.uk; 9 pm. **Accommodation:** 5 rooms, from £95.

LYDFORD, DEVON   1–3C

The Dartmoor Inn   **£ 49**   ❷❷❷
Moorside EX20 4AY   (01822) 820221
Recently refurbished, this "really delightful" old moorside inn "continues to deliver fine fare using the best local produce"; overnight guests also benefit from a "wonderfully imaginative breakfast!" / **Details:** www.dartmoorinn.com; on the A386

Tavistock to Okehampton road; 9.30 pm; closed
Mon L & Sun D. **Accommodation:** 3 rooms,
from £95.

LYME REGIS, DORSET   2–4A

**Hix Oyster and Fish
House**   **£ 54   ❷❸❶**
Cobb Rd DT7 3JP   (01297) 446910
"Glorious views over Lyme Bay" reward a trip to
Mark Hix's "fun and casual" glass-fronted cliff-top
venture, nowadays a major destination; on most
accounts the "extremely fresh and simple" seafood
matches up well too, even if "it's priced for the
tourist crowd". / **Details:** www.restaurantsetcltd.co.uk;
10 pm.

LYMINGTON, HAMPSHIRE   2–4C

Egan's   **£ 50   ❷❷❸**
24 Gosport St SO41 9BE   (01590) 676165
With its "delicious" food and "friendly staff", this
long-running bistro "remains consistently good";
"after London prices, we were astonished by the
value for money". / **Details:** 10 pm; closed Mon &
Sun; no Amex; booking: max 6, Sat.

LYMM, CHESHIRE   5–2B

The Church Green   **£ 54   ④⑤⑤**
Higher Ln WA13 0AP   (01925) 752068
Many reports on this inn run by an ex-Dorchester
chef; most do praise it for "good" and "imaginative"
cuisine, but a sizeable minority speak of
disappointing meals, and "indifferent" service.
/ **Details:** www.aidenbyrne.co.uk; 9.30 pm, Fri & Sat
10 pm, Sun 7.45 pm; no Amex.

La Boheme   **£ 41   ❷❷❷**
3 Mill Ln WA13 9SD   (01925) 753657
"A lovely French restaurant transported to the heart
of Cheshire!" – this family-run establishment
attracts consistently positive reports, not least as
quite possibly "the best place in the area for a
special occasion". / **Details:** laboheme.co.uk; Mon-Sat
10pm; Sun 9pm; closed Mon L & Sat L.

LYNDHURST, HAMPSHIRE   2–4C

**Hartnett Holder & Co
Lime Wood Hotel**   **£ 41   ❸❸❸**
Beaulieu Rd SO43 7FZ   (02380) 287177
Angela Hartnett's début in the "super-swish"
country house hotel dining market impresses most
reporters with its "innovative" cuisine (and a
"tremendous-value set lunch" in particular) and its
"amazing choice of wines"; reports are not yet quite
consistent, though – for critics, this is an
establishment "which nearly works, but not quite".
/ **Details:** www.limewoodhotel.co.uk; @limewoodhotel;
11 pm.

MADINGLEY, CAMBRIDGESHIRE   3–1B

Three Horseshoes   **£ 51   ④❸❸**
High St CB23 8AB   (01954) 210221
This "charming" pub (complete with "lovely"
conservatory), has long been a staple of Cambridge
undergrads and their parents; it continues to please
most reporters, but is also perennially accused of
going "downhill".
/ **Details:** www.threehorseshoesmadingley.co.uk;
@Madingley_3hs; 2m W of Cambridge, off A14 or
M11; 9.30 pm, Sun 8.30 pm.

MAIDENHEAD, BERKSHIRE   3–3A

**Boulters Riverside
Brasserie**   **£ 51   ❼**
Boulters Lock Island SL6 8PE   (01628) 621291
"A top tip for a sunny day" – this waterside
operation has a magnificent location, perched on
the Thames; the cheaper brasserie is a better bet
than the downstairs restaurant.
/ **Details:** www.boultersrestaurant.co.uk; @boultersuk;
9.30 pm; closed Mon & Sun D; no Amex.

The Royal Oak   **£ 68   ❸❶❷**
Paley St SL6 3JN   (01628) 620541
Parkie's "beautifully restored" pub draws a big fan
club from far and wide thanks to its "seriously
good" cooking, and "excellent" service (that's "coped
well with the recent extension"); even fans, however,
concede that it's "pricey".
/ **Details:** www.theroyaloakpaleystreet.com;
@theroyaloakpaleystreet; 9.30 pm, Fri & Sat 10 pm;
closed Sun D; children: 3+ .

MALMESBURY, WILTSHIRE   2–2C

The Old Bell Hotel   **£ 63   ❼**
Abbey Row SN16 0BW   (01666) 822344
The dining room of one of England's oldest hotels, in
the shadow of Malmesbury Abbey, is tipped for its
"friendly" staff and "lovely setting", and the Sunday
lunch menu is "excellent" too.
/ **Details:** www.oldbellhotel.com; 9 pm, Fri & Sat
9.30 pm. **Accommodation:** 33 rooms, from £115.

MANCHESTER, GREATER
MANCHESTER   5–2B

Akbar's   **£ 31   ❷❷❷**
73-83 Liverpool Rd M3 4NQ   (0161) 834 8444
"De rigeur on a visit to Manchester" – this "bustling
and large Pakistani" serves "amazing and plentiful
food that's great value for money"; "there's often
justifiably big queues, as there's no booking", but
"switched on service means that even when it's
thronging, you don't wait long".
/ **Details:** www.akbars.co.uk; 11 pm, Fri & Sat
11.30 pm; D only; need 10+ to book.

Albert Square Chop House   **£ 45** ④❸❸
The Memorial Hall, Albert Sq M2 5PF
(0161) 834 1866
"Imagine Balthazar-NYC-meets-the-Rovers Return!";
this new sibling to Sam's and Mr Thomas's inspires
mixed opinions – fans say it's "the best so far", and
like its "classic" Traditional cuisine "with a twist", but
others find it all a bit too "rough 'n' ready".
/ Details: www.albertsquarechophouse.com;
@chophouseAlbert; 9.45 pm, Sun 8.30 pm.

Albert's   **£ 49** ④④④
120-122 Barlow Moor Rd M20 2PU
(0161) 434 8289
"For a slow and fashionably laid back evening of
food matched by good cocktails" fans tip this "very
trendy" and "noisy" West Didsbury hang-out,
although its detractors say it's "over-rated and
mediocre". / Details: www.albertsdidsbury.com;
@alberts_dids; 10 pm; no Amex.

Albert's Shed   **£ 46** ④④❷
20 Castle St M3 4LZ (0161) 839 9818
"A very popular Mancunian destination by the
canal" in Castlefields; there's "a great buzz about
the place", although arguably the food is only
"average". / Details: www.albertsshed.com; 10 pm, Fri
10.30 pm, Sat 11 pm, Sun 9.30 pm; no Amex.

Armenian Taverna   **£ 36** ❸❸❸
3-5 Princess St M2 4DF (0161) 834 9025
"I went back after 20 years, and found it not
changed at all" – it may offer nothing startling, but
this city centre veteran is still tipped as a venue that
"always delivers".
/ Details: www.armeniantaverna.co.uk; 11 pm; closed
Mon, Sat L & Sun L.

Aumbry   **£ 64** ❷④❸
2 Church Ln M25 1AJ (0161) 7985841
"An oasis of top-level cooking in North
Manchester"; this "tiny temple to fine food" in Prestwich wows all of the many reporters who comment on it with its "exceptional",
"experimental" cuisine and "impeccable" service;
"minute" portions, though, can take the gloss off the
experience. / Details: www.aumbryrestaurant.co.uk;
9.30 pm; closed Mon, Tue L, Wed L, Thu L & Sun;
SRA-67%.

Australasia   **£ 58** ❸❸❷
1 Spinningfields M3 3AP (0161) 831 0288
Arguably it's "theatrical, OTT, somewhat pretentious
and a little expensive", but this "laid back", "trendy
clubby" basement hot spot is "just the place to
impress someone", and there's substance to its
"stunning" pan-Asian cuisine.
/ Details: www.australasia.uk.com; 10.45 pm.

Chaophraya,   **£ 47** ❷❸❸
Chapel Walks M2 1HN (0161) 832 8342
"By far the best Thai restaurant in Manchester";
with its "diverse and interesting" menu, and
"relaxed" vibe, this "large and efficient" city-centre
venture is a very consistent crowd-pleaser; it's noted
for a "good-value lunch".
/ Details: www.chaophraya.co.uk; 10.30 pm.

City Cafe   **£ 53** ❶
One Piccadilly Pl, 1 Auburn St M1 3DG
(0161) 228 0008
"The bland name doesn't do much to attract
custom", but this hotel brasserie has a convenient
location near Piccadilly Station, and is generally
tipped as a "reliable" destination.
/ Details: www.cityinn.com; 10 pm.
Accommodation: *285 rooms, from £79.*

Croma   **£ 34** ❸❷❷
1-3 Clarence St M2 4DE (0161) 237 9799
"Still the most enjoyable place in the city-
centre";near the Town Hall, this flagship of a "busy"
and "reliable" local pizza chain is "like Pizza
Express on steroids" (for whom the founders used
to work), according to its massive local fan club.
/ Details: www.cromapizza.co.uk; 10 pm, Fri & Sat
11 pm.

Dimitri's   **£ 45** ❷❷❷
1 Campfield Arc M3 4FN (0161) 839 3319
"It's hard not to order too much!" – they serve
"great meze" at this "always reliable", very
"relaxed" Greek café, interestingly housed in a
Victorian arcade, off Deansgate; the Didsbury
offshoot is "not as good".
/ Details: www.dimitris.co.uk; 11.30 pm.

Dough   **£ 35** ❷❷④
75-77 High St M4 1FS (0161) 8349411
"Imaginative, wholesome, reasonably priced food
and good wines in an upmarket canteen setting" –
a Northern Quarter pizzeria that's "worth a visit".
/ Details: www.doughpizzakitchen.co.uk; 11 pm.

East Z East Hotel Ibis   **£ 35** ❷❷④
Charles St M1 7DG (0161) 244 5353
City-centre Punjabi which delivers "authentic",
"unusual" and "well-cooked" fare, and is a notably
"consistent" venture too; there's another branch at
Riverside (Blackfriars St) which even offers "free
valet parking"! / Details: www.eastzeast.com;
11.15 pm, Fri & Sat 11.45 pm, Sun 10.45 pm; D only.

Evuna   **£ 43** ❸❷❸
Deansgate M3 4EW (0161) 819 2752
"Quality tapas", and "some amazing wines"; in a
city-centre still short of worthwhile places to eat, this
"excellent bar" is a handy standby that's "great for
a business lunch"; it generates an impressive volume
of positive survey feedback.
/ Details: www.evuna.com; 11 pm, Sun 9 pm.

The French Restaurant
Midland Hotel **£70** **❶❶❸**
Peter St M60 2DS (0161) 236 3333
*"Finally Manchester gets a restaurant whose
ambition is matched by the skill of the kitchen!" –
Simon Rogan's "really hits the heights" with the
"intriguing" relaunch of this famous Edwardian hotel
dining room, hailed as "superb all-round", not least
for its "clever" and "extraordinary" cuisine.
/ Details: www.qhotels.co.uk; 10.30 pm, Fri & Sat
11 pm; D only, closed Mon & Sun; no jeans or trainers;
children: no children . Accommodation: 312 rooms,
from £145.*

Gaucho **£70** **❷❹❸**
2a St Mary's St M3 2LB (0161) 833 4333
*"Great if you've won the lottery, or play for Man
U..." – this glitzy steakhouse, near House of Fraser,
is priced "very highly by Northern standards", but
even cost-conscious reporters concede it serves
"outstanding steak".
/ Details: www.gauchorestaurants.com; 10.30 pm,
Fri & Sat 11 pm.*

Glamorous **£38** **❸❹❹**
Wing Yip Bus' Centre, Oldham Rd M4 5HU
(0161) 839 3312
*"Usually bustling with the Chinese community" –
this large, slightly "chaotic" venue, above the
Ancoats branch of the Wing Yip supermarket
empire, offers "varied and flavourful dim sum
(served all day), plus a wide variety of standard –
and far from standard – mains".
/ Details: www.glamorous-restaurant.co.uk.*

Great Kathmandu **£36** **❶❸❹**
140 Burton Rd M20 1JQ (0161) 434 6413
*"Manchester's best place for a curry"; this long-
established West Didsbury stalwart has an
"interesting" menu (with Nepalese specials) and
wins high praise for its "brilliant" dishes at "very
reasonable" prices (and in "big portions" too).
/ Details: www.greatkathmandu.com; midnight.*

Green's **£42** **❸❸❸**
43 Lapwing Ln M20 2NT (0161) 434 4259
*Fans still find this West Didsbury veggie a "lovely"
destination serving "outstanding" food; since its
recent expansion, though, critics can find it "noisy",
"uninspired" and – paradoxically – rather
"crammed" too. / Details: www.greensdidsbury.co.uk;
Sun-Wed 9.30 pm, Thu-Sat 10 pm; closed Mon L;
no Amex.*

Grill on the Alley **£51** **❹❷❸**
5 Ridgefield M2 6EG (0161) 833 3465
*This city-centre venture is a "popular", "bustling"
sort of spot, which most reporters judge a
"reasonable all-rounder" or better; critics, though,
can find it rather "noisy" and "brash", and the
occasional "disappointing" meal is not unknown.
/ Details: www.blackhouse.uk.com; @GrillManc;
11 pm.*

Jem & I **£42** **❷❸❸**
1c School Ln M20 6RD (0161) 445 3996
*"It lives in the Lime Tree's shadow, but it's better!",
claim fans of this Didsbury bistro (whose owner
used to work at its rival); its menu, if "limited",
certainly wins high ratings, and prices here are "very
reasonable". / Details: www.jemandirestaurant.co.uk;
10 pm, Fri & Sat 10.30 pm; no Amex.*

Katsouris Deli **£14** **❷❸❸**
113 Deansgate M3 2BQ (0161) 819 1260
*"Great food and great value" – this city-centre
fixture may 'just' be a deli, but all reports agree that
it's "well worth queuing for"; the Bury offshoot,
similarly, offers "fabulous food, and some of the best
coffee around". / Details: L only; no Amex.*

Koh Samui **£39** **❶**
16 Princess St M1 4NB (0161) 237 9511
*On the fringe of Chinatown, a long-established Thai
basement tipped for cooking that can be "very
good"; excellent value lunchtime menu.
/ Details: www.kohsamuirestaurant.co.uk; 11.30 pm;
closed Sat L & Sun L.*

The Lime Tree **£47** **❷❷❸**
8 Lapwing Ln M20 2WS (0161) 445 1217
*"South Manchester's best and most reliable
restaurant"; few reporters can avoid commenting on
the "incredible consistency" of this "casual" and
"friendly" Didsbury brasserie, which has now been in
business for over a quarter of a century.
/ Details: www.thelimetreerestaurant.co.uk; 10 pm;
closed Mon L & Sat L.*

Little Yang Sing **£37** **❷❸❸**
17 George St M1 4HE (0161) 228 7722
*The basement little brother of the famous oriental
(in fact, its original premises) won very high ratings
this year, for cooking that's never worse than
"reliable", and its most ardent fans insist is "the
best in Chinatown".
/ Details: www.littleyangsing.co.uk; 11.30 pm, Fri
midnight, Sat 12.30 am, Sun 10.45 pm.*

The Lowry
The Lowry Centre **£39** **❶**
Pier 8, Salford Quays M50 3AZ (0161) 876
2121
*"Good, by the standards of such places" – this
Salford art venue's dining facility is tipped for its
"consistently good pre-theatre menu"; "there are
lots of regular visitors, though, so it would be nice if
they changed the menu more often!"
/ Details: www.thelowry.com; 45 min prior to start of
the latest performance; L only, D on performance nights
only.*

The Mark Addy **£42** **❷❹❺**
Stanley St M3 5EJ (0161) 832 4080
*"Hilariously ugly place, but the food is spot-on!";
considering the "slightly run-down" appearance of
this gastroboozer by the Irwell, it's striking how*

many reports confirm that its nose-to-tail cuisine is consistently "bold and well executed".
/ **Details:** www.markaddy.co.uk; @themarkaddy; 10 pm, Fri & Sat 10 pm, Sun 6 pm; closed Sun D; no Amex.

Michael Caines
ABode Hotel **£ 66** **❷❷④**
107 Piccadilly M1 2DB (0161) 200 5678
Especially worth seeking out for its "bargain set lunch", this basement outpost of the Gidleigh Park chef, near Piccadilly Station, has become known as one of the city's most "classy" culinary operations; the interior is "stark" however, and one or two reports are "underwhelming".
/ **Details:** www.michaelcaines.com; 10 pm; closed Sun; no shorts; 8+ to go through Events.
Accommodation: 61 rooms, from £79.

Mr Thomas's Chop House **£ 45** **❸❸❸**
52 Cross St M2 7AR (0161) 832 2245
"Still the best steak 'n' kidney pud"; for "great traditional cooking", and in "excellent portions" too, this city-centre Victorian boozer is a "good place to know about" – most local business types already do!
/ **Details:** www.tomschophouse.com; 9.30 pm, Sun 8 pm.

Oast House **£ 37** **❷❷❷**
The Avenue Courtyard, Spinninglfields M3 3AY
(0161) 829 3830
"A hugely successful new(ish) entrant to the Manchester scene"; the food at this (supposedly) olde worlde pub, in a modern office development, may be "very simple", but all reports agree it's "first-rate". / **Details:** www.theoasthouse.uk.com; 10.30 pm.

Piccolino **£ 47** **❸❷❷**
8 Clarence St M2 4DW (0161) 835 9860
"A good option for a simple meal"; near the Town Hall, this "very pleasant" outlet of the national Italian group "manages to retain a unique identity, despite being part of a chain".
/ **Details:** www.piccolinorestaurants.co.uk/manchester; 11 pm, Sun 10 pm.

Red Chilli **£ 25** **❷④④**
70-72 Portland St M1 4GU (0161) 236 2888
"Searingly hot and unusual, but utterly delicious" Sichuanese dishes, make this "out of the ordinary" Asian, "the best in the slowly growing regional Chinese food scene in Manchester"; "it's never going to win any awards for decor!"
/ **Details:** www.redchillirestaurant.co.uk; 11 pm; need 6+ to book.

Room **£ 51** **❸❸❶**
81 King St M2 4AH (0161) 8392005
This "friendly" and "funky" restaurant on the first floor of a "splendid" High Victorian building is putting in a more "professional" performance of late; top cocktails too.

/ **Details:** www.roomrestaurants.com; 10 pm, Sat 11 pm; closed Sun.

Rose Garden **£ 41** **❶❷❸**
218 Burton Rd M20 2LW (0161) 478 0747
William Mills is "a chef with skill and imagination", and "combines varied local ingredients to wonderful effect", at his small and "minimalist" West Didsbury restaurant "in a cleverly converted shop" – it's starting to make big waves locally.

Rosso **£ 52** **❶**
43 Spring Gdns M2 2BG (0161) 8321400
"It may be part-owned by Rio Ferdinand, but it's not up to much"; it's a shame that this potentially "magnificent" city-centre room is not better run; it's tipped for its set lunch menu's that's "good value", and "more innovative than the à la carte"!
/ **Details:** www.rossorestaurants.com; @rossorestaurants; 11 pm.

Sam's Chop House **£ 45** **④❸❸**
Back Pool Fold, Chapel Walks M2 1HN
(0161) 834 3210
With its "old-fashioned" British fare (corned beef hash, for instance), this pubbily-styled and sometimes "crowded" city-centre spot is a bit of a "throwback", whose hefty "comfort food" pleases most reporters; but it leaves critics cold – "I'm amazed by the positive reviews"!
/ **Details:** www.samschophouse.com; @chophousesams; 9.30 pm, Sun 8 pm.

San Carlo **£ 40** **④④❷**
40 King Street West M3 2WY (0161) 834 6226
A city-centre Italian where the food is "formulaic", the service sometimes "shocking", and the tables "rammed together"; why, then, is it "bustling" at all hours? – must have something to do with the "show" provided by all those "WAGs" and other "minor celebrities"! / **Details:** www.sancarlo.co.uk; 11 pm.

San Carlo Cicchetti **£ 49** **❷❷❷**
42 King Street West M3 2QG (0161) 839 2233
"If you can get over the fact that you are eating in a former shop window" (House of Fraser, FKA Kendal's), this "buzzy" Italian tapas bar is a "really good" all-rounder (and arguably the best informal place to eat in the city-centre); there's a "great buzz", too – especially at lunchtime.
/ **Details:** www.sancarlocicchetti.co.uk; 11 pm.

Second Floor Restaurant
Harvey Nichols **£ 57** **❸④❸**
21 New Cathedral St M1 1AD (0161) 828 8898
For a "relaxed quality experience" – be it a break from consumerism, or the Supper Club Menu – this department store dining room has a fair few fans; it's no bargain, however.

/ **Details:** www.harveynichols.com; 9.30 pm; closed Mon D & Sun D; SRA-60%.

63 Degrees £ 59 ❸❸❸
20 Church St M4 1PN (0161) 832 5438
"Proper French food at last!"; the Moreau family's Northern Quarter newcomer has made quite a splash... although even fans of the "lovely" cooking can find portions "minuscule", and prices "hefty". / **Details:** www.63degrees.co.uk; 10.30 pm, Fri 11.30 pm; closed Mon, Sat D & Sun.

Solita £ 40 ❸❸❸
37 Turner St M4 1DW (0161) 839 2200
A Northern Quarter adherent to the "dirty food" movement, this steak 'n' burger joint scores plusses with its "innovative" burgers (the 'Big Manc' is a particular hit); social media followers, though, can find its "continual self-praise" rather hard to stomach! / **Details:** www.solita.co.uk; 10 pm, Fri-Sat 11pm, Sun 9pm.

Soup Kitchen £ 15 ❶
31-33 Spear St M1 1DF (0161) 236 5100
In the Northern Quarter, a tip for "top-quality soups at sensible prices" (and for the "good-value meal-and-pint deal" too); this is an event venue too, and goes on till 4am at weekends.
/ **Details:** www.soup-kitchen.co.uk; @SoupKitchen; 9 pm; closed Mon D, Tue D, Wed D & Sun D.

Stock £ 53 ❸❹❶
4 Norfolk St M2 1DW (0161) 839 6644
The "delightful building" (the city's old Stock Exchange) provides an "impressive" backdrop to a meal at this city-centre venue, for either business or romance; its "solid traditional Italian cuisine" won much more consistent praise this year too.
/ **Details:** www.stockrestaurant.co.uk; @stockrestaurant; 10 pm; closed Mon & Sun.

Tai Pan £ 35 ❶
81-97 Upper Brook St M13 9TX
(0161) 273 2798
A Longsight Chinese tipped for its "consistently good value, as evidenced by the number of Chinese locals and students who eat here". / **Details:** 11 pm, Sun 9.30 pm.

Tampopo £ 30 ❸❸❸
16 Albert Sq M2 5PF (0161) 819 1966
"Knocks the spots off Wagamama"; near the Town Hall, this "buzzy" and "fun" noodle bar is a "reliable" destination whose "fast and tasty" dishes continue to please all who comment on them.
/ **Details:** www.tampopo.co.uk; 11 pm, Sun 10 pm; need 7+ to book.

Teacup On Thomas Street £ 23 ❸❸❸
53-55 Thomas St M4 1NA (0161) 832 3233
"A haven of relaxation, herbal infusions and cake in the heart of the party district!" – this Northern Quarter café also has quite a reputation as a breakfast stop, with "lovely egg dishes".
/ **Details:** www.teacupandcakes.com.

This & That £ 12 ❶❸⑤
3 Soap St M4 1EW (0161) 832 4971
"Without doubt the best-value food in Manchester"; "you can stuff yourself for a fiver" at this Northern Quarter Indian diner/takeaway, whose "un-Anglicised everyday curries" are a local lunchtime legend; "you don't go for the atmosphere".
/ **Details:** www.thisandthatcafe.co.uk; 4 pm, Fri & Sat 8 pm; no credit cards.

Wing's £ 51 ❷❷❷
1 Lincoln Sq M2 5LN (0161) 834 9000
With its "impressive" cooking, this celeb-friendly Chinese, near the Town Hall, "challenges Yang Sing in every department", and remains a top city-centre destination; it does take some flak for its prices, however – critics say they're "inflated by the feeling that this is 'the place to be'".
/ **Details:** www.wingsrestaurant.co.uk; 11 pm; closed Sat L; children: 11+ after 8 pm Mon-Fri, 21+ D.

Yang Sing £ 42 ❶❷④
34 Princess St M1 4JY (0161) 236 2200
"Still Manchester's best and, on the right day, most authentic Chinese" – Harry Yeung's Chinatown "stalwart" (est 1977) has shown "a welcome return to form" in recent years; the dim sum and banquets, in particular, can be "astonishingly good".
/ **Details:** www.yang-sing.com; @yangsing; 11.30 pm, Sat 12.15 am, Sun 10.30 pm.

MANNINGTREE, ESSEX 3–2C

Lucca Enoteca £ 37 ❶
39-43 High St CO11 1AH (01206) 390044
Tipped for its "generous pizzas and salads", this out-of-the-way Italian receives a thumbs-up from all reporters, and it offers "very good value" too.
/ **Details:** www.luccafoods.co.uk; 9.30 pm, Fri & Sat 10 pm; no Amex.

MARGATE, KENT 3–3D

The Ambrette £ 45 ❶❷❸
44 King St CT9 1QE (01843) 231 504
"No curry, just excellent Kentish fusion fare!"; Dev Biswal's "unique" brand of Indian-based cuisine – with its "subtle but distinctive flavours" – "ticks all the boxes" for fans of his "affordable" Old Town spot. / **Details:** www.theambrette.co.uk; @the_ambrette; 9.30 pm, Fri & Sat 10 pm; closed Mon.

GB Pizza £ 28 ❶❶❷
14a Marine Drive CT9 1DH (01843) 297 700
"Amazing", "Naples-style, wood-fired" pizzas ("with extremely thin crispy bases and delicious toppings") are not the only attraction of this seafront spot – it has its own "quirky charm" and you get "wonderful views over the Harbour Arm".

Australasia

Katsouris Deli

Sam's Chop House

/ *Details: www.greatbritishpizzacompany.wordpress.com; 9.30 pm; closed Sun D.*

MARLBOROUGH, WILTSHIRE   2–2C

The Harrow at Little
Bedwyn   **£ 75 ❶❷❷**
Little Bedwyn SN8 3JP (01672) 870871
It may be "impossible to find", but Sue & Roger Jones's "pretty" venue is "well worth the trip into deepest Wiltshire", for cooking that's "exciting and full of flair"; service (from Mrs) is "charm itself", and "the wine list is exceptional, particularly when it comes to Australia".
/ *Details: www.theharrowatlittlebedwyn.co.uk; 9 pm; closed Mon, Tue & Sun; no trainers.*

MARLOW, BUCKINGHAMSHIRE   3–3A

Adam Simmonds
Danesfield House Hotel   £ 91   ❷④❸
Henley Rd SL7 2EY (01628) 891010
"The star here is the cooking" – Adam Simmond's cuisine offers "a true culinary experience", not least a "wonderful" tasting menu – at this "spacious" Thames-side dining room ("you could drive a coach and horses between the tables!"); service though can grate, and contribute to a "lack of ambience".
/ *Details: www.danesfieldhouse.co.uk; 3m outside Marlow on the A4155; 9.30 pm; closed Mon, Tue L, Wed L & Sun; no jeans or trainers.*
Accommodation: *62 rooms, from £159.*

Aubergine
Compleat Angler   £ 75   ❷❷❷
Marlow Bridge SL7 1RG (01628) 405405
With its "impeccable" service, and "excellent views over the Thames", the "posher" of the two restaurants in this luxury hotel is "expensive, but otherwise hard to fault"; tasting menus come particularly recommended.
/ *Details: www.atozrestaurants.com; 10.30 pm, Sun 9.30 pm; no shorts.* **Accommodation:** *64 rooms, from £150.*

Hand & Flowers   £ 77   ❷❸④
West St SL7 2BP (01628) 482277
"We're big fans, but how it got two Michelin stars is a mystery"; Tom Kerridge's "fantastic twist on traditional British food" makes his "uncomfortably crowded" pub an "all-time favourite" for many reporters, but star No 2 can make it seem "unbelievably over-rated", and it's also more "big headed" nowadays.
/ *Details: www.thehandandflowers.co.uk; 9.30 pm; closed Sun D.* **Accommodation:** *4 rooms, from £140.*

The Royal Oak   £ 42   ❸❷❸
Frieth Rd, Bovingdon Grn SL7 2JF
(01628) 488611
With its "consistently good food", this "very informal" but "efficient" Chilterns pub-restaurant is hailed as a "welcoming and reliable" destination by

---

all who comment on it.
/ *Details: www.royaloakmarlow.co.uk; @royaloakSL7; 9.30 pm, Fri & Sat 10 pm.*

The Vanilla Pod   £ 65   ❶❷❸
31 West St SL7 2LS (01628) 898101
"Sublime" Gallic cooking, served in an "intimate" setting that's "rather like someone's dining room" – Michael MacDonald's establishment induces "complete contentment" is almost all who comment on it. / *Details: www.thevanillapod.co.uk; 10 pm; closed Mon & Sun.*

MASHAM, NORTH YORKSHIRE   8–4B

Black Sheep Brewery
Bistro   £ 34   ❶
Wellgarth HG4 4EN (01765) 680101
"An excellent stop-off, offering a good beer selection, and hearty fare"; this "very friendly" large café in the heart of the well-known brewery is a top tip for some straightforward "Yorkshire hospitality".
/ *Details: www.blacksheep.co.uk; @blacksheepbeer; 9 pm; Sun-Wed L only, Thu-Sat L & D; no Amex.*

Samuel'sSwinton Park
Hotel & Spa   £ 71   ❷❷❷
HG4 4JH (01765) 680900
"What a fantastic setting!" – in a "stately" country house hotel, this "romantic" dining room with "gothic overtones" offers "exquisite food" and a "seductive" wine list, and wins recommendations from all who comment on it.
/ *Details: www.swintonpark.com; @SwintonPark; 9.30 pm, Fri & Sat 10 pm; closed Mon L; no jeans or trainers; booking: max 8; children: 8+ at D; SRA-82%.* **Accommodation:** *31 rooms, from £185.*

MATLOCK, DERBYSHIRE   5–2C

Stones   £ 44   ❷❷❷
1C Dale Rd DE4 3LT (01629) 56061
"Just very good food at excellent prices, in a lovely venue" – Kevin Stone's chic town-centre restaurant attracts a hymn of praise from all who comment on it. / *Details: www.stones-restaurant.co.uk; 9 pm; closed Mon, Tue & Sun; no Amex; no shorts.*

MELBOURNE, DERBYSHIRE   5–3C

Bay Tree   £ 48   ❶
4 Potter St DE73 8HW (01332) 863358
A top tip for "special-occasion dining at a very reasonable price!" – a "consistent" and "friendly" family-run veteran, where champagne breakfasts are a highlight.
/ *Details: www.baytreerestaurant.co.uk; 9.30 pm; closed Mon, Tue & Sun D.*

MELLOR, LANCASHIRE   5–1B

Shajan   £ 32   ❷❸❸
Longsight Rd, Clayton-le-Dale BB1 9EX
(01254) 813640

"Perfect for a family meal, a special night or a takeaway" – this vast and *"very popular"* Southfork-style Indian has quite a name for its *"consistently good"* curries. / **Details:** *8m E of Preston on A59; 11.30 pm.*

MELLS, SOMERSET   2–3B

The Talbot Inn   **£ 46** ❷❷❶
Selwood St BA11 3PN (01373) 812254
Don't let the fact that it's associated with a TV chef (James Martin) put you off – the "beautiful" dining room of this grand old inn offers a "wonderful" culinary experience comprised of "memorable" food and "impeccable" service.
/ **Details:** *www.talbotinn.com; 9.30pm.*

MICKLEHAM, SURREY   3–3B

The Running Horses   **£ 53** ④⑤④
Old London Rd RH5 6DU (01372) 372279
'Surrey's dining pub of the year 2013' (according to the GPG) generated a lot of survey feedback; much of it lauds its "excellent" food and "obliging" style, but service can be "very slow", and a number of reporters feel performance is "average all-round".
/ **Details:** *www.therunninghorses.co.uk; off A24 near Dorking or Leatherhead; 10.30 pm, Sun 10 pm.*
Accommodation: *5 rooms, from £110.*

MILFORD ON SEA, HAMPSHIRE   2–4C

Verveine Fishmarket Restaurant   **£ 53** ❷❷❸
98 High St SO41 0QE (01590) 642 176
*"The range of fresh fish is stunning" at this fishmonger offshoot, where most reports extol its "impeccable" preparation and "charming" service; its robbed of top marks, however, by one or two reporters who feel the cooking's "slightly fussy" and "trying too hard". / **Details:** www.verveine.co.uk; 9.30 pm; closed Mon & Sun; no Amex.*

MILFORD ON SEA, HAMPSHIRE   2–4C

La Perle   **£ 46** ❶
Lymington SO41 0QD (01590) 643 557
"A delightful and very reasonably-priced Gallic bistro/restaurant"; it's tipped as "one to watch in an area that needs more good dining experiences".
/ **Details:** *www.laperlemilford.co.uk; 9 pm; closed Mon L & Sun.*

MILNTHORPE, CUMBRIA   7–4C

No. 17   **£ 44** ❶
17 Park Rd LA7 7AD (01539) 564 831
*This "very trendy" new venture, divided between a café-bar and more formal restaurant, inspires rather variable reports; it's still a handy tip, though, in an area "otherwise lacking any sort of restaurant"! / **Details:** www.no17parkroad.com; @No17ParkRoad; 8.45 pm; closed Sun D.*

MISTLEY, ESSEX   3–2D

The Mistley Thorn Hotel £ 42 ❸❸❸
High St CO11 1HE (01206) 392 821
*Sherri Singleton's gastropub-with-rooms impresses most reporters with its "very good" all-round standards, included fish-based cuisine realised to a "massively impressive" standard; the occasional critic, though, can find standards a touch "hit-and-miss". / **Details:** www.mistleythorn.com; @mistleythorn; 9.30 pm; no Amex.*
Accommodation: *8 rooms, from £80.*

MOLD, FLINTSHIRE   5–2A

Glasfryn   **£ 41** ❸❸❸
Raikes Ln CH7 6LR (01352) 750500
*A "typical, large Brunning and Price pub set in its own grounds, with great views"; this outpost of the leading local gastropub group is particularly recommended as an "ideal venue for a pre-Theatr Clwyd dinner". / **Details:** www.glasfryn-mold.co.uk; 9.30 pm, Sun 9 pm.*

MONTGOMERY, POWYS   2–

Checkers   **£ 64** ❶❷❷
Broad St, Powys SY15 6PN (01686) 669 822
All the more "unexpected" in a "gastronomic desert", this "beautiful" restaurant-with-rooms provides "outstanding" food from "extremely talented" chef, Stephane Borie, who trained (with one of his co-owners) at the Waterside Inn; all reporters agree – "put it on your list!", as it's "well worth a visit".
/ **Details:** *www.thecheckersmontgomery.co.uk; @checkerschef; 9 pm; closed Mon, Tue L & Wed L; children: D 8+.* **Accommodation:** *5 rooms, from £125.*

MORECAMBE, LANCASHIRE   5–1A

Midland Hotel   **£ 51** ❸④❸
Marine Road central LA4 4BU
(01524) 424000
*"A superb view over the bay" rewards visitors to this famous Art Deco hotel; it's not what you could call a foodie destination, but the cooking is "not at all bad". / **Details:** www.englishlakes.co.uk; 9.30 pm, Fri & Sat 10 pm; booking essential.*
Accommodation: *44 rooms, from £94.*

MORETON-IN-MARSH, GLOUCESTERSHIRE   2–1C

Mulberry Restaurant
The Manor House Hotel £ 67 ❶
High St GL56 0LJ (01608) 650501
Critics may find the food "lacks excitement", but this "beautiful hotel" (with "gorgeous grounds") is strongly tipped nonetheless as a "good value" destination, especially for lunch.

/ **Details:** www.cotswold-inns-hotels.co.uk; 9.30 pm;
D only, ex Sun open L & D.

MORSTON, NORFOLK   6–3C

Morston Hall   **£ 87 ②③②**
Main Coast Rd NR25 7AA   (01263) 741041
"Can't recommend it highly enough" – the
consistent verdict on Galton Blackiston's "first-class"
country house hotel, where the "exciting" cuisine
features "contrasting and challenging flavours";
"well-matched wine flights" too.
/ **Details:** www.morstonhall.com; between Blakeney &
Wells on A149; 8 pm; D only, ex Sun open L & D.
Accommodation: 13 rooms, from £330.

MOULSFORD, OXFORDSHIRE   2–2D

**The Beetle & Wedge
Boathouse**   **£ 45   ④③①**
Ferry Ln OX10 9JF   (01491) 651381
A "delightful" Thames-side location (the inspiration
for the 'Wind in the Willows') – "incredible on a
sunny day" – which makes it particularly worth
seeking out this rôtisserie in a former boathouse; the
food generally pleases too, but really "this place is
all about its position".
/ **Details:** www.beetleandwedge.co.uk; on A329
between Streatley & Wallingford, take Ferry Lane at
crossroads; 9.45 pm. **Accommodation:** 3 rooms,
from £90.

MOUSEHOLE, CORNWALL   1–4A

2 Fore Street Restaurant £ 43   ②②①
2 Fore St TR19 6PF   (01736) 731164
"A good find" – "lots of fresh seafood daily specials"
are the highlight you might expect at this diminutive
bistro, and some seats enjoy a "good view over the
harbour" too; for nice days, there's also "a sunny
little walled garden".
/ **Details:** www.2forestreet.co.uk; 9.30 pm.
Accommodation: 2 rooms, from £250 pw.

MURCOTT, OXFORDSHIRE   2–1D

The Nut Tree Inn   **£ 54   ①①③**
Main St OX5 2RE   (01865) 331253
"A fabulously understated restaurant with an
excellent sommelier and fantastic tasting menu!";
almost all reports on Michael North and Imogen
Young's "stunning" thatched gastroboozer are a
hymn of praise – "one of the most enjoyable meals
I've had in years", for instance.
/ **Details:** www.nuttreeinn.co.uk; 9 pm, Sun 3 pm.

MUTHILL, PERTH AND KINROSS   9–3C

Barley Bree   **£ 51   ②②②**
6 Willoughby St PH5 2AB   (01764) 681451
"A wonderful restaurant-with-rooms", run by a
French chef and his wife, offering a "delicious and
beautifully cooked" menu using "quality local
produce"; popularity with visitors from Gleneagles

and beyond, though, can sometimes make it "too
noisy". / **Details:** www.barleybree.com; @barleybree6;
9 pm Wed-Sat, 7.30pm Sun; closed Mon & Tue;
no Amex. **Accommodation:** 6 rooms, from £105.

NAILSWORTH, GLOUCESTERSHIRE   2–2B

Wild Garlic   **£ 49   ③③④**
3 Cossacks Sq GL6 0DB   (01453) 832615
Matthew Beardshall serves up some "unusual and
tasty" food – including, yes, some "interesting wild
garlic-based dishes" – at this small restaurant-with-
rooms. / **Details:** www.wild-garlic.co.uk;
@TheWildGarlic; 9.30 pm, Sun 2.30 pm; closed Mon,
Tue, Wed L & Sun D; no Amex. **Accommodation:** 3
rooms, from £75.

NAIRN, HIGHLAND   9–2C

Boath House Hotel   **£ 96   ②①①**
IV12 5TE   (01667) 454896
"A blissful oasis"; this imposing country house hotel
offers a "relaxing and top class experience"
combining Charlie Lockley's "outstanding" cuisine,
with "excellent and very obliging" service, in a "very
elegant" setting. / **Details:** www.boath-house.com;
7.30 pm; no Amex; no jeans or trainers.
Accommodation: 8 rooms, from £300.

NANT-Y-DERRY, MONMOUTHSHIRE   2–2A

The Foxhunter   **£ 53   ③③④**
NP7 9DN   (01873) 881101
"A truly wonderful experience, each and every time"
– TV chef, Matt Tebbutt's small village-restaurant
remains a hit with most reporters, who praise its
"sensitive" local cooking and "charming" staff;
feedback is limited, though, and the occasional off
day not unknown. / **Details:** www.thefoxhunter.com;
9.30 pm; closed Mon & Sun D. **Accommodation:** 2
cottages rooms, from £155.

NANTGAREDIG, CARMARTHENSHIRE 4–4C

Y Polyn   **£ 42   ②①③**
SA32 7LH   (01267) 290000
A "delightful little country restaurant run by
enthusiastic owners" which "never fails to please"
with its "excellent local produce, cooked with
imagination"; lunches offer particular value – "good
job it's a 40 mile drive or we would be there every
week!" / **Details:** www.ypolyn.co.uk; @PolyNation;
9 pm; closed Mon & Sun D.

NARBERTH, PEMBROKESHIRE   4–4B

Ultracomida   **£ 33   ②③③**
7 High St SA67 7AR   (01834) 861491
"Lovely food, inexpensive, and with beautiful flavours
too" – there's little not to like about the "Spanish
with a Welsh twist" dishes on offer at this
communal-tables tapas bar, behind a "thoughtfully
stocked deli". / **Details:** www.ultracomida.co.uk;
10 pm.

NETHER BURROW, CUMBRIA   7–4D

The Highwayman   £ 42   ❷❷❸
LA6 2RJ   (01524) 273338
*"A nice surprise to find such a high standard of food
in the wilds"; as a top spot for "good post-fell
walking fodder", you're unlikely to do much better
than the "wonderful food" on offer at this outpost of
the Northcote-based Ribble Valley Inns chain.
/ Details: www.highwaymaninn.co.uk;
@highwayman_inn; 8.30 pm, Fri & Sat 9 pm, Sun
8 pm.*

NETHER WESTCOTE, OXFORDSHIRE   2–1C

The Feathered Nest Inn   £ 65   ❷❷❷
OX7 6SD   (01993) 833 030
*"Stylish and soigné", this Cotswolds gastropub in a
"beautiful setting", "hidden away down winding
lanes", is worth seeking out for its "refined" cuisine.
/ Details: www.thefeatherednestinn.co.uk;
@FeatheredNestInn; 9.15 pm; closed Mon & Sun D.*
Accommodation: 4 rooms, from £150.

NEW MILTON, HAMPSHIRE   2–4C

Vetiver
Chewton Glen   £ 87   ❷❷❷
Christchurch Rd BH25 6QS   (01425) 275341
*This "gorgeous" country house hotel "keeps
evolving" and its "wonderful" dining room wins
acclaim for many "outstanding" meals; as ever,
however, there's an undercurrent of opinion
suggesting the cooking is a bit "unspectacular"…
well "at these prices anyhow".
/ Details: www.chewtonglen.com; @chewtonglen; on
A337 between New Milton & Highcliffe; 10 pm.*
Accommodation: 70 rooms, from £310.

NEWARK, NOTTINGHAMSHIRE   5–3D

Café Bleu   £ 49   ❶
14 Castle Gate NG24 1BG   (01636) 610141
*Still tipped as the "best in town", an ambitious
bistro which does a good local trade; service can be
"iffy", though, and the volume of support from
reporters isn't a patch on yesteryear.
/ Details: www.cafebleu.co.uk; 9.30 pm; closed Mon &
Sun D; no Amex.*

NEWBURY, BERKSHIRE   2–2D

The Crab at Chieveley   £ 57   ❷❸❷
Wantage Rd RG20 8UE   (01635) 247550
*After a somewhat patchy spell, this "excellent
seafood restaurant" – with a glorious but decidedly
landlocked location – is winning praise for its
"imaginative and satisfying" cuisine (especially à la
carte). / Details: www.crabatchieveley.com; M4 J13 to
B4494 – 0.5 mile on right; 9.30 pm.*
Accommodation: 14 rooms, from £99.

NEWCASTLE UPON TYNE,
TYNE AND WEAR   8–2B

Blackfriars Restaurant   £ 48   ❶
Friars St NE1 4XN   (0191) 261 5945
*It's not just the "lovely" location, in a monastic
courtyard, that makes this city-centre operation of
interest – it's also tipped for some "superb" cooking,
including "really excellent fish".
/ Details: www.blackfriarsrestaurant.co.uk; 10 pm;
closed Sun D; SRA-78%.*

Broad Chare   £ 44   ❸❸❷
25 Broad Chare NE1 3DQ   (019) 1211 2144
*Terry Laybourne's well-known gastropub, off the
Quayside, attracts plenty of reports, most in praise
of its "lively" style, "straightforward" fare and "really
fine draught ales"; downstairs in the bar they serve
"tasty titbits" (Glaswegian tapas) – upstairs a more
ambitious menu. / Details: www.thebroadchare.co.uk;
@_thebroadchare; 10 pm; closed Sun D; no Amex.*

Café 21   £ 62   ❷❷❷
Trinity Gdns NE1 2HH   (0191) 222 0755
*"Still the most popular place in town" – Terry
Laybourne's "always packed" flagship, just off the
Quayside, remains reporters "go-to destination" for
a meal combining "unfailing", quite "classical"
cooking in a "very buzzy" ("very noisy") setting.
/ Details: www.cafetwentyone.co.uk; 10.30 pm, Sun
9.30 pm.*

Café 21
Fenwick   £ 38   ❶
39 Northumberland St, First Floor NE1 7DE
(0191) 260 3373
*"Always reliable" – this department store
café/restaurant is consistently tipped as "a good
place for a break from shopping".
/ Details: www.cafetwentyone.co.uk; 0; L only.*

Café Royal   £ 44   ❸④④
8 Nelson St NE1 5AW   (0191) 231 3000
*Much comment on the "recent change of layout", at
this "popular" grand café by Grainger Market,
although "it's done nothing to make it quieter!"; for
breakfast, or a coffee and snack, it's still "always
good". / Details: www.sjf.co.uk; @caferoyalsjf; 6 pm;
L only; no booking, Sat.*

Caffè Vivo   £ 43   ④❸❷
29 Broad Chare NE1 3DQ   (0191) 232 1331
*This "Terry Laybourne-style Italian" ("ie not very")
makes an "excellent standby", and just off the
Quayside too; even fans, though, may concede that
"standards fluctuate a bit".
/ Details: www.caffevivo.co.uk; @caffevivo; 10 pm;
closed Mon & Sun.*

The Cherry Tree   £ 48   ❸④❸
9 Osborne Rd NE2 2AE   (0191) 239 9924
*A former telephone exchange provides the "smart"
and striking setting for an ambitious Jesmond*

restaurant many locals regard as quite a "classic"; service has its ups and downs, but the food – on most reports – is "consistently good".
/ **Details:** www.thecherrytreejesmond.co.uk; 10 pm, Sun 9 pm.

Dabbawal £ 35 ❷❷❸
69-75 High Bridge NE1 6BX (0191) 232 5133
A "great-value" newcomer with a handy location "around the corner form the Theatre Royal", offering "Indian street food at its best" – "ideal for a quick, tasty meal", and the staff are "wonderful with children" too. / **Details:** www.dabbawal.com; 10.30 pm; closed Sun.

David Kennedy's Food Social
The Biscuit Factory £ 43 ❸❷❸
Shieldfield NE2 1AN (0191) 2605411
Although yet to attain the heights or consistency of his previous venture, Black Door, David Kennedy's "popular art gallery/restaurant" is still "worth seeking out", and the early evening menu in particular is "great value".
/ **Details:** www.foodsocial.co.uk; 9.30 pm; closed Sun D.

Francesca's £ 34 ❸❷❶
Manor House Rd NE2 2NE (0191) 281 6586
"Standard unfussy Italian food" comes at brilliant prices at this "cheap as chips and very cheerful" Jesmond Dene pizzeria, which "oozes" atmosphere.
/ **Details:** 9.30 pm; closed Sun; no Amex; no booking.

Hotel du Vin et Bistro £ 47 ❶
Allan Hs, City Rd NE1 2BE (0191) 229 2200
With its "extensive" wine list and "excellent and knowledgeable sommeliers", this outpost of the hotel-bistro chain, up above the quayside, is tipped as "pricey but worth it for special occasions".
/ **Details:** www.hotelduvin.com; 10 pm, Sun 9.45 pm.
Accommodation: 42 rooms, from £150.

Jesmond Dene House £ 68 ❸④❷
Jesmond Dene Rd NE2 2EY (0191) 212 6066
"Buried deep in the wooded gorge that slices through Jesmond", Terry Laybourne's Arts & Crafts country house hotel certainly has a "lovely" setting; its "rich" cuisine (and "great choice of wines") pleases most reporters too, but let-downs are not unknown. / **Details:** www.jesmonddenehouse.co.uk; @Nicky_Sherman; 9.30 pm, Fri & Sat 10 pm.
Accommodation: 40 rooms, from £144.

Pan Haggerty £ 53 ❶
21 Queen St NE1 3UG (0191) 221 0904
Near the Quayside, a small restaurant tipped by a number of reporters for its "great-value set lunch"; the ambience, though, can sometimes seem lacklustre. / **Details:** www.panhaggerty.com; @panhaggerty; 9.30 pm; closed Sun D.

Pani's £ 30 ❸❷❷
61-65 High Bridge NE1 6BX (0191) 232 4366
"A bit of a legend locally" – a visit to this "really buzzy" Sardinian café can be "quite a whirlwind experience", but "their good manners would put the Ritz to shame", and the "cheap and cheerful" fare offers "top value". / **Details:** www.paniscafe.co.uk; 10 pm; closed Sun; no Amex; no booking at L.

Paradiso £ 40 ❸❶❷
1 Market Ln NE1 6QQ (0191) 221 1240
A "traditional trattoria in the heart of the city", offering "great value" overall; the welcome is always "fantastic" too, with children, in particular, "treated like kings". / **Details:** www.paradiso.co.uk; 10.30 pm, Fri & Sat 10.45 pm; closed Sun.

Sachins £ 37 ❸❷❸
Forth Banks NE1 3SG (0191) 261 9035
"The most authentic Indian in Newcastle" – this long-established Punjabi near Central Station inspires the odd gripe, but overall is recommended by all who comment on it.
/ **Details:** www.sachins.co.uk; 11.15 pm; closed Sun.

Six
Baltic Centre £ 50 ❷❸❷
Gateshead Quays, South Shore Rd NE8 3BA
(0191) 440 4948
"Stunning views over the Tyne" ("especially from the Ladies!") are a particular attraction of this sixth-floor Gateshead dining room; "the food varies between good and very good".
/ **Details:** www.sixbaltic.com; @six_baltic; 9.30 pm, Fri & Sat 10 pm; closed Sun D.

A Taste of Persia £ 30 ❷❷④
14 Marlborough Cr NE1 4EE (0191) 221 0088
"You don't visit for its looks", but this "cracking" family-run Persian scores top marks for its "high-quality" dishes – and it's "ridiculously cheap" to boot. / **Details:** www.atasteofpersia.com; 11 pm; closed Sun.

Tyneside Coffee Rooms
Tyneside Cinema £ 25 ❸❷❶
10 Pilgrim St NE1 6QG (0191) 227 5520
"A North East institution", this long-established café, in an Art Deco cinema building, enjoys "almost cult status" locally; "haute cuisine isn't the point" – "comfort food is", and the "always buzzing" atmosphere is hard to beat.
/ **Details:** www.tynesidecinema.co.uk; 9 pm; no Amex.

Vujon £ 44 ❶❷❸
29 Queen St NE1 3UG (0191) 221 0601
"If you want a great Indian experience in Newcastle, you should try Vujon" – "the food is stunning, you can taste every individual spice".
/ **Details:** www.vujon.com; 11.30 pm; closed Sun L.

| NEWENT, GLOUCESTERSHIRE | 2–1B |

Three Choirs Vineyards £ 48 ❷❷❸
GL18 1LS (01531) 890223
A "beautifully located" dining destination in the
lovely heart of the famous vineyard; the wines are a
big feature – the food is always at least "enjoyable",
and some reporters would be more generous in
their praise. / **Details:** www.threechoirs.com; 8.45 pm;
no Amex. **Accommodation:** 8, & 3 lodges rooms,
from £120.

| NEWMARKET, SUFFOLK | 3–1B |

Thai Street Cafe £ 38 ❶
26-28 High St CB8 8LB (01638) 674123
A handy town centre tip – a "good" and "cheap"
place, offering "great Thai food, especially at
lunchtime". / **Details:** www.thaistreetcafe.co.uk;
10 pm; no Amex.

| NEWPORT, PEMBROKESHIRE | 4–4B |

Llys Meddyg £ 51 ❷❷❷
East St SA42 0SY (01239) 820008
"An absolute jewel" say fans of this restaurant-with-
rooms whose "charming" setting incorporates a
number of dining areas (including a gorgeous
garden); "wonderful food" from "excellent local
produce" is provided by "fantastically friendly" staff.
/ **Details:** www.llysmeddyg.com; 9 pm; D only in winter,
L & D in summer; no Amex. **Accommodation:** 8
rooms, from £100.

| NEWTON LONGVILLE, BUCKINGHAMSHIRE | 3–2A |

Crooked Billet £ 44 ❸❸❸
2 Westbrook End MK17 0DF (01908) 373936
It's the "extensive and interesting" wine list (from
which any wine can be ordered by the glass) which
particularly makes it worth seeking out the
Gilchrists' thatched inn, on the fringes of Milton
Keynes; the food, though, is "consistently good" too.
/ **Details:** www.thebillet.co.uk; 9.30 pm, Fri & Sat
10 pm; D only, ex Sun open L only.

| NEWTON ON OUSE, NORTH YORKSHIRE | 8–4C |

The Dawnay Arms £ 46 ❶
YO30 2BR (01347) 848345
In a "lovely setting" by the River Ouse, a Georgian
inn tipped for "gems aplenty on the specials board"
(and an "excellent" children's menu too).
/ **Details:** www.thedawnayatnewton.co.uk; 9.30 pm,
Sun 6 pm; closed Mon & Sun D.

| NEWTON-IN-BOWLAND, LANCASHIRE | 5–1B |

The Parkers Arms £ 42 ❶❷❷
BB7 3DY (01200) 446236
Kathy Smith and Stosie Madie's venture, in a rural
pub, takes local sourcing "almost to an extreme", to
produce "quality, unfussy food" at "unbeatable-
value" prices; "if you found this on a byway in
France, you'd come back saying things like 'only in
France'!" / **Details:** www.parkersarms.co.uk;
@parkersarms; 8.30 pm, Sun 6.30 pm; closed Mon.
Accommodation: 4 rooms, from £77.

| NEWTOWN, CHEW MAGNA, BRISTOL | 2–2B |

The Pony and Trap £ 45 ❷❸❸
BS40 8TQ (01275) 332 627
"Great locally-sourced pub food", and "lovely"
service, and all in a "scenic" setting too, win high
praise for Josh Eggleton's consistent inn.
/ **Details:** www.theponyandtrap.co.uk;
@theponyandtrap; 9.30 pm; closed Mon; no Amex.

| NOMANSLAND, WILTSHIRE | 2–3C |

Les Mirabelles £ 43 ❶❷❸
Forest Edge Rd SP5 2BN (01794) 390205
"A wonderful find in such an out-of-the-way place";
it's not only the "beautiful New Forest setting"
("ponies grazing") which delights at this "first class"
fixture – "Claude the proprietor is a sommelier of
note" and the "excellently sourced" wines are
matched by "the most delicious" classic French
cuisine. / **Details:** www.lesmirabelles.co.uk; off A36
between Southampton & Salisbury; 9.30 pm; closed
Mon & Sun.

| NORDEN, LANCASHIRE | 5–1B |

Nutter's £ 53 ❸❸④
Edenfield Rd OL12 7TT (01706) 650167
"Impressive food in generous portions" (plus
"enthusiastically explained wines") makes "local
celebrity chef" Andrew Nutter's manor house
restaurant very popular with most reporters; the
occasional dissenter, though, finds it "average" and
"overpriced". / **Details:** www.nuttersrestaurant.com;
between Edenfield & Norden on A680; 9 pm; closed
Mon.

| NORTH UIST, WESTERN ISLES | 9–A2 |

Langass Lodge £ 44 ❶
Loch Eport HS6 5HA (01876) 580285
"The hotel at the end of the world!… and none the
worse for that!"; there are two dining rooms, both
tipped for their "lovely" fish – "you eat what they, or
you, have caught". / **Details:** www.langasslodge.co.uk;
8.45 pm; D only; no Amex. **Accommodation:** 11
rooms, from £95.

| NORTHALLERTON, NORTH YORKSHIRE | 8–4B |

The Cleveland Tontine £ 58
DL6 3JB (01609) 882 671
Formerly known as 'McCoy's at the Tontine', this
popular local institution moved into new ownership
just as our survey for the year was closing; in the

circumstances, an appraisal will have to wait until next time. / **Details:** www.theclevelandtontine.co.uk; near junction of A19 & A172; 9 pm, Fri & Sat 9.45 pm, Sun 8 pm. **Accommodation:** 7 rooms, from £130.

NORTHAW, HERTFORDSHIRE   3–2B

The Sun at Northaw   **£ 54**   ❸❹❸
1 Judges Hill EN6 4NL   (01707) 655507
A village gastropub serving some "outstanding" dishes from an "interesting locally-sourced menu"; it can seem quite "expensive", though, and service sometimes seems a little "stretched".
/ **Details:** www.thesunatnorthaw.co.uk; 10 pm; closed Mon & Sun D; no Amex.

NORTHLEACH, GLOUCESTERSHIRE   2–1C

Wheatsheaf Inn   **£ 47**   ❷❸❸
GL54 3EZ   (01451) 860244
This "terrific" gastropub-with-rooms (with a "lovely garden") is "both stylish and laid back" ("dogs, humans, babies, no problem"), and attracts a crowd that's "buzzy, but not local", with its "delicious" food, "stunning" wines and "good real ales".
/ **Details:** @wheatsheafgl54; 9 pm, Sat & Sun 10 pm. **Accommodation:** 14 rooms, from £140.

NORTON, SHROPSHIRE   5–4A

Hundred House   **£ 49**   ❶
Bridgnorth Rd TF11 9EE   (01952) 730353
Perhaps not inspiring, but this ancient inn remains a top tip locally for "consistent" and "solid" English cooking (including "good-quality meat in good portions"). / **Details:** www.hundredhouse.co.uk; on A442 between Bridgnorth & Telford; 9.30 pm. **Accommodation:** 10 rooms, from £99.

NORTON, NEAR MALMESBURY, WILTSHIRE   2–2B

The Vine Tree   **£ 45**   ❶
Foxley Rd SN16 0JP   (01666) 837654
Top tip locally for those in search of a "great country pub" near the M4 (and one offering a "very extensive menu" too).
/ **Details:** www.thevinetree.co.uk; @TheVineTree; 9.30 pm, Fri & Sat 10 pm; closed Sun D.

NORWICH, NORFOLK   6–4C

The Gunton Arms   **£ 45**   ❷❶❶
Cromer Rd, Thorpe Mkt NR11 8TZ
(01263) 832010
"The perfect weekend hideaway" – this gastropub-with-rooms is set "in an amazing location on the edge of a deer park", and serves "hearty steaks" and so on, cooked on an open grill; all-in-all it's "exceptional value for money".
/ **Details:** www.theguntonarms.co.uk; 10 pm; no Amex. **Accommodation:** 8 rooms, from £95.

Last Wine Bar   **£ 45**   ❸❷❸
70-76 St Georges St NR3 1AB
(01603) 626626
This "jolly" and "well-established" bistro and wine bar, in a former shoe factory, is a top local standby, with an "extensive list covering many regions"; there's nothing startling on the food front, perhaps, but its "consistency" is impressive; a brasserie offshoot inspires mixed reports.
/ **Details:** www.thelastwinebar.co.uk; @LastWineBar; 10.30 pm; closed Sun.

Roger Hickman's   **£ 64**   ❷❷❸
79 Upper St. Giles St NR2 1AB
(01603) 633522
"Easily the best food in Norwich"; this "small and perfectly formed" venue, run by David Adlard's former head chef, is now "at a standard deserving national recognition"; only real complaint? – "it's getting ever more difficult to secure a table".
/ **Details:** www.rogerhickmansrestaurant.com; 10 pm; closed Mon & Sun.

Waffle House   **£ 34**   ❶
39 St Giles St NR2 1JN   (01603) 612790
A "reliable place to stop off for a snack"; the lunch menu is "particularly good value" – "arrive early for a table". / **Details:** www.wafflehouse.co.uk; 10 pm; no Amex; need 6+ to book.

NOSS MAYO, DEVON   1–4C

The Ship Inn   **£ 42**   ❸❸❷
PL8 1EW   (01752) 872387
This "attractive" inn offers "excellent views at high tide", and cosy "roaring fires"; on the menu – "British pub grub staples", with "great fish" a highlight. / **Details:** www.nossmayo.com; 9.30 pm, Sun 9 pm.

NOTTINGHAM, NOTTINGHAMSHIRE   5–3D

Atlas   **£ 27**   ❷❷❸
9 Pelham St NG1 2EH   (0115) 950 1295
"Everything that could be said about Atlas has been said over the years, but quite simply it's the natural choice for anyone wanting a quick lunchtime bite"… and the "best coffee in Nottingham" while they're about it! / **Details:** www.atlasdeli.co.uk; 4 pm, Sat 5 pm; L only.

Cast   **£ 34**   ❶
The Playhouse, Wellington Circus NG1 5AN
(0115) 852 3898
By the Playhouse, a handy tip for a "very good" and sensibly priced pre-theatre meal; of late, however, the food has been a touch more "variable" than usual. / **Details:** www.nottinghamplayhouse.co.uk; 10 pm, Sun 6 pm; no Amex.

334

Chino Latino
Park Plaza Hotel   **£ 55**   **❷❸❸**
41 Maid Marian Way NG1 6GD   (0115) 947 7444
"Stunning food always" is an unlikely find at this ambitious Asian-fusion hang-out, bizarrely located off the foyer of a boring looking, central hotel; "the decor looks tired, but in the dark it still works well!" / Details: www.chinolatino.co.uk; 10.30 pm; closed Sun.

The Cumin   **£ 38**   **❷❷❸**
62-64 Maid Marian Way NG1 6BQ
(0115) 941 9941
"Far better than the average Indian" – this "well-run" and "always-busy" city-centre establishment serves the "best biryani around", and vegetarians and vegans are also "well catered for". / Details: www.thecumin.co.uk; 10.45 pm; closed Mon L, Tue L, Sat L & Sun.

Delilahs   **£ 29**   **❶**
12 Victoria Street NG1 2EX   (0115) 948 4461
A "nice and buzzy" deli, tipped for its "snacks, wine and coffee"; it is "greatly expanded" since it moved into a "stunning" former bank building in recent times, but it can still be "hard to get a table". / Details: www.delilahfinefoods.co.uk; @delilahfinefood; 7 pm, Sun 5 pm; no Amex.

4550 Miles From Delhi   **£ 33**   **❸❷❸**
Maid Marian Way NG1 6HE   (0115) 947 5111
Prominently situated on a big central highway, this large Indian offers a "vast menu selection", and – though "noisy" – wins praise for its "efficient service and always great food". / Details: www.milesfromdelhi.com; @4550Nottingham; Mon-Thu 10 pm, Fri & Sat 11 pm, Sun 10.30 pm; no Amex.

French Living   **£ 41**   **④❸❷**
27 King St NG1 2AY   (0115) 958 5885
"The real thing... a genuinely French bistro with few airs and graces but simple and excellent food"; not everyone's impressed, admittedly, but even critics admit that you "can't complain about the prices", particularly the "great-value" early bird deal. / Details: www.frenchliving.co.uk; 10 pm; closed Sun; no Amex.

Hart's   **£ 50**   **❶❶❷**
Standard Ct, Park Row NG1 6GN
(0115) 988 1900
"Back to its best… if not better!"; established in 1997, this "airy", "friendly" and "relaxed" modern brasserie, near the castle, is perhaps provincial England's most "reliable" city-centre restaurant, and – under chef Dan Burridge – the cooking in recent times has been "consistently excellent". / Details: www.hartsnottingham.co.uk; 10 pm, Sun 9 pm. Accommodation: 32 rooms, from £125.

Iberico   **£ 35**   **❷❷❷**
The Shire Hall, High Pavement NG1 1HN
(01159) 410410
"Proper" tapas, plus "slick" and "friendly" service (and also a "particularly good-value" weekday express lunch) make this "hidden-away" but "lively" cellar a big favourite locally; they've recently expanded into nearby Derby, so let's "hope that doesn't take their eye of the ball"! / Details: www.ibericotapas.com; 10 pm; closed Sun; no Amex; children: 12+ D.

Kayal   **£ 34**   **❷❷❸**
8 Broad St NG1 3AL   (0115) 941 4733
Fans "just love" this mini-chain outlet, which specialises in Keralan cuisine; its "delicious" dishes offer "a reminder of just how right Indian food can be when you move away from the mainstream rubbish". / Details: www.kayalrestaurant.com; 11 pm, Sun 10 pm.

The Larder on Goosegate £ 44   **❶**
1st Floor, 16 -22 Goosegate NG1 1FE
(01159) 500 111
An interestingly-housed venture, "in the original Boots shop", tipped for its "consistently good" food in general (and "great steaks" in particular). / Details: www.thelarderongoosegate.co.uk; 10 pm; closed Mon & Sun.

MemSaab   **£ 39**   **❷❷❸**
12-14 Maid Marian Way NG1 6HS   (0115) 957 0009
"Big, glitzy Indian" in the city-centre serving "a great mix of traditional and modern cuisine, including the best grilled dishes"; the odd regular say it's "less imaginative" since a management change-over in 2012, but overall it remains highly rated for its "fine dining at bargain prices". / Details: www.mem-saab.co.uk; near Castle, opposite Park Plaza Hotel; 10.30 pm, Fri & Sat 11 pm, Sun 10 pm; D only; no shorts.

Mistral   **£ 40**   **❶**
2-3 Eldon Chambers NG1 2NS   (0115) 941 0401
"A lovely little bistro with reliably good food, plenty of choice, good service and prices"; it doesn't thrill everyone, but even the least-impressed reporter would concur that it's a "good-value" tip. / Details: 11 pm, Sun 7.45 pm; no Amex.

Petit Paris   **£ 33**   **④❸④**
2 Kings Walk NG1 2AE   (0115) 947 3767
A "very reliable" Continental restaurant in "first floor" premises, attracting particular praise for its "excellent-value" lunch and pre-theatre menus… especially as "this can, for a small supplement, be extended to include virtually the entire menu"! / Details: www.petitparisrestaurant.co.uk; near Theatre Royal; 10 pm; closed Sun.

Restaurant Sat Bains   **£ 109 ❸❹❸**
Lenton Ln NG7 2SA   (0115) 986 6566
*"Under the flyover and pylons is a strange setting"
for this renowned restaurant-with-rooms, near the
city limits; Sat Bains is "a really down-to-earth guy",
but his cooking is "stunning" and "continually
surprising" – "inventive without being plain stupid";
"it's expensive for the Midlands" (and this location)
however. / **Details:** www.restaurantsatbains.com;
8.30 pm, Fri & Sat 9.45 pm; closed Mon & Sun;
children: 12+.* **Accommodation:** *8 rooms, from £129.*

Tarn Thai   **£ 41   ❼**
9 George St NG1 1BU   (0115) 959 9454
*A curious lack of feedback of late for this Thai tip,
handily located just off the Lace Market; it can seem
"too large and loud", but all reports rate the food
good or better. / **Details:** www.tarnthai.co.uk;
10.30 pm, Fri & Sat 11 pm.*

Victoria Hotel   **£ 33   ❸❷❷**
Dovecote Ln NG9 1JG   (0115) 925 4049
*A "large and friendly" pub handy for Beeston station
– a hit with all who comment on it thanks to its
"tasty, ample and promptly-served" grub (including
a "good-quality veggie menu"), served alongside a
"a very fine choice of beers".
/ **Details:** www.victoriabeeston.co.uk; 9.30 pm, Sun-Tue
8.45 pm; no Amex; children: 18+ after 8 pm.*

The Wollaton   **£ 41   ❸❸❸**
Lambourne Drive NG8 1GR   (0115) 9288610
*A popular gastropub, where "you can eat in the bar
or restaurant"; the dishes, which feature "a lot of
local sourcing", are "very well prepared", and there
are "good deals" too.
/ **Details:** www.thewollaton.co.uk; 9 pm, Fri & Sat
10 pm, Sun 8.30 pm.*

World Service   **£ 54   ❷❷❷**
Newdigate Hs, Castlegate NG1 6AF
(0115) 847 5587
*"In a lovely historic building, with ephemera from
around the globe", this professional "oasis" (with
cute courtyard, and "excellent cocktails") is a huge
hit locally; the perennially ambitious cuisine "has
misses as well as hits", but fans say it's worth
persevering for when its "superbly innovative" ideas
pay off. / **Details:** www.worldservicerestaurant.com;
10 pm; closed Sun D, except bank holidays; children:
10+ at D.*

OARE, KENT   3–3C

The Three Mariners   **£ 40   ❷❷❸**
2 Church Rd ME13 0QA   (01795) 533633
*"The difficulty in booking speaks for itself", says one
of the many fans of this "very popular gastropub
overlooking a creek", where "fabulous fresh fish" is
the menu highlight; service is "really helpful and
friendly" too.
/ **Details:** www.thethreemarinersoare.co.uk; Mon-Thu
9pm, Fri-Sat 9.30 pm, Sun 9 pm; no Amex.*

OBAN, ARGYLL AND BUTE   9–3B

**Ee-Usk (Seafood
Restaurant)**   **£ 46   ❸❸❶**
North Pier PA34 5QD   (01631) 565666
*A "fantastic situation on the North Pier" ("with full-
height windows and amazing views") adds wow-
factor to this popular restaurant; on most accounts
the food is "wonderful" too, but it "did not live up to
expectations" for absolutely everyone this year.
/ **Details:** www.eeusk.com; @eeuskoban; 9 pm;
no Amex; children: 12+ at D.*

Manor House Hotel   **£ 56   ❸❷❷**
Gallanach Rd PA34 4LS   (01631) 562087
*This Georgian villa on the harbour provides a
"comfortable and civilised" experience, incorporating
high quality cooking; quibbles tend to be minor –
that's it's "a bit expensive", a little "staid", or serves
"portions that are rather large".
/ **Details:** www.manorhouseoban.com; Follow the signs
to the ferry terminal, the hotel is 200 yards past it on
the right; 8.30 pm; children: 12+.*
Accommodation: *11 rooms, from £195.*

Seafood Temple   **£ 44   ❶❷❶**
Dungallan Pk, Gallanach Rd PA34 4LS
(01631) 566000
*"An outstanding location perched above Oban Bay",
with "stunning views" provides the setting for this
exceptional, small, family-run restaurant, extolled in
all reports for its "perfect" and "generous" seafood
dishes. / **Details:** www.obanseafood.com; D only.*

OCKHAM, SURREY   3–3A

The Black Swan   **£ 47   ❸❸❷**
Old Ln KT11 1NG   (01932) 862364
*"A busy pub with a good buzzy vibe" and "plenty of
well-kept ales" – less of a foodie destination than a
good all-rounder, it's often noted as a family-friendly
sort of place. / **Details:** www.blackswanockham.com;
@blackswancobham; 9.30 pm, Fri & Sat 10 pm, Sun
6.30 pm.*

OCKLEY, SURREY   3–4A

**Bryce's at the Old School
House**   **£ 51   ❷❸④**
Stane St RH5 5TH   (01306) 627430
*"An unusually landlocked place to find an excellent
seafood restaurant!"; as ever, this converted
schoolhouse defies the odds with some of the "best
seafood and fish outside London"; the dining room is
a little "dark" for some tastes however.
/ **Details:** www.bryces.co.uk; 8m S of Dorking on A29;
9.30 pm; no Amex.*

OLD HUNSTANTON, NORFOLK   6–3B

The Neptune   **£ 68   ❶❶❷**
85 Old Hunstanton Rd PE36 6HZ
(01485) 532122

"Fabulous food on a par with anything in London", and "relaxed yet attentive service" too makes the Mangeolle family's "sophisticated" 18-century coaching inn very "difficult to fault".
/ **Details:** www.theneptune.co.uk; 9 pm; closed Mon, Tue-Sat D only, Sun open L & D; children: 10.
Accommodation: 6 rooms, from £120.

OLDSTEAD, NORTH YORKSHIRE   5–1D

Black Swan   **£ 73   ❶❷❸**
YO61 4BL   (01347) 868 387
"Do they think they're a gastropub or a posh restaurant?" this "pampering" venture (near Byland Abbey) serves "gorgeous", "very proficient" cooking in "very comfortable surroundings", but can also seem a trifle "overpriced" or "stiff".
/ **Details:** www.blackswanoldstead.co.uk; 9 pm; closed Mon L, Tue L & Wed L; no Amex.

ONGAR, ESSEX   3–2B

Smith's Brasserie   **£ 60   ❸❷❸**
Fyfield Rd CM5 0AL   (01277) 365578
"There is simply no other venue in Essex in which to eat fish!", say fans of this well-known destination, praising its "amazing cooking"; it "can get busy and chaotic", however, and even fans can find it "overpriced".
/ **Details:** www.smithsbrasserie.com; left off A414 towards Fyfield; Mon-Fri 10 pm, Sat 10.30 pm, Sun 10 pm; closed Mon L; children: 12+.

ONICH, HIGHLAND   9–3B

Loch Leven Seafood Café £ 46   ❷❸❸
PH33 6SA   (01855) 821048
"Now a mandatory detour from the A82!"; with a "stunning view across Loch Leven", this waterside café is a "seafood-lover's dream", and with a "terrific wine list" to match; the "Billy Bunter-sized seafood platters are the thing to go for", but there's a short list of alternatives too.
/ **Details:** www.lochlevenseafoodcafe.co.uk; 9 pm; no Amex.

ORFORD, SUFFOLK   3–1D

Butley Orford Oysterage £ 37   ❷❸④
Market Hill IP12 2LH   (01394) 450277
"Little seems to have changed over the 50 years in operation!"; how to improve, though, on a "basic" formula that's essentially all about "locally caught fish without fuss"? – well, perhaps the "school dining room"-style space could be jollied up just a bit? / **Details:** www.butleyorfordoysterage.co.uk; on the B1078, off the A12 from Ipswich; 9 pm; no Amex.

The Crown & Castle   **£ 50   ❷❸❸**
IP12 2LJ   (01394) 450205
This "delightful" gastropub-with-rooms (co-owned by celebrity hotelier Ruth Watson) pleases all reporters with "excellent" local fare – "especially the fish

dishes"; it has a "wonderful coastal setting" too.
/ **Details:** www.crownandcastle.co.uk; on main road to Orford, near Woodbridge; 9 pm, Sat & Sun 9.15 pm; no Amex; booking: max 10; children: 8+ at D.
Accommodation: 21 rooms, from £135.

Jolly Sailor   **£ 39   ⓞ**
Quay St IP12 2NU   (01394) 450243
"Chelsea with a whiff of ozone!" – this popular pub in a pretty village is tipped for "robust" cooking in "large" portions; "it's worth the wait... but it can be quite a wait!" / **Details:** www.jollysailororford.co.uk; 9 pm; no Amex. **Accommodation:** 3 rooms, from £95.

ORKNEY ISLANDS, ORKNEY ISLANDS

The Creel   **£ 54   ❶❷❶**
St Margaret's Hope, South Ronaldsay KW17 2SL   (01856) 831311
"Great use of local ingredients to produce top-class dishes" – this "tiny restaurant-with-rooms" is hailed in all reports for its "superb" cooking (especially fish and seafood), and its "very kind" service.
/ **Details:** www.thecreel.co.uk; off A961 S of town, across Churchill barriers; 8 pm; D only; closed Jan-Mar; no Amex. **Accommodation:** 3 rooms, from £110.

ORPINGTON, KENT   3–3B

Osteria da Fabrizio   **£ 43   ⓞ**
254 High St BR6 0LZ   (01689) 874 488
Tipped as a "really authentic" and "well-priced" destination, this "friendly" but "slightly echoey" Italian lurks – "Tardis-like" – behind a deli.
/ **Details:** www.dafabrizio.co.uk; @DaFabrizio11; 11 pm, Sun 9 pm; closed Mon D.

Xian   **£ 30   ❶❶❸**
324 High St BR6 0NG   (01689) 871881
"By far the best Chinese for miles around"; this "lighthouse in the gloom" always "comes up trumps" with its "authentic flavours" and "efficient and no-nonsense service overseen by the friendly maitre d'" – "the fact that you have to book ahead, even midweek, is testimony to its quality".
/ **Details:** 11 pm; closed Mon & Sun L.

OSMOTHERLEY, NORTH YORKSHIRE   8–4C

Golden Lion   **£ 41   ⓞ**
6 West End DL6 3AA   (01609) 883526
A village inn tipped for its "well-cooked" food; "always a nice feel" too.
/ **Details:** www.goldenlionosmotherley.co.uk; 9 pm; closed Mon L & Tue L; no Amex. **Accommodation:** 5 rooms, from £90.

OSWESTRY, SHROPSHIRE   5–3A

Sebastian's   **£ 55   ❷❸❸**
45 Willow St SY11 1AQ   (01691) 655444
A restaurant-with-rooms which inspires impressively consistent praise for its "satisfying" and "well-

balanced" Gallic-inspired cuisine; "anywhere that's supplied desserts for the Orient-Express must be doing something right!"
/ **Details:** *www.sebastians-hotel.co.uk; 9.45 pm; D only, closed Mon & Sun; no Amex.* **Accommodation:** *5 rooms, from £75.*

OXFORD, OXFORDSHIRE   2–2D

Al-Shami   £ 28 ❷❸④
25 Walton Cr OX1 2JG   (01865) 310066
"Oxford's best Lebanese!"; this "great-value" Jericho spot "seems to have got even better" of late, offering "beautifully spiced and smartly presented" mezze with a wine list "to suit all wallets"; the atmosphere spans all options from "intimate" (window tables) to "exuberant" (out at the back).
/ **Details:** *www.al-shami.co.uk; 11.30 pm; no Amex.* **Accommodation:** *12 rooms, from £60.*

Anchor   £ 45 ❶
2 Hayfield Rd OX2 6TT   (01865) 510282
A North Oxford local tipped as "probably the best" gastropub in town (with "excellent fish" a highlight); "good family area" too.
/ **Details:** *www.theanchoroxford.com; @theanchorinn; 11 pm; no Amex.*

Ashmolean Dining Room £ 50 ④❸❶
Beaumont St OX1 2PH   (01865) 553 823
"An unsurpassed rooftop location with splendid views of the dreaming spires" is the main draw at this "very pleasant lunch spot"; the food is "decent" by institution standards too (ie somewhat "dull", and at "inflated prices").
/ **Details:** *www.ashmoleandiningroom.com; 10 pm; closed Mon, Tue D, Thu D & Sun D.*

Atomic Burger   £ 30 ❷❷❸
96 Cowley Rd OX4 1JE   (01865) 790 855
*"Very quirky, hip and cool!"; this "comic-style burger bar" (like a "mini-MEATliquor in Oxford") is "bursting with students" – "but try it, it's better than it sounds!"; burgers come with a "mind-boggling array" of sides, including "delicious chilli and garlic 'sci-fries'"! / **Details:** www.atomicburger.co.uk; 10.30 pm; no Amex.*

Aziz   £ 33 ❸❸❸
228-230 Cowley Rd OX4 1UH
(01865) 794945
"Others try, but none comes near" – this staple Cowley Road curry house remains an ever-popular standby; top menu choice if you're a veggie? – "anything involving pumpkins"!
/ **Details:** *www.aziz.uk.com; 11.30 pm, Sat midnight; closed Fri L.*

Big Bang   £ 35 ❷❷❷
42 Oxford Castle Quarter OX1 1AY
(01865) 249413
"Real mash, proper gravy, authentic sausages, tasty veg and big portions, all served by the charming and

charismatic owner, Max" – that's the deal at this "friendly" bangers 'n' mash spot which is a "great independent".
/ **Details:** *www.thebigbangrestaurant.co.uk; opposite Cocktail Bar Raoul's; 10.30 pm; no credit cards.*

The Black Boy   £ 45 ❷❸❸
91 Old High St OX3 9HT   (01865) 741137
In Headington, a "contemporary dining pub", which attracts consistent praise for its "reliable" and "good-quality" cooking.
/ **Details:** *www.theblackboy.uk.com; 9 pm; no Amex.*

Bombay   £ 23 ❷❶④
82 Walton St OX2 6EA   (01865) 511188
"Delicious" food and you can "bring your own alcohol" too – no surprises that this tiny Jericho Indian "tends to get packed with students in term-time"; it may be "slightly more expensive" than some of its neighbours, but it "remains good value".
/ **Details:** *11 pm; closed Fri L; no Amex.*

Branca   £ 43 ❸❷❸
111 Walton St OX2 6AJ   (01865) 556111
*"Still maintaining high standards", this "lively" Jericho staple's food stays "simple and focused... like the best Italian cooking" ("it's not just pizza, although they are good"); further boons include "good offers", and a "fabulous terrace" for when the sun shines. / **Details:** www.branca.co.uk; 11 pm; no Amex.*

Brasserie Blanc   £ 46 ❸❸④
71-72 Walton St OX2 6AG   (01865) 510999
*"Still the best brasserie in Oxford by far"; this "very competent" outlet of what's now a national chain "outstrips other branches"; why? – "Raymond himself is regularly on site, keeping standards and service on track". / **Details:** www.brasserieblanc.com; 10 pm, Sat 10.30 pm, Sun 9.30 pm; SRA-64%.*

Browns   £ 41 ④④❸
5-11 Woodstock Rd OX2 6HA
(01865) 511995
*"Forty years on and still reliable and good value for money" – so say long term fans of this seminal branch of the famous British brasserie chain (who feel the "new tapas area is a good addition"); feedback remains as divided as ever, however, and numerous critics find it thoroughly "second rate" nowadays. / **Details:** www.browns-restaurants.com; 11 pm, Fri & Sat 11.30 pm, Sun 10.30 pm.*

Cherwell Boathouse   £ 44 ❷❸❶
Bardwell Rd OX2 6ST   (01865) 552746
"Evolved from the cheap 'n' cheerful boathouse of my student days…"; the "impossibly romantic" riverside setting has always been the killer feature of this stalwart venture, but the "improving" food more often lives up to the other "particular highlight" – a wine list "with great variety and some fantastic prices".

/ *Details: www.cherwellboathouse.co.uk;*
@cherwellboathouse; 9 pm, Fri & Sat 9.30 pm.

Chiang Mai   £ 43   ❷❷❷
Kemp Hall Passage   OX1 4DH   (01865) 202233
"Incongruously located", in a "strangely laid out"
and "rickety" medieval building, down an alleyway
off the high, this "relaxing" venture remains one of
the town's most "reliable" destinations, thanks to its
"fresh and aromatic" Thai dishes; "the only problem
is it's always full…"
/ *Details: www.chiangmaikitchen.co.uk; 10.30 pm.*

Edamame   £ 31   ❷❸❸
15 Holywell St   OX1 3SA   (01865) 246916
A "welcome escape from Oxford's many chain
restaurants", this hole-in-the-wall venture satisfies
almost all reporters with "outstandingly fresh
Japanese food, lovingly prepared and reasonably
priced"; downsides? you "often have to wait", and
"you always share tables".
/ *Details: www.edamame.co.uk; 8.30 pm; L only, ex*
Thu-Sat open L & D, closed Mon & Tue; no Amex;
no booking.

The Fishes   £ 43   ❸❸④
North Hinksey   OX2 0NA   (01865) 249796
A "family-friendly" venue, with a lovely waterside
setting on the fringe of the city, with a "great
summer garden", where food can be ordered picnic-
style – results are "decent" if, on some reports, "a
bit pricey". / Details: www.fishesoxford.co.uk;
@fishesoxford; 9.45 pm; SRA-58%.

Gee's   £ 55   ④④❸
61 Banbury Rd   OX2 6PE   (01865) 553540
This north Oxford venture in a Victorian glasshouse
has "undergone a revamp, taking it back to its
former informality"; the occasional fan does find it
"fun and glamorous", with "food much better than
a year ago", but other reporters rue a
"disappointing fall from grace".
/ *Details: www.gees-restaurant.co.uk; 10 pm, Fri & Sat*
10.30 pm.

The Magdalen Arms   £ 42   ❷❸❸
243 Iffley Rd   OX4 1SJ   (01865) 243 159
"Now Oxford's best"; offering "London gastropub
excellence closer to home", this outpost of the Big
Smoke's Hope & Anchor is a "meat-eater's
paradise" noted for "robust, flavoursome food";
"service is a touch slow, but they know their stuff".
/ *Details: www.magdalenarms.com; 10 pm, Sun*
9.30 pm; closed Mon L; no Amex.

Malmaison   £ 51   ❼
3 Oxford Circle   OX1 1AY   (01865) 268400
Certainly a top tip if you're looking for an
"interesting" venue – a hotel dining room located in
a former prison; the cooking inspires the odd 'off'
report, but most feedback is positive.
/ *Details: www.malmaison.com; 10 pm; 6+ need to*
book. Accommodation: 94 rooms, from £160.

My Sichuan   £ 38   ❶④④
The Old School, Gloucester Grn   OX1 2DA
(01865) 236 899
"Super-authentic, vivid and clean Sichuanese
flavours" gives "no concession to non-Chinese
patrons" at this former school building, by the bus
station, where often "the conversation of diners and
waiters is predominantly in Mandarin"; service an
be "slightly flakey". / Details: www.mysichuan.co.uk;
11 pm.

The Nosebag   £ 28   ❸❸❸
6-8 St Michael's St   OX1 2DU   (01865) 721033
This central favourite is one of the best-value
eateries in town... "where else for a hearty main
with three dollops of decent salad to leave you full
and content – for less than the price of a pizza?";
lunchtimes, unsurprisingly, can be "chaos".
/ *Details: www.nosebagoxford.co.uk; 9.30 pm, Fri &*
Sat 10 pm, Sun 8.30 pm.

The Old Parsonage   £ 57   ❸❷❶
1 Banbury Rd   OX2 6NN   (01865) 292305
"The food can be very good, although never exciting,
but the more is lovely…"; this old stone building
(plus gorgeous courtyard) houses a "very pleasant
hotel and tea room" and is just the job for a "great
Sunday brunch", a "good-value lunch", or "very
civilised afternoon tea"
/ *Details: www.oldparsonage-hotel.co.uk; 10.30 pm.*
Accommodation: 30 rooms, from £220.

Pierre Victoire   £ 43   ❷❸❸
Little Clarendon St   OX1 2HP   (01865) 316616
"As close to good-priced French bistro food of
decent quality as you'll find" – this mega-popular
survivor of a nowadays defunct chain is
"unpretentious", "authentic", and "always bursting
at the seams". / Details: www.pierrevictoire.co.uk;
11 pm, Sun 10 pm; no Amex.

Quod
Old Bank Hotel   £ 46   ❸④❸
92-94 High St   OX1 4BJ   (01865) 799599
This city-centre venture is always "full of the
jeunesse dorée being fed by mater and pater"; it's
"not a gourmet choice", but one which "usually
delivers" on the food front; service, though, can be
"slow". / Details: www.oldbank-hotel.co.uk; 11 pm,
Sun 10.30 pm; no booking at D. Accommodation: 42
rooms, from £137.

Shanghai 30s   £ 39   ❼
82 St Aldates   OX1 1RA   (01865) 242230
In an Elizabethan building opposite Christ Church,
this Chinese restaurant occupies the site of former
age old favourite 'Elizabeth' (long RIP); nowadays,
however, it's mainly tipped for a "great-value" set
lunch. / Details: www.shanghai30s.com; 10.30 pm;
closed Mon L.

Sojo **£ 40** **❶❶④**
8-9 Hythe Bridge St OX1 2EW
(01865) 202888
"Brilliant food, both Sichuan and Shanghainese" (the former "mind-alteringly hot"), plus very "willing" owners inspire massive approval for this "small and buzzy" venture, where "at least half the clientele appear to be Chinese".
/ Details: www.sojooxford.co.uk; 10.30 pm, Sun 9.30 pm.

Turl Street Kitchen **£ 30** **❷⑤❸**
16 Turl St OX1 3DH (01865) 264 171
"Value is unbeatable" at this central, "not for profit" café, which serves "simple", "healthy and organic" scoff from a short daily changing menu in a "laid back" fashion, to "students making use of the free wifi"; arrive early – "dishes run out later on".
/ Details: www.turlstreetkitchen.co.uk; @turlskitchen; 10 pm.

The Vaults And Garden Cafe **£ 17** **❸❸❸**
University Church of St Mary the Virgin, Radcliffe Sq OX1 4AH (01865) 279112
An "excellent choice for a reliable and cheap lunch with a lively atmosphere" and "bang in the middle of Oxford", too; this veggie-friendly self-service joint – a large vaulted room – is a "great hang-out", and so popular it's "often hard to find a seat".
/ Details: www.thevaultsandgarden.com; @VaultsandGarden; 6 pm; L only.

OXTED, SURREY 3–3B

The Gurkha Kitchen **£ 32** **❶❷❸**
111 Station Road East RH8 0AX
(01883) 722621
"A fabulous place to eat thanks to its stunning food" – this family-run Nepalese has maintained "consistently high standards over many years".
/ Details: 11 pm, Sun 10 pm; no Amex.

OXTON, CHESHIRE 5–2A

Fraiche **£ 87** **❶❶❷**
11 Rose Mount CH43 5SG (0151) 652 2914
"An amazing culinary delight in an unlikely setting"; "exciting", "exquisite"… – the plaudits for Marc Wilkinson's "ever more innovative" cuisine go on and on (and it's "ridiculously cheap too, given the technique involved"); "just wish it was easier to get a table…" / Details: www.restaurantfraiche.com; 8.30 pm, Sun 7 pm; closed Mon, Tue, Wed L, Thu L, Fri L & Sat L; no Amex.

PADSTOW, CORNWALL 1–3B

Margot's **£ 49** **❶❷❷**
11 Duke St PL28 8AB (01841) 533441
"Forget Rick Stein – if you're going to eat out in Padstow, Margot's is a delight!"; Adrian Oliver "makes it all look so easy with the simple, but

superb food which emerges from his tiny kitchen: 19 covers, 1 chef, 1 waitress, no problems!"
/ Details: www.margotsbistro.co.uk; @adrian_margots; 9 pm; closed Mon & Sun.

Paul Ainsworth at Number 6 **£ 67** **❶❷❷**
6 Middle St PL28 8AP (01841) 532093
"Continuing to outshine Rick in Padstow"; Paul Ainsworth's "fun" backstreet restaurant achieves higher ratings for its fish cooking than anywhere in the Stein empire, thanks to its "meticulous" cuisine and its "friendly and informative" service.
/ Details: www.number6inpadstow.co.uk; @no6padstow / paulainsw6rth; 10 pm; closed Mon & Sun; no Amex; children: 4 yrs +.

Rick Stein's Café **£ 42** **❷❸❸**
10 Middle St PL28 8AP (01841) 532700
Critics snipe that it's "boring" at the price, but Rick's "informal and buzzy" spin off is for the vast majority of reporters a worthy No. 2 to his main HQ thanks to its "bustling" style and its "delicious fresh fish, unfussily presented".
/ Details: www.rickstein.com; 9.30 pm; no Amex; Only for D. Accommodation: 3 rooms, from £100.

Rojanos **£ 45** **❷❸❷**
9 Mill Sq PL28 8AE (01841) 532796
"Another refurbishment and a new menu at this popular venture has only added to its success"; Paul Ainsworth's "little gem" continues to wow reporters with "very well-prepared" Italian staples, and an ambience which "bustles just as much as the port it's located in". / Details: www.rojanos.co.uk; @rojanos; 9.30 pm; no Amex.

St Petroc's Hotel & Bistro **£ 56** **④④❸**
4 New St PL28 8EA (01841) 532700
There are fans of Rick's crowded bistro who say it's a "lovely" venue that's "more enjoyable than the Seafood!"; its ratings were lacklustre this year, however, with a feeling that "is has neither the charm of the café, nor the prosaic competence of the flagship". / Details: www.rickstein.com; 10 pm; no Amex. Accommodation: 10 rooms, from £150.

Seafood Restaurant **£ 82** **❶❶❷**
Riverside PL28 8BY (01841) 532700
"Fish simply-served" and "seafood as it should be" – Rick Stein's "outstanding" but "unpretentious" (and sometimes rather "cramped") waterside HQ has waxed and waned over the years, but is currently on a high – "as devoted fans of his on TV, this place is The Holy Grail for us, and it was everything we hoped for!" / Details: www.rickstein.com; 10 pm; ; no Amex; booking: max 14; children: 3+. Accommodation: 16 rooms, from £150.

Stein's Fish & Chips **£ 34** **❸⑤⑤**
South Quay PL28 8BL (01841) 532700
There are "always queues", but this is perhaps not

Cherwell Boathouse

Malmaison

The Magdalen Arms

the TV chef's finest outlet – the fish is "very good" but "on the expensive" side, while service can be somewhat "inefficient" and the interior's a mite "grotty". / **Details:** www.rickstein.com; 9 pm; no Amex.

PARKGATE, CHESHIRE   5–2A

The Boathouse   £ 41   ❷❷❷
1 The Pde CH64 6RN   (0151) 336 4187
"Beautiful views over the River Dee estuary, well-prepared and filling food, friendly service, good beer…" – supporters can see no end to the virtues of this marsh-side fixture; "always ask for a table in the conservatory".

PAXFORD, GLOUCESTERSHIRE   2–1C

The Churchill Arms   £ 43   ❷❸❸
GL55 6XH   (01386) 594000
This "lovely" Cotswold pub wins diners' hearts with its "imaginative" menu, and service that's generally pretty "reliable" too.
/ **Details:** www.thechurchillarms.com; off Fosse Way; 11 pm; no Amex. **Accommodation:** 4 rooms, from £85.

PEEBLES, SCOTTISH BORDERS   9–4C

Cringletie House   £ 58   ❶
Edinburgh Rd EH45 8PL   (01721) 725750
A "wonderful country house hotel", tipped for its "very accomplished" cuisine, and "style to match".
/ **Details:** www.cringletie.com; between Peebles and Eddleston on A703, 20m S of Edinburgh; 9 pm; D only, ex Sun open L & D; booking essential.
Accommodation: 13 rooms, from £80.

PENALLT, MONMOUTHSHIRE   2–2B

Inn at Penallt   £ 44   ❶
NP25 4SE   (01600) 772765
"A lovely place to stay in the Wye Valley"; this pretty village pub consistently pleases reporters, and it's tipped for its "great food" too.
/ **Details:** www.theinnatpenallt.co.uk/; 9 pm; closed Mon, Tue L & Sun D; no Amex. **Accommodation:** 4 rooms, from £75.

PENARTH, VALE OF GLAMORGAN   1–

Fig Tree   £ 40   ❶
The Esplanade CF64 3AU   (029) 2070 2512
In a one-time Victorian beach shelter, a restaurant tipped for "very good food" generally, and "excellent lunchtime value" in particular, and it all tastes best "on the veranda overlooking the sea".
/ **Details:** www.thefigtreepenarth.co.uk/; 9.30 pm; closed Mon & Sun D; no Amex.

PENZANCE, CORNWALL   1–4A

The Honey Pot   £ 22   ❷❷❷
5 Parade St TR18 4BU   (01736) 368686
"Still the best of its type in town" – this simple

---

central café serves "top notch" coffee, cakes and light bites, and "stays relaxed even when it's doing a roaring trade… which is frequent". / **Details:** L only, closed Sun; no credit cards.

PERSHORE, WORCESTERSHIRE   2–1C

Belle House   £ 50   ❶
Bridge St WR10 1AJ   (01386) 555055
Tipped as "the best in the area", a town-centre restaurant (and traîteur) where lunch, in particular, can be a "very enjoyable" experience.
/ **Details:** www.belle-house.co.uk; 9.30 pm; closed Mon & Sun.

PERTH, PERTH AND KINROSS   9–3C

Cafe Tabou   £ 49   ❸❶❷
4 St John's Pl PH1 5SZ   (01738) 446698
"You could be in France" (except the chef and owner are Polish!) at this "lovely, warm and welcoming" venture – a "good value", "cheek-by-jowl" bistro, serving "unpretentious and robust" Gallic classics. / **Details:** www.cafetabou.com; 9.30 pm, Fri & Sat 10 pm; closed Mon D & Sun; no Amex.

Deans at Let's Eat   £ 51   ❶
77-79 Kinnoull St PH1 5EZ   (01738) 643377
"A diamond in the rough" – a town centre restaurant tipped for its "very good" cooking from an "interesting" and "diverse" menu; "friendly and well-informed" staff too.
/ **Details:** www.letseatperth.co.uk; 9 pm; closed Mon & Sun; no Amex.

63 Tay Street   £ 58   ❷❸❸
63 Tay St PH2 8NN   (01738) 441451
Graham Pallister's "top quality", "interesting" cooking "avoids the easy trap of being a 'posh' restaurant cliché" at this "friendly but smart" fixture, in the town centre.
/ **Details:** www.63taystreet.co.uk; on city side of River Tay, 1m from Dundee Rd; 9 pm; closed Mon & Sun.

PETERSFIELD, HAMPSHIRE   2–3D

JSW   £ 70   ❷❸④
20 Dragon St GU31 4JJ   (01730) 262030
Jake Saul Watkins has "maintained or exceeded the highest standards over the years", with the "imaginative, yet classic" cuisine at his former coaching inn; "pity about the ambience", though, of this "stark" room – it's "a bit like eating in a library". / **Details:** www.jswrestaurant.com; on the old A3; 8 min walk from the railway station; 9 pm; closed Mon, Tue & Sun D; children: 5+ D.
Accommodation: 4 rooms, from £95.

PETTS WOOD, KENT   3–3B

Indian Essence   £ 34   ❶❷❸
176-178 Petts Wood Rd BR5 1LG   (01689) 838 700

"An amazing find for this area"; this "superb" suburban newcomer, from Atul Kochar – of Benares (Mayfair) fame – has become an immediate hit thanks to his "outstanding" Indian cuisine; the dining room, though, is "cramped" and sometimes "loud". / **Details:** *www.indianessence.co.uk; 10.45 pm, fri & sat 11 pm, sun 10.30 pm; closed Mon L.*

Uskudar　　　　　　　**£ 32**　**❼**
61 Queensway BR5 1DQ　(01689) 820055
Top tip locally as a "meat-eater's paradise" – "a great little Turkish restaurant with great food and a funky interior". / **Details:** *www.uskudar.co.uk/; 11 pm; no Amex.*

PETWORTH, WEST SUSSEX　　　　　　3–4A

The Noahs Ark Inn　　**£ 44**　**❷❸❶**
Lurgashall GU28 9ET　(01428) 707346
According to pretty much every report, this is an "outstanding" all-rounder – "a traditional pub, with food worthy of a decent restaurant", "great beers", and a "perfect village setting" on "a village green worthy of Midsomer". / **Details:** *www.noahsarkinn.co.uk; 9.30 pm, Sun 3 pm; closed Sun D.*

PICKERING, NORTH YORKSHIRE　　　8–4C

The White Swan　　　**£ 46**　**❷❸❸**
Market Pl YO18 7AA　(01751) 472288
"Great gastropub food" (including "excellent local seafood") comes "reasonably priced" at this elegantly understated coaching inn which, of late, has been a hit with all who comment on it. / **Details:** *www.white-swan.co.uk; 9 pm.* **Accommodation:** *21 rooms, from £150.*

PINNER, GREATER LONDON　　　　3–3A

Friends　　　　　　　**£ 52**　**❹❷❷**
11 High St HA5 5PJ　(020) 8866 0286
"Still going strong", Terry Farr's "intimate" venture in an "historic building on the high street" continues to strike most (if not quite all) reporters as a "perfect local restaurant". / **Details:** *www.friendsrestaurant.co.uk; 9.30 pm; closed Mon & Sun D.*

L'Orient　　　　　　**£ 44**　**❸❷❸**
58 High St HA5 5PZ　(020) 8429 8488
Featuring an "excellent choice of different menus from the East", a suburban restaurant of more than usual interest, thanks to its impressive all-round standards. / **Details:** *www.lorientcuisine.com; 10 pm, Sat 11 pm, Sun 10 pm; closed Mon, Tue-Fri D only, Sat & Sun open L & D; no Amex.*

PLEASINGTON, LANCASHIRE　　　5–1B

Clog and Billycock　　**£ 43**　**❹❸❸**
Billinge End Rd BB2 6QB　(01254) 201163
"Clever" pub grub "with a strong and fresh regional accent" served in a "real pub atmosphere" wins

---

fans for Ribble Valley chain gastropub; "high expectations were not met" for quite a few critics, however – "what could be great is often mediocre". / **Details:** *www.theclogandbillycock.com; 8.30 pm Mon-Thu, Fri & Sat 9 pm, Sun 8 pm.*

PLUMTREE, NOTTINGHAMSHIRE　　5–3D

Perkins　　　　　　　**£ 48**　**❼**
Old Railway Station NG12 5NA
(0115) 937 3695
"Good food" makes this local restaurant a handy enough tip in a not over-provided area; it can sometimes seem a bit "pricey", though. / **Details:** *www.perkinsrestaurant.co.uk; @PerkinsNotts; off A606 between Nottingham & Melton Mowbray; 9.30 pm; closed Sun D.*

PLUSH, DORSET　　　　　　　2–4B

Brace of Pheasants　　**£ 42**　**❷❷❷**
DT2 7RT　(01300) 348357
"Well worth seeking out" ("you'll need the satnav"), this "hidden treat" of an inn wins acclaim all round, not least for its "gourmet pub food", including the "imaginative" treatment of game you might hope for. / **Details:** *www.braceofpheasants.co.uk; 9.30 pm.* **Accommodation:** *4 rooms, from £95.*

PLYMOUTH, DEVON　　　　　　1–3C

The Barbican Kitchen Brasserie　　　　　**£ 47**　**❸❹❸**
60 Southside St, The Barbican PL1 2LQ
(01752) 604448
This "excellent Barbican restaurant", located in the old Plymouth Gin distillery, earns mostly positive reports for "good-value" fare and its "bright and spacious" setting; service can be "a bit perfunctory", though, and critics find food standards a touch variable. / **Details:** *www.barbicankitchen.com; 10 pm.*

Chloe's Gill Akaster House　　**£ 59**　**❸❸❸**
Princess St PL1 2EX　(01752) 201523
"One of the better places in Plymouth", this "smart" bistro is "ideally suited for theatre-goers" and – "with the ivories tinkling in the background" – quite a popular destination for romance too. / **Details:** *www.chloesrestaurant.co.uk; 10 pm; closed Mon & Sun.*

Rhodes at The Dome　　**£ 40**　**❹❺❸**
Hoe Rd PL1 2NZ　(01752) 266600
This smart new restaurant (and wedding venue) – now the UK's only 'GR' branded restaurant – has "stunning views across Plymouth Sound"; fans say the cooking is "pretty good" too, but there's a feeling that "after a shaky start it still needs a good shake to up its game" – "come on Gary!" / **Details:** *www.rhodesatthedome.co.uk/; 9.30 pm, sat & sun 10 pm.*

Rock Salt £ 42 ❷❸❷
31 Stonehouse St PL1 3PE (01752) 225522
*This tiny former backstreet pub "in one of the
town's less salubrious locations, down by the docks"
is nowadays "a great café bistro" – an "all things to
all people" destination, where "they make you
welcome, and serve some of the tastiest food in
town". / **Details:** www.rocksaltcafe.co.uk;
rocksaltcafeuk; 11pm.*

Tanners Restaurant £ 68 ❶❷❷
Prysten Hs, Finewell St PL1 2AE
(01752) 252001
*"Fine local ingredients are married with first class
wines", at the Tanner Brothers' "atmospheric" small
restaurant – undboutedly the city's best; even fans
can find it pricey, but set menus offer "astonishing
value". / **Details:** www.tannersrestaurant.com;
9.30 pm; closed Mon & Sun.*

POLKERRIS, CORNWALL 1–3B

Sams on the Beach £ 46 ❷❸❶
PL24 2TL (01726) 812255
*"Great casual dining in a superb beach location" –
this seaside diner is a "favourite holiday lunch spot";
it does do pizza, but the highpoint is the seafood –
"so fresh and simple, but beautifully cooked".
/ **Details:** www.samsfowey.co.uk; 9 pm; no Amex.*

POOLE, DORSET 7–3D

Branksome Beach £ 50 ④❸❷
Pinecliff Rd BH13 6LP (01202) 767235
*A "lively restaurant on the seafront"; it's
"reasonably-priced" (at least "for a beachside
Sandbanks venue") and attracts very positive
feedback, albeit more for the "stunning" location
than the "OK food and service".
/ **Details:** www.branksomebeach.co.uk.*

Guildhall Tavern £ 52 ❷❶❸
15 Market St BH15 1NB (01202) 671717
*"A great find" in the underserved harbour district –
this "very welcoming" Gallic brasserie serves "top-
class food" (especially "for fish lovers"); more than
one fan, though, sees the "Happy Eater-style menu"
as a sign that this fine dining venue is "not too sure
of its niche". / **Details:** www.guildhalltavern.co.uk;
10 pm; closed Mon & Sun; no Amex.*

Storm £ 49 ❷❸④
16 High St BH15 1BP (01202) 674970
*Pete & Frances Miles's restaurant may be a touch
"basic", but it's a "relaxed" and "friendly" sort of
establishment offering an "excellent" range of fish
dishes, and "good puds" too.
/ **Details:** www.stormfish.co.uk; 9.30 pm, Fri & Sat
10 pm; closed Mon L, Tue L & Sun L.*

PORT APPIN, ARGYLL AND BUTE 9–3B

Airds Hotel £ 73 ❶❷❸
PA38 4DF (01631) 730236
*One touring reporter had their "best meal in
Scotland" at this comfortable hotel, by Loch Linnhe
– both food and service are always very highly
rated, and there are "magical views" from the
window tables. / **Details:** www.airds-hotel.com;
@AirdsHotel; 20m N of Oban; 9.30 pm; no jeans or
trainers; children: 8+ at D. **Accommodation:** 11
rooms, from £290.*

PORT ISAAC, CORNWALL 1–3B

Outlaw's Fish Kitchen £ 35 ❸❶❷
1 Middle St PL29 3RH (01208) 881138
*Stepping into the shoes of the Harbour Restaurant
(RIP), Cornwall's biggest foodie name opened in
autumn 2013 in these bijou premises, aiming for a
relaxed style, and with chef Paul Ripley producing a
tapas-y seafood menu. / **Details:** www.outlaws.co.uk.*

PORTHGAIN, PEMBROKESHIRE 4–4B

The Shed £ 39 ❷④④
SA62 5BN (01348) 831518
*"Heartily recommended" – this "unusual" venture,
"picturesquely located" right by the harbour, offers a
"real variety" of fish 'n' chips, alongside a full à la
carte. / **Details:** www.theshedporthgain.co.uk; 9 pm;
no Amex; Booking essential.*

PORTHLEVEN, CORNWALL 1–4A

Kota £ 45 ❷❷❷
Harbour Head TR13 9JA (01326) 562407
*"A quality all-round experience in a picturesque
harbour location" – this seaside venture provides (on
nearly all accounts) "excellent food with an
antipodean twist from an exciting and eclectic
menu". / **Details:** www.kotarestaurant.co.uk; 9 pm;
D only, closed Sun-Tue; no Amex. **Accommodation:** 2
rooms, from £70.*

PORTMAHOMACK , HIGHLAND 9–2C

The Oystercatcher £ 57 ❷❷❸
Main St IV20 1YB (01862) 871560
*"Worth a trip north of Inverness", say fans, this
"very casual bistro", on the water's edge, where
"very fresh seafood is generously served";
"surprisingly good wine list" too.
/ **Details:** www.the-oystercatcher.co.uk; 10 pm; closed
Mon, Tue, Wed L & Sun D. **Accommodation:** 3
rooms, from £77.*

PORTMEIRION, GWYNEDD 4–2C

Portmeirion Hotel £ 62 ④④❶
LL48 6ET (01766) 772440
*The hotel at the centre of Sir Clough Williams-Ellis's
Italianate replica village is a "unique" and
"fabulous" location, with fine estuary views and quite*

a culinary reputation; but numerous repeat visitors were nonplussed by lacklustre recent meals – "essentially 'posh catering' and not worth the trek". / **Details:** www.portmeirion-village.com; off A487 at Minffordd; 9 pm. **Accommodation:** 14 rooms, from £185.

PORTSMOUTH, HAMPSHIRE   2–4D

abarbistro   **£ 40   ❸❷❸**
58 White Hart Rd PO1 2JA   (02392) 811585
Living up to its name, a "buzzy" dining room in a former pub where the menu features some "interesting" specials, and results are "consistently good". / **Details:** www.abarbistro.co.uk; midnight, Sun 10.30 pm.

Le Café Parisien   **£ 29   ❶**
1 Lord Montgomery Way PO1 2AH
(023) 9283 1234
Top tip near the University, but this "very popular" daytime coffee shop can just be too "busy" – "get there early for the specials".
/ **Details:** www.lecafeparisien.com; Mon-Fri 5.30 pm, Sat 4 pm; closed Sun; no Amex.

Loch Fyne   **£ 43   ❸❸❸**
Unit 2 Vulcan Buildings PO1 3TY
(023) 9277 8060
This chain outlet attracts a surprising volume of survey feedback, all of which is positive; "possibly the best of the Loch Fynes I've visited", says one reporter, and it benefits from a "large al fresco seating area" too.
/ **Details:** www.lochfyne-restaurants.com; 10.30 pm.

Relentless Steak &
Lobster House   **£ 45   ❷❸④**
85 Elm Grove PO5 1JF   (02392) 822888
A real "gem", this "popular" Southsea surf 'n' turf spot may look "like an upmarket chippy", but its cuisine – which includes fish straight from the sea that day – is "fresh, well cooked and substantial"; book ahead. / **Details:** 9.30 pm.

Restaurant 27   **£ 55   ❷❷❸**
27a, Southsea Pde PO5 2JF   (023) 9287 6272
"The best restaurant in Portsmouth by far!", say fans of this "intimate" local – the exterior may be a touch "unprepossessing", but all reports laud its "fabulous" food, and its "pleasant and efficient" service. / **Details:** www.restaurant27.com; 9.30 pm; closed Mon, Tue, Wed L, Thu L, Fri L, Sat L & Sun D.

PRESTBURY, CHESHIRE   5–2B

Bacchus   **£ 52   ❷❷❸**
The Village SK10 4DG   (01625) 820009
Run by the team behind the erstwhile local hero Moss Nook (RIP), a restaurant unanimously praised by reporters for its "great ambience, service, and – most importantly – food!"
/ **Details:** www.bacchusprestbury.co.uk;

@bacchusprestbur; 9.30 pm, Fri & Sat 10 pm; closed Mon & Sun D.

PRESTON BAGOT, WARWICKSHIRE   5–4C

The Crabmill   **£ 45   ❸❷❸**
B95 5EE   (01926) 843342
A large, modern gastropub with "a wonderful countryside setting", and conveniently placed for M40 motorists too; there's a "good outside dining space for when the weather behaves", and the interior is "always busy", thanks not least to the "wide and interesting menu".
/ **Details:** www.thecrabmill.co.uk; @lvlycrabmill; on main road between Warwick & Henley-in-Arden; 9.30 pm; closed Sun D; no Amex; booking essential.

PRESTON CANDOVER, HAMPSHIRE   2–3D

The Purefoy Arms   **£ 46   ❷❸❷**
RG25 2EJ   (01256) 389 777
This may look "just like a typical village pub", but "this is very much a restaurant", and one where the "Spanish chef's background shows through"; the "food seems to improve on every visit" too… which is creating a "growing reputation" locally.
/ **Details:** www.thepurefoyarms.co.uk; @thepurefoyarms; 10 pm; closed Mon & Sun D.

PRESTON, LANCASHIRE   5–1A

Bukhara   **£ 31   ❶❷❷**
154 Preston New Rd PR5 0UP
(01772) 877710
"Always a joy"; this "homely" Indian inspires high praise for its "genuine, freshly prepared" food and its "very friendly" staff; no alcohol, but "who needs that with so many fresh and interesting dishes" on the menu? / **Details:** www.bukharasamlesbury.co.uk; 11 pm; D only; no Maestro.

PWLLHELI, GWYNEDD   4–2C

Plas Bodegroes   **£ 64   ❷❷❶**
Nefyn Rd LL53 5TH   (01758) 612363
It's the "wonderful" setting – overlooking a "beautiful garden", with "sheep roaming in the distance" – which makes the Chowns' restaurant-with-rooms a "special" experience; the cooking is also "very sound" and, includes some "brilliant vegetarian options".
/ **Details:** www.bodegroes.co.uk; @bodegroes; on A497 1m W of Pwllheli; 9.30 pm; closed Mon, Tue-Sat D only, closed Sun D; no Amex; children: not at D.
Accommodation: 10 rooms, from £130.

QUEENSBURY, MIDDLESEX   3–3A

Regency Club   **£ 30   ❷④❸**
19-21 Queensbury Station Pde HA8 5NR
(020) 8905 6177
"Some of the best Indian food bar none", plus Bollywood on the big screens – what more could you want in a suburban restaurant?; it can feel a bit

"crowded", though. | Details: www.regencyclub.co.uk; 10.30 pm; closed Mon L.

QUEENSFERRY, CITY OF EDINBURGH 9–4C

Dakota Forth Bridge   **£ 53** ❷❷❷
Ferrimuir Retail Pk EH30 9QZ
(0870) 423 4293
"Handy for business travellers", or "in the middle of nowhere"? – the "strange" location of this hotel dining room, on the south tip of the Forth Road Bridge, may divide opinion, but the "inspired" food attracts uniform praise.
| Details: www.dakotaforthbridge.co.uk; 10 pm; booking essential. Accommodation: 132 rooms, from £99.

RADLEY GREEN, ESSEX   3–2B

The Cuckoo   **£ 46** ❷❸❸
CM4 0LT (01245) 248946
In a canny bit of marketing, this hard-to-find, rural restaurant, in a row of old cottages, offers a 'ladies who lunch' menu which often finds favour with reporters; it's "always a good experience" – if a "noisy" one at times!
| Details: www.cuckooradleygreen.co.uk; On the A14 between Ongar and Chelmsford; 8.45 pm, Fri-Sat 9 pm; closed Mon & Sun; no Amex.

RAMSBOTTOM, LANCASHIRE   5–1B

Ramsons   **£ 60** ❶❶❸
18 Market Pl BL0 9HT (01706) 825070
"Gone are the sparkly tabletops, naked men on the walls and general informal feel" – Chris Johnson's long-running staple is now a "very smart" venue where a new chef cooks "exceptionally well", while the "exclusively Italian wine list" is still "superb"; service "can be overbearing" but also "entertaining".
| Details: www.ramsons-restaurant.com; 9.30 pm; closed Mon, Tue L & Sun D; no Amex.

RAMSGATE, KENT   3–3D

Age & Sons   **£ 43** ❶❸④
Charlotte Ct CT11 8HE (01843) 851515
The "exceptional" quality of Toby Leigh's menu, featuring "interesting twists on classic British dishes" commends this "light" dining room to most reporters; even fans can find it "overpriced", however, and critics sense a drift in standards.
| Details: www.ageandsons.com; 9.30 pm; closed Mon & Sun D; no Amex.

RAMSGILL-IN-NIDDERDALE, NORTH YORKSHIRE   8–4B

Yorke Arms   **£ 89** ❶❶❷
HG3 5RL (01423) 755243
"OMG, what truly amazing food"!; Frances & Gerald Atkins's grand inn is a "picture-postcard building" with a "beautiful location" in a "quiet Dales village";
for once it's Mrs who's the chef, and her "brilliant attention to detail" shines through in "perfect" seasonal cuisine. | Details: www.yorke-arms.co.uk; 4m W of Pateley Bridge; 8.45 pm; no Amex. Accommodation: 16 rooms, from £200.

READING, BERKSHIRE   2–2D

Cerise
Forbury Hotel   **£ 63** ❶
26 The Forbury RG1 3EJ (01189) 527770
This "quiet and peaceful" venture is popular with business types, and tipped for its "very good value-for-money" weekday lunch menu.
| Details: www.theforburyhotel.co.uk; 10 pm. Accommodation: 23, 17 apts rooms, from £150.

London Street Brasserie   **£ 57** ❸❸❷
2-4 London St RG1 4PN (0118) 950 5036
"A reliable choice amongst the chain pubs and restaurants"; this "lovely find" – with its "good food" and its "nice canalside location" is particularly popular in the summer months.
| Details: www.londonstbrasserie.co.uk; 10.30 pm, Fri & Sat 11 pm.

REIGATE, SURREY   3–3B

La Barbe   **£ 48** ❸❷❸
71 Bell St RH2 7AN (01737) 241966
"Wonderful, authentically French atmosphere, staff who know their stuff, and great food"; now in its fourth decade, this Gallic staple pleases most reporters, though there has been the occasional report of "patchy" cooking of late.
| Details: www.labarbe.co.uk; @LaBarbeReigate; 9.30 pm; closed Sat L & Sun D.

Tony Tobin @ The Dining Room   **£ 62** ④④④
59a High St RH2 9AE (01737) 226650
A "welcome slice of fine dining in Reigate"; this TV chef's venture combines "good cooking" with "good front-of-house"; critics, though, can find the whole set-up rather "staid", and complain of "top-end London prices" too.
| Details: www.tonytobinrestaurants.co.uk; @cheftonytobin; 10 pm; closed Sat L & Sun D.

REYNOLDSTON, SWANSEA   1–1C

Fairyhill   **£ 64** ❶
SA3 1BS (01792) 390139
Still, under new chef Neil Hollis, a limited number of reports on this once-celebrated country house hotel, "remotely located" on the Gower Peninsula; it's tipped nonetheless for a menu which "if not the most adventurous, is flawlessly executed".
| Details: www.fairyhill.net; 20 mins from M4, J47 off B4295; 9 pm; no Amex; children: 8+ at D. Accommodation: 8 rooms, from £180.

RHOSCOLYN, ANGLESEY   4–1C

The White Eagle   **£ 41**   ④❸❸
LL65 2NJ   (01407) 860 267
The "lovely food and setting" (with sea views from
some tables) make finding this "out-of-the-way" spot
a "real pleasure"; a couple of reports, however,
suggest that it's been "slipping" of late – hopefully
just a blip! / **Details:** www.white-eagle.co.uk; 9 pm;
no Amex.

RICHMOND, SURREY   3–3A

The Dysart Arms   **£ 60**   ❷❷❷
135 Petersham Rd TW10 7AA
(020) 8940 8005
"A great gastropub perfectly placed next to
Richmond Park for walking off the calories" – this
"beautiful" Arts & Crafts pub, in Petersham, has
many charms, including "surprisingly good food"
(some of which "they send a forager out for").
/ **Details:** www.thedysartarms.co.uk; 9.30 pm; closed
Sun D; no Amex; children: 12+ after 8 pm.

RIPLEY, SURREY   3–3A

Drakes   **£ 87**   ❶❶④
The Clock Hs, High St GU23 6AQ
(01483) 224777
"Fantastic" cooking – in an "unusual" and
"challenging" style you might not necessarily expect
in Surrey – is making a huge hit of Steve Drake's
village-restaurant; even in the face of all this culinary
excitement, though, the room remains "rather dull".
/ **Details:** www.drakesrestaurant.co.uk; 9.30 pm; closed
Mon, Tue L & Sun; no Amex; booking: max 12.

RIPON, NORTH YORKSHIRE   8–4B

Prima Pizzaria   **£ 24**   ❶
33 Kirkgate HG4 1PB   (01765) 602034
Near the Cathedral, a "cheerful" pizzeria tipped for
its "wide menu selection" and "good value"; it's
"always busy". / **Details:** 10.30 pm; D only; no Amex.

RIPPONDEN, WEST YORKSHIRE   5–1C

El Gato Negro Tapas   **£ 41**   ❶❷❷
1 Oldham Rd HX6 4DN   (01422) 823070
"Some of the best tapas in the UK" and "in an
unexpected (converted pub) location" too – no
wonder fans are full of praise for this "friendly
family-run business"; it's also of note for an
excellent-value "weekday special tapas deal".
/ **Details:** www.elgatonegrotapas.com; 9.30 pm, Fri &
Sat 10 pm, Sun 7.30 pm; closed Mon, Tue, Wed L,
Thu L, Fri L & Sun D.

ROADE, NORTHAMPTONSHIRE   3–1A

Roade House   **£ 46**   ❷❶❸
16 High St NN7 2NW   (01604) 863372
"For many years, the finest dining destination near
Northampton" – this smart, purpose-built

establishment is "reliably good" and "good value"
too. / **Details:** www.roadehousehotel.co.uk; 9.30 pm;
closed Mon L, Sat L & Sun D; no shorts; booking
essential. **Accommodation:** 10 rooms, from £82.

ROCK, CORNWALL   1–3B

Dining Room   **£ 56**   ❶❷❸
Pavilion Buildings, Rock Rd PL27 6JS
(01208) 862622
"A very pleasant surprise"; chef Fred Beedle, serves
up "interesting and enjoyable flavour combinations"
in "smart surroundings" at his family-run venture;
fans say "it's a very close second to Outlaw's!"
/ **Details:** www.thediningroomrock.co.uk; 9 pm; closed
Mon, Tue, Wed L, Thu L, Fri L, Sat L & Sun L; no Amex;
children: 10+.

Restaurant Nathan Outlaw
The St Enodoc Hotel   **£ 123** ❶❶❷
Rock Rd PL27 6LA   (01208) 863394
"The finest fish restaurant in the UK", according to
this year's survey – Nathan Outlaw takes "zingingly
fresh" seafood and treats it "with respect and
intelligence", to create "simple, yet beautifully
crafted" dishes; the interior is a touch "anodyne",
but the views of the Camel estuary are "fabulous".
/ **Details:** www.nathan-outlaw.co.uk; 9 pm; D only,
closed Mon & Sun; no Amex; no shorts; Essential;
children: 12+ D. **Accommodation:** 20 rooms,
from £130.

ROCKBEARE, DEVON   1–3D

Jack in the Green Inn   **£ 48**   ❸❷❸
London Rd EX5 2EE   (01404) 822240
"What a gastropub should be", offering "delicious
food" and an "unhurried, relaxed atmosphere".
/ **Details:** www.jackinthegreen.uk.com;
@JackGreenInn; On the old A30, 3 miles east of
junction 29 of M5; 9.30 pm, Sun 9 pm; no Amex.

ROMALDKIRK, COUNTY DURHAM   8–3B

The Rose & Crown   **£ 40**   ❷❷❶
DL12 9EB   (01833) 650213
A "lovely well-appointed inn, with very comfortable
accommodation, set in a delightful village in the
heart of the English countryside"; "seriously good"
food and "super-willing service" complete its winning
formula. / **Details:** www.rose-and-crown.co.uk; 6m
NW of Barnard Castle on B6277; 9 pm; D only, ex Sun
open L & D; children: 7+ in restaurant.
Accommodation: 14 rooms, from £150.

ROSEVINE, CORNWALL   1–4B

Driftwood Hotel   **£ 70**   ❶❷❷
TR2 5EW   (01872) 580644
This cliff-top hotel dining room not only offers
spectacular views, but "wonderful" food made with
local produce to provide a supremely "relaxed and
enjoyable experience".
/ **Details:** www.driftwoodhotel.co.uk; off the A30 to

Truro, towards St Mawes; 9.30 pm; D only; booking: max 6; children: 10+. **Accommodation:** 15 rooms, from £170.

ROWDE, WILTSHIRE   2–2C

The George & Dragon   £ 43 ❸❷❷
High St SN10 2PN   (01380) 723053
"A lovely pub dining room, with an emphasis on fresh fish" – something of a "surprise find", in the middle of nowhere, and offering a "great welcome" too. / **Details:** www.thegeorganddragonrowde.co.uk; @_thegandd; on A342 between Devizes & Chippenham; 10 pm; closed Sun D; no Amex. **Accommodation:** 3 rooms, from £65.

ROWHOOK, WEST SUSSEX   3–4A

Chequers Inn   £ 48 ❸❷❷
RH12 3PY   (01403) 790480
"A cut above the other gastropubs on the Surrey/Sussex border"; in a "lovely" old cottage "tucked away in a quiet location", this is a "charming" and "unpretentious" sort of spot with "well-cooked, straightforward food". / **Details:** www.chequersrowhook.com; 9 pm; closed Sun D; no Amex.

ROWSLEY, DERBYSHIRE   5–2C

The Peacock   £ 73 ❶❶❷
Bakewell Rd DE4 2EB   (01629) 733518
A "high class" of cooking that's "unexpectedly good" wins top marks for this "charming and historic" inn, which has "exceptional staff to boot"; some nights see the service only of a simple bar menu, but it's "still good". / **Details:** www.thepeacockatrowsley.com; 9 pm, Sun 8.30 pm; children: 10+ at D. **Accommodation:** 15 rooms, from £160.

RYE, EAST SUSSEX   3–4C

The Ambrette at Rye   £ 41 ❶④④
24 High St TN31 7JF   (01797) 222 043
"A perfect mix of Indian fine dining and local produce" (like rabbit or venison) underscores the "subtle" and "refreshing" approach at this "outstanding" venture, on the south coast; service can be "slow" however, and the room is "a little soulless". / **Details:** www.theambrette.co.uk; @the_ambrette; L only; closed Mon.

Landgate Bistro   £ 44 ❷❷④
5-6 Landgate TN31 7LH   (01797) 222829
This "low-key" but well-known stalwart bistro has earned a very "loyal local following" with its "first-class" fare, "cooked by a truly independent-minded chef"; it's also praised for the "best front of house for miles around". / **Details:** www.landgatebistro.co.uk; 9 pm Sat 9.15 pm; closed Mon, Tue, Wed L, Thu L, Fri L & Sun D; no Amex.

Mermaid   £ 53 ❸❸❷
Mermaid St TN31 7EY   (01797) 223065
You won't find a setting much more "historic" than this old smugglers' inn (which has quite a grand dining room); the food has always seemed a bit incidental, but most recent reports have been very positive; "good ales" too. / **Details:** www.mermaidinn.com; 9.30 pm; no jeans. **Accommodation:** 31 rooms, from £150.

Tuscan Kitchen   £ 48 ❷❷❸
8 Lion St TN31 7LB   (01797) 223269
"Don't tell anyone as bookings for this peerless restaurant are hard to come by!"; with its "decent, meat-focussed Tuscan fare", this "busy" but "helpful" establishment is a real hit (practically) all those who comment on it. / **Details:** www.tuscankitchenrye.co.uk; 11.30 pm; closed Mon, Tue, Wed L & Sat L.

**Webbe's at The
Fish Cafe   £ 43 ❷❸❸**
17 Tower St TN31 7AT   (01797) 222226
"Just the thing for a coastal town – a truly good fish restaurant"; Paul Webb's town-centre venture may have a "limited menu", but "it's well worth it, for what you get", and the scallop tasting menu, in particular, is "excellent"; service, though, is occasionally a bit "haphazard". / **Details:** www.thefishcafe.com; @webbesrye; 9.30 pm.

SALFORD, GREATER MANCHESTER   5–2B

Damson   £ 57 ❷❷❸
Orange Building, Media City UK M50 2HF
(0161) 751 7020
"A real find"; this first-floor newcomer near Media City makes an ideal business rendezvous thanks to its "calming" and "spacious" decor and its "beautifully presented" cuisine. / **Details:** www.damsonrestaurant.co.uk; Mon-Thu 9.30pm Fri & Sat 10pm; closed Mon L, Tue L, Wed L, Thu L, Sat L & Sun D.

SALISBURY, WILTSHIRE   2–3C

Anokaa   £ 41 ❶❷❸
60 Fisherton St SP2 7RB   (01722) 414142
Despite its "uninviting high street location", this "proper upmarket Indian" inspires rave reviews for its "delicate" and "flavoursome" cuisine; some dishes have "western influences"… but "fear not ye dyed-in-the-wool Indophiles, the classics are in there too!" / **Details:** www.anokaa.com; @eatatanokaa; 10.30 pm; no shorts.

Jade   £ 36 ❷❸④
109a Exeter St SP1 2SF   (01722) 333355
"Have yet to find a better Chinese in these parts"; the "very well-prepared" dishes ("sea bass and lobster are especially good") at this long-running Cantonese continue to score high praise; the wine

list, though, "could do with an update".
/ **Details:** www.jaderestaurant.co.uk; 11.30 pm; closed Sun; no Amex.

SALTAIRE, WEST YORKSHIRE   5–1C

Salts Diner   **£ 33**   ❸❷❷
Salts Mill, Victoria Rd   BD18 3LA
(01274) 531163
An "ideal place for a good meal after an absorbing intellectual session in the galleries"; this restaurant in a "wonderful old mill" (a UNESCO World Heritage site) serves some "excellent" food… but "oh, if only they could do something about the noise!" / **Details:** www.saltsmill.org.uk; 2m from Bradford on A650; L & afternoon tea only; no Amex.

SALTHOUSE, NORFOLK   6–3C

Cookies Crab Shop   **£ 21**   ❷❺❸
The Grn, Coast Rd   NR25 7AJ   (01263) 740352
A "strange, quirky, olde-worlde" '50s hang-over – diners have been known to "get dripped on" when it rains, and service can be "grumpy" too; however, the food – with seafood salads the highlight – is "brilliant" and "great value" too.
/ **Details:** www.salthouse.org.uk; on A149; 7 pm; no credit cards.

SANCTON, EAST YORKSHIRE   8–

Star   **£ 42**   ❸❸❹
King St   YO43 4QP   (01430) 827269
An "upmarket dining pub", praised by most (if not quite all) reporters for its "consistent quality and good value" – "just the place for a celebratory lunch, a quiet dinner-à-deux, or a quick bar meal and a pint brewed in their own microbrewery".
/ **Details:** www.thestarsancton.co.uk; Tue-Sat 9.30pm Sun 8pm; closed Mon.

SANDSEND, NORTH YORKSHIRE   8–3D

Estbek House   **£ 58**   ❷❷❷
East Row   YO21 3SU   (01947) 893424
An "excellent restaurant-with-rooms, right on the front" specialising in fresh fish "cooked precisely and imaginatively", and with "outstandingly helpful" service; a catch? – even ardent fans can find it a little "complacent and unchanging".
/ **Details:** www.estbekhouse.co.uk; 9 pm; D only; no Amex. **Accommodation:** 5 rooms, from £125.

SAPPERTON, GLOUCESTERSHIRE   2–2C

The Bell at Sapperton   **£ 48**   ❷❷❷
GL7 6LE   (01285) 760298
A "friendly" Cotswold gastropub that attracts consistent praise for its "good simple food" (with "quirky and exciting puddings" a highlight).
/ **Details:** www.foodatthebell.co.uk; from Cirencester take the A419 towards Stroud, turn right to Sapperton; 9 pm, Fri & Sat 9.30 pm, Sun 7.30 pm; no Amex.

SAWLEY, LANCASHIRE   5–1B

The Spread Eagle   **£ 46**   ❼
BB7 4NH   (01200) 441202
"Gets a bit busy, but well worth the wait" – this Ribble Valley coaching inn is tipped for the quality of its "wide-ranging menu from pub grub through excellent specials".
/ **Details:** www.spreadeaglesawley.co.uk; 9.15 pm, Sun 7.15 pm. **Accommodation:** 7 rooms, from £80.

SCARBOROUGH, NORTH YORKSHIRE   8–4D

Lanterna   **£ 47**   ❷❷④
33 Queen St   YO11 1HQ   (01723) 363616
Pepped up by a recent refurbishment, this "well-run family restaurant" delivers "superb seafood" in an "Italian country-style"; both daily specials and seasonal menus rate mention.
/ **Details:** www.lanterna-ristorante.co.uk; 9.30 pm; D only, closed Sun; no Amex.

SEER GREEN, BEACONSFIELD , BUCKINGHAMSHIRE   3–3A

The Jolly Cricketers   **£ 51**   ❷❷❸
24 Chalfont Rd   HP9 2YG   (01494) 676308
This "lovely, relaxed" village pub is a solid all-rounder, offering "delicious" food, "superb wines" and "helpful staff"; "gorgeous" pudding a highlight.
/ **Details:** www.thejollycricketers.co.uk; @jollycricketers; 11.15 pm, Fri & Sat midnight; closed Sun D.

SENNEN COVE, CORNWALL   1–4A

Beach Restaurant   **£ 46**   ❷❷❷
TR19 7BT   (01736) 871191
"A light and airy glass and wood building on a cliff" is the vantage-point for "lovely views" over the harbour, beach and surfers at this seaside venue, whose menu "includes lots of seafood, but with something for everyone including kids"; beware "ferocious" enforcement of rules in the adjoining car park! / **Details:** www.thebeachrestaurant.com; @beachsennen; 9 pm; no Amex.

SEVENOAKS, KENT   3–3B

The Vine   **£ 50**   ④④❸
11 Pound Ln   TN13 3TB   (01732) 469510
The odd report of "slow service" and "sometimes disappointing food" notwithstanding, reporters are pretty clear that this is "the best Sevenoaks can offer"; the new conservatory extension has "improved the ambience" too.
/ **Details:** www.vinerestaurant.co.uk; 9.30 pm; closed Sun D; no Amex.

SHALDON, DEVON   I–3D

Ode   **£ 58   ❷❶❸**
Fore St TQ14 0DE   (01626) 873977
*"Tiny but full of enthusiasm" – this "lovely" spot "in
a quaint village" uses "only sustainable and organic
ingredients" to "excellent" effect; its offshoot Café
Ode, with sea-view, also gets the thumbs up.
/ Details: www.odetruefood.co.uk; 9.30 pm; D only,
closed Sun-Tue; booking essential; SRA-90%.*

SHALFORD, SURREY   3–3A

The Seahorse   **£ 44   ❸❷❸**
52-54 The St GU4 8BU   (01483) 514 351
*Just outside Guildford, a village inn offering "above-
average" food that's "well-presented"; it's an
"accommodating" sort of place too (including for
kids). / Details: www.theseahorseguildford.co.uk;
10 pm, Fri & Sat 10.30 pm, Sun 9 pm.*

SHEFFIELD, SOUTH YORKSHIRE   5–2C

Artisan   **£ 47   ❷❷❷**
32-34 Sandygate Rd S10 5RY   (0114) 266 6096
*Richard Smith's good-value "neighbourhood
restaurant" is praised in all reports for "quality
cooking"; just "make sure you leave room for pud!"
/ Details: www.artisansheffield.co.uk; 9.30 pm; closed
Mon L, Tue L, Wed L, Thu L & Sun D; no Amex.*

The Cricket Inn   **£ 46   ❶**
Penny Ln S17 3AZ   (0114) 236 5256
*"Whether eating inside or out", this popular local, by
a cricket pitch, is tipped for its "good pub grub and
cracking Sunday lunch".
/ Details: www.relaxeatanddrink.co.uk;
@cricketinnshef; Mon-Sat 9.30 pm, Sun 8 pm;
no Amex.*

The Milestone   **£ 45   ❸❸❸**
84 Green Lane At Ball St S3 8SE
(0114) 272 8327
*"It's worth hopping on the tram" to get to this
"buzzy" gastropub "in a formerly industrial area",
say fans of this "sensibly straightforward and good-
value" spot. / Details: www.the-milestone.co.uk;
@TheMilestone; Mon-Sat 10 pm, Sun 9 pm; no Amex.*

Moran's   **£ 49   ❷❸④**
289 Abbeydale Road South S17 3LB
(0114) 235 0101
*"A bit out of town but well worth the trip", this
Abbeydale spot is often "buzzing" – the attraction?
– food (especially steak) that's "more-than-
reasonably priced", and served by "welcoming" staff
too. / Details: www.moranssheffield.co.uk; 9 pm;
closed Mon, Tue-Fri L & Sun D; no Amex.*

Nonna's   **£ 46   ❷❷④**
535-541 Eccleshall Rd S11 8PR
(0114) 268 6166
*Always "buzzing", this "trendy" Eccleshall Italian
impresses practically all reporters with "incredibly*

generous" portions of "beautifully thought out" and
"authentic" fare (including "some dishes you don't
often see"). / **Details:** www.nonnas.co.uk;
@NonnasCucina; 9.30 pm, Sat & Sun 9.45 pm;
no Amex.

Nosh   **£ 10   ❶❷④**
69 Division St S1 4GE   (0114) 272 8951
*"It looks like a transport caff down an alley", but
this "backstreet noodle bar" dishes up "fabulous
value" and "excellent, hot, generous food"; "for the
price and quality, you don't expect too much service
or ambience"; BYO. / Details: noshretail.co.uk; 6 pm,
Sun 5 pm; L only; no Amex.*

The Old Vicarage   **£ 86   ④⑤④**
Ridgeway Moor, Ridgeway S12 3XW
(0114) 247 5814
*If it hadn't long held a Michelin star, we'd probably
pass over this "pricey" stalwart; given the accolade,
though, it's worth recording how strongly the
(modest) feedback it inspires suggests it's decidedly
"resting on its laurels".
/ Details: www.theoldvicarage.co.uk; 9.30 pm; closed
Mon, Sat L & Sun; no Amex.*

Rafters   **£ 55   ❸❸④**
220 Oakbrook Rd, Nether Grn S11 7ED
(0114) 230 4819
*This "cosy" and "intimate" Ranmoor staple "never
fails to please", offering "quality food at reasonable
prices" (not least "black pudding to die for").
/ Details: www.raftersrestaurant.co.uk; 10 pm; D only,
closed Tue & Sun.*

Silversmiths   **£ 36   ❶**
111 Arundel St S1 2NT   (0114) 270 6160
*Varied reports on a lively bar/restaurant in the city-
centre's 'Cultural Quarter' tipped for its "improved"
standards in recent times, and its "pre-theatre good
value in particular"; "with a bit more polish, it could
be a real gem!"
/ Details: www.silversmiths-restaurant.com;
@Silversmiths; 11.30 pm, Fri & Sat midnight; D only,
closed Mon & Sun; no Amex.*

SHEFFORD, BEDFORDSHIRE   3–1A

Black Horse at Ireland **£ 48   ❶**
Ireland SG17 5QL   (01462) 811398
*A "recently refurbished" former pub with a "lovely"
conservatory dining area tipped for its "well
executed", "beautifully presented" cooking; one or
two regulars, however, feel "standards have dropped
in the last few years".
/ Details: www.blackhorseireland.com; 9.30 pm, Fri &
Sat 10 pm; closed Sun D. Accommodation: 2 rooms,
from £55.*

SHELLEY, WEST YORKSHIRE   5–2C

Three Acres   **£ 56   ❸❸❸**
Roydhouse HD8 8LR   (01484) 602606
Out on the moors, this long-established inn remains

a "deservedly popular" destination, thanks to its "wonderful" cooking; even fans note that "it's becoming a bit expensive" however, and the odd critic feels its decor in particular "needs a refresh".
/ **Details:** *www.3acres.com; 9.30 pm; no Amex.*
Accommodation: *16 rooms, from £125.*

SHENLEY, HERTFORDSHIRE   3–

White Horse   **£ 46** ❷❷❸
37 London Rd WD7 9ER   (01923) 853054
"Really very good pub food in very comfortable dining rooms with incredibly attentive service" – this large gastropub inspires lots of reports, and almost all of them are consistently very positive.
/ **Details:** *www.whitehorseradlett.co.uk; 10 pm, Sat 10.30 pm.*

SHERBORNE, DORSET   2–3B

The Green   **£ 51** ❷❸❸
The Green DT9 3HY   (01935) 813821
"Still the best in Sherborne and its environs"; this informal restaurant offers cooking with "real wow-factor" – and it's only on the up since a recent change of management.
/ **Details:** *www.greenrestaurant.co.uk; @greensherborne; 9 pm; closed Mon & Sun.*

SHERE, SURREY   3–3A

Kinghams   **£ 50** ❸❸❸
Gomshall Ln GU5 9HE   (01483) 202168
This "lovely cottage" in a "fairytale village" has a set-up that's as "old-fashioned" as it sounds, but all reports concur that it's a "reliable" and "welcoming" destination with "sensible" prices.
/ **Details:** *www.kinghams-restaurant.co.uk; off A25 between Dorking & Guildford; 9 pm; closed Mon & Sun D.*

The William Bray   **£ 50** ❸④❷
Shere Ln GU5 9HS   (01483) 202 044
A posh venture in a historic pub, with a "contemporary feel" and serving "very good" food that's "reasonably-priced by stockbroker belt standards"; service, though, can sometimes be "slow". / **Details:** *www.thewilliambray.co.uk; 10 pm; no Amex.*

SHINFIELD, BERKSHIRE   2–2D

L'Ortolan   **£ 96** ❸❷❸
Church Ln RG2 9BY   (0118) 988 8500
"Brilliant" cooking is all part of the formula that makes dining at Alan Murcheson's "stylish" former rectory a "real treat", say most reporters; the minority which finds the whole approach "pretentious", though, never quite goes away.
/ **Details:** *www.lortolan.com; @lortolan; 8.30 pm; closed Mon & Sun.*

SHIPBOURNE, KENT   3–3B

The Chaser Inn   **£ 43** ❸❸❷
Stumble Hill TN11 9PE   (01732) 810360
"Does it say on the tin and then some!"; this "lovely" country inn pleases almost all reporters with its "fresh pub grub" in general, and "fabulous" weekend breakfasts in particular.
/ **Details:** *www.thechaser.co.uk; 9.30 pm, Sun 9 pm.*

SHIPLAKE, OXFORDSHIRE   2–2D

Orwells   **£ 56** ❷❸❸
Shiplake Row RG9 4DP   (0118) 940 3673
Out in the "lush countryside" of the Thames Valley, a "consistently good" and "imaginative" restaurant in a "delightful old building"; it's particularly worth seeking out for its "amazing-value set lunch".
/ **Details:** *www.orwellsatshiplake.co.uk; 9.30 pm; closed Mon & Sun D, except open on Bank Hols.*

SHIPLEY, WEST YORKSHIRE   5–1C

Aagrah   **£ 37** ❷❷❸
4 Saltaire Rd BD18 3HN   (01274) 530880
"Good Pakistani food at value-for-money prices" and staff who "really go the extra mile" – that's the "winning formula" of this "swish" HQ of a local chain which remains "as popular as ever"; the "amazing" variety of the upstairs buffet wins particular praise. / **Details:** *www.aagrah.com; 11.30 pm; closed Sat L.*

SHIRLEY, DERBYSHIRE   5–3C

The Saracen's Head   **£ 30** ❶
Church Ln DE6 3AS   (01335) 360 330
This "nicely arranged pub" (with a "pleasant area outdoors for summer") is tipped for "always reliable and occasionally outstanding" food – and in sufficient portions to "satisfy ravenous teenagers" too! / **Details:** *www.saracens-head-shirley.co.uk; 11 pm, Sun 10.30 pm; no Amex.*

SKENFRITH, MONMOUTHSHIRE   2–1B

The Bell at Skenfrith   **£ 51** ❷❸❷
NP7 8UH   (01600) 750235
"The setting alone is worth the trip", but this remote country inn also gains points for "creative food that draws on locally available produce" and an "intriguing cellar" too; all in all, "a great weekend getaway". / **Details:** *www.skenfrith.co.uk; on B4521, 10m E of Abergavenny; 9.30 pm, Sun 9 pm; no Amex; children: 8+ at D.* **Accommodation:** *11 rooms, from £110.*

SLEAT, HIGHLAND   9–2B

Kinloch Lodge   **£ 91** ❷❷❷
IV43 8QY   (01471) 833333
The "shades of Downton" setting provides a "wonderful" backdrop to a meal at the ancestral home of the Macdonald of Macdonald; it's not all

about faded baronial splendour though – chef Marcello Tully creates "brilliant dishes with a distinctive style". / **Details:** www.kinloch-lodge.co.uk; @kinloch_lodge; 9 pm; no Amex. **Accommodation:** 19 rooms, from £99.

SMALL HYTHE, KENT   3–4C

Swan English Restaurant £ 53   ④④❷
Tenterden Vineyard TN30 7NG
(01580) 761616
"Chapel Down winery already produces excellent wine but now it has its own restaurant too"; the food can be "average", but most reporters leave satisfied, aided by the "wonderful" location "overlooking the vineyard", and good "buzz". / **Details:** www.loveswan.co.uk/chapeldawn; @swanchapeldown; 9.30 pm; closed Mon D, Tue D, Wed D & Sun D.

SNAPE, SUFFOLK   3–1D

The Crown Inn   £ 39   ❷④❸
Bridge Rd IP17 1SL   (01728) 688324
"A good choice if you are visiting the Maltings"… this typical Suffolk pub is recommended for use of "fresh and very local produce" ("some home-grown"), and "gorgeous lobster" too. / **Details:** www.snape-crown.co.uk; off A12 towards Aldeburgh; 9.30 pm, Sat 10 pm, Sun 9.30 pm; no Amex. **Accommodation:** 2 rooms, from £90.

SONNING-ON-THAMES, BERKSHIRE   2–2D

The Bull Inn   £ 53   ❼
High St RG4 6UP   (0118) 969 3901
A "picturesque" inn, "name-checked in 'Three Men in a Boat'", though actually a short walk uphill from the river, tipped for "hearty food", "great real ale" and a "good-value wine list". / **Details:** www.bullinnsonning.co.uk; off A4, J10 between Oxford & Windsor; 9.30 pm. **Accommodation:** 7 rooms, from £110.

The French Horn   £ 82   ❷④❶
RG4 6TN   (0118) 969 2204
"Calm, gracious, reassuringly expensive and consistently excellent" – the imperishable charms of this grand and traditional Thames-sider are a fixed point in a changing world, as is the "extensive" wine list… which even includes some options described as "sensibly-priced"! / **Details:** www.thefrenchhorn.co.uk; 9.30 pm; booking: max 10. **Accommodation:** 21 rooms, from £160.

SOUTH SHIELDS, TYNE AND WEAR   8–2B

Colmans   £ 33   ❷❷❸
182-186 Ocean Rd NE33 2JQ
(0191) 456 1202
"Still the best for quality of both fish and chips on Tyneside!" – this "classic" large-scale chippy (est 1926) is deemed "expensive but worth it" by almost all who comment on it.

/ **Details:** www.colmansfishandchips.com; L only; no Amex; SRA-70%.

SOUTHAMPTON, HAMPSHIRE   2–3D

Coriander Lounge   £ 34   ❼
130-131 High St SO14 2BR   (02380) 710888
In this under-provided city, an high street Indian tipped for "really tasty" food, and "very friendly" service too. / **Details:** www.corianderlounge.com; 11pm, Sun 10pm; booking essential on weekends.

Kuti's   £ 32   ❸❸④
37-39 Oxford St SO14 3DP   (023) 8022 1585
Part of a small Hampshire chain, this "upmarket Indian" has won plenty of local support, thanks to a "varied menu" that's "conventional, but always delivers"; "go hungry to take full advantage!" / **Details:** www.kutis.co.uk; 11.30 pm.

SOUTHPORT, MERSEYSIDE   5–1A

Bistrot Vérité   £ 42   ❷❷❸
7 Liverpool Rd PR8 4AR   (01704) 564 199
"A buzzy little French bistro", in Birkdale Village; all reports confirm its "authentic" charms, so it's not surprising that it can get "very busy". / **Details:** www.bistrotverite.co.uk.

The Vincent Hotel   £ 41   ❷❸❷
98 Lord St PR8 1JR   (01704) 883800
A "trendy, modern hotel", which serves up a "variety of dishes from sushi to Italian"; a "great venue for people-watching" too. / **Details:** www.thevincenthotel.com; 10 pm. **Accommodation:** 60 rooms, from £93.

SOUTHROP, GLOUCESTERSHIRE   2–2C

The Swan at Southrop   £ 50   ④④❸
GL7 3NU   (01367) 850205
"It has a really pretty, perfect pub interior", but views still diverge on this prominent Cotswold gastroboozer, which changed hands last year; on most accounts, however, "the new owners are now getting the hang of it". / **Details:** www.theswanatsouthrop.co.uk; 10 pm; closed Sun D; no Amex.

SOUTHSEA, HAMPSHIRE   2–4D

Garage Lounge   £ 30   ❸❸❷
1 Albert Rd PO5 2SP   (023) 9282 8432
"Southsea's popular retro coffee shop", in an "old garage", serving "tea, coffee, cakes and substantial snacks"; its "cool" charms make it a "favourite" for some reporters, even though there's "no booze". / **Details:** @garagelounge1; 11 pm.

SOUTHWOLD, SUFFOLK   3–1D

The Crown
Adnams Hotel   £ 54   ④④❷
90 High St IP18 6DP   (01502) 722275

"When it's good, it's very very good", but this famous Adnams pub has somewhat "lost its way"; it still has a brilliant atmosphere and "top notch wines", but "the food rarely shines" nowadays, and for it you pay "London prices".
/ **Details:** www.adnams.co.uk/stay-with-us/the-crown; 9 pm; no Amex. **Accommodation:** 14 rooms, from £160.

Sole Bay Fish Company £26 ❶❷❸
22e Blackshore IP18 6ND (01502) 724241
"A gem at the harbour", offering "wonderful crustacea and all things fishy, mostly cold" – don't forget to take your own bread and wine; "if it's raining, avoid the leaks – it's all part of the fun!"
/ **Details:** www.solebayfishco.co.uk; closed Mon.

Sutherland House £52 ❷❷❷
56 High St IP18 6DN (01502) 724544
"Delightful service, lovely seafood, very accommodating…" – a typical report from the Banks family's "quaint and comfortable" restaurant in this cute seaside town.
/ **Details:** www.sutherlandhouse.co.uk; @SH_Southwold; 9.30 pm; closed Mon (winter). **Accommodation:** 3 rooms, from £150.

The Swan £52 ❹❹❸
The Market Pl IP18 6EG (01502) 722186
This "ever-popular, classy hotel owned by Adnams brewery" serves "generally sound" food in a "comfortable", rather "traditional" style; critics, though, feel that it's somewhat "overhyped" nowadays, and that its whole approach needs an overhaul.
/ **Details:** www.adnams.co.uk/stay-with-us/the-swan; @swansouthwold; 9 pm; no Amex; no jeans or trainers; children: 5+ at D. **Accommodation:** 42 rooms, from £185.

SPARSHOLT, HAMPSHIRE   2–3D

The Plough Inn £45 ❸❸❸
SO21 2NW (01962) 776353
"A perfect place for this inn crowd!" (geddit) – this "reliable" boozer is a consistent crowd-pleaser, offering "good basic home cooking".
/ **Details:** www.theploughsparsholt.co.uk; 9 pm, Sun & Mon 8.30 pm, Fri & Sat 9.30 pm; no Amex.

SPEEN, BUCKINGHAMSHIRE   3–2A

The Old Plow £63 ❷❷❸
Flowers Bottom Ln HP27 0PZ
(01494) 488300
Critics may find the interior a little "dated", but there's no doubt that this "well-hidden" inn offers some "excellent" dishes (especially fish), using the "very best ingredients".
/ **Details:** www.yeoldplow.co.uk; 20 mins from M40, J4 towards Princes Risborough; 9 pm; closed Mon & Sun.

SPELDHURST, KENT   3–4B

George & Dragon £45 ❸❸❷
Speldhurst Hill TN3 0NN (01892) 863125
"A lovely old pub", where the food – much of which is "locally sourced" – ranges from "good" to "excellent". / **Details:** www.speldhurst.com; @GDSpeldhurst; 9.30 pm; closed Sun D; no Amex.

ST ALBANS, HERTFORDSHIRE   3–2A

Barrissimo £14 ❸❷❷
28 St Peters St AL1 3NA (01727) 869999
This "lively" café offers "excellent coffee and snacks" (especially the "delicious panini"); fans also appreciate the "friendly management" and "nice background jazz". / **Details:** 5.30 pm, Sun 4 pm; L only; no credit cards.

Darcy's £52 ❸❸❸
2 Hatfield Rd AL1 3RP (01727) 730777
"Welcoming, busy and consistent", this local fixture offers some quite "inventive" dishes in a "handy" central location, and is a "staple" for those with kids in tow; it also gives rise to the odd "very average" report, however.
/ **Details:** www.darcysrestaurant.co.uk; 9 pm, Fri & Sat 10 pm.

Lussmanns £43 ❷❷❸
Waxhouse Gate, High St AL3 4EW
(01727) 851941
Although it shares an aesthetic with "Prezzo/Café Rouge-type places", this "fab, family-run fish restaurant" by the abbey stays "a cut above" the competition thanks to a "varied and imaginative" menu. / **Details:** www.lussmanns.com; @andreilussmanns; 10 pm, Fri & Sat 10.30 pm, Sun 9 pm; SRA-72%.

St Michael's Manor £53 ❹❸❶
Fishpool St AL3 4RY (01727) 864444
In its "delightful riverside setting" (and "with lovely grounds to enjoy in good weather"), this hotel dining room is a consistently popular destination… even if the food is "agreeable, rather than memorable".
/ **Details:** www.stmichaelsmanor.com; near the Cathedral; 9 pm. **Accommodation:** 30 rooms, from £130.

The Waffle House
Kingsbury Water Mill £26 ❹❹❷
St Michael's St AL3 4SJ (01727) 853502
From the "fantastic breakfast choice" to the constantly-changing "sweet and savoury menus", this local institution – in a "beautiful" old watermill – continues to please; diverge from the basic waffle, though, and "add-ons make this an expensive experience". / **Details:** www.wafflehouse.co.uk; 6 pm; L only; no Amex; no booking.

ST ANDREWS, FIFE   9–3D

The Doll's House
Restaurant   **£ 42 ❸❷❷**
3 Church Sq KY16 9NN (01334) 477422
*"For over 20 years this unpretentious spot has
consistently offered freshly-cooked food to a high
standard"; even a reporter who says it's "not the
best restaurant in town" notes that "it is the best
value". / **Details:** www.dolls-house.co.uk.*

Seafood Restaurant   **£ 68 ❷❹❷**
The Scores, Bruce Embankment KY16 9AB
(01334) 479475
*"Super-fresh seafood in a stunning glass-sided cube,
with wonderful views of the Firth of Forth" – that's
the deal that makes this "futuristic" venture a
"delightful" experience for all who comment on it.
/ **Details:** www.theseafoodrestaurant.com; 10 pm;
children: 12+ at D.*

Vine Leaf   **£ 46 ❶**
131 South St KY16 9UN (01334) 477497
*"You have to find it first", but loyal fans say "you've
entered another world" when you visit this cute,
long-established bistro, tipped for its "good
selection" of dishes.
/ **Details:** www.vineleafstandrews.co.uk; 9.30 pm;
D only, closed Mon & Sun.*

ST AUSTELL, CORNWALL   1–4B

Austells   **£ 41 ❶❶❷**
10 Beach Rd PL25 3PH (01726) 813888
*"A wonderful place, with terrific food"; Brett
Camborne-Paynter's "marvellous" restaurant,
deserves wider acclaim – service is "attentive and
friendly", the cooking is "fabulous (especially the
local fish)", and "the open-plan kitchen provides
theatre". / **Details:** www.austells.co.uk; Tue-Sun 10pm;
closed Mon.*

ST DAVIDS, PEMBROKESHIRE   4–4A

Cwtch   **£ 45 ❷❷❷**
22 High St SA62 6SD (01437) 720491
*The "best restaurant in St Davids"; locals have
already cottoned on to this "up and coming" town-
centre bistro, where "wonderful local fish" is cooked
with aplomb by chef Andy Holcroft.
/ **Details:** www.cwtchrestaurant.co.uk; 9.30 pm; D only.*

Warpool Court
Warpool Court Hotel   **£ 50 ❶**
SA62 6BN (01437) 720300
*Mark Napper has returned to the stoves of this
charmingly located seaside hotel three decades into
a career which has given him wide experience
elsewhere; the relaunched dining room is already
being tipped for the quality of its cuisine.
/ **Details:** www.warpoolcourthotel.com; 9 pm; D only.
Accommodation: 22 rooms, from £140.*

ST IVES, CORNWALL   1–4A

Alba Restaurant   **£ 42 ❷❷❷**
The Old Life Boat Hs, Wharf Rd TR26 1LF
(01736) 797222
*"Superb fresh fish" (especially the "exceptional crab
linguini") is the highlight at this "comfortable and
classy restaurant", and it offers "amazing harbour
views" too, if you get a table at the front; only
quibble? – "a slight tendency to over-complication".
/ **Details:** www.thealbarestaurant.com;
@albarestaurant; 10 pm; closed Mon L & Sun L.*

Alfresco   **£ 51 ❶❷❷**
Harbourside Wharf Rd TR26 1LF
(01736) 793737
*"Stunning food in a perfect location!"; the volume of
reports is not huge, but the consistency of feedback
on this "relaxed" and "friendly" harbour-side
seafood specialist is impressive.
/ **Details:** www.stivesharbour.com; on harbour front;
9.30 pm; no Amex.*

Porthgwidden Beach
Café   **£ 41 ❷❷❷**
Porthgwidden Beach TR26 1PL
(01736) 796791
*With its "great setting" overlooking a small beach,
this seaside café serves some "stunning food" –
particularly the "beautifully cooked fish" and
"fabulous" puddings; "they could be a little lighter
with the clotted cream, but this is Cornwall!"
/ **Details:** www.porthgwiddencafe.co.uk; 9.30 pm;
no Amex; booking: max 10.*

Porthmeor Beach Cafe   **£ 35 ❸❷❶**
Porthmeor Beach TR26 1JZ (01736) 793366
*An "unbeatable holiday food experience"… this
beach café near the Tate scores praise for its
"amazing views" and "well-priced dishes" for
breakfast, lunch, dinner or a light snack.
/ **Details:** www.porthmeor-beach.co.uk; 9 pm; D only.
Closed Nov-Mar.; no Amex.*

Porthminster Café   **£ 48 ❷❷❶**
Porthminster Beach TR26 2EB
(01736) 795352
*"Interesting and different seafood variations, served
in a setting to die for" – this famous beachside
restaurant is, for its many fans, a destination "to
dream about"; the odd critic, however, is beginning
to fret that the "perfect" location is seen as just "a
licence to print money".
/ **Details:** www.porthminstercafe.co.uk; 10 pm;
no Amex.*

The Seafood Café   **£ 38 ❷❷❸**
45 Fore St TR26 1HE (01736) 794004
*"A good concept" – you choose your fish at the
counter, along with how you want it prepared at this
clean and bright operation – an "uncomplicated"
but "always reliable" formula.
/ **Details:** www.seafoodcafe.co.uk; 10.30 pm; no Amex.*

Seagrass **£ 42** 🅣
Fish St TR26 1LT   (01736) 793763
A harbour-view restaurant, strongly tipped for the "fabulous" results from its "interesting" menu; more reports please. / Details: www.seagrass-stives.com/; 10 pm; no Amex.

Tate Cafe
Tate Gallery **£ 34** 🅣
Porthmeor Beach TR26 1TG   (01736) 796226
Tipped for its "wonderful location, perched overlooking the town and beaches", the contemporary art gallery's top-floor café offers a "good range of light lunches", and "delicious coffee". / Details: www.tate.org.uk; L only; no Amex.

ST LEONARDS-ON-SEA, EAST SUSSEX   3–4C

St Clement's **£ 46** ❷❸❸
3 Mercatoria TN38 0EB   (01424) 200355
"As Jay Rayner said, everyone deserves a local like this"; a "long-term favourite" (and not just of celebrity scribes), Nick Hales's "lovely little" place has an accent on "interesting seafood and fish". / Details: www.stclementsrestaurant.co.uk; 9 pm; closed Mon, Tue & Sun D; no Amex.

ST MAWES, CORNWALL   1–4B

Hotel Tresanton **£ 63** ❷❶❶
27 Lower Castle Rd TR2 5DR
(01326) 270055
"Fantastic views over St Mawes" help make Olga Polizzi's fashionable hotel "one of the most romantic locations in the UK", "especially if you can get out on the terrace"; the food is "fine and elegant" too, albeit not much of a bargain. / Details: www.tresanton.com; 9.30 pm; booking: max 10; children: 6+ at dinner. Accommodation: 31 rooms, from £245.

ST MERRYN, CORNWALL   1–3B

The Cornish Arms **£ 36** ❷❸❸
Churchtown PL28 8ND   (01841) 520288
A perfect holiday pub ("avoid the obvious busy periods when it gets too crowded") – Rick Stein's inn may serve a "predictable" menu, but the "simple" fare (mussels, crab salad) is of very "high quality", service is "delightful" and it has a "great, casual atmosphere". / Details: 8.30 pm; no Amex.

ST MONANS, FIFE   9–4D

Craig Millar @ 16
West End **£ 60** ❷❷❶
16 West End KY10 2BX   (01333) 730327
"Accomplished cooking which sees Fife's wonderful larder utilised superbly" wins all-round praise for this "beautifully situated fine dining restaurant", "right on the harbour". / Details: www.16westend.com; 9 pm; closed Mon & Tue; children: 5+.

STADHAMPTON, OXFORDSHIRE   2–2D

The Crazy Bear **£ 57** ❸❷❶
Bear Ln OX44 7UR   (01865) 890714
Let's be honest, it's the "wacky" interior which makes this "exotic" institution "unforgettable", but a visit to this "crazy" Anglo/Thai establishment (one dining room for each) still generally pleases overall. / Details: www.crazybeargroup.co.uk; 10 pm; children: Not D FRi, Sat. Accommodation: 17 rooms, from £180.

STAMFORD, LINCOLNSHIRE   6–4A

The George Hotel **£ 68** ❸❷❶
71 St Martins PE9 2LB   (01780) 750750
This vast, "historic" coaching inn pleases traditionalists with its "silver service from venerable, heavyweight trolleys" bearing "the rib of beef of olde England and good wines"; the fare can seem a touch "bland and formulaic", though, and some prefer the "less pricey" Garden Room, or courtyard in summer. / Details: www.georgehotelofstamford.com; 10 pm; jacket and/or tie; children: 8+ at D. Accommodation: 47 rooms, from £125.

STANLEY, PERTHSHIRE   9–3C

The Apron Stage **£ 42** ❶❷❸
5 King St PH1 4ND   (01738) 828888
"A hidden countryside gem"; this "converted front room of a terraced house" may be "tiny" (and "cramped"), but it has a "big reputation" locally for cuisine "to give the big names a run for their money" – "very popular with the locals, so book well in advance". / Details: www.apronstagerestaurant.co.uk; 9.30 pm; D only, closed Mon–Wed & Sun; children: 12+.

STANTON, SUFFOLK   3–1C

Leaping Hare Vineyard **£ 44** ❷❸❸
Wyken Vineyards IP31 2DW   (01359) 250287
"Super local vinos and bubbly" are evidently the highpoint at this "beautifully converted" barn, but it's a "terrific hit" all-round, thanks to its "wonderful style" ("very Martha Stewart, but great for romance") and "imaginatively cooked", "locally sourced" fare. / Details: www.wykenvineyards.co.uk; 9m NE of Bury St Edmunds; follow tourist signs off A143; 5.30 pm, Fri & Sat 9 pm; L only, ex Fri & Sat open L & D; SRA-74%.

STATHERN, LEICESTERSHIRE   5–3D

Red Lion Inn **£ 37** ❷❷❸
2 Red Lion St LE14 4HS   (01949) 860868
With "spartan and unpretentious surroundings", this "fantastic traditional pub" near Belvoir Castle attracts less press than the Olive Branch, its Clipsham sibling; that's a shame, as – with its "great foodie ideas" and "excellent-value" set deals – it just

"seems to get better and better".
/ **Details:** *www.theredlioninn.co.uk; 9.30 pm; closed Sun D; no Amex.*

STOCKBRIDGE, HAMPSHIRE   2–3D

Clos du Marquis   **£ 52** ❷❷❸
London Rd SO20 6DE   (01264) 810738
A *"very good country restaurant serving genuine French fare"*, to which diners feel they could *"happily return again and again"*; slight reservation – the odd reporter feels that the decor *"could use a makeover"*. / **Details:** *www.closdumarquis.co.uk; 2m E on A30 from Stockbridge; 9 pm; closed Mon & Sun D.*

Greyhound   **£ 56** ❷❷❸
31 High St SO20 6EY   (01264) 810833
The *"new management have flipped it from good to much better"*, says one of the fans of this notably *"reliable"* inn, where a *"classy"* menu that's *"strong on fish"* is served up by *"well-informed"* and *"attentive"* staff.
/ **Details:** *www.thegreyhoundonthetest.co.uk; 9 pm, Fri & Sat 9.30 pm, Sun 9 pm; booking: max 12.* **Accommodation:** *7 rooms, from £100.*

Thyme and Tides   **£ 31** ❸④④
The High St SO20 6HE   (01264) 81 01 01
"A café, deli and fishmonger rolled into one"; offbeat as it may sound, the locals say *"it does well on all three counts"*, not least its *"interesting"* dishes, and *"very good coffee"*.
/ **Details:** *thymeandtidesdeli.co.uk/; closed Mon; no Amex.*

STOCKCROSS, BERKSHIRE   2–2D

The Vineyard at
Stockcross   **£ 101** ❸❸❷
RG20 8JU   (01635) 528770
With *"over 300 wines by the glass!"* – the California-biased list is *"like no other in the world"* – oenophiles get very excited by a visit to Sir Peter Michael's *"professional"* contemporary-style operation; Daniel Galimiche's food – *"imaginative"* and *"delicious"* as it is – has to work hard to keep up! / **Details:** *www.the-vineyard.co.uk; from M4, J13 take a34 towards Hungerford; 9.30 pm; no jeans or trainers.* **Accommodation:** *49 rooms, from £190.*

STOCKPORT, LANCASHIRE   5–2B

Damson   **£ 53** ❷❷❷
113 Heaton Moor Rd SK4 4HY
(0161) 4324666
This ambitious suburban (Heaton Moor) gem is the epitome of a *"very good neighbourhood restaurant"*, winning consistently high ratings for its quality cooking and stylish interior; its new spin-off in the Salford Media City is likewise highly praised (see also). / **Details:** *www.damsonrestaurant.co.uk; 9.30 pm, Fri & Sat 10 pm; closed Mon L & Sun D.*

STOKE HOLY CROSS, NORFOLK   6–4C

The Wildebeest Arms   **£ 47** ❸④④
82-86 Norwich Rd NR14 8QJ
(01508) 492497
This little village pub serves *"very impressive gastropub fare, especially for such an out-of-the-way place"*. / **Details:** *www.animalinns.co.uk; @wildebeestarms; from A140, turn left at Dunston Hall, left at T-junction; 9 pm.*

STOKE ROW, OXFORDSHIRE   2–2D

The Crooked Billet   **£ 54** ❶❷❷
Newlands Ln RG9 5PU   (01491) 681048
"Out of the way, but well worth the trip", this *"superb"* Chilterns pub-restaurant offers the complete package – an *"olde worlde atmosphere with very good food and wine without any fuss"*; indeed, the consistency of the positive feedback is impressive. / **Details:** *www.thecrookedbillet.co.uk; off the A4130; 10 pm, Sat 10.30 pm.*

STOKE-BY-NAYLAND, SUFFOLK   3–2C

The Crown   **£ 42** ❷❷❷
Park St CO6 4SE   (01206) 262346
"A rare treat in this very rural area"; the cooking at this *"perennial favourite"* may be *"superb"*, but it's the *"unbelievable"* wine list and *"walk-in fine wine store"* which really excite reporters; fortunately, it's also a *"great place to stay"*.
/ **Details:** *www.crowninn.net; @CrownInnSuffolk; on B1068; 9.30 pm, Fri & Sat 10 pm, Sun 9 pm.* **Accommodation:** *11 rooms, from £130.*

STONE IN OXNEY, KENT   3–4C

Crown   **£ 39** ❶
TN30 7JN   (01233) 758302
This village inn is tipped in part for its *"enthusiastic"* style; surprise menu star? – *"delicious, fresh pizzas"*. / **Details:** *9 pm; closed Mon & Sun D; no Amex; children: 12+ evening.*

STONOR, OXFORDSHIRE   2–2D

Quince Tree   **£ 43** ❷❸❷
RG9 6HE   (01491) 639039
"Pub, restaurant, café and deli" – this *"stylish"* and *"confident"* operation pleases all who comment on it, in particular as *"a lovely place for coffee and a cake, or a light lunch"*.
/ **Details:** *www.thequincetree.com/; 9.30 pm; closed Sun D.*

STOW ON THE WOLD,
GLOUCESTERSHIRE   2–1C

The Old Butchers   **£ 44**
Park St GL54 1AQ   (01451) 831700
This outfit in an old butcher's shop reopened in September 2013 and we haven"t, therefore, given it a rating; in the past it's been very consistent, so

*here's hoping that the owners' new venture – The Fox at Lower Oddington – doesn't take their eye off the ball. / **Details:** www.theoldbutchers.com; on the main road heading out of Stow on the Wold towards Oddington; 9.30 pm, Sat 10 pm; closed Mon & Sun; Max 12.*

STRACHUR, ARGYLL AND BUTE 9–4B

Inver Cottage Restaurant £46 ❶
Stracthlachlan PA27 8BU (01369) 860537
*"Miles from anywhere", and in a "lovely" setting too, beside Loch Fyne – a "good and consistent" restaurant, tipped for its "divine" seafood. / **Details:** www.invercottage.com; 8.30 pm; closed Mon & Tue; no Amex.*

STRATFORD UPON AVON, WARWICKSHIRE 2–1C

Lambs £45 ④❸❸
12 Sheep St CV37 6EF (01789) 292554
*"Straightforward", "useful", "predictable" – this "always reliable" stalwart (the most commented on place in town) has an attractive location, a formula which "suits pre-theatre dining", and staff who are "always willing to speed up service for curtain-up". / **Details:** www.lambsrestaurant.co.uk; @lambsrestaurant; 9.30 pm; closed Mon L & Tue L; no Amex.*

No. 9 £45 ❷❷❸
9 Church St CV37 6HB (01789) 415 522
*"Innovative and tasty food cooked by a skilled and considered chef", wins praise for this half-timbered house – "it's not as characterful as some Stratford restaurants, but the quality of the cooking makes up". / **Details:** no9churchst.com; 9.15 pm; no Amex.*

The Oppo £45 ❸❷❸
13 Sheep St CV37 6EF (01789) 269980
*A staple choice for a pre-theatre meal; the food is "consistently good" and well-priced, and the service is "excellent" and "speedy". / **Details:** www.theoppo.co.uk; 10 pm, Sun 9.30 pm; closed Sun L; no Amex; booking: max 12.*

Rooftop Restaurant Royal Shakespeare Theatre £46 ④④❷
Waterside CV37 6BB (01789) 403449
*"The main pleasure here is the view", but the food is "perfectly decent" too, say fans of this "surprisingly good theatre restaurant"; service, though, varies between "lackadaisical" and over-attentive – "every member of staff who passed the table stopped to ask if everything was OK"! / **Details:** www.rsc.org.uk/eat; 9.45 pm; no Amex.*

The Vintner £40 ❸❷❷
4-5 Sheep St CV37 6EF (01789) 297259
A "wonderful restaurant set in a quirky medieval building", in "a great location in the centre of Stratford"; despite its popularity with the pre-theatre

*crowd, service always manages to remain "friendly and attentive". / **Details:** www.the-vintner.co.uk; 9.30 pm, Fri & Sat 10 pm, Sun 8.30 pm; no Amex.*

STUCKTON, HAMPSHIRE 2–3C

The Three Lions £60 ❷❷❸
Stuckton Rd SP6 2HF (01425) 652489
*"Everything a rural gastropub should be in terms of food and service"… this "comfortable, unpretentious" (perhaps "unadventurous") New Forest restaurant continues to score high marks all round; it's "also a nice place to stay". / **Details:** www.thethreelionsrestaurant.co.uk; off the A338; 9 pm, Fri & Sat 9.30 pm; closed Mon & Sun D; no Amex. **Accommodation:** 7 rooms, from £105.*

STUDLAND, DORSET 2–4C

Shell Bay £45 ❷❸❶
Ferry Rd BH19 3BA (01929) 450363
*"First class seafood in a scenic location overlooking Poole Harbour"; this "pretty minimal" spot provides "wonderful sea views" – "especially at sunset, on the terrace" – and is "pleasant in every way and highly recommended". / **Details:** www.shellbay.net; near the Sandbanks to Swanage ferry; 9 pm.*

SUMMERHOUSES, COUNTY DURHAM 8–3B

Raby Hunt £73 ❶❷❷
DL2 3UD (01325) 374237
*"Top-class dining in a rural setting"; "plate after plate of delicious, beautifully presented food" rewards all reporters who visit James Close's "amazing" restaurant-with-rooms "in a part of the country that has nothing else like this". / **Details:** www.rabyhuntrestaurant.co.uk/; 9.30pm; closed Mon, Tue & Sun.*

SUNBURY ON THAMES, SURREY 3–3A

Indian Zest £42 ❷❸❷
21 Thames St TW16 5QF (01932) 765 000
*Manoj Vasaikar's "lovely" venue occupies a large, rambling villa, decorated in colonial style; service is "courteous", and its "subtle and elegant" nouvelle Indian cooking is "excellent value for money". / **Details:** www.indianzest.co.uk; 11 pm.*

SUNNINGDALE, BERKSHIRE 3–3A

Bluebells £64 ❷❶❷
Shrubs Hill SL5 0LE (01344) 622 722
*A "nice place for midweek nosh and a natter" – this "very popular" roadside fixture is "not much from the outside, but lovely inside with open fires in winter" (and outside tables in summer); highpoints include "faultless service", and the "remarkable value" set lunch. / **Details:** www.bluebells-restaurant.com; 9.45 pm; closed Mon & Sun D.*

SURBITON, SURREY   3–3A

The French Table   **£ 56**   **❶❷④**
85 Maple Rd KT6 4AW   (020) 8399 2365
A "consistently wonderful" suburban beacon which
"punches above its weight" with its "cracking" and
"genuine" Gallic cooking; even fans of its
"outstanding" cuisine, however, can find the setting a
bit "cramped" or note that "acoustics are a
problem". / **Details:** www.thefrenchtable.co.uk;
10.30 pm; closed Mon & Sun.

Red Rose   **£ 29**   **❷❸❸**
38 Brighton Rd KT6 5PQ   (020) 8399 9647
Fans are "never disappointed with the food", at this
reliable suburban curry house; there is growing local
competition from "trendy" rivals, but, it "always
seems to be buzzing".
/ **Details:** www.redroseofsurbiton.com; 10.30 pm.

SUTTON GAULT, CAMBRIDGESHIRE   3–1B

The Anchor   **£ 46**   **❷❷❸**
Bury Ln CB6 2BD   (01353) 778537
"Off the beaten track" with "a fascinating location
in the fens", this "warmly welcoming" inn has
changed hands of late; on most accounts there's still
"no better gastropub in East Anglia" thanks to
"varied and imaginative" cuisine that "would grace
a top restaurant".
/ **Details:** www.anchorsuttongault.co.uk; 7m W of Ely,
signposted off B1381 in Sutton; 9 pm, Sat 9.30 pm, Sun
8.30 pm; no Amex. **Accommodation:** 4 rooms,
from £79.5.

SWANSEA VALLEY, POWYS   1–1C

Pen y Cae Inn   **£ 39**   **❷❷❷**
Brecon Rd SA9 1FA   (01639) 730100
Billing itself as a 'restaurant and gallery', this is an
all-too-rare sort of Welsh destination – a
"delightfully friendly" place (for kids too), offering
accomplished modern cuisine in "tranquil"
surroundings; "nice views" too.
/ **Details:** www.penycaeinn.com/; @penycaeinn; 9 pm;
no Amex.

SWANSEA, SWANSEA   1–1C

Castellamare   **£ 62**   **❷❷❷**
Bracelet Bay, Mumbles Rd SA3 4JT
(01792) 639408
"A table next to the window, overlooking the
Mumbles lighthouse is a real bonus", if you visit this
large Italian restaurant, which inspires impressively
consistent reviews (not least for "the best tiramisu
anywhere"); "good-value set lunch" too.

Didier And Stephanie   **£ 38**   **❷❶❸**
56 Saint Helen's Rd SA1 4BE   (01792) 655603
A "small French restaurant" near Brangwyn Hall,
offering a "superb culinary experience"; its
"intimate" atmosphere makes it the "perfect choice

for a date" too. / **Details:** 9.15 pm; closed Mon &
Sun; no Amex; booking essential.

SWINBROOK, OXFORDSHIRE   2–2C

Swan   **£ 50**   **❷❸❸**
OX18 4DY   (01993) 823339
"Imaginative well cooked pub food in an beautiful
riverside setting"; this "nice old Cotswold inn" –
owned by Debo, youngest of the Mitford sisters, and
adorned with family photos – is a real all-round
crowd-pleaser.
/ **Details:** www.theswanswinbrook.co.uk; 9 pm, Fri-Sat
9.30 pm.

TAPLOW, BERKSHIRE   3–3A

The Terrace
Cliveden House   **£ 97**   **④❷❷**
Cliveden Rd SL6 0JF   (01628) 668561
Now under the same ownership as Chewton Glen,
this famously "grand" country house hotel makes an
"amazing" destination for some reporters; critics
find the style a bit "corporate", though, and it still
has yet to establish its credentials as a seriously
foodie hotspot, although, as we go to press, the
arrival of new chef André Garrett may change all
that. / **Details:** www.clivedenhouse.co.uk; 9.30 pm;
no trainers. **Accommodation:** 38 + cottage rooms,
from £252.

TAUNTON, SOMERSET   2–3A

Augustus   **£ 46**   **❷❶❸**
3 The Courtyard, St James St TA1 1JR
(01823) 324 354
With a chef and maître d' came from the defunct
Castle Hotel diningroom, this "beautifully-formed"
bistro "was always going to be good", say fans –
from the "sophisticated but simple cooking" to the
"superb staff", it's a great all-rounder whose "only
downside is that the room feels a bit too clinical".
/ **Details:** www.augustustaunton.co.uk; 9.30 pm; closed
Mon & Sun; no Amex.

Brazz
Castle Hotel   **£ 38**   **❶**
Castle Bow TA1 1NF   (01823) 252000
"Not as busy as previously which might indicate
locals are not as impressed"… this "former
favourite" seems to have gone somewhat downhill
of late, although overall it's still tipped for
"wholesome, freshly cooked food" at "sensible"
prices. / **Details:** www.brazz.co.uk; 10 pm.
Accommodation: 44 rooms, from £230.

The Willow Tree   **£ 51**   **❸❸④**
3 Tower Ln TA1 4AR   (01823) 352835
A "beacon in a culinary desert"; Darren Sherlock's
"good value" restaurant has been trading for a good
few years now, but it's still "very consistent".
/ **Details:** www.thewillowtreerestaurant.com; 9.15 pm;
D only, closed Sun & Mon; no Amex; Essential, max. 6.

TEDDINGTON, SURREY   3–3A

Imperial China   £ 39   ❷④④
196-198 Stanley Rd   TW11 8UE
(020) 8977 8679
Oddly, in deepest suburbia, you can "feel like you're in Hong Kong" at this, at peak times, "insanely packed" destination; "excellent dim sum" and service that's "not great" only adds to the general impression of authenticity.
/ **Details:** www.imperialchinalondon.co.uk; 11 pm, Fri & Sat 11.30 pm, Sun 10 pm.

Retro   £ 48   ❶❶❷
114-116 High St   TW11 8JB   (020) 8977 2239
"A smart but casual bistro, with a dynamic personality"; a "flamboyant" maitre d' is just part of the formula that makes this "a terrific local" – other plusses include "colourful" decor and "a short menu that delivers again and again".
/ **Details:** www.retrobistro.co.uk; Tue-Sat 11pm; closed Mon & Sun D.

TEIGNMOUTH, DEVON   1–3D

Crab Shack   £ 28   ❶❷❸
3 Queen St   TQ14 9HN   (01626) 777956
"Seafood doesn't get any fresher" than at this beachside shack, where "Mrs runs the shack, Mr catches the crabs"; book early though – "over a four week period, I found it impossible to get a table on any night at all!"
/ **Details:** www.crabshackonthebeach.co.uk/; 9 pm; closed Mon & Tue; no Amex.

TENTERDEN, KENT   3–4C

The Raja Of Kent   £ 35   ❶
Bibbenden Rd   TN30 6SX   (01233) 851191
Less feedback than we would like, but this Bangladeshi restaurant is tipped for its "original and delicious curries" (such as with game and fish), as well as the more standard offerings.
/ **Details:** www.therajaofkent.com; midnight.

TETBURY, GLOUCESTERSHIRE   2–2B

Calcot Manor   £ 67   ❷❷❷
GL8 8YJ   (01666) 890391
Reports on the "more formal" and "romantic" main restaurant of this family-friendly country house hotel have been a model of consistency of late; they almost invariably confirm that the food is typically "very good". / **Details:** www.calcotmanor.co.uk; junction of A46 & A4135; 9.30 pm, Sun 9 pm. **Accommodation:** 35 rooms, from £280.

Gumstool Inn
Calcot Manor   £ 44   ❸❷❸
GL8 8YJ   (01666) 890391
Even those dissing the "upmarket" pub-style of the "casual" dining option at this country house hotel as "like a glorified Harvester", concede the cooking is "pretty good", and it's "a great destination for adults and kids". / **Details:** www.calcotmanor.co.uk; @Calcot_Manor; crossroads of A46 & A41345; 9.30 pm, Sun 9 pm; no jeans or trainers; children: 12+ at dinner in Conservatory. **Accommodation:** 35 rooms, from £240.

THELWALL, CHESHIRE   4–2B

Little Manor   £ 43   ❸❶❷
Bell Ln   WA4 2SX   (01925) 261703
Very consistent feedback on this outpost of the Brunning & Price gastropub chain, which has a "superb location" and "large, secluded outdoor area"; "friendly and attentive" service is exemplary, and there's a "great menu choice" too.

THORNBURY, GLOUCESTERSHIRE   2–2B

Ronnie's   £ 45   ❷❸❸
11 St Mary St   BS35 2AB   (01454) 411137
Ronnie Faulkner's venture in a 17th-century barn offers "standard dishes with a twist" which, say regulars, "never disappoint"; set menus offer "excellent value" too.
/ **Details:** www.ronnies-restaurant.co.uk; @ByRonnie; Tue-Thu 9.30 pm, Fri & Sat 10.30 pm; closed Mon & Sun D; no Amex.

THORNHAM, NORFOLK   6–3B

Lifeboat Inn   £ 48   ❶
Ship Ln   PE36 6LT   (01485) 512236
New owner Marco Pierre White "has poured welcome new life into this salty old sea dog", say fans of this celebrated pub; overall, though, ratings tend to suggest that there's "nothing at all special" about the place.
/ **Details:** www.maypolehotels.com/lifeboatinn/; 20m from Kings Lynn on A149 coast road; 9.30 pm; D only, ex Sun open L & D; no Amex. **Accommodation:** 13 rooms, from £104.

The Orange Tree   £ 46   ❶
High St   PE36 6LY   (01485) 512 213
A good number of reporters give this coastal gastropub top marks for cooking; dishes can be complex and are beautifully presented.
/ **Details:** www.theorangetreethornham.co.uk; 9.30 pm; no Amex. **Accommodation:** 6 rooms, from £89.

TILLINGTON, WEST SUSSEX   3–

The Horse Guards Inn   £ 40   ❷❷❶
Upperton Rd   GU28 9AF   (01798) 342 332
"Looks like another typical village pub, but once inside WOW!" – this "professional" and "buzzing" rustic boozer has a fantastic atmosphere; and the cooking is – "it's steady, yet always imaginative".
/ **Details:** www.thehorseguardsinn.co.uk; 9 pm, Fri & Sat 9.30 pm; no Amex; SRA-63%.

TIMBLE, NORTH YORKSHIRE   5–1C

The Timble Inn   **£ 47** ❶❷❸
LS21 2NN   (01943) 880530
"Half way up a hill", in the Dales, this "absolutely
stunning little country inn" is a "very can-do sort of
a place" which offers "delicious" food (and
"immaculate" accommodation too).
/ **Details:** www.thetimbleinn.com; 9.30 pm; closed
Mon, Tue, Wed L & Sun D; no shorts.

TITCHWELL, NORFOLK   6–3B

Titchwell Manor   **£ 49** ❷④④
PE31 8BB   (01485) 210 221
Some of "the best food on the North Norfolk coast"
is to be had at this Victorian farmhouse/hotel, for a
quarter of a century in the ownership of the Snaith
family; the "very imaginative" cuisine includes some
"great seafood". / **Details:** www.titchwellmanor.com;
@TitchwellManor; 9.30 pm. **Accommodation:** 29
rooms, from £95.

TITLEY, HEREFORDSHIRE   2–1A

Stagg Inn   **£ 49** ❶❶❷
HR5 3RL   (01544) 230221
It's "still a local pub… just" (with a "tiny" bar), but
the main attraction these days at this country
hostelry is Steve Reynolds's "superlative food" – with
particular plaudits going to the "best bread and
butter pudding ever"! / **Details:** www.thestagg.co.uk;
@TheStaggInn; on B4355, NE of Kington; 9 pm; closed
Mon & Sun D. **Accommodation:** 6 rooms,
from £100.

TOBERMORY, ISLE OF MULL,
ARGYLL AND BUTE   9–3A

Café Fish   **£ 43** ❶❷❷
The Pier PA75 6NU   (01688) 301253
"It's a long trip to get there", but this "small, but
amazingly located" venue (former ferry company
offices, overlooking the harbour) offers "a fantastic
dining experience" – "I've never found fish as
fresh!" / **Details:** www.thecafefish.com; 10 pm; Closed
Nov-Mar; no Amex; children: 14+ after 8 pm.

TOOT BALDON, OXFORDSHIRE   2–2D

The Mole Inn   **£ 47** ❷❷❷
OX44 9NG   (01865) 340001
"More gastro than pub, a pleasant and cheerful
establishment, with a lovely garden, in a tiny village
near Oxford", which attracts almost unmitigated
praise from all who comment on it.
/ **Details:** www.moleinn.com; 9.30 pm, Sun 9 pm.

TOPSHAM, DEVON   1–3D

The Galley   **£ 48** ❷❶❷
41 Fore St EX3 0HU   (01392) 876078
"Fresh fish dishes from Lyme Bay and the River
Exe" from an "ever-changing" menu win plaudits for

this restaurant with a "great setting", in this seaside
town; plus great "South African wines".
/ **Details:** www.galleyrestaurant.co.uk; 9 pm; closed
Mon & Sun; booking essential; children: 12+.

TORCROSS, DEVON   1–4D

Start Bay Inn   **£ 33** ❷❷❸
TQ7 2TQ   (01548) 580553
"The best fish 'n' chips", creates a constant crush at
this beachside pub, which specialises in locally-
caught seafood – "some of it only comes from a
couple of hundred yards away!"
/ **Details:** www.startbayinn.co.uk; on beach front (take
A379 coastal road to Dartmouth); 10 pm; no Amex;
no booking.

TORQUAY, DEVON   1–3D

Elephant Restaurant &
Brasserie   **£ 72** ❷❷❸
3-4 Beacon Ter, Harbourside TQ1 2BH
(01803) 200044
This first-floor restaurant "gem" is "just too good to
be true", say fans of Simon Hulstone's magical way
with "great local ingredients"; other merits include
"harbour views" from the bar and "attentive"
service; downstairs, "simple but tasty brasserie
fare". / **Details:** www.elephantrestaurant.co.uk;
9.30 pm; closed Mon & Sun; children: 14+ at bar.

No 7 Fish Bistro   **£ 52** ❷❷❷
7 Beacon Ter TQ1 2BH   (01803) 295055
"No standing on ceremony" at this unpretentious
establishment – just "unbeatable fish" in an
"extremely easy and comforting" setting; it's
"extremely busy throughout the year".
/ **Details:** www.no7-fish.com; 9.45 pm; D only Sun-Tue.

TOTNES, DEVON   1–3D

Willow   **£ 33** ❷❸❸
87 High St TQ9 5PB   (01803) 862605
A "break from the norm", this "mobiles-not-allowed"
restaurant serves "healthy vegetarian food" ("much
of it organic"); it's also tipped for live music and
'Indian' nights; cash only. / **Details:** 9.30 pm; closed
Mon D, Tue D, Thu D & Sun; no credit cards.

TREEN, CORNWALL   1–4A

Gurnards Head   **£ 45** ❶❷❶
TR26 3DE   (01736) 796928
Given its "terrific" cliff-top location and "lovely laid-
back and convivial atmosphere", it's easy to be
wowed by this remote and "chilled" pub; its
"serious" cooking is an attraction in itself, though,
nowadays "mixing unusual flavours, without losing
sight of local produce and specialities, to inspired
effect". / **Details:** www.gurnardshead.co.uk;
@gurnardshead; on coastal road between Land's End &
St Ives, near Zennor B3306; 9.30 pm; no Amex.
Accommodation: 7 rooms, from £90.

TRING, HERTFORDSHIRE   3–2A

Olive Limes   **£ 36   ❶❷❷**
60 High St HP23 5AG   (01442) 828283
*Overlooking Tring Park, a slick Indian restaurant,
praised by a small but enthusiastic fan club for its
"amazing" cooking. / Details: www.olivelimes.co.uk;
11 pm, Fri & Sat 11.30 pm.*

TROUTBECK, CUMBRIA   7–3D

Queen's Head   **£ 46   ❷❷❸**
Townhead LA23 1PW   (01539) 432174
*A "brilliant Lakeland pub", now under new
management; even the odd sceptic concedes that
it's "not a bad option in a tourist area", while most
reports enthuse about its "interesting menu" and
"welcoming" feel.
/ Details: www.queensheadhotel.com; A592 on
Kirkstone Pass; 9 pm; no Amex. Accommodation: 15
rooms, from £120.*

TUDDENHAM, SUFFOLK   3–1C

Tuddenham Mill
Tuddenham Mill Hotel   **£ 62**   ④⑤④
High St IP28 6SQ   (01638) 713 552
*"Amazingly innovative cooking from a rising star", or
"pretentious", "tasteless", and, in short, a "disaster"?
– as with last year, view remain unusually starkly
divided on this attractively housed dining room.
/ Details: www.tuddenhammill.co.uk;
@Tuddenham_Mill; 9.15 pm. Accommodation: 15
rooms, from £205.*

TUNBRIDGE WELLS, KENT   3–4B

The Black Pig   **£ 50   ❶**
18 Grove Hill Rd TN1 1RZ   (01892) 523030
*"A solid gastropub", "really handy" for the railway
station and major department store; it's a "bit
old-fashioned to be called trendy, though (even in
Tunbridge Wells!)" / Details: @BlackPigTW; 9 pm,
Fri & Sat 9.30 pm; no Amex.*

Hotel du Vin et Bistro   **£ 49**   ④④❷
Crescent Rd TN1 2LY   (01892) 526455
*"More like a club", really, the impressive Victorian
premises of this HdV branch make a "very
comfortable" place to while away a lunchtime ("or,
indeed, to spend an afternoon"); shame, though, that
the "wholesome" food so determinedly "plays
second fiddle" to the "extensive" wine list.
/ Details: www.hotelduvin.com; 10 pm, Fri & Sat
10.30 pm; booking: max 10. Accommodation: 34
rooms, from £120.*

Signor Franco   **£ 43   ❷❸❷**
5a High St TN1 1UL   (01892) 549199
*"Alas, Signor Franco himself has gone to that great
restaurant in the sky", but his spirit lives on at this
popular and long-standing Italian stalwart still run
by his family, where the food is "as good as ever",*

*perhaps even better. / Details: 10.45 pm; closed
Mon & Sun D; no Amex.*

Thackeray's   **£ 67   ❸④④**
85 London Rd TN1 1EA   (01892) 511921
*Elegantly-housed in a Regency villa near the town-
centre, Richard Phillips's acclaimed destination has
long been the pre-eminent restaurant locally; it's
undoubtedly worth seeking out for its "outstanding-
value" lunch menu – overall though, reports (on
both food and service) are quite up and down.
/ Details: www.thackerays-restaurant.co.uk;
@Thackeraysrest; 10.30 pm; closed Mon & Sun D.*

TUNBRIDGE WELLS, KENT   3–4B

Giggling Squid   **£ 26   ❷❸④**
57 Calverley Rd TN1 2UY   (01892) 545499
*"No fuss Thai" (part of a growing chain), serving "a
small selection of tapas dishes, as well as the
traditional offerings"; "if you want something quick
and not too pricey, it's great".
/ Details: www.gigglingsquid.com/branches/tunbridgew
ells.html.*

TUNSTALL, LANCASHIRE   7–4D

Lunesdale Arms   **£ 37   ❶❷❸**
LA6 2QN   (01524) 274203
*A real all-rounder, Emma Gillibrand's smart inn is
praised in all reports for cooking "of real quality",
and at prices that make it "excellent value for
money". / Details: www.thelunesdale.co.uk; 15 min
from J34 on M6 onto A683; 9 pm; closed Mon.*

TUXFORD, NOTTINGHAMSHIRE 5–2D

Mussel and Crab   **£ 42   ❷❷❷**
Sibthorpe Hill NG22 0PJ   (01777) 870 491
*A "little gem"; an "excellent cross between a
gastropub and fish restaurant", its winning formula
includes "deliciously-prepared seafood" and a "good
wine list". / Details: www.musselandcrab.com; 10 pm,
Sun 9 pm; no Amex.*

ULLSWATER, CUMBRIA   7–3D

Sharrow Bay   **£ 100 ❸❸❷**
CA10 2LZ   (01768) 486301
*Fans say the new owners of this famous country
house hotel, with its "magnificent" Lakeland views,
are "maintaining excellent standards" (including its
reputation for "the best puds ever"); the style is
rather "dated", of course… but isn't that why
people like it? / Details: www.sharrowbay.co.uk; on
Pooley Bridge Rd towards Howtown; 8 pm; no jeans or
trainers; children: 10+. Accommodation: 18 rooms,
from £175.*

UPPER BUCKLEBURY, BERKSHIRE   2–2D

Bladebone Inn   **£ 42** ❷❷❸
Chapel Row RG7 6PD   (0118) 971 2326
"An excellent pub, serving a wide range of locally sourced cooking, many local beers and a fantastic wine list" – "beef and lamb dishes are particularly well cooked and presented".
/ **Details:** www.thebladeboneinn.com/; 9 pm; closed Mon & Sun D; no Amex.

UPPER SLAUGHTER,
GLOUCESTERSHIRE   2–1C

Lords of the Manor   **£ 95** ❷❷❶
GL54 2JD   (01451) 820243
In a "lovely" Cotswolds hotel, this dining room offers a "wonderfully clever fusion of tastes", and a wine list "you could spend hours with"; it's perhaps unsurprising that prices are on the high side.
/ **Details:** www.lordsofthemanor.com; 4m W of Stow on the Wold; 8.45 pm; D only, ex Sun open L & D; no jeans or trainers; children: 7+ at D in restaurant.
Accommodation: 26 rooms, from £199.

UPPINGHAM, RUTLAND   5–4D

The Lake Isle   **£ 50** ❶
16 High Street East LE15 9PZ   (01572) 822951
A "trusted treat" in a tiny market town, tipped for "excellent-quality" mains, "delicious desserts" and an "extensive" (though somewhat "pricey") wine list. / **Details:** www.lakeisle.co.uk; past the Market place, down the High Street; 9 pm, Fri & Sat 9.30 pm; closed Mon L & Sun D. **Accommodation:** 12 rooms, from £75.

VENTNOR, ISLE OF WIGHT   2–4D

The Hambrough   **£ 81** ❷❷❷
Hambrough Road PO38 1SQ   (01983) 856333
Relatively few reports of late on dining at this "lovely" hotel, by the sea; its ambitious cuisine, though, is still generally hailed as "exquisite".
/ **Details:** www.robert-thompson.com; 9.30 pm; closed Mon & Sun; no Amex. **Accommodation:** 7 rooms, from £170.

The Royal Hotel   **£ 60** ❶❷❷
Belgrave Rd PO38 1JJ   (01983) 852186
"Exceptional for a grand old hotel!" – this "picturesque" Victorian four-star has an "elegant" dining room on quite a scale, serving "100% reliable silver service cuisine" that can be "stunning".
/ **Details:** www.royalhoteliow.co.uk; 9 pm; children: 3+. **Accommodation:** 54 rooms, from £170.

VERYAN-IN-ROSELAND, CORNWALL   1–4B

Dining Room
The Nare Hotel   **£ 68** ❶
Carne Beach TR2 5PF   (01872) 501111
We suspect you'd never be allowed to build a hotel nowadays in the stunning seaside location enjoyed by this country house-style operation; those who like their dining in a notably traditional style tip it for its "superb cuisine without pretence".
/ **Details:** www.narehotel.co.uk; @TheNareHotel; 9.30 pm; D only; jacket & tie; Booking essential; children: 7+. **Accommodation:** 37 rooms, from £270.

WADEBRIDGE, CORNWALL   1–3B

Bridge Bistro   **£ 40** ❷❷④
4 Molesworth St PL27 7DA   (01208) 815342
Run by a husband-and-wife team "with great care and skill", this "gem" of a restaurant is praised in all reports for its "excellent" locally sourced cuisine (which, as you would expect, is "very strong on fish"). / **Details:** www.bridgebistro.co.uk/; 9 pm; closed Mon & Sun; no Amex.

WALBERSWICK, SUFFOLK   3–1D

The Anchor   **£ 42** ❸❺❸
Main St IP18 6UA   (01502) 722112
Fans applaud the "sophisticated" cooking at this popular inn, which boats a "good wine list" and well-kept ales too; erratic (and sometimes "abysmal") service, however, helps lead some reports to suggest it's "not as good as it used to be."
/ **Details:** www.anchoratwalberswick.com; 9 pm.
Accommodation: 10 rooms, from £110.

WARLINGHAM, SURREY   3–3B

Chez Vous   **£ 40** ❷❸④
432 Limpsfield Rd CR6 9LA   (01883) 620451
"A new hotel and restaurant in an area that's a bit of a desert"; all reports confirm that the cooking is "of top quality" (though the wine list can seem "a little restricted"). / **Details:** www.chezvous.co.uk.

WARWICK, WARWICKSHIRE   5–4C

The Art Kitchen   **£ 43** ❷❷④
7 Swan St CV34 4BJ   (01926) 494303
The food comes "hot and spicy", and "usually really fast", at this "thoroughly enjoyable" and consistently well-rated town-centre Thai.
/ **Details:** www.theartkitchen.com; 10 pm.

The Saxon Mill   **£ 42** ④④❶
Coventry Rd, Guys Cliffe CV34 5YN
(01926) 492255
Entrancing views of the mill race from the terrace make this, above all, a "wonderful summer evening venue" – the food, though, is "consistently reasonable" too. / **Details:** www.saxonmill.co.uk; 9.30 pm, Fri & Sat 10 pm, Sun 9 pm.

Tailors **£ 53** ❷❹❸
22 market place CV34 4SL (01926) 410590
"A real gem"; with its "visionary" food, this former town-centre shop "goes from strength to strength", and receives nothing but the highest praise from its army of local fans.
/ **Details:** www.tailorsrestaurant.co.uk; 9 pm; closed Mon & Sun; no Amex; children: 12+ for dinner .

WATERGATE BAY, CORNWALL 1–3B

The Beach Hut
Watergate Bay Hotel **£ 45** ❶
On The Beach TR8 4AA (01637) 860543
"What a position, right on the beach, and good food too" – the "relaxing" charms of this "bustling", "California-style" establishment win it a tip as "the best place ever" for family dining (even if "the menu does make no particular concessions to kids").
/ **Details:** www.watergatebay.co.uk; 9 pm; no Amex.
Accommodation: 69 rooms, from £105.

Fifteen Cornwall
Watergate Bay Hotel **£ 80** ❷❷❶
TR8 4AA (01637) 861000
"A superb location overlooking Watergate bay" adds considerable appeal to Jamie O's stylish, "fun and informal" operation, by the beach; fans say the food is "excellent" too, but even they can feel "taken advantage of" by the "whopping prices – more City than Cornwall"! / **Details:** www.fifteencornwall.co.uk; @fifteencornwall; on the Atlantic coast between Padstow and Newquay; 9.15 pm; children: 7+ for dinner.

WATERMILLOCK, CUMBRIA 7–3D

Rampsbeck Hotel **£ 76** ❸❷❷
CA11 0LP (01768) 486442
"Simple but excellent food in perfect surroundings"; all reports on this country house hotel, on the shore of Lake Ullswater, concur that it is an "impressive" destination all-round – "deserves to be better known". / **Details:** www.hotel-lakedistrict.com; next to Lake Ullswater, J40 on M6, take A592 to Ullswater; 8.30 pm; no Amex; children: 8+. **Accommodation:** 19 rooms, from £110.

WATERNISH, HIGHLAND 9–2A

Loch Bay **£ 45** ❶
Stein IV55 8GA (01470) 592235
A lochside bistro, tipped for "superb fish straight from the sea" and "the best chips in the country"!; the owners rent two former fishermen's cottages nearby; open Easter to mid-October.
/ **Details:** www.lochbay-seafood-restaurant.co.uk; 22m from Portree via A87 and B886; 8m from Dunvegan; 8.30 pm; closed Mon, Tue L, Wed L, Thu L, Fri L, Sat & Sun; no Amex; children: 8+ in the evening.

WATH-IN-NIDDERDALE,
NORTH YORKSHIRE 8–4B

Sportsman's Arms **£ 50** ❸❷❸
HG3 5PP (01423) 711306
"Excellent pub food, a cut above the rest"; in a pretty Dales village, this "eager-to-please", very traditional destination is well worth seeking out.
/ **Details:** www.sportsmans-arms.co.uk; take Wath Road from Pateley Bridge; 9 pm, Sun 8 pm; no Amex; booking essential. **Accommodation:** 11 rooms, from £120.

WEDMORE, SOMERSET 2–3A

The Swan **£ 43** ❷❷❷
Cheddar Rd BS28 4EQ (019) 3471 0337
"Fantastic attention to detail" in all departments attracts a paean of praise for this "buzzy", recently grooved-up inn, not least for its "fab" locally-sourced cuisine, its "friendly" service and "reasonable prices". / **Details:** www.theswanwedmore.com; 10 pm, Sun 9 pm; closed Sun D; no Amex; SRA-69%.

WELFORD ON AVON,
WARWICKSHIRE 2–1C

The Bell Inn **£ 45** ❶
Binton Rd CV37 8EB (01789) 750353
A "very good gastropub in the middle of nowhere", tipped for a menu that's "more extensive than your average pub", and at "reasonable prices" too.
/ **Details:** www.thebellwelford.co.uk; 9.30 pm, Fri & Sat 10 pm.

WELLS NEXT THE SEA, NORFOLK 6–3C

Globe **£ 40** ❶
The Buttlands NR23 1EU (01328) 710206
"Another gem in Chelsea-on-Sea"; this Adnams inn is tipped for its "good helpings of superior pub food", and its "friendly" atmosphere too.
/ **Details:** www.holkham.co.uk/globe; 9 pm; no Amex.
Accommodation: 7 rooms, from £100.

WELLS, SOMERSET 2–3B

Goodfellows **£ 59** ❷❸④
5 Sadler St BA5 2RR (01749) 673866
"Best fish ever, and – if you sit downstairs – you can watch them cook it !"; Adam Fellows's "small but pleasant restaurant" (with "excellent patisserie" and café attached) generally inspires impressive reviews, though critics do find it rather "cramped".
/ **Details:** www.goodfellowswells.co.uk; 9.30 pm; closed Mon, Tue D & Sun.

Old Spot £ 46 ❷❷❸
12 Sadler St BA5 2SE (01749) 689099
*Ian Bates's "great old-fashioned pub" impresses all
reporters, thanks to its "delicious" modern British
grub, and its "wonderful selection of real ales" too;
an attractive space, it features "a view of the
cathedral from the back of the room".
/ Details: www.theoldspot.co.uk; 9.15 pm; closed Mon,
Tue L & Sun D.*

WELWYN, HERTFORDSHIRE   3–2B

Auberge du Lac
Brocket Hall £ 89 ❸❹❸
AL8 7XG (01707) 368888
*"Best at lunchtime, so you can take in the setting" –
this restaurant with lake views (and many tables al
fresco) has "one of the prettiest locations"; critics
can find the whole style of the place "pretentious",
though, and the service, usually "friendly", can have
its ups and downs. / Details: www.brocket-hall.co.uk;
on B653 towards Harpenden; 9.30 pm; closed Mon &
Sun; no jeans or trainers. Accommodation: 16 rooms,
from £175.*

The Wellington £ 44 ❸❷❷
1 High St AL6 9LZ (01438) 714036
*This pub-like venture pleases most reporters with its
"buzzy" atmosphere and its impressive range of
Aussie wines; on most accounts the food is
"fabulous" too, but a couple of regulars do note that
"quality can vary from month to month".
/ Details: www.wellingtonatwelwyn.co.uk; 10 pm;
no Amex. Accommodation: 6 rooms, from £100.*

WEST BRIDGFORD,
NOTTINGHAMSHIRE   5–3D

Larwood And Voce £ 43 ❸❸❷
Fox Rd NG2 6AJ (0115) 981 9960
*Gastropubs by football pitches don't always have
the best reputation, but this "relaxed" and "family-
friendly" spot by Trent Bridge, part of a local chain,
"keeps standards high even on match days"; brunch
is a highlight. / Details: www.larwoodandvoce.co.uk;
@larwoodvocepk; 9 pm, Sun 5 pm; closed Sun D.*

WEST CLANDON, SURREY   3–3A

The Onslow Arms £ 43 ❸❹❸
The St GU4 7TE (01483) 222447
*"Good-value food, slow service" – often the theme of
commentary on this large inn, recently refurbished.
/ Details: www.onslowarmsclandon.com; 10 pm, Fri &
Sat 10.30 pm; children: 18+ after 7.30pm.*

WEST HOATHLY, WEST SUSSEX   3–4B

The Cat Inn £ 45 ❸❷❷
Queen's Sq RH19 4PP (01342) 810369
*"A hugely popular pub, with reliably good food" –
this "professionally-run" and "hospitable" village
boozer inspires impressively consistent praise.
/ Details: www.catinn.co.uk; 9 pm, Fri-Sun 9.30 pm;
closed Sun D; no Amex; children: 7+.
Accommodation: 4 rooms, from £110.*

WEST MALLING, KENT   3–3C

The Swan £ 52 ❸❸❸
35 Swan St ME19 6JU (01732) 521910
*"Such a gem"; even former critics of this local
restaurant (with a nice garden) feel that "there have
been clear improvements" of late, particularly the
"excellent" new brunch; it still takes flak, however,
for a "big plate, small meal" approach, that can
make it seem "very expensive".
/ Details: www.loveswan.co.uk; @swanwm; 11 pm, Sun
7 pm.*

WEST MEON, HAMPSHIRE   2–3D

The Thomas Lord £ 43 ❸❷❷
High St GU32 1LN (01730) 829244
*Now part of a small group, this "very relaxing and
friendly" village inn, in the South Downs National
Park, continues to impress with its "sound" cooking;
"the new owners have a lot to live up to", however,
and the food can seem a little "less adventurous"
nowadays. / Details: www.thethomaslord.co.uk; 9 pm,
Sat 9.30 pm.*

WEST MERSEA, ESSEX   3–2C

The Company Shed £ 32 ❶❹❸
129 Coast Rd CO5 8PA (01206) 382700
*"Spanking fresh fish served in a shack on the edge
of the beach"... and so what if you have to bring
your own bread and wine? – all reports confirm that
this mega-famous seaside destination offers
"simplicity at its best"; get there early to beat the
queues. / Details: www.the-company-shed.co.uk;
4 pm; L only, closed Mon; no credit cards; no booking.*

West Mersea Oyster Bar £ 37 ❷❸❸
Coast Rd CO5 8LT (01206) 381600
*If you're looking for that "authentic seaside
experience", seek out the "very good seafood" (plus
"fish 'n' chips to die for") on offer at this estuarial
fixture, whose bright, IKEA-style decor contrasts with
that of the famous 'Shed', nearby.
/ Details: www.westmerseaoysterbar.co.uk; 8.30 pm;
Sun-Thu closed D; no Amex; no shorts.*

WEST WITTON, NORTH YORKSHIRE   8–4B

The Wensleydale Heifer   **£ 56**   ❷❷❷
Main St DL8 4LS   (01969) 622322
"It shouldn't work but it bloomin' does!"; from the "lovely rooms", to the "excellent food", and "charming service", this "really rather superb seafood restaurant" in "the middle of deepest, remotest North Yorkshire" delights all of the many who comment on it.
/ Details: *www.wensleydaleheifer.co.uk; 9.30 pm; booking required.* **Accommodation:** *13 rooms, from £130.*

WESTCLIFF ON SEA, ESSEX   3–3C

Toulouse   **£ 49**   ❶
Western Esplanade SS0 8FE   (01702) 333731
"A surprisingly nice restaurant in a dismal location"; this sea-front venture (housed in a pair of former public conveniences, geddit?) is tipped for its "comforting and tasty food", especially from the "good-value early-evening menu"; service is "very professional" too.
/ Details: *www.toulouserestaurant.co.uk; 9.30 pm, Sat 9.30, Sun 7 pm; closed Mon L.*

WESTFIELD, EAST SUSSEX   3–4C

The Wild Mushroom   **£ 45**   ❶❷❸
Westfield Ln TN35 4SB   (01424) 751137
"An unusual place to find somewhere as good as this"; this "comfortable" country establishment (it's a "proper restaurant – amuse bouches, linen napkins, china plates, petits fours") wins praise for its "exceptional use of local ingredients"; set lunch is "excellent value".
/ Details: *www.webbesrestaurants.co.uk; 9.30 pm; closed Mon, Tue & Sun D.*

WESTON SUBEDGE,
GLOUCESTERSHIRE   2–

The Seagrave Arms   **£ 46**   ❶
Friday St GL55 6QH   (01386) 840 192
On the edge of the Cotswolds, a pub-cum-restaurant tipped for the "interesting" use it makes of "good fresh local produce"; "sweeping views" and a "good range of beers" too.
/ Details: *www.seagravearms.co.uk; 9 pm; closed Mon.*

WHALLEY, LANCASHIRE   5–1B

Food by Breda Murphy   **£ 38**   ❶❶❷
41 Station Rd BB7 9RH   (01254) 823446
An "excellent small deli and restaurant", overseen by a "genuinely friendly" Irish host – a Ballymaloe-trained chef whose fish pie "surpasses that of Rick Stein", and who creates an "amazing choice of cakes and scones too"; shame it's usually "not open in the evening".
/ Details: *www.foodbybredamurphy.com; 5.30 pm; closed Mon & Sun, Tue-Sat D; no Amex.*

The Three Fishes   **£ 40**   ❷❷❸
Mitton Rd BB7 9PQ   (01254) 826888
The original Ribble Valley Inn is "still the best" of the Northcote-based group, showcasing as it does "consistent delivery of honest regional food"; highlights include "excellent" fish pies and "amazing" burgers.
/ Details: *www.thethreefishes.com; 8.30 pm, Fri & Sat 9 pm, Sun 8 pm.*

WHEATHAMPSTEAD,
HERTFORDSHIRE   3–2A

L'Olivo   **£ 53**   ❸❷❸
135 Marford Rd AL4 8NH   (01582) 834 145
"If you are looking for a traditional Italian restaurant you can't go wrong here" – for supporters it's simply "fantastic", and even the worst critics of this "busy and buzzy" spot concede that it's a "solid" sort of destination.
/ Details: *www.lolivo-restaurant.com; 9.30 pm; D only, closed Mon & Sun.*

WHITBY, NORTH YORKSHIRE   8–3D

Greens   **£ 48**   ❸❸❸
13 Bridge St YO22 4BG   (01947) 600284
"Fantastic" cooking of "fish straight from the quayside" inspires largely positive reports for this ground-floor bistro (with more formal restaurant above); its ratings are undercut, however, by those who say it's "not as good as it was".
/ Details: *www.greensofwhitby.com; 9.30 pm, Fri & Sat 10 pm.*

Magpie Café   **£ 40**   ❶❷④
14 Pier Rd YO21 3PU   (01947) 602058
"Still the best fish and chips in the world" – this "amazingly efficient" harbour-side legend (one of the UK's best-known restaurants) is "in a class of its own"; "it's best visited off-season, as the queues can be appalling". **/ Details:** *www.magpiecafe.co.uk; 9 pm; no Amex; no booking at L.*

Trenchers **£ 39** ❷❸❸
New Quay Rd YO21 1DH (01947) 603212
*"How do you compete with the Magpie?!" – well
this "elegant" venue has for years, and earns plenty
of superlatives for "amazingly good fish and non-
greasy chips", and it's "not as pricey as its rival"
either! / Details: www.trenchersrestaurant.co.uk;
8.30 pm; need 7+ to book.*

WHITEBROOK, MONMOUTHSHIRE 2–2B

**The Crown at
Whitebrook** **£ 79**
NP25 4TX (01600) 860254
*This celebrated restaurant-with-rooms has had a
torrid time of late, with its closure under
administration, and subsequent re-opening; let's
hope that it rises again, with Blanc protégé Chris
Harrod at the helm.
/ Details: www.crownatwhitebrook.co.uk; 2m W of
A466, 5m S of Monmouth; 9 pm; children: 12+ for D.
Accommodation: 8 rooms, from £145.*

WHITSTABLE, KENT 3–3C

Birdies **£ 38** ❷❸❸
41 Harbour St CT5 1AH (01227) 265337
*"The only reason I go to Whitstable"; this "nice local
French-style restaurant" doesn't inspire a huge
number of reports, but they are all very positive; a
"very good-value set lunch" is a highlight.
/ Details: 9.15 pm; closed Mon L & Tue; no Amex.*

Crab & Winkle **£ 43** ❷❸❸
South Quay, Whitstable Harbour CT5 1AB
(01227) 779377
*In a "lovely" setting overlooking the harbour, this
basic, café-like outfit has made quite a name for
itself with "good fresh fish" and "imaginative"
seafood that's "reasonably priced"; a "busy" place,
though, it can get very "noisy" at times.
/ Details: www.crabandwinklerestaurant.co.uk;
9.30 pm; closed Mon & Sun D; no Amex.*

East Coast Dining Room **£ 52** ❸❸④
101 Tankerton Rd CT5 2AJ (01227) 281180
*Encouraging reports on this "interesting" new
restaurant (which has quite a local pedigree) "at the
less fashionable end of town" make it 'one to
watch'; you get a "fine lunch" for the set price.
/ Details: eastcoastdiningroom.co.uk/; 9 pm; closed
Mon, Tue, Wed D & Sun D.*

JoJo **£ 31** ❷⓿⓿
2 Herne Bay Rd CT5 2LQ (01227) 274591
*A "favourite which never disappoints"; since shifting
to larger premises near the sea two or three years
ago, this 'Meze, Meat & Fish Restaurant' is even
more "fantastic", combining "wonderful, tapas-style
food" and a popular BYO option, with a superbly
"vibrant" atmosphere.
/ Details: www.jojosrestaurant.co.uk; 8.30 pm; closed
Mon, Tue, Wed L & Sun D; no credit cards.*

Pearson's Arms **£ 48** ❸❸❸
The Horsebridge, Sea Wall CT5 1BT
(01227) 272005
*An offshoot of Thackeray's in Tunbridge Wells, this is
a "busy" spot not far from the water (with "good
views" from the upstairs room); the "seafood is
always very fresh", there's an "excellent-value set
lunch", and "children eat free on Sundays –
amazing"!
/ Details: www.pearsonsarmsbyrichardphillips.co.uk;
@pearsonsarms; 9 pm, Fri & Sat 9.30 pm, Sun
8.30 pm; closed Mon D.*

Samphire **£ 46** ❷❷❷
4 High St CT5 1BQ (01227) 770075
*This "always-busy" all-day venture offers "an
interesting take on modern British and locally-
sourced" fare and, thanks not least to the
"unhurried service", is also "a place to linger".
/ Details: www.samphirerestaurant.co.uk;
@samphirewhit; 10 pm; no Amex.*

The Sportsman **£ 49** ⓿⓿❷
Faversham Rd, Seasalter CT5 4BP
(01227) 273370
*"Oh, how looks can deceive!"; Stephen Harris's
phenomenal operation, "on the edge of a bleak bit
of coast", appears nothing more than "a somewhat
run-down and windswept seaside tavern"; it was the
survey's No.1 pub-like pub, however, thanks to its
"perfect" food, which makes "brilliant use of local
ingredients".
/ Details: www.thesportsmanseasalter.co.uk;
@sportsmankent; 9 pm, Sun 2.30 pm; closed Mon &
Sun D; no Amex; children: 18+ in main bar.*

Wheelers Oyster Bar **£ 44** ⓿❷⓿
8 High St CT5 1BQ (01227) 273311
*"Some of the best food I have ever eaten!"; it's
"worth a trip from London" for the "oh-so special"
experience of eating at this "unique" and "really
fun" 16-seat "institution" (est. 1856), where the fish
and seafood are almost invariably hailed as
"exquisite" – "book months ahead"; if you want, you
can BYO too.
/ Details: www.seewhitstable.com/Wheelers-Whitstabl
e-Restaurant.html; 7.30 pm, Sun 7 pm; closed Wed;
no credit cards.*

Whitstable Oyster
Fishery Co.   **£52** ❷④❸
Royal Native Oyster Stores, Horsebridge CT5
1BU (01227) 276856
"Seafood doesn't need to be fancier than this" – this
famous characterful institution is brilliantly located
on the beach, and lives up to its name with
"excellent oysters" in particular; other fare, however,
is "not special" at the "OTT" prices, and staff (do
they "dress down"?) "need proper training".
/ **Details:** www.whitstableoystercompany.com;
8.45 pm, Fri 9.15 pm, Sat 9.45 pm, Sun 8.15 pm.

WILLIAN, HERTFORDSHIRE   3–2B

The Fox   **£45** ❷❸❸
SG6 2AE (01462) 480233
"Unusual and ambitious dishes, which mostly work"
– this "friendly" gastroboozer is hailed in most
reports as offering a "step up" from the more
standard offerings. / **Details:** www.foxatwillian.co.uk;
@FoxAtWillian; 1 mile from junction 9 off A1M; 9 pm;
closed Sun D; no Amex.

WILMSLOW, CHESHIRE   5–2B

Chilli Banana   **£39**
71 Water Ln SK9 1BQ (01625) 539100
"Never disappointed in a decade of visits!" – this
pleasant Thai really impresses its fans, so let's hope
it thrives in this new location to which it moves
(from the Kings Arms Hotel) in late-2013.
/ **Details:** www.chillibanana.co.uk; 10.30 pm; closed
Mon, Tue-Thu D only. **Accommodation:** 7 rooms,
from £60.

WINCHCOMBE, GLOUCESTERSHIRE   2–1C

5 North Street   **£65** ❶❷❸
5 North St GL54 5LH (01242) 604566
Marcus Ashenford's "ingenious" cooking that's
"innovative and interesting without becoming
pretentious" makes his (and wife Kate's) restaurant
in "quiet" former tea-rooms a consistently
outstanding destination; the lunchtime menu is
"astounding value".
/ **Details:** www.5northstreetrestaurant.co.uk; 9 pm;
closed Mon, Tue L & Sun D.

Wesley House   **£55** ❷❷❸
High St GL54 5LJ (01242) 602366
A restaurant in a Tudor house, praised for its
"relaxed and civilised atmosphere" and some
"surprisingly varied and imaginative cooking for a
place hidden away in a quaint Cotswold village";
"you can feel a bit cut off if your table is in the
conservatory". / **Details:** www.wesleyhouse.co.uk;
@Wesley_House; next to Sudeley Castle; 9 pm; closed
Mon & Sun D. **Accommodation:** 5 rooms, from £90.

WINCHESTER, HAMPSHIRE   2–3D

Bangkok Brasserie   **£37** ❷❷❸
33 Jewry St SO23 8RY (01962) 869 966
"Always busy, always with a buzz" – this "light, airy
and spacious" restaurant has won a big local
following with its "brilliant range of traditional and
more unusual Thai and pan-Asian dishes".
/ **Details:** www.bangkokbrasserie.co.uk; 10.30 pm.

The Bengal Sage   **£36** ❶❷❸
72-74 St George's St SO23 8AH
(01962) 862 173
For a "seriously good curry", head to this
"consistently outstanding" Indian two-year-old,
unanimously hailed for its "very creative", "locally
sourced and delicious" cuisine.
/ **Details:** www.thebengalsage.co.uk; 10.30 pm;
no Amex.

The Black Rat   **£56** ❷❸❸
88 Chesil St SO23 0HX (01962) 844465
"Adventurous" cooking ("modern British at its
best!") wins adulatory reviews for this "gastronomic
delight" – a "converted pub on the outskirts of the
city"; "service could be improved" a little though.
/ **Details:** www.theblackrat.co.uk; 9.30 pm; closed
weekday L; children: Weekend L only.

The Chesil Rectory   **£55** ❸❷❷
1 Chesil St SO23 0HU (01962) 851555
Plenty of positive feedback on this "quaint old
building" ("all wonky floors and low ceilings") in the
city-centre; its dishes include "much locally sourced
fare" to often "impressive" effect, and the wine list is
"very interesting" too; a quibble? – it's "a bit
expensive". / **Details:** www.chesilrectory.co.uk;
@ChesilRectory; 9.30 pm, Sat 10 pm, Sun 9 pm;
children: 12+ at D.

The Chestnut Horse   **£47** ④④❶
Easton Village SO21 1EG (01962) 779257
No one doubts that this is a "lovely old pub", but it
has been generating rather mixed reports in recent
times; fans insist that it "ticks all the boxes", but
some regulars complain of "diminished value for
money". / **Details:** www.thechestnuthorse.com;
@CHESTNUT_HORSE; Junction M3 Newbury exit
right hand lane; 9.30 pm, Sun 8 pm; no Amex.

Hotel du Vin et Bistro   **£53** ④❸❷
14 Southgate St SO23 9EF (01962) 841414
For fans, "the original Hotel du Vin has maintained
the highest standards", including a "great
atmosphere" and an "exceptional, multi-faceted
wine list"; critics, however, focus on the fact that the
food "doesn't live up to the surroundings".
/ **Details:** www.hotelduvin.com; @HdV_Winchester;
9.45 pm; booking: max 12. **Accommodation:** 24
rooms, from £145.

Kyoto Kitchen £ 34 ❶❷❸
70 Parchment Street SO23 8AT
(01962) 890895
"One of Winchester's newer restaurants, but already a standard-bearer"; this Japanese debutante "brings London standards to this sleepy town", serving "absolutely amazing sushi and other wonderful dishes" – "you'd have to go a long way to beat this". / Details: www.kyotokitchen.co.uk/; 10.30 pm.

The Avenue
Lainston House Hotel £ 79 ❸❷❸
SO21 2LT (01962) 776088
"Expensive, but a great location"; this grand (and arguably somewhat "staid") country house hotel is undoubtedly "impressive", and most (if not quite all) reporters don't begrudge the cost for romance or "proper fine dining".
/ Details: www.lainstonhouse.com; 9.30 pm, 10 pm Fri & Sat. Accommodation: 50 rooms, from £245.

The Old Vine £ 41 ❸❸❸
8 Great Minster St SO23 9HA
(01962) 854616
A "hugely popular pub, with restaurant and rooms, near the cathedral"; the cooking places "a big emphasis on local ingredients", and it's complemented by a wine selection that's "second to none". / Details: www.oldvinewinchester.com; @oldvinewinch; 9.30 pm, Sun 9 pm; children: 6+. Accommodation: 5 rooms, from £100.

Wykeham Arms £ 49 ❸❷❶
75 Kingsgate St SO23 9PE (01962) 853834
"How all pubs should be"; in the heart of the city, this ancient and "unique" venture has "an atmosphere of very comfortable prosperity" (especially in the "candlelit Jameson room"); many fans report that, after a patchy period, the food is "on the up". / Details: www.fullershotels.com; between Cathedral and College; 9.15 pm; children: 14+. Accommodation: 14 rooms, from £139.

WINCHESTER, CUMBRIA 7–3D

First Floor Café
Lakeland Limited £ 32 ❷❸❸
Alexandra Buildings LA23 1BQ
(015394) 47116
Run by the famous purveyors of kitchen equipment, a dining room – headed up by ex-Gavroche head chef Steven Doherty – where "standards are maintained"; the word is out, though – brace yourself for a "long wait for a table".
/ Details: www.lakeland.co.uk; 6 pm, Sat 5 pm, Sun 4 pm; no Amex.

Gilpin Lodge £ 85 ❷❷❷
Crook Rd LA23 3NE (01539) 488818
"A wonderful meal in beautiful surroundings"; pretty much all reports agree that a visit to the tasteful dining room of this luxurious but "relaxed" country

house hotel includes some "stunning" cooking.
/ Details: www.gilpinlodge.co.uk; 9.15 pm; no jeans; children: 7+. Accommodation: 20 rooms, from £255.

Holbeck Ghyll £ 91 ❷❷❶
Holbeck Ln LA23 1LU (01539) 432375
"A superb location overlooking Windermere" helps make this "stylish Arts & Crafts hotel" a "special experience"; it's "pricey but worth every penny" for the "exquisitely presented" traditional cuisine – "the lady on the next table actually cried when she started her chocolate dessert!"
/ Details: www.holbeckghyll.com; 3m N of Windermere, towards Troutbeck; 9.30 pm; no jeans or trainers; booking essential; children: 7+ at D. Accommodation: 25 rooms, from £190.

Hooked £ 47 ❶
Ellerthwaite Sq LA23 1DP (015394) 48443
A fish restaurant of fairly recent vintage, tipped for its "small but interesting" menu; service, though, does seem to have its ups and downs.
/ Details: www.hookedwindermere.co.uk/; 8.30 pm, Fri & Sat 9 pm; D only, closed Mon; no Amex.

Jerichos £ 52 ❶
College Rd LA23 1BX (01539) 442522
Since last year's review, this restaurant with rooms "now opens on Saturdays only" and bills have been hiked up too; although there are still fans of its "top notch" cuisine, there's a collective feeling that "if the new hours continue and the prices persist this view will change". / Details: www.jerichos.co.uk; 9 pm; closed Mon, Tue, Wed, Thu, Fri, Sat L & Sun; children: 12+. Accommodation: 10 rooms, from £85.

Linthwaite House £ 76 ❶
Crook Rd LA23 3JA (01539) 488600
Reports on this hotel above Windermere remain scarcer than we'd like, but its dining room is again tipped for "well-presented fare of a high standard", and it offers "the service and ambience one should expect of a well-run country house".
/ Details: www.linthwaite.com; near Windermere golf club; 9 pm; no jeans or trainers; children: 7+ at D. Accommodation: 30 rooms, from £180.

The Samling £ 85 ❶
Ambleside Rd LA23 1LR (01539) 431922
An interregnum in the kitchen seems to have upset reports on the dining experience at this romantic, lake-view country house hotel, hence we've passed on a rating until a new chef is firmly established at the stoves. / Details: www.thesamlinghotel.co.uk; @theSamlingHotel; take A591 from town; 9.30 pm. Accommodation: 11 rooms, from £150.

WINDSOR, BERKSHIRE	3–3A

Al Fassia £ 39 ❷❸④
27 St Leonards Rd SL4 3BP (01753) 855370
A *"family-friendly"* restaurant long tipped for its
"excellent Moroccan food".
/ **Details:** www.alfassiarestaurant.com; 10.15 pm, Fri &
Sat 10.30 pm, Sun 9.45 pm; closed Mon L; Booking
recommended Fri & Sat.

The Greene Oak £ 45 ❼
Deadworth Rd, Oakley Grn SL4 5UW
(01753) 864294
A handy tip on the outskirts of the town, and
somewhat removed from the tourists – *"a great
gastropub, with lovely food, really friendly service,
and a cracking wine list"*.
/ **Details:** www.thegreeneoak.co.uk; 9.30 pm.

WINTERINGHAM, LINCOLNSHIRE	5–1D

Winteringham Fields £ 108 ❷❸❷
1 Silver St DN15 9ND (01724) 733096
"Fast becoming a destination of choice" once again
– this rural restaurant-with-rooms (in the middle of
nowhere) is re-establishing its reputation for *"all-
round excellence"*, with *"divine"* cuisine and all-
round attention to detail; even fans, however, note
prices are a bit *"daft"*.
/ **Details:** www.winteringhamfields.co.uk; 4m SW of
Humber Bridge; 9 pm; closed Mon & Sun; no Amex.
Accommodation: 11 rooms, from £180.

WISWELL, LANCASHIRE	5–1B

Freemasons at Wiswell £ 56 ❶❷❷
8 Vicarage Fold Clitheroe BB7 9DF
(01254) 822218
It *"represents itself as a country pub, yet the main
competition is with nearby Northcote Manor!"*; this
"cosy, multi-roomed old inn", in an attractive Ribble
Valley hamlet, remains rather under the radar –
despite Steven Smith's extremely *"classy"* cooking
(*"it should have a Michelin star"*).
/ **Details:** www.freemasonswiswell.co.uk; Tue-Thu
9 pm, Fri & Sat 9.30 pm, Sun 8 pm; closed Mon;
no Amex; 8+ have to pre-order.

WIVETON, NORFOLK	6–3C

Wiveton Bell £ 46 ❼
Blakeney Rd NR25 7TL (01263) 740 101
A *"smart gastropub"* serving *"pub meals in a bistro
style"*, complete with *"friendly"* service, and a *"nice
log fire in winter"*. / **Details:** www.wivetonbell.co.uk;
@wivetonbell; 9 pm; no Amex. **Accommodation:** 4
rooms, from £75.

WOBURN SANDS, BUCKINGHAMSHIRE	3–2A

Purple Goose £ 46 ❷❶❸
61 High St MK17 8QY (01908) 584385
A *"small independent restaurant in the High
Street"*, with *"food that's a notch up from gastropub
standards, but at similar prices"*; *"the chef takes
great pride in his menu and often greets guests at
the end of the meal."*
/ **Details:** www.thepurplegoose.co.uk/; 9.30 pm; closed
Mon, Tue L, Wed L & Sun D; no Amex.

WOBURN, BUCKINGHAMSHIRE	3–2A

Birch £ 47 ❼
20 Newport Rd MK17 9HX (01525) 290295
A *"popular and busy"* gastroboozer tipped by most
(if not quite all) who report on it as *"a rare
certainty in a culinary desert"*.
/ **Details:** www.birchwoburn.com; between Woburn
and Woburn Sands on the Newport rd; 9.30 pm; closed
Sun D; booking: max 12, Fri & Sat.

The Black Horse £ 49 ❼
1 Bedford St MK17 9QB (01525) 290210
A *"cosy pub"*, in a *"picturesque setting on the
common"*, tipped for its *"good Sunday roast"*; the
"senior citizen meals are a real bargain" too
apparently (although the most enthusiastic report is
from a 21-year old!)
/ **Details:** www.blackhorsewoburn.co.uk; 9.45 pm, Sun
9 pm; SRA-58%.

Paris House £ 93 ❷❷❸
Woburn Pk MK17 9QP (01525) 290692
"If you're lucky you get deer grazing" as you enter
this *"idyllically located"* Tudor house, where chef Phil
Fanning wins adulation for his *"clever, original and
un-clichéd"* cuisine; the interior doesn't match the
external loveliness, however, and the odd reporter
leaves un-wowed generally.
/ **Details:** www.parishouse.co.uk; on A4012; 8.30 pm;
closed Mon, Tue L & Sun D.

WOLVERCOTE, OXFORDSHIRE	2–2D

The Trout Inn £ 44 ④⑤❷
195 Godstow Rd OX2 8PN (01865) 510930
With its *"fantastic riverside setting"*, this *"lovely"* old
favourite – made famous by Inspector Morse –
"was once an authentic spit-and-sawdust pub", but
has *"got rid of the casual drinkers"* in recent times;
"such a beautiful location should do better",
however – standards can be very *"erratic"*.
/ **Details:** www.thetroutoxford.co.uk; 2m from junction
of A40 & A44; 10 pm, Fri & Sat 10.30 pm, Sun 9 pm.

WOLVERHAMPTON,
WEST MIDLANDS   5–4B

Bilash   **£ 52 ②②③**
2 Cheapside WV1 1TU (01902) 427762
"What a find!" (and bang in the middle of town,
too); Sitab Khan's family-run fixture "elevates the
standard of Indian available in this town to Premier
League level"… even if the "innovative" cuisine does
come "at a price". / Details: www.thebilash.co.uk;
@thebilash; 10.30 pm; closed Sun.

WOODLANDS, HAMPSHIRE   2–4C

Terravina
Hotel Terravina   **£ 57 ⓿⓿❸**
174 Woodlands Rd, Netley Marsh, New Forest
SO40 7GL (023) 8029 3784
The "astonishing" wine list is the "particular
highlight" at Gerard (founder of Hotel du Vin) and
Nina Basset's hotel dining room on the edge of the
New Forest, but its "superb" cuisine and "very high
standard" of service make it an all-round hit with
reporters. / Details: www.hotelterravina.co.uk;
9.30 pm. **Accommodation:** 11 rooms, from £160.

WOODSTOCK, OXFORDSHIRE   2–1D

The Feathers Hotel   **£ 69 ④④❸**
Market St OX20 1SX (01993) 812291
After such good reports last year, this famous,
luxurious inn has not maintained this momentum of
late; fans praise its "quirky" style (including a "lovely
new outside terrace") and "delicious" cuisine, but
doubters find it "very inconsistent", and "struggling
to justify the prices". / Details: www.feathers.co.uk;
8m N of Oxford on A44; 9 pm; no jeans or trainers.
Accommodation: 21 rooms, from £199.

WOOLHOPE, HEREFORDSHIRE   2–1B

Butcher's Arms   **£ 40 ❼**
HR1 4RF (01432) 860281
New owner Phil Vincent took this "welcoming" half-
timbered inn over from Stephen Bull in late 2013;
he has his work cut out to maintain the "routinely
inventive" style of the former régime – fingers
crossed! / Details: butchersarmswoolhope.com;
Tue-Sat 9pm; closed Mon & Sun D.

WORMINGHALL,
BUCKINGHAMSHIRE   2–1D

Clifden Arms   **£ 36 ❷❸❸**
75 Clifden Rd HP18 9JR (01844) 339273
"Excellent cooking, in a charming location"; this
family-friendly thatched inn is quite an all-rounder,
but reports suggest that it's the accomplished food
("making good use of local sourcing") which is the
special attraction. / Details: www.theclifdenarms.com;
9 pm; closed Mon. WORTHING, WEST SUSSEX
3–4A

The Fish Factory   **£ 38 ②②④**
51-53 Brighton Rd BN11 3EE (01903) 207123
"Glorified fish 'n' chips, but very tasty!" – this
"enthusiastic", "simply decorated" and "fairly
priced" venue inspires upbeat reports from all who
comment on it.
/ **Details:** www.protorestaurantgroup.com; 10 pm.

WRINEHILL, CHESHIRE   5–2B

The Hand and Trumpet   **£ 46 ❸❸❷**
Main Rd CW3 9BJ (01270) 820048
A Brunning & Price gastropub, serving up "superb
food in generous portions" (and with "good options
for vegetarians" too) – even so, the occasional critic
can find it a touch "overpriced".
/ **Details:** www.brunningandprice.co.uk/hand; 10 pm,
Sun 9.30 pm; no Amex.

WRINGTON, SOMERSET   2–2B

Ethicurean   **£ 46 ⓿②⓿**
Barley Wood Walled Garden, Long Ln BS40
5SA (01934) 863713
Adjacent to a Victorian kitchen garden, a "simple"
restaurant serving "exquisite" dishes created from
"brilliantly sourced local ingredients"; "on a fine
summer's evening, this must be one of the most
beautiful places in the UK to eat" too!
/ **Details:** www.theethicurean.com; Fri/Sat 11.30pm;
Sun 2.30pm; closed Mon, Tue D, Wed D & Thu D.

WYE, KENT   3–3C

The Wife of Bath   **£ 52 ②④④**
4 Upper Bridge St TN25 5AF (01233) 812232
In a small village, a restaurant-with-rooms where all
reports agree on the "very good" standards of the
cooking; "unhelpful" or "lackadaisical" service
"spoilt" the experience for quite a few reporters this
year, however. / **Details:** www.thewifeofbath.com;
@TheWifeofBath2; off A28 between Ashford &
Canterbury; 9.30 pm; closed Mon, Tue L & Sun D;
no Amex. **Accommodation:** 5 rooms, from £95.

WYKE REGIS, DORSET   2–4B

Crab House Café   **£ 44 ❷❷❷**
Ferrymans Way, Portland Rd DT4 9YU
(01305) 788867
"In an area where many of the food outlets are
dire", this "great little place by the bay" really stands
out; "if all you want is freshly caught fish beautifully
prepared, this is the spot for you".
/ **Details:** www.crabhousecafe.co.uk; overlooking the
Fleet Lagoon, on the road to Portland; 9 pm, Sat
9.30 pm; closed Mon L & Tue; no Amex; 8+ deposit of
£10 per head.

WYMONDHAM, LEICESTERSHIRE   5–3D

The Berkeley Arms   £ 45   ❷❷❸
59 Main St LE14 2AG   (01572) 787 587
"Consistently busy, and deservedly so" – this
"buzzy" inn attracts only positive reports, for its
"fabulous and relatively sensibly priced" cooking
(from an ex-Hambleton chef) and "smiling" service.
/ Details: www.theberkeleyarms.co.uk;
@TheBekeleyArms; 9 pm, Sat & Sun 9.30 pm; closed
Mon & Sun D.

YEADON, WEST YORKSHIRE   5–1C

Murgatroyds   £ 34   ❶❷❸
Harrogate Rd LS19 7BN   (0113) 250 0010
A spacious and "good value" canteen, tipped for
"some of the best fish 'n' chips in Yorkshire".
/ Details: www.murgatroyds.co.uk; 9.30 pm.

YORK, NORTH YORKSHIRE   5–1D

Ate O'Clock   £ 43   ❼
13A, High Ousegate YO1 8RZ
(01904) 644080
"A good bistro in central York", tipped for its
"interesting" menu and "good value".
/ Details: www.ateoclock.co.uk; 9.30 pm, Mon 9 pm;
closed Mon L & Sun; no Amex.

Bettys   £ 45   ❻❷❷
6-8 St Helen's Sq YO1 8QP   (01904) 659142
This famous room remains "the last word in
Edwardian-style elegance" for most reporters, who
also praise its "lovely" cakes and "Swiss-influenced"
light bites made from "first-class ingredients"; it's
also a "tourist must", though, and queues are
omnipresent. / Details: www.bettys.co.uk; 9 pm;
no Amex; no booking, except Sun.

The Blue Bicycle   £ 54   ❹❸❸
34 Fossgate YO1 9TA   (01904) 673990
As so often in the past, reports on this prettily-
housed river-view dining room are notably up-and-
down; fans insist it offers "fine" ("predominantly
fish") cooking and "friendly" and "attentive" service,
but results can be pretty "average" too.
/ Details: www.thebluebicycle.com; 9.30 pm, Sun
9 pm; closed Mon - Wed L; no Amex; booking: max 8
Sat D. Accommodation: 6 rooms, from £175.

Café Concerto   £ 43   ❼
21 High Petergate YO1 7EN   (01904) 610478
In a prime location by the Minster, this classic
café/bistro is an "ideal lunch spot" that's tipped
above some of the more obviously touristy
competition, thanks to its "fresh and imaginative"
cuisine. / Details: www.cafeconcerto.biz; 9.30 pm;
booking: max 6-8. Accommodation: 1 room, at
about £175.

Cafe No. 8 Bistro   £ 45   ❷❸❸
8 Gillygate YO31 7EQ   (01904) 653074
In a city "full of '70s-style bistros", this "friendly"
establishment near the Minster is a "breath of fresh
air"; although the kitchen may be "minuscule", the
food is "alchemic". / Details: www.cafeno8.co.uk;
9.30 pm; no Amex.

City Screen Café Bar
City Screen
Picturehouse   £ 33   ❼
Coney St YO1 9QL   (01904) 612940
A useful destination, with some al fresco tables
beside the river, tipped for its "good selection" of
dishes, including "plenty of vegetarian options".
/ Details: www.picturehouses.co.uk; 9 pm; no Amex;
no booking.

Delrio's   £ 41   ❼
10-12 Blossom St YO24 1AE   (01904) 622695
This "nice staple Italian" – a cellar restaurant and
bar near the station, with al fresco dining in good
weather – is tipped as "well worth a visit"; brace
yourself, though, for seating "which some might call
cosy". / Details: www.delriosrestaurant.com;
10.30 pm; D only, closed Mon.

Il Paradiso Del Cibo   £ 35   ❷❹❸
40 Walmgate YO1 9TJ   (0190) 461 1444
"A great place… but it risks being spoilt by being
featured in too many places!"; this very "good-
value" Sardinian is "not for you if you like quiet and
calm", but the food is "excellent", and staff "fit the
Italian stereotype of charm and warmth".
/ Details: www.ilparadisodelcibo; 10 pm.

Le Langhe   £ 46   ❶❹❸
The Old Coach Hs, Peasholme Grn YO1 7PW
(01904) 622584
Fans praise "some of the best food for miles
around" at Octavio Bocca's "above-average"
restaurant and deli; the menu is "not particularly
extensive", and service "a bit hit and miss", but –
"for authentic Italian dishes in a simple but very
pleasant atmosphere" – it's "hard to beat".
/ Details: www.lelanghe.co.uk; @lelanghe; midnight;
closed Mon, Tue, Wed, Thu & Sun; no Amex.

Melton's   £ 51   ❷❷❹
7 Scarcroft Rd YO23 1ND   (01904) 634 341
"Bullseye!" – Michael Hjort's "utterly dependable"
venture in a "gentrified suburb just outside the city
walls" is spot on for "superb" locally sourced food
matched by an "extensive" wine list; "they also train
their staff…" / Details: www.meltonsrestaurant.co.uk;
@Meltons1; 9.30 pm; closed Mon & Sun; no Amex.

Middlethorpe Hall   **£ 75**   ⊙
Bishopthorpe Rd   YO23 2GB   (01904) 641241
"Wonderful gardens" set the scene at this country
house hotel, in an estate on the edge of the city,
tipped by a loyal fanclub for its "high standard" of
cooking. / **Details:** www.middlethorpe.com; 9.30 pm;
no shorts; children: 6+. **Accommodation:** 29 rooms,
from £199.

Mumbai Lounge   **£ 31**   ❷❸❸
47 Fossgate   YO1 9TF   (01904) 654 155
"Subtle spicing" and "presentation that's way above
average" again win praise for this "consistently
excellent" Indian, in the city-centre.
/ **Details:** www.mumbailoungeyork.co.uk; 11.30 pm,
Fri & Sat midnight; closed Fri L.

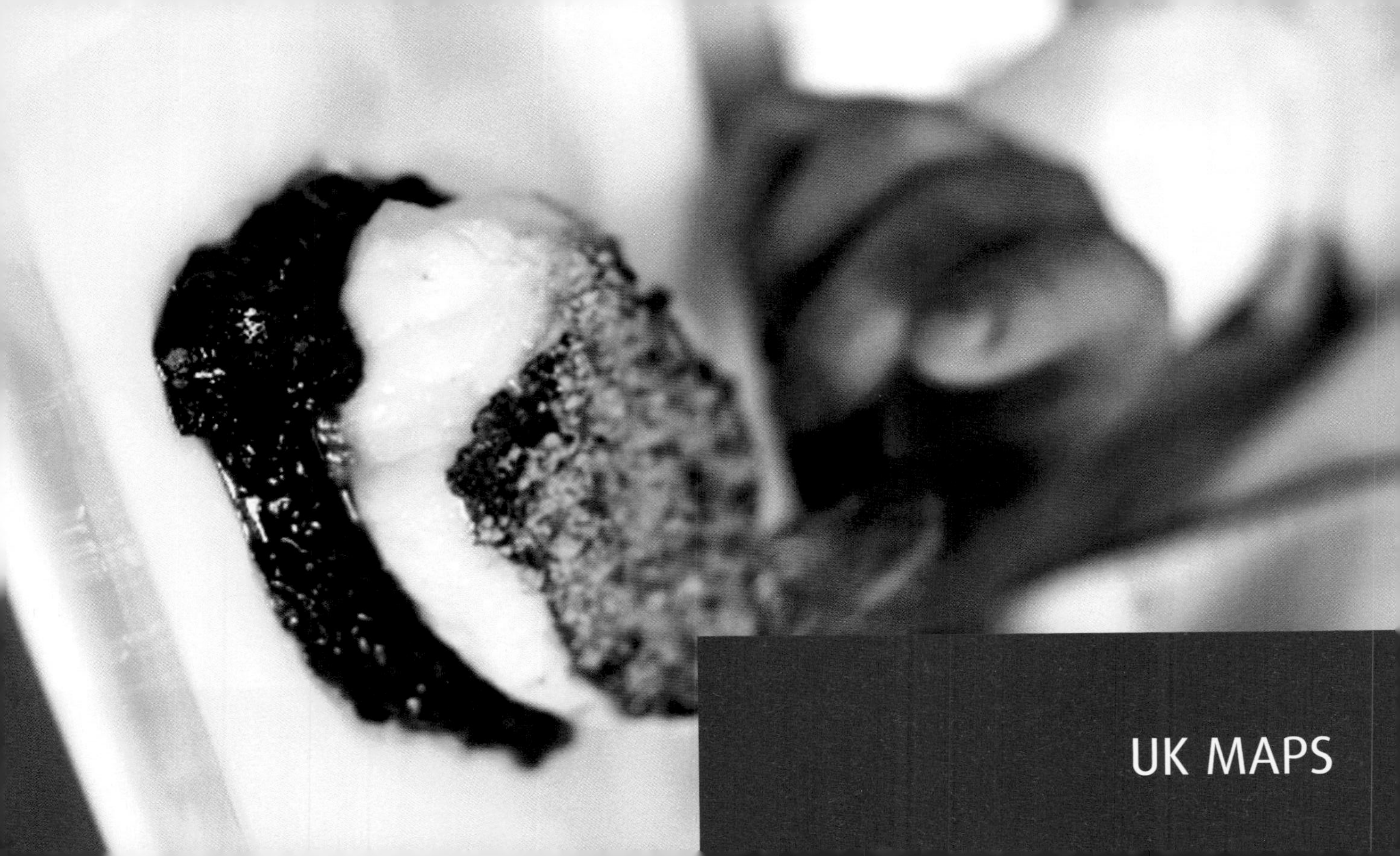

UK MAPS

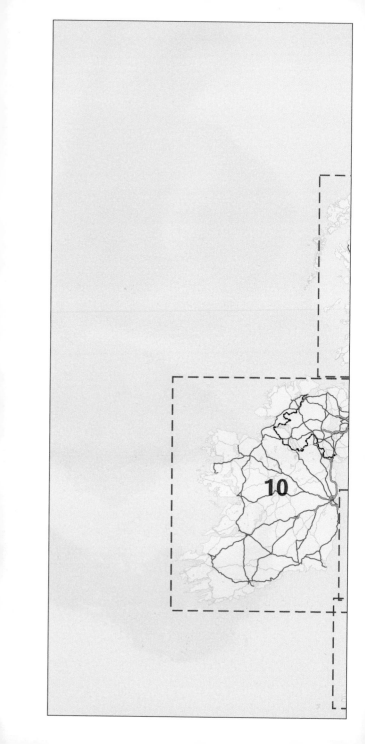

10

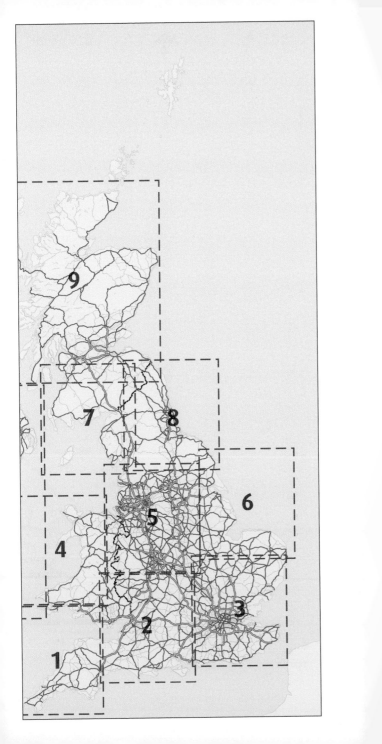

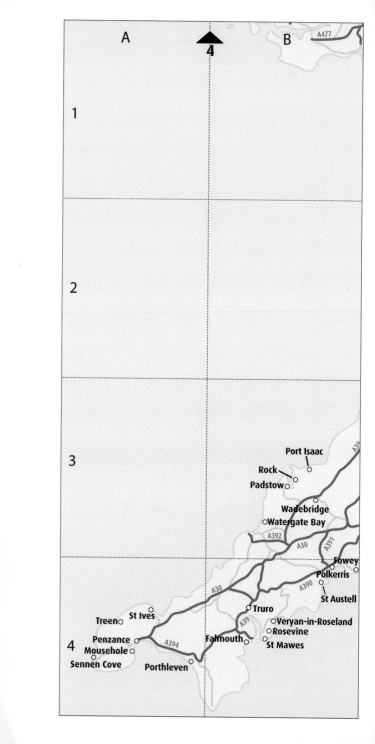

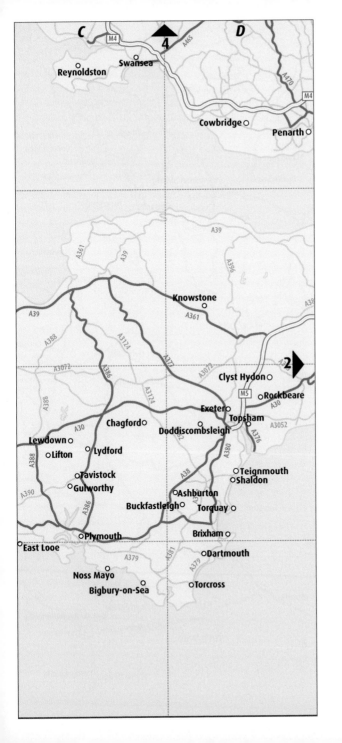

MAP 2

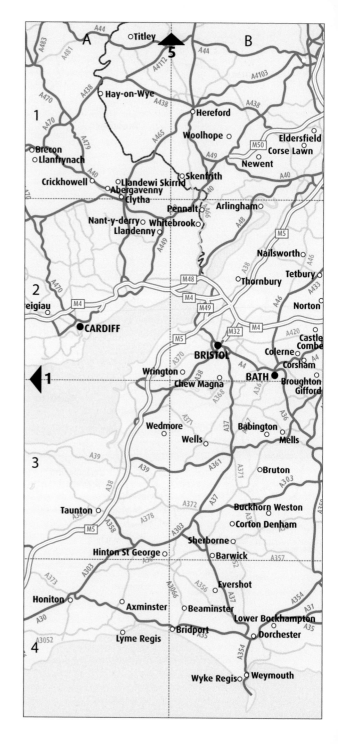

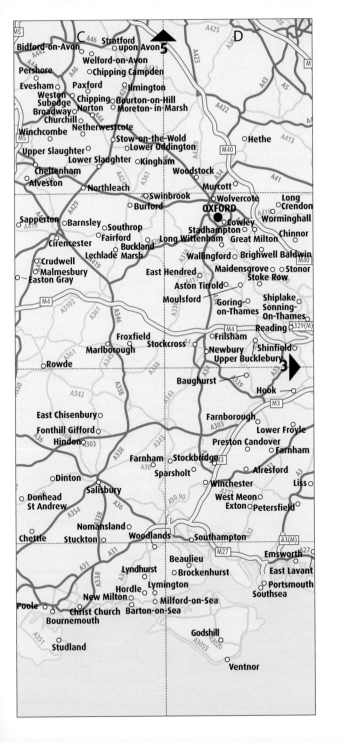

MAP **2**

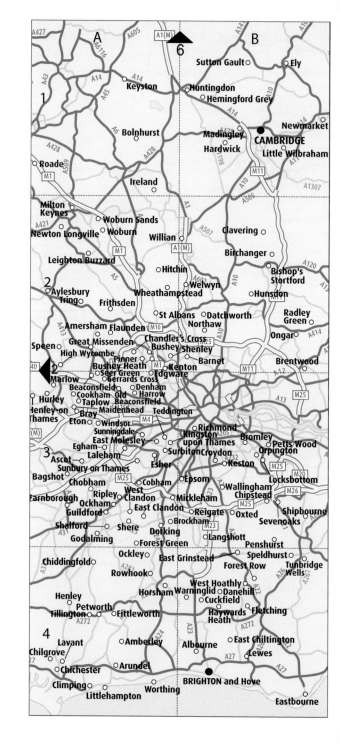

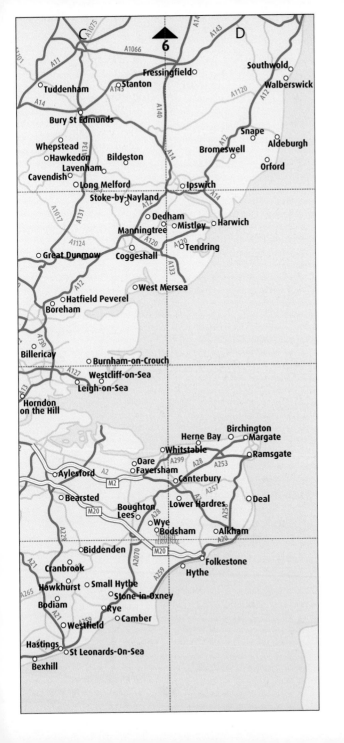

MAP **4**

	A	B
1		
2		
3		
4		Newport Porthgain St Davids Broad Haven Narbeth

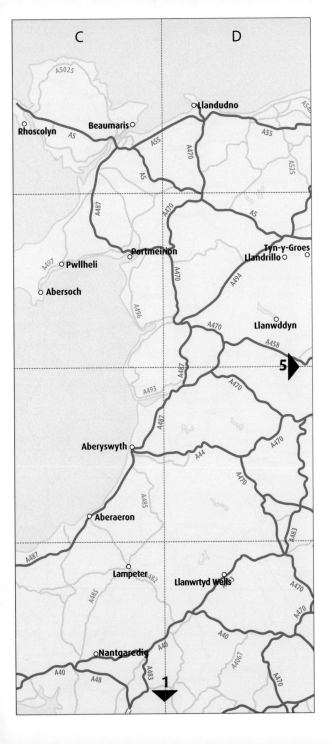

MAP 4

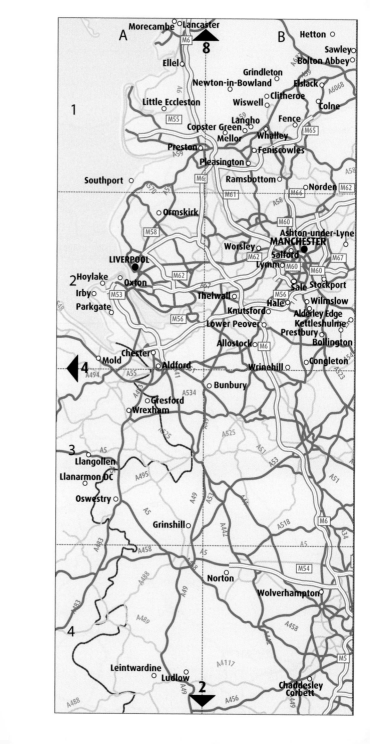

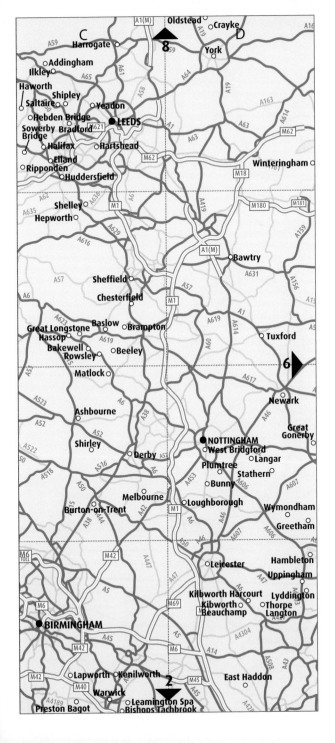

MAP **5**

MAP 6

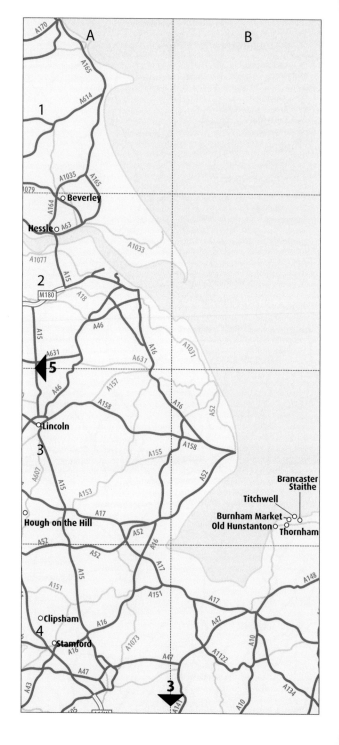

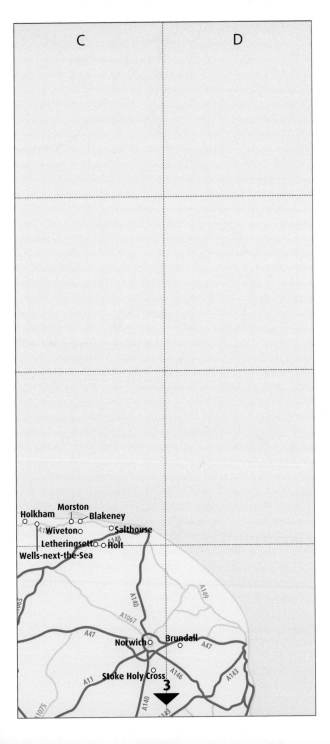

MAP 6

C

D

Holkham
Morston
Blakeney
Wiveton
Salthouse
Letheringsett
Holt
Wells-next-the-Sea

A148

A149

A140

A1067

A47

Norwich
Brundall
A47

A11

Stoke Holy Cross
A146
A143

3

A140

A143

A1075

A1075

MAP **7**

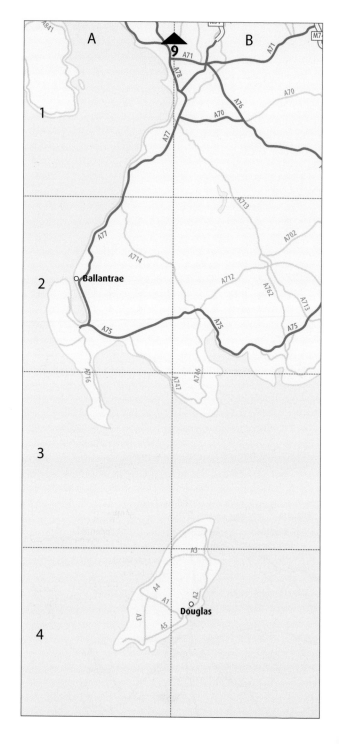

A 9 B

1

A77

A77 A714

2 ○ **Ballantrae** A712 A75

A75

3

A3

A4 A2
A1
Douglas
4 A3
A5

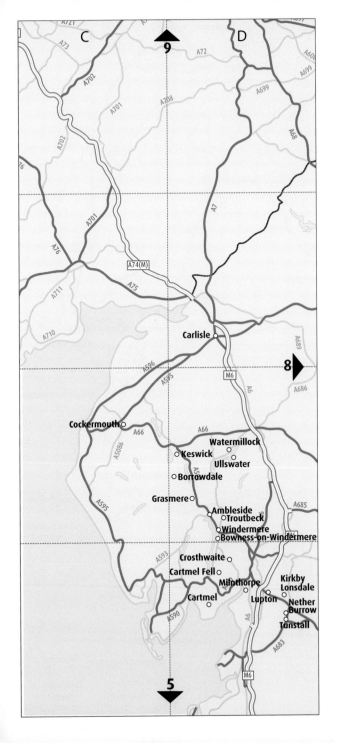

MAP 7

MAP 8

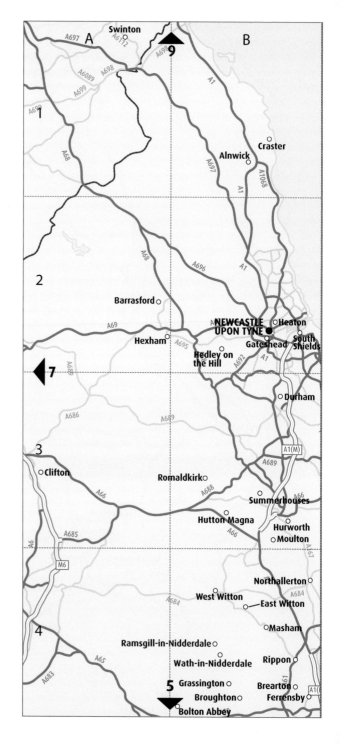

MAP 8

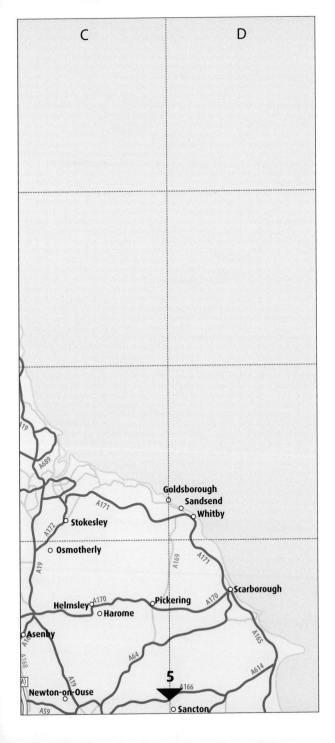

MAP **9**

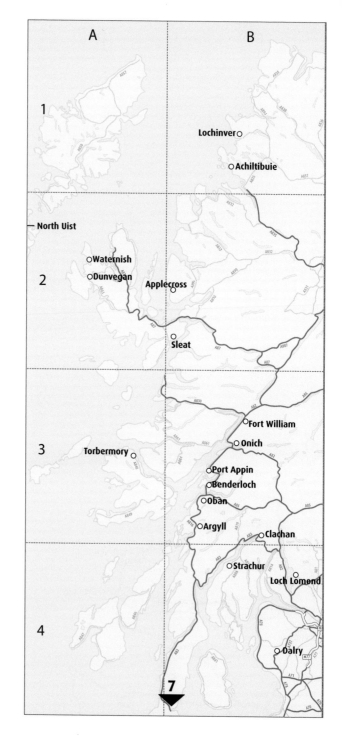

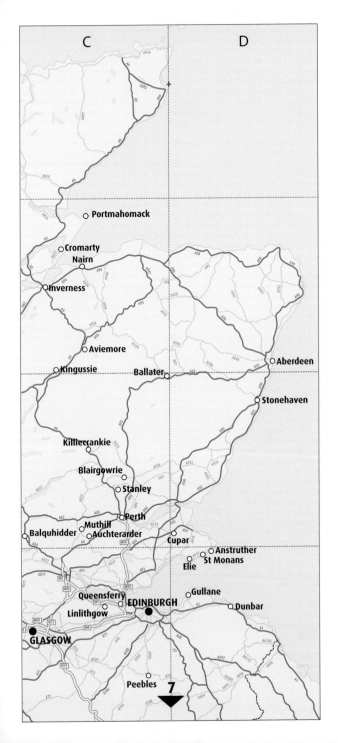

MAP 9

C   D

Portmahomack

Cromarty
Nairn
Inverness

Aviemore
Kingussie   Ballater   Aberdeen

Stonehaven

Killiecrankie

Blairgowrie
Stanley

Perth
Muthill
Balquhidder   Auchterarder
Cupar
Anstruther
St Monans
Elie

Queensferry   Gullane
Linlithgow   EDINBURGH   Dunbar

GLASGOW

Peebles   7

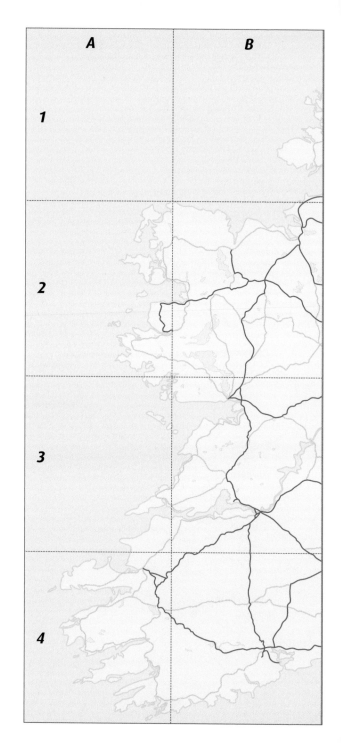

MAP **10**

A   B

1

2

3

4

MAP **10**

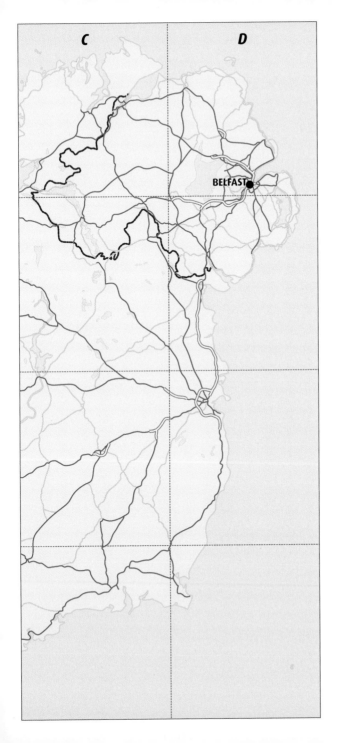

C

D

BELFAST

ALPHABETICAL INDEX

ALPHABETICAL INDEX

ALPHABETICAL INDEX

ALPHABETICAL INDEX

ALPHABETICAL INDEX

ALPHABETICAL INDEX

413

NEW ZEALAND

L'Arche Kapiti	Parapraumu	1998

ARGENTINA

El Arca Buenos Aires	Buenos Aires	2003

BANGLADESH

L'Arche Mymensingh	Mymensingh	2003

EGYPT

Al Fulk	El Minia	2003

UKRAINE

L'Arche Kovcheh	Lviv	2007

LITHUANIA

Project Betzatos bendruomene	Vilniaus	2008

KENYA

Project L'Arche Kenya	Nyahururu	2009

CROATIA

Project L'Arche Zagreb	Zagreb	2009

KOREA

Project L'Arche Korea	Seoul	2004

PALESTINE

Project Ma'an lil-Hayat	Bethlehem	2008

List updated in June 2011. For more details, visit www.larche.org.